SOUL OF THE QUR'AN

SOUL OF THE QUR'AN

(Volume 1)

Muhyadheen Muhammad Irumbuzhi

KALPAZ

Soul of The Qur'an: Volume- 1
(Explanation of the Holy Qur'an)

ISBN: 978-81-7835-813-0

Published in 2010 in India by
Kalpaz Publications
C-30, Satyawati Nagar,
Delhi-110052
E-mail: kalpaz@hotmail.com
Phone : 9212729499

Printed at : G. Print Process,

"Certainly those who believe from among Muslims, those who are Jews, Christians, Sabeans, anyone who believes in Allah and Last Day, and acts honorably will receive their reward with their Lord and there shall be no fear and for them will not be grieved". (2: 62; 5: 69)

CONTENTS

Preface

Adhikr (Soul of the Qur'an) is a splendid Book, no falsehood shall approach it either before or after, since it's a revelation from the One, Who is Wise, Praiseworthy as mentioned in the verse 41:42. It's the best interpretation of the Qur'an specified in the verse 25:33.

Today, unfortunately every faction of people by considering the body and meaning of the Book without Its Soul are deviated from the straightpath, and each group rejoice with what they have. By identifying oneself, Lord and the aim of life utilizing the Soul of the Qur'an; bloodshed, terrorism and other mischievous activities can be wiped out and human harmony can be formed. Due to the mischievous activities of mankind, the end of the World is hurrying. Prophet has taught: *'The Dooms day will not happen until ten crucial signs appear, by appearance of which, no soul shall benefit with her belief'*. Soul of the Qur'an is the Device to postpone the appearance of Anti-Christ (Masseh-A-Dajjal); one of the ten crucial signs. It's the Shield and Safeguard for any individual not to include among the hypocrites and those who associate others in the Dominion of Allah, mentioned both in the verses 33:60 and 33: 73 who will be killed by the second coming of JESUS.

Soul of the Qur'an is the Food, Cloth and Sight of the human soul. It's the inevitable duty of every person to utilize and convey It to the entire mankind irrespective of nation or religion. Remember that It's the Balance and Trust to keep the Earth in its equilibrium as well as the Universe. Since It's the Message of the Lord, copyright of this Book ***(Soul of the Qur'an)*** is not to be reserved. So anyone can translate, print and publish It. As per the verse 15:9, it is revealed by the Lord and He Himself will preserved It. Beware, whoever hide and reject after receiving Soul of the Qur'an, they are the only fuel of the Hellfire from the mankind.

Irumbuzhi **Muhyadheen Muhammed Irumbuzhi**

With the name of Allah, the Impartial, the Compassionate.

INTRODUCTION

What we call 'I', 'you' etc. are not the visible physical body! On the contrary, it is '*Nafs*'- soul. Body is the vehicle to travel for the soul. It is an earthen 'frame or a mould' developed by the Supreme Creator by mixing the sperm and ovum of father and mother respectively. When Adam- the first man was created; the entire soul of men till the Last Day were created from the single soul in the Paradise itself. So the soul of all mankind is the one as told in the verses 4:1; 7:189 and 39:6. Taking out their progeny which exists till the Last Day from the napes of Adam's children, the Creator asked each one of them: "Am I not your Lord, the Owner?" Then each of them replied: "Of course, we witness for it". By doing this covenant everybody admitted that the authority for giving rules and regulations to entire mankind is their Lord only. Afterwards, they were made lifeless and sent back to the nape of Adam. Read together the verses 7: 172-173.

By making the oath in the verses 91:1-6, on the apparent six matters- sun and its hot light; consequent moon and resplendent light; the appearance of bright day; the darkening of night; the canopied sky; the earth shaped like an ostrich's egg- Allah says in the verses 7-10: He evenly balanced the soul and gave its false way and good way. Then whoever purifies (identifies himself) will prosper, while whoever neglects to do so-doesn't identify- will fail. The verse 76: 3 says: "Indeed We gave the man freedom to select either the way of grateful or ungrateful". In the verse 90: 10 it is told: "Then we guided the man by two stars (two ways) one to the Hell and the other to the Paradise". Allah became Impartial by teaching man Soul of Qur'an which contains both ways of Satan (falsehood) and the way of Allah (Truth) from the Paradise itself as told in the verses 55: 1-4. As per the verse 10: 100, no one becomes a believer without Allah's permission i.e. the Soul of Qur'an. Therefore it is the duty of each individual (man or woman) to confirm that he is grateful i.e. a believer by utilizing the Soul of Qur'an.

The Body:

The Creator made the body of Adam from "sounding", "adhesive" and "foul smelling" black clay as a potter shaping a pot as told in the verse 15: 26. Then the '*Rooh*'- spirit (Life + soul) of the Creator was blown into the body as told in the verses 15: 29 and 38: 72. Then Eve, the mate of Adam was created from the soul of Adam. It is told in verse 4:1 that from "her", "her" mate was created. In Qur'an the soul of both male and female, and the body of women are used in feminine gender, whereas the body of men is used in masculine gender.

Before men were created, the vicegerents of Allah on earth were '*Jinns*'- sprites whose bodies were created from flame as per the verse 15: 27. Afterwards when they all became transgressors on earth without bearing Lord's representation, Angels wiped out them completely under the leadership of *Iblis*. At that time, *Iblis* who belongs to *Jinn* as per the verse 18: 50, had not turned to be a rebel. After this, men were created in Paradise in order to depute them to the earth as Allah's vicegerents. The saying in the verse 45: 13 that, "**everything** is given to the man from their Lord" means He has taught the man the Soul of Qur'an which is the constitution, ways and practices of the Impartial Lord as well as the knowledge of past, present and future. Since mankind was taught the 'Software' of the Universe which is the Balance and Trust to keep the Universe in its equilibrium, the control of everything is given to him and he is honored above all creatures. So it is the duty of mankind to keep the Universe in its equilibrium by utilizing the Soul of Qur'an. But the only one among each thousand to the Paradise will take this respon sibility. Such a believer who is teaching and conveying the Soul of Qur'an which is food, cloth and sight of human soul to entire mankind is not present in all over the world, then Dooms Day will occur. Read together the verses 22: 65 and 35: 45.

When the spirit of the Creator was blown in Adam, Allah commanded the assemblage of Angels including Iblis to make '*Sujood*'- prostration to Adam. Everybody made *Sujood* except Iblis. He was arrogant that he who was made of flame couldn't make *Sujood* in front of Adam who was made of mud. Following this, he was cursed and denied mercy, and finally he was expelled from the Paradise. Consequently, he requested Allah that he should be given an opportunity to tempt and deviate man from the Straight path. Allah gave him the opportunity till a fixed day, and also gave him all the facilities needed, as told in the verses 17: 62-64. Read together the verses 4: 116-121and 7: 16-17.

Then Allah told: Oh, Adam! Reside in the Paradise yourself and your mate. Eat fruits from the Paradise as both of you wish. But neither you nor your mate should eat the fruit of the particular tree. If you do so, you will be included among wrongdoers. Then satan betrayed them and told them: Your Lord has not prohibited you regarding this tree, except both of you won't become Angels or immortal. Again satan swore to them: Definitely, I am one among your well-wishers as per the verses 7: 19-21. He won over them by tempting in this way. When both of them tasted the fruit of that tree, their private parts were revealed and began to hide those parts with the leaves from the Paradise. Their Lord called them both and asked: Didn't We prohibit you regarding that tree? Didn't We also tell you that satan is surely the clear enemy to both of you? Read together the verse 7: 22. Adam, who felt sorry in heart, was given words from Allah for return into the Straight path by repenting as per the verse 2:37. As per the verse 7:23 both of them prayed: Our Lord, we have done wrong to ourselves. If You don't forgive us and if You don't shower your Mercy upon us, we will definitely be included among the losers. Allah accepted their repentance. Indeed He is the Oft Forgiving; Merciful. By this event Allah taught mankind the parable of life on earth and the nature of the satanic temptations.

When Allah sent men down to the earth from Paradise, He said: "Get you down all from here; if the Guidance has come to you from Me, then anyone who follows My Guidance, on them there shall be no fear and for them will not be grieved, is told in the verses 2: 38 and 20: 123. With the rhythmic balance of the wind, Adam carrying all the children up to the Last Day on his nape and Eve were descended into the Earth as explained in the verse 2:164.

The Creation of Human Body:

Allah asks in the verse 76: 1 "Hasn't a long period passed for men, when he was nothing worth mentioning." This is to say that at the time of creation of Adam itself, all the souls till the Last Day has been created in the Paradise. Then the Creator decides the period, nation, tribes, parents and sex through which the individuals should be brought on Earth. Read together the verse 2: 28.

First father and mother ate food material produced from soil which contained the elements of soil. From this, blood is formed. And from its essence the Creator produced semen containing sperm and ovum (*Nuthfa*).The word *Nuthfa* is used for sperm as well as ovum. The verses 86: 5-7 says: So let every man observe what he has been created from? He is created by the water ejected from the fathers' '*Swulb*' (testicles in the case of men-early stage it was in between the ribs) and mothers' '*Thara-ib*' (pelvis region of women). And in the verse 76: 2 says: Indeed We have created man from the mixture '*Nuthfa*' of male and female. After staying 40 days in the womb of mother as '*Nuthfa*'-embryo, then 40 days as '*Alaqa*'-clot and again 40 days as '*Mudhu'gha*'- clinging mass of flesh. The 'soul' situated in fathers nape is carried to the fetus in mother's womb during fourth month through Angels. Read together the verses 22: 5; 23: 12-14 and 32: 7-9. Prophet taught as an answer to a Jew's question that, the bones and nerves are formed from the '*Nuthfa*' of father, whereas blood and flesh are formed from the '*Nuthfa*' of mother. If man is compared to a computer, his body is the hardware, life is the power (electricity) and soul is the software.

The History of Men:

Adam and Eve continued to live on earth by utilizing the Soul of Qur'an which is taught from Paradise itself as explained in the verse 2: 213. Gradually, the children of Adam were deviated due to temptation of satan and became those who lost the aim of life. When most of them became wrongdoers, Allah sent Prophets who convey glad tidings from Allah to believers and warning to disbelievers. Ten generations from Adam to *Nooh* lived according to the Soul of Qur'an taught from the Paradise. In due course, according to the development of society, when men were trapped by satan, and there was nobody to represent as the vicegerent of Allah, He sent Messenger *Nooh*. Who is also known as 'Manu and Noah', and revealed for the first time the Scripture in its bodily form. The Book is only revealed to the Messengers, not to the Prophets as told in the verse 57: 25. As a result of *Nooh's* instructions with the Reminder, only a few from his people believed. When Allah, the Knower of past, present and future understood that nobody will further believe, He commanded *Nooh* to pray to Him for a decision between believers and transgressors. As a result of this, through a flood which was spread in all areas of human inhabitance, Allah destroyed all of them and saved *Nooh* and believers in an ark. All the men today on Earth are the successors of those who escaped in the ark. Read together the verses 11: 48; 17: 3 and 36: 41.

A section of those who escaped were settled in Iraq. Gradually when they were seduced and became idol worshipers as well as wrongdoers, Allah sent *Ibrahim* as a Messenger. He insisted people about one Deity, but the people including his father decided to kill by throwing him into burning fire. Allah saved him from it as told in the verse 21: 69. The predecessors of "Aryans", who finally arrived in India seeking pastures for grazing cattle, were from Iraq. The similarity between the worship practices of *Ibrahim* such as the dress style for *Hajj*, composite around *Ka'aba* keeping left etc., and the dress style and composite around temple keeping left of Brahmins may be due to the above reason. According to the command of Allah, the first child *Isma'el*, and his mother *Hajara* were brought to Mecca where the *Ka'ba* is situated and they settled there. Afterwards *Ibrahim* went back to Palestine. When the reserve water was over, *Hajara* ran between 'Safa' and '*Marva*' hills seven times in search of water for the child, and finally '*Zum-zum*' fountain was burst and flowed under the foot of the child. When *Isma'el* was fourteen years old, Allah ordered Ibrahim that his son should be sacrificed. When he was ready even for that Allah called him and told: "Enough, you have fulfilled the command! Now sacrifice this goat instead." When he was triumphant in all these ordeals, Allah showed him the foundation of the *Ka'ba*, the Allah's first house on earth, which was constructed for the worship of Allah and had been dilapidated in the flood at the time of *Nooh* as told in the verse 3:96. *Ibrahim* and *Isma'el* together built up the *Ka'ba*. Read together the verses 2: 126-127. According to the verses 14: 35- 36 though Prophet *Ibrahim* prayed not to include himself and his children among idol worshipers, gradually the children of *Isma'el* had gone astray and installed up to 360 idols at the *Ka'ba*, which is constructed for the worship of Allah alone.

Prophet *Yoosuf*, the son of Prophet *Ya'qoob* (also known as *Isra'el*), the grand son of Prophet *Ishaaq* who was the second son of Prophet *Ibrahim;* was thrown in to the well by his brothers. He was recovered by the caravan and sold in Egypt. In due course, Prophet *Yoosuf* became the ruler of Egypt and he brought his father *Ya'qoob* and all his family members to Egypt and settled there. Thus the children of *Isra'el* arrived in Egypt. Gradually, the teachings of Prophet *Yoosuf* were forgotten by the people including the children of *Isra'el* and they themselves immersed in cow worship and other immoral deeds. The Pharaohs from '*Qibthi*' race became the Egyptian rulers and they suppressed the children of *Isra'el* and made them slaves. Then Prophet *Moosa* was sent by Allah to save them from Pharaohs.

Though *Moosa* and *Haroon* conducted spiritual instructions in Egypt for years, only one among the Pharaoh's people became the believer. Finally, Allah saved *Moosa* and the children of Isra'el by parting the sea as told in the verse 26: 63; bestowed them with so many bounties and honored more than any other people. More than half of Prophets who have been specifically mentioned in Qur'an, including two Messengers *Moosa* and Jesus from among '*Ulul-Azm*' are included in the children of Isra'el. Prophet *Sulaiman* who has been given the most prowess, dignity and majesty; and Prophet *Davood* and three pairs having father and son as Prophets also included them. Before deploying Prophet Mohammad, the leadership of world was in the hand of children of Isra'el. But they gradually became arrogant; concealed the Holy Book; assassinated some of the Prophets and even tried to kill Jesus.

By hiding the *Thourath* -Book from Allah- the Jewish priests lived as white colored graves and led the people to live without soul. Though Eisa preached against their exploitation and misguiding, the children of Isra'el were not ready to believe. (For details see gospel of Mathew: 23:1-36.) Only thirteen disciples from among them were ready to follow Eisa. The Jewish priests influenced the Roman Governor to crucify Eisa and at last they decided to crucify him. But the Mighty exalted Allah raised Jesus to Heaven bodily. As explained in the verses 4: 157-158 Allah raised him by whirlwind to the heaven and transformed *Surjjas*' face (one of the disciple) as that of Eisa, then the Roman soldiers captured *Surjjas* and he was crucified. The rest of the twelve disciples trembled by facing the situation i.e. the disbelief of the people, the mocking and spy work of Jewish priests, the partiality of Roman rulers etc; could not explain to the people the fact that Eisa was raised up by the Lord of worlds. Afterwards they could not work together in a place; they disintegrated and continued preaching the Message individually in different places. Meanwhile 'Paul' -one of the Jew, among the enemy of *Eisa* came as an self declared 'apostle' and started to preach a new way of belief against the Message and teaching of *Eisa* under the support and permission of Jews and Roman rulers. Thus they became different groups and deviated from the Straight path. Read together the verses 3: 52-55.

After Jesus, when the world became dark and was about to be destroyed, Allah deployed Prophet Mohammad (who has been mentioned as 'Kalki' in the Hindu Scriptures and as the 'steward' or 'the soul of truth' in the Bible) as the last Prophet and Messenger of Islam. The ignorance of the morally degraded children of *Isma'el* became so dark that both male and female were encompassing the *Ka'ba* in the nude. In a situation in which it was impossible to live contacting the outer world, Mohammad started to live in *Hira* cave lonely. It was then that "*Jibreel*", the Messenger from the Angels arrives with Qur'an- the right divine message. Read together the verses 53: 1-17 and 81: 19- 27. It was told Prophet

Mohammad to read out first five verses from *Sura* 96, and when Prophet replied: "I am not one who reads", *Jibreel* embraced Prophet and then breathlessly, the Soul contacted Paradise. Subsequently he read Qur'an taught from Paradise. Then in various situations, the sending down of Qur'an was completed in 23 years, step by step.

Are all 'Religions' true? :

Islam, natural religion is the submission of will and whole life to the Creator, or a lifestyle codified under the shadow of the whole divine Book, satisfied by Allah for entire mankind from the beginning to the Last as explained in the verses 3: 19, 85. Messengers were deputed from mankind in order to live according to the Book and to explain content in detail. In order to turn people's attention to Allah and to frighten them, some tests such as famine, calamities and terrifying wars were tried; and some divine miracles were shown through Prophets. Even with extreme opposition, a small group of people accepted this way of life and eventually the religion of Allah established here.

Gradually, the hypocrites among prominent persons and priests themselves presented the divine miracle as the gift of Prophets; distorted religion according to their whims and interests and thus tried to put in force a new lifestyle. The Prophets were started to consider as incarnations of Allah and sons of Allah, and attributed a share in the powers and rights of Allah. In earlier days, Veda was transferred to generations through oral statements. Later years, hypocrites began to write books distortedly interpreting certain parts without considering whole Veda and adding untruths. Without trying to learn Veda's soul, they taught the common people that Heavenly reward can be attained by 'eating its body' (mere reading without trying to understand the messages). Then they introduced the books such as Upanishads, gospels, mythologies and religious rituals written by their own hands as the basis of the life. Since man is hasty and hedonistic, they were prepared to follow the shortcuts made by the above said people. Subsequently various kinds of thoughts and philosophies were originated which resulted into partiality and a complex of meaningless practices and rituals. As a result of this, the *Islam* (the way of life satisfied by the Lord, from Adam to the last men) became just a religion. Then, in order to show Straight path to men Allah introduces His scripture in another language through another Messenger. People who have been entirely detracted having false pride as the followers of the previous Prophet will be in the forefront in opposing this scripture and new Messenger!

All existing religious practices in the world including the traditional religion of Muslims are rejecting and denying the Qur'an. Those who dedicate their lives and pray to Allah or '*Yehova*' or '*Jagadeeshwar*' are believers, and those who pray, worship, chant and pay offerings to His creations such as *Prophet muhammed, Badar* Martyrs, *Muhyadheen Sheikh*, Jesus, Saints, *Moosa, Uzair*, Rama, Krishna and Buddha are disbelievers, whichever may be their caste, religion, dress or nationality. Whoever invokes any creatures other than the Creator is invoking only the cursed satan is mentioned in the verses 4: 116-117. The inmates of the hellfire are those who hide and reject the Qur'an verses after receiving It. The non-Muslims who have not received The Soul of Qur'an will not be considered as disbelievers. Qur'an is the only Scripture for entire mankind after its codification till the end of the world as per the verses 7: 157-158. The Soul of Qur'an is the words and guidance from the Creator of entire mankind including Hindus, Jews, Christians, Muslims, Atheists etc. and One who controls them and provides air, water, light and soil for them. Qur'an is the ultimate form of the previous scriptures, which testifies and confirms previous Holy books and preserves them. Scriptures have been revised without having any changes in the basic principles, just as college and school text books are being revised periodically. And this revision has been made not as separate books for Hindus, Christians and Muslims.

Today in the entire society the natural Islam is reflected comparatively more in Hindus, Christians and even in Atheists than Muslims; if anyone observes through the light of Qur'an. Since Prophet Mohammad is the last Prophet and Qur'an exists in the same language form as it was presented, there does not arise the need of new book or messenger. When the Muslims deviate from the principles of Qur'an and reach the state of ignorance by darkening their entire life, the result will be the end of the world. Before that, Allah will bring again Jesus into the world in order to emphasize the reality of Islam for the entire world. Qur'an and Prophet Mohammad are Mercy as mentioned in the verses 21:107and 25:1. Muslims all over the world except in *Hijas* (the Provinces *include Mecca* and *Madeena*) will be misled by *Maseeh-A-Ddhajjal* (Anti-Christ) who comes before Jesus. By the second coming of Jesus, Islam -the Lord's way of life- will be put into force, and onwards everybody will realize that Islam is the only comprehensive and complete way of life.

The Book (Al- Kithab):

The Creator of all who created Heaven and earth and all the things in between them from nothingness, is the Omniscient. And Qur'an being, His wise words are the knowledge of three times-present, past and future. One third of Qur'an verses are concerned with past, one third with present and one third with future- the warning of the events to be happened. First of all, He documented and kept the Qur'an in a safe compact disc which is the constitution of the Universe and the ways and practice of all time which is called "*Al-Kithab*"-The Book. Read together the verses 56: 77-78 and 85: 21-22.

The Scripture was periodically revealed from the Paradise to the Earth having the same soul with different bodies. That is to say, if the body of Bhagavatgeetha is Sanskrit, the body of *Thourath* is Hebrew, the body of *Injeel* is Aramaic, and the body of Qur'an is Arabic, the soul (*Adhikr*) is the same. Qur'an means The Book for repeated reading. So all the scriptures revealed is Qur'an. As per the verses 15: 90-91 it can understand that the previous Book revealed was The Qur'an .The '*Zaboo*r' (Psalm) mentioned in the verses 4:163 and 21:105 is Qur'an itself. Only the difference is it was in poetical form. '*Adhikr*' means the soul of the Book in ones heart's language. It is the food, cloth and sight of human soul as told in the verses 6:104 7:26; 11: 88. Prophet taught that what is meant by seven verses mentioned in 15:87 is '*Ummulkithab*'- *Fathiha*. Both in the verses 13:39 and 43:4 it is mentioned that *Ummulkithab*-mother of the Book- is with Allah. If all messengers have been presented with Qur'an only, Alkithab which consists of both Qur'an and Ummulkithab itself was presented to Prophet Mohammad.

Ar-Rooh (The spirit):

As per the verses 4: 171; 15: 29; 32: 9; 38: 72 it is told that all the men including Prophet Jesus have been given 'Rooh' from the 'Rooh' of Creator. As per the verses 16: 102; 26: 193; 78: 38 the Angel *Jibreel* has been mentioned as 'Rooh'. In the verses 16: 2 and 42: 52 Qur'an has been mentioned as 'Rooh'. If the Soul of Qur'an is the soul of the Book and the meaning is its life, then 'Rooh' is *'Kalimath'* combined by soul and life.

What is the difference between sleep and death?

Sleep is a minor death. During sleep only soul is departed from the body and life is not departed as explained in the verses 6: 60 and 39: 42, while in death both the soul and life are departed. That means *'Rooh'*- Spirit- is departed. One has the soul, only when the remembrance about of Allah is maintained with the Soul of Qur'an. Those who don't have it are in the state of sleep; they have only life without soul. This is the reason for saying that the hypocrites who knowingly hide the Soul of Qur'an are equal to killed people as told in the verses 2:99; 63: 4; 80: 17.

What is Qur'an?

In the verse 36: 69 says: This is nothing but a '*Dhikr*' and a clear Qur'an. '*Dhikr*' mentioned here is the 'Soul of Qur'an and the Arabic text is its body. When the servant contacts with his Master through the opening Sura '*Fathiha*' which is the mother of Qur'an (*Ummul Qur'an*), there is a request "Show us the Straight path". As an answer to this, Qur'an-the Straight path as mentioned in the verse 6: 126 which includes the verses from *Sura Baqara* to *Sura An-nas* is given. There are 114 *Suras* in Qur'an. Since there is not completely mentioned a specific subject in a particular *sura*, it can't be called a chapter or lesson. Entire sentences in Qur'an which contains 6236 verses are highly philosophical and independent. The verse is called '*Ayath*'. '*Ayath*' has the meaning such as sign, divine miracle and evidence. In other words, each verse of Qur'an is a sign.

Codification:

The Angel *Jibreel* appeared and vested The Qur'an into the heart of Prophet Mohammad and the Prophet who did not know to read and write wanted some of his followers who were literate, to record those verses in such and such *Suras*. They recorded them accordingly. In certain situations a *Surath* was revealed as a whole. Every year in the month of *'Ramdhan'* in which Qur'an was revealed, *Jibreel* used to hear by making Mohammad read Qur'an. In this way, during the last *'Ramdhan'* of Prophet's life, he made Mohammad read Qur'an and heard it twice. During the evening of the Prophet's life, religious renounce originated under the leadership of the pseudo prophet *'Musailimathul kadhab'*. Then during the rule of *Aboobaker*-the first *Khaleefa*- a war took place with them. In this war, a lot of Qur'an by hearted believers became martyrs. Due to fear that Qur'an may be lost unless it is preserved in the form of a Book, it was codified during the period of *Aboobaker* by the encouragement of *Umer.* Those who had Qur'an by hearted were assembled together under the leadership of *Zaid-ibn-Thabith*, one of the writers, and also called to bring the scripts available with them written in leather scrolls, palm leaves and bones. By comparing all these scripts with the by hearted Qur'an the first edition of the book form of Qur'an which is seen today, was formed. That edition was entrusted with the Prophet's wife *Hafza* in order to preserve. The manuscripts copies had with others were compared and confirmed with this edition. Gradually, when Islam was spread into various countries, more editions of Qur'an became necessary. Thus during the period of *Usman* eight imprints were taken and sent to various countries. Reading regulations were made not to lose congruence of ideas due to changes in the reading of Qur'an when the languages of the different countries varied. Through the verses 75:16-19 Allah says: "Move not your tongue concerning the Qur'an to make haste with. It is for Us to collect It as well as how to recite It. So when We have recited It (through *Jibreel*) follow Its method of recitation. It is then We who must explain It". The verse 20:114 says: exalted is Allah, the true controller. Do not hurry while reading the Qur'an before its revelation has been accomplished for you. But pray "Oh my Lord! Increase me the knowledge". The verse 15: 9 says: "Indeed We Ourselves have sent down the Reminder -Soul of Qur'an; just as We are safeguarding It". So it's clear that Qur'an should be read, learn and taught according to the codified order from *Sura Baqara* downwards.

The Soul of Qur'an (Adhikr)

Adhikr-The Soul of Qur'an is the only Book revealed from the paradise. It is a splendid book, no falsehood shall approach It either before or after codification since it is a revelation from the one who is wise, Praiseworthy. Nothing has been told to you except what has been told Messengers before you. Whoever hides *Adhikr* after receiving It will have severe punishment. See the verses 41: 41-43. Through the verse 21: 24 Allah command Prophet to say, "This is '*Adhikr*' (The Message) with me and the Message as well as whoever came before me". Allah has never told that the body of Qur'an will be preserved eternally; on the other hand, it is told that the *'Adhikr'* (soul) will be preserved as told in the verse 15:9.

The verse 38: 8 says: Has *'Adhikr'* been revealed just to him among us? Nay, they are in doubt about the *'Dhikree'*; rather they have not tasted any torment! Here as well as in the verses, 18: 100 and 20: 14, 124; '*Dhikree*' means only The Soul of Qur'an. The '*Adhikra*' mentioned in the verses 6: 90; 7: 2; 11: 120; 51:55 and 89:23 also means The Soul of Qur'an. The word '*Adhikr*' is mentioned about 100 places in Qur'an. In all these places, '*Adhikr*' is the Soul of Qur'an. Through the verse 63: 9 by addressing the believers Allah says: Your property or children should not obstruct you from '*Dhikrillah*'; if anybody acts in that way, then such will be the losers. Here '*Dhikrillah*' means Allah's Remembrance, but the message is only the Soul of Qur'an. Because the remembrance of Allah is possible anywhere he is. Then what is meant by the '*Dhikrillah*' is the assemblage where is explaining the Soul of Qur'an; or the '*Qutuba*' (Speech) mentioned in 62: 9. So '*Qutuba*' must be the explaining of the Soul of Qur'an. It is told in the verse 29: 45 that, 'the Remembrance of Allah with Soul of Qur'an is the greatest'.

The Ticket (Thadhkirah)

The Soul of Qur'an is the Ticket to anyone who likes to return to the paradise. Both the verses 73:19 and 76:29 say indeed this is a Ticket for anyone who wishes to adopt a way to his Lord. But as per the verse 69:48 it is told that it will be used as a ticket by the heedful only, means the one who follow the Soul of Qur'an. As per the verse 39:33 it is told that he who reaches the Truth and he makes it truthful, such are the only heedful. As per the verses 74:49-51 it is told about the disbelievers that what is wrong with them that they flee from the '*Tadkirah*' as if they were affrighted wild donkeys running away from a roaring lion? As per the verse 26:212 it is told that indeed satans have been prevented from hearing the Soul of Qur'an, but not from hearing the body or meaning of Qur'an.

The Guidance (Huda)

In the verse 20:123 it is told that should Guidance ever come to you from Me, then anyone who follows My Guidance shall never stray away nor be regretted. Guidance is The Book which is come forever from Allah. The Soul of Qur'an is the only Guidance to entire mankind as per the verses 2:2, 38,185. Even though the Soul of Qur'an is revealed as the Guidance for all worlds, the believers only accept It as the Guidance. The verses 7:52, 203; 16:64 etc ends as the Soul of Qur'an is the Guidance and Mercy for the people who believe. The Impartial Lord will not punish any people unless they received the Guidance. The verse 17:15 says, whoever accept the Guidance is for his own benefit; who goes astray by rejecting It, then the soul makes her own loss: No bearer of burdens can bear the burden of another: and nor would We punish until We had sent a Messenger.

The Criterion (Furqan)

The Criterion-*Furqan* is the Soul of Qur'an by which the only way to Paradise and different ways to Hell in entire life can be separated or the Truth and false in all places and time can be distinguished. Both in the verses 2:185 and 25:1 it is told that Qur'an is sent down as Guidance or warnings to entire world and a Criterion for discriminating Truth and untruth. *Furqan*, the Soul of Qur'an, is the touchstone to recognize the way of Allah and the ways of satan.

The Explanation (Bayan)

The verse 3: 138 says, The Soul of Qur'an is an Explanation –*Bayan*, for mankind, as well as the Guidance and Instruction for the heedful. Both in the verses 6:38, 16: 89 it is told that the Soul of Qur'an is explained everything and is a Guidance, a Mercy, and good news for those who submit everything to Allah. To the Prophet not only Qur'an, but other unrecorded divine message has also been revealed. The verses 53: 2-3 it is told that "Prophet won't pronounce of his own desire, and it is no less than divine message received through inspiration". So the life and sayings of the Prophet Mohammad is the explanation of Qur'an indeed from Allah. But as per the verse 4: 64 it is ordered that if the saying of Prophet is contradicting against any word of Qur'an should not be accepted. Through the verse 7: 203 Allah orders the Prophet to say: I follow only what has been inspired in me by my Lord. In all the verses such as 17: 41; 18: 54; 30: 58 and 39: 27 it is told that We have explained all sort of examples for mankind in this Book. Read together in the verse 75: 19

The Balance (Meezan)

The verse 42: 17 says that He is the One who has sent down the Book with the Truth, and as the Balance. In the verse 57: 25 Allah says that surely We send Our Messengers with clear signs and send down with them the Book and the Balance- scales of Justice. Here all the three words- the clear signs, the Book and the Balance mean the Soul of Qur'an. So the Qur'an is the Balance to keep the Universe in its equilibrium, but only believers will utilize It as the Balance throughout life. Whoever not makes judgement in his individual, family and social life as per the Soul of Qur'an, such are the disbelievers wrong-doers and transgressors according to the verses 5: 44, 45 and 47 respectively.

The Truth (Haq)

Through the verse10: 108 Allah orders the Prophet to say: "Oh mankind! The 'Truth' has reached you from your Lord! Anyone who accepts It as Guidance is guided only for his own sake; while any soul who strays away, will only become loss at her own risk, for I am not a custodian over you. The verse 39: 41 says "We have sent down you the Book with 'Truth' for mankind. Anyone who is guided will be so for his own sake, while anyone who goes astray will only stray because of it as well, you are not a custodian over them". If not utilize the Soul of Qur'an as Balance or Truth in this world, there will not be any weight on the Day of Judgment as explained in the verses 7: 8-9. In the verses like 34: 26 ; 39: 69, 75 it is told that the judgment will be made with Truth-The Soul of Qur'an among them on the Day of Judgment.

The Justice (Qisthw)

Through the verse 5: 8 by calling believers Allah says, act steadfast for Allah under the shade of Qur'an, as witnesses with the Justice. What is meant by this is: You do Justice with Qur'an. The meaning of '*Qisthw*' told in verses such as 4: 135 and 57: 25 is definitely the Soul of Qur'an. The verses 5: 42, 49: 9 and 60: 8 end as indeed Allah like those who do justice with The Soul of Qur'an. Both in the verses 17: 35 and 26: 182 it is told that you should weigh with '*Qisthwasul Musthaqeem*' -means, indeed you should weigh with the balance of justice which is the Straight path.

The Insight (Baswa'er)

In the verses 6: 104; 7: 203 and 45: 20 it is told that the Soul of Qur'an is the Insight for entire mankind; and if anybody uses It, the benefit will be for himself; and also if anybody pretends to be blind regarding It, the harm will be for his own soul. Insight means the instrument which shows to each soul -male or female- her seat in the hereafter whether it is in Hell or in Paradise. This is also an instrument which shows in advance whether one sees the ugly face of satan or the pleasant face of Allah at the time of death i.e. by utilizing The Soul of Qur'an as Insight one can analyze whether he belongs to the party of satan or the party of Allah.

The Proof (Burhan)

The Proof the clear light mentioned in the verse 4: 174 as well as the Mercy, Bounty and the Straight path mentioned in the verses 4: 175 is The Soul of Qur'an. Only for those who can quote a word from Qur'an as a proof for any matter, Qur'an will argue in favor and will stand as a witness for them. The verse 28: 75 says We shall drag a witness out of every community and We shall say: "bring on your proof"! Then they will realize that indeed the Truth belongs to Allah while whatever they were inventing has left them in the lurch. In the verse

21: 24 three names '*Burhan*', '*Haqq*' and '*Dhikr*' is used for The Soul of Qur'an. Therefore each individual should have a proof from the Soul of Qur'an to clear their activities in front of His Lord in the Day of Judgment.

The Light (An-Noor)

In the verse 24: 35 it is told that Allah is the Light of Heaven and Earth. Through the verses 5: 16-17 say, indeed a Light and clear Book have been brought to you from Allah with which He will guide any one who seeks His approval along the ways of peace; He leads them out of darkness into the light by His Permissions, and guides them to the Straight path. The Light, the Permission and Straight path mentioned in the verses 5: 16-17 is the Soul of Qur'an. The verse 7: 157 ends as, those who follow the Light which is sent down with the prophet; such will be the only prosperous. The Light mentioned in the verse 64: 8 is also the Soul of Qur'an. By burning the satanic habits such as pride, jealousy, arrogance, selfishness etc with the Light-the soul of Qur'an, one can fulfill the aim of life. Read together the verse 42: 52. Knowledge, Guidance and enlightening Book mentioned in both verses 22: 8 and 31: 20 is the Soul of Qur'an

Goal of life is to go back to Allah ie.to the Paradise itself by burning all the satanic characteristics such as arrogance, envy and pride with the Light, the Soul of Qur'an. Both in the verses 9: 32 and 61: 8 it is told that hypocrites try to extinguish the light by blowing with their mouth; but Allah will indeed perfect His light. As per the verse 66: 8 the believers prayer will be always that "Our Lord, perfect our Light for us, and grant us forgiveness; indeed you are capable of everything".

The Witness (Shahid)

As per the verse 11: 17 Allah says that what about some one who is upon a clear Evidence from his Lord and to whom a witness from Him is reciting while *Moosa's* Book remain before It, as a Guide and a Mercy? Such persons believe with it; anyone from the factions rejects It, then fire is promised to him, so you should not be in any doubt about It. Indeed It is the Truth from your Lord. Yet many among men do not believe. The verse 2: 121 ends as, whoever hides The Soul of Qur'an such are the only losers. Through the verse 2: 140 Allah ask "who is more unjust than those who hide The Soul of Qur'an-the witness from Allah?" As per the verse 6:19 both Allah and The Soul of Qur'an is great witness. Through the verses 2: 143 and 22: 78 it is commanded that believers should understand

Prophet Mohammad from the Soul of Qur'an and should witness that life to the entire mankind.

The Wisdom (Hikmath)

The soul of Qur'an is mentioned as Wise reminder in the verse 3:58. In the verse 11: 1 it is told that this is a Book with full of philosophical verses, further it is explained in detail. This Book is sent down from the One who is Wise, Encompassed all. It is told in the verse 2: 269 that He gives Wisdom to anyone He wishes and anyone He gives Wisdom to, receives an abundant Boon. It is told in the verse 36: 2 that Qur'an is full of Wisdom. Otherwise '*Hikmath*' is called the ability to understand Qur'an verses by combining and comparing with similar verses. In the verse 31: 12 it is told that *Luqman* has been endowed with Wisdom in order to acknowledge his gratitude to Allah.

The Advice (Mouidhath)

The verse 16: 125 says, invite to your Lord's way with '*Hikmath*' and best Advice. Here the '*Hikmath*' means the highly philosophical and wise verses of Qur'an. The verse10: 57 says, Oh mankind! Advice has been come to you from your Lord, healing for whatever is in your chests; plus Guidance and Mercy for believers. So in the case of believers '*Mouidhath*' is best advice and in the case of mankind it's warning. '*Mouidhath*' is used as lesson in the verse 2: 66. As per the verse 3: 138 '*Mouidhath*' is used as best advice. In the verse 24: 34 it is told that: We have already sent down to you verses making things clear, an illustration from the story of people who passed away before you and a best advice for those heedful. What is meant by '*Mouidhath*' is similar observance and figure of the '*Hikmath*' verses of Qur'an for today's which having clear in ideas and full of wisdom. In the verse 25: 33 the '*Mouidhath*' is mentioned as the best explanation.

The Healing (Shifa')

If it is told in the verse 10: 57 that Qur'an is Healing for entire mankind, it is told in the verse 41: 44 that Qur'an is the Guidance and Healing for those who believe. In the verse 17: 82 it is told that there are Healing and Mercy with Qur'an for believers; but for wrongdoers it cause nothing but loss over loss. If it is told in the verse 9: 124 that the Qur'an will increase the faith of believers, it is told in the verse 125 that for hypocrites -those who have disease in their hearts, it will increase filth over filth. The verse 69: 50 says: Indeed Qur'an is a cause of sorrow for disbelievers. So one will become a believer only if he is convinced with the Soul of Qur'an by which he has to clear all doubts in all matters.

The Mercy (Rahmath), the Bounty (Fadhl)

Both in the verses 2:105 and 3: 74 Allah says, For His mercy He specially chooses whom He pleases, for Allah is the Lord of Bounties unbounded. Here what is meant by Mercy and Bounty is the Soul of Qur'an. Through the verse 10: 58 Allah commands Prophet to say: let them rejoice with the Bounty and Mercy of Allah that is better than anything they are earning. While explaining this, Prophet taught: *'among you the best one is those who learn and teach the Soul of Qur'an'*. The Prophet also taught: *Qur'an is prosperity, after that there is no poverty; and without It there is no prosperity*. The verse 76: 31 says, He will admit anyone He wishes in to His Mercy, while He has kept prepared painful torment for wrongdoers. Through the verse 47: 24 Allah asks: Do they not then earnestly seek to understand and be proud with the Qur'an, or are their hearts locked up about it? Through the verse 67: 22 Allah asks: then someone who walks prone on their face better guided than someone who walks properly along a Straight path? Those who are living despicably in this world after receiving Qur'an and without having something to cling to, they will be dragged into the Hell prone on their faces; and they are the people who have gone astray and will be in a most evil plight as mentioned in the verses 17: 97-98 and 25: 34. Read together the verses 3:79 and 4: 113.

The Forefront (Imam)

Both in the verse 11: 17 and 46: 12 the Qur'an and *Thourath* are mentioned as Imam-leader- and Mercy. As per the verse 17: 71 it is told: On the Day of Judgment We shall call together all mankind with their respective leaders. Those who are given their record in their right hand will read it with pleasure. And they will not be dealt with unjustly in the least. The verse 72 continues as: Those who were blind towards the Imam in this world will be more blinded in the Hereafter, and most astray from the path. See the explanation 2: 6-7. The verses 17: 13-14 say: We have tied every man's fate around his neck; and We shall produce a book for him on the day of judgement that he will find it as an illuminated open book. It will be said to him: 'Read your own book: sufficient is yourself this Day to make out an account of you'. The book mentioned in the verses 18: 49; 39: 69 and 45: 28-29 is the same. Therefore, whoever hears, reads, thinks and discuses with others about the Soul of Qur'an throughout his entire life, his book of deeds will be worth-reading and gaining weight in the balance. They are the people who receive the Book in the right hand. The Prophet taught: *You should keep up Qur'an in forefront of you as Imam. Qur'an is from Allah and withdraws into Him. If you make it behind, it will push you into Hell.* In all the verses such as 7: 170; 29: 45 and 35: 29 it is commanded to give first preference to The Soul of Qur'an than any other deed including '*swalath*'(Five time's Prayer).

The Safeguard (Muhaimin)

As per the verse 59: 23 Allah and 5: 48 The Soul of Qur'an is '*The Muhaimin'*. It means safeguard, preserve, protect, supervise, maintain and support etc. Then what we understand by saying, 'Qur'an is the Safeguard of the Book' is that the essence of all divine learning contained in previous books is vested in the Soul of Qur'an. The Soul of Qur'an will exist safely till the end of the world. Though the verses of Allah and the human sayings are intermingled in the existing previous Scriptures, through the witness of The Soul of Qur'an they can be understood distinctly. Therefore, The Soul of Qur'an will safeguard the believer and his family, houses, property from all disasters in this world and from the Hell in the Hereafter.

The Speech (Hadeeth)

The verse 4: 78 ends as, what is wrong with such these people that they cannot understand this Speech. Both the verses 4: 87, 122 end with a question that whose speech can be truer than Allah's? The verses 7: 185 and 77: 50 end with a question: then what Speech after this will they go to believe in? The verse 45: 6 ends as, what Speech will they believe after rejecting Allah and His verses? All the *Hadeeth* specified in above verses as well as specified in verses 52: 34 and 68: 44 means The Soul of Qur'an. The best speech specified in verse 39: 23 is also the Soul of Qur'an. The best Speech is the words of Allah, which is the Soul of Qur'an. At the same time the sayings of Prophet is *Hadiya* -the explanation of Qur'an which is received beyond reason. But today, the Book bearers who could not distinguish between the soul and body, consider the sayings of the Prophet as *Hadeeth*, and thus make both the sayings of Prophet and Qur'an false. In other words, in order to understand the Qur'an, Qur'an itself is enough. But *Hadiya*, the saying of Prophet is to understand its explanation. For example, Qur'an has told about the prayer of the soul. But the prayer (*swalath*) in which body also participates, is explained as the teaching of Prophet. Through the verse

20: 14 Allah ordered Prophet and believers to establish regular *swalath* in order to preserve the Soul of Qur'an. Then, without reading The Soul of Qur'an which is the Speech or news of the Creator for entire mankind; if anyone reads any other things like news paper, organizational publications, literary books, material education books etc, he is ungrateful and disbeliever. Read together the verses 2: 23-24.

The Ways and Practice (Sunnath)

The Ways and Practice of Allah is Qur'an itself. In another sense, Qur'an is the knowledge of the past, present and future of the all knowing Lord. In the verse 17: 77 it is told that this was Our practice with the Messengers We sent before you. You will find no changes in our ways. In the verse 33:61 Allah says about hypocrites and their blind followers: cursed people, whenever and wherever they are found, they shall be seized and slain one by one. Then the verse 62 continues: such is Allah's practice with those who have passed on before; you will never find any change in Allah's practice. Through the verse 35: 43 Allah asks, are they only waiting for what happened to primitive people? Yet you will never find any change in Allah's Practice, nor will you ever find any postponement for Allah's Practice.

The verse 68: 4 says; indeed you have been with tremendous character. Here mentioned 'tremendous character' is the character of Qur'an. The practice of Prophet also was indeed Qur'an. But today by ignoring the '*Hadeeth*' and '*Sunnath*' of Allah, Muslims follow the books written by His creatures. Moreover they blame the believers that they are without '*Hadeeth*' and '*Sunnath*'. If a people do injustice to their Prophets or reject the verses of Allah, they cannot continue in that place for a long time. Either Allah's punishment will destroy them, or any other people will conquer them. Or else the followers of Prophet will survive them. This will definitely be the Practice of Allah to Muslims who live by ignoring the Soul of Qur'an. If the people are not trying to implement and propagate Allah's Book, Allah will substitute another people in their place who are ready for it as explained in the verse 4: 133.

The Message (Risalath)

The verse 5: 67 says; Oh Messenger! Deliver whatever has been sent down to you by your Lord. If you do not do so, you will not have conveyed His Message. Allah will defend you from mankind: certainly Allah will not guide the people who hide the Soul of Qur'an. As per the verse 7: 62 Prophet *Nooh* told his people: I delivered my Lord's Messages to you and counseled you sincerely. I know something from Allah that you don't know. As per verses 7: 68 Prophet 'Hood', 7: 79 Prophet *Swalih* and 7: 93 Prophet *Shuhaib* said that Oh my people! I have delivered my Lord's Messages to you, and counseled you sincerely, then why should I grieve over a disbelieving people? The Soul of Qur'an is the Message from Paradise for the entire creatures from the Creator of all. Then whoever received, read and understood It but not molded their life accordingly will have to return Hell, the home of disbeliever satan. Generally whatever may be the language of a message (visa, appointment order etc.) which has been received for achievement in material life, man is cautious enough to understand it and work accordingly. While the 'Letter' of the Creator in ones heart's language is received but not using and not giving others to use, then he will be the ungrateful and the lost one as explained in the verse 6: 26.

The Trust (Amanath)

The verse 33: 72 says: We did indeed offer the Trust to Heaven and Earth and to the mountains. Yet they refused to carry It, and shrank back from It. But men accepted It; he has been unjust and ignorant. The verse 73 continues: the purpose of the '*Amanath*' revealed is to punish the hypocritical men and hypocritical women, and men and women who associate others with Allah. However Allah relents with believing men and believing women, Allah is forgiving Merciful. It is told in both verses 23: 8 and 70: 32 that the succeeding believers will preserve their trusts and their pledges. Since the Soul of Qur'an is the Trust and Balance to keep the Universe in its equilibrium, Muslims, the carriers of It if not ready to utilize It and not giving other people to utilize It as the Balance and Trust in order to keep the universe in its equilibrium; Allah will entrust It to a people who will not hide It as mentioned in the verse 6: 89. Today, the believers should utilize all their times, property and all other blessings for learning and teaching the Soul of Qur'an-The Trust.

The Interpretation (Thafseer)

Through the verse 25: 33 Allah says, they will not come to you with any question –example, unless We will bring you the Truth and the best Interpretation, so that nobody need ask such question till the Day of Judgment. From this we can understand that the true Interpretation of Qur'an is from Allah and not from prophet or any other persons. The verse 4: 105 says, We have sent the Book down to you with the Truth so that you may judge among mankind as Allah intends.

As per the command of the verse 20: 114, whenever begin to hear, think and tell about the Soul of Qur'an, one should politely pray by his mind: "Oh my Lord, increase me knowledge". Qur'an should be explained with Qur'anic verses and the Prophet's sayings. So one who explains Qur'an should never say, 'my opinion is this'. But he should consider that Allah is explaining through His servant. The explanation of Qur'anic verses as in today's situations is called '*Mouidath*'. In other words, '*Mouidath*' -similar examples and figures of the Wisdom verses- is the interpretation as explained in the verse 3: 138.

What for Qur'an?

The Soul of Qur'an is meant for identifying the losers such as the disbelievers, wrongdoers, arrogant, *mujrims*(madmen), transgressors, sinners, aimless men, heedless men, doubters, frustrated ones, associates, forgers, rejecters, mischief makers, squanderers, repudiators, aggressors, trespassers etc. and not to include in those groups. Also meant to travel through the only way of Paradise without falling in Hell, being entrapped by satan or '*Thagooth*' -Arrogant force.

For getting response to the appeals and for accepting *swalath*, *zakkath*, fasting and *hajj* etc, there are two conditions specified in the verse 2: 186. (1). follow the Soul of Qur'an as should be followed (2). Believe in Allah as per the Soul of Qur'an submitting. The literate can only become believer with the Soul of Qur'an-the permission of Allah as told in the verse 10:100. Both the verses 13:14 and 40:50 end as 'the prayer of disbelievers will not increase except astray'.

Both in the verses 18:57 and 32: 22 it is told that who does more wrong than one who is reminded the verses of his Lord in his heart's language, then turns away from them, forgetting the deeds which his hands have sent forth? Indeed We shall exact due retribution to such *Mujrims*. As per the verses 28: 48 the disbelievers say "(about Qur'an and *Thourath*) 'double sorcery' to back each other up" and they say: "we disbelieve in everything". As per the verses 49-50 Allah commands Prophet to say: "bring a Book from Allah's presence which will be better Guide than either of them, so that I may follow It, if you are Truthful". If they do not respond to you, then know they are merely following their own whims. Who is more misguided than someone who follows his own whim without having any Guidance from Allah? Indeed Allah will not guide such wrongdoing people to the Straight path.

It is told in the verses 2: 6-7 as to the disbelievers who knowingly hide the Soul of Qur'an, is the same whether you warn them or do not warn them, they still will not believe. Allah has sealed their hearts and hearing; and over their sights hangs a veil; and for them have grievous torment. The verse 63: 6 says: It is the same whether, you ask for their forgiveness or not ask for their forgiveness, Allah will never forgive them, indeed Allah will never guide such transgressing people. The verse 9: 67 ends as indeed the hypocrites, they are the transgressors. Both in the verses 9: 68 and 13: 25 it is told that on them is the curse and for them is the terrible home. In the verse 39: 63 Allah says: Those who hide the verses of Allah, such are the losers. And in the verse 2: 99 it is told: None hide the verses of Allah except who are transgressors. The verse 7: 102 says: We did not find any agreement was ever kept by most of them, although We did find most of them as transgressors. Through the verse 59: 19 by addressing the believers Allah says: you should not be like the people who forgot Allah, when they forgot Allah, they forgot themselves. Such are only the transgressors. The believers keep Allah in their hearts with the Soul of Qur'an as explained in the verses 2: 152; 3: 190-191; 4: 103. Both in the verse 63: 4 and 80: 17 it is told that the hypocrites who hide the Soul of Qur'an are killed by Allah. The verses 51: 10-11say those who live as intoxicated and careless after getting the Soul of Qur'an are killed. The verse 41: 41 says, certainly those who hide the Soul of Qur'an when it is come to them will have severe torment.

Those who hide the clear Proofs and Guidance, after We have made It clear in the Book for mankind will have Allah's curse and that of those who are entitled to curse; except on those who repent, reform and say openly before what he was hiding; I will accept their repentance, for I am the Receiver of repentance, the Merciful, is told both in the verses 2: 159-160; 3: 86-89. Then the verse 2: 161 says, surely those who are disbelievers and die as '*Kuffar*' ,they are the ones on whom the curse of Allah the Angels and of all humankind. In the verse 4: 140 Allah says: He will collect the hypocrites who quote Qur'an verses out of place, distort them and hide them, and also the disbelievers who listen to it -all together in the Hell. As the verse 4: 145 the hypocrites will go to Hell even without trial. The verse 46: 35 ends with the question shall any people will be destroyed except those who are transgressors? As well as the verse 6: 47 ends as: will any be destroyed except the people who are wrongdoers? In short, the world will end when all the people will become wrongdoers or transgressors. Therefore, the only way to prolong the life of the Universe is to convey the Soul of Qur'an to entire mankind.

The verse 7:40 says, "indeed those who reject Our verses and treat them with arrogance, will not open the gates of Heaven, nor will they enter the Paradise until the camel can pass through the eye of the tailor's needle. Such is the reward for the *Mujrims"*. The verse 10: 17 says, then who does more wrong than the one who invents a lie against Allah, or rejects His verses without trying to understand, indeed, He will not allow to prosper such *Mujrims*. In Qur'an more than fifty verses mention about the *Mujrims*. In all these places *Mujrims* include the hypocrites who knowingly hide the Soul of Qur'an, and the *fujjar*- plural of fajir- who eat the body of Qur'an without trying to understand the soul. When believers recite the verse 1: 7: "Not the path upon whom your wrath happened", they should bear in mind the way of hypocrites and when they say: "And not who go astray" they should bear in mind the way of *fujjar* who follow blindly hypocrites.

To form Faith in Allah:

As per the verse 59: 23 Allah is the believer. To become a believer the knowledge about Him submitting by 6236 verses should be formed. Since Allah is impartial by teaching the Soul of Qur'an which contains the only way to Him and different ways of satan. The believer who represents Him on earth should consider the Soul of Qur'an as the Balance and Trust to keep the Universe in its equilibrium and propagate It throughout the world. Those who hide and reject The Soul of Qur'an which is the Food, cloth and sight of the human souls are hypocrites and disbelievers Since they are serving the disbeliever satan, they are the inmates of Hell from among mankind as mentioned in the verses 2: 39, 9: 68, 48:6 etc. Therefore to distinguish the way of the Lord and satan in every time and place The Soul of Qur'an should be utilized as Criterion and Insight. In Qur'an there are ninety nine verses which describe satan.

One may become heedful by keeping Allah in his heart with the Soul of Qur'an, or may become '*muhsin*'-one who lives under the light-Soul of Qur'an. To understand character and nature of the winners such as forerunners -Those who enter the Paradise without trail, virtuous men, reformers, justice men, devotees, men of patience, men of perseverance, heedful, truthful, honorable men who entered the Paradise and to follow them, the Ticket- Soul of Qur'an is a must.

The verse 16:97 says: whether man or woman whoever do honorable deeds and he is a believer, indeed We will give him a pure glorious life in this world and We will give reward according to their best deeds in this world. Today the best deed is to learn and teach the Soul of Qur'an. Read together the verse 40:40.

To form Faith in Angels:

The Angels are a peculiar creature, created from the light. They are all believers who do not disobey Allah In anything He commands them. And they do whatever they ordered to. They are considered as the governing servants of the Universe. They are also acting as the messengers to convey the Message from the Lord to human messengers. To put it brief the Soul of Qur'an should be utilized as Insight to fulfill the belief in Angels i.e. who are Angels? Do they know the hidden things? What is their role in the governing system of Universe? What is their connection with man? How they differ from *Jinns*? What is their peculiarity from other creations etc? In Qur'an there are ninety nine verses which describe the Angels. Read together the verses13:13; 16:2; 19:64.

To understand about *Jinns,* the Soul of Qur'an is necessary. They had been created from the flames of fire before human being. Just like men they have freedom either to be grateful or ungrateful. For each and every man there is a *Jinn* companion staying as his soul mate. In brief, nobody can become a believer without reforming his Soul mate, who whispers in the breast of mankind, with the Soul of Qur'an as specified in the verses 114: 4-6. Read together the verses 43: 36-39 and 50: 27-30.

To form Faith in Books:

When we understand the contents of Qur'an as a whole, then only the belief in Book is formed. From the Lord of the world, only one Book has been sent down to Earth. The soul of the Book is the same, where as only the bodies are different. See the explanation 2: 2. If the books sent down during different periods include the rules and regulations for those particular periods, the soul of Qur'an which testifies and safeguards the previous books is for the entire mankind. See the explanation 5: 48.The soul of Qur'an as mentioned in the verses 41: 43 is a Splendid Book which explained all things; it is invisible, unique and impossible to undergo corrections and amendments. Through the verses 2: 23-24 and 10:

38 Allah has challenged to produce a *Sura* similar to that of 114 *Suras* in Qur'an. Subsequently Qur'an has told that even if men and *Jinns* work together it will be impossible for them to accept that challenge. The verse 21: 10 says: "We have sent down a Book for you. In which you have been remembered. Then will you not utilize your intelligence?" Prophet taught that whoever identified him self, he recognized his Lord. Then it is clear that this Book is meant for recognizing the Lord, oneself and aim of life. As per the verses 8: 22 and 55 in the sight of Allah the worst creatures are those who act as deaf and dumb without using their intelligence to understand the Soul of Qur'an. Read together the verse 98:6. In order to desist from the forbidden of Qur'an, one should know Its contents. As per the verse 54: 17 it is made very easy to understand the Soul of Qur'an.

To form Faith in Prophets:

All the Prophets were from human beings deputed by the Lord of the worlds to show a life way namely Islam-only life way satisfied by the Lord- as explained in the verses 2:136; 3:19, 85. Even though more than hundred and twenty four thousand Prophets have been dispatched, among them only three hundred and thirteen were appointed as messengers. The first messenger is Prophet *Nooh* and the last is *Muhammad.* Among the Prophets and messengers only twenty five are mentioned by name in Qur'an. As per the verse 57:25 all the messengers have been given 'The message', whereas the Prophets were following the concerned message. Even some Prophets have been assassinated by the transgressing people, not any messengers have been assassinated. It is when we follow and testify them by seeing their life from the Soul of Qur'an, only the faith in Prophets and messengers are formed. The quintessence messages of all previous books and Prophets are assembled in the Soul of Qur'an and Prophet Mohammad. As per the verses 7:158; 21:107; 34: 28 etc, Prophet Mohammad is dispatched as a Messenger as well as Mercy for all worlds from the time of his appointment till the Last Day of the world. As per both in the verses 2: 146 and 6: 20 it is told that those who are given the Book will know the Prophet as they know their own sons. Today the believers who holdfast the Soul of Qur'an with their molar teeth can only lead and witness of the Prophet's life in the society. Other Muslims by hiding Allah and prophet in the soul of Qur'an they are actually inviting *Maseeh-A-Ddajjal-* the thirtieth pseudo prophet. Among this boar people specified both in the verses 25:18 and 48: 12, the hypocritical disbelievers will enter the Hell without trail while the *fujjar* disbelievers who follow them blindly will be led to the Hell after trail. Read together the verses 4: 145 and 39: 71.

To form Faith in the Hereafter:

The believers in the Hereafter are those who are always living here with a mind that, on the Day of judgement both man and woman individually should have to answer about all moments of his fourth phase of life. If anybody living here without that awareness, their own hearings, sights, hands, skins, legs, and even earth will be witnessing against them as per the verses 17: 36; 36: 65; 41: 19-24; 99: 4-5 etc. One third of Qur'an verses explain the scenes that are to happen in the Hereafter. In the verse 2: 4 it has been told that the succeeded heedful are having steadfast belief of the Hereafter. Where the *Mujrims* will hang their heads before their Lord, and will say: Our Lord! We have observed and heard; so send us back we will act honorably; indeed we are convinced, is warned in the verse 32: 12. As per the verses 39: 69 and 75: on that day the scale of judgement will be the Soul of Qur'an. So the believers will utilize the Soul of Qur'an as the Balance and scale in this world itself considering the verse 16:64 and the Lord as impartial. See explanation 1: 3.

To form the Belief that Good and Bad is from Allah:

Impartial Allah by teaching the Soul of Qur'an from the paradise itself each and every human soul is given the ways of good and bad. Good way leads to Allah and Paradise where as bad ways lead to satan and Hell fire. Whenever having the remembrance of Allah with the Soul of Qur'an then only good things occur while in a situation forgetting Allah by ignoring the Soul of Qur'an bad things occur. In condition of forgetting Allah he will be trapped by the soul mate-satan.

As per the verse 8: 24, in believers Allah slips in between him and his heart; whereas in disbelievers stays satan- his soul mate. And therefore all deeds of disbelievers will become useless as mentioned in the verses 18: 103-105; 25: 21-23 and 47: 8-9. Since the control of all things is in the hand of Allah, there will not occur any disturbance, disasters and accidents from any creatures including satan without knowledge and permission of Lord of the worlds. The knowledge and permission of Impartial Lord is the Soul of Qur'an. Therefore the believers who utilize the soul of Qur'an as the Shield and Safeguard, not any bad thing or disaster will occur for them. As per the verse 4:78, it is told that when hypocrites achieve something good they will say: It is from Allah and when they are affected by something bad, they say: It is from you (Prophet). Oh Prophet! You say: All things are from Allah. What happened to these people that they fail to understand this speech? Then the verse 79 continues: whatever good happens to you is from Allah and whatever bad happens to you is from yourself i.e. from your soul mate -satan. It is told in all the verses such as 9: 51; 10: 61; 11: 6; 17: 13-14; 22: 70; 27: 75; 34: 3; 35: 11; 36: 12; 57: 22 that all the things happening in the Heaven and Earth and in between these in living and non-living things including man have been determined before hand by the Creator, and those have been recorded in the Book, that is the Soul of Qur'an.

Through the verse 36:69, after saying what is Qur'an, the verse 70 says: Qur'an is sent down in order to give warning to anyone who are alive, and that the charge may be proved against disbeliever who hide and reject It. But today most of the Muslims read Qur'an to the dead and near the graveyard. This is just opposite to the purpose for which the Qur'an is revealed. It is told in the verse 6: 36 that indeed only those who listen will respond to you. As to the dead, Allah will raise them up, and then unto Him will they return. That means, the Prophet or anyone can't make hear the dead. The verses 30: 52-53 say: Indeed, you cannot make the dead hear; nor even make the deaf hear the appeal, if they have turned their backs on it. No one can guide the blind out of their straying: only the one who believes in Our verses and they are committed to live in peace can be guided. The disbelivers don't consider what the Prophet has taught: *If you recite Qur'an without knowing the contents even in swalath, will be darted away from Islam as an arrow is darted away from its bow; and the recited Qur'an will witness and argue against you.* See the explanation 4: 43, 6:36

Who is the Kafir –disbeliever that Qur'an portrays?

Those who do not believe with Allah as submitting the Qur'an verses, those who approve Qur'an but do not approve the sayings of the Prophet –which is the explanation of the Qur'an, those who approve some Messengers of Allah but do not approve some others, those who do approve certain Qur'an verses but reject other verses, those who use the verses revealed in *Mecca* but do not use what is revealed in *Madeena* and vise versa or those who don't use the Soul of Qur'an as the Ticket to Paradise, after receiving It -such are the true disbelievers. Allah has kept prepared such disbelievers a humiliating punishment, is told in the verses 4: 150-151. Through the verse 2: 85 it is warned that for those who believe in some verses and disbelieve in other verses of Qur'an, have disgrace in this world and grievous punishment in the Hereafter. The disbelievers specified in the verses 41: 26-28 are those who will say to the common people, do not listen to this Qur'an and chatter away while it is being explained, so you will be succeeded. They are the enemies of Allah as well as the believers. Such will be the Fire as a reward since they have been repudiating with the verses of Qur'an. The disbelievers specified in the verses 41: 29 are the common Muslims who follow blindly the hypocritical disbelievers.

As per the verse 7: 37 The most unjust people are the ones who after receiving Qur'an, hide and distort It or who does not try to understand what It is. At the time of death, they will witness against themselves that they were indeed disbelievers, and as per the verse 6:130 they will witness against themselves on the day of judgement. As per the verse 39: 59 to those who reject and hide the Soul of Qur'an, at the time of death Allah will tell them 'Of course My verses came to you, yet you rejected them and acted proudly, and you were among disbelievers?' Read together the verses 39: 71-72. Those who had a veil upon their eyes towards the Soul of Qur'an and those were unable to hear It are the disbelievers, is told in the verses 18: 100-101, and as per the verses 20:124-127 they will be resurrected as blind on the Day of judgement. As per the verse 67: 10 they will say in the Hereafter: 'If we had heard the Soul of Qur'an and had thought utilizing the intelligence, we would not have become inmates of the blaze. The verse 5: 67 ends as indeed Allah will not guide the people of disbelievers who are hiding the message of Allah-the Soul of Qur'an. The verse 109: 6 commands the Prophet and the believers to say disbelievers who hide Allah in the Soul of Qur'an and serving the satan: 'For you your way of life and for me the True way of life i.e. Islam.

Who are the Wrongdoers?

Those who distort the Qur'anic verses from Allah's intention or reject His verses are the most wrongdoers as per the verse 6:21. And as per the verse 10: 17 it is told that indeed He will not lead to prosper such wrongdoers and *mujrims*. Allah asks through both the verses 29: 68 and 39:32 as then who is more in the wrong than one who invents a lie about Allah or rejects the Truth- the soul of Qur'an- after it has come to him? Will there not be place of abode in Hell for such disbelievers? See the explanation 2: 124. If anyone who adopt the hypocrites or *fujjar* as their sponsors, they are the wrongdoers. The verses such as 5: 51; 6: 144; 28: 50; 46: 10 end as certainly Allah will not guide such wrongdoing people. The verse 32:22 says, who is more in the wrong than someone who has been remembered with his Lord's verses, then neglect them; We will avenge on such *mujrims.*

Who are the Mujrims -mad men?

The verse 7: 40 says certainly those who reject Our verses and feel too arrogance towards them, the gates of Heaven will not be opened for them, nor will they enter the Paradise until a camel can pass through the eye of tailor's needle. Thus We reward *mujrims*. It is warned in the verse 34: 32 that the hypocritical leaders will ask on the day of judgement to the weaklings who follow them blindly here: did we block you off from the Guidance once it came to you? Rather you yourself were *mujrims*. As per the verse 26: 99 the weaklings who lived blindly following the hypocritical leaders will say: it has only been *mujrims* who have led us astray. And as per the verse 37: 33 about both the hypocritical leaders and their weaklings who become partners in torment on that day, Allah will tell: Thus We deal with such *mujrims*. It is warned through the verse 45: 31 to those who live here aimlessly hiding and rejecting the Soul of Qur'an, on the Day of judgement will tell them: You were such *mujrim* people. Through the verses 36: 59-62 the scene of *mujrims'* trial is portrayed: step aside today, you *mujrims,* did I not pledge with you, Oh children of Adam, not to serve satan? He is an open enemy of yours and serve Me alone- this is the Straight path. He has led numerous mobs of you astray. Haven't you been thinking using intelligence? Therefore the *mujrims* are those who are having intelligence but not utilizing their intelligence for thinking the aim of life. In Qur'an fifty places about *mujrims* are mentioned. All these places the aimless hypocrites and the heedless followers belong to *mujrims* and both of them are compared to a dog which will not change its attitude whether you attack or not, as explained in the verses 7:175-176.

Who are the Hypocrites-transgressors?

The Soul of Qur'an- the food, cloth and sight of the Soul and the instrument to identify ourselves the Creator Lord and the aim of life will not be hidden except by the transgressors, is told in the verse 2: 99. As per the verse 59:19 it is told, those who have forgotten their own souls as well as Allah, such are the transgressors. And the verse 9: 67 ends as certainly the hypocrites are the transgressors. The hypocrites are the enemies of Allah as well as believers, is told in the verse 63: 4. As per the verse 9: 80 if Prophet seeks forgiveness for them seventy times over, Allah would never pardon them i.e. because they disbelieve in Allah and His messenger. Allah does not guide such transgressing people. The verse 63:6 ends as: Certainly Allah does not guide such transgressing people. As per the verse 9: 95 hypocrites are filthy, so neglect them and vide verse 9: 125 The Soul of Qur'an will increase them filth over filth and they are died while they are disbelievers. As per the verse 9: 84 the believers should not seek forgiveness or pray for the hypocrites since they are died as disbelievers and transgressors. Read together verses 9:53-55 and 17: 82.

Who are the Associates in the dominion of Allah- Mushriks?

Those people who know to utter 'Allah' in Arabic form while they are leading a life without considering Allah, as it should be considered are the associates. They are reciting the verse 2: 255, "as Allah! There is no Deity except Him, the Living, the Eternal! Neither slumber nor sleep overtake Him and whatever in the Heavens and whatever in the Earth belongs to Him. Who is there to intercede with Him except with His permission? He knows what lies before them and what is behind them, while they embrace nothing in knowledge except whatever He may wish. His seat extends farover Heaven and Earth; preserving them both does not overburden Him. He is the Sublime, the Almighty!" But in the practical life they consider intercessors and other patrons to Allah to bring them closer to Him. The Trust- the soul of Qur'an- is revealed in order to punish the hypocritical men and women and associating men and women is told in the verse 33: 73. Read together the verses 48: 6 and 98: 6. These associates are mentioned as '*kuffar*' in the verses 9: 73 and 66: 9, and as 'rejectors' of the Qur'anic verses in the verses 2: 39; 5: 10, 86; 57: 19; 64: 10 etc. The '*kuffar*' mentioned in the verses 9: 123 and 48: 29 include both hypocrites and associates; as well as both of them are the mentioned '*fujjar*' in the verses 82: 14 and 83:7. When the believer recites the verse 1: 7 'Not the path upon whom Your wrath happened. And who are gone astray should remember in mind that not in the way of the hypocrites and the associates who follow blindly them. To put it brief, there are only two parties, one is Allah's party-the believer one in each thousand from Adam to Last day belongs to this party- the other is satan's party-all Muslim organizations in different parties belong to this party, and they are nine hundred and ninety nine in each thousand. Read together the verses 2: 176; 23: 51-53; 30: 31-32.

Who are the People of the Book (Ahlul Kithab)?

During the time of Prophet before codifying Qur'an as the Book, the Jews and Christians were considered as the people of the Book. After codifying Qur'an as a Book, the bearer of It are only considered the people of Book since It is meant for entire mankind as per the verses 7: 158 and 25: 1. Today, '*Adhikr*'- the Soul of Qur'an- mentioned in the verses 41: 41-43 is the only Book from Wise and Praiseworthy Allah for entire mankind. Then whoever leads a life against the do's and don'ts of It after receiving It are the disbelievers, wrongdoers, transgressors and the inmates of the Hell from mankind.

Why Qur'an?

Apart from other creatures, the man endowed with intelligence is deputed to earth to act as the vicegerent of the Impartial Lord in order to keep the Universe in its equilibrium. The Soul of Qur'an is considered as the Trust and Balance for that purpose. But Muslims-the bearers of Qur'an - are bearing It as burden carrying donkeys neither utilizing The soul of Qur'an nor giving to other people for utilizing. By seeing the Muslims-the boar people- mentioned in the verse 25:18 as forefront in all satanic evil deeds; other people not even enquire about the Soul of Qur'an. Actually all the mischief burden of the sins occurring in the world should have to bear the hypocrites who are hiding the Soul of Qur'an knowingly. Read together the verses 6: 26 and 20: 99-100.

All men like peaceful life. For this, they accept various rules and regulations except that of Lord's. Such rules and regulations made by men instead of reducing unjust, selfishness, partiality, schisms, mischief, blood-shed, communalism, chauvinism, racism, envy, haughtiness, arrogance, snobbery, pretending superficiality, owing to illegally consuming money of the people through liquors, ganja, narcotics, prostitution, sodomy, fornication, murder, rape, theft, fraud, robbery, incendiary, smuggling, hoarding, black-marketing, adulteration, manipulation in weight and measure, interest, hawala, gambling, bribing and corruption; and also to deliver men from the demonic beliefs such as sorcery, black magic, astrology, horoscope and omen which are the footsteps of satan can be seen increasing day by day all over the world. The only solution to reduce all these mischief and evil deeds is to implement the rules and regulations of soul of Qur'an-the three times Knowledge of all the Three Time Knower, the Lord of the worlds. With It, man can identify the aim of life, can form the unity of the human harmony and can lead the prescribed lifetime peacefully for mankind as well as for other creatures.

The Soul of Qur'an is the only weapon against terrorism and to stop bloodshed. Then the question will be how it is possible. By teaching the Soul of

Qur'an one can identify himself, the aim of life and man has no choice or power to select his nation, tribes, parents, religion, sex, age or era to take birth or death etc. Thus to identify that, none of the creature except the Creator -the Owner of the soul and Maker of the body, has power to slay anyone. Anyone who kills any person without for another soul or for causing mischief in the land, then it will be as if he had killed all mankind. Anyone who spares life acts as if he had granted life to whole mankind is told in the verse 5: 32. By teaching the Soul of Qur'an to everyone make aware that the computer software is fixed around his neck and on the Day of Judgment it will be produced as an illuminating spread open Book to him and will say: read your book, and today it is enough yourself for your account, as specified in the verses 17: 13-14; 18: 49 and 45: 28-29.

To do '*Jihad*' as it should be done: Today Muslims as well as Non-Muslims have same misconceptions about the Islam and Jihad. Actually Muslims are commanded to lead and witness the life of Prophet Mohammed among the mankind as per both the verses 2:143 and 22:78. Prophet was a living example of the Soul of Qur'an. Gradually Muslims deviated from the Soul of Qur'an by the influence of other religious people especially Jews and Christians and are following them inch by inch and cubit by cubit as prophesized by Prophet. By hiding and rejecting the Soul of Qur'an the Muslims are falsifying Prophet and Islam and are involved in terrorist and mischievous activities all over the world. If any Non-Muslim hates and rejects the Soul of Qur'an and Prophet by seeing the way of life of Muslims, a believer who represents the Impartial Allah cannot blame them. Therefore, it is the inevitable duty of believer to convey the Soul of Qur'an – Message of Lord – to the entire mankind irrespective of religion or nation in order to justify Islam and Prophet.

'*Jihad*' means to utilize all the will and power to fulfill the aim of life. The aim of life is to act on earth as a vicegerent of the Lord, prepare Paradise on earth and inherit the Paradise by death. During the period of Prophet, fighting with body, weapons and wealth were included in '*Jihad*' as told in the verses 9: 111 and 61: 10. But today the '*Jihad*' is only with the Soul of Qur'an to the disbelievers who hide and reject It- the food, cloth and sight of the human soul- as specified in the verses 9: 73 and 25: 52. Thus to fulfill the Prophet's teaching that: *The best one among you is the one who learns and teaches the Soul of Qur'an*. Since the non- Muslims are not preventing the propagation of the Soul of Qur'an and there is no compulsion in the religion as per the verses 2: 256 and

10: 100, there is no '*Jihad*' against them. The verse 9: 6 says: If one of the associates from non-Muslims should ask you for protection, then grant him asylum until he has heard Allah's speech, then escort him to where he can find peace and safety; that is because they are the people who do not know the Soul of Qur'an- the real knowledge. The verse 48: 29 says that Mohammad is the Messenger of Allah, and those who with him are strict hard against the '*kuffar*' and compassionate each other. The '*kuffar*' specified in this verse as well as in the verses 9: 68, 73, 123; 66: 9 are those who repeatedly hiding or rejecting the Qur'anic verses.

The hypocrites have the same characters of Jews in primitive days as told in the verse 5: 41-42. Both of them have been killed by Allah as per the verses 9: 30 and 63: 4 respectively. The Jews introduced the anti-Islamic communal unity, and then today the hypocrites are trying and arguing to implement the same among Muslims. They are ready to any evil coalition for getting power. Today, hypocrites and '*kuffar*' by hiding and rejecting the Soul of Qur'an are actually inviting Anti Christ- *Maseeh-A-Dajjal*. By the second coming of Jesus, the false lord *Dajjal* will be killed. Then the cursed hypocrites and their followers having disease in their hearts as well as the Jewish agitators in Madeena will be killed implementing the command of the verses 33: 60-61. Read together the verses 33:72-73 and 48: 6

By awakening the people with the Soul of Qur'an and thereby forming the unity of mankind enable to preserve the ecology of the Earth and Universe. It is also essential to keep the mountains in their own places, which has been placed as nails in order that Earth may not be shaken and thus help the nature for maintaining in its equilibrium. And there by to lead a peaceful life here till the duration of life which Allah has fixed to each creatures. It is also essential to recognize whole mankind- whether believer or disbeliever- and to lead the life of a believer by satisfying others with the satisfaction of the Creator and hate others in the wrath of Allah.

The verse 53: 39 says that men can have nothing but what he aims for. During whatever work is done, Allah looks into his heart. Allah evaluates that work by seeing the state of his mind. Believers are those who remember Allah in their heart with humility and fear, by witnessing that Allah knows the condition of hearts. Through the verse 7:205 it is commanded to remember Allah by the soul with humility and fear without even murmuring with the tongue always, irrespective of morning and evening and not to be included among heedless people who does not approve that Allah does know the state of hearts.

According to the verse 13:28, to become '*Nafsu-muthmainna*'– the soul which acquired peace and tranquility- the Soul of Qur'an is inevitable and such will only be the prosperous. The verses 89: 27-30 say: "Oh! The soul, which has acquired peace and tranquility, you come back to your Lord well pleased yourself, and with Him; you serve Me; enter My Paradise; to include among those who fulfill their aim of life".

All the Bounties of Allah such as air, water, light, soil are deserved to all men alike. But His greatest Mercy and Bounty is the Soul of Qur'an which is the guide from Him, the touchstone of discriminating truth and untruth, and the complete form of The Book, if not utilize and not give others to utilize, the torment will be severe to such worst people. Therefore today, to become a believer, no need to change ones name, dress and religion as it is told in the verses 2: 62 and 5: 69. Since there is not a group of believers who live witnessing the life of the Prophet, today's non-Muslims can go to Paradise, if they live without doing wrongs, and forming true belief on the basis of the Soul of Qur'an. Allah has warned the believers in the verses 30: 31-32 that you should not become associates -*Mushriks,* by joining in the various Muslim organizations. Read explanation 2: 137, 176.

Which are the seven phases of Man?

The man first created in the Paradise has seven stages. While the first man Adam was created, the entire mankind(soul) till last day was created and Allah made covenant from each man by asking that "am I not your Lord"? They all told "yes, we do witness" as explained in the verses 7:172-174. Then sent them down to the Earth by depositing in the nape of Adam as explained in the verse 2:38. And that soul passes from Adam through the succeeding generations till it reaches the father of the specified child which has to take birth on that period. This is the second stage. Through the verse 76: 1 Allah asks: "Hasn't a long period passed for men; while he was nothing worth mentioning". When the growing embryo with the presence of life alone attains four months in the womb of the mother, the soul which is situated in the nape of its father is transferred to the womb through an Angel. Thus the child gets Soul + life - *rooh*. The third stage starts here and ends at when the child attains 15 years old. Any child expires before attaining 15 years old will return to the Paradise. From the 15 year old until death is the fourth stage. During sleep, only soul departs; while on death both the soul and life – *rooh* departs from the body. The aim of life of each individual in the fourth stage is to identify the Creator, oneself, and to prepare Paradise in order to inherit It in the seventh stage by utilizing the Soul of Qur'an as the Light, Insight and instrument as explained in the verse 3:136, 4:1, 7:43, 21:10. Fifth stage is known as *Bursaq*, which extends from death to the day of Resurrection as explained in the verse 23:100. Sixth stage is the Day of Judgment which is as long as 50,000 years of this worldly life as explained in the verse 70:4. Whoever prepares Paradise by utilizing the Soul of Qur'an in the fourth stage will inherit It in the seventh stage. Whoever not receives the Message of Lord - Soul of Qur'an- during the worldly life will be sent to any other world other than Paradise or Hell by the Lord of the worlds. Whoever hides and rejects the food and cloth of human soul - Soul of Qur'an- after receiving It will be the fuel of Hell as explained in the verses 2:24, 39; 254 4:150 -151 etc. For further explanation see the Soul of Qur'an Volume I.

The goal of Life:

No man has power to choose his destiny on earth such as, when one should be born, in which nation, where, in which tribe, in which race, to which parents, in which sex etc. The aim of deputing down men to the earth till a period is to build up Paradise utilizing the Light- Soul of Qur'an-, recognizing oneself and his Creator. The verse 67:2 says: It is He Who created death and life in order to find out which of you is doing deeds by seeing Him. Both the verses 11: 7 and 18: 7 are having the same message. The Prophet has taught that what is meant by '*Ihsan*' is *be you as if you see Allah even though you don't see Allah, He is seeing you.* Or be '*Muhsineen*', those who are living under the Light. In the verses 16: 90 Allah has commanded Justice and *Ihsan*; and in the verse 128 it is told: Allah is with those who keep Him in their hearts and with those who live under the Light.

Mankind is deputed to earth on their fourth phase in order to testify them. Then the Hell or Paradise is earned by the individuals. Allah- the Impartial- never sends anybody either to Hell or Paradise. In the verse 3: 185 says: Every soul shall have a taste of death. And on the Day of Judgment you will be paid your full recompense. Only he who is saved far from the Fire and is admitted to the Paradise by himself will have attained the aim of life. The life of this world is nothing except a feast of deception. It is notable the words told in the verse 14: 1, 'by the Permission of their Lord'. In another sense, everybody should acquire Straight path by asking their Lord. All the Prophets including Prophet Mohammad or any other great persons are not at all able to lead any person to the Straight path as per the verses 2: 272; 16: 111and 28: 56.

In the Hereafter the believers residing in the Paradise will call out: Praise is to Allah Who has guided us to this Way. Never could be having found Guidance, had It not been for the Guidance of Allah. Indeed It was the 'Truth' that the Messengers of our Lord brought to us. They will be called out: There is the Paradise, which you may inherit as reward for your deed in the worldly life. See the verse 7: 43. The verse 32:19 says: those who believe and convey the belief to others will abide Paradise as hospitable home, that is for their doings in this world. The verses 3: 136; 29: 58 and 39: 74 end as what a blissful wages will be for the workers doing good deeds in the world. Those who reside in Paradise praise Allah for leading them in the Straight path.

The Hell also is acquired by oneself. All the verses 3:181; 8: 50 and 22: 9 point to the fact 'you taste the torment of burning Fire.' Then verses 3: 182; 8: 51; 22: 10 say: That is what your hands send for you ahead and indeed Allah is no one to harm to His servants. Through the verse 59: 18 Allah addresses the believers and says; keep Allah in hearts and let everyone look to what provision he has sent forth for tomorrow (hereafter). Through the verse 78: 40 it is warned against the Day when any man will see whatever his own hands have sent on ahead, the disbelievers will say: Woe unto me! If I was only dust. The verse 4: 42 is also with the same message. Read together the verses 2: 94-95 and 62: 6-7

Community (Ummath) and People (Quom):

The difference between community and people can be understood with the Criterion -the Soul of Qur'an. The entire mankind from the appointment of Muhammad as messenger till the Last day belongs to his 'community', whereas the 'people' include addressees of prophet's time and nominal Muslims up to the last day, who are not following prophet's way of life-the Soul of Qur'an. Just like all other messengers Muhammad also will witness against 'the people' on the Day of Judgement as told in the verses 25: 18, 30 and 48: 12. The inmates of the Hell are coming from 'the people' who hide and reject the Soul of Qur'an as specified in the verses 2: 39; 5: 10 and 58: 19. The people who hide and reject the Soul of Qur'an is compared to a dog which will not change its attitude whether it is disturbed or not as per the verse 7: 176, and as per the verse 62: 5 they are compared to burden bearing donkeys and Jews, and the verse ends as 'Allah will not guide such wrong doing people'. It is told in the verse 13: 11 that Allah does not change what any people may have until they change whatever they themselves have. 'The people' at the time of their death will witness against themselves that they were disbelievers as per the verse 7: 37, and on the Day of Judgement as per the verse 6: 130. This boar people who ignore the Soul of Qur'an will welcome and accept antichrist *Maseeh-A-Ddajal* as prophet and later even as their lord. By second coming of *Eisa*, he will kill *Ddajjal*, and all non-Muslims belonged to Muhammad's community will approve *Eisa* and *Islam*. Then the hypocrites and those who have a disease in their hearts specified in the verse 33: 60 who hide and reject the Soul of Qur'an as well as falsify prophet and *Islam* will not find any shelter or hiding places anywhere in the world. They will be killed and thus the command of the verses 4: 91; 9: 123 and 33: 61will be implemented. For more explanation read the verses 4: 157-159

Will the prophet witness against the muslims?

"And the day when We shall call a witness from every community to testify against them, and We shall call you to testify against this people: that is why We have sent down to you a Book (Qur'an) which explains everything clearly. That is a Guidance, a blessing and good news for those who submitted everything for Allah." (16:89).

As per the verse 39:69, on the Day of Judgment Allah will bring the Prophets and witnesses and will judge among them with the "Truth"-the soul of Qur'an; and any one will not be dealt wrongfully. The Prophets deputed to each people will witness either in favor or against them. After the Prophets, the believers who follow the Soul of Qur'an and witness the Prophet's life will witness in favor or against the people. Eventhough all mankind from Prophet Mohammed to the last day will come under Prophet's "Ummath" -community; only Muslims will come under Prophet's "Qoum" -people. On the Day of Judgment, Prophet will not witness infavor or against the non-Muslims; where as he will witness only against his own people by name – Muslims. The verse 25:30 says, and the Messenger will say:" my Lord, surely this my own people has assumed this Qur'an as out-dated",ie they neglected and migrated from the Soul of Qur'an. Read together the verses 25:27-29. The verse 43:44 says "In fact this Qur'an is a reminder for you and your people; and both of you will be questioned about It". As per the verse 25:18, on the Day of Judgment, the saint people whom this people considered here as the interceders and mediators to Allah-the Knower of three times- will say against them that "they were a worthless bore people due to living by forgetting the Soul of Qur'an". About the hypocrites during the Prophet's time in Madeena, it is told that they were a worthless bore people in the verse 48:12.

For those who touch or read Qur'an without following Its do's and don'ts will witness and argue against them; whereas who read the Soul of Qur'an and follow the do's and don'ts as much as he can, then the Qur'an will witness and argue in favor of him. As per the verse 11:17 whoever hides the Soul of Qur'an - the utmost witness -from among different groups of Muslims, then the Fire is promised to him. Note that, it is not told in the verse 'whoever hides It from among mankind', instead told that 'from among different groups of Muslims'. See explanation 6:19. The verse 17:15 says, anyone who took the Guidance – Soul of Qur'an - then he is guided for his own soul; and anyone who strays away, then only strays against her own soul. No bearer of burden shall bear other's burden. We have never acted as a punisher until We have dispatched a Messenger. There is no justification for Allah to punish the Non-Muslims who come under the "Ummath" - community - of Prophet, since today there is not a group of believers who witness the complete life of Prophet. But the literates among them who didn't utilize The Soul of Qur'an as the weapon to stop the bloodshed and terrorism even after receiving It also will be sent to the Hell along with the Muslims who hide and reject the Soul of Qur'an. But if they realize the Truth by reading The Soul of Qur'an and convey It to others, then after the interrogation they will be sent along with those who didn't receive Soul of Qur'an to any other world than the Hell and the Paradise. Those who wish to return to the Paradise should utilize Soul of Qur'an as the Ticket.

Dheen (Religion) and Shariath (Practical deeds):

'*Dheen*' is related to the Soul whereas the *'Shariath'* is related to the body. '*Dheen*' is the same every time as explained in the verses 3: 19, 85; whereas the *'Shariath'* -practical deeds- differ time to time. Even early period and the later period of prophet Muhammed, 'Shariath'-practical deed is different. '*Dheen*'-the religion- is related to the individual, whereas *'Shariath'* is demanded to the group of believers. Today, since there is no group of believers anywhere in the world, there is no way to implement '*Islamic Shariath'*. During this time it is taught by the prophet to the believer here and there to remain by holding fast the Soul of Qur'an with his molar teeth. Without forming the belief with the Soul of Qur'an, no *'Shariath'* -practical deeds- will be accepted as explained in the verse 2: 186.

The Exalted Book- apart from the falsehood:

Qur'an which has explained everything has never told step by step, yet Qur'anic verses never contradict to another. Then we should study and compare the various verses of Qur'an and try to understand It. In Qur'an all the matters have been repeated in more than one place, that is why it is called '*Mathaanee*' as specified in the verses 15: 87 and 39: 23.

The commands of certain verses were not applicable at the period of Prophet;it becomes applicable during later. For e.g.: (1) the verse 25: 52 says: therefore you should not obey the disbelievers who hide the Soul of Qur'an. Strive against them with the utmost strenuousness with the Qur'an. Here mentioned the disbelievers are hypocrites. All the wars undergone during the period of the Prophet were with the weapons such as sword, shield, arrow, bow and spear. But today there is no group of believers, and hence no killing or war. Instead there is only '*Jihad*' with the Soul of Qur'an. (2) Through the verses 4: 91; 9: 123 and 33: 61 the group of believers have been ordered to kill the hypocrites, wherever and whenever they meet them. But this command has not been implemented yet. This will be implemented only after the second coming of Jesus. Nobody has ruled yet making Mecca as the capital, though Mecca is the centre of the world. This also will be implemented by the coming of Jesus.

Some of the verses implemented during the time of the Prophet can't be implemented today, for e.g.: (1) the woman and the man guilty of fornication shoud be flogged with a hundred stripes, let a party of the believers witness for their punishment. This command said in the verse 24: 2 can't be implemented today. Because, there is no group of believers and the punishment should be carried out by those who are not doing sins. Prophet Jesus has taught: "Let them throw stones who have not sinned". So, we can understand that the punishment in *Islam* during the period of Jesus was also killing by throwing stones, if married man and married woman fornicate. This has also been implemented during the period of Prophet Mohammad. But later in future years especially today, it is impossible to implement it. The reason is that there is only a few who has not done that sin including sodomy, a guilt which is harder than adultery and even against the nature, though Prophet Mohammad has taught that one who does sodomy and one who is subjected to sodomy should be killed. Today the approach towards men and women engaged in fornication is as prescribed in the verses 4: 15-16. (2) Liquor eradication was carried out in different stages. For the first time in the verse 2: 219 says, in each of them (liquor and gambling) is great sin as well as some benefit. But sin is greater than the benefit. Then drinking became less with the command through the verse 4: 43 that "Don't approach *swalath* with a mind of intoxication". Finally according to the verses 5: 90-91, liquor was completely prohibited with a command: "Indeed liquor is filth; you should give it up". But today we can see that last two verses' commands are not obeyed either by those who do *swalath* or not. So it is only possible to advise them to stop drinking by explaining the Soul of Qur'an as told in the first command.

When forming a decision in any matter, all the verses revealed in that matter should be considered. For e.g.: (1) Through the verse 17: 23 it is ordered: You must be kind to parents whether one or both of them attain old age in your life, don't say a word of contempt to them nor repel them. But through the verse 31: 15 and 29: 8 it is ordered that if those parents strive to make you associate others with Allah by things of which you have no knowledge, don't obey them. Keep them company under the shadow of the Soul of Qur'an only and you follow the path of those who returned to Allah. Through the verse 9: 23, Allah says by calling the believers: Do not take your fathers and your brothers as protectors if they prefer disbelief to belief. Anyone of you do so, then such are the wrongdoers. The verse 58: 22 says, you will not find any people who believe in Allah and the Last Day, showing affection for anyone who resists Allah and His Messenger, even though their own fathers, their sons, their brothers, or anyone in their family connections. With those He will engrave faith on their hearts, assist them with a spirit from Himself, and will enter them in to the Paradise beneath which rivers flow, to live there in forever. Allah has pleased them while they will be pleased with Him, such are only Allah's party. Indeed, Allah's party will only be prosperous. The verse 9: 113 says: It is not suitable for the Prophet and those who believe that they should pray for forgiveness for those who associate others with Allah, even though they are close relatives, after it is cleared to them that they are indeed the inmates of the Hades. But the verse 46: 17-18 say: Anyone who says to his believing parents: "Phooey on you! Do you promise me that I will come forth from my grave while generations have passed on before me?"- And while they both implore Allah's help: "It will be too bad for you! Believe: Indeed Allah's promise will come true", he merely says: "Those are only legends about primitive men". Such are the ones among the nations of *Jinns* and humans who have passed away before them, against who the sentence will be justified, they will be the losers. In short, Allah has taught each person through various orders and prohibitions which should be kept in different occasions. The believers -the vicegerents of Allah- will have His character. In the case of hypocrites who deliberately do wrong, Allah will never forgive. To those who do wrong unknowingly, Allah may forgive. The verse 4: 17 says: Repentance holds with Allah for those who do evils due to ignorance, then repent shortly after, to them Allah will turn to; and Allah is Wise, All Knowing. And the verse 18 says: Repentance is not there to such people who continue to do evils until death faces one of them. And he says, now have I repented indeed, and not for those who hide Qur'anic verses, die as hypocrites. Read together the verses 9: 55, 85 and 125. Prophet taught: When an evil is seen, prevent it with your hands; if that is not possible, prevent it with your tongue; if that also is not possible, hate them with your mind; if that also is not done, he doesn't have even an atom of faith. Allah will not forgive or guide those who not utilize the Soul of Qur'an -the Exalted Book, apart from the falsehood mentioned in the verses 41: 41-42, even after receiving It.

How to read:

The inspiration for the inception of this interpretation (*Thafseer*) "The Soul of Qur'an" is to call the men to the Creator by giving the contents of Qur'an in their hearts' language, and to prepare them individually to answer before the Lord on the Day of Judgment. Here Qur'anic verses are explained with Qur'anic verses and with the sayings of the Prophet which are Its interpretations. An attempt has been made to point out similar examples of each verse as '*Mouidhath*' suitable for today. This has been carried with a prayer to exclude my own views or ideas any where else, and to explain as intended by the Lord. If there is any mistake notified, I request you to point out them after reading the whole contents.

Warning:

The Soul of Qur'an is not simply to keep in your cupboard; You should consider that It is your Lord's Speech and He caused to reach the Book to you. If you don't find time to read and understand this Book or you didn't follow after reading It, tomorrow in the court of Allah, your hand that touched this Book, your eyes that saw this Book, and your skin, all will witness and argue against you. While the Prophet has taught that the Best Speech is the Book of Allah, reading any other book or other periodicals, without reading the Soul of Qur'an is not suitable for a true believer.

Remember:

Satan prevents you only from the soul, not from reading the body or meaning of Qur'an. So when you start reading It, seek refuge from him to Allah- the all Hearing, all Knowing. Allah has given satan the ability to prevent you by making boredom, making you feel sleepy, making you short of time and dragging other problems into your way. As well, when you begin to follow It, the human satan will try to ridicule and isolate you. So beware of him, also take refuge from him to your Lord regarding the temptation, menace and all the destructive activities.

You go on reading the Soul of Qur'an praying heartily: "My Lord! Increase me in my knowledge" remembering the doubts you have. As you are involved in the conversation between your Lord and you, the answers to your doubts will be receiving gradually. If you have not received answers for your doubts in the first reading, continue the reading, you will definitely get the answer before finishing your reading. Direction for reading various verses combined together and reading the explanation should be strictly followed by checking the references, as and when required. In other words, if there are three verses which have been directed to read altogether with a verse, then those three together will give new idea besides the ideas in them. This is the meaning of what has been said that the explanation of Qur'an will never end whether It is written or told. In order to read the Soul of Qur'an the best time should be selected, and we should approach It without pre-judgment with the innocence of a new born baby. If there are any unclear doubts even after completing the reading of the entire contents, you should not hesitate to ask and learn from those who know the Soul of Qur'an. I would like to remind you that every body has the commitment to convey this message which is meant for the entire creatures of the Lord, without any discrimination in caste, religion, nation etc. To carry out this task, each and everybody can take part in this venture by taking Its copies and translating into various languages.

Oh our Lord! Give us the opportunity to understand the Soul of Qur'an and to follow as It should be followed and as You have intended. Oh Lord, lead us out of darkness to the Light with the Light-The Soul of Qur'an, Oh, the Light of the Heaven and Earth. Bless us to utilize the Soul of Qur'an, so that It will witness and argue in favor us and not against us! Our Lord! Enter us to the Paradise together with the forerunners and virtuous with the Ticket, oh the One Who sent down the Ticket, Oh the Virtuous, Merciful.

With the name of Allah, The Impartial, The Compassionate,

1. Al-Fathiha

Surath Fathiha is the preface to Qur'an. This Surath was revealed at Mecca. Prophet taught that this is the glorious Surath. The verse 15: 87 says: We have bestowed up on you the seven oft-repeatedly coming verses and the glorious Qur'an. Prophet taught that Fathiha is the *Ummul-Kithab* or the *Ummul Qur'an*- Mother of the Book. The message of whole Qur'an is contained in these seven verses. Fathiha and the last two verses of *Surath Baqara* are the two lights which have not been given to any other Prophets, except Prophet Muhammad. These are given at the Paradise on the night of *Isra'-Wal-Mihraj* –ascension to the Paradise and meeting with The Lord. While the servant asks for Guidance to his Lord through Fathiha, the Qur'an verses 2: 1 to 114: 6 are given as the answer.

I seek refuge with Allah from Satan, the outcaste one.

It is commanded through the verse 16: 98: "Whenever you read the Qur'an, seek refuge with Allah from Satan, the outcast". Prophet prayed as: *"I seek refuge with Allah, All-Hearing, All-Knowing regarding the temptation and frightening of the cursed Satan as well as the evil practices like magic and sorcery of him"*. This prayer is also an implementation of the verses 23: 97-98 -i.e. My Lord; I seek refuge with You from the temptations of Satans. Also I seek refuge with You, my Lord from he accompanied and even approach me.

Before men created, *Jinns* were the vicegerents of The Lord on Earth. *Iblis* was their leader. Then all the members become transgressors without being a single believer, the angels under the leadership of *Ibilis* wiped out them. Then Allah created men, breathed from His Spirit and ordered the assemblage there including the angel to do *Sujoodh*-'prostrate'- before him. Then all of them except *Iblis* prostrated as specified in the verses 15: 26-31. As per the verse 15: 32 Allah asked: *"Iblis*, what is wrong with you for not among those who made prostrated?" He said I am no one to prostrate before a human being You have created from ringing clay, from moulded slime. Then Allah said get out of here, for you are an outcast on you having the curse until the Day of repayment. Then he asked: My Lord was it not your intension that I didn't prostrate? So give me respite till the Day of Resurrection. Allah said: You have been given respite till the Day of Repayment. When he asked for more respite Allah said: while Adam is given a child; you will also be given a child. You can reside in their heart, travel through blood. Read together the verses 7: 17-18; 17: 64. Thus *Iblis* became Satan. Then satan said: My Lord, you have made me gone astray aimless. So I will show them the life of Earth alluring, and I will make them aimless of life except those who live only for saving You and who are Your innocent servants. Allah said: This is My Straight path. You can seduce anybody except those who live as My representative –vicegerent- keeping Me in their heart with the Soul of Qur'an which is the food and cloth of the soul. No influence or authority you will have over My servants except such as put themselves in the wrong way and follow you. Then Hell is the promised abode for you and your followers. Read together the verses 15: 27-43; 38: 82-85. In the verses 4: 117-118 it is told that if anybody calls up on except Allah, he calls up the doubting, cursed Satan only. Allah has cursed him. Satan said: that I will indeed take a great majority of Your servants. As the explanation of this verse Prophet has taught: *In each and every thousand, nine hundred and ninety-nine will be fallen in the temptation of Satan. This is meaningful, fixed and well-known.* Through the verse 8: 24 Allah says addressing the believers: Know that Allah comes in between you and your heart. I.e. whoever remembers Allah with the Soul of Qur'an always in their all walking, sitting and lying, then Allah is with them and they are the only believers. Those who forgot Allah are hypocrites tempted by satan. In the verse 7: 27 Allah says: Indeed We made the Satans as protectors to those who are not believers. As per the verse 40: 40: Nobody will become a believer without making his Jinn companions a believer. The only instrument to make one's soul mate a believer is the Soul of Qur'an which is made very easy to understand with ones hearts language.

Satan belongs to Jinn as per the verse 18: 50 and disbeliever as per both the verses 2: 34, 38: 74 does not prevents man from reading the body of the Qur'an or Its life-meaning-, but prevents only from the Soul of Qur'an since It cause to rise man's rank among all other creatures. Prophet taught: You recite Qur'an, only when your reciting is in harmony with your heart. When both of them (heart and reciting) are apart, stop reciting and mind in your business. The teaching of Prophet is applicable to all men from that day to the Last Day. So, the meaning of what Prophet taught is that satan will try to deviate the attention of even the companions of the Prophet who knew the contents of Qur'an into other fields, then Qur'an should not be recite. Prophet taught that *Qur'an is a document either in favor or against you. So if Qur'an is read without soul, the read Qur'an will witness and argue against the reader.* Prophet also taught us that the most evil person among the people is the one who recites the body of Qur'an without trying to understand Its contents and he will be darted away from Islam just like the arrow is darting from the bow.

Through the verse 25: 29 it is warned against a scene which one wails that satan prevented me from the Soul of Qur'an after It has reached to me; satan was a great betrayer to man. So those who read the body of Qur'an without trying to understand the content will admit on the Day of Judgment that satan prevented him from the Soul of Qur'an. Through the verses 43: 36-39 it is warned that whoever has shown indifference regarding the Soul of Qur'an which is useful for the remembrance of Most Gracious, intimate a companion to him. And that satan companions will hinder them from the Real Path. But they will think that they are in the Straight Path. And thus when both of them come to Us they will say: Oh woe to us! How better it would have been had there a distance of two easts (east and west) between us. Then you are indeed the most evil companion. Thus both the evil doers (Man and his Jinn companion) shall be partners in the punishment. Read together the verses 59: 16-17.

Remember that it has not been ordered to recite '*Bismi*' when we start to recite Soul of Qur'an which is the speech of Allah; it has been ordered to seek refuge with Allah for not preventing us from understanding It as Allah intends.

Prophet used to pray three times in the morning and evening as: 'I seek protection with all His '*Kalimath*' –explanation- from all evils that Allah has created. Here, the refuge seeking is not with Qur'an, but with '*Kalimath*' which is the Spirit of Qur'an.

With the name of Allah, the Impartial, the Compassionate,

Believers should start any action with the name of Allah Who is the Impartial, the Compassionate. There is a scene in the verse 27: 30 in which the letter of

Prophet *Sulaiman* sent through the bird leader 'Woodpecker' is read out to the chiefs in the court of Queen *Sheeba*, the worshipper of sun. The letter is as follows: "Indeed it is from *Sulaiman*. This is begun with the name of Allah, the Impartial, the Compassionate". It is only in the verse 27: 30 that '*Bismi*' is considered as a verse in Qur'an. Prophet used to pray three times morning and evening as: "With the name of Allah, with which never will happen any mishap anywhere either on Earth or in the sky, and He is the All-hearing, All-knowing." Whenever you are doing any job whether it be entering latrine, sexual intercourse, eating food, getting into the vehicle, going out of the house or looking at the mirror etc. you have to remember Allah with your soul. You should not utter '*Bismi*' loudly to convince others. Any activity which is not begun with '*Bismi*' i.e. remembering Allah with heart, whether it be in swalath, sacrifice or any other job, it will turned as the service to satan. Read together the verses 6: 119-121and 11: 41.

1. Praise be to Allah, the Lord of all worlds.

The verse has been repeated in two places as same and as the part of the verse in three places.

(1) 6: 45:- In the verses, 6: 42-44 say: "We have sent Messengers to many nations before you. And We have afflicted them with suffering and adversity in order that they might show humility. When the calamity reached them from Us, instead of becoming humble, they became more arrogant. Satan made their sinful acts seem alluring to them. But when they forgot the warning that they received, We opened to them the doors of all blessings. In the midst of that enjoyment when they were making merry without expressing thankfulness to Allah and forgetting themselves, all of a sudden We called them to account. Then look! They became like desperate Iblises. We cut off the tap root of those wrongdoers, and Praise is to Allah, the Lord of all worlds". Here the believers praise Allah who destroyed the wrongdoers, and to keep the Earth in its equilibrium so that His creatures can live with peace, calm and quiet.

(2) 10: 10:- In the verses 10: 7-8 Allah says: Indeed, those who do not keep hope on their meeting with Us, are pleased and satisfied with the life of this world, and those who heedless with Our verses, their final abode is Hell. That Hell they have earned in the present world. Indeed, those who believe and work righteousness, their Lord will guide them because of their faith to the

Straight Path. Beneath them will flow rivers in Gardens of bliss. There in the Paradise their calling will be, "Glory is to You, oh Allah!" And their greeting will be "peace, peace". The closing of their all talking will be: All praises be to Allah, the Lord of all worlds. The character of those who enter the Paradise will be like this: whether happy or sad, they will always and everywhere keep the remembrance of Allah, by hold fasting The Soul of Qur'an. Read together the verses 2: 152; 3: 191; 4: 103; 62: 10.

(3) 37: 182:- Associates who lived in Mecca used to consider Angels as the daughters of Allah and *Jinns* as the sons. See the verse 6:100. They had attributed a blood-relationship between Him and the *Jinns*. But the *Jinns* knew quite well that they should indeed appear for judgment before Allah. Allah is free glorious from all the things they ascribe to Him, is told in the verses 37: 158-160. About Angels in the verses 37: 164-166 it is told: Indeed, there is none of us except having an acknowledged status. We are ready to stand in row. Indeed, we are those who glorify Allah. After explaining in the verses 171-173 that what measures Allah has taken in the previous Prophets, then in the verses 174-179 what policy Prophet Muhammad has to take, the Surath ends by declaring that your Lord is the Purest and free from what they ascribe to Him; peace be on the emissaries! Praise is to Allah, the Lord of all worlds.

(4) 39: 75:- The trumpet will be sounded, whoever is in the Heaven and whoever is on Earth except those whom Allah intended will swoon and fall down. Then when it will be blown a second time, they will be standing up and looking around. The Earth will shine through its Lord's Light. The record of deeds as mentioned in the verses 17: 13-14; 18: 49 will be placed open. The Prophets and the witnesses will be brought in, and judgment will be pronounced with the Soul of Qur'an. And to every soul will be repaid in full whatever it has earned, He is quite aware of what they are doing. The disbelievers will be driven along to Hell in crowd and when they reach the Hell, the doors of It will be automatically opens and Its keepers will ask: "Did not Messengers come to you from among yourselves, reciting your Lord's verses to you, and warning you about meeting of this Day of yours?" They will say: "Of course, but the sentence about torment has still come due for disbelievers." Then it will be told: "Enter Hell's gates to remain there. Then how evil is the abode for the arrogant! See the verses 39: 69-72. Note that these verses make clear that Kafirs –disbelievers, are only those who reject Qur'an after receiving It.

Those who have heeded their Lord will be driven along to the Paradise in crowds. Until just as they come up to It, then Its doors will be opened by Prophet Muhammad. Its keepers will tell them: "Peace is upon you! You have done well. So enter it to remain there." And they will say: "Praise is to Allah, who has held true to His promise for us, and let us inherits the Earth. We can dwell in the Paradise as we will. Then how Excellent reward for those who work!" You will see the Angels surrounding the Throne, glorifying their Lord's praise. Judgment will be pronounced among the creatures with the Soul of Qur'an. And there will be a pronouncement: "Praise is to Allah, the Lord of all worlds!"

(5) 40: 65:- Allah is the One Who has granted you the Earth to settle down on, and the sky built as a canopy, and has shaped you. He has made your shapes handsome and provided you with wholesome things. Such is Allah your Lord. So blessed is Allah, the Lord of the worlds. He is the living; there is no deity except Him. So appeal to Him sincerely, living exclusively for Him. Praises be to Allah, the Lord of all worlds. See the verses 40: 64-65. Prophet was praying: *Praise is to Allah in all states - except the state of Hell.*

The sixth, eighteenth, thirty forth and thirty fifth Suras begin with praising Allah.

The verse 45: 36 says: Then all the praise is to Allah, Lord of the Heavens and Lord of the Earth, the Lord of all worlds. The verse 30: 18 says: by Indicating the time of swalath: To him is all praise, in Heavens and on Earth; in the late after noon or after the supper and when you are at noon hour. As per the verse 14: 39 Prophet *Ibrahim* says: Praise is to Allah Who has granted me in old age *Isma'el* and *Is'haq*. The verse 7: 43 the believers who entered in the Paradise will say that: praise is to Allah, Who has guided us to this bliss. Never could we have found Guidance, had It not been for the Guidance of Allah.

Through the verse 23: 28 Allah commands to Prophet *Nooh*: When you have embarked on the ark -you and those with you say: "Praise is to Allah, Who has saved us from the people of wrongdoing. As per the verse 27: 15 both Prophets *Dawood* and *Sulaiman* declared: Praise is to Allah who has favored us above many of the believing servants. The verse 27: 59 Prophet is ordered to say: Praise be to Allah and peace be upon His servants whom He has chosen and as per the verse 33: 93: Praise be to Allah who will soon show you His signs, so that you shall know them. Your Lord is not heedless of all that you do. As per the verse 35: 34 the believers entered in Paradise will say: "Praise is to Allah, who has lifted sadness from us. Our Lord is Forgiving, Appreciative. The verse 29: 63 says: if you ask them who it is that sent down rain from the sky, and gives life there with to the Earth after Its death, they will certainly reply: "Allah!" say: "Praise be to Allah!" But most of them do not understand. Read together the verses 16: 75 and 39: 29. The verse 28: 70 says: He is Allah; there is no Deity except Him! Praise belongs to Him from the very first as well as in the Hereafter. Discretion is His, and to Him will be all you returned.

The verse 15: 98 says: Glorify your Lord's praise and be one among who prostrates. The verse 110: 3 says: Then Glorify your Lord's praise and beg Him for forgiveness, since He is so Relenting. In the verse 17: 44 Allah says: The seven Heavens and Earth, as well as whoever is in them, Glorify Him. Nothing exists unless it Glorify His praise; yet you do not understand their Glorification. Still He has been Forbearing, Forgiving. The verse 24: 41 says: have you not seen how everyone in Heaven and Earth Glorifies Allah, even to the birds lined in flight. Each knows its swalath and how to Glorify Him. Allah is aware of whatever they do.

After the swalath when we say 33 times "*Alhamdulillah*" - Praise be to Allah, we should bear in mind the message of all the verses mentioned above. Since all the praise is to Allah is a declaration, it should be said aloud.

Rubb –The Lord: - The word '*Rubb*' means Creator, Guardian, and the Owner Who has the authority to preserve and destroy. If the beginning of Surath Fathiha is with a declaration of praise to '*Rubb*', the last Surath *Annas* begins by commanding to say: I seek refuge with the Lord, King and the Deity of mankind. The verses 7: 172-173 say, when Adam was created in the Paradise, all the human beings till the Last Day also was created, and they were all asked individually. Am 'I' not your Lord? Then all of them said: Of course, we do testify. This incident is called covenant. This covenant is taken from everybody in order not to say anybody: We were heedless about it on the Day of Judgment; or our forefathers made associates in the dominion of Allah; were we not the descendants after them? Are You then destroy us for the deeds of men who were following falsehood?

Wa'ad -The promise, on the Day of Judgment there will be questioned about the covenant, is the promise. Read together the verse 2: 27.

Al alameena –All worlds: Here without saying '*alam*', -the world- told '*alameena*' -all worlds, means the Creator of Angels, *Jinns*, mankind in this and the Hereafter worlds, and all the living and non-living things; it also means Guardian and the only Lord Who is capable of sustaining and destroying. The phrase; 'the Lord of all worlds' as mentioned 42 times in the Qur'an. As per the verses 20: 49-52 Pharaoh asked: "Who is Lord for both of you, oh *Moosa*?" *Moosa* told: "Our Lord is the One Who has given everything its on constitution; then guided it." He asked: "What was the attitude about the earlier centuries?" *Moosa* told: "Knowledge concerning them rests in a book with my Lord. My Lord neither misses anything, nor does He forget.

Today the Muslims in general, who have received Qur'an and are conducting swalath bodily without the participation of Soul, are doing similar activities against the do's and don'ts of Qur'an. They keep the false notion that they will enter the Paradise and all non Muslims will go to Hell. Some of them ask where the abode of non-Muslims is after death! The answer for all of them is: Allah is not only the Lord of the worlds such as Paradise and Hell; but He is the Lord of many other worlds. The non-Muslims who have not received Qur'an will not go to the Hell. Then those who hide and reject the Soul of Qur'a'nic verses will go to Hell as per the verses 5: 10, 86. Allah the Lord of all worlds may send the non-Muslims to some other worlds than the Muslims are sending! Only the believers who utilize the Soul of Qur'an as the Ticket will return to the Paradise.

2. The Impartial, the Compassionate.

'*Ar 'rahman*' means: Most Gracious, Impartial- One Who Himself not sends anybody to Paradise or Hell, One Who does good both to the submitters as well as the rejecters, or one who does more good to the rejecters who forgot Him and not approve of Him. The meaning of '*Ar 'raheem*' is: The Compassionate Most Merciful, One who does goodness particularly to the believers who have submitted themselves to Him in the Hereafter. '*Rahman*', the particular noble good name of Allah, not will be approved by the hypocrites and those who associate others with Allah. But they always approve and quote the good name '*Raheem*'.

The Impartial:- The verses 43: 33-35 say: Were it not that all men might become of one even way of life, We would provide for everyone who denies The Impartial, silver roof for their houses, stair-cases to go upstairs, doors to their houses, and coaches to recline on and all the adornments with gems. But all these are nothings but enjoyment of the present life. The Hereafter, in the sight of your Lord is for the heedful people". The verse 25: 60 says: if they are told to prostrate before the Impartial, they will ask: Who is this *Rahman*? Do we prostrate to whom you command? It merely increases their disdain. The verse 13: 30 says: thus We have sent you to a community- communities have passed long before it- so you may recite to them what We have inspired you with even though they disbelieve with the Impartial. Say "He is my Lord there is no deity except Him. On Him do I entrust and towards Him my repentance. The verse 2: 163 says your Deity is the one Deity alone. There is no Deity except Him, the Impartial, the compassionate. The verses 27: 30; 41: 2, 59: 22 also end as He is the Impartial, the compassionate.

The verses 55: 1-4 say: The Impartial! Who taught the Qur'an Created men (bodily on Earth), has taught him the explanation of Qur'an. Then it is clear that the Impartial is the One Who taught men the Soul of Qur'an from the Paradise and the explanation after sending to the Earth. Through the verse 43: 45 Allah commands Prophet to ask to the Messengers whom He sent before that "did He appoint any deities other than The Impartial, to be worshipped? The verses 43: 19-20 say: They consider Angels who are the servants of Impartial as females! They say: "If the Impartial had so wished, we would not have worshipped them. Through the verse 43: 81 Allah commands to tell: "If the Impartial had a son, I would be the first to serve him." Whenever the disbelievers saw the Prophet, they treated him not except with ridicule. They ask: Is this the one who talks about your Deity? They conceal the message of Qur'an which generate the remembrance of Impartial Allah, is told in the verse 21: 36. And as per the verse 21: 42 Allah commands to ask: Who shields you night and day and from the Impartial, indeed they are evasive about the Reminder of their Lord.

The verse 25: 26 says: true control will belong to the Most Gracious on that Day; it will be a harsh Day for disbelievers. The verse 26: 5 says: No reminder ever comes to them as a renewal from the Most Gracious, except they shun it. The verse 36: 11 says: Indeed you will only warn to one who follows the Soul of Qur'an, and fears the Most Gracious unseen. As per the verse 50: 33 the Paradise will be brought up a short distance to the heedful who lives in awe of the Most Gracious even though unseen, and comes with a repentant heart. It is told in the verse 67: 3; You not see any discrepancy in the creation of Impartial. Through the verse 67: 19 Allah asks: Have they not watched the birds flapping their wings in rows above them. No one holds them up except the Most Gracious! He is observant of everything. The verse 67: 29 says: "Say it will be the Most Gracious. We believe with Him, and on Him do we rely. You will know who is in plain astray". The verse 17: 110 says: You call upon Allah or you call upon *Rahman*. By whatever name you call upon Him it is well. It is to Him belongs the most beautiful names.

In the verse 19: 58, after describing about some of the Prophets Allah says: Whenever the verses of the Impartial were recited to them, they drop down to prostrate by weeping. As per the verse 19: 61: To those who fear Most Gracious unseen, are promised with the Paradise of eternity. The verse 19: 87 says, they will possess no power of intercession except for someone who has already fulfilled the covenant from the Impartial. As per the verse 88, the disbelievers say that the Impartial has adopted a son. The verse 20: 50 ends as, the Most Gracious settled on the Throne.

The compassionate: - Through the verse 7: 32 asks: Who has forbidden Allah's amenities which He has produced for His servants and the wholesome things from His provision? Say: "On Resurrection Day they will be exclusively for those who have believed during worldly life. The verse 39:53 says: My servants who have acted extravagantly against themselves still do not despair of Allah's Mercy. Allah forgives all offences. He is the Forgiving, the Merciful. As per the verses 39: 54-55 there are two conditions for forgiving, that one should distinguish the mistakes and wrongs; with the Criterion; the Soul of Qur'an tell them to the Most Merciful by mind and afterwards justly follow the Soul of Qur'an. Allah has given only a part of a hundred from His Mercy to all the creations of the worlds. And the remaining ninety nine parts are with Him. The love and mercy which the creations show here is a part of that mercy bestowed by Allah.

Rahmath (Mercy):- In both verses 6:12 and 54 Allah said that He has prescribed mercy as His stable character Himself. By explaining the history of Prophet *Moosa* and Pharaoh through the verses 26: 10-66, the history of Prophet *Ibrahim* and his people through the verses 26: 69-102, the history of Prophet *Nooh* and his people through the verses 26: 105-120, the history of Prophet Hood and his people *Aa'd* through the verses 26: 123-138, the history of Prophet *Swalih* and his people *Thamood* through the verses 26: 141-157, the history of Prophet *Looth* and his people through the verses 26: 160-173, the history of Prophet

Shuaib and his people through the verses 26: 176-189 Allah say that is a sign, though most of them are not believers. Yet your Lord is the Powerful, the Merciful. Through the verse 26: 217 Allah commands Prophets to rely on the Powerful, the Merciful.

The verses 28: 16; 34: 2; 41: 32; 42: 5; 46: 8; 49: 5, 14; 57: 28; 58: 12; 60: 7, 12; 64: 14; 66: 1; 73: 20 end as Allah is the Forgiving, Merciful.

In the verses such as 6: 157; 7: 52, 203; 12: 111; 16: 64 it is told that Soul of Qur'an is the Guidance and a Mercy to believers. As per the verse 11: 28 Prophet *Nooh* told to his people: Oh my people, I have a clear sign from my Lord. I also receive '*Mercy*' from Him. But you are blind regarding It. Shall we compel you to accept It while you dislike It? As per the verse 11: 63 Prophet *Swalih* told the same matter to his people. As per the verse 11: 88 Prophet *Shuaib* asked to his People: "My people, have you considered whether I bear any explanation from my Lord? He has provided me with the '*Best sustenance*' from Himself. As per the verse 11: 94 it is told: We saved Shuaib and those who believed with him with the '*Mercy* from Us'. As per the verses 11: 118-119 it is told: The people will not cease to dispute except the one who utilize your Lord's Mercy. The Mercy and the Best sustenance mentioned in the above all verses is The Soul of Qur'an.

Through the verses 10: 85-86 Allah taught the believers to pray as: On Allah do we rely our Lord, do not turn us in to a trial for wrongdoing people, save us with Your '*Mercy*' from such disbelieving people.

It is told in the verse 35:2, there is no withholding any 'Mercy' that Allah may open for mankind. The verse 25: 48 says, He is the One Who has send the winds as heralds announcing His '*Mercy*', We send pure water down from the sky. Here mentioned Mercy is rain. The verse 30: 21 says: Among His signs is that He has created spouses for you from among yourselves, so that you may console yourselves with them. He has planted affection and 'Mercy' between you; in that there are signs for the people who think and reflect. The verse 30: 36 says: Whenever We let mankind taste 'Mercy' they are glad about it; yet if any evil should strike them because of what their hands have sent on ahead, they become despair. Through the verse 33: 17 Allah commands Prophet to ask: "Who is there to shield you from Allah if He should wish any evil for you or wants Mercy for you?" They will find no any patron or helper besides Allah. The verse

33: 43 ends as, Allah is Merciful with believers. As per the verse 7: 151 Prophet *Moosa* prayed: "Oh my Lord! Forgive me and my brother. Admit us to Your Mercy. You are the Most Merciful of those who show Mercy. As per the verse 12: 87 Prophet *Ya'qoob* says to his sons: You should never give up hope of Allah's Mercy. Indeed no one despairs of Allah's Mercy, except the disbelieving people. As per the verse 12: 92, *Yoosuf* told to his brothers: "This day, there is no revenge on you. Allah will forgive you. He is the Most Merciful of those who show Mercy.

As per the verse 15: 56 Prophet *Ibrahim* says: No one despairs about his Lord's Mercy except those who go astray. The verses 2: 143; 16: 7, 47; 22: 56, and 57: 9 end as: To all mankind Allah is Gentle and Merciful. As per the verse 59: 10 believers will pray as: Our Lord, forgive us and our brethren who have preceded in faith, and do not place any rancor in our hearts concerning those who believe. Our Lord, You are Compassionate Merciful.

As per the verse 21: 83 Prophet *Ayyoob* prayed as: "Adversity has afflicted me, while You are the Most Merciful of the Mercy granting." The believers' prayer is mentioned in the verse 23: 109 as: Our Lord, we believe, so forgive us and have Mercy on us; You are the best One to show Mercy. As per the verse 7: 23 Adam couple prayed: Our Lord! We have wronged to our own souls. If you do not forgive us and do not bestow Your Mercy upon us, we shall certainly among the losers. As per the verse 11: 47 Prophet *Nooh* prayed: My Lord, I take refuge with You from asking You something I have no knowledge about. If You do not forgive me and show me Mercy, I would become among the losers.

The Prophet taught about a woman who was a prostitute in an earlier society. Using her shoes, she gave water to an extremely thirsty dog, and due to this Mercy, Allah made her among the inhabitants of Paradise. But a hypocritical woman of the same society tied up and starved a cat causing its death by preventing it to prey on Allah's Earth. And that cruel act made her among the inmates of the Hell. In brief, only believers will understand the Mercy of Allah and his Prophet, and do Mercy accordingly to others.

3. Master of the Day of Judgment.

The Day on which each and every man should have to answer individually about each moment of the worldly life from fifteenth age till death before his Lord, Lord Allah-they ever watchful, without slumber or sleep, having no beginning or end, without having similes or example; irresistible, omnipotent and omniscient. That is the Day of Judgment. On that Day skins, hearings and sight of disbelievers-enemies of Allah- will witness against them as told in the verses 41: 19- 24. The verse 36: 65 says: That Day We shall set a seal on their mouth. And their hands will speak to Us, and their feet bear witness to all they have earned. That day the tongues, private parts, wombs etc. will submit its record. Read together the verses 4: 1, 17: 36, 24: 24. The Day the Earth will submit its record as per the verse 99: 4. In brief, One third of the verses in Qur'an reveal the scene of the Day of Judgment.

Through the verses 2: 48, 123, by addressing the Israelis, Allah teaches entire mankind: Heed a Day when no soul will compensate any other soul in any way. Intercession will not be accepted from her, nor will any alternative be taken for it they will not be helped. The verse 2: 281says: Heed a Day when you will be brought back to Allah; then every soul will be paid in full according to whatever it has earned, and they will not be treated unjustly. As per the verse 3: 9 those who have versed knowledge will pray as: Our Lord, you will be gathering mankind together on a Day. There is no doubt about; Allah will never go back on promises. The verse16: 111 says: On that Day each soul will come to plead for itself, and every soul will be repaid according to whatever it has done and they will not be wronged. Read together the verse 3: 30. It is told in the verse 78: 40: On a Day when any man will see whatever his own hands have sent on ahead, and the disbeliever will say: "If I were only dust! Read together the verse 4: 42. As per the verses 4: 41, 16: 89 and 39: 69 on the Day of Judgment Prophets and believers will be brought as witness against each community and people. Moreover each individual's record fastened around their neck as per the verses 17: 13- 14 will produce as an illuminating spread open Book and will say: Read your book; today it is enough yourselves to see your account. The verse 18: 49 says: The book will be produced and you will see the *mujrims* apprehensive. They will say: "Woe to us! What kind of a book is this? It omits nothing either small or large unless it is accounted for. They will find whatever they have done present there, even though you're Lord will not harm anyone. The book mentioned in the verses 35: 11; 36: 12; 45: 28-29; 78: 27-29 also is the same.

The verse 16: 38-39 says, they have sworn by Allah with their most solemn oaths that Allah will not rise up anyone who dies. Nonetheless it is a promise truly binding on Him, even though most men do not realize it. In order to explain to them what they have been differing over, and so those who disbelieve may know that they have been lying. The verse 45: 22 says, Allah has created Heaven and Earth for a true purpose, and so every soul will be rewarded whatever it has earned, and they will not be harmed. The verse 34: 3 says those who disbelieve say: "The hour will not come up on us". Say: "Of course, by my Lord; it will come to you through the knower of the unseen". No atom's weight in either Heaven nor on Earth nor anything less than that nor larger escapes Him, unless it is in a clear book. Read together the verses 10: 52-53; 64: 7. As per the verses 3: 91; 5: 36; 10: 54; 13: 18; 39: 47 it is told: Even if those who hide the Soul of Qur'an owned whatever is on Earth plus its like besides, in order to redeem themselves from torment by means of it on Resurrection Day, it would not be accepted from them, they will have painful torment. In both the verses 9: 55 and 85 Allah says, about the hypocrites, do not let their wealth nor children dazzle you; Allah only wants to punish them by means of them during worldly life and for their souls to perish while they are disbelievers. About such hypocrites it is told in the verse 9: 125: The Soul of Qur'an will add filth to their existing filth and they will die while they are still disbelievers. Both in the verses 6: 130 and 7: 37 it is told that those who twist or reject the Qur'an verses will witness against themselves that they were disbelievers on the Day of Judgment.

The verse 5: 109 says, on that Day Allah will assemble His Messengers and say: "What response have you received?" They will say: "We possess no knowledge; You are the only knower of all unseen things!" Read together the verse 7: 6. As per the verses 5: 116-120, there is a description of the scene in which Prophet Jesus has been specifically questioned. Through the verses 6: 28; 32: 12; 40: 11 it is warned: The *mujirims* who do not utilize themselves and not give to others the Soul of Qur'an when they are set before the Fire, will say: "Woe unto us! Our Lord, if we might only be send back and had not rejected our Lord's verses and we had been believers".

The death scene of wrongdoers is portrayed in the verse 6: 94 as: You have all come to Us individually now, just as We created you in the first time. You have left behind what We bestowed on you, nor do We see your intercessors along with you, whom you claimed to be Allah's associates for your affairs. And all relations between their partners will be cut off from you, and what you have been claiming has merely led you astray. The verses 18: 48, 19: 80, 95 also teach that each one has to reply before their Lord individually. Believers should meet Allah pleasantly; whereas the disbelievers meet the satan sadly at the time of death as told in the verses 75: 22-24. The *mujrims* will not see Allah on the Day of Judgment also. The verse 83: 15 says, indeed they will be screened off from their Lord on that Day.

The verses 38: 55, 59-64 say: For the wrongdoers who lived transgressing the limit will have an evil place of final return. To those who went first to the Hell, Allah will say: here is a troop rushing headlong with you. Then those who are in Hell will say: "no welcome for them, truly they shall burn in the fire". The followers will say: "no, you too, no welcome for you. It is you who have come before us. How evil is this place to stay in! The followers will say: "our Lord! They are our predecessors; add to them a double punishment in the Fire". They will ask: "what happened to us? Here, we don't see men whom we used to consider among the evil persons. Did we treat them in ridicule or have our eyes failed to perceive them? "Certainly, that is just and true, the mutual arguments of the people of the Fire.

The verses 37: 50- 56 say, some of the dwellers of Paradise will step forward to question someone among them will speak up and say: I had an intimate companion on the Earth. He used to ask me: Are you among those who make true Qur'an? Do you believe that when we have died and become dust and bones, will we be called to account? Then Allah will ask him: would you like to see him? Then he will look down, and will see his companion in the midst of the Hades. Then the Paradise dweller will say: By Allah! You almost ruined me, if it were not for my Lords favor; I would have been made to appear with you. The verse 31: 33 says: Oh mankind, heed your Lord and dread the Day when no parent will make aments for his child nor will any offspring make aments in any way for his parent. Allah's promise is true, so do not let worldly life deceive you, nor even let the deceiver deceive you concerning Allah. As per the verses 80: 34-42, on that day each and everyone will flee from his brother, his mother and his father, his mate and his children. All of them will have enough to look after very much of their own affairs. Some faces will be beaming on that Day laughing, rejoicing while other faces will be covered with grime on that Day. Soot will over shadow them. Such are the hypocrites and *fujjaar*. Through the verses 70: 11-14 it is warned: It is a Day when *mujrims* will desire to ransom himself from that Day's torment through his children, his wife, his brother, his family circle which has sheltered him, and everyone who is on Earth if might then save him.

In the verse 17: 72, it is warned: Those who were blind to the Soul of Qur'an in this world will be blind more in the Hereafter. In the verses 89: 23-24 also there is a warning that the Day when Hell is brought face to face man will be remembered that, had I used the Soul of Qur'an how better it would have been, and he will regret that I have wasted my life for nothing. Read together the verses 18: 100-101, 44: 10-14. The verses 25: 24 says the inhabitance of the Paradise will have the best residence and finest lodging on that Day. The verses 36: 53-54 say, there will be only a single blast and then they will all be assembled in Our presence. On that Day no soul will be harmed in anyway, and you will be rewarded only for what you have been doing. As per the verses 36: 55-58 continues: Indeed that Day the inhabitants of the Paradise will be happily at work on that Day. They and their spouses will relax on coaches in shady nooks; they will have fruit there and they shall have anything they request. "Peace will be a greeting from the Merciful Lord!" The verses 59-64 say: "Step aside today, you *mujirims!* Did I not hold covenant with you, oh children of Adam, not to serve satan? He is an open enemy of yours. And to serve Me alone, that is the Straight Path; he has led a numerous mob of you astray. Then were you not utilizing your intelligence? This is Hell, which you were threatened with! Roast in it today because you have disbelieved.

Therefore, when we recite the third verse of Fathiha, we should have to keep in mind to include us with the people mentioned in the verses 36:55-58 and not to include among the dwellers of the Hell mentioned in verses 59-64. The verses 82: 13-16 says: Certainly, the virtuous shall be in bliss, and the *fujjar* will be in Hades, they shall roast there on the Day of Judgment; they will never be led out of It. Then through the verses 82: 17-18 Allah asks: What do you know about the Day of Judgment? Again, what do you know about the Day of Judgment? Then the verse19 says: It is the Day when no soul shall have power to do any helps or harm to another. That day all the command will be with Allah only! On the Day of Judgment the whole of the Earth will be in Allah's hand, and the Heavens will be rolled up in His right hand, then He will say: I am the Monarch, I am the Arrogant and I am the Dictator. Where are the monarchs on the Earth? Where are the arrogant persons? Where are the dictators? On that Day all of them will be presented as naked, barefooted and without circumcision before Allah. It will be asked: who holds control today? Allah alone, the Dictator. Read the verses 39: 67, 40: 16.

The verses 14: 48-51 say: On the Day the Earth will be changed to different Earth and so will be the Heavens. All the men will be exposed before Allah, Who rules everything. On that day you can see that the *mujrims* (madmen) are bound together in fetters. Their garments there will be of liquid tar, and faces will be covered with fire. That day has been fixed so that Allah may requite each soul according to its deserts. Indeed Allah is swift in calling to account. The verses 11: 18-23 say: Who does more wrong than those who invent a lie about Allah? Those will be turned over to their Lord and witnesses will say: "These are the ones who lied about their Lord". Does not Allah's curse rest on wrongdoers, those who obstruct Allah's way and attempt to make it crooked, and are disbelievers in the Hereafter? Those will not prevent anything from happening on Earth nor will they have any patrons besides Allah. Torment will be doubled for them. They have not been enabled to hear not have they been observing the Soul of Qur'an. Such are the ones who have lost their own souls, while whatever they were inventing has led them astray. No doubt they will be indeed the losers most in the Hereafter. Indeed those who believe perform honorable deeds and humbled themselves by mind to their Lord, such are the inhabitance of the Paradise; they will live in It forever. As per verse 7: 44 it is told: The companions of the Paradise will call out to the companions of the Fire: "We have indeed found the promises of Lord to us true. Have you also found your Lord's promises true?" The inmates of the Fire will say: "Yes". Then an announcer among them will call out: "Allah's curse rests on wrongdoers. Who obstruct Allah's path and try to make it crooked, and are disbelievers in the Hereafter".

Therefore, those who wish to escape on the Day of Judgment has to utilize the Soul of Qur'an as Insight, Balance, Proof, Guidance, Light, Trust, Truth, Ticket, Safeguard and there upon make It Argue, Witness and Intercede in favor of him, not against him.

4. We do serve only for You and we do seek help only from You.

The group of believers from Prophet Adam to the Day of Judgment who are mentioned in the verses 5: 56 and 58: 22 whether they are alone or together, say when they pray: We are living only for You, or living as Your representatives, and for that in any situations we seek only Your help. Though all mankind and *Jinns* were deputed to the Earth to live as Allah's representatives, only the believers are ready to bear that. All others are the bearers of Satan's representation, and are included in Satan's party as mentioned in the verse 58:19. The verses 51: 56-57 say: I have never created *Jinns* and men except them have to serve Me alone; I do not want any sustenance from them nor do I need them to feed Me. The verse 67: 2 says: He is the One Who created death and life in order to test which of you is the finest in action, He is the Powerful, the Forgiving. Read together the verses 11: 7; 18: 7.

Prophet taught: "What is meant by '*Ihsan*'- existing in the consciousness that as like you see Allah, though you do not see Him, He is seeing you". That means existing in remembrance of Allah in all walking, sitting and lying- always and everywhere with the Soul of Qur'an.

As per the verses 38: 82- 83 Satan said to Allah: "Then by Your power, I will make all of them aimless astray except Your servants among them who serve for You only. This conversation between Allah and Satan is mentioned in the verses 4: 117-120; 7:12-18; 15: 39-43, 17: 62-65 etc. Then in the verses 38: 84-85 Allah said: "Such is the truth, and the truth do I say, certainly I shall fill Hell with you and any of them who follow you". This fact is also mentioned in the verses 11: 118- 119; 32: 13. Thus one who approves Allah as Perfect and Independent of anything, but all creatures are depended upon Him, he is the sincere, innocent servant of Allah, such believer number is one out of thousand as specified in the verse 4: 118.

The one who always exists remembering Allah by hold fasting The Soul of Qur'an firmest rope specified both in the verses 2: 256 and 31: 22 is serving Allah and he can help Allah by propagating It among all world. Such that the Soul of Qur'an will act as a shield and safeguard for him from all the disasters in this world as well as from the Hell. As told in the verses 9: 67, 59: 19 and 32: 14 the one, who are living by hiding and rejecting the Soul of Qur'an and Allah with an aimless and heedless mind that He doesn't see and watch, is serving Satan. Anyone feared or obeyed others disobeying Allah is serving satan. The verse 3: 102, by calling the believers says: You should keep Allah in hearts as it should be kept, and you shouldn't be dying except in peace submitting all to Him. By forgetting Allah whoever calls or invokes great people who are just the creation of Allah; fear their curse will be affected; make offerings in order to propitiate and hope their recommendations or intercession-all these include under the serving of Satan. Prophet *Ibrahim* as per the verses 6: 81-82, Prophet Muhammad as per the verses 7: 194-195, Prophet *Nooh* as per the verse 10: 71 and Prophet Hood as per the verses 11: 54-56 challenged the associates of their period concerned to plot away against them.

The verse 40: 60 says: Your Lord has said: "Appeal to Me; I shall respond to you. The one who are too arrogant to serve Me, will enter Hell abjectly. Here the 'worship' is prayer. The verses 25: 17-18 say: On that Day He will summon them along with whatever they have been worshiping instead of Allah and He will ask: "Were you the ones, who led these servants of Mine astray, or did they stray away by themselves?" Then the great men will reply: "Glory is to You!" We would never take on any patrons beside You! However You let them and their forefathers enjoy things until they forgot the Soul of Qur'an and became a worthless boar people. It is told in the verse 48: 12 that the hypocrites are indeed a worthless, boar people. As per the verse 14: 30 it is commanded the believer to tell such boar people that, enjoy yourselves, certainly your return will be to the Fire. Read together the verse 39: 8. The verse 10: 18 says: Instead of Allah they serve what neither harms nor benefits them, and they say: "These are our intercessors with Allah". Say: "Do you notify Allah about something in Heaven and on Earth that He already doesn't know? Glory is to Him; exalted is He over whatever they associate with Him. And the verses 28- 29 say: On the Day, We will summon them altogether, then We shall tell those who has associated: "Stay where you are, you and your associates!" We will sort them out, and their associates will say: "You weren't serving us. Allah suffixes as a witness between us and you. We were heedless that you were even serving us. In the verses 16: 86- 87 say: When those who have associated (others with Allah) see their associates, they will say: "Our Lord, these are our 'associates', whom we appealed to instead of You". They will toss the statement back at them: "Indeed you are lying". They will proffer their surrender to Allah on that Day, while anything they were inventing will leave them in the lurch. Read together the verses 4: 172, 18: 110; 41: 37- 38.

Ilah- Deity: The verse 21: 25 says: "We did not send any Messenger before you unless We inspired him with the fact 'there is no deity except Me', then worship Me". Here, worship is the recognition of Allah as the only Deity. The verse 16: 2 says: He sends down Angels with the spirit of His command on any of His servants He may wish: "Warn mankind that there is no Deity except Me"; so heed Me. And it is told in the verse 16: 36 that We have dispatched a Messenger to every community saying: Serve Allah alone and turn aside from the arrogant ones.

Deity means, the One who can seek refuge and help, upon whom one can entrust, only to whom one can afraid, on before Him one has to reply about his life. Whoever calls anyone as deity other than Him; whoever lives to convince others will be the worship for satan. For the '*Thagooth*' see the verse 2: 257. The verse 16: 51 says: Do not adopt two deities, there exists only one Deity; if you are only revere Me alone. As per the verse 2: 133, when death approached Prophet *Ya'qoob*, he called his sons and asked: what will you serve after I am gone?" They replied: "We shall serve your Deity and the Deity of your forefathers *Ibrahim*, *Ismaeel* and *Is'haq*; the single Deity alone and we are all submitted peacefully to Him". The verse 20: 98 says: "Your Deity is Allah alone; there is no Deity except Him, He comprehends all things in His knowledge. As per the verse 5: 116, when Allah questioning Jesus as: Have you told the people that adopt me and my mother as two deities instead of Allah? Then Jesus will reply: "Glory is to You! I could never say what I had no right to say! If I had told it You would indeed have known it. You know what is in my mind, while I do not know anything that in Yours. Indeed, You are the only Knower of all unseen things.

Prophet taught: "Prayer, that is the worship". In the verses 16: 20- 21 Allah say: "Those whom they invoke instead of Allah do not create a thing, while they themselves have been created; dead, lifeless, they don't even perceive the time when they will be raised up again. Then the verse 22 says "Indeed your deity is the Deity alone! Those who don't believe with the Hereafter have hearts which refuse to accept this, while they are over pride. By saying through the verse 35: 13 the one who you appeal instead of Allah, don't control a wisp. Then the verse 35: 14 says: "If you should appeal to them, they will not hear your appeal. While even though they hear it, they wouldn't respond to you. On the Day of Judgment they will deny your associating others with Allah. No one notifies to you such things except the One Who is acquainted of all things". The verse 22: 73 says: Oh you mankind, a parable has been composed, so listen to it! Indeed those whom you appeal to other than Allah will never create a fly, even though they combined together to do so. Yet the fly should snatch anything away from them, they would have no power to recover it from it. Alas! Both the seeker and the sought are weak. The verses 29: 41-42 say: Those who enlist other p ether the verse 59: 21. The verse 35: 28 ends as: Yet, only among His servants who learned the Soul of Qur'an, fear Allah, even though Allah is Powerful, Forgiving. The verse 67: 12 says: Indeed the ones who live in fear of their Lord even though He is unseen will have forgiveness and great reward. Read together the verses 23: 1-10; 36: 11; 98: 8.

Those who obey the hypocritical scholars, priests and leaders, who judge against the revelation of Allah; i.e. against the Soul of Qur'an, are the worshipers of satan. Read together the verses 2: 166-167; 9: 30- 31. Through the verses 19: 44 Prophet *Ibrahim* says by calling his father: "Oh my father! Serve not Satan; for Satan is a rebel against the Impartial". And in the verse 45, Oh my father! I fear lest some torment from the Impartial should afflict you, since you choose satan as your protector.

Both in the verses 22:40 and 47:7 Allah says: If anyone helps Allah, Allah will help him also, and his foot will be kept in the Straight Path firmly. Today, to help Allah means teach mankind the Soul of Qur'an in order to recognize Allah, themselves, the aim of life, thus make truthful the teaching of Prophet that the best among you is the one who learns and teaches the Soul of Qur'an. Through the verse 39: 64 Allah tells the Prophet to ask, "Oh, you ignorant ones, do you order me to live and serve other than Allah? Through the verses 6: 56 and 40: 66 Allah orders the Prophet to say: "Indeed I am forbidden to worship those- other than Allah- whom you call upon. In the verses 6: 88 and 39: 65 it is told: "If any one associate others in the dominion of Allah, all their deeds will be in futile and they will be the losers. That is why through the verse 63: 9 Allah calls believers and say: Neither your property nor your children prevent or obstruct you from the Soul of Qur'an, by which remembrance of Allah can only be maintained and anyone does so, such are the losers. Through the verses 10: 104- 106 Allah orders the Prophet to say: "If you are in doubt about '*Dheen*'- my way of life-, I do not live and serve for what you live and serve other than Allah. But I live only for Him who shall cause your death. And I am ordered to be among the believers. I am also ordered to set my face towards this '*Dheen*' with true sincere and not be among those who associate partners with Allah and also ordered not to call and pray anybody other than Allah. If I do so, I will be certainly among the wrongdoers. Read together the verse 6: 52.

Through the verses 109: 1-6 Allah orders the Prophet and the believers to say: "Oh, you disbelievers who hide and reject the Soul of Qur'an after receiving It: I do not serve, what you serve; nor are you serving, what I serve! I will not worship what you have worshiped. Neither will you worship what I worship. For you, your way of life, while for me the True way of life. In the verse 98: 5 Allah says: They have been not commanded to worship except for Allah alone. Also they have been commanded to establish *swalath* and practice regular charity. That is the right and straight '*Dheen*'- way of life. The verses 39: 2- 3: "We have sent the Book down to you with the Truth, so serve Allah sincerely, making whole life to Him. Pure religion belongs to Allah alone! The ones, who take on other patrons instead of Him, say that "we don't serve them except to bring us closer to Allah in homage." Truly Allah will judge among them about whatever they have been differing over; Allah does not guide who is a disbelieving liar. The verses 22: 11- 13 say: There are some men who serve Allah along the border line: if any some good should happen to him, he accepts it calmly, while if some trial should strike him, he turns over on his face in despair. He loses this world as well as the Hereafter i.e. such as obvious loss. He appeals to something that neither harms nor yet benefits him, instead of Allah that is extreme astray; he appeals to someone whose harm is closer than his benefit. How wretched is such a patron!

It is told the verse 17: 23 that your Lord has decreed that you should serve nothing except Him. The verse 20: 14 says: "Indeed I am Allah alone, there is no Deity except Myself, So serve Me and keep up *swalath* to remember Me by. After explaining about some of the Prophets, in the verse 21: 92 Allah says: "Indeed this community of yours is a single community, while I am your Lord, so worship Me alone. In the verse 22: 71 Allah says: "Yet instead of Allah they worship something for which no authority has been sent down and about which they have no knowledge. There is no any helper for such wrongdoers. It is told in the verse 19: 49: "When *Ibrahim* moved away from his own people and what they worshiped besides Allah, Allah bestowed on him *Is'haq* and *Ya'qoob* and each made a Prophet. Read together the verses 21: 69- 72.

The verse 23: 117 says, "Any one who appeals to any other deity along with Allah, has no proof for it. His reckoning rests only with his Lord. Disbelievers will not succeed. It is told in the verse 25: 68 that the most beloved servants of Allah do not appeal to any other deity besides Allah; nor kill any soul whom Allah has forbidden except with truth and they will not fornicate. The verse 28: 88 says; "do not appeal any other deity along with Allah: there is no deity except Him. Everything is perishable except His face! Discretion belongs to Him, and to Him will you all be returned.

The verse 35: 40 says: "have you ever seen your associates whom you appeal to instead of Allah? Show me what they have created on Earth. Or have they a partnership in Heavens? Or have We given them a book? Have they come upon any explanation from It? Rather wrongdoers nothing promises one another except delusions. The verse 31: 30 says, "That is because Allah is the truth while anything they appeal to instead of Him is false. Allah is the Sublime, the Great. The verse 7: 194 says, "Those you appeal instead of Allah are servants just like yourselves. Appeal to them so they may respond to you if you are so truthful! The verse 27: 91 says I have only been ordered to serve the Lord of this region which He has hallowed. He possesses everything. And I have been ordered to be a Muslim-who submitted everything to Allah in peace.

The verse 29: 17 says, "You serve only images instead of Allah, and thus creating falsehood. The ones you serve instead of Allah do not control any sustenance for you, so seek sustenance from Allah Himself and serve Him; act grateful towards Him; To Him will you be returned. And the verse 56 says, "Oh, My servants who believe! Truly, My Earth is vast, if you are Me alone are worshipping! Read together the verse 2: 21. The verse 13: 36 says: Those whom We have given the Book to are happy with what has been sent down to you; yet among the groups there are some who disagree part of It. Say: "I am only ordered to serve Allah and not associate any thing with Him. To Him do I call you, and towards Him will be my retreat. As per the verse 12: 108 it is ordered Prophet to Say: "This is my way. I am inviting you to Allah. I and who follow me are upon an Insight. Glory is to Allah and I am not among the associates. Read together the verses 28: 85- 88.

Addressing mankind through the verse 16: 114 Allah says: "Eat any lawful, wholesome things Allah has provided for you with, and be grateful for Allah's favors, if you are worshipping Him alone. Addressing the believers through the verse 2: 172 Allah says: "Eat any lawful, wholesome things Allah has provided for you with, and be grateful for Allah's favors, if you are worshipping Him alone. The verses 36: 74- 75 say, "They have adopted other deities instead of Allah, so that might be helped. They still cannot achieve their help; yet they stand up as a troop against them when they all gathered together. Read together the verses 46: 5-6. As per the verse 21: 112 Prophet said: "My Lord will judge with Truth", and "our Lord is the Impartial - Most Gracious whose help is sought against what you ascribe.

It is only to Allah, the Lord of the worlds that believers ask regarding any matter. Then Allah, Creator of all fulfills it through others. That is the idea of what Prophet taught to pray: *Oh Allah, there is nobody who prevents what You give; and nobody to give what You prevent. There is none who cancel what You have judged, and nobody is there who amends Your judgment. No arrogance or pride of an egoist will be of any use with You.*

It is commanded through the verses 17: 56-57 to say: "Invoke those whom you claim besides Him: they do not control any means of removing harm from you, nor for changing it". Such are whom they appeal to, crave access to their Lord vying to be nearest. They hope for His Mercy and fear His torment. Your Lord's torment is something to beware off! Read together the verse 5:35. So if anyone appeals to any creatures whether they are Angels, Prophets, saints or anybody else than the Creator as the intercessors or recommenders, seeking accessibility of *satan*. Crave accessibility of Allah is by doing good deeds, turning back from doing evils, even though there is a chance to do so; by thinking that Allah is observing every thing. Prophet taught that once there was storm and rain three members of the children of Israel took refuge in a cave. Then the entrance of the cave was closed by a hanging rock, so that they couldn't get out of the cave. They sought the accessibility of Allah by quoting good deeds done by each of them. Thus by raising the rock each time one by third opening the entrance of the cave, Allah saved them. It is taught a prayer by *Hadeeth Qudsee*: *"Oh, You the one Who ever lives Oneself and makes all others alive, with Your Mercy I seek help"*. Otherwise seeking '*Waseela*'-craving accessibility is remembering by mind the favors bestowed during the incidents of Prophet's life. Read together the verses 10: 103, 21: 88, 30:47.

Prophet taught, when it is said, "Praise be to Allah, the Lord of all worlds. Then Allah will say: My servant has praised Me properly. When the servant says the Most Gracious, the most Merciful, *Allah* will say: My servant has approved Me properly. When the servant says: "Master of the Day of Judgment", Allah will say: "My servant has honored Me properly. When the servant says: "We do serve only for you and we do seek help only from You". Allah will say: that is the covenant between Me and the servant. So certainly I will give what the servant is asking. Therefore when we recite this verse, we should pray by heart as: "Include me among the one out of each thousand and among those who lives, serves, represents and worships you alone; even though it may be disgusting for the disbelievers and associates".

5. Guide us along the Straight path.

The verses 15: 39-43 say: satan who refused to prostrate before man told to Allah: "Oh my Lord, since You have made me aimless, I will make things on Earth seem attractive to them; I will make them all aimless astray, except Your sincere servants who serve You alone. Allah told, "This is indeed the way that leads straight to Me. You shall have no authority over My sincere servants except such as who became aimless astray themselves. And Hell is the promised abode for all of them together. The verse 17: 65 says: "Indeed, My servants you will have no authority over them; your Lord suffices as a Trustee. The verse 36: 61 says: And you serve Me alone, this is the Straight Path.

The quintessence of Qur'an is the Straight path. It is the Ticket to reach Allah by crossing the bridge over the Hell. As per the verse 2: 38 when everybody was sent down to Earth from the Paradise, Allah said: "If the Guidance has come to you from Me, then any one who follows My Guidance, on them there shall be no fear and for them will not be grieved. It is told in the verse 2: 185 that Qur'an is the Guidance for the entire mankind. Without the Soul of Qur'an nobody become believer and only from believers *swalath*, Fasting and Hajj etc. performed will be accepted as told in the verses 2: 186, 7: 8-9, 18: 103-106. It is told both in the verses 17: 82 and 41: 44 that Qur'an is Guidance and Healing for the believers. The verse 6: 126 says: "And this is the Straight Path of your Lord, indeed We have detailed the verses for the people who remember with heart. All verses 2: 142, 213 and 10: 25 end as Allah guides whom He indents to the way that is Straight. The Impartial Allah by teaching the Soul of Qur'an containing the ways to the Paradise as well as the Hell has given to each soul. Therefore Allah bestows Straight path only to those who ask to Him. Through the verses 13: 27-28 Allah commands to say: "Indeed Allah lets anyone who wishes go astray, and guides anyone who turns to Him; i.e. those who pray "my Lord, increase in my knowledge" then read and follow the Soul of Qur'an, the Straight path. The verse 16: 37 says, even if you are eager to guide them, Allah still does not guide someone who misleads himself and they will not have any helpers. Read together the verse 7: 178. It is told in the verse 3: 101: "Whoever holds firmly Allah is already guided to the Straight Path". To hold firmly Allah means to hold firmly the rope of Allah, the Soul of Qur'an. Read together the verses 3: 103 and 4: 174-175.

In the verse 6: 39 Allah say, "Those who reject Our verses are deaf and dumb in the midst of darkness. Allah lets anyone He wishes to go astray, while He sets anyone He wishes upon the Straight path. The verses 39: 32- 33 say: who is more in the wrong than someone who lies about Allah and denies the Truth i.e. The Soul of Qur'an after It has come to him. Is there not place in Hell for such disbelievers? Those who received the truth and made It truth are the heedful. Read together the verses 6: 87, 161, 29: 68 As per the verse 16:76 Allah says the parable of two men, "One of whom is dumb and cannot do anything, and he is a nuisance to his master. Wherever he sends him on an errand, he brings no good. Is he equal to someone who commands with justice and he is on the Straight Path. As per the verse 16:121 it is told that Allah has chosen Prophet *Ibrahim* and has guided to the Straight path. As per the verse 11: 56 Prophet *Hood* has told that indeed my Lord is on the Straight Path. The verse 28: 56 says, "Indeed you do not guide someone you love. But Allah guides anyone He wishes. He is quite aware as to who are guided. Read together the verse 16: 125. The verse 2: 272 revealed as an answer to a question whether charity can be given to non-Muslims; Allah says: Their Guidance is not given to you. But Allah guides whom He wishes. Through the verses 81: 27- 29 Allah say that this Qur'an is nothing except a Reminder to awake all the worlds for anyone of you who wishes to live on Straight path. Yet, you will only wish whatever Allah, the Lord of the World may wish. It is told in the verse 14: 1 that Qur'an is sent to Prophet Muhammad down in order to lead mankind out of the darkness in to light- by the Permission of their Lord- to the way of the exalted in Power and self praise worthy. Here mentioned 'Permission' is the Soul of Qur'an. 'Their Lord's Permission' means each individual has to pray by mind 'my Lord, increase me in knowledge' as told in the verse 20: 114 then read and follow the Soul of Qur'an. As per the verse 22: 24 the heedful have been guided to a wholesome way of speech as well as guided along the Praise Worthy's path. Here mentioned both wholesome way of speech and the Praise Worthy's path are the Soul of Qur'an. The verse 22: 54 ends as, "Indeed Allah acts as a guide to the Straight path for those who believe". The verses 36: 3-5 say, certainly, you are belongs to the Messenger along the Straight path, revealed from the exalted in Power, Merciful. The verse 42: 52 ends as, "And indeed you guide men to the Straight path". The verse 40: 73 ends as, "indeed you are inviting them to the Straight path."

Prophet Muhammad led the life of Qur'an. The verses 43: 43-44 say, "So hold on to whatever has been revealed to you; indeed you are on a Straight Path.

And certainly It is the Reminder for you and your people and both you will be questioned about It." Through the verse 67: 22 Allah asks, "Is then one who walks headlong, with his face groveling, better guided, or one who walks evenly on a Straight Path. And the verse 25: 34 says, "Those who do not walk with their heads upright even after receiving Qur'an will be gathered to Hell prone on their faces. Indeed they are in the worst place and the most astray. In the verse 7: 16 Allah warns mankind as told by satan, "since You have made me aimless astray, I will sit for them along the Straight path". The Prophet has taught in *Hajjathul Vida'* that one should remain by biting the Soul of Qur'an-the Straight Path- with the molar teeth during when there is not having the leader and party of believers.

In brief, the Soul of Qur'an is the Straight Path from the first man to the last. It is given as the reply to the servant's request 'guide us to the Straight Path'. On reciting this verse of Fathiha in *Swalath*, anyone if not utilizing the Straight path which is the Soul of Qur'an; enters in to the next *swalath* again and again is joking Allah-their Lord. Such people's *swalath* will not only be accepted, but also will cause to depart from the '*Dheen*' faster than an arrow depart from the bow. In the Hereafter they will be thrown in to the Hell in the shape of dogs, pigs, monkeys etc. Read together the verses 2: 66, 4: 43, 5: 60.

6. The path of those whom You have favored.

"The path of those whom you have favored" means the way of all Prophets, Truthful, Martyrs and Honorable men. The verses 4: 68- 69 say: Anyone who obeys Allah and the Messenger such are with those whom Allah has favored, such as Prophets, Truthful, Martyrs and Honorable men. How fine are such companions? That is the Bounty from Allah; it is enough for Allah to be aware. The verse 57: 19 says: "Those who believe in Allah and in His Messengers such are the Truthful and testify Qur'an verses and Prophet's life. In front of their Lord, they have their reward and their own light, while those who hide and reject Our verses will become the inmates of Hades".

All believers from Adam to the Day of Judgment belongs to Allah's party specified in the verses 5: 55- 56 and 58: 22. It is told in the verse 63: 8 that, "Honor belongs to Allah, His Messenger, and believers; even though hypocrites do not realize it". All the Prophets are believers. But all the believers are not Prophets. Through the verse 10: 104 Allah orders the Prophet to say, "I am commanded to be one among the believers. In the verse 7: 143 Prophet *Moosa* declares that I am the first among the believers. As per the verses 37: 81,111,132 it is told that he was one among My believing servants respectively about *Nooh, Ibrahim,* and *Ilyas*; and in the verse 122 says both *Moosa* and *Haroon* were two of Our believing servants. As per the verse 12: 24 Allah says: Prophet *Yoosuf* was one of Our sincere and purified servants. As per the verse 19: 51 it is told that *Moosa* was sincere, Messenger and Prophet. The verse 10: 103 Allah says, "Then We will save Our Messengers and those who believe; it is thus Our duty to save believers!" The verse 30: 47 ends as, 'it is the duty for Us to support believers!' The verse 21: 88 ends as, 'thus We save believers!' As per both in the verses 15: 40 and 38: 83 it is told that satan cannot deviate the sincere servants of Allah. The verse 16: 99 says: surely satan has no authority upon the believers who trust in their Lord. The way of Allah is the way of Messengers, i.e. The Soul of Qur'an. Read together the verse 9:65. Both through the verses 2: 143 and 22: 78 it is ordered the believers that they should witness Prophet's life among the people by leading the life of the Prophet.

Truthful- Those who make the Qur'an truth: - The verse 9: 119 says: "Oh believers heed Allah and stand by those who make Qur'an truth". The verse 49: 15 says: Surely, believers are the ones who believe with Allah and His Messenger; then never doubt and strive for Allah's sake with their property and persons in the Straight path; such are the truthful. Today the 'Jihad' is only with the Soul of Qur'an and that is to those who hide It. The verse 25: 52 says: Therefore you obey not the disbelievers who hide the Soul of Qur'an and make Jihad- Strive against them with It.

Witnesses- Martyrs: - The Witnesses means the Martyrs during Prophet's time; whereas today they are those who witness the life of Prophet as well as Qur'an to entire mankind. The saying of Jesus disciples is mentioned in the verse 3: 53 as: Our Lord! We believe in what You have sent down and have followed the Messenger, so enroll us among the witnesses. About the men who say we are the helpers of Allah, the verses 5: 83-84 say: When they listen to what has been sent down to the Messenger, you will see their eyes well up with tears because of the Truth they recognize. They say: "Our Lord, we believe, so enroll us among the witnesses! Why should be we not believe in Allah and any Truth that has come to us? We wish for our Lord to admit us along with the Honorable people.

Honorable men- Heedful:- In the verses 2: 130; 16: 122 and 29: 27 it is told about Prophet *Ibrahim* that Allah chose him in this world while in the

Hereafter he will be among the Honorable men. As per the verse 26: 83 it is told that *Ibrahim* prayed: 'Oh my Lord, bestow Wisdom on me, and acquaint me among the Honorable men!' As per the verse 37: 100 Prophet *Ibrahim* prayed: "My Lord! Bestow me from the Honorable men". The verse 37: 112 says: We gave him glad news about *Is'haq* -a Prophet- among the Honorable men. The verse 6: 85 says: The descendents of *Ibrahim* such as *Zakariyya*, *Yahya, Eisa* and *Ilyas* all were among the Honorable men. As per the verse 12: 101 Prophet *Yoosuf* prayed: "Unite me with the Honorable men; and as per the verse 27: 19 Prophet *Sulaiman* prayed: 'Oh my Lord, admit me, by Your Mercy among Your Honorable servants. The verse 29: 9 says: Those who believe and do honorable deeds, surely We shall admit them among the Honorable. And about Prophet *Yoonus* Allah says in the verse 68: 50: Then his Lord chose him and included him among the Honorable men. The verse 21: 72 ends as: Each one- Prophets We made into Honorable men. And about *Looth* the verse 75 says: And We admitted him to Our Mercy; surely he was among the Honorable men. And in the verses 85: 86 say about *Isma'el, Idrees* and *Zul-kifli* (*Ezkiel*), that We admitted them in Our Mercy, surely they were among Honorable men. And the verse 105 says that, 'indeed My Honorable servants will inherit the Earth. It is told in the verse 28: 27 that the father-in-law of *Moosa* told him: You will find me, Honorable men, if Allah so wishes. In the verse 3: 39 it is told about Prophet *Yahya* that he is a leader having self control and a Prophet among the Honorable men. In the verse 46 it is told about Prophet *Eisa* that he was among the Honorable men. In the verses 113- 114 Allah says: Some persons of the Book were Honorable people who learned and followed Book; enjoined right and forbid evil and were among the Honorable men.

In the verses 40: 7-8, it is mentioned that Allah's throne bearing Angels and that stand around Him will seek forgiveness for those who believe, and pray for their entrance in to the Paradise which has been promised to them along with their Honorable children, mates and fathers. The verses 13: 19- 23 say: "Is some one who knows whatever has been sent down to you from your Lord is truth, like someone who is blind? Surely, prudent persons will remember It by heart. Those who fulfill Allah's covenant and do not break the agreements, who transmit anything Allah has ordered to be transmitted, and dread their Lord and fear the worst Reckoning, who persevere in seeking satisfaction of their Lord and keep up *swalath* and spent whatever We have provided them both secretly and publicly, and ward of evil with Best- the Soul of Qur'an. Those will have the compensation of the final home i.e. the Paradise of eternity which they will enter, as well as anyone who has acted honorably from among their forefathers, their spouses and their off springs. Angel will come in on them in every gate. When Prophet greeted Allah in the Paradise on the occasion *Mihraj Night*, Allah replied: "Oh Prophet, Allah's protection has to you, also His Mercy and Blessings". Then Prophet asked: "Let your protection be on all of us, the Prophets, and also on all Your Honorable servants". The verse 7: 196 says: "Indeed my Protector is Allah Who revealed this Book and He will choose only the Honorable men".

Through the verse 63: 10 Allah says to the believers: "Spend something from whatever We have provided with before death comes to one of you. Then he says: "My Lord! If you would only delay things for me for a short while, then I will make the Truth and become Honorable. It is told in the verse 2: 11- 12 that when the believers say to the hypocrites: "Do not make mischief on the Earth", they say: "Certainly we are the honorable"; beware, surely they are the mischief doers, but they do not realize it. So believers have to pray in their prostates especially in the last prostrate as; '*Oh, my Lord, by your Great Mercy- Soul of Qur'an, let's include among the Honorable servants'*.

7. **Not the path upon whom Your wrath happened; and who gone astray.**

That is, not in the path of Jews and hypocrites whom Allah has already killed due to their knowingly hiding Qur'an verses. They are those upon whom Allah's wrath and curse happened. Not in the way of the Christians who have gone astray by portraying Eisa as one of the trinity-father, son and Holly spirit, which is against the teachings of Prophet *Eisa*. Today the one who gone astray are '*fujjar*' who are rejecting the Soul of Qur'an and following blindly hypocrites.

Not in the path of hypocrites men and women, who are transgressors and the '*kuffar*' to whom Allah has cursed and kept prepare the Hellfire as specified in the verses 9: 67,68, The '*kuffar*' mentioned both in the verses 9: 73 and 66: 9 are also the gone astray people. The Soul of Qur'an, the Trust and Balance for preserving the Universe in its equilibrium has been revealed in order to punish the hypocrites men and women and those who associate others in Allah's dominion, and also to receive the repentance of believers, men and women, is told in the verses 33: 72- 73. Those men or women who associate others in Allah's dominion mentioned in this verse, are belonged to the people who gone astray. The verse 98: 6 say, "Indeed those who hide the Truth among the people of the Book and the '*mushrikeen*'- those who associate others in Allah's dominion will be in Hell-fire. They dwell in forever. They are the worst of creatures of Land". Since today the Book is Qur'an, hiders of the Truth mentioned here is the hypocrites, and the '*mushrikeen*' are the people who gone astray. The verse 4: 140 ends as 'Certainly Allah will gather all the hypocrites and disbelievers into Hell'. Here, the hypocrites are those who hide, ridicule or distort the Qur'an verses in their speech, and the disbelievers are those who sit listening them and they are the people who gone astray. The believers should pray that they should not be included in both of them. Read together the verse 48: 6

The disbelievers mentioned in the verses 41: 26- 28 are the hypocrites who forbid common people from the Soul of Qur'an. They are the enemies of Allah and they have to dwell the Hell for ever; as the reward, for they were repudiating the Qur'an verses. In the verse 63: 4 it is told that the hypocrites are the enemies of Allah and believers; so beware of them. The disbeliever mentioned in the verse 41: 29 is the people who have gone astray following these hypocrites as leaders. Tomorrow they will say; "Our Lord, show us those who have led us astray. Let us tramp them and propitiate our anger- instead of having lived as inferior and as their followers in the world. As per the verse 33: 12 it is told that the hypocrites and those whose heart contains malice were saying; "Allah and His messenger have promised us nothing except delusions." Here mentioned 'those whose heart contains malice' is the people who have gone astray following the hypocrites. Both in the verses 33: 1, 48 Allah say addressing Prophet, 'you do not obey the disbelievers and hypocrites.' The disbelievers mentioned in these verses are those who have gone astray. The verses 22: 3- 4 says, "Among men there are such as dispute about Allah without any knowledge –means the Soul of Qur'an, and they follow every willful satans. It has been written down concerning anyone he befriends that he shall mislead him and Guides him to the torment of the Blaze. Read together the verses 22: 8, 31: 20 and 21.

The hypocrite leaders are human devils and wrongdoers who have lost their aim of life. They belong to the '*ghaveen*'. Read together the verses 6: 112 and 7: 175. Those who follow them are heedless and they belong to '*ghafileen*'. The hypocrites know that the Soul of Qur'an is the Straight path but they did not only utilizing It as the Straight path and also not allow the heedless people to utilize It. The hypocrites will fall in to the bottom of Hell without even trial as told in the verse 4: 145, and the gone astray people will be led to the Hell after reckoning as told in the verses 39: 71-72. Read together the verses 7: 179, 18: 100-101 and 67: 6 - 11. The death scene of both the gone astray people and hypocrites portrays in the verse 39: 59 as: "Rather of course My verses came to you but you rejected them and acted proudly and you were among the disbelievers. Here, the rejected people are heedless, gone astray people and acted as proudly are the hypocrites. Allah says both of them are among the disbelievers. Both of these people will witness against themselves that they were disbelievers at the time of death as per the verse 7: 37 and on the Day of Judgment as per the verse 6: 130. In the verses 16: 106- 109 Allah say, "Any one who after accepting faith in Allah utters unbelief, and his heart remaining firm in unfaith on them there will be wrath from Allah. They will have dreadful torment. That is because they cherish worldly life rather than the Hereafter. Indeed Allah will not guide such disbelieving people. Those are the ones whose hearts, hearing and eye sight Allah has sealed off. Those are the heedless. There is no doubt, in the Hereafter they lost everything. Here mentioned heedless include both the hypocrites and the gone astray people. The verse 60: 13 says, "Oh who you believe, do not patronize any people upon whom Allah's angry happened; they despair of the Hereafter justas *'Kuffar'* despair of the inmates of tombs. Here, upon whom Allah's angry happened are the hypocrites and the *'kuffar'* is the people who gone astray.

The verse 16: 37 says, even if you are eager to guide them, then surely Allah does not guide the one who made astray himself and they will not have any helpers. The verse 30: 29 says, rather, the wrongdoers follow their own whims without having any knowledge. Then who will guide someone whom Allah has let go astray? And they will not have any helpers. They are the hypocrites whom Allah has killed. Read together the verse 7: 176. Through the verses 25: 43- 44 Allah asks, "Have you seen some one who takes his own whim or will as his deity? Would you act as a trustee for him? or do you reckon that most of them listen or utilize their intelligence? Certainly they are nothing except like cattle. Nay; they are even further astray from the Straight Path". Through verse 45: 23 Allah asks, "Have you seen some one who has taken his whim as his deity, Allah knowingly leads him go astray? And made a seal upon his hearing and heart, and places a covering over his eyesight. Who will guide him instead of Allah? Will you not utilize the Soul of Qur'an? Note that if anyone not utilizes the Soul of Qur'an after receiving It they are the blind, deaf and dump and their lodging will be the Hell. Through the verses 39: 36- 37 Allah asks, "Is not Allah enough for His servants? They try to frighten you with the ones they worship instead of Him while anyone whom Allah lets go astray, then he will not be guided; and no one can gone astray others whom Allah guides. Is Allah not exalted in powerful, the wielder of revenge?

The verse 39: 41 says, "Indeed We have sent you down the Truth for mankind. Then anyone who utilizes Guidance benefits his own soul, while anyone who goes astray will only stray because of it as well. You are not set over them to dispose of their affairs. The verses such as 6: 104, 10:108 and 27:92 are having the same message. The verse 28: 50 says, if they do not respond to you, you know that they are merely following their own whims. Who is more astray than someone who follows his own passions without having any Guidance from Allah? Allah does not guide such wrongdoing people. The verse 85 says, indeed the one who has charged you with this Qur'an will return you the best destination, Paradise. You do say, "My Lord knows very best that has brought true Guidance and who is in plain astray.

The verse 33: 36 ends as anyone who disobeys Allah and His Messenger has wandered off into manifest astray. The verse 5: 12 ends as, "Having received true path, if anyone among you denies It has gone astray from the most Straight path. Through the verse 77, Allah commands the Prophet to say addressing the people of the Book, "Do not exaggerate in your religion beyond the truth, nor follow the whims of the people who have already gone astray and mislead many as they stray from the only Straight Path. This verse addresses the Christians. The person who has already gone astray and misled many as they stray refers to Jews. The only Straight path means the Soul of Qur'an. Today the '*mouidath*' of this verse to the believer is not to follow the whims of the hypocrites who have already gone astray and misled many common Muslims as they stray. The verse 4: 136 ends as, one who hides with Allah, His Angels, His Books, His Messengers and the Day of Judgment in Qur'an already gone far astray. The verse 4: 167 says: "Those who hide faith and object the people from Allah's way have indeed strayed far away from the Straight Path.

The verse 2: 161 says, "Those who hide Qur'an and die as '*kuffar*', on them is Allah's curse, and then curse of Angels and of all mankind. In the verses 37: 62- 68 after explaining the food and drinks of Hell-dwellers, Allah says in the verse 69- 71, "For generations they have gone astray". And then yet they went scurrying along in their footsteps, and surely most of the men gone astray before them also. As per the verses 23: 105- 107 Allah will ask those who are roasted in the Hell, "Were not My verses recited to you, and you were rejecting them?" they will reply," our Lord! Our misfortune over whelmed us, and we became a people astray. Our Lord! Let us go out of here. If we ever should return to disobedience, then we would indeed be wrongdoers.

In the verse 28: 15 when Prophet *Moosa* struck the man with his fist and causes to die, then *Moosa* said, "This is some of satan's work; Indeed he is an obvious enemy and plain misleader." As per the verse 26: 19, pointing out the above incident Pharaoh told to Prophet *Moosa*, "When you committed the deed you did so you are one among the disbelievers". Then in the verse 20, *Moosa* reply, "if I did it, I was one among the astray." And as per the verse 86 Prophet *Ibrahim* asked, "My Lord, forgive my father, surely he is the one among who gone astray. As per the verse 93: 7 Allah says to Prophet, "I found you straying, and then I gave you Guidance". The verse 62: 2 says, He is the One Who has dispatched a Messenger from the unlettered people among themselves, to recite His verses to them, purify them and teach them the Book and wisdom, even though previously they were in plain astray. Therefore we can understand that for those who didn't receive the Soul of Qur'an and hence they are straying for Guidance, can beseech Guidance to Allah for them, and for who won't arouse in spite of awakening them and those who have gone astray, and become heedless cannot beseech for forgiveness. Read together the verse 7: 179. And in the case of hypocrites the believers cannot beseech even Guidance.

Conclusion: - Prophet taught that *without 'Fathiha' there is no swalath 'and it is the mother of the Book.* The seven verses of Fathiha contain the whole message of Qur'an. For those who are performing *swalath* absent minds are having the '*waile*' valley in the Hell, is told in the verses 107: 4-5. The prayer of beloved servants of Impartial is explained in the verse 25: 65 as, Our Lord, avert us from the torment of Hell (by the Soul of Qur'an) certainly, Its punishment is a penalty for those who perform *swalath*, fasting and *Hajj* etc. which did not prevent them from doing evil and forbidden deeds. According to the verses 9: 53- 54 neither the charity nor the prayer of hypocrites will be accepted. The reason is, 'they have concealed Allah and His Messengers in the Soul of Qur'an, they have no remembrance of 'Allah' in their prayer, and they do not spend in the way of Allah except with hate." There for whenever believer recites this verse he should remember by mind not includes the way of the hypocrites as well as the gone astray peopie who blindly follow them. Read together the verses 4: 142-143.

Allah, make us believers with your permission-The soul of Qur'an and bestow us, to follow the truth as It should be followed, and enter us the Paradise with the Fore-runners, Victorious, with the Ticket ,Oh the One Who sent down the Ticket, Oh the Virtuous and Merciful. Our Lord, do not include us among the hypocrites and rejecters who will be the fuel of the Hell from Mankind.

With the name of Allah, the Impartial, the Compassionate.

2. Al-Baqara

This *Madeena*-revealed Surath is the largest one in Qur'an consisting of 286 verses. Prophet taught that everything has a peak point and the peak point of Qur'an is *Al-Baqara*. The glorious verse of Qur'an known as the 'Verse of throne' (*AyathulKursiyy*) is 255th and the longest verse in Qur'an is 282. Both *Al-Baqara* and *Ali-Imran* is together known as '*Zahravan*'- means two flower gardens. Prophet taught: *"You should learn and teach Al-Baqara and Ali-Imran; certainly they are two flower gardens. Those who learn those Suraths with content will be provided shades to them as two canopies of clouds or two turbans or two wings of a bird on the Day of Judgment"*.

Allah delivered the children of Israel who were immersed in cow adoration in Egypt from the Pharaohs and his folks by splitting the sea. They encamped in desert 'Siena'. By the direction of Allah, Prophet *Moosa* went to the 'Mount-Thwoor' to receive the *Thourath* by appointing his brother *Haroon* as the representative. This time, under the leadership of *Samiriyy*, the people melted all their ornaments and molded a calf. Satan gave it a mooing sound. They began to worship it. Since cow adoration were dissolved in their very heart, Allah ordered them to sacrifice a cow which is used to worship and has characteristic trait is specified in the verses 67-71. From this event, this surath got the name *Baqara*-which means 'the cow'. This surath teaches that Satan's footsteps like cow adorations, blindly following the way of forefathers, selfishness, racialism, lusts, nationalism, communalism, partiality etc. should be wiped out from one's heart by the Soul of Qur'an and thus should keep Allah in heart.

With the name of Allah, the Impartial, the Compassionate,

1. Alif Lam Meem

The abbreviated letters which form the verse is belonged to allegorical verses mentioned in the verse 3: 7. Since the Qur'an has explained all things in detail, this verse is also explained. *'Alif'* means Allah- from whom the Qur'an is sent down, *'Lam'* means the Angel *'Jibreel'*- through whom It is sent down, *'Meem'* means Prophet Muhammad- to whose heart, It is sent down as specified in the verses 26: 192-194.

2. That Book, no doubt about It, is Guidance to those who are heedful

'That Book' means *Al-kithab*- The book consisting of Glorious Qur'an and The *Ummulkithab*- The mother of the Book specified both in the verses 13: 39; 43:4. The mother of the Book is known as Fathiha. The verses 85: 21-22 say "This is a majestic Qur'an inscribed in a compact disc preserved in Paradise. It is the only Book which is sent down to the Earth as Scripture. Even though Its body is in different languages and is revealed in different times, Its soul –*Adhikr*- is the one and same just like that of human being. The verses 56 :77-82 say that this is indeed a Qur'an most noble and respectable, in a Book well guarded and preserved which none shall touch except those who are purified, revelation from the Lord of all worlds; is it such a speech that you would consider with little importance? Are you making your food that you reject It? The verse 32: 2 says "This is the revelation of the Book in which there is no doubt, is from the Lord of worlds." If all messengers were given only the Qur'an that is Soul of Qur'an, Prophet Muhammad was given complete *Al-kithab*- containing both *Fathiha* and Qur'an as specified in the verse 15: 87

The verses 41: 41-43 say: Those who hide the Soul of Qur'an when it comes to them, they shall have a severe punishment and indeed it is Book of exalted Power. No falsehood shall enter in It either before or after Its codification. It is sent down by One full of wisdom and worthy of all praise. Nothing is said to you that were not said to the Messengers before you. The verse 21: 24 says: This is the Message with me and the Message of those before me, but most of them know not the Truth and so they neglect It. The verse 16: 44 says: "We have sent down the Reminder to you that you may explain clearly to mankind what was sent down to them and that they may reflect to those who have not heard. The verse 15: 9 says: Indeed We have revealed this *'Adhikr'* -soul Qur'an; and We will surely preserve it Ourselves.

Muthaqeen-Heedful: - only those who follow Qur'an as Guidance are the heedful. Otherwise who live under the Light- the Soul of Qur'an are the heedful. The verse 16: 128 says: "Certainly Allah is with those who keep Him in their heart and those who live under the Light. The verse 39: 33 says: "And the one who comes with the truth and then makes it true- they are the heedful. The verse 69: 48 says: "Surely, this Qur'an is a Ticket for heedful. Both the verse 73: 19 and 76: 29 say: "Certainly the Soul of Qur'an is a Ticket for one who seeks path to his Lord." To put it briefly, only the heedful should utilize the Soul of Qur'an as a Ticket and Guidance.

3. Those who believe in the unseen, keep up prayer steadfastly and spend in charity out of whatever We have provided them.

'*Ghaib*'-unseen: - Non perceptible to the senses beyond the materialistic matters presented in the Soul of Qur'an. In Other words by using the 'Insight' identify Allah and satan, see the state of death, life in the grave, Resurrection, the Day of Judgment, their seat in the Hereafter, Paradise, enjoyment in the Paradise, the Hell, severe punishment in the Hell, their bodily shape in the Hell etc.

Once Prophet asked to his companions, *who are the excellent among believers? They replied: that might be us since we follow you and battle along with you. Prophet asked, what happened to you? I am among you and Qur'an is being revealed to me. They asked: 'then are they be the Angels?' Prophet replied: 'the Angels!' they are the nearest to Allah and do not do evils. Are they be the other Prophets? Replied, how they might be since they are receiving inspiration. They asked, and then who are they? Prophet replied, they are the people after you, who see and follow me from the Book -The soul of Qur'an- between two covers.* The verse 36: 11 says "Certainly your admonition may be listened such one who follows the Soul of Qur'an and fears the Impartial unseen then to such one, give glad tidings of forgiveness and a reward most honorable." Read together the verses 67: 12-13. Both verses 2: 146 and 6: 20 say those to whom We have given the Book know him- the Prophet -more than they know their own sons.

The '*swalath*' is the conversation between the Soul and the Owner of the soul. The Soul of Qur'an and the Owner of the Soul are the same. Therefore prayer is to be conducted for establishing the Soul of Qur'an or the remembrance of Allah as told in the verse 20: 14. The five times *swalath* at stated time are obligatory only for the believers as mentioned in the verse 4: 103. Prophet and believers are commanded first to do '*Thilawath*' of Qur'an and then perform *swalath*.

Thilawath:- The recitation of Qur'an with response and convey the message to others is called *Thilawath*. When it is mentioned about believers, virtuous and Paradise dwellers ask Allah by hearts to include among them, when it is mentioned about hypocrites, disbelievers and Hell dwellers asking not to join with them. Read together the verse 2: 44. The verse 29: 45 says "Recite with response whatever has been revealed to you from the Book and then perform *swalath*, certainly the *swalath* restrains from shameful and evil deeds; and the remembrance of Allah with the Soul of Qur'an is the most important. And Allah knows whatever you industrialize or produce". The verse 7: 170 says "And those who holdfast the Book and keep up *swalath*, we shall never waste such reformers' reward". The verse 35: 29 says "Certainly those who recite Qur'an with response keep up *swalath* steadfastly and spend from whatever We have provided for them secretly and publicly are in hope for a business which will never fail. Read together the verses 8: 2-4; 39: 22-23. Since the compiled Qur'an was unavailable during Prophet's time, they used to perform *swalath* to implement the command of the verse 20: 14.

The aim of life is to purchase or build the Paradise by using all the favors provided by Allah. The verse 102: 8 says, and then you shall be questioned about all the favors. The Soul of Qur'an is the greatest favor as per the verse 10: 58. Prophet taught *"Among you the best one is who learns and teaches Soul of Qur'an"*. Therefore the believers shall utilize their wealth, offspring, time, influence, hearing, sight, speech, position etc. to learn and teach the Soul of Qur'an. The verse 63: 9 says to believer: "Your wealth and offspring shall not prevent you from the Soul of Qur'an, whoever does so, such are the only losers". Read together verses 17:36, 32: 15-16.

4. And who believe in what has been sent down to you as well as sent down before you and they have convinced belief with Hereafter.

Prophet taught *"Those who follow the prohibitions of Qur'an as permissible things don't believe with Qur'an"*. Therefore the one who don't know the Soul of Qur'an can not believe in Qur'an. Allah says in surath *Qamar* four times that certainly We have made the Qur'an very easy to understand with hearts, Is there any one to receive admonition? Belief in the previous scriptures is formed only by understanding that scriptures using the Soul of Qur'an as *Furqan*- Criterion. Certain words mentioned in Qur'an may be explained in other Scriptures.

E.g.:- (1) Circumcision is not mentioned in Qur'an, but is mentioned in Bible as Abraham was undergone circumcision and his elder son Ismael also at the age of thirteen. (2) In Qur'an only '*Al-Maseeh*' is mentioned (See the verse 3:45). That word is used for both Jesus and *Maseeh-A-Dhajjhal*. The details of *Maseeh-A-Dhajjhal* may be found in the Bible under the caption "coming of Anti-Christ." For details see explanation 4:155-159.

Through the verse 4: 136 Allah says by calling the believers "You who believe, believe in Allah, His messenger and the Book which He has sent down to His messenger as well as the Book sent down previously. Anyone who disbelieves with Allah, His Angels, His books, His messengers and the Last Day has gone far astray from the Truth. In this verse it is mentioned to believe in the Book that had been sent before the Qur'an to previous Prophets and then Allah says "Those who disbelieve His 'books' (plural of the Book) have gone far astray from the Truth". Therefore we should understand that the Soul of all the books revealed is the same while its body (language) may vary from age to age. See explanation 2:2.

The people of assurance in the Hereafter are those who keep Allah in their heart, fearing Allah unseen and thinking that He is watching every situation and in everywhere. And know that they have to answer about each and every second of their life individually after fifteenth age on the Day of Judgment. The verse 45: 20 says that the Soul of Qur'an is the Insights for entire mankind, Guidance and Mercy for those people who have convinced belief.

The verse 32: 12 says: If you only could see how *Mujrim*s will hang their heads before their Lord: "Our Lord, we have observed and heard; so send us back to the Earth! So that we may do good deeds; certainly we have become the convinced believers!" Prophets are speaking for the sake of Allah, so are the believers. When there is not even a believer to do so, then Allah will send a Monster to speak for Allah as one of the ten signs of the Last Day. The verse 27: 82 says, We shall bring forth a Monster (*Dabathul'ardh*) from the Earth which will speak to them that 'mankind have no convinced belief in Our verses'. Here, instead of saying 'Bi *Ayathillahi*' which means 'with the verses of Allah', '*Bi Ayathina*' means 'with Our verses of Qur'an' is used i.e. Monster is speaking for the sake of Allah. And this Monster neither begets nor is begotten.

Through the verse 5: 50 Allah asks "Do they then seek after a judgment of the Days of Ignorance? But who is finer in judgment than Allah for a people who have convinced belief?" Read together the verses 27: 1-3 and 32: 24.

5. Such are on true Guidance from their Lord; and such will only be successful.

"Oh Allah! Include us among those who are guided with the Soul of Qur'an and include us with those who attain prosperity". Prophet taught that those who recite the first five verses, the 'verses of Throne' and following two verses, and the last three verses from this surath; satan will not approach them and their family members, since they are under the guardianship of Allah. The first five verses of surath *Luqman* are of the same contents of these verses. The verse 7: 157 ends as "Those who believe in Prophet, honor him, help him, and follow the Light which is sent down with him, such will be only successful. The verse 9: 88 says, but the messenger and those who believe along with him do struggle with their wealth and persons; such will have even better things; such will be successful.

Today there is no war or slaughtering with weapons, instead only *Jihad* with the Soul of Qur'an to those who hide It and propagate the Soul of Qur'an among entire mankind in their heart's language in order to help them for identifying themselves, the aim of life in order to stop bloodshed and to make peace and harmony. So the Soul of Qur'an is the mightiest weapon for *Jihad* today. The verse 24: 51 says "The reply of the believers when they are invited to Allah and His messenger in order to judge among them is: We have heard and we have obeyed. Such are only who will attain prosperity. Read together verses 23: 1 -11

6. Certainly as for those who hide the Truth, it is the same to them whether you warn them or you do not warn them, they still will not believe.

The hiders of truth mentioned here are the hypocrites. The verse 63: 6 says that it is the same, whether you ask for their forgiveness or not ask for their forgiveness, Allah will never forgive them, indeed Allah will never guide such transgressing people. The verse 9: 67 ends as indeed the hypocrites-they are the transgressors. The verse 10: 33 says, thus has the word of your Lord proved true in regards to the transgressors that surely, they will not believe. The verse 40: 6 says: And thus shall the word of your Lord be proved true against the disbelievers; certainly they are the inmates of Hellfire. The verse 7: 193 says: If you invite them to Guidance -Soul of Qur'an, they will not follow you. It will be the same for you whether you call them or keep quiet. The verses 36: 10-11 say, it is the same about them whether you warn them or warn them not, they will not believe. Certainly your warning may become useful to one who follows the Soul of Qur'an. Therefore to such one, convey the glad news of forgiveness and an honorable reward. Both the verses 5: 67 and 16: 107 end as, indeed Allah will not guide who hide and reject the Soul of the Qur'an. In the verse 9: 37 says, Allah guides not the people of disbelievers who transpose the prohibited months of fighting (Today those who transpose the day of celebration of *Eid*, performance of *Hajj*, fasting etc.). The verses 9: 24, 80 and 61: 5 end as: And Allah will never guide the people who are transgressors.

7. Allah has sealed their hearts and hearing and over their sight there hangs a veil and for them have grievous punishment.

The hypocrites have the faculties of hearing, sight and intelligence. But they will not utilize these faculties to understand the Soul of Qur'an in order to fulfill the aim of life. In the verse 7: 179 says: "Certainly, We have destined many *Jinns* and human beings for Hell; they have hearts with which they do not understand, and eyes with which they do not see the Insight, they have ears with which they do not hear. Such are like livestock; rather they are even worse than them, such are the only heedless". They have hearts with which they do not try to understand what is, what for and why Qur'an? They have eyes with which they see not the Soul of Qur'an. They have ears with which they hear not the Soul of Qur'an. The verses 18: 100-101 say: We shall bring the Hell near to the disbelievers on the Day of Judgment; they are those whose eyes had been under a veil to see the Soul of Qur'an, and had been unable to hear It. The verse 50: 22 warns, one who has a veil on his eyes about the Soul of Qur'an in this world, that veil shall be removed on the Day of Judgment, and will tell him, this Day your sight is so sharp to see all. The verses 20: 124-126 say, whoever lives by neglecting the Soul of Qur'an, indeed for him has a narrowed life in this world, and he shall be resurrected as blind on the Day of Judgment. That Day he will ask, oh my Lord! Why did you resurrect me blind, when I had sight in the material world? Then Allah will say: just like that you had come upon Our verses, then you forgot them, like that you also have been forgotten this Day. The verses 17: 97-98 say: One whom Allah guides is truly guided. He whom Allah leaves astray, for such will you find no protector, no helper besides Him. We shall bring them together prone on their faces blind, dumb and deaf. Their abode will be Hell. Whenever its flame dies down, we shall make it blaze up. That is their reward since they hide and rejected Our verses and for saying that when we are reduced to bones and ant-hill should We really be resurrected. Asking of disbelievers mentioned in every other places in Qur'an as: If we are reduced to bones and mud or dust, should we really be resurrected, but in this verse as well as 17: 49 say 'bone and ant-hill'. Prophet taught, *when there is no leader (Imam) or party of believers, the believer should go to forest and remain by biting the bottom of a tree till death.* Remember that in such occasion the dead body is not being buried. Thus it becomes '*rufath*' -ant-hill. Where this advice is for illiterate people, and literate people have to remain by biting the Soul of Qur'an with their molar teeth. In the verse 8: 22 says: Indeed the worst beast in the sight of Allah is the deaf and dumb who think not using their intelligence. The verses 6: 25-26 says, among them there are some who listen to you, but We have made a wrappings on their hearts, so they understand not the Soul of Qur'an and a veil on their ears; if they see everyone of the verses, they will not believe in them. When they come to you they will say, these are nothing but tales of ancients. They forbid the people from Qur'an as well as themselves, thereby they do not destroy any one other than themselves, but they perceive not. Read together the verses 17: 45-46 and 18: 57

8. Among the people there are some who say, We believe with Allah and Last Day while they are not believers.

This verse illustrates the condition of the majority of Muslims today. Those who haughtily boast that we learn and teach Qur'an are actually disbelievers and they are the fuel for the Hell as taught by Prophet in the explanation of the verse 3:10. The verse 49:14 commands to Prophet to say the *Bedouin-Arabs*, when they said we have believed: yet you have not believed, instead you say we are Muslims -committed ourselves live in peace, while '*Eemaan*' –the Soul of Qur'an, not has entered in your hearts. If you obey Allah and His messenger, it will not go waste your deeds, Allah is ever Forgiving, most Merciful. The verse 5:41 says: "Oh Prophet does not let those who rush off in to disbelief grieve you among those who say we believe with their lips, but whose hearts have no faith, and those from among the Jews. The habit of such hypocrites is mentioned in the verse 48:11 as they say some thing with their tongues that is not in their hearts. Read together the verses 63: 1-11 and 58:8.

9. They would like to deceive Allah and those who believe, actually they deceive none except themselves but they do not perceive it.

The hypocrites are the enemies of Allah and the believers as told in the verses 41: 26-28 and 63:4. They fear the believers; it is because they are certainly men devoid of aim of life as told in the verse 59:13. Believers should select Allah, His messenger and other believers as their guardians and protectors. In the verse 9:16 Allah asks the believers, "Do you think that you would be left alone while Allah has not yet known those among you who struggle utmost in the path of Allah and take none as protectors and guardians except Allah, His messenger and believers". Through the verse 9:23 Allah commands to the believers: "Don't take your fathers or brothers as protectors if they prefer disbelief to belief. If any of you do so such are only the wrongdoers". They do their deeds with body without the participating their souls. Therefore, their body will bear witness against themselves. Read together the verses 17:36 and 41:19-24. Hypocrites are the transgressors who identified Allah and themselves from the Soul of Qur'an but hide the truth from the people, as told in the verse 2: 99. Those who hide the Soul of Qur'an have been killed as told in the verse 80: 17.

10. Their hearts contain a disease so Allah has increased their disease, they will have painful punishment because they have been lying.

When the hypocrites come to the Prophet, they say: We bear witness that you are indeed the messenger of Allah. Yes, Allah knows that you are indeed the messenger and Allah bears witness that the hypocrites are indeed liars, is told in the verse 63: 1. The verse 9: 107 ends as: "Certainly they (hypocrites) are liars". It is mentioned in the verse 36: 15 that three messengers were deputed to a city and the rejecters said to those messengers: "the most Gracious has not sent anything down; you are only lying and thereby they rejected them". As per the verses 29: 12-13 these hypocritical disbelievers tell those who believe: "Follow our path, we will bear your mistakes. They will not bear their mistakes in any way: they are such liars. However they will carry their own loads and others loads besides their own. They will be questioned on Resurrection Day about what they have produced. Read together the verses 16: 24-25. Prophet taught: *The visible features of hypocrites are: Lying on speak, deceiving on believe, discarding the agreements.* They are human satan who undeservingly boast as anchorites not follow the Soul of Qur'an after knowing It. They deceive the common people and lead them to Hell. They say to common people by mere recitation of Qur'an without understanding the Soul will be deserved to get reward from Allah. Prophet taught about them: *"Their scholars are the worst of beasts under the sky"*. Those are the people upon whom the wrath of Allah happened, told in the verse 1: 7. Read together verses 4: 91; 9: 123 and 33: 60. The only medicine to cure the hypocrisy which is the disease of soul and thereby to strengthen the faith is the Soul of Qur'an. See the verse 8: 4.

11. Whenever someone tells them not to make mischief on Earth, they say: we are certainly reformers.

12. Be know, certainly they themselves are the mischief makers but they perceive it not.

The Soul of Qur'an is only device to stop mischief making on Earth and to shun all evils, bloodshed and thereby establish human unity and peace. The hypocrites they don't use It as well as do not give others to utilize it; lead and show a life just against It to the people. By hiding the Soul of Qur'an actually they fill fire in their bellies as told in the verse 2: 174. Whoever makes mischief and bloodshed on Earth, its burden should be carried by such Hypocrites before Allah-The Just. Their similitude is that of 'donkey' and 'Jews' who carries the Qur'an as told in the verse 62: 5, and that of a 'dog' as told in the verse 7: 176. The world will come to an end when mankind becomes hypocrites without any believer. Read together the verses 6: 47and 46: 35.

13. When someone tells them: "Believe just as other people believe." They say: "Do we believe just as the foolish believe?" Surely they are the fools though they do not realize it!

Mankind has to undergo trial on the life. While comparing the hypocrites, the believers are possessed with a little livelihood. Believers give more importance to the life in the Hereafter where as the hypocrites prefer the life of this world. Therefore the hypocrites' allegation on believers is saying that they are fools and they do not know how to enjoy the life. About such hypocrites in the verses 9: 67-68 say: Hypocritical men or women resemble one another, they command evil, forbid just and clench their fists, and they forgot Allah, so He has forgotten them. Certainly hypocrites are only the transgressors. Allah has promised Hellfire for hypocrites whether they are men or women and for those who reject the verses one by one: It will be enough for them. Allah has cursed them and they will have constant punishment. Read together the verse 6: 112. They are not considering Allah's good name '*Rahman*' -The Impartial. All the happenings which take place on the world are already decided and recorded in the Book as per the verses 10: 61; 34: 3; 57: 22 and that Book is the Soul of Qur'an. Then the believers will utilize the Soul of Qur'an as the Balance, Criterion and Insight to separate good and bad. Allah makes trial to recognize those who are believers and those who are hypocrites as told in the verse 29: 11. Thus the battle of *Uh'd* is taken place in order to identify who are the believers and who are the hypocrites -as told in the verses 3: 166-167. Since Allah is the knower of all times, to identify Allah means to identify the believers who are the vicegerents of Allah.

The Hypocrites think that their wealth and prestige are the blessings of Allah as they are in truth. But through the verses 9: 55, 85 say don't let their wealth and children astonish you, Allah only wants to punish the hypocrites by means of them during this world, and let their souls perish while they are the disbelievers. It is told in the verses 7: 48-49 that the men who distinguish the companions of Fire and the companions of Paradise, will say to the hypocrites on the Day of Judgment: "Your strength of group and your arrogance in the world are not profited to you. And the men whom you swore that Allah with His Mercy would never bless, they are told to enter the Paradise. See the explanation 1: 2, 7.

14. Whenever they meet those who believe, they say: "We believe"; but when they are alone with their devils they say: "certainly we are with you; we were only joking".

These opportunistic hypocrites, when they are in proximity to the believers establish *swalath*, fasting, *Hajj* etc, but they don't remember Allah, are not conscious to answer before Allah about each moment of the worldly life Here. They boast that they have studied all the contents of the Qur'an so Allah has announced them a grievous torment. Read together the verses 31: 5-6 and 63: 5-6.

Prophet taught, "Many hypocrites from my people recite Qur'an and the hypocrites who recite Qur'an are compared to 'Mint', the taste of which is bitter and smell is attractive". The hypocrites who do not recite Qur'an are compared to '*Nuxvomica*' fruit, both its taste and smell is bitterer. The hypocrites are filth (impure) as told in the verse 9: 95. As per the verse 9:125 Qur'an will increase nothing except filth to their existing filth, and they will die while they are still disbelievers. The satan mentioned here are the hypocritical leaders who are men devils. They know the Soul of Qur'an, but not follow It, instead they forbid It to their disciples. They shall go to the bottom of Hell fire even without trial as per the verse 4:145. These hypocrites and '*fujjar*' are *mujrims*. Read together the verses, 7: 40, 10: 17 and 32: 22. See the explanation 1:7 and 2:6.

15. Allah will jock with them and let them go on wandering arrogantly in their blind fashion.

They are pretending sleepiness, concealing the Soul of Qur'an. So they are followed by satan and hence they are the human devils dragging the common people to the Hell. They are intoxicated by the ornaments and decorations of the Earth and they live in their own whims. They will say good and attractive words to the common people while abstain to practice themselves. They will recite Qur'an with response and pretend crying without following the teachings of Qur'an, as told in the verse 2:44. Through the verse 7:185 Allah asks what speech after this Qur'an will they then believe? And the verse 186 says anyone who Allah lets go astray will have no guide; He leaves them in their trespasses with arrogance and they are wandering aimlessly. Certainly the Hell fire will be rewarded as abode to such rebellious hypocrites is warned in the verses 78: 21-22. And in the verses 27-28 it is told, that is because they are not expecting the trial in the Hereafter and repeatedly rejecting Our verses.

16. Such are the ones who have purchased astray instead of Guidance, while their bargain does not profit them, nor have they been guided.

Prophet taught in the explanation of the verse 2:185 that if anybody seeks Guidance other than from Qur'an, he will be retreated from the Guidance. The verse 35: 29 says "Certainly those who recite Qur'an with response, keep up *swalath* steadfastly and spend whatever We have provided them secretly and openly are in hope the business which will never fail. Through the verses 61:10-11 Allah says to the believers, Oh you who believe, shall I inform you about a bargain that will save you from painful torment? You should believe with Allah and His messenger and strive strenuously in Allah's ways with your property and persons; that will be better for you if you know. Today the '*Jihad*' is to learn and teach the Soul of Qur'an. See explanation the verses 1:5 and 2:5.

17. They may be compared to someone who kindles a fire, and ones it lights up whatever lies around him, Allah takes away their Light and leaving them in utter darkness. They do not utilize The Insight.

18. Deaf, dumb and blind, they will never return to the right path.

For people who exist in darkness when a candle ignites and spread its light around them and then when it is extinguished they will not have even their former sight in darkness. Like that these hypocrites when they got the light of Allah which is Qur'an, they neither utilize It nor permit others to utilize It. The verses 9: 32-33 say, they want to extinguish out Allah's light with their mouths, while Allah refuses except that His light must be perfected, no matter how disbelievers may hate it. He is the One who has sent His messenger with Guidance and the true religion so he may cause it to prevail over all other religions, no matter how associates in the dominion of Allah may hate it. Read together the verses 61: 7 and 8.

The blessings like hearing, sight, wisdom which Allah bestowed upon them, will not be utilized to see Allah through the Light of Soul of Qur'an and thereby to fulfill the aim of life of returning to the Paradise. So their return is to the Hellfire. It is because they hide the Soul of Qur'an knowingly; which will stand witness and argue against them. Certainly the blessings like hearing, sight etc shall be questioned as per the verses 17: 36 and 102: 8. The hearings, sights and skins of these enemies of Allah will stand witness against them on the Day of Judgment, is warned in the verses 41: 19-24.

19. Or to a rain cloud from the sky containing darkness, thunder and lightning; they stick their fingers in their ears to ward of death because of the thunder claps, and Allah is encompassed with such disbelievers.

20. Lightning almost snatches their sight away: each time it flashes they walk along it, while when darkness settles down on them, they stand still. If Allah so willed, He would take away their hearing and eyesight; certainly Allah is capable of everything.

When it is warned to the hypocrites by quoting the verses of Qur'an which is Allah's Light, they come to the conclusion that it is necessary to study, follow the Soul of Qur'an, and thereby purify the life. But when they are not hearing the classes explaining the Soul of Qur'an, they will rush to more darkness and Hell. They don't have the prayer and deed to complete the Light and rush to the Paradise removing their arrogance by burning with the Soul of Qur'an like the innocent believers. Their similitude is portrayed in the verses 74: 49-51 as, and then what is the matter with them that they turn away from this admonition like frightened donkeys running from roaring lion? Both verses 15:12 and 26: 200 say, that We penetrate the Soul of Qur'an in to the hearts of *mujrims* like a heated iron bar.

The verse 36: 11 says: "Those who follow the Soul of Qur'an and fear the Impartial seeing from the Soul of Qur'an, such one has forgiveness and most honorable reward. The Soul of Qur'an is mentioned as the Light in the verses such as 4:174; 5:15; 7:157, 42: 52 and 64: 8. The verse 36: 66 says: "If it had been Our will, We could surely blotted out their eyes thus they are groping to the path, but how could they have seen?" The verse 67 says: "If it had been Our will, We could have transformed them in their places; then they should have been unable to move or could they have returned to?" When one is died by thunder bolts, stands like statue and falls down only when they are touched. The believers always remember Allah and they don't fear the catastrophes and the natural calamities like thunder bolts, electric shock, Earth quake, tsunami, typhoons etc. since they don't fear death. They are the one who are preparing Paradise here for the Hereafter. They utilize the Soul of Qur'an as Insight. See the verse 6: 104. Certainly Allah has encompassed the rejecters of faith who perverse and they never believe since Allah has killed them. They go to Hell without trial as mentioned in verse 4:145. See the explanation 2: 4-7.

21. Oh you mankind! Serve your Lord, who created you as well as those before you; so that you may become heedful.

22. The One Who has made the Earth as a carpet for you, and had the sky built as a canopy above you and sent water to pour down from the sky and brought forth fruit by means of it as sustenance for you. Don't set up rivals for Allah while you know better.

Allah addresses the entire human beings through this verse. Allah created human beings in the Paradise and sent down to the Earth to live as His vicegerent, but only the believers accept that command. Allah entrusted the bearers of Qur'an to deliver this Message to entire mankind in order they to become heedful. Only believers do this inevitable duty by conveying the Soul of Qur'an. Hence those who received the Qur'an, but hide and reject without conveying to others are vicegerents of satan. Satan belongs to disbelievers as told in the both the verses 2: 34, 38: 74. Therefore disbelievers' soul-mate is satan. The satan tempts the men to celebrate several observances and obeisance by adulterating natural life. After entering the *swalath* if there is no remembrance of Allah, then *swalath* will become for the satan. For those who perform *swalath* without consciousness is promised '*Wail*' -The severe torment part of the Hell, as told in the verses 107: 4-5. To become the whole life to the Lord Allah, one should have to mould the faith under the Soul of Qur'an and to follow its do's and don'ts; such people are called 'heedful'. The verses 2: 63, 179, 183, 6: 153 and 7: 171 also end as, for that you might become heedful. Read together the verses 2: 186; 13: 18 and 14: 22. See the explanation 1:4 and 2: 4.

23. If you are in any doubt about what We have sent down to Our servant, then bring a Surath like It and call in your witnesses besides Allah if you are so truthful.

Allah has repeated this challenge in the verse 10: 38. There are 114 Suraths in Qur'an. Allah challenges entire mankind to bring forth such a Surath til the Last day. In the verse 11: 13 Allah has challenged to bring forth ten Surath forged like unto Qur'an. Allah challenges through the verse 17: 88 that if the entire mankind and *Jinns* will gather together to bring something like this Qur'an, they would never bring anything like It, even if they help and support one another. It is told in the verse 52: 34 'if it be they speak truth then bring a same speech like unto Qur'an'.

Qur'an is the official news paper to the all creatures from The Creator. The verses 10:38, 11:13, 35, 32:3 and 46: 6 begin by asking "do they say he has forged It". Nobody has succeeded in confronting this challenge till today. It proves that Qur'an is revealed from Allah through the illiterate Prophet. The verses 69: 44-47 says, if he invent any false statement saying about Us, We would have hold him by the right hand and will cut off his main artery, then no one of you would have then prevent him from the punishment of Allah. The Soul of Qur'an is the only Book revealed from the paradise. It is a splendid Book, no falsehood shall approach It from either before or after codification since it is a revelation from the one who is Wise, Praiseworthy is told in the verses 41: 41and 42

24. Then if you do not -and you will never do so heed the Fire whose fuel is mankind and stones which has been kept prepared for disbelievers.

Qur'an is the Guidance for entire mankind from the Lord and Ticket to reach back to Him. Those who do not utilize It after getting, they shall never return to the Paradise. The verse 66: 6 says: Oh believers! Save yourselves and your families from Hellfire, whose fuel is men and stones, in the charge of fierce and mighty Angels who never disobey Allah's command and who promptly do what they are commanded to do. The death scene of disbelievers through the verse 39: 59 is portraing as: "Nay, but there came to you my verses and did reject It, you became arrogant and you were among the disbelievers". In the verses 36: 69-70 say, this is nothing but a Soul of Qur'an and the clear body of Qur'an with which may give warning who are alive, and such that the word of punishment may be proved on disbelievers. Since Allah is the Impartial He will not enter anyone Hell without bearing witness that they were disbelievers against themselves as told in both verses 6: 130, 7: 37. The verse 22:51 says those who strive against our verses to frustrate them, they will be companions of the Fire and in the verse 57 it is told those who hide and reject Our verses, there shall be humiliating punishment for them. In brief, those who hide and reject the Soul of Qur'an after receiving It are the disbelievers and will be the fuels of the Fire, even though they perform *swalath*, spend charity, fasting, hajj etc. Read together the verses 39: 32, 71, 57: 19 and 64: 10. See explanation 2: 17-18.

25. Proclaim to those who believe and perform honorable deeds that they will have gardens beneath which rivers flow. Each time they are provided with fruits from it for their sustenance, they will say: "this is what we were provided with before!" For they are given things in similitude and have clean-living spouses there. They will live in it forever.

The Qur'an is sent down as a Healing and Mercy to the believers, but it does not increase to the wrongdoers anything except loss. Read together the verses 17: 82 and 41:44. In the Paradise, each time they are given to eat various kinds of fruits in similitude but different in taste, they will say this one is we ate now, and so bring other than this. Read together the verses 6: 99, 141. Spouses in the Paradise have no menses and other unpurified state or an excreta. In a Paradise there are at least 12 rivers as mentioned in the verse 47:15.

26. Allah does not hesitate to compare things to a mosquito nor to anything bigger than it. Those who believe realize that it is the truth from their Lord, while those who disbelieve say: "what does Allah means by this similitude? By such a similitude Allah goes astray many and guides many. But none does He cause thereby to go astray except the transgressors.

27. Those who break Allah's covenant after it has been established and cut aside whatever Allah has ordered to be joined, and cause mischief on Earth, such will be the only losers.

This is the reply for the disbelievers of all times who mocks the quoting of insects as similitude, such as fly in the verse 22: 73, spider in the verse 29: 41, bee in the verse 14: 68, ant in the verse 27: 18 etc. The verse 13: 25 says: Those who have broken Allah's covenant after having reminded it and intercepted what Allah has commanded to be transmitted, and do mischief on Earth will have the curse and theirs will be the worst home.

The Transgressors are those who do not keep the covenant made with Allah from the Paradise mentioned in the verses 7: 172, 173 after having reminded through the Qur-an. The verse 7: 102 says: We found no men true to their covenants who were destroyed in the towns before, but most of them We found transgressors. The verse 2: 99 says: "No one hide the verses of Allah except those who are transgressors. The verse 39: 63 says: Those who hide the verses of Allah, such are the only losers. The following verses such as 9: 53, 67; 10: 33; 24: 55; 32: 18; 57: 16, 26-27; 59: 19; 61: 5 and 63: 6 are also mentioned about transgressors. Prophet taught that believers are those who live keeping the covenant and who pray the '*Sayidul Isthigfar*'- the most exalted prayer to seek forgiveness, at the beginning of night and day and so they will enter the Paradise whenever they die.

Oh Allah! You are my Lord, no Deity except You, You have created me, I am your servant and I am living with that covenant and a promise as well as I can, I seek refuge to You about the evil that I produce, I present before You the blessings that you bestowed upon me (keep remembering the blessings in heart). I present before You my sins, so may You forgive my sins. Certainly, no one is to forgive my sins except You. Those who live remembering such covenant in this world, they will get the Paradise which is promised through the Prophets. It will be asked again by Allah, pertaining to the covenant when He gathers all together on the Day of Judgment. That is the promise mentioned in the verse. Allah says in the verse 50: 31 that the Paradise will be brought near to the heedful no more far distant, and in the verse 32 says this is what was promised for those who keep the '*Sayidul Isthigfar*' prayer and repeatedly penitent one.

28. How can you disbelieve in Allah? When you once were dead and He furnished you with life? Then He will cause you die once more, then bring you back to life again; unto Him you be returned.

As per the verses 7: 172, 173, all souls are created in the Paradise. When asked: Am I not your Lord? All of them individually replied: 'Of course' we do testify. After buying such covenant from each one they were sent back to the nape of Adam and then the first birth on Earth happened. That is why it is told as: Then We gave you life instead of saying as then We created you. The verse 22: 66 says: It is He who gave you life on Earth, then He will cause you to die, then He will again give you rebirth from the Earth; truly man is the most ungrateful creature. That means they do not become grateful and identify the Creator by utilizing the soul of Qur'an and do not construct Paradise in this world and thereby fulfill the aim of life. A scene is warned in the verse 40: 11 when the rejecters stand near the Hell and say: "Our Lord! You have let us die twice and have revived twice, now we have identified our sins and then is there any way to go out? Here it is told about the death first that we have died twice means the first creation took place in the Paradise, then after taking covenant made first death and kept in the nape of Adam; the second death will occur in Earth. 'We have born twice' means the first birth occur on Earth and the second birth will be in the Hereafter.

Allah says in the verses 7: 24-28, when He sent mankind from Paradise to Earth: "Get you down with enmity between yourselves (i.e. hypocrites are the enemies of believers), on Earth will be your dwelling place and your means of livelihood for a time, therein shall you die and from it shall you be taken out once again. Read together the verse 20: 55. The verse 16: 78 says: It is Allah who brought you forth from the wombs of your mothers when you knew nothing and He gave hearing, sight and intelligence so that you may become grateful. The verse 39: 6 says: "He creates you in the wombs of your mothers in stages one after another in three veils of darkness. Such is Allah, your Lord, and to Him the dominion belongs, but there is no Deity except Allah, then how can you turn away from this Allah". In the verse 53: 32 says: He knows you well when He planted you on Earth and when you are hidden in your mother's wombs. Therefore, hold not yourselves purified. He is quite aware as to who has done his duty. Do not purify oneself means one should not be boast and arrogant without the Truth-the Soul of Qur'an and follow not ones own whims. Read together the verse 64: 6 and 96: 6-7. One can not act and tell as self-sufficient without–the Soul of Qur'an- the prosperity and the proof.

After quoting directly visible events in verses 91: 1-6, Allah says in verses 7-10: "By the soul and Him who perfected it then inspired its own wrong and its own right, indeed anyone who purifies it (identify himself) will prosper and indeed anyone who corrupts it (fail to identify himself) will be the failure. Read together the verses 57: 14-15 and 90: 10. One can purify himself By utilizing the soul of Qur'an as Balance and Criterion.

29. He is the One who has created everything that is on Earth for you; then He soared up to Heaven and fashioned it as seven Heavens. He has perfect knowledge of everything.

The verses 25: 59, 32: 4; 50: 38 etc. say, Heavens, Earth and all between them are created in six days. The verse 41: 9 asks: is it that you deny Him Who created the Earth in two days? And do you setup rivals to Him since He is the Lord of all worlds. He set on the Earth mountains and bestowed all things and measured their in its sustenance (considering the interest and necessities of creatures). All these happened in four days as a reply to those who ask, is told in the verse 41: 10. Then He soared up to the Heaven while it was still a haze, and told both it and the Earth: "come either obediently or reluctantly". They both said: "We do come together in willing obedience" is told in verse 11. He completed them as seven firmaments with in two days, and He inspired its own order in each Heaven is told in the verse 12. The verse 21:30 says: Have not those who disbelieve seen how Heaven and Earth were once joined together as one mass and thus We split them asunder? (Established as we see now) and We have made every living beings from water for surviving, will they still not believe? Read together the verses 13: 2-3; 23: 17; 67: 3 and 71: 15.

30. Remember the occasion when your Lord said to the Angels that I am going to place a vicegerent on Earth, they said: Will you place therein one who will do mischief on it and shed blood, while we glorify Your praise and sanctify You? He said I know what you do not know.

Even though all men are deputed to the Earth as vicegerents of Allah, only the believers do so. Mankind is deputed not only to praise and sanctify Allah, but to identify themselves, Allah-the Impartial Lord and thereby to construct Paradise Here utilizing the Soul of Qur'an. See the verses 2: 28; 3:136, 182, 185 and 31: 12. The verse 21:10 says: We have sent down a Book to you that contain your Reminder, will you not utilize your intelligence. Reminder means one which reminds who are men, soul, body, where he was first created, for what he is deputed to the Earth, birth, death, sleep, difference between sleep and death, who will go to Paradise and Hell etc. in ones heart language. Men and *Jinns* are independent creatures and Allah accepts the praises and prayers only from the believers among them. The Angels have no freedom for selection. They will not defy Allah and they only obey Him. Men and *Jinns* are given freedom for selection. That is why they are distinguished as the vicegerents of Allah. Before mankind, *Jinn* were deputed to Earth as the vicegerents of Allah. See the verse 15: 27. Without the participation of soul, the deeds and observances like speech, recitation of Qur'an, prayer, fasting, *Hajj, Zakath* etc will not be accepted. Not only that their skin, hearing, sights etc. will stand witness against them on the Day of Judgment as told in the verses 41: 19-24. The Soul of Qur'an is a must to participate the soul in all deeds since it is the cloth, food and sight of human soul. All beings declare the praises and celebrate the glory of Allah as told in the verses 17: 44 and 24: 41. Each one is taught its own mode of prayer and praises. So the men who are blessed with the intelligence have to celebrate and praise the Lord heartlier and it is their duty to keep the Universe in its equilibrium by utilizing the Soul of Qur'an- the Trust and Balance. The Soul of Qur'an is the only instrument to shun the mischief on Earth like bloodshed, racialism, communalism, nationalism, selfishness and to establish the harmony and unity of mankind. Read together the verses 11: 57 and 24: 55. See the explanation 2: 6-7, 24.

31. And He taught Adam the names of every thing; then presented them to the Angels, and said: "Tell me the names of these, if you are so truthful".

32. They said: "Glory is to You; we have no knowledge except what ever You have taught us. Certainly You are the Knower, the Wise".

33. He said: "Oh Adam, tell them their names", once he had told them their names He said: "Did I not tell you that certainly I

know the unseen in Heaven and Earth? And I know whatever you disclose and what ever you have been hiding".

Mankind has been created in the best of calendar-stature as the shade of Allah, and deputed them to Earth as His vicegerents. But only the believers who consider the Allah as the Impartial will carry the vicegerent by utilizing the Soul of Qur'an and return to Allah, the Believer by His stature and character. Believer is one of the finest names of Allah mentioned in the verse 59: 23. The disbelievers will return to the Hell, the house of satan in the form of different creatures like dogs, swine, bandicoots, monkeys, snakes, scorpions etc. Both in the verses 2: 34; 38: 74 it is told that satan belongs to disbeliever. The verses 95: 4-6 say: "We have indeed created man with the finest calendar, then abase him to the lowest; except for those who believe and do honorable deeds -for them have the reward never withheld. The verse 17: 70 says: We have indeed dignified the children of Adam and We transported them in both land and sea. And We have provided them the good and pure sustenance, conferred them over many of those whom We have created. The verses 64: 2-3 say: He is the One Who created you all, and among you there is disbeliever and there is believer, and Allah is observing whatever you do. He created Heaven and Earth with Truth and aim, made your shape best one and to Him is your final return. The verse 23: 14 ends as: then blessed be Allah the best of Creators. Qur'an being the knowledge of all time - past, present and future, by teaching Qur'an He dignified men than the Angels. Read together the verses 55: 1-4.

As per the verse 2: 116 disbelievers say: Allah has adopted a son, Glory is to Him. Nay, to Him belongs all that in Heaven and Earth, all things are devoted to Him..The verse 3: 191 says: The wise men remember Allah while standing, sitting and lying on their sides, and meditate on the creation of Heaven and Earth. They pray that our Lord! Not in vain have You created Heaven and Earth, Glory be to You! So shield us from the torment of fire.

The verse 7: 143 says, Prophet *Moosa* wanted to see Allah, and when Allah manifested Himself to the mount, He made it a dust and *Moosa* fell down in swoon. When he recovered his sense he said: Glory to You, to You I turn in repentance and I am the first to believe. The pagans in Mecca attribute sons and daughters without any knowledge. Therefore He is above what they attribute to Him- told in the verse 6: 100. The dwellers in Paradise always pray: Oh Allah! Glory be to You -is told in the verse 10: 10. In the verse 9: 31 says: There is no

Deity except Allah, Praise and Glory to Him, far is He from having partners they associate with Him. The verses 10: 18; 16: 1; 30: 40 and 39: 67 end as: Glory to Him and far is He above the partners they attribute Him. Through the verse 12: 108 Allah commanded Prophet to say: This is my way, I do invite you unto Allah; I and anyone who follows me up on an Insight. Glory is to Allah and I am not among the associates. Therefore, any believer who follows the Prophet has to follow the Soul of Qur'an –The Insight.

As the thunder bolts glorify Allah's Praises, the Angels who work behind it also glorify His Praises with awe -is told in the verse 13: 13. The verse 17: 1 says: Glory to who did take His servant for a journey by night from the '*Masjidhul-Haram*' (Mecca) to '*Baithul-Muqadhiss*' (Jerusalem). The verse 17: 44 says: "The seven Heaven and Earth and all beings there in declare His Glory. When the pagans in Mecca wanted some divine wonders as a proof for the Prophethood of Muhammad, Allah commanded the Prophet to reply: "Glory be to my Lord, am I anything but a human Messenger?" is told in the verses 17: 90-94. The verse 21: 22 ends as: Then Glory is to Allah!-the Lord of the Throne, beyond what they describe. The verse 21: 87 says: When Prophet *Yunus* cried to Allah from the stomach of whale under the depth of darkness as, there is no Deity except You, Glory be to You, I have indeed become among wrongdoers. On hearing the scandal about the believers, Allah advised the believers through the verse 24: 16 as, "why did you not when you heard it say: We aught not this, Glory be to You, this is a most serious slander? On the Day of Judgment, Allah will gather them together as well as those whom they worship besides Allah, He will ask: Were it you who lead my servants astray or did them astray from the path themselves? They will reply; Glory is to You, not suitable was it for us that we should take protectors other than You. But You did bestow on them and their forefathers sustenance till they forget the Soul of Qur'an; they were a people of boredom (worthless) -is told in the verses 25: 17-18. When all are gathered together on the Day of Judgment, Allah asks the Angels: Were it you (Angels) that these men used to worship? They will reply: Glory is to You, You are our protector and not they. Nay, but they worshipped the *Jinns* and most of them believed in them -is told in verses 34: 40-41. The verse 27: 8 ends as: Glory is to Allah, the Lord of all worlds. The verse 36: 36 says: Glory is to Allah who created in pairs all things and that the Earth produces as well as in themselves and other things of which they have no knowledge. And in the verse 36: 83 says: Glory is to Him in whose hand is the dominion for all things and to Him will you be returned. Allah taught a prayer through the verses 43: 13-14 when alight a vehicle: "Glory is to Him Who has subjected this vehicle to us. Unless He had not subjected this vehicle we couldn't have use it. Indeed once we must return to our Lord". The verse 43: 82 says: Glory is to the Lord of Heaven and Earth, the Lord of the Throne, above of what they ascribe to Him. In the verse 67: 29 says: A people who have been destroyed their crops, prayed at last: Glory is to our Lord; indeed we have been among the wrongdoers. The Suraths 57, 61 and 59 begin as whatever is on the Heaven and Earth has already declared the Praise and Glory of Allah. The suraths 62 and 64 begin as whatever is in the Heaven and Earth does declare the Glory of Allah. Surath 87 begins with a command that Glorify the name of your Lord, the All -Highest. Through the *Surath* 110 commands: When comes the help of Allah and victory and you we can see the mankind entering Allah's '*Dheen*'(Islam) in droves; then Glorify your Lord's praise and beg Him for forgiveness, since He is so Relenting! Therefore not only the 'victory of Mecca' but whatever the victory they attain, the Prophet and believers do glorify their Lord's praises only. After each swalath, when we glorify Allah by saying '*Subhanallah*' in 33 times, we have to keep in mind the contents of all above verses.

34. Remember the occasion that We told to the Angels: prostrate you all before Adam. They all prostrated themselves except Iblis. He refused and acted proudly, he was among disbelievers.

He (*Iblis*) was one among the disbelievers is told in the verse 38: 74 and he was one among the *Jinns* told in the verse 18: 50.

35. And We said: Oh, Adam settle down in the Paradise, both you and your wife, and eat freely from it anywhere either of you may wish, yet don't approach this tree lest you become wrongdoers.

36. Satan made them stumble over it and had those both expelled them from where they had been living. We said: "clear out some of you as enemies of others. You will have resting place and a enjoyment for a while".

Read together the verses 7:19-20, 24. Men and satans are enemies to each other, as well as hypocrites are enemies to believers. As per the verse 63:4 it is told about hypocrites: they are the enemies, so beware of them. Both satans and hypocrites are the enemies of Allah and believers. Read together the verse 41:

28. Just like in men, there are both believers and disbelievers among *Jinns*. Read together the verses 6: 112 and 114: 6. Therefore it is the duty of man to make his soul mate a believer with the soul of the Qur'an, otherwise both of them has to go to Hell as mentioned in the verses 43: 36-39 and 59: 16-17.

The verse 50: 27-29 say, the Jinn companion will say on the Day of Judgment, "our Lord, I did not make him haughty deliberately but he himself was far away from the soul of the Qur'an. Allah will say that in My presence, you should not dispute and argue with each other, I had already promised you this occasion; the word will not be changed within My presents and nor am I unjust towards My servants. Read together the verses 41: 25-26. Whoever constructs Paradise Here they will inherit it in the Hereafter and all others who received the Soul of Qur'an but living aimlessly will go to Hell. Read together the verses 3: 136 and182. Through the verse 7:27 Allah says, "Oh you children of Adam, do not let satan tempt you just as he turned two your ancestors out of the Paradise", striping them off their clothing of heedfulness in order to show them their private parts. He and his tribe watch you from where you do not see them. We have placed devils as patrons for those who do not believe. As per the verse 8:24 by calling the believers Allah says, know you that Allah is with you in between you and your hearts whenever you stand remembering Him with the Soul of Qur'an, the Allah -the Believer is present with one, his soul-mate also become Believer.

37. Then Adam received words from His Lord, and he turned towards Him, certainly He is the Relenting, the Merciful.

38. We said: "Get you down all from here! If the Guidance has come to you from Me, then any one who follows My Guidance, on them there shall be no fear and for them will not be grieved.

Adam identified his sins and so he experienced mental distress but he could not express it by words. Then the Lord Who knows the state of hearts gave the words as told in the verse 7: 23. And both Adam and Eve prayed as, "Our Lord! We have wronged ourselves, if you don't forgive us and don't grant mercy, we'll become among losers". The Lord Who has forgiven sins of both of them; deputed children of Adam to Earth till the Last Day in order to trial. Those who got chance to do error but don't do error and live here witnessing as His vicegerent can return to Paradise. For that the parent must teach their children the Guidance, i.e. the Soul of Qur'an before the age of 15th and they all have to live following

It. Those who did sins before receiving the Soul of Qur'an but after receiving It if confess secretly by hearts all the sins to Knower of heart's state and thereby following the do's and don'ts of Qur'an in the best way, can return to the Paradise after trial.

The Guidance mentioned in the verse 2: 38 is the same as mentioned in the verses 2: 2, 185; 20: 123. The verse 7: 35 says: Oh children of Adam! Whenever there come to you Messengers from among you explaining one by one to you My verses, those who keep Allah in their hearts and purify their deeds, on them there shall be no fear and for them will not be grieved. All the verses 2: 62, 112, 274, 277; 5: 69; 6: 48; 10: 62; 38: 61; 41: 30, 32 and 43: 57, 58 also end as on them there shall be no fear and for them will not be grieved.

Therefore by mere reading or reciting the Soul of Qur'an with response will not achieve virtue; instead one should utilize It as Guidance, Balance, Light, Proof, Ticket, Criterion and Insight.

39. And those who hide and reject with Our verses, such are the inmates of the fire; they shall remain in it for ever.

The message of both these verses 2: 38 and 39 is included in the verse 57: 19 as those who believe in Allah and His Messenger, they are the truthful and the true witnesses in the sight of their Lord; they shall have their reward and their light. But those who hide and reject Our verses; they shall be the inmates of Hades.

Both verses 5: 10 and 86 say: As for those who hide and reject Our verses, they shall be the inmates of Hades. In the above mentioned verses those who hide the verses of Qur'an denote Hypocrites, and those who reject the verses denote the *Fujjar* -plural of *Fajir*, i.e. those who eat the body of Qur'an without trying to understand the contents.

The verse 7: 36 says: But those who deny Our verses and treat them with arrogance, such are the inmates of Fire to live therein forever. The verse 7: 40 says: Certainly those who reject Our verses and treat them with arrogance; their admission into Paradise will be as impossible as the passing of a camel through the eye of a tailor's needle. That is how We shall reward to the *Mujrims*. Here those who arrogant about the verses are the Hypocrites while those who reject the verses are *Fujjar*. The *Mujrims* include both of them. See explanation 1: 7 and 2: 24.

40. Oh children of Israel! Remember the favors which I bestowed upon you and fulfill the covenant with Me, I will fulfill My covenant with you and if you fear in mind Me alone.

Israel is another name of *Ya'qoob*, the grandson of Prophet *Ibrahim*. Prophet *Yoosuf*, the son of Prophet *Ya'qoob* was thrown into a well by his own brothers, caravan of travelers hold him out from the well and sold him in Egypt. In the due course, he became the ruler of Egypt. Then he brought his father and other family members to Egypt and provided home and sustenance. Thus the Children of Israel came to Egypt. Gradually that people including the children of Israel forgot the teachings of Prophet *Yoosuf*, and involved in cow adoration and other immoral activities .The Pharaohs who belonged the native clan '*Qibthi*' became the rulers suppressed and enslaved the children of Israel, the migrants to the Egypt. Then, Allah appointed Prophet *Moosa* to release them.

These verses address the Jews in *Madeena* at the time of Prophet: "Actually the favors bestowed upon their forefathers about 1500 years before at the time of Prophet *Moosa* are mentioned. This is because, the Jews in *Madeena* were proud and argued that we are following the footsteps of our forefathers on a straightway and they boasted that our hearts were overflowing with the contents of Scripture revealed upon us, so we are no need of another Book for our Guidance.

Today this verse reflects the condition of Muslims who proud that they are following Prophet and his companions. But they hide and reject the contents of Qur'an, belie the Prophet and his true followers in front of the public, follow the cursed Jews and astray Christians at the time of Prophet. The covenant made with Allah is explained in the verses 2: 27-28. In the verse 16: 91 says: Break not your oaths and covenants after you have confirmed them. Indeed you have made Allah your witness and certainly Allah knows all that you do. The verse 17: 34 says: don't approach near to orphan's wealth except to improve it until he attains the age of full strength and fulfill every covenant; every covenant will be questioned. Both the verses 23: 8 and 70: 32 say: the succeeding believers will preserve their trusts and their covenants. See the explanation 2: 39.

41. And believe in what I sent down confirming what you already have, and be not the first to conceal it and you should not sell my verses for a petty price, if you keep only Me in your hearts.

Qur'an is revealed to justify and safeguard the message of the whole Books revealed before. The coming of Prophet Muhammad and Qur'an was indicated in all the Scriptures came before. The verse 3: 81 says: Allah took the covenant with the Prophets, saying: "Now that you have been given the Book and Wisdom; there will come to you a Messenger who will confirm that which is with you; you will have to believe in him and help him in his mission." Then He asked "Do you affirm this covenant and agree to take this heavy responsibility?" The Prophets replied, "Yes, we do affirm." Allah said: "Very well, bear witness to this and I too bear witness with you". Read together the verse 6: 20. See explanation 2: 2-4.

The verse 2: 174 says: Surely those who conceal what Allah has revealed in the Book and sell it for petty price shall swallow nothing but fire into their bellies. On the Day of Resurrection Allah will neither speak to them nor purify them and they shall have painful punishment. The verse 3: 199 says: There are some among the people of the Book who truly believe in Allah and what has been revealed to you and what has been revealed to them before you. They humble themselves before Allah and do not sell the revelations of Allah for a petty price. For them, there will be a reward from their Lord. Surely Allah is very swift in settling the accounts. Read together the verse 3: 187.

Today, the Muslims especially the hypocrites are the first in hiding the Soul of Qur'an. So they will be admitted Hell fire immediately after their death even without trial as told in the verse 4: 145. Read together the verses 3: 10; 9: 55 and 125.

42. And you don't clock the Truth with falsehood nor hide the Truth while you realize It.

The verse 10:108 says: (Oh Muhammad, declare to mankind) "Indeed the Truth has come to you from your Lord! Any one who accepts It as a Guidance is only for his own sake, while anyone who strays away from It will only become astray its own risk; for I am not a custodian over you". The Truth mentioned here as well as in the verses such as 2: 119, 147; 3: 60; 7: 8; 39: 41, 75; 42: 17. -is the Soul of Qur'an only that is the food, cloth and sight of human soul. That is why it is told "its own risk" instead of "souls own risk" feminine in gender.

The Truth is the way of Allah and the falsehood is the way of satan. "Don't clock the Truth with falsehood" means: - don't overlay anything that Qur'an reveals, don't confound Qur'an with falsehood; that is not to change the intention of the verse revealed, not change the meaning of the verses that Allah has indented. The habit of Jews during the time of Prophet and the hypocrites of today is illustrated in the verse 3:78 as: There are some among them who twist their tongues around concerning the Book so that you will reckon them as from the Book while it is not from the Book. They say: "it is from Allah", while it is not from Allah. They knowingly tell lie about Allah. Read together the verse 2: 78 79 and 3: 71.

43. And keep up swalath, pay the welfare tax and obey along with those who bow their heads.

Here 'obey' means to follow the do's and don'ts of Qur'an and thus enter to the party of Allah. The verse 22: 77 says: "Oh believers! Obey, prostrate yourselves serve your Lord and do good deed so that you may attain prosperity". The verse 3: 43 says: "Oh *Mariyam* worship the Lord devoutly, prostrate yourself and obey along with those who bow their heads". Here also the meaning is not bow down in *swalath* with those who bow down. But some hypocrites misquote this verse as a proof to follow hypocrites in *swalath* whom Allah has already killed.

44. Are you ordering people to be virtuous, while you forget it yourselves, even as you recite the Book? Will you not then think by using your intelligence?

This character of Jews of *Madeena* is having today the hypocrites. Prophet taught: Read Qur'an only when Its content is understood. "*You Recite the Qur'an when your hearts are involved and reconciled with Its contents, when they separate (heart and recitation), you stand up and go away*". Otherwise the recited Qur'an will witness and argue against you. Since the codified Qur'an was not available at time of Prophet, he used to perform *swalath* for recitation of Qur'an. Read together the verse 20: 14. All the verses especially the verses 7: 170; 29: 45; 35: 29 instruct to give first preference for *Thilawath* (propagation of Qur'an) then only for *swalath*. Even the hypocrites do *Thilawath* by pretending, crying to show the people, they will not achieve virtue with It. They have been killed by Allah and commanded the party of believers to kill them as told through the verses 4: 91; 9: 123; 33: 61. The hypocrites are liars and say what they don't doing. Their leaders will say Islam and Qur'an are good things, and you don't evaluate *Islam* by seeing us. The verses 61: 2-3 say: "Oh you believe!

Why say you which you do not do, grievously hateful in the sight of Allah that you say which you do not do". The *Thilawath* of these verses are given below.

"Oh Allah be not join us with such people, and join us with those who follow the Soul of Qur'an as it should be followed, make the Qur'an as a witness and arguing for us, not against us. And enter us to the Paradise with forerunners, virtuous and victorious one with the Ticket, oh You sent down The Ticket".

Through the verse 36: 62 Allah warns a scene on the Hereafter, He will ask those who don't use their intelligence, satan led astray a great multitude of you, then did you not have been thinking? The rejecters, who don't utilize the Soul of Qur'an after receiving It, they will reply the keepers of Hell on the Day of Judgment: Had we but heard the Soul of Qur'an or used our intelligence, we should not now be among the companions of blazing Fire, is warned in the verse 67: 10. The verses 3: 65; 6: 32; 7: 169; 10: 16; 11: 51; 12: 109; 21: 10, 67; 23: 80; 28: 60; 37: 138 also end as, 'will you not then think by using your intelligence?' See explanation 2: 3, 24.

45. Seek help through patience and swalath, since it is exacting except for the submissive.

46. Who assume they will meet their Lord, and that they will return to Him.

Patience, sacrifice and tolerance mean to stand firmly and courageously in truth by assigning all to the Lord, and understand that all the oppositions in the way of truth, all difficulties, hardships, miseries, diseases and losses in wealth and body occur in the knowledge of Allah and lead a life in such a consciousness that Allah has deputed mankind to Earth in order to under go a trail. The way of Prophet at the time of all hardships and difficulties was to conduct an interview with the Lord through the *swalath*. Performing *swalath* with out the participation of soul, not only be accepted, but also causes to be darted from the *Dheen* as an arrow is darted from bow. For such the 'Wail' -the severe torment part of Hell will be rewarded as per the verses 107: 4-5. Indeed the accepted *swalath* restrains from shameful and evil deeds as mentioned in the verse 29: 45. It is told in the verses 23:1-2, indeed the successful believers are those who submissive in their *swalath*. The verse 24: 41 says, all things including living things as well as non livings are taught its own mode of *swalath* and how to glorify Him. Read together the verse 17:44. All the living beings have souls and they are praying with their souls whereas only human beings and *Jinns* have been given intelligence, and so only both of them shall be questioned about the life here. The verse 59:19 says that be not like those who forgot Allah, as a result Allah caused them to forget themselves, it is they who are the transgressors. The customs of all Prophets were that they were ever quick in emulating good deeds and called Us with hope, fear, and submission mentioned in the verse 21: 90. Such believers will pray like this: "Oh Allah! Make us fearing You, submissive before You, bowing our heads only before You and ever remembering You with the Soul of Qur'an. See explanation 2: 3-5.

47. Oh children of Israel! Remember My favor which I bestowed upon you that I have preferred you over the rest of the worlds.

This verse as well the next verse again is repeated in the verses 2: 122, 123. The blessings that Allah bestowed upon the children of Israel are explained in the consequent verses. Not only the children of Israel but the children of Adam are also excelled by the blessings of Allah. Since half of the twenty-five Prophets mentioned in the Qur'an including Prophet *Moossa* and *Eisa* who belonged to '*Ulul Azm*' (Prophets- *Nooh, Ibrahim, Moosa, Eisa* and *Muhammad* are known as '*Ulul Azm*') came from children of Israel.

The Prophets *Davood* and *Sulaiman* were given such prowess, splendor, dominion which were not given to anyone in the world. The three pairs of Prophets both father and son came among them. Thus, before the deputation of Prophet Muhammad, the leadership of the world was in the hands of children of Israel. See explanation 2: 33.

48. Heed a day when no soul will compensate for any other soul in any way intercession will not be accepted from him, nor will any alternative be taken for it. They will not be helped.

This verse pictures the Day of Judgment. That day, each and everyone -man and woman- should answer individually about their life in this world, before the Lord. In the verse 31:33Allah says: Oh mankind! do your duty to your Lord and fear a Day when no father can avail aught for his son; nor a son avail aught for his father. Verily the promise of Allah is true, so do not let worldly life deceives you, nor the chief deceiver deceives you about Allah. The verses 6: 164, 17:15,

35: 18 and 39: 7 say that no bearer of burden can bear the burden of another. In the verses 44: 40-42 Allah says, certainly the Day of sorting out is the time appointed for all of them. The Day when no protector can avail his client in aught and no help can they receive except such as Allah's mercy. Certainly He is the Mighty, Merciful. Read together the verse 6: 94. See explanation 1: 3.

49. And remember when We rescued you from Pharaoh's folk, they had been subjecting you to the worst torment, slaying your sons and sparing your women, therein was an awful testing from your Lord.

Here all, the Jews at the time of Prophet are addressed as 'children of Israel'. That is because the Jews in *Madeena* were with vain glory that they followed their forefathers without astray and they do not need what Prophet brought. Just like that the Muslims today show haughtiness that they are following Prophet and his companion. But actually they do not have any relation to their lives. The message of this verse is reflected in the verses 7: 141 and 14: 8. Read together the verses 28: 4, 40: 37-40, 44: 30.

50. And remember We divided the sea for you and thus saved you, while We drowned the Pharaoh's folk as you were looking on.

The history of Prophet *Moosa* is explained in many places in Qur'an. Pharaoh, the dictator and autocrat declared that he was the Lord highly exalted, and he divided his subjects in to two sects, suppressed one sect, i.e. the children of Israel, let their women live and slaughtered their sons and thereby did mischief on Earth. This was due to the fear from satan's erroneous notions that a man from the children of Israel takes hold of his kingship. But Allah gave inspiration to the mother of *Moosa* to suckle the child, put him to a box and cast into river. The people of Pharaoh picked the box from the river and brought to the palace. When they opened it they found the child. The wife of Pharaoh (*Assia*) told do not slay him for he be a comfort of the eyes for me as well as for you and may adopt him as a son. As a result, Pharaoh gave a proclamation inviting people to suckle the child and *Moosa's* sister came up (she was chasing the box). She said: "shall I point out you about a house that will feed and bring him up for you". Thus Allah fed *Moosa* by his own mother. After the feeding age he was entrusted to the palace and brought up there with the whole facilities. And when he reached his full age and was firmly established, entered into the city, and found two men fighting, one of his own people and other of his foes (*Qibthi*). As an answer to the appeal of the man of his own people, *Moosa* struck the man of *Qibthi* and he has been killed. *Moosa* remembered it was an act of satan because of not having remembrance of Allah while striking. He sought forgiveness from Allah and Allah forgave him. Next morning, when he was in the city to enquire about the matters, fearfully and vigilantly, saw the man who had appealed his help the day before was fighting with another man and called again for his help. *Moosa* told, you are truly one erring manifestly. When he tried to separate him, the man turned against *Moosa* and asked: "Is it your intention to slay me as you slew a man yesterday". At that time came a man running from the farthest end of the city and told to *Moosa* that he was being enquired for retaliation. Hearing this, in a state of fear, hiding from them and praying to Allah, he migrated to *Madyan*. When he arrived at *Madyan* he found a group of men watering their flocks. As he saw two women keeping back their flocks, *Moosa* watered their flocks. Women informed their father about this. One of them came back to *Moosa*; who was sitting and asking the help of Allah in a desperate mood. She said: "Father invites you to give reward for having watered". As he arrived at home, their father enquired everything about *Moosa*. He wedded one of the two daughters on the condition that he had to work with them for eight years.

After completing ten years there, *Moosa* was returning to Egypt with his family. Then he saw a light from the 'mount *Thwoor*', he went to that direction. When he reached there, Allah spoke to him and deputed him as a Prophet. Allah gave two miracles to *Moosa*, one was to change his staff which was used to fell leaves for goats into a snake by the permission of Allah and the second one was when he sticks his hand under his armpit it will come white without any blemish. Allah deputed *Haroon* (*Moosa's* half brother) as the demand of *Moosa*. Thus Moosa and Haroon came to Pharaoh with the signs of Allah, invited Pharaoh into the Lord of all worlds. See the verses 28: 1-40. Seeing the signs instead of accepting Allah Pharaoh became more arrogant and told: "*Moosa* and *Haroon* were sorcerers". Pharaoh invited the entire sorcerers for a competition with *Moosa*. When *Moosa* succeeded in the competition, all the sorcerers fell into prostration by declaring: "We believe in the Lord of *Moosa* and *Haroon*". Pharaoh declared cut off their hands and feet on opposite sides and to crucify them. The chiefs from his palace asked pharaoh whether he is letting Moosa and *Haroon* to do mischief on Earth excluding him and his deities. As a reply, pharaoh ordered again to let the women to live and slaughter their sons from the children of Israel. Fearing the punishment of pharaoh, only a few youth believed. Allah commanded *Moosa* and *Haroon* that the believers should establish *swalath* centering their own home. Since pharaoh became transgressing hypocrite and he never accepts the truth, even after he had shown several signs, Allah commanded to *Moosa* to pray as: "To expel his treasures and wealth and every kind of honorable positions and make his heart hard, so that he will not believe until he faces a severe punishment". As a reply to his prayer, Allah commanded Moosa to travel with the children of Israel by night itself. Pharaoh with his troops chased them. When Moosa reached on the shore of Red sea, Allah commanded to strike the sea with his staff. So it was divided and each separate part of water became like a huge, mountain. Read together the verse 26: 63. Thus children of Israel crossed the sea through a dry path as described in the verse 20: 77 Allah ordered to leave the sea as a furrow as per the verse 44: 24. When the Israelites looking fearfully towards the opposite shore, pharaoh and his troops reached in the middle of the sea, overwhelmed and drowned by attaching the two mountain of water. Pharaoh declared when 'the spirit (soul + life)' reached his throat: "I believe that there is no deity except Allah, Whom the children of Israel believe in and I am one among those who submit whole to Him". Allah replied: "Ah at now, you had disobeyed before and been a mischief-maker! However today we will save your body only so you may be a sign to anyone who comes after you. Yet many people are quite heedless of Our verses. Read together the verses 10: 83-92.

Approximately 2800 years Allah kept the body of pharaoh in the sea and today it is in the Egyptian museum. This verse (regarding the body of Pharaoh) becomes a sign for those who are in search of the contents of remaining 6235 verses out of total verses of Qur'an 6236. Read together the verses 7: 103-127; 20: 37-52 and 26: 10-66.

51. Remember when We appointed with Moosa for forty nights, then you took the calf as God after he had left and you became wrongdoers.

52. Then later on We still pardoned this you, so that you might become grateful.

The verse 2: 56, 185; 3: 123; 5: 6, 89; 8: 26; 16: 16, 78; 22: 36; 28: 23; 30: 46; 35: 12 and 45: 12 also end as: "so that you might become grateful".

53. When We gave Moosa the Book and the standard, so that you might become rightly be guided.

The verses 2: 150; 3: 105; 7: 158; 16: 15 and 43: 10 also end as: "You might become rightly be guided".

54. And remember Moosa told to his people: "Oh my people, indeed you have wronged yourselves by accepting the calf. So turn towards your Maker in repentance and kill your own selves; that will be better for you with your Maker; then He will relent towards you, since He is the only relenting, the Merciful.

Allah saved the children of Israel by splitting the sea. Later, Allah appointed *Moosa* for an interview thirty days in order to give Guidance to them and completed the period adding ten more to become forty days. Read together the verse 7: 142. Before *Moosa* went up he gave charge of the people to *Haroon*. But the children of Israel, under the leadership of *Samiryy*, put all ornaments in to the fire for melting. *Samiryy* brought out of the fire the mould of a calf. Satan gave it a mooing sound. *Samriyy* told: "This is your Deity as well as the Deity of *Moosa*, but *Moosa* has forgotten to inform you. *Haroon* had already told them: "Oh my people, you are only being tested by means of it. Certainly your Lord is the 'impartial'. So follow me and obey my command". They said: "We will never quit being devoted to it until *Moosa* returns to us". They tried to kill and suppress *Haroon*. Allah informed *Moosa* about the worship of calf. So *Moosa* returned to his people in a state of anger and sorrow and he threw away the stone discs (Ten commandments- *Thourath*). He seized his brother *Haroon* by his head and beard, dragged him and said: "What you have done in my place and in my absence. Did you make haste in the matter of your Lord?" *Haroon* replied: "Oh son of my mother! Seize me not by my head. I feared otherwise you should say that you have caused a split among the children of Israel by not waiting for your word. They tried to weaken, suppress and even to slay me. Therefore make not the enemies either rejoice over my misfortune or count you me among the people of wrongdoers". Then Moosa prayed "Oh my Lord, forgive to me and my brother, admit us to Your mercy, certainly You are the most merciful of those who show mercy. Read together the verses 7: 150 and 20: 83-94.

Moosa ordered *Samriyy*, the Hypocrite, under whose leadership they molded the calf, to get out of the place by saying: "touch me not (believe me not)". They burned and scattered the calf in to the river. See the verses 20: 95-98. Allah ordered through *Moosa* that all the rebellious of Israelites for making the calf should kill each other. Consequently unlimited slaughtering taken place and nearly 70,000 people were killed. Among those who were killed innocently got the reward of a martyr in the way of Allah, as taught Prophet.

Similar events have taken place in previous '*Shareat*'. E.g:- The deviated Israelites devoted the goddess '*Ba'al*'. In the time of Prophet *Illyas* who was deputed to them. And under his leadership two groups of people conducted a sacrifice. As a proof for the acceptance of sacrifice a fire came from sky and burned the sacrificed animal. By remembering this Jews in *Madeena* at the time Prophet *Muhammad* as per the verse 3: 183 told that: "Allah took our promise not to believe in a messenger unless he showed us a sacrifice consumed by fire". The same event had occurred as a proof for accepting the sacrifice by Adam's children. Read together the verse 5: 27. The Creator of soul known as '*Khaliq*' –The Creator, and the Maker of body is known as '*Barie*'-The Maker. From these events we can understand that there is no forgiveness for those who do evils knowingly and Allah will take revenge against them. Since the believers are the vicegerents of Allah they have an attitude of revenge only against the hypocrites who conceal the Truth knowingly. If we see a sin, prevent it by our hand, if it's not possible prevent it by our tongue, if it's also not possible, then hate it at least by mind. If anybody has not at least the habit of hating the sin by mind, there won't be a minute atom of belief in him, as taught by Prophet. See explanation 2: 2 and 38.

55. And remember when you said: "Oh Moosa, we will never believe in you until we see Allah openly", the thunder bolts caught you while you were looking on.

56. Then We raised you up after you had died, so that you might become grateful.

When the children of Israel wanted to see Allah with their own eyes, *Moosa* went to the mount '*Thwoor*' with seventy representatives from twelve tribes; Allah seized them with a Tremor. And they fell down. Then *Moosa* prayed: "My Lord, even though You may have wished to wipe them out and my self earlier, are You wiping us out just because what some fools among us have done? It is only Your manner of testing: You let anyone You wish to go astray by means of it, and let anyone You wish to be guided. You are our Patron. So pardon us and show us mercy. You are the best pardoner. Read together the verse 7: 155. Then Allah gave them rebirth. Allah raised the mount *Thwoor* over them as an umbrella as if that was going to fall on them. Allah said to them: "Hold firmly what We have given to you and bring ever to remembrance what is therein, in order to become heedful, is told both in the verses 2: 83 and 7: 171. The verse 76: 3 says: "Certainly We showed the man either of the two ways -grateful or ungrateful. Read together verses 64: 2; 90: 10 and 91: 7-10. Each individual is constructing his/her own Paradise or Hell in this world. Anyone who constructs Paradise here by using Soul of Qur'an can inherit Paradise after his death. While those who lived here aimlessly by neglecting the Soul of Qur'an will go to the Hell. Allah, the Impartial, not causes anyone to go either Paradise or Hell. It is warned in the verse 14: 22 that there will be no chance for blaming even satan for ones own wrongdoings. See explanation 1: 2 and 2: 28

"Oh Allah, make us remembering You and showing gratitude to You. Shower Your blessings to return to You as a new born baby by ruminating and confessing our sins by utilizing the Soul of Qur'an".

57. And remember We spread the clouds out to shade you, and sent down "Manna" and "Selva"-Quails for you: "Eat some of good things which We have provided you with!" They didn't harm Us, but it was themselves whom they harmed.

The same content of this verse has come as a part of the verse 7:160. "They didn't harm Us, but it was themselves whom they harmed" means, since Allah is impartial, it is the duty of each individual to construct Paradise or Hell. Goodness is from Allah and bad is from your soul mate satan as told in the verses 4: 78-79. Without making the Soul mate believer with the Soul of Qur'an only effect bad things. The verses 16: 33, 118; 29: 40 and 30: 9 end as: "They wronged not with Us or We wronged not with them, but it was themselves whom they harmed." The verse 43: 76 says: "Still We will not harm them, rather they have already harmed them selves". The verse 10: 106 says: "Nor appeal to something that will neither benefit nor harm you, instead of to Allah. If you should do so, you would be then among the wrongdoers. Read together the verse 6: 52.

58. And remember We said: "Enter this town and eat wherever you may wish in it at your leisure. Enter the gate prostrating and by

saying: "Hithwathun" (relive us)! We will forgive your mistakes and give even more to those who act kindly.

'Enter the gate prostrating' does not means or on the face in turn it means to enter the city as 'well-wishers' to the people of that city and instructing them to live by obeying the do's and don'ts of Allah i.e. following the Book. '*Hithwathun*' means to utter the word of '*Thouheed*'-saying no deity except Allah, seeking forgiveness to Allah and saying peace to the residents. Read the verses 4: 154 and 7: 161.

59. Yet those who do wrong altered the statement to something else than what had been told them, so We sent a scourge down from the Heaven on those who did wrong since they have acted so transgress.

The children of Israel were told to enter the Palestine which was the Promised Land for them. From among them twelve chiefs were sent to observe the land. They returned and all except two said: Verily, the people of that land are of exceeding strength; we shall never enter there until they leave the city. If they leave, then we shall enter. But the God fearing two men said: "Enter you that land. When once you are in, victory will be yours, and on Allah put your trust if you have faith". Then they said, "We shall never enter the city as long as they are there, go you and your Lord and fight, while we sit here". Then *Moosa* said, "Oh my Lord, I have power only over my self and my brother, so separate us from this rebellious people". Allah said: "For forty years that land is prohibited for them and they will wander through that land in distraction. Therefore, sorrow you not over this rebellious people". Read together the verses 5: 20-26; 7: 161-162 and 29: 34.

60. And remember when Moosa asked for water for his people, We said "strike the rock with your staff!" So twelve springs gushed forth from it, each group of people knew their drinking spot: "Eat and drink from Allah's provisions and do not cause any havoc on Earth, as if you were mischief-makers".

The verses 57-60 are also repeated in the verses 7:160-162.

61. And remember when you said: "Oh Moosa we will never stand with one kind of food, appeal to your Lord, to produce whatever

the Earth will grow for us such as its vegetables, cucumbers, wheat, cauliflower, lentils, onions etc"; He said: "Do you want to exchange some thing common place for something that is better"? Go to Egypt to get what you asked for. And humiliation and poverty were stamped up on them and became victims of the wrath from Allah. That was because they had disbelieved Allah's verses and killed the Prophets without having any just. That happened because they disobeyed and had acted so defiant.

As per the verse 5: 26 it is told to them to perch and stay in Palestine, but they were not ready for that. Allah proclaimed, they will wander in distraction on Earth and Palestine is forbidden for them for forty years. At the same time as per the verse 26: 59; 44: 28, a group among them returned to Egypt and stayed there enjoying gardens, springs, cultivation, castles and honorable positions which had relished by Pharaoh and his folks. But gradually when they became ungrateful and arrogant their unity was broken and poverty and disgrace were raised on them.

The children of Israel have illegally killed several Prophets. They slaughtered Prophet *Yahya* and presented his head putting on a tray in order to satisfy a danseuse in the palace. They have killed some of the Prophets by pelting stones, by submerging on the pond of mud, by cutting with sowing sword. Even they boasted that they have killed Prophet Jesus. Read together the verse 4: 157. The verse 3:21 says: Those who hide the verses of Allah, slay Prophets and slay those who teach Just to mankind announce to them a grievous torment. Today the verses of Allah are only the verses of Qur'an. Today the meaning of killing Prophet is to accept the Prophets' name, but not follow their way of living. And falsely present their way of life. Today only the Muslims have this behaviour. Therefore, they became victims of curse and wrath of Allah and people. There are disgrace and dishonor up on them every where in the world. This is because they don't follow the Soul of Qur'an which is sent down by Allah to entire mankind. They forbid It to others and conceal It themselves. Read together the verses 6: 26; 9: 67-68; 16: 106-107; 33: 61. The only remedy for this disgrace and hardship is to return to the Soul of Qur'an and there by submit and live only for Allah. The verse 4: 42 says: On the Day of Judgment, those who hide the Qur'an and disobey the Prophet would like to have the Earth leveled off while they are still remain under in it; Allah will never conceal even a single word of them. The verses 3: 112 and 5: 78 also end as: that happened because they disobeyed and had acted so defiant. See the explanations 1: 7 and 2: 24.

62. Certainly those who believe from among Muslims, those who are Jews, Christians, Sabeans, anyone who believes in Allah and Last Day, and acts honorably will receive their reward with their Lord and there shall be no fear and for them will not be grieved.

This verse is repeated as the verse 5: 69. The verse 49: 13 says: Oh mankind, certainly We created you from a single pair of male and female, and made you into different nations and tribes so that you may recognize one another. Certainly the most honored of you in the sight of Allah is heedful; Allah is Well aware, Well acquainted. This verse teaches that it is not necessary to change the names and clothes to become a believer. In other sense, in Islam there is no baptism, but only change in belief. Whatever and wherever man does a work, Allah looks the state of his heart and gives reward based on it. The verse 53: 39 says: And surely the man shall have nothing except he aims for. Prophet taught, deeds are evaluated by its aim. Without Allah's Permission-the Soul of Qur'an- nobody becomes a believer as told in the verse 10: 100. No one enter the Paradise unless he is a believer as per the verse 40: 40. Since today there is no group of believers anywhere in the world there is not compulsory to practice the *shariath* laws but it is ordered to holdfast the Soul of Qur'an with molar teeth to any person who literate. Read together the verses 16: 96-97 and 20: 112. See explanation 2: 21-22 and 38-39.

63. And remember when We have made an agreement with you by raising the mount Thwoor above you. Hold firmly which We have given you and remember what it contains, so that you may become heedful.

The verse 7:171says, We raised the mount *Thwoor* as an umbrella and they thought it was going to fall on them and said, hold firmly to what We have given you and bring ever to remembrance what is therein so that you might become heedful. Even though in that time it was commanded to the children of Israel to hold fast *Thourath* and bring ever remembrance there in, today since the Soul of Qur'an is the only Book for entire mankind his heart's language one should learn and follow It to become heedful. See explanations 2: 2, 55 and 56.

64. Then even after that you turned back and if Allah's Bounty and His Mercy had not upon you, you would have turned out to be the losers.

In this verse as well as in the verses 4: 83,113; 10: 58, 24: 10, 14, 20, 21 Allah's Bounty and Mercy means the Soul of Qur'an. See explanation 2: 38.

65. Yet you knew which of you had been transgressed on the Sabbath, so We told them, "become apes despised and hatred".

66. We set them up as an illustration of what had come before them and what would come after them, and as a good advice for the heedful.

As per the verse 16:124, the Jews transposed the day of weekly festival to Saturday which Allah ordained on Friday in 'Islam'. Some of the Jews settled on the shore of '*Aila*' who lived by fishing followed an unwritten dictum that no job should be carried out on Saturday. But fishes came in lumpsum numbers to a canal on Saturdays. So they made a blockade to prevent the fishes returning and they fished on next day. Thus they did against the teaching that Allah looks in to the state of heart while doing any deeds. Due to their repeated transgression their bodies were transformed into apes. This event is explained in the verses 7:163-166. Read together the verses 4:147-154.

The lesson of this incident is whoever does this type of deeds forgetting Allah -the Knower of the states of hearts, their punishment will be severe just like this. Qur'an is the Guidance and good advice for the heedful as told in the verse 3:138. The verse 10: 57says, Oh mankind, there has come to you an Admonition and Instruction from your Lord. The 'verse 11: 120 says, to you there came the Truth as well as an Instruction and Message of remembrance to people who believe. Here the Truth, Instruction and Message of remembrance denote only the Soul of Qur'an. Even though the Qur'an is an Instruction for mankind, only the heedful accept It as an Admonition and Instruction. It is told in the verse 16:125 that call mankind to the path of your Lord with '*Hikmath*' and with the '*Mouidhathul-Hasnath*'. Here mentioned '*Hikmath*' means clear explained Qur'an verses' and the '*Mouidhathul-Hasnath*' means similar examples or commands and forbidden of clear verses of Qur'an. The '*Hikmath*' and '*Mouidhathul-Hasnath*' denotes the Truth and the best interpretation respectively mentioned in the verses 25: 33.

Some examples for '*Mouidhath*' are given below. If the Muslims, the bearers of the Qur'an under take the following activities, they shall be resurrected as apes, bandicoots and dogs etc. in the Hell. Allah will not transform their body shape in this world because of the Prophet's prayer.

(1) As against the dictum to the verses 2: 229-230, to say three '*Thwalaqs*' -Husband says the word of divorce three times at a time, and later he thinks that it should not have been done, and then he wants to take back her, there is a condition said, i.e. she has to be married by another and if that man divorces her normally for natural reasons, then only the former husband can marry her. But many Muslims today take back the three times divorced wife after making her married first to any other man, then make her divorced.

(2) Without quoting the last part of the verse 62: 5 i.e. how evil is the similitude of people who reject the verses of Allah and Allah never guides such type of wrong doers, by quoting only the first part of the verse and says the similitude of Jews who carry *Thourath* is that of a donkey and it is not applicable to the Muslims. Whereas actually today Allah's verses are only the verses of Qur'an and the carriers of It are the Muslims.

(3) Not pay attention to what Allah gives as a similitude of dogs to hypocrites -who hide the Soul of Qur'an and the common Muslims who deny understanding what is, what for, and why Qur'an? After receiving It through the verses 7: 176. And to oppose and menace those who warns them by quoting such verses.

(4) Not pay attention to what Allah said in the verse '2: 174' i.e. surely those who conceal any part of the Book which Allah has revealed and those who sell His verses for miserable price (for material gain -such as accept salaries for conducting sermons and acting Imam for *swalath*, recitation of Qur'an to the dead, accept money by making amulets and talisman by writing Qur'an verses on it and accept commission of dowry etc.); shall filling nothing except fire into their bellies. On the Day of Resurrection Allah will neither speak to them nor purify them and they shall have painful punishment.

(5) Not pay attention to what Allah said in the verse 3: 103 i.e. hold together the Rope of Allah -The Soul of Qur'an and become one party and be not divided. But they divide in to several organizations and enjoy each one as they are in truth

and considered others in astray. Read together the verses 23: 51-53 and 30: 30-32

67. And remember Moosa told his people: "Certainly Allah commands you to sacrifice a cow". They asked: "do you take us for a laughing stock?" He said: "I seek refuge with Allah lest I become so ignorant".

68. They said: "appeal to your Lord for us, to explain to us what a type of cow she is"? He said: "Certainly He says she should be neither too old nor too young, but of an age in between. Then do as you are ordered".

69. They said: "Appeal to your Lord for us, to explain to us what color she is". He said: "Certainly He says that she is a bright yellow cow. Her color gladdens those who look at her".

70. They said: "Appeal to your Lord for us, to explain to us what she is like. Cows seem all alike to us and we should be guided properly if Allah so wishes".

71. He said: "He says that she is a cow which has not been used to plough the Earth or to irrigate any crops; she is sound and has no blemish on her". They said: "Now you are telling the truth", and they slaughtered her though they almost had not done so.

The devotion towards had dissolved in their heart of the children of Israel as they were involved in cow adoration in Egypt. That is why satan helped them to mould a calf with a mooing sound from the pit which is used for melting ornaments. They were commanded to sacrifice a cow with golden color without blemish in order to wipe out the devotion towards such cows for ever. This *Surath* got the name "The Cow" considering on this event.

72. And remember you killed a soul and quarreled over it. But Allah was bound to bring forth whatever you had hidden.

73. We said: Strike him with some part of it. Thus Allah revives the dead and shows you His signs. So that you may think utilizing your intelligence.

There were existed a custom that when a murder occurred, the chiefs of the clans shall wash their hands on a cow, as like to say that they have no share in the murder. It was commanded to kill a cow like that of they devoted. At the time of sacrifice there was a dead body of a man of which the killer had not identified. Then Allah told to strike the dead body with some parts of killed cow. Thus Allah brought the dead back to life in order to say about the killer. Through this event it is proven that Allah has the power to bring forth whatever people conceal. By reviving the dead man by means of striking with the part of killed cow, nine hundred and ninety-nine people out of thousand believed that the cow is the Deity and has the power to bring forth the dead to life even after it is killed. Thus Allah separates the believers and disbelievers by this type of incidents.

Man is given the intelligence to do deeds by thinking and using it. Deeds without consciousness shall not be accepted. If the word 'you' is used in the verse, 'so that you may think utilizing your intelligence', is about Jews in previous times today the word 'you' is applicable to the Muslims only, because they are the people who read, hear and touch the Qur'an. The verses 2: 232, 6: 151, 12: 2, 24: 61, 40: 67, 43: 3, 57: 17 also end as, "you might become men of thinking". See the explanation 2:44.

74. Even after that your hearts were hardened and became stony, and even harder yet, for there are some stones which rivers gush out of and there are others which water comes forth from when they spilt open, and there are still others which sink down by fearing Allah. And Allah is not heedless of what you are doing.

The children of Israel who were the ancestors of Jews in *Madeena* at the time of Prophet were witnesses of all the signs (divine wonders) that Allah shown through Prophet *Moosa*. But they repeatedly forgot that and involved in evils and arrogance. They became cruel without having any tenderness and mercy. The Jews in *Madeena* had the same character of their forefathers. That is why through the verses like 5: 51 Allah says: "Oh you who believe, do not accept Jews or Christians as patrons; some of them act as patrons for one another. Any of you who make friends with them becomes one of them. Indeed Allah does not guide such a wrong doing people".

Today the word 'you' referred in the part of the verse 'Allah is not heedless of what you are doing' is applicable to Muslims especially the hypocrites among them. As per the verse 63: 4 it is such hypocrites whom Allah had killed; and shall have curse and wrath on them and Allah commanded to the party of believers if there is to kill them through the verses 4: 91, 9: 123, 33: 60-61. The verses 2:85,140,149, 3:99 also end as "Allah is not heedless of what you are doing". Both the verses 11:123 and 27:93 end as, "your Lord is never heedless of what you are doing". Through the verse 10: 88, Allah commanded to Prophet *Moosa* to pray to give hardness to the heart of Pharaoh who was the hypocrite, such that he will not believe until he sees a painful torment. It is told in the verse 39: 22, "woe to those whose hearts are hardened against the Soul of Qur'an. Such people are in clear astray".

Allah asks through the verse 57: 16 "Oh believers, has not the time arrived for you even now to become your hearts in humble with fear of Allah in to the remembrance of Allah through the Soul of Qur'an? You should not become like those whom the Book was given before. Long ages passed over them and their hearts grew hard, for many among them were transgressors". Read together 22: 52-53. See explanation 2: 26 and 27.

75. Are you so hope for them to believe for your own sake while a group of them had already heard Allah's words? Then they distort with it knowingly after It understood to them.

Today the hypocrites among the Muslims have the character, which had been the character of Jews at the time of Prophet. It teaches the believers who belong to the party of Allah that they do not expect these hypocrites will ever return to belief or become the followers of Qur'an. Read together the verses 10:33 and 40:6. See explanation 2: 6-7.

All these verses portraits the character and conduct of Jews and hypocrites. Today all the leaders of Muslim organizations have this behavior. That means they twist the verses of Qur'an in order to protect the interest of their organizations. Read together the verses 2: 14, 3: 78, 4: 46 and 5: 13, 40-41.

76. Whenever they meet with those who believe, they say: "We believe", while when some of them go off privately with one another, they say: "Will you report something to them which Allah has disclosed to you, so they may dispute with you about it in the presence of your Lord? Will you not then think by using your intelligence?

77. Do they not realize certainly Allah knows anything they hide and anything they display?

When the Jews meet with the believers, they will say: "Qur'an is Truth which agrees and justifies what is told in our Scripture. But when they go off privately with one another", they were asking whether the reference about the Qur'an and the Prophet included in their Scripture –*Thourath*, had been to the notice of believers unknowingly? Thus are you giving a chance to them (believers) to argue with informed truth before the Lord tomorrow? We can see the same character of hypocrites in the verses 2: 14-15. They maintained this character because of their disbelief. Allah, the Knower of all times has already recorded what is happening both in Heaven and Earth in the Book is told in the verses like 9: 51, 10: 62 and 11: 6. The explanation of "Will you not then think by using your intelligence?" is given in the verse 2:44.

78. Some of them are illiterate and do not know the Book except having their own guessing and they neither follow except conjectures.

Today Qur'an is the only Book. The men referred as illiterates and do not know the Book in this verse are the common Muslims who try not to understand what is, what for, and why Qur'an? The verse 49: 12 says "Oh you believe! Avoid conjectures as much. Certainly conjectures in some cases are sin".

It is told in the verses 41: 21-23, Tomorrow, on the Day of Judgment, they will say to their skins, why do you bear witness against us? Their skins will say: "Allah who grants speech to everything has given us speech. He created you in the first place and to Him are you being returned. You did not mere expect lest your hearing, eyesight or your skins would bear witness against you, did you suppose that Allah does not know so much about whatever your doing. That conjecture of yours which you concerned about your Lord has ruined you. So you have awakened among the losers". The verse 6:116 says to Prophet and believers, if you obey the majority of people, they will lead you away from the Straight path of Allah; most of them not follow except guessing and many of them maintain except conjectures.

In the verse 6: 148 Allah says regarding the Muslims of today who live without the Soul of Qur'an, which is the real knowledge: "You follow nothing but conjecture. Certainly you are merely guessing". The verse 10: 36 says: "Most of them follow nothing but conjecture, truly conjecture can be no avail against truth, and through the verse 10: 60 Allah asks, what will be the guessing of those who invent a lie about Allah on the Day of Resurrection? Certainly Allah possesses Bounty for mankind, yet most of them are not grateful. The verse 10: 66 says: "Does not in the Heaven and anyone on Earth belong to Allah? What do those follow, who appeal to associate instead of Allah? They merely follow conjecture and they are only guessing. Read together the verses 38: 27; 48: 6, 12 and 53: 23, 28. See explanation 2: 4-5, 45 and 46.

79. Then, the 'Wail' is for those who write the Book down with their own hands, and say: "This is from Allah", for selling it for a petty price. So the 'Wail' is for them for what their hands have written. And 'Wail' is for them whatever they earned.

This verse portraits the behavior of the hypocrites who twist the Qur'an, shuffle It, hide It, quote It to establish wrong meaning, quote It for firming his ideas against what Allah has intended, quote Qur'anic verses for establishing the satanic ways like communalism, selfishness, nationalism and organizational partiality, to confuse the common man by quoting only a part verses in stead of complete verses, misquote the verses as a proof to establish satan's works like sorcery, incantation, omens; justify those who recite the Qur'an to dead and accept money; to publish books to obstruct the common man from the Soul of Qur'an. These hypocrites -the leaders of the Muslim organizations, will be in the dam depth of Hell as told in the verse 4:145. They will have 'Wail' -the severe torment valley of Hell, which is earned by them.

These hypocrites compel the common man to perform "*swalath*" without teaching them the Soul of Qur'an and thus drag to Hell. They quote the verses 18: 109, 31:27 and say even they have the full knowledge in Arabic language do not know the explanation of Qur'an since It will never exhaust by writing or saying. Therefore, they teach the common man to recite Qur'an, perform *swalath* and to follow them. But Allah asks in four places through the *Surath* 54: "We have indeed made the Qur'an easy to understand with heart, but who is there to receive the admonition". They neglect the teaching of Prophet that not to recite Qur'an with out understanding its contents, and for who do so will be the worst one among the people. In conclusion these hypocrites are the man devils who obstruct man openly from the Soul of Qur'an. See explanation 1: 7 and 2: 11-12.

80. And they say: "The fire will not touch us except for a few numbered days". Say: "Have you taken an agreement from Allah? If so Allah

never breaks His agreement? Or are you saying something about Allah which you really do not know".

The Jews boasted that they are the beloved servants of Allah and reserved people for Paradise. They even boasted, even if they entered in the Hell, they will have to stay there only for forty days, the duration of cow adoration. Read together the verses 2: 94-95; 62: 6-7. Today only the disbelievers among Muslims have this character and argument. In this verse the meaning of 'few numbered days' is forty days and in verse 2: 184 it is 29 or 30 days and in 2: 203 it is three days. A group of hypocrites who undeservingly proud as the men of Qur'an argue that the few numbered days referred in Qur'an is below seven days and therefore fasting during the month of *Ramadan* is needed only for three days. They are quoting the verse 2: 203 as the proof for their argument neglecting both verses 2: 80, 184. This verse demands all men not to tell about Allah without quoting or knowing the Soul of Qur'an. The verse 2:169 says that satan merely orders you to commit evil and shocking deeds, and to say what you do not know about Allah. It is warned through the verse 6: 93 that at the time of death of the rebellious hypocrites and *fujjar* i.e. wrongdoers, they will be pushed to Hell by saying that enjoy the shameful torment of Hell since you had been talking about Allah without the Soul of Qur'an, and were arrogant to the verses of Qur'an. Read together the verses 4: 43 and 7: 28. See explanation 2: 27.

81. Nay, anyone who earns evil and encompassed in evil, those will become inmates of the Fire; therein shall they abide forever.

The verse 4: 123 says: Neither your (Muslims) desires, nor of the people of the Book prevail, whoever does devil will be requited accordingly, nor will he find besides Allah any protector or helper. And in the verse 124 says, anyone who does good deeds under the Soul of Qur'an, whether it is a man or woman provided that he is a believer, will enter the Paradise and they will not be harmed a speck. This verse also teaches that each person individually earns Paradise or Hell from this world. Read together the verse 16: 97. See explanation 2: 39.

82. And those who believe and perform honorable deeds will be the inhabitants of the Paradise, therein shall they abide forever.

Believers are those who identified Allah, themselves and the aim of life through the Soul of Qur'an. The heedful men are those who follow the do's and don'ts of Qur'an. See explanation 2: 62.

83. Thus We made an agreement with the children of Israel: "You shall serve Allah alone and treat your parents kindly, and near relatives, orphans and the needy, and speak the best word to the people, and keep up swalath and pay the welfare tax"; then you turned except a few of you, and even now you are neglecting that agreement.

Nobody is to be loved except under the love of Allah and maintain Allah's anger to anybody. 'To speak the best word' means to speak with the Soul of Qur'an which contains the do's and don'ts of Allah. Just like the children of Israel at the time of Prophet *Moosa* who broke the agreement with Allah, the Jews in front of Prophet also didn't obey the agreement. Today the Muslims are living neglecting the do's and don'ts of Qur'an and there by they also disobey the covenant made with Allah and agreements made with other people. The majority of the Muslims have the same character of Jews in *Madeena* towards the Qur'an even though they are reciting these verses. The verse 32: 22 says: "And who does more wrong than one to who are recited the verses of his Lord in the hearts language and then turns back there from it, certainly We shall revenge to such *mujrims*". The verse 43: 67 says: On the Day of Judgment all brotherly relationships will be in foes one another except with those who lived under the Light of Qur'an. And the verse 68 it is told to the believers who follow the Soul of Qur'an in this world: "Oh My servants, no fear shall be on you today, nor shall you grieve". The verse 69 says: "Those who believe in Our verses and submitted all to Us are the honorable men. Read together the verses 18: 57 and 20: 124-127.See explanation 2: 21.

84. So We made an agreement with you: "Shed not blood among you, nor drive one another out of your homes"; Then you solemnly ratified that agreement and to this you were witnesses (even now).

When Prophet arrived at *Madeena*, there were Jews clans like '*Banunadheer*', '*Bnuquraidha*', '*Banu-Quainuqaa*' and Arabic clans like '*Ouse*' and '*Khazraj*'. It was made a contract that Jews should live according to their Scripture and Muslims to live according to Qur'an and encounter the public enemies together. In the verse 3: 81 says: "Remember, Allah took agreement from all the Prophets saying: Have I not given you a part of the Book and wisdom", then a messenger came to you to confirm what you already had, so you might believe with him and support him. Allah asked: "Do you agree and take this agreement as binding on you"? They said: "we agreed it". He said: "Then bear witness and I am with you among the witnesses". Read together the verse 3: 187. See the explanation 2: 27.

85. After this it is you the people who go on killing one another and driving a group of you from their homes, backing one another up against them out of sin and enmity. If they are brought to you as captives, you ransom them, while it has been forbidden for you even to expel them! Thus do you believe in part of the book and disbelieve in another part of It? What reward has anyone of you who does so, except disgrace during worldly life, while on Resurrection Day they will be driven off to the harshest torment? And Allah is not heedless of what you are doing.

The Jews in *Madeena* neglecting the agreement with Allah and His messenger, united two groups for opposing and driving off the third group from their homes, cities and they plotted to seize their wealth. Thus they were brought in front of the chief of the tribes as captives, accepted ransom as bribery then released them. Thus they lived fighting and quarrelling with one another without unity. But today, the Muslims everywhere in the world are divided into several groups and are leading a life in enmity. They do not use themselves the Book for entire mankind and do not give It to others to utilize. Therefore they should have to bear the sins of other people along with their own and has to go to Hell, is warned in the verse 6: 26. The verses 4: 151 says: Such are the true disbelievers and We have reserved a humiliating punishment for them. They are the people in different organizations among Muslims as specified in the verse 4: 150.

The word 'you' told in the part of the verse 'Allah is not heedless of what you are doing' refers today only to the readers of Qur'an. The verses 22: 8 and 31: 20 say: "There are men such one dispute about Allah without knowing the Soul of Qur'an". The verse 22: 9 says, those who partially bending one side in order to lead others astray from Allah's path without the whole Soul of Qur'an, such one will have disgrace in this world while we shall let him taste the torment of burning on the Day of Judgment. And the verse 10 says, this Hell is because of the deeds which your hands sent forth; certainly Allah is not unjust to His servants. The verses 15: 89-91 say, just like for those to whom We sent warners who divided the Qur'an into arbitrary parts, We sent you too. Say: "Verily I am a clear Warner", but Muslims who read such verses are commanded to be united as one party as per the verse 3: 103; are divided into several groups. All organizations of Muslim except one are considered as associates as per the verses 23: 51-53 and 30: 31-32 and belongs to the party of satan. Read together the verses 2: 176-177 and 6: 158-159. Those who don't follow the Soul of Qur'an after getting It shall have disgrace in this world and severe torment on the Day of Judgment, is told in the verses 2: 114; 16: 27; 39: 25-26 and 41: 10.

86. Such are the ones who purchase worldly life instead of the Hereafter; punishment will not be lightened for them and nor will they be helped.

Read together the verse 2: 175. See explanation 2: 16.

87. Verily, We gave Moosa the Book and followed him up with a succession of messengers. We gave Eisa, the son of Maryam clear Evidence and strengthened him with the Holy Spirit. Yet every time some messenger comes to you with what you yourselves do not desire, do not you act so arrogant? One group you have rejected, while another group you are killing.

'The Holy Spirit' means the Angel *Jibreel*. Just like all other people, the spirit of Prophet *Eisa* is from Allah. The body of Prophet *Eisa* formed by the Word of Allah "To be" as per the verse 4: 171. The verse 16: 102 say: "The Holy spirit has brought It down with Truth from your Lord to brace those who believe and as Guidance and Good news for Muslims. The verse 26: 193 says, 'the faithful spirit has brought It down' and it is told about *Jibreel* in the verses 81: 19-21 as: it is a statement by a honorable messenger possessing strength established by the One enthroned who is to be obeyed and more than that is trust worthy. And 'the spirit' is told in the verse 78: 38 is also *Jibreel*.

'One group you have rejected, while another group you are killing' told in the verse is applicable only to ones who read the Qur'an. Since the way of life of all messengers were the Soul of Qur'an, by hiding and rejecting It, Muslims of today are really rejecting and killing messengers. By accepting the names and adornment of messengers without witnessing their life, actually they are serving satan, the cursed one. It is very clear that Muslims everywhere follow these kinds of life. Read together the verses 2: 253 and 5: 110. It is clear that as per the verse 5: 11 the Jews and as per the verse 9: 74 the hypocrites in *Madeena* were trying to kill Prophet *Muhammad*. See explanation 2: 1-2 and 6.

88. And they say our hearts are covered over, rather, Allah has cursed them because of their disbelief, so a little do they believe.

The Jews in *Madeena* behaved to Prophet and to the believers in such a manner that "They have in their hearts even the wrapper of the Book. Therefore, they don't want anything more". Today, when the believers say Muslims to learn and teach the Soul of Qur'an, their response is also like that, especially of the hypocrites among them. The verse 4: 155 says, because of their repeated breaking of the covenant, hiding of Allah's verses, killing of the Prophets without any just, and their saying arrogantly "our hearts are covered over", instead, Allah has stamped them with their disbelief, they only believe a little.

Today, these characters of Jews in *Madeena* are only seeing in hypocrites all over the world who live arrogantly and boastfully on Earth in an attitude that they have studied the Qur'an completely. They are the enemies of Allah, so Allah has killed them and the believers should treat them as their enemies as told in the verse 63: 4. Those who treat the verses with arrogance are the Hypocrites, mentioned both in the verses 7: 40 and 39: 59. It is told in the verse 7: 146 that those who behave arrogantly as scholars in the Earth without the Soul of Qur'an, I will turn them away from My verses. See explanation 2: 6-7 and 14.

'A little do they believe' told in the verse also means, "a few among them will only believe" that is one in every thousand as explained in the verse 4: 118.

89. Whenever a Book has come to them from Allah to confirm what they already have -where as previously they had been seeking victory over those who disbelieve- so whenever something they can recognize is brought to them, they disbelieve in it. Then the curse of Allah lies upon the disbelievers.

90. How wretchedly have they sold their own souls by disbelieving in what Allah has sent down to them, insolent envy that Allah should sent down some of His Bounty on any of His servants He may wish. They have brought an exchange of anger up on anger on themselves. The disbelievers will have shameful torment.

The Jews in *Madeena*, before the coming of Prophet, said to the Arabs tribes among them (*Ouse, Khazraj*), there is a reference about coming of a Prophet in our Book and when he comes we would join with him and succeed over upon you. But when Prophet came with Qur'an confirming the Book with them, they concealed the Book and became forerunners of opposing him. The Jews did not believe in Qur'an, because of their anger and selfishness that Prophet *Muhammad* has come from *Ismael* progeny instead of *Is'haq*and thereby they lost their souls. But today, only the Muslims all over the world conceal the Soul of Qur'an and falsify the Prophet and saying boastfully that they are the bearers of Qur'an and followers of Prophet. Their similitude is that of a donkey and Jews told in the verse 62: 5 and that of a dog, which lolls out his tongue whether you attack or not, told in the verse 7:176. There shall have Allah's curse, the curse of Angels and whole the mankind on this kind of rejecters of verses, is told in the verses 2: 159-161 and 3: 86-88.

Today the Muslims are divided into several organizations instead of forming a single party by holding the Soul of Qur'an, each of them has taken their organizations as criterion instead of the Soul of Qur'an which is the touch stone to separate truth and false. *swalath*, charity, fasting, hajj etc: will not be accepted without the Soul of Qur'an. The disbelievers are from among the Muslims who hide and reject the Soul of Qur'an. The hypocrites who knowingly hide the Soul of Qur'an shall have wrath upon wrath and will go to Hell even without trial as told in the verse 4:145. See the explanation 1: 7 and 2: 41-42.

91. Whenever someone tells them: "believe in what Allah has sent down"; they say: "we believe in what has been sent down to us", while they disbelieve in what has come after that, even though It is the truth confirming what they already have with them. Ask: "Why did you kill Allah's Prophets previously, if you are really believers"?

Today, this question is applicable to the Muslims only. If the Muslims, the bearers of Qur'an, are really believing in It, they should be the just and the best among all the people and should be fit to take leadership of them. They are responsible to witness the life of Prophet among them as per both verses 2: 143 and 22: 78. Instead how did you fall into utter failure through disgrace and are being hatred by others? All Prophets are believers. Only those who lead the life of Prophets are included in the party of Allah, the only party to Paradise.

The verses 2: 93, 248, 278; 3: 139, 175; 5: 23, 57, 112; 7: 88; 8:1; 9:13; 11: 86; 24: 13; 57: 8 end as, 'If you are really believers'. See explanation 2: 40-44

92. And certainly Moosa came to you with Evidences; then later on you adopted the Calf, and became wrongdoers.

As a reply to the argument of Jews in *Madeena* that they are in truth and followers of their forefathers, the arrogant policy of their ancestors is memorizing here. Today, the Muslims who are falsely prided that they are leading the life of Prophet are obliged to take this verse as '*Mouidath*'-moral. They, instead of blindly imitating the life of forefathers should lead a life under the shade of Qur'an which Allah has sent down as the Guidance, there by only they may succeed Here and the Hereafter. Read together the verses 2: 170; 5: 104; 31: 21; 43: 21-23. See explanation 2: 18.

93. Remember when We made agreement with you and raised up the mount 'Thwoor' over you, "hold firmly whatever We have brought you and listen"; they said: "We listen and disobey and their hearts were sucked of the (spirit of) Calf because of their disbelief. Ask how wretchedly your faith commands you, if you are really believers?"

The children of Israel led a haughty life breaking the covenant and agreement made with Allah due to Calf adoration that sucked in their inner heart. The Jews in *Madeena* who came to Prophet told: "We hear and yet we disobey" instead of saying: "we hear and we obey". Read together the verse 4: 46. When it is told to the Muslims to lead a life under the shadow of Qur'an, they shall have a false prestige that they have studied It and believed in It. Instead of Calf they installed different organizations and the way of forefathers in their inner hearts. When such disbelievers are thrown to Hell they will reply to the questions of Its keepers, "had we but listened the Soul of Qur'an or used our intelligence of thinking, we should not be among the inmates of Blazing fire". See the verses 67:6-10. Read together the verses 39: 59, 71 and 36: 62. Allah says in the verse 5: 81: "If the Jews had believed with Allah and the Prophet, and in what is revealed to him, never would they have taken hypocrites as friends and protectors, but most of them are transgressors". Today the Muslims, who are proud of the bearers of Qur'an, have this character of Jews. Hypocrites will come only from them, because today the Book of Allah is only the Qur'an. Read together the verse 11:17. See explanation 2: 61, 73-76.

94. Say, if a Home in the Hereafter with Allah is exclusively yours instead of other people's, then long for death if you are so truthful.

The verses 2: 23, 28, 31, 111; 3: 93, 168, 183; 6: 40, 143; 10: 48; 11: 13; 27: 64, 71; 32: 28; 34: 29; 36: 48; 44: 36; 45: 25; 46: 4; 49: 17; 56: 87; 62: 6; 67: 25; 68: 22 are also end as "if you are so truthful".

95. They will never long for it, because of what their hands have already prepared. Allah is well knower with such wrongdoers.

This character and attitude of Jews in *Madeena* at the time of Prophet is now having with the Muslims in everywhere. Allah, the most Merciful is Impartial. That means, He will never send anyone to Hell or Paradise. Allah created men in the Paradise and gave each soul its own wrong and right i.e. the Soul of Qur'an. And truly he succeeds who recognizes and purifies herself (the soul), and he who fails to recognize herself shall fail, is told in the verses 91: 7-10. The man is given the freedom to select either the way of grateful or the ways of ungrateful, is told in the verse 76: 3. Through the verse 59: 18, by calling the believers Allah says: "Let every soul (men or women) look to what their hands have prepared for tomorrow (the Hereafter)". It is told in the verse 62: 7 in that time the Jews; but today, the hypocrites who never long for death because of their hands have already prepared is Hell. It is asked through the verse 18: 57; who does more wrong than one who is remembered their Lord's verses in their hearts language, then turns away from the verses forgetting what his hands have already prepared.

"It is told in the verse 8: 49: "The hypocrites and those in whose hearts is a disease say: Their religion has deceived the believers" and the verse 50 portraits the scene when the Angels take the souls of this hypocrites who are disbelievers at the time of their death strike their faces, backs and will be told to taste the torment of the Blaze. And the verse 51 says; that punishment your hand has prepared for you ahead yet, indeed Allah is no one to harm any of His servants. The verse 52 says; that is because they hide and reject the verses of Allah. The verse 53 says; Allah will never change the Grace which He has bestowed on a people until they change themselves. Read together the verses 7: 37-38 and 13: 11. Believers will never fear death because they spend time, wealth and all other blessings to learn and teach the Soul of Qur'an and thus they have taken the Ticket to their Lord in Paradise. They lead a life remembering the aim of life, Allah well-pleased with them and they with Allah as told in the verses 5: 119; 9: 100; 13: 28; 58: 22; 89: 27-30 and 98:6.

The verses 3: 181-182; 22: 10; 26: 48; 59: 18; 78: 40; 89: 23-24 say: Whatever they have earned in this world will get the same in the Hereafter. It is told in the verse 25: 23: "Whatever deeds they did in this life without the Soul of Qur'an as proof, We shall place such deeds before them and make it floating dust scattered about. See explanation 2: 24, 39.

96. You will find them the people most eager to live, even compared with those who associate others with Allah, each one of them would like to live on for a thousand years! Yet it would never save anyone from torment, even should he live that long. And Allah is observant of whatever they do.

The Jews who lost the aim of life satisfied with the life of this world. They wished for a thousand years of a Heavenly life here. But their long life did not useful for them to identify their sins with the light of the Book and repents to return Paradise as a newborn child. If we take the '*Mouidhath*' (moral teaching) of this verse, today the condition of Muslims, the bearers of Qur'an, is the same. If we take the Soul of Qur'an as the 'Insight' we can see the Muslims are most joyful ones, spendthrift and fear death while comparing with other people in every matter. This is because their hands sent forth are Hell instead of Paradise. About such hypocrites Allah says in the verse 9: 82; then you laugh a little and cry a lot as a reward for what you have been earning. Today the Muslims are forerunners in all evils and back in doing good. While the bloodshed and mischief occur anywhere in the world; its punishment will have to bear on the Day of Judgment, by the Muslims who carries the Qur'an just like donkeys, especially the hypocrites who knowingly hide the Soul of Qur'an. But they do not identify It. Alas! What a patience they show towards Hell. See the verses 2: 174-176.

'Those who associate others with Allah' referred in the verse are the common people among Muslims of today. The hypocrites wish for a long life more than them. While the hypocrites are those who will welcome and help pseudo prophet anti-Christ *Maseeh-A-Dhajjhal*; the common men among the Muslims will select his Paradise. By the second coming of *Eisa*, he will kill Maseeh-A-Dhajjhal and seventy thousand Jewish leaders, then all the people such as Hindus, Christians and all other non-Muslims will approve *Eisa* and *Islam* and they will kill the hypocrites and those in whose hearts is a disease in order to implement the command of the verses 33: 60-61 in to practice. Prophet taught the believers to select the Hell of *Maseeh-A-Dhajjhal*. He also taught to stay by biting the Soul of Qur'an with the molar teeth during that period. Only the believers will do and follow this command. See explanations 2: 6-7, 90.

97. Say: "Whoever is an enemy to Jibreel, he has brought It down to your heart by Allah's permission, to confirm what came before It and as Guidance and Good news for believers.

The verse 16: 102 ends as: "This Qur'an is a Guidance and Good news to those who submitted whole things to Allah". As per the verse 2: 185, even though Qur'an is sent down as Guidance for entire mankind, It will be utilized as Guidance and Good news only by those who follow It understanding Its soul. The verses 7: 52, 203; 12: 111 and 16: 64. also end as: "Qur'an is a Guidance and Mercy for those people who believe". The verse 27: 77 is: "Verily Qur'an is a Guidance and Mercy for believers". The verses 6: 157; 10: 57; 27: 2; 31: 3 and 41: 44 say: Qur'an is Guidance, a Mercy, Good news and Healing for believers. But Qur'an will increase filth over filth and loses to the hypocrites and wrongdoers are told respectively in the verses 9: 125 and 17: 82. The Qur'an is the cause of sorrow for disbelievers as told in the verse 69: 50. See explanation 2: 2, 5 and 62.

98. Who is an enemy of Allah and His Angels, and His messengers, as well as Jibreel and Meechaeel! Then Allah is an enemy of such disbelievers.

The Jews considered *Jibreel* as their enemy, because he brings the revelation to Prophet. Whoever shows enmity towards Allah, His Angels, His Messengers, they are the rejecters of faith (disbelievers) and Allah is an enemy to such disbelievers. A group among Jews approached Prophet and sought explanation for four things and they told that if you give clear reply for the questions, we will confirm you as Prophet and believe with you.

(1) What Israel (Prophet *Ya'qoob*) had forbidden to himself before the revelations of the *Thourath*? Prophet replied: "When a disease affected Prophet *Ya'qoob*, he shunned his favorite meat and milk of camel as an offering he made before". Then they said: "Oh Allah! it is right", then Prophet witnessed Allah upon them.

(2) How does the water of man and woman (semen) vary? Prophet replied: "Male water is dense and white colored, whereas female water is thin and yellow colored. In whose ejaculation takes place first, the child born is in his/her facial

feature. If the male ejaculation takes place after that of female, by Allah's will the child will be a boy and if female ejaculation occurs after that of male, by Allah's will the child will be a girl". Then they said: "Oh Allah! It is right", then Prophet witnessed Allah upon them. From this teaching, we can understand that those men who have self control by not having the ejaculation before the women's can decide their child as boy.

(3) Explain to us who is the illiterate Prophet and who is his '*Valiyy*'-helper- from Angels referred in the *Thourath*? Prophet replied: "Prophet is the one when his eyes are sleeping, his heart doesn't sleep. And his '*Valiyy*'-helper-is *Jibreel*. Allah has deputed no Prophets without *Jibreel* as the helper". Then they replied: "Here we differ". If there anybody else from Angels except *Jibreel*, we follow and confirm you because *Jibreel* is our enemy. When they said this Allah revealed the verse 2: 98.

(4) Tell us about thunder and lightening? Prophet replied: "When the Angel *Meechaeel*, who is in charge of clouds, split the clouds and from its friction there arrives fire as lightening and sounds as thunder.

Really just like the Muslims today, the Jews in *Madeena* did not have the enmity towards Angels, Prophets, and believers, lest their enmity was towards the Truth -Qur'an. It is told in the verse 6: 33; yet they are not rejecting you, but the wrongdoers are repudiating with Allah's verses. The hypocrites who prevent common men from hearing the Soul of Qur'an are the enemies of Allah, is told in the verses 41: 26-28 and the common men from Muslim also belong to disbelievers according the verse 41: 29. Both of them have fire as eternal home. It is only because they rejected the verses of Allah, is told in the verses 41: 26-28. Read together the verses 7: 49-51 and 41: 40-44. See explanation 2: 6, 39.

99. We have sent you down clear verses; and none conceal them except those who are transgressors.

The verse 9: 67 ends as, 'indeed the hypocrites, they are the transgressors.' Those who hide the verses of Qur'an are the hypocrites. They forgot Allah and themselves as told both in the verses 9: 67 and 59: 19. The verse 6: 49 says, those who reject Our verses and being transgressors, Our punishment will alight on them. It is told in the verse 29: 47 that "none repudiate with Our verses except the disbelievers". As per the verse 48 they are talkers of vanities and in the verse

49 it is told this Qur'an is self evident in the chest of those endowed with knowledge and none repudiate and deny with our verses except the wrongdoers. The verse 46: 35 ends with a question: "Shall any people be destroyed except the people of transgressors?" The verse 80: 17 says, those men have been killed who hide the Soul of Qur'an. And in the verse 63: 4 it is told: "Hypocrites have been killed", and in the verses 51: 10-11 It is told: "Those who live as intoxicated and aimless after getting Qur'an are killed.

Today under the light of Soul of Qur'an we can see that these transgressed hypocrites are the Imams-leaders to conduct *swalath*- of every Masjid all over the world. Therefore it is impossible for a believer to follow them. When we recite the verse 1: 7: "Not the path upon whom your wrath happened", we have to keep in mind not to include with these hypocrites. Being an answer to a question of *Hudaifathul-Yamani* Prophet taught; when there is no single party of Muslims and Imam-leader- as believer, the illiterate believers have to bite firmly the bottom of a tree and exist like that till death. But according to the command of Prophet on the day of departure pilgrimage, those who are literate should bite firmly the Soul of Qur'an with their molar teeth. See explanation 1: 7 and 2: 6, 7, 39.

100. Each time they made a covenant, a group of them shrug it off. Rather, most of them do not even believe.

The transgressors are those who break covenant made with Allah in the Paradise. The meaning of 'each and every time' is when they are warned by whichever verses, they don't obey and they break the covenant with creatures which they made by witnessing Allah. If anyone fails to judge by the Soul of Qur'an in individual, family and social life are transgressors told in the verse 5: 47. See explanation 2: 8-16, 26-28.

101. Whenever a Messenger from Allah has come to them to confirm what they already had, a group of those who were given the Book have tossed Allah's Book behind their backs as if they didn't know.

102. They followed whatever the devils recited concerning Sulaiman's control, Sulaiman didn't disbelieve. But the devils disbelieved, teaching mankind sorcery, and what was sent down to Harooth and Marooth, two Angels at Babylon. Neither of them would teach anyone unless they first said: "Certainly we are only a temptation,

so don't disbelieve"! They learned from both of them what will separate a man from his wife. Yet they do not harm anyone through it except with Allah's permission. They learn what will harm them and does not benefit them. They know that anyone who deals in it will have no share in the Hereafter; how wretched is what they have sold themselves for, if they only knew.

The devils had spread the news that the control of Prophet *Sulaiman* existed with witchcrafts like sorcery, magic etc. Allah bestows the abilities of Prophet *Sulaiman*, where as sorcery is taught by satan. When the people of Babylon involved in such kind of sorcery taught by satan in order to fulfill their desires, Allah deputed the Angels *Harooth* and *Marooth* in the form of man to teach sorcery as a trial for them. They teach them by saying: "Verily we are a trial for you, and therefore be not disbelieved". They used this device-sorcery- to discord the wife from her husband and thereby enable to setup illegal relationship. Actually no one can harm anybody without Allah's permission not only by sorcery but also in any way. This is from the belief that good and evils are coming from Allah. But that people learned this trick which is harmful to enjoy material world and thereby lost Hereafter. Prophet taught that those who are involved with the sorcery, they don't get even the smell of Paradise. This verse teaches that sorcery is there and those who teach and involved in it are human satans. There are satans among men and *Jinns* as told in both verses 6: 112 and 114: 6. The satan has no authority over those who believe and put their trust in their Lord is told in the verse 16: 99. The believers who live with the remembrance of Allah entrusting all in their Lord will not be affected by sorcery and anything from anyone. Did the sorcery affect the Prophets? The reply is 'yes'. When the sorcerers who were called by Pharaoh for the competition with Prophet *Moosa* threw down their ropes and rods, they seemed to be snakes moving towards *Moosa*. *Moosa* felt in his mind a sort of fear as told in the verses 20: 66-67. In the verse 38: 41 we can see that Prophet Ayyoob cried to his Lord: Verily satan has afflicted me with distress and suffering. As per the verse 21: 83, years after he prayed again to his Lord: Verily distress have seized me, You are the most merciful of those among merciful. Then Allah replied by removing the distresses and bestowed His Bounties upon *Ayyoob* as per the verses 38: 42-44. Read together the verses 21: 84.

The *Jinn* satans afflicted sorcery to Prophet Muhammad through a hypocrite, the men satan. Read together the verse 25: 31. This is happened in order to send down the remedy as prevention from sorcery to the believers. Thus *Surath* '*Annas*' and '*Falaq*', which are called together "*Muavidatheini*" - the two *Suraths* to seek refuge from satanic evils - were sent down. Those who follow the completed form of Qur'an, any evil will never affect them. Prophet was reciting the *Suraths* '*Ikhlas*' and '*Muavidatheini*' at least 12 times in a day -three times after the *swalath-al-Fajr*, *Maghrib* and before going to sleep; one time each after every other *swalaths*. Besides this he had prayed and sought refuge from all the evils by Allah's 'complete words'. The 'complete words' referred here is the '*Rooh*' of Qur'an which can not be completed by saying or writing. No danger will happen wherever in the sky and on Earth with the remembrance of Allah. Allah knows and hears all things. Believers remember Allah in their walking, sitting and laying down on their sides and live only for Allah as His vicegerent. Read together the verses 2: 152, 3: 190-191 and 4: 103.

No sorcery and temptation shall affect the human devil hypocrites because Allah has already killed them. It is told in the verse 19: 83: "Satans are deputed to disbelievers to fulfill their desires". Both in the verses 6: 43 and 27: 24 it is told that the satan made whatever they were doing seem attractive to them. It is told in the verse 58: 10: "Certainly secret council are only by satan in order to cause grief to the believers, but he can't harm them in the least except as Allah permits". Then believers put their trust in Allah Who is the Lord of satan as well as has the control of all dominions. Read together the verses 7: 201-202. Prophet taught, those who approach the fortune tellers -the agents of satan from men- to know the unseen things, hear very carefully what they say and act accordingly what they said, didn't believe in what Allah has revealed to Prophet Muhammad i.e. in Qur'an. Strictly speaking, the people who are gone from the Soul of Qur'an are involved in satanic belief like magic, omen, Sorcery etc. and are subjected to the exploitation of hypocrites. Today the believers using the exalted Soul of Qur'an as a Shield and Safeguard will not affect sorcery or any other disasters. See explanation 1: 4 and 7.

103. If they had only believed and heedful, a recompense from Allah would have been better, if they only knew.

104. Oh you who believe! Do not say "Raaeinaa" –herd us; and say instead "Undhurna" –watch over us, and listen. And the disbelievers will have painful torment.

Even though the word "*Raaeinaa*" is having the meaning like 'look to us', 'consider us', it is also used as the word of fun and has the meaning like 'a man with rough behavior', 'barbarian', 'herd us' and 'fool'. This word was widely used as joke by the Jews and hypocrites who came to Prophet to hear the teaching of Qur'an. If the word pronounced as "*Raaeenaa*" with prolonged sound is having the meaning 'our shepherd'. Therefore Allah commanded the believers to use the word "*Undhurna*" -watch over us -the word in any case will not become a joke or not having a twisted meaning. Those who use the word (*Raaeenaa*) again after this command are the disbelievers and they shall have a painful punishment. Today, the hypocrites, the victims of Allah's wrath and curse occurred use these kinds of words towards the believers who are teaching the Soul of Qur'an.

Allah says in the verse 64: 16, so fear Allah as much as you can, listen to the Qur'an carefully and obey it, and spend in charity for the benefit of yourselves, and those who feel secure from their own souls selfishness, such are the only successful, and the verse 17 says, if you advance Allah a handsome loan, He will compound it for you and He will grant you forgiveness, for Allah is Appreciative, Lenient". If anyone does not obey the demand "listen carefully" while hearing the Soul of Qur'an, they will tell on the Hereafter: "If we had only listened and had utilized our intelligence of thinking, we would not have become inmates of the Blazing fire", is warned in the verse 67:10.

The character of the Prophet and the believers are prescribed in the verse 2: 285 as, they will say that we heard and we obeyed. The verse 7:179 says, "Many men and *Jinn* who are distained for Hell, whom have hearts wherewith they think not about the aim of life, they have eyes wherewith they do not read the Soul of Qur'an, they have ears wherewith they hear not the Soul of Qur'an, they are like cattle. Nay, more gone astray, such are the only heedless." See explanation 2:6-7 and 18.

105. Neither those People of Book who disbelieve, nor associate others with Allah would like any good from your Lord to be sent down to you and Allah will particularly select anyone he wishes for His Mercy, and Allah possesses splendid Bounty.

During the time of Prophet, the Jews, Christians and hypocrites in *Madeena* showed hostility towards Qur'an. But today the hypocrites among the Muslims who learn and teach the meaning and body of Qur'an without the soul, and the '*fujjar*' who eat the body of Qur'an show hostility to the Soul of Qur'an as well as to the believers. They will not utilize the Soul of Qur'an as the Balance, Standard and Insight, and so for them it will increase loss over loss.

The words referred in the verse- '*Khair*' -the best. '*Rahmath*'-mercy, '*Fadhl*' –Bounty is only the Soul of Qur'an. Prophet taught; the best one among you is the one who learns and teaches the Soul of Qur'an. He also taught, when you return from the place of "*swalath*", alight by your left leg and ask Allah for His bounty. The following verses 3: 74, 174, 8: 29, 57: 21, 29, 44: 5, 7 and 62: 4 also end as, "Allah possesses the Splendid Bounty". See explanation 2: 99.

106. We do not cancel any verse nor let it be forgotten; instead We bring something better than it or else something similar, Do you not know that Allah is capable of everything?

107. Do you not know that Allah alone holds control over Heaven and Earth and you have no patron nor any helper besides Allah?

Read together the verse 2: 2. According to the teaching of Qur'an only the Book with single soul and different bodies are revealed from first to the last i.e. "*Adhikr*" which is the soul of Qur'an. It is told in the verse 41: 43 that, nothing has been told to you except what has been told Messengers before you. Read together the verses 16: 44 and 21: 24. The people of ancient scripture asked Prophet, "If it is so, is it enough to maintain *Thourath* and *Injeel*, is there in need of a new Scripture?" Allah the knower of the secrets in Heaven and earth knows the rules and regulations of the people in each ages of time. The scriptures sent down in a particular age are exclusively for those ages. But the Qur'an which included the contents of all scriptures came before It and has the rules and regulation for entire people to the last Day. Qur'an which confirms the scriptures that came before It and guarding It safely as told in the verses 5: 48 and 06: 156-157.

Even in Qur'an the instructions in verse, which came first, has amended or limited by the verses that came later. E.g. it is prescribed when death approaches any of you; if he leaves any wealth that he make a bequest to parents and next of kin according to reasonable usage. This is due for the heedful told in the verse 2:180 has limited when the law of inheritance revealed in *Surath An-Nisa*' that no bequest for inheritors and bequest is only one third of the total wealth. The annihilation of liquor made stage by stage through the verses 2: 219, 4:43 and 5:90 are also examples for this.

In brief, Allah the knower of all times has revealed the unique Qur'an as a warning to all worlds and no falsehood can approach It from before or behind It as told in the verse 41:41-42. Allah asks Prophet Muhammad in the verse 22:70, "Know you not that Allah knows all that is Heaven and on earth and indeed it is all recorded in a Book and that is easy for Allah".

It is said in the verse 22: 52, "Never did We send a Messenger or Prophet before you but when he framed a desire satan threw some vanity into his desire, but Allah will cancel anything that satan throws in, and Allah will confirm and establish His verses, certainly Allah has full knowledge and wisdom". Nothing will happen in Heaven and earth and even in men except what Allah has decreed before, told in the verses such as 9: 51, 10: 61, 11: 6, 34: 3, 35: 11, 57: 22 and 64:11. Allah alone is the protector and helper to Prophets and believers. Satan is the protector and helper to hypocrites and *Fujjar*. Is not Allah, the Lord of all creatures including satan, enough for His servant asked in the verse 39:36. Then, the believers live depending only on Allah, in the same manner how you will live if you are brought to earth as a son of Adam. Those who live just like that depending exclusively on Allah is become believers. Then only you might become the acceptor of Allah as "*Aswamad*". (See the content of Sura '*Ikhlas*'). See the explanation 1: 4, 2: 98, 102.

108. Or do you (all) want to question your Messenger just as Moosa was questioned previously? Then anyone who exchanges faith for disbelief has strayed from the Straight path.

The demand of Moosa's disciples to see Allah manifestly, their question pertaining to the colour and the age of the cow to be sacrificed; When they had provided '*Manna* and *Salva*' as food they were not satisfied with that, instead they wanted vegetables like onion, cucumber as food, are examples for such questions. The Jews and hypocrites of Madeena and their followers asked Prophet several questions like this. They demanded to give Qur-an as a codified Book just like what was given to Moosa or to conduct sacrifice burned by the fire coming down from the sky are some of the examples for this. Therefore, Allah commanded the believers in the verse 5: 101, "Ask not questions about anything while revealing Qur'an which if made plain to you may because you trouble. Several matters Allah has forgiven to you not revealing". E.g. when it is revealed the verses pertaining to Hajj they asked, is it necessary to observe Hajj every year? That time this verse sent down. Read together the verses 5: 60-61.

Today the disbelievers among the Muslims have this character. When it is said to them that only one party, Allah's party from beginning to last of mankind goes to Paradise and all other parties belong to satan's party goes to Hell. They do not accept this even though they are warned by verses of Qur-an. They accepted disbelief instead of faith and strayed from the only Straight path. The verses 5:12, 60, 77; 28:22; 60:1 also ends in the meaning that the only one and Straight path to Heaven. This straight path is the only way to Paradise of Allah's party (believers) from first to last. Read together the verse 58: 22. This way is the whole contents of Qur'an and all other ways are to Hell. All of them are the party of satan told in 58: 19. See the explanation 1:5.

109. Many people of the Book would like to turn you back after your faith, out of envy for themselves, even though the truth has been explained to them. So pardon them and over look till Allah comes with His command. Certainly Allah has power over all things.

Since this was the character of Jews and Christians who are the people of Book towards believers in the old, now the non believing Muslims have this character. When it is said to them no one will become a believer, and never go to Paradise without the ticket- the contents of Qur'an, and all Muslim parties are to be united holding firmly the soul of Qur'an, and not to be divide by quoting the verse 3: 103. They don't accept that and will try to return the believers to their parties, *Madhabs*, *Fiq'h* Books which are made by men and to their belief. Prophet taught the believers to hold fast the Qur'an by their molar teeth and to wait until the coming of Jesus who will put in to practice the do's and don'ts of Qur'an. Read together the verses 3: 69; 9: 113; 42: 14-15 and 98: 4. See the explanation 2: 105.

110. And steadfast in swalath and pay the welfare tax you will find any good you have sent on a head for your own sake you shall find it with Allah. Surely Allah is watching what you do.

The verse 59: 18 says, Oh you who believe keep Allah in hearts and let every soul watch out for whatever it has sent on a head for tomorrow and fear Allah, Allah is acquainted anything you do. It is only to the believers are commanded to perform *swalath, Zakath* and fasting. No deeds shall be accepted without the soul of Qur-an. The group of *swalath* with is only commanded to the party of believers. Not only the *swalath* but what ever deeds will be accepted only from the believers. The disbelievers, wrongdoers and transgressors are coming exclusively from Muslims told in the verses 5: 44, 45, and 47.

The word '*aathuzakath*' in the verse is translated as pay welfare tax. Actually it means you bring purifications activities that are not only for the wealth but also for the Soul, body and place. The verses 87: 14-15 say, anyone who purifies himself, remember his Lord's name and then keep up *swalath* will prosper. Purification is possible with the soul of Qur'an only. That is the message of the prophet's teaching that *the best and noble among you is the one who learn and teach the soul of Qur'an.* Read together the verses 9: 103; 73: 20. See the explanation 1: 7, 2: 28 and 95.

111. And they say, none will enter the Paradise except he be a Jew or a Christian. These are only their wishful desires. You say: bring on your proof if you are so truthful.

The verse 27: 64 ends as: Is there any Deity along with Allah, bring on your proof if you are so truthful. The Jews were saying that no one will enter the Paradise without being Jews .And Christians were saying no one will enter Paradise without being Christians. Today the Jews and Christians are not saying so. Instead different parties of Muslims maintain this belief. The *Burhan*-evidence or proof- and *Noor*-light- told in the verse 4: 174 is the Soul of Qur'an. This verse teaches the necessity of Qur'anic verse as a document for every matter. It is told in the verse 23: 117: "If any one invokes any other Deity along with Allah, has no proof for it, his reckoning rests only with his Lord, certainly such disbelievers will not succeed". It is told in the verse 28: 75: "From each people We shall draw a witness and then say them, bring on your proof, then they shall realize that the truth belongs only to Allah and whatever they were inventing without the proof of Qur'an made them astray.

It is told in the verse 21: 24: "have they still adopted other Deity instead of Him, say, bring on your proof. This is the Reminder for any one who is with me, as well as the Reminder for whoever came before me. But most of them do not recognize Truth and so they neglect It. Read together the verses 12: 24 and 28: 32.

112. Rather, anyone who submits his persons peacefully to Allah and is living seeing Allah will get his reward from his Lord. On them there shall be no fear, and for them will not be grieved.

Those who live keeping remembrance of Allah in their all walking, sitting, lying on their sides and submit their whole heartily to Allah whichever religion they belongs, can return to Paradise. There is no conversion of religion in Islam but only accept the true belief. '*Muhsins*' are those who live seeing Allah under the Light-the Soul of Qur'an. See the explanation 2: 62.

113. The Jews say the Christian have nothing to stand up on while the Christians say the Jews have nothing to stand up on, yet they quote and argue from the same Book, likewise those who do not know anything make a statement similar to theirs, then Allah will judge between them on the Day of Judgment concerning how they have been differing.

Though both the Jews and Christians learn and teach the same Book- the Bible, the Jews were saying Christians are strayed and Christians were saying the Jews are strayed. Allah says, those who do not know the soul of Book were saying like this in all the times. Today the Book is only the Soul of Qur'an, and its bearers are the Muslims. They are grouped into different parties and each party find fault one another and argue for their own rightness. Both the verses 23: 53 and 30: 32 end as each party are delighting what they possess with themselves. Only Allah's party from Adam to the last day is only in on the Straight path. Believers will select this party. Whoever differ from the Soul of Qur'an and are involved in different parties are associates and disbelievers, and all belong to the satan's party. The verse 16: 64 says, we have not sent down the Book to you except to explain to them what they are differing over and as a Guidance and Mercy for the people who believe. So the believers should utilize the Soul of Qur'an as the Balance to differentiate between the path of Allah and satan in all places and all times in this world. The Truth –the Soul of Qur'an- will be the Balance for the judgment on the Day of Judgment, is told both in the verses 39: 69 and 75. Read together the verses 25: 18, 30.

The verse 16: 39 says, that the Day of Judgment is determined in order to explain to the people what they have been differing over, and so those who disbelieve may know that surely they have been lying. The verse 32: 25 says: "Certainly your Lord alone will sort them out on the Day of Judgment concerning whatever they have been differing over. The verse 22: 69 says: "Allah will judge between you on the Day of Judgment concerning what you have been disagreeing about". Through the verse 39: 46 Allah says to pray as, "Oh Allah, the Originator of Heaven and Earth, knowing the unseen and the visible, you will judge among your servants concerning whatever they may have been differing about". So guide us with the Soul of Qur'an in whatever they have been differing to the Straight path. Certainly none is there to lead Straight Path except You. Read together the verses 10: 93; 16: 124; 22: 17; 36: 3 and 45: 17.

114. Who is more in the wrong than someone who prevents from Allah's masjids from remembering His name in it and attempts to ruin them? Such persons should not enter them except in fear; for them have disgraces in this world as well as a great torment in the hereafter.

'*Masjid*' means the places for '*sujood*', i.e., prostrate. Prophet taught: *all the places except the graveyard and lavatory are masjids for my community.* The verse 72: 18 says, certainly, the *masjids* belong to Allah, so you do not appeal to any one with Allah. But today, Muslims are deviated in to different sects and each sect constructs their own *masjids*. Thus they are astrayed from the Straight Path. In Islam *masjids* are considered as Allah's houses .Today, no such *masjids* are there any where in the world. Instead all the *masjids* are turned in to satan's house, since they neglect the Soul of Qur'an. Because of this, today, there exists a situation that no one can enter the *masjids* without fear. About the *swalath* of Meccan associates at *Ka'ba* is told in the verse 8: 35 as their *swalath* at the house consist only of whistling and clapping. (It will be told to them) then taste torment since you have disbelieved. Today there is no remembrance of Allah in the *masjids* with the Soul of Qur'an, instead there prevails only shouting and calling neglecting the verse 7: 205. Thus all the *masjids* in the world have become just like as Prophet taught i.e. *their masjids will be huge concrete buildings, but they are strayed from the Guidance.*

The verses 9: 17-18 say: It is not suitable for the associates to be vouchsafes of Allah's *masjids*, since they act as witnesses for their own disbelief. Such are the one whose all deeds are in vain and they will remain forever in the Fire. Verily, the *masjids* of Allah shall be vouchsafed by such one who believes in Allah and the Last Day, keeps up prayer and pays the welfare tax and should not dread anyone except Allah. Perhaps those may be the ones who submit to Guidance. The verse 22: 40 says: If it were not because Allah repels some men by means of others, then Monasteries, churches, synagogues and Masjids where Allah's name is commemorated frequently would have been demolished.

Certainly Allah helps anyone who helps Him indeed only Allah is Strong, Powerful. It is not suitable for the believers to perform '*swalath*' by following the hypocrites and associates as *Imam.* Since today in all the *masjids* either hypocrites or associates are the *Imams* –leaders. So the believers today as taught by Prophet should not go to *masjids* for *swalath*. Such harmful *masjids* as told in the verses 9: 107-108 should be demolished. Read together the verses 33: 1, 73 and 48: 6. See explanation 1: 7; 2: 7, 85.

115. To Allah belongs the East and West. Wherever you may turn, there is Allah's face (proximity). Certainly Allah is Boundless, All knowing.

The verse 2:177 begins as "virtue does not mean to turn your, faces towards the East or West". This verse is revealed as a reply to the hypocrites who do not accept the change of *Qibla*. This verse also teaches the believers till the Last Day that do not enter the *masjids* for *swalath* if it is strayed from Guidance, instead they can perform *swalath* in hole and cave. Allah is with you wherever you may be and He observes well all that you do. Read together the verses 57: 4 and 58: 7. See explanation 2:107.

116. They say: "Allah has adopted a son". Glory be to Him! Rather He owns whatever is in Heavens and Earth; all things are devoted to Him.

The Jews say that *Uzair* is the son of Allah, the Christians say that Jesus is the son of Allah as told in the verse 9: 30. Meccan idolaters believed Angels as the daughters and *Jinns* as the sons of Allah as per the verses 6:100 and 43: 17-19. All the things in Heaven and Earth and in between them belong to Allah and devoutly obey to Him. Neither the Jesus nor the Angels, those nearest to Allah disdain to serve or worship Allah, is told in the verse 4: 172. Read together the *Surath Ikhlas*.

The verse 19: 92 says; it is not proper for the Impartial to adopt a son. The verse 93 says; everyone who is in Heavens and Earth not coming to the Impartial most Gracious except as a servant. The verse 30: 26 says: To Him belongs every being that is in Heaven and Earth and are all devoutly obedient to Him. Read together the verses 2: 238; 3: 17; 33: 35; 66: 12. See explanation 2: 29 and 33.

117. The Originator of the Heaven and Earth, whenever He decrees an affair, He merely tells it: 'Be!' and it is.

The verse 6: 101 says; Originator of Heaven and Earth, how can He have a son while He has no consort? He created everything and is Aware of everything. Read together the 16: 40; 19: 35; 21: 30; 36: 82 and 40: 68. See explanation 2: 107.

118. Those who do not know say if Allah would only speak to us or a sign brought us! Likewise those before them said the same as they are saying; their hearts are all alike. We have explained verses for the people who have convinced belief.

Today those who do not know the Soul of Qur'an which is made very easy to understand by ones heart as told in the verse 54: 17, ask such questions like who is Allah? Who is Prophet? Who are men? What is the soul? What is his body? Where is he created? Where is the first birth? Where is the second death? What is the aim of life? What is Qur'an? What for Qur'an? Why do we use Qur'an? Where is the Paradise? Who will go to Paradise? Where is Hell? Who will go to Hell? Those who don't try to understand the answers for such questions given above through the Soul of Qur'an after they have received It, are the aimless and heedless people. This Qur'an is a great sign for those who endowed with knowledge as told in the verses 29: 47-51. It is told in the verse 4: 153: The children of Israel wanted *Moosa* to show them Allah directly. The verse 6: 109 says they swear by Allah with their stiffest oaths that if a sign were given them, they would believe in it. Say: "Signs belong only to Allah". What will make you perceive that even when they are given them, they will still not believe? The verse 6: 111 says; even though We were to send Angels to them and the dead were to speak to them and we gathered together all things before their very eyes, they still would not believe unless Allah so wishes; yet most of them act so out of ignorance. As per the verses 25: 21-23, those who don't expect to meet Us say: "Why are not Angels sent down to us, or we are allowed to see our Lord?" They act too arrogant of themselves and strut around quite insolently. Some day they shall see the Angels! There will be no good news for *mujrims* on that day and they will say: 'If there an unseen barrier forbidden between Angels and us'. We shall advance up on whatever deeds they have performed and turn it into scattered dust. Read together the verses 18: 103-106. See explanation 2: 1-5, 55 and 99.

119. Indeed, We have sent you with the Truth as a Herald and a Warner: You will not be questioned about the inmates of Hades.

It is impossible for Prophet to make any one to the Guidance or wickedness. The verse 5: 99 says: The duty of Messenger is nothing except to deliver the Message, while Allah knows whatever you disclose and whatever you hide. Read together the verse 5: 67. Prophet is deputed to witness the life of Qur'an among the people and those who follow his life, consider the Prophet as a herald and for others he is a Warner. No questions shall be asked to Prophet that why this much people entered in the Hell. Each one should ask Guidance to Allah as told in the verses 13: 27 and 14: 1. And each of them has to save themselves from the Hell. Read together the verses 2: 272; 3: 128-129 and 10: 108.

120. Neither the Jews nor the Christians will ever be satisfied with you, until you follow their lifestyle. Say: Indeed, the Guidance of Allah that is the only Guidance. If you follow their whims after the knowledge which has come to you, you would not have any patron or helper against Allah.

Verily Allah's Guidance that is the only Guidance told in the verse 6: 71 also. It is told in the verse 3: 73 to say; indeed the Guidance means Guidance of Allah. If the attitude of the people of the Book during the period of Prophet was as mentioned in the verse, today this attitude is found among Muslims all over the world towards the believers. If they were warned by Prophet's teaching that only one out of each thousand go to Paradise and nine hundred ninety nine to Hell. Hence, the one who led a life holding firmly the Soul of Qur'an can go to the Paradise. This verse warned the believers that those who follow their own lusts or the way of majority after receiving the knowledge which is the Soul of Qur'an, they are the only losers in the hereafter. Read together the verses 6: 116; 17: 73-75. By explaining about the change of *Qibla,* Allah says in the verse 2: 145 that if you follow their vain desire after the knowledge has reached to you; indeed, you would then be among the wrongdoers. The verse 5: 49 says, judge you between them with what Allah has revealed and not follow their vain desires, but beware of them lest they seduce you from any of that which Allah has sent down to you and if they turn away, be assured that for some of their offences, it is Allah's purpose to punish them. Indeed most of the men- nine hundred and ninety nine out of thousand as the teaching of Prophet- are transgressors. Allah says in the verses 10: 15-16, when Our clear verses are recited to them, those who do not hope on their meeting with Us say, "Bring us a Qur'an other than this or make some amendments in this". Say to them, it is not up to me to change it since it is not from my own accord, Verily I follow nothing except what is inspired to me. I fear torment on an awful day if I should disobey my Lord. Say if Allah had so wished I would not have recited it to you nor advised you about It. I spend for a lifetime among you before receiving It. Won't you think by using your intelligence? Read together the verses 13:37, 18:28, 42:15. See explanation 1: 5, 2: 2 and 38.

121. Those to whom We have given the Book recite It in the way It should be recited. Such men believe with It. And anyone who hides It, then such ones, will be the only losers.

The verse 63: 9 says: "Oh you, who believe, let not your property or children prevent you from the Soul of Qur'an. If any do like that, then such ones will be the only losers". The verse 7: 178 is the third verse which ends as: Then such ones will be the only losers. At the time of revealed this verse the people of the Book were the Jews and Christian. They should understand Qur'an from their Book and should follow the life way of Qur'an. Today the Book is only Qur'an for entire mankind, and so those who are given It recite It in a manner as It should be recited. Recite means, read and deliver the message to entire mankind. The verses 28: 52-53 say: The ones to whom We gave the Book previously, believe in It. And whenever It is recited to them, they say: We believe in It; It is the Truth from our Lord. Indeed we have already committed to Allah in peace. See the explanation 2: 44.

Those any one who hide Our verses, such one are the only losers has told in the verse 39: 63. Prophet taught that: *the one who observe the forbidden things in Qur'an as permissible don't believe with It.* The similitude of the hypocrites and the *Fujjar* who reject the verses of Qur'an is that of a dog, which does not amend its attitude whether it is disturbed or not as told in the verse 7: 176. The verse 7: 177 says: Evil is the similitude of such people who belie and reject Our verses and they are doing wrong to their own souls. Read together the verses 9: 23-24 and 29: 4. It is told in the verse 11: 17 that if any one from different organizations among Muslims conceal the Soul of Qur'an, then Fire will be his promised abode. Therefore Oh Prophet! Be not then in doubt in the matter of Qur'an, verily It is the Truth from your Lord. But many among men are not believers. See the explanation 2: 24, 39, and 99

122. Oh children of Israel! Remember My favor which I bestowed upon you and how I preferred you to all other people in the world.

123. Then heed a Day when a soul shall not avail another and no compensation will be accepted, no any intercession benefits it, and they will not be helped.

The children of Israel are the sons of Prophet *Ya'qoob*; the son of Prophet *Is'haq* who was the second child of Prophet *Ibrahim. Ibrahim* is known as "the father of Prophets". The Children of Israel were proud and rejoiced that they are in the way of Truth like their forefathers. Then, the lifestyle of their forefathers such as *Is'haq*, *Isma'el, Ibrahim* are mentioning in the continuing verses, that was a people who has passed away, they shall have what they earned and you shall have what you earned and you shall not be asked about what they did as told in the verses 2:134,141. See the explanation 2:28, 47 and 48.

124. And remember that His Lord tested Ibrahim by means of certain words, and he fulfilled them, He said: "I am going to make you in to a leader for mankind. He asked; "what about my offspring?" Allah said; My pledge does not apply to wrongdoers.

When *Ibrahim* called his father and people to Allah and avoiding idolatry worship, the government under the leadership of *Namrood* prepared a fire pit. When they were not able to throw *Ibrahim* to the middle of the fire pit, they used pellet bow and threw him. *Ibrahim* consoled himself by saying; Allah is enough for me as a custodian of my affairs. He did not show worried ness, and then Allah made the fire cool and safety. Read together the verses 21:65-70, 29:24. As a result of his continuous prayer, son *Isma'el* was given to him in his old age as told in the verse 14:39. Allah commanded to take that son and his wife *Hajara* to *Ka'ba* to stay there. Were even water was not available. While exhausting water *Hajara* mounted *Safa* and then run to *Marva* seeking water several times. Lastly the gushing of *Zum-Zum* happened from beneath the footsteps of the child. When Allah commanded to sacrifice his son *Isma'el* on his 14 years of age, Prophet *Ibrahim* prepared for that. Allah gave a goat instead of his son and He maintained that great sacrifice as an observance-*Sunnath-* to the succeeding generations. Read together the verses 37:100-109 and 60:4. See the explanation 2:40.

125. Remember that We set up the House as a resort for mankind and a sanctuary. And adopt Ibrahim's station as a place for prayer. We entrusted with Ibrahim and Isma'el with cleaning out My

house those who circle around it, secluded praying, bowing and prostrating.

As per the verses 3: 96-97 the first House of worship set up for mankind is the one at Mecca (ie. *Ka'ba*). It is full of Blessings and Guidance for all the worlds. There are the clear signs such as *Ibrahim's station*; anyone who enters it he will be secured. The stone in which *Ibrahim* stepped and stood to construct *Ka'ba* on which his footprint marked, is preserved in a glass case near *Ka'ba* is known as *Ibrahim's station*. To perform *swalath* near it is virtuous. But when there is over crowded it is enough to perform *swalath* wherever possible in the Sacred *Masjid*. Read together the verse 22: 28. See explanation 2: 41-43.

126. And remember that Ibrahim prayed: My Lord! Make this countryside safe, and provide any of its people who believed in Allah and the last day with fruits of all kinds. Allah said, "Even anyone who disbelieves, I will let enjoy things for a while, then drive him along towards the torment of fire-what an evil returning place."

As per the verse 2:124 when *Ibrahim* asked Allah to make his offspring leader as well as him, Allah replied that it is not applicable to wrongdoers among them. Due to this Ibrahim prayed to provide all kinds of fruits only to those who believe in Allah and the last Day. But Allah said, all kinds of food and convenience in this life would be given to the disbelievers also. Then after the death, they will be pushed in to the Hell. Guidance and its leadership will be given only to believers. But foodstuffs and power will be given to disbelievers also. Allah commanded through the verse 14:30 to say to the disbelievers who set up equals to Allah and prevent people from the Soul of Qur'an, enjoy this material life, for verily your return will be the fire. The verse 39:8 ends as say: enjoy with your disbelief for a little while, for verily you are the inmate of fire.

Place of return: - All human beings came to the Earth from Paradise. If anyone wishes to return to Paradise he must utilize the Soul of Qur'an as the Ticket. Both the verses 73:19 and 76:29 say indeed this is a Ticket for anyone who wants to adopt a way unto his Lord. The verses 3:196-197 say, do not let it deceive you those who disbelieve bustle around the land, it is short enjoyment; and then their refuge will be the Hell. What an evil cradles! Read together the verses 14:35-37. The verses 3:162; 8:16; 9:73; 22:72; 24:57; 57:15; 58: 8;

64:10; 66: 9 and 67: 6 also end as, what an evil returning place! See the explanation 2: 26.

127. And remember Ibrahim along with Isma'el rose up the wall on the foundation for the House and prayed. Our Lord! Accept this from us, indeed You are the All-Hearing, All-Knowing.

Ka'ba is the first place of worship on Earth since the time of Prophet Adam. Its entire wall except the foundation was destroyed in the flood at the time of Messenger *Nooh*. Allah commanded both Prophet *Ibrahim* and *Isma'el* to construct that wall. It is told in the verse 22: 26, "Remember that We pointed out the site of the House to *Ibrahim* in order to construct a House saying, "Do not associate anything with Me" and purify My House for those who circle around it, and those who stand there praying and bowing on their knee and prostrating".

This verse teaches that whatever deeds we are doing should be for the sake of Allah, praying Him to accept that deed. Otherwise the deeds will turn to satan and one has to reply to Allah for wasting time. Any physical deeds without the participation of the soul will not be accepted and be punished.

128. Our Lord! Make both of us all submitted to You and make a community from our offspring who submitted all to You. And show us our ceremonies and You turn towards us, for verily You are so Relenting, Merciful.

129. Our Lord! Send a Messenger in among them from among themselves who will recite Your verses to them and teach them the Book and Wisdom! He will purify them; indeed You are the Powerful, the Wise!

Allah answered for this prayer approximately after 2500 years by deputing Prophet Muhammad. "Indeed you are the Powerful, the Wise" means Allah the omniscient decides earlier what ever happens on Earth and He is unquestionable, totalitarian, despotic and dictator to decide when, where, and how things to be happened. On the Day of Judgment when all will be reckoned especially Prophet Eisa, his reply in the verse 5: 118 ends as, 'Verily if you do punish them, they are your servants, if you do forgive them, Indeed You are the Powerful, the Wise". That is the verse which Prophet Muhammad was unable to complete in one day night *swalath* and he spent in the *swalath* by crying. Read together the verses

62: 2-3. The verses 40: 8 and 60: 5 also end as, "Indeed you are Powerful, the Wise".

The verses 3: 67-68 say that *Ibrahim* was neither a Jew nor a Christian, but he was truth seeker, a committer all to Allah and he was not among the associates in the dominion of Allah. Certainly the closest people to *Ibrahim* are those who follow him, as well as this Prophet -Muhammad- and those who believe. Allah is believer's patron. Today only the believers among the Muslims follow the way of Prophet *Ibrahim* as well as Prophet Muhammad and all other Muslims by name, accept the way of Jews, Christians and associates in the dominion of Allah. Read together the verse 2:151. After explaining about some of the Prophets Allah says in the verse 21:92, "verily this community of yours is a single community; while I am your Lord therefore serve Me alone".

130. And who would shrink away from the life way of Ibrahim except someone who fools himself? We selected him during worldly life, (to propagate My message), while in the Hereafter he will be among the honorable ones.

The verses 16: 120-122 say that Indeed *Ibrahim* alone was a community himself devoted to Allah seeker of truth and he was not among one who associates others in the dominion of Allah; Grateful for His favors, Allah chose and guided him to the Straight Path. We gave him a fine thing in this world, and he will be among the honorable in the Hereafter. Though the Jews, Christians and idolaters reject all other Prophets, they did not reject Prophet *Ibrahim,* but like the Muslims of today they didn't follow the life way of Ibrahim which is the life way of Prophet Muhammad and true believers. The verse 16:123 says, then We inspired you: follow the way of Ibrahim, the truth seeker; and he was not among associates. See explanation 1: 6.

131. So when his Lord told to him: 'Be the one who submit all to Allah', he said: I have already submitted myself peacefully to the Lord of the all worlds.

'To become Muslim' means, to submit oneself and all the blessings like wealth, house, children, parents, spouses, hearing, sights, intelligence etc. to the Lord. See explanation 1: 1, 4.

132. Ibrahim commissioned upon his sons with it (Islam) and so did Ya'qoob: "My sons, certainly Allah has chose for you this Dheen. Then you do not die except in the state of submitting all to Allah.

Islam is the system of life which the Creator satisfied for all creatures from Adam to the Last Day. It is told in the verse 3: 19 that the religion acceptable with Allah is Islam and in the verse 3: 85 it is told: "If anyone seeks (accepts) a way of life other than Islam, never will it be accepted from him and in the Hereafter he will be among the losers". Prophet taught that: *All men take birth as Muslims that is in Islam-nature. It is their parents, who make them Jews, Christians, Majoosi or idolaters.* Each man has to reply in front of their Lord about the entire life after their age of fifteenth. Therefore those who die before the age of fifteen will be considered as Muslims and shall enter the Paradise. No one can enter Paradise who dies after the age of fifteenth unless he utilizes the Ticket which is the Soul of Qur'an. See the explanation 2:121. That is why Prophet taught that it is the duty of parents to teach their children the Soul of Qur'an before their age of fifteenth. Otherwise both the children and parents will be gathered in the Hell. The scene is warned in the verse 7: 38 as the children will say pointing their parents: "Our Lord, these people had misled us, so give them double torment from the fire!" Allah will say: "Each shall have double, even though you do not realize it". The verse 3: 102 says, Oh you who believe! Keep Allah in your hearts as He should be kept, and should not die except in the state of all submitted to Allah. That is in the state of innocent or in the state of new born child.

If there prevails no Islamic system of life in the country, one can enter the Paradise if he believes with Allah and establish the remembrance of Allah always like the believer mentioned in *Surath Yaseen* or as the seven companions of the Cave mentioned in *Surath Kahf* or as the sorcerers who believed in Allah after the competition with Prophet Moosa in the assemblage of Pharaoh. If one is illiterate and the Soul of Qur'an is not received, he may live in forest or cave or hole keeping the remembrance of Allah alone can also enter Paradise. Today since every one is literate; one may live as believer by remembering Allah always with the Soul of Qur'an in their standing, sitting and laying and can die peacefully and enter the Paradise. See the explanation 2: 62.

133. Or were you present as death appeared for Ya'qoob, when he asked to his sons "what will you serve after I am gone?" They replied: "We shall serve your Deity and the Deity of your

forefathers Ibrahim, Isma'el and Is'haq; the single Deity alone and we are all submitted peacefully to Him".

Ilah-Deity: - The One to whom can seek refuge and help, upon whom one can put trust, only whom one can afraid; on before Him one has to reply about his life. See explanation 1:4.

134. That is a community which has already passed away; They will have whatever they have earned, and you will have whatever you have earned, you will not be questioned about what they have been doing.

Each one gets whatever he has earned here in the Hereafter. So each individual has to prepare Paradise in this world in order to inherit it in the Hereafter. The children will not be questioned about their parents. But the parents will be questioned about their children. Therefore, it is the duty of parents to teach their children the Soul of Qur'an which is the Ticket to the Paradise. Read together the verses 7: 37-38.

This verse is also repeated as the verse 2: 141. The verse 52: 21 says: "And We shall unite together the believers and children who have followed them in faith. We will not deprive them of any action of theirs in any way; each man is a guarantee for whatever he has earned. The verses 74: 38-39 say; every soul will be held as a guarantee for anything he has earned except the companions of Right. It is told in the verses 13: 23 and 40: 6 that the Right Hand companions of the Paradise shall get their righteous offspring, fathers and spouses in the Paradise. No prayer, *swalath* or other deeds will be accepted without being a believer with the Soul of Qur'an. So what should one do to get his parents in the Paradise who had died before getting the Soul of Qur'an? The answer for this is to propagate the Soul of Qur'an to entire mankind and advise them to lead a life under the Light of Qur'an. And pray earnestly for the entrance of their parents to Paradise. Thus Allah, the knower of states of mind fulfills the desires of believers who are the companion of Right hand mentioned in the above verse. The verses 90: 19-20 say: "Those who conceal Our verses they are the companions of Left Hand. Upon them a Fire will hem them in". See the explanation 2: 112.

135. They say: "Become Jews or Christians: you will then be guided, say: Rather, the truth seeker Ibrahim's way of life is the true one and he was not among the associates.

The Jews and Christians in *Madeena* said separately that one should be rightly guided if he follows only their way of life. Today the argument of the different Muslim organizations is also the same. They are divided in to sects as several religions thus they are become 'associates' by joining different organizations instead of the single one, Allah's party as mentioned in the verses 21:51-53, 30: 30-32. They follow not the way of *Ibrahim* or Prophet Muhammad; on the contrary they follow the ways of Jews and Christians. Prophet taught: *In the final days of the material world, the Muslims will follow the Christians and Jews very closely. At that time the believers should maintain their belief even living in cave or hole by holding the Soul of Qur'an with their molar teeth. i.e. They should abstain from the flow of majority Muslims.*

The Jews got the nation of Israel by terrorist activities such as kidnapping the diplomats, killing, bargaining and destroying the Embassies and important places by bombing. These types of terrorist activities, in 1948 under the leadership of Britain and America a nation was formed in the name of Isra'el for the Jews who were scattered around the world until 1947. The Muslims of today as taught by Prophet follow the terrorist activities of Jews to get the country, Palestine. The only device to maintain peace on Earth and to annihilate bloodshed is the Soul of Qur'an by which one can identify himself, his Lord and the aim of life. But today, the Muslims forbid It to others and keep away from It themselves as told in the verse 6: 26. Today there is no killing or war. But there is only utmost strive with the Soul of Qur'an against disbelievers who hide It as told in the verse 25: 32. The verses 3: 67, 95; 6: 161; 16: 123 also end as: he was not among the associates. See explanation 2: 111-113 and 120.

136. Oh believers! All of you say : "We believe in Allah and what has been sent down to us, and what has been sent down to Ibrahim, Isma'el, Is'haq, Ya'qoob and their tribes and what was given to Moosa and Eisa and what was given the other Prophets from their Lord. We do not discriminate about anyone of them and we are all submitted with peace to Him.

The verse 3: 84 is also with the same message. Here the tribes means the twelve tribes mentioned in the verse: 7: 160:- i.e. the offspring's of the ten children of Prophet *Ya'qoob*, and two children of Prophet *Yoosuf*. All Prophets were sent for one mission that is to propagate there is no Deity except Allah and all Prophets came in Islam. The verse 21: 25 says, We did not send any Messenger before you except We inspired him with the fact that there is no Deity except Me, so serve Me alone. The verses 16: 2, 36 also have the same message. The only Book that came from first to last is *Al-Kithab* -the Book, even though Its body is different the soul is the same. Today it is the Soul of Qur'an. Read together the verse 41: 41-43. See explanation 2: 2.

In this verse believers are to proclaim whereas in the verse 3: 84 Prophet or the believer is commanded to proclaim so. Then whoever says and believes that Prophet Muhammad established the religion of Islam and he is the Prophet exclusively for Muslims is disbeliever. Both verses 7:158 and 34: 28 say, Prophet Muhammad is sent to entire mankind as a Messenger and it is told in the verse 21:107 that Prophet Muhammad has not been sent except as a mercy for all worlds. See explanation 1:6.

137. Then if they believe the same as you believe with, they are rightly guided, while if they turn back they will only fall in to schism. Allah will suffice for you against them and He is the all Hearing, the all Knowing.

Those who follow the Soul of Qur'an as Guidance are the real believers. Those who take some part from Qur'an and avoid the rest, like not accepting the whole tree of Islam but holding a branch of It are in schisms or dissension. According to the verses 4: 150-151 they are the true disbelievers. It is told in the verse 2:176 that those who seek the causes of dispute in the Book are in a schism and far away from the Truth.

The verse 5: 67 says, Oh Messenger! Deliver what ever has been sent down to you from your Lord. If you do not do so, you will not have conveyed His Message. And Allah will defend you from mankind. Indeed Allah will not guide such a people who hide the Soul of Qur'an. The verses 15: 94-95 say "Go ahead with Qur'an as you are commanded and neglect those who associate others in the dominion of Allah. Certainly sufficient are We for you against the scoffers".

Believers are the one who are helping the Impartial Allah by conveying his message for entire mankind in order to utilize as the Balance and Trust to keep the Universe in its equilibrium and for them the Soul of Qur'an the Safeguard and Shield from all disasters as well as the Hell. The verse 25: 31 says, such as We have made for every Prophet an enemy from the *Mujrims* but enough is your Lord to guide and help. It is taught by *Hadith Qudsi*: *"So those who live with remembrance of Allah, never will come a mishap anywhere either on the Earth or in the sky, and He is all Hearing and all Knowing."* Read together the verses 3:103; 21: 92-93; 38: 12 and 41: 52. See explanation 2: 38 and 39.

138. Such is Allah's design! Who is better than one who accepts the design of Allah and is living only for Him?

This verse opposes the ceremony of Baptism of Christians that existed in the time of Prophet. In Islam there is no conversion of religion, but only to accept the true belief and way of life. See explanation 2:112. Really no one has the power or right to select his time, nation, community, religion, parents, sex etc... This verse calls all mankind to become the one among Allah's party which is the only party enters the Paradise. The believers will say by mind that: 'Yes, we are nothing, we own nothing as ours. We are servants.' And all things belong to the Lord of Worlds.

Among the mankind from Adam to Last Day a party belongs to Allah as told in the verse 58: 22, while all other organizations among Muslims are belonged to the party of satan as told in the verse 58:19. Those who have not receive the Criterion to distinguish the party of Allah and satan will not enter either the Paradise or the Hell but the Lord of worlds may send them to any other world. The member of the party of Allah will live or serve Allah only as His representatives. That is only one from each thousand as taught Prophet in the explanation of the verse 4:118 and others will represent the disbeliever satan and will live or serve him. See explanation 1: 4.

139. Say: "Do you argue with us about Allah while He is our Lord and your Lord as well? We have our deeds while you have yours deeds, and we are sincere to Him only".

Today this verse is the reply for the majority of Muslims who have gone astray from the Straight path and argue about Allah with the believers who are living by holding firmly the Soul of Qur'an. The character of believers in the Book is described through the verse 28: 55 as whenever they hear any gossip they shun it and say: "we have our deeds while you have your deeds. You can seek your way. We do not engage the way of ignorant people". Allah commands Prophet and believers to say through the verse 6: 71: "Should we appeal to something that can neither benefit nor harm us, instead of to Allah? Shall we turn on our heels after that Allah has guided us, bewildered like someone whom the devils have enticed away on Earth, while his companions are calling him to Guidance: Come to us? Say, indeed the Guidance of Allah is the only Guidance. We have been ordered to submit ourselves peacefully to the Lord of worlds". Through the verse 109: 6 Allah commands the Prophet and the believers to declare to the disbelievers: You have your way of life, while I have the True way of life.

It is told in the verses 15: 39-40 and 38: 82-83 that satan has taken an oath to Allah that he will lead them all astray aimless to the Hell except for those among them who are Your sincere servant. It is told in the verse 12: 24 that verily *Yoosuf* belongs to one of Our innocent servants. Therefore the believers who follow the life of Prophets belong to the innocent servants. When We say the verse 1:4: "We do serve only for You and we do seek help only from You", we have to keep in mind that 'make us innocent ones who serve only for You' i.e. the one in thousand to the Paradise.

140. Or do you say that Ibrahim, Isma'el, Is'haq, Ya'qoob and the tribes were Jews or Christians? You ask: "Are you more knowledgeable than Allah?" Who is more unjust than some one who hides the Witness from Allah which he holds? And Allah is not heedless of what you are doing.

Today the question is to the different organizations of Muslims who themselves are divided as separate parties is that whether Muhammad, *Ibrahim, Isma'el, Is'haq, Ya'qoob* and their believing followers were following your way of life or the way of one out of thousand who is living by holding firmly the Soul of Qur'an.

Witness from Allah: - the witness from Allah mentioned here is about the *Thourath* and *Injeel* which were present in the hands of Jews and Christians in *Madeena*. See explanation 2: 101. Today the witness is the Soul of Qur'an only for entire mankind. And those who hide the witness from Allah are more unjust. That is why Allah told respectively in the verses 5: 44, 45 and 47 that those who do not judge with what Allah has revealed are the disbelievers, wrongdoers and transgressors.

Prophet taught that: *Qur'an is witness either in favor of you or against you.* The Qur'an will bear witness in favor to those who understand the Soul of Qur'an, follow It and make It truthful. The Qur'an will bear witness against those who neglect It and lead a life against Its rules and regulations, after receiving It. Today Muslims who hide this 'Witness' are mad men and rebellious one as told in the verses 7: 40; 10: 17 and 32: 22. The word 'Witness' is used for Allah as well for Qur'an in both verses 5: 83 and 6: 19. It is commanded to Prophet

Muhammad to live as a witness to Allah and Qur'an through both verses 33: 45 and 48:8. It is commanded to believers through both in the verses 2:143 and 22: 78 that they have to witness the life of Prophet among the public.

The verse 89:14 says, Allah is closely watchful all things. The verse 57: 4 says, He is with you where ever you may be. The verse 6:103 says that no Vision can grasp Him but He grasps all Visions. Neither slumber nor sleep can seize Him, is told in the verse 2: 255. In the verse 50: 16 it is told that We are nearer to them than their jugular vein. The verse 67: 13 says whether you hide your words or make it known, He certainly has the full knowledge of the secrets of all hearts. The verse 8:24 says, Oh believers! Know that Allah comes in between the soul and heart of you. In brief it is impossible to have any thought in anywhere and any times without Allah's knowledge. Read together the verses 22: 70; 35: 11; 41: 53 and 46: 12-13. See explanation 2:121.

141. That is a community which has already passed away; They will have whatever they have earned, and you will have whatever you have earned, you will not be questioned about what they have been doing.

See the explanation 2: 134. *Ibrahim, Isma'el, Is'haq*, the offspring's of *Ya'qoob* and believers are included in the party of Allah. They shall get their reward for their deeds. But if you-Jews and Christians in *Madeena*- are in their ways, you must be included in one party and live only for Allah as His vicegerents. Whoever constructs Paradise here, they will inherit eternal Paradise as the reward. Others who received the Book but hide Its contents will get the Hell as reward. The *Mouidhath* of this verse is Prophet and believers are included in a single party and they are living for Allah only. But you-the Muslims of today, are divided into several parties and there by become party of satan and you are only cause mischief and bloodshed on Earth. As a result you will be entered in to the Hell. See explanation 1: 7 and 2: 23-24.

142. "Some foolish people will ask whatever turned them away from the direction (Qibla) toward which they used to face?" Say: "To Allah belongs the east and the west; He guides whomever He wishes towards the Straight path".

143. Thus We have made of you a community justly balanced. That you may act as witnesses for mankind, such as the Messenger witnessed for you. We appointed Qibla towards which you used to face so We might know the one who is following the Messenger, from those who would turn on their heels. Indeed that event (appointment of Qibla) was a serious matter except for those whom Allah has guided! And Allah not intends to make your faith fruitless. Certainly Allah is Kindness, Merciful with mankind.

144. Certainly We see you shifting your face towards the sky, So We shall appoint a Qibla (direction) for you which you will feel satisfied with; So turn your face towards the sacred Masjid wherever you (all) may be, turn your face towards it. And certainly those were given the Book known well that It is the Truth from their Lord; while Allah is not heedless what they are doing.

Ka'ba in Mecca, the first House of Allah for the worship of entire mankind on Earth, is constructed by Prophet *Ibrahim* and son Prophet *Isma'el*. Then Islam was propagated through the Prophets like *Is'haq*, the son of *Ibrahim*, *Ya'qoob*, the son of *Ishaaq*, *Yoosuf* the son of *Ya'qoob*, *Moosa*, *Haroon*, *Davood*, *Sulaiman*, *Zakaria*, *Yahya* and Eisa. The Jews who argued that they were the loving people of Allah being the children of these Prophets boasted that we crucified Prophet Eisa. Read together the verses 4:157-158. Really what happened was that Allah raised him bodily to Him. The Christians who argue that they are the followers of '*Ansaries*' -who helped Prophet Eisa to propagate Islam the life way of Allah- gradually strayed. Read together the verses 3: 52-53 and 61: 14. Later they were deviated and maintained a deformed belief that Eisa is the son of God or God is the three in one -the son, the father and the Holy Spirit. Read together the verses 4:171-172; 5:17, 72.

The offspring's of Prophet *Isma'el* in Mecca gradually strayed and installed about 360 idols of great peoples including Prophet *Ibrahim*, Prophet *Isma'el*. And their deeds became in a stage that they had to be destroyed. Thus when whole world become darkened, Allah deputed Prophet Muhammad with Qur'an, the Light and Mercy to whole worlds as told in the verses 4: 174-175. The *Qibla* (direction) for the Prophets and believers migrated to *Madeena* was the *Masjid* in Plasteen- i.e. '*Baithul-Muqadhis*'. This is because he and believers have to make good relation to the bearers of Book than the associates of others in the dominion of Allah. Read together the verses 2: 221 and 5: 5. Muhammad who was deputed as Prophet in his fortieth year of age was compelled to migrate to *Madeena* in his fifty-three year of age. In *Madeena* there about 17 months he performed *swalath* turning towards *Baithul-Muqadhis* as *Qibla*. The Jews and Christians in *Madeena* often asked Prophet and his followers that your way of life is completely a new one, then why should you continue *Baithul-Muqadhis* as your *Qibla* even now? According to the verse 2: 129 Muhammad is deputed as Prophet as the result of the prayer of Prophet *Ibrahim* -the father of Prophets. And Prophet Muhammad had great desire to be the *Ka'ba* as the *Qibla.* The Meccan pagans were asking to the Prophet that you are arguing, you are following the life way of *Ibrahim* and *Isma'el*, then why you are not accepting the house of *Ka'aba* as *Qibla*?

Then Allah made prophet praying changed the Qibla to Ka'ba in Mecca, which is the centre of all nations. The Jews and Christians as well as the hypocrites questioned this changing of *Qibla*. Then it is told through this verse to say them that Allah belongs to east and west and Allah has the power to take whatever decisions and put them in to practice. Those who believe in Allah- the only one Deity do not have any doubt in the changing of *Qibla*. As a result of this changing of *Qibla,* the leadership of world is transferred from the children of Israel to the Arabs, in the lineage of Prophet Isma'el. See explanation 2: 115 and 136.

Even the Hypocrites among the Muslims in *Madeena* were unable to accept this changing of *Qibla*. Allah, the Knower of all times, appointed *Baithul-Muqadhis* as *Qibla* in order to identify disbelievers among the Muslims to Prophet and believers. The Hypocrites alleged that the changing of *Qibla* is Prophet Muhammad's single -mindedness and he turns according to his whims and fancies. Today, those who believe and say that changing of *Qibla* is the result of Prophet's prayer also are not true believers. On the other hand, the true believer having the belief that the changing of *Qibla* is from Allah and He put it in to force being the reply for the Prophet's prayer. They accept *Qibla* for all matters like *swalath*, fasting, *Eid*, *Arafa day*, *Hajj* and all their life round the clock will be concentrating the *Ka'ba* as the *Qibla*. To memorize this '*Thwawaaf*' i.e. going round up the *Ka'ba* is made.

Allah does not intend to be in vain the belief of people through the changing of *Qibla*. On the other hand, it is intended to understand the practice and way of

Allah, there by increase their belief, to identify Allah and Prophet by using their intelligence.

'Justly balanced people' means modest people, middle people and people living under the Soul Qur'an- the Light etc. The Prophet's way of life was Qur'an- the Justice. Therefore, to witness Prophetic life means to mould a life with the do's and don'ts of the Soul of Qur'an and thus introduce the Prophet among the public as a mercy for all. Only the believers will do this. The verse 22: 78 says: "It is He Who has named you Muslims accepters of Islam both in this Book and before in order that the Prophet must be witness for you and you must be witness for mankind". Allah says by calling Prophet in the verse 33:45, "Truly We have sent you as a witness, a bearer of glad tidings and a Warner". Verily We have sent you as a witness, to witness the life which Allah has satisfied as a bringer of glad tidings for those who witness you and as a Warner to others, is told in the verse 48: 8. Allah says in the verse 28:78, "And from each people We shall bring a witness and We shall say to them produce proof for your life, then they shall know that certainly the Truth is with Allah alone". Here mentioned both the Truth and Proof is the Soul of Qur'an. See explanation 1:5 and 2:111-113.

145. Even though you brought any evidence to the people of Book they would not follow neither your 'Qibla' nor you follow their 'Qibla' and they will not follow one another's 'Qibla'. If you were to follow their whims after the knowledge has come to you, certainly you would be among the wrongdoers.

Today the Book is only the Soul of Qur'an for entire mankind. But the bearers of Qur'an neither try to understand and follow It nor give other people to utilize It. They without considering *Ka'ba* as the *'Qibla'* observing their Fasting, *Eid* in separate days as that is against in Mecca. Allah says by calling the believers through the verse 3:100, "If you obey any group among the Muslims they would turn you back in to disbelievers after you have believed". Today this verse is saying to the believers who follow the Prophet that they should not change the day of fasting, *Arafa* and *Eid* as that of in *Qibla* and if they follow the desires of majority of Muslims after the knowledge has reached to them, they will be among the wrongdoers. Read together the verse 6:116. See explanation 2:120.

146. Those to who We have given the Book recognize It just as they recognize their own sons. And certainly a group of them conceal the truth even though they know It.

The Jews and Christians who were given Book knew even more as they know their own sons that the change of '*Qibla*' is from Allah and *Ka'ba* in Mecca has to become the '*Qibla*', which is the house of Allah constructed by Prophet *Ibrahim* and Prophet *Isma'el* and it is also the centre of the world. A group among them is concealing the truth deliberately. The preposition 'Hu' in the word "*Yahrifoonahu*" of this verse may have six meanings. All the meanings are considerable also.

(1) Allah: - those who are given the Book should know Allah more than they know their own sons.

(2) Satan: - those who are given the Book should know satan more than they know their own sons.

(3) Prophet Muhammad: - those who are given the Book should know Prophet Muhammad more than they know their own sons.

(4) Change of '*Qibla*': - those who are given the Book should know that the Change of '*Qibla*' is from Allah more than they know their own sons.

(5) The Soul of Qur'an: - those who are given the Book should know the soul of Book more than they know their own sons.

(6) Himself: - those who are given the Book should know him more than they know their own sons.

Today the Book for the entire mankind is the Soul of Qur'an. Therefore; from the Soul of Qur'an one should understand Allah, satan, Prophet, the reality in changing of '*Qibla*', the soul of the Book and the soul and body of man etc... The verse 21:10 says; Verily We have sent down a Book to you in which about you is remembered, will you not then think by using your intelligence?

The verse 6:20 says those to whom We have given the Book know Him just as they recognize their own sons; yet those who have lost their souls will never believe. i.e. those who do not recognize themselves the Lord and the aim of life utilizing the Soul of Qur'an will not believe.

147. The Truth comes from your Lord, then you should not be the one among the doubtful.

Truth mentioned in the verse is Soul of Qur'an. It is commanded to Prophet to say in the verse 10: 108: "Oh you men, now Truth has come to you from your Lord. Then those who are guided by utilizing It is only for his own sake; while any one astray away It, will only become lost at her own risk. I am not the custodian of your affairs. There shall not be any doubt regarding any matters for those who received the Truth –The Soul of Qur'an. The verse 15: 99 says: "And then you live for your Lord until there come unto you the certainty. The only way to get certainty is the Soul of Qur'an. It is told in the verse 69: 51: "Certainly it is the Truth of assured certainty and in the verse 56: 95 it is told: Verily only this is - Qur'an- the very Truth of assured certainty. The verse 13: 28 says: "Know, by the Soul of Qur'an do hearts get peace and tranquility". Allah commands Prophet through the verses 38: 67-68 to say, certainly this is a supreme Message about which you do turn away. The verses 7: 8-9 say, the weight on the Day of Judgment will be to the Truth, and then who made the scale heavy will be only prospered; while those whose scales are light are the ones who have lost their souls because of their blindness towards the verses of Qur'an i.e. they lost their deeds without having any weight. It is told both in the verses 39: 69, 75 that the Truth will be the Balance on the Day of Judgment. And the verse 16: 64 says, We have not sent down the Book for you except to explain to them in what they are differing over, and as a Guidance and Mercy for the people who believe. Therefore the believers should utilize the Soul of Qur'an as the Balance in this world. This verse is repeated in 3: 60. For those who showed tediousness and aloofness towards the verses of Qur'an, all their deeds gone astray and become fruitless, is told in the verses 47: 8-9. It is Allah Who has sent down the Book which is the Truth and Balance, is told in the verse 42: 17. And in the verse 57: 25 also says, Qur'an is the Balance. Therefore those who do not utilize the Soul of Qur'an as Balance and Proof in this world, there shall not be any weight for their deeds record in the Hereafter. Allah commands Prophet through the verse 34: 49 to say, "the Truth has arrived and falsehood never start or repeat". The believers should always pray as, oh Allah! Let us not be included among the doubters about the Truth. See explanation 2: 119.

148. Everyone has a goal to which He turns him. So compete in doing good deeds. Wherever you may be, Allah will bring all together; Certainly, Allah is Capable of everything.

Those who utilize the Soul of Qur'an which is the Guidance increases the Guidance and bestows on them self-control power as told in the verse 47:17. The most Merciful Allah is Impartial. He will never make any one to Paradise or Hell. Each one has a goal. The goal of believers would be to return to Paradise itself. They stand always for the achievement of that goal. Their thought, speech, deeds and heritage are useful to the creatures and will be in the form of Allah has satisfied. In order to achieve this virtue one has to observe the teaching of Prophet: *Among you the best one is, the one who learns and teaches the Soul of Qur'an.* The verse 53: 39 says, "And man has nothing except the deeds with intention". Whatever deeds we do, Allah looks to the hearts of us and all our deeds get acceptance by looking to the states of hearts. This is the truth that Prophet taught: *do not recite the Qur'an without knowing Its contents.* The *swalath* without the remembrance of Allah is to satan.

'So compete in doing good deeds' means you gush in order to understand and convey to others the Soul of Qur'an which is the Ticket to Paradise. Prophet taught in the explanation of the verse 4:118 that *in every thousand, nine hundred and ninety nine go to Hell and one only goes to the Paradise.* Therefore, those who didn't take the Soul of Qur'an as the Guidance and as a Ticket will not include among the one to the Paradise and all his deeds will be fruitless. See the explanation 2: 120 and121. The verse 9:100 says, those came forward first as an answer to the invitation to the Truthful Faith among the *Muhajirs* –migrants-and *Ansaries* –helpers- and those who follow them in the best way, Allah is well pleased with them and they with Him. Allah has prepared for them Paradise under which rivers flow, they dwell therein forever. That is the supreme triumph. The *Sabiqeens* –forerunners- are those who go to Paradise without trial since they completed their reckoning from here utilizing the Soul of Qur'an as the Balance and considering Allah as the Impartial. They are a small sect among the earlier people and very few in the later times, is told in the verses 56:10-14. For them the doors of Paradise are kept open, as told in the verse 38: 50. See the explanation 2: 3, 28, 106 and 107.

149. To wherever you started forth, turn your face towards the scared Masjid. That is indeed the Truth from your Lord. Allah is not heedless what you are doing.

150. To wherever you started forth, turn your face towards the scared Masjid; wherever you may be, turn your faces towards it, so that

people will not have any argument against you, except for those among them who are wrongdoers. So fear them not, but fear Me, so I may complete My favors towards you in order that you should become rightly guided one (for that purpose the 'Qiblas' is assigned).

The life of believers should always be concentrated on Allah. The *Qibla* is made as a symbol of Allah. It is made in order to form unity and harmony among mankind. Hence, not only in the case of *swalath* but also in starting Fasting, celebration of *Eid*, the day of *Hajj*, *Arafa* etc. one should turn towards '*Qibla*' in order to form unity and harmony throughout the world. Therefore, the believers not only turn by vision but also turn by mind towards *Qibla*. Prophet taught that *there is virtue in looking to Ka'ba and Qur'an, since Ka'ba is the symbol of Allah and Qur'an is the words of Allah*. *Qibla* is appointed in order that the believers should become like one body in all subjects and their complete attention will be always towards one center and one goal. Whatever signs or proof bring to the rebellious wrongdoers, they will never believe and approve the *Qibla*. So the believers shall never fear or obey these rebellious rejecters but fear and obey only Allah. The religion Islam visualizes one Creator, one world, one Qibla, one Prophet, one day festival, one day *Arafa*, one day Hajj and one day in the entire world of life. As per the verse 5: 3 these splendid Mercy was completed in '*Hajjathul-Vidaa*' - farewell pilgrimage.

Gradually deviation started in Islam and today there are several groups or parties among Muslims and all are belonged to satan's party. Today there is no group of believers, i.e. Allah's party -the only party from the beginning to end of the world which will be prospered. The ignorance, Dark Age superstition etc. that existed before the arrivals of Prophet Muhammad have become widely spread today among Muslims in several forms. The *Maseeh-A-Dhajjhal* will be coming to annihilate Islam and to implement rebellion in the entire world except the region '*Hijas*' i.e. *Mecca* and *Madeena*. Then *Eisa* will come to introduce Islam and Prophet Muhammad to those who have not touched, not heard or not learned the Qur'an and he will govern by making *Ka'ba* as the capital of the entire world. That day the entire world will recognize Islam. Prophet Muhammad used to pray three times after performing *swalath 'maghrib'* and '*Faj'r'* as I am pleased with Allah being my Lord, Islam being my '*dheen*' -way of life and Prophet Muhammad being the Messenger. The verses 2:53; 3:103; 7:158; 6:15 and 43:10 also end as in order that you should become rightly guided one.

151. Just as We have sent a messenger to you from among yourselves to recite My verses to you, and to purify you and teach you the Book and wisdom and to teach you what you didn't know.

This means that the purpose of appointment of Prophet Mohamed and *Qibla* are the same. The purpose of appointing the Prophet is told in the verse 2:143. 'The Messenger to you from among yourselves' means the offspring's of *Isma'el*, illiterate people as well as the illiterate Prophet. In order to purify them and to teach them what is in the Book and wisdom and the knowledge about all things to become a single party of Allah and to establish the harmony of single community. For this purpose the *Qibla* was also appointed. The purpose of the Book revealed is to purify themselves and others, to stop bloodshed and mischief and such a way to keep the Universe in its equilibrium. See explanation 2:129-132.

152. Then you do remember Me, I will remember you, be grateful to Me and not to be ungrateful with Me.

To remember Allah means to stay always in the conscious that Allah knows the states of chests. In other words keep Allah in hearts with the Soul of Qur'an. Those who remember Allah in standing, walking, sitting and laying on their sides are the prudent person who utilize their intelligence, is told in the verses 3: 190-191. Through the verse 20:14 it is commanded that the five times *swalath* is prescribed to maintain the remembrance of Allah or to keep up the Soul of Qur'an. The verse 4: 103 says, once you have finished the *swalath*, remember Allah while standing, sitting and laying on your side even when you are at peace and tranquility, still keep up the *swalath*, certainly the *swalath* is a timely prescribed duty for the believers. The verses 62: 9-10 say, Oh you who believe! When you are called for *swalath* on the day of *Jumua* –Friday, hasten to the remembrance of Allah and leave all worldly commerce. That will be better for you if you are only realized it. Once *swalath* has been performed, then disperse through out the land and seek Allah's bounty. Remember Allah frequently so that you may prosper. The verse 29: 45 says, Recite whatever has been revealed to you from the Book and then keep up *swalath*: certainly *swalath* restrains one from shameful and evil deeds and maintaining the remembrance of Allah with the Soul of Qur'an is the greatest and Allah knows what ever you producing. The verse 7:170 says, and those who hold fast the Book and keep up *swalath* certainly We shall never make fruitless the wages of such reformers. So first preference will be given to the Soul of Qur'an, and then only the Prayer, *swalath*, fasting, charity, *Hajj* such deeds will be accepted as told in the verse 2:186. The verse 76: 3 says, Allah has given each man his freedom to select one of the two ways either to be grateful or ungrateful. The verse 7: 205 commands the Prophet and believers that remember your Lord with your soul in humility and fearing in the very inner and without saying Allah by your tongue. Any deeds without the participation of the soul not only be accepted, but will be punished. The Qur'an introduces Allah as the Knower of states of heart. And so you be not among the heedless like thinking that Allah hears only if said by tongue. The remembrance of Allah is only possible with the Soul of Qur'an that is why it is told in the verse 63:9 that 'Oh you believers, let neither your wealth nor your children distract you from the Soul of Qur'an, if any one does so, such are the only losers.' In order to prevent the remembrance of Allah, satan prevent men from the Soul of Qur'an which can understand from the verses 5: 90-91; 7: 175; 25: 29; 43: 36 and 58: 19. In the verse 47:7 Allah says by calling believers: If you help Allah, He will help you and plant firmly your foot steps in the way of Truth. To help Allah means to convey the message of Allah- the Soul of Qur'an. Read together the verse 36: 10-11 and 61: 14. See explanation 2: 99.

"*Oh Allah let us include among the people who remember You and are grateful to You and not include in the people who forget you and reject you*". Prophet taught the believers to pray like this: "*Oh Allah includes me among the one who remembers you and thankful to you and serve you in the best way*".

153. Oh you who believe, seek help with patience and swalath. Certainly Allah is with those who keep patient.

Whatever needs shall be asked in the *swalath* to the Lord. Prophet taught that *"the servant is the most proximate to his Lord on sujood -prostration, in his life, therefore, you aught to strive in sujood."* To strive in prostration means to ask whatever our needs to the Lord, by understanding that if our needs are not answered in the prostration, it shall never be answered anywhere else. The verse 96:19 says, of course do not obey him; you prostrate and come closer. There is prescribed *swalath* for all matters in Islam. The *swalath*, which does not prevent shameful and wicked deeds, shall not only be accepted, but also will be caused for punishment as told in the verses 11: 87; 29: 45 and 107: 4-5. Prophet taught that you should never recite the Qur'an even in the *swalath* without knowing its content. He has foretold about a bore people *who will recite Qur'an but it will never get down from their throat to their heart and there by they depart out from the religion as the arrow departs out from the bow"*. Therefore the greatest thing is to maintain the remembrance of Allah and that will achieve only by the Soul of Qur'an.

Patience: - To be in a state that Allah sees and knows every thing. Either any matter of evils or goodness is from Allah. And we should put our trust on Allah in all occasions and critical situations like disease, disaster, fear, opposition in the way of Truth. One should be in conscious that Allah is only my Lord, and I am His servant; Allah deputed me to Earth to live as His vicegerents and I have to return to Him without any anxiety. Prophet has taught: *patience is the half of the faith.* As per the verse 31: 17 *Luqman* advised his son: "My dear son keep up regular *swalath*, command what is just by Qur'an and forbid what is wrong by Qur'an and endure patiently whatever may afflict you; indeed that shows determination in handling matters. In the verse 21: 55 says, after mentioning Prophets *Ayyoob, Isma'el, Idrees*, and *Dhul-kiflee*, Allah says, all of them are men of constancy and patience. Allah has prepared forgiveness and great reward for men and women who are patient and constant, is told in the verse 33: 35. The verse 46: 35 says, be patient just as those messengers who were steadfast patient do not try to hurry up for them since they will scene to have lingered for only an hour of day light on the Day when they shall see what they have been promised. So deliver the message! Yet will it be wiped out except the people of transgressors. The verse 8: 46 also end as: Certainly Allah is with those who keep patient. The verse such as 2: 249 and 8: 66 ends as Allah is with those who keep patient. It is mentioned about patient the verses 3: 146; 13: 24; 16: 126; 42: 43; 59: 1-3 etc. See explanation 2: 44-46.

154. And you do not say: "They are dead!" About anyone who is killed in the way of Allah. Rather they are living even though you do not perceive it.

The battle of *Badr* took place in order to show whether the truth is in the side of believers or idolaters as told in the verses 8: 19 and 41. The battle of *Uh'd* to identify the hypocrites and the believers among the Muslims as told in the verses 3: 166-167. This verse is revealed as a reply to the sayings of hypocrites about the martyrs that if they had obeyed us and kept away from the battle, they would not have been killed. The believers should not think about those who are killed in Allah's way as dead. They rejoice in the bounty provided by Allah in

Paradise with regard to those left behind who have not joined them (participated in the battle but have not become martyrs) in their bliss, on them there is no fear nor have they cause to grieve as told in the verses 3: 168-172. But there are some strayed people among Muslims who believe that they will get help by invoking and giving offerings to the martyrs besides Allah. Through the verse 35: 14 to those who keep these kind of belief and observances as replies: If you invoke them they will not listen to your call and if they were even to listen they cannot reply. On the Day of Judgment they will reject your association of others in Allah's dominion. The verses 36:74-75 say and they have adopted others as deity instead of Allah so that they may be helped by them. They still cannot help them and they will stand like an army against them while they are assembled together on the Day of Judgment. The verses 46: 5-6 say, who is more astray than someone who appeals to someone who will not respond to him until Resurrection Day instead of to Allah, they are heedless about the fact that they are being appealed to. When mankind is summoned, they will become enemies of theirs and renounce their own worship. Through the verse 7: 192 Allah asks: "Do they associate something with Him that has never created anything, while they themselves have been created?" The verses 16: 20-22 say, those whom they invoke instead of Allah do not create a nothing, while they themselves have been created; dead, lifeless, they do not even perceive the times when they will be raised up again. Your Deity is the One Deity only! Those who do not believe in the Hereafter have hearts which refuse to accept and they are over proud.

The verses 25:17-18 say, some day He will summon them along with whatever they have been worshiping instead of Allah He will ask: "Were you the ones who led these servants of Mine astray, or did they stray away by themselves?" They will say: "Glory be to You! We would never take on any patrons besides You! However You let them and their forefathers did bestowed livelihood until they forgot the Soul of Qur'an and they became a boar, worthless people. Then hiding all of these verses the hypocritical leaders say to their blind followers strayed people that it is permissible to appeal give offerings to great souls and martyrs. But the scene that they will keep aloof from them may read in the explanation of the verses 2: 166-167. The hypocrites think that death is a loss, and they will go to Hell after their death even without reckoning as told in the verses 9: 84-85. But the believers since they follow the Soul of Qur'an will enter the Paradise after their death and begin their real life. See explanation 2: 6-7 and 99.

155. Certainly We shall test you with something of fear, hunger, shortage of wealth and persons and crops and products. And announce glad tidings to those who keep patient.

156. Those who say, whenever some calamity strikes them: "Indeed we belong to Allah, and are returning to Him".

157. Such are the people upon whom their Lord's Blessings and Mercy are bestowed and they are the ones who are rightly guided.

The verses 29:2-3 say, "do men reckon that they will be left alone just because they say: 'we believe', without being tested. Certainly We have tested those before them, indeed Allah has to know those who are true and those who are false". The verse 76:2 says, certainly We created mankind from a drop of mingled sperm of men and ovum of women in order that We have to test him. Mankind who are created in the Paradise are deputed to Earth in order to seek and find out the Creator, to identify themselves and to construct Paradise here by utilizing all the blessing which the Creator have bestowed and thereby fulfill the goal of life. This world is a trial and every one's fate is determined and enrolled on their neck as told in the verses 17:13-14. The verse 3:185 says: "Every soul will taste death and your earning will be completely repaid on the Day of Judgment. Anyone who is saved himself from the fire and made entered in to the Paradise will be triumphed and this worldly life is nothing except a little enjoyment of deception. The verse 186 says, You will be tested by means of your wealth and through your own selves, and you will hear much abuse from those who were given the Book before you, as well as those who associates others with the dominion of Allah. If you are patient and heedful that is the way of steadfast.

The Soul of Qur'an is the Insight which shows all three times - past, present and future matters in ones heart's language. The believers by utilizing this Insight will pray to their Lord and thereby amend their fate by the will of Him. Prophet taught, the fate will not be changed except without prayer. So each one individually should pray to their Lord and thereby has to determine that they are the one to the Paradise. That is the meaning of saying 'by the permission of their Lord' in the verse 14:1.

But two conditions are mentioned in the verse 2: 186 for the acceptance of prayer.

1) Respond to the call of Allah. 2) Believe in Allah as it should be believed. 'To believe in Allah as it should be believed' means to understand Allah as

submitted through 6236 verses of Qur'an. To give answer to the call of Allah means to follow the Guidance mentioned in the verse 2: 38. Those who live following the Guidance, the Soul of Qur'an, are the rightly guided one. The verse 11: 6 says, there is no living creature on Earth except its sustenance is with Allah. Allah knows its resting place and where it will reach last (Godown). All has recorded in a clear Book. It is told in the verse 11:7, He is the One Who created the Heaven and Earth in six days in order to test you which of you is best in conduct. Before that His throne –control, was on water. The fact that mankind is created for testing is also told both in the verses 18:7 and 67:2. The verse 3:173 says When it is said to the believers, verily mankind has gathered against you, so fear them, then it will increase their faith and they will say: "For us Allah is sufficient and He is the best Custodian" Read together the verses 21: 35; 47: 31 and 57:22. See explanation 2: 147- 148.

158. Certainly Safa' and Marva are among the symbols of Allah. So anyone who goes on pilgrimage to the House or visits it will not be blamed if he runs along between them. And with anyone who volunteers some good, Allah is Appreciative, Aware.

Once '*Hajara*'-the mother of Prophet *Isma'el-* climbed the mount *Safa* and looked around for water for her child. Finding no water there she ran and climbed to mount *Marva* and looked around for water. She repeated this for seven times. Meanwhile '*Zum-Zum*' gushed forth from the foot steps of child. Keeping in memory of this 'running of *Hajara'* it is included in the observance of Hajj and *Umra*. In the slope of these two mountains, walking was too speedy, that is why it is called running. Today to denote the place, it is marked by a tube light green in color. One has to run when he reaches that place rather than walking.

In the course of time, the ancestors of Isma'el who became astray from the path of their forefathers began to worship idols. They installed 360 idols in *Ka'ba*, one idol named '*Isaf*' fixed on the mount *Safa* and another idol named '*Na-ila*' on mount *Marva'*. The idols '*Isaf'* was of a man, while '*Na-ila'* a woman. Both of them had fornicated in *Ka'ba* not respecting its sacredness, Allah transformed them into stone. About this fact in the verse 36: 67 Allah says: If it had been Our Will We would have fixed in their place so that they would not able to move forward and backward. There are other examples for such events in the ancestral community. For example those who were on the day of Saturday disobeying its sacredness, Allah transformed them into apes as explained in the verse 2: 66. The Jews who ate from *Maeda* -tray containing food, which was sent down as a reply to the prayer of Prophet Jesus, and rejected after eating were transformed into swine as explained in the verse 5: 60. By denoting the type of invoke and worship of the disbelievers in the verse 35: 14, Allah says that if they were too listen they can't answer your call, one can understand from that verse that Allah will make to hear the idols and buried people the movements takes place here as a torture. But today, due to the prayer of Prophet Muhammad this kind of torments are postponed to the Hereafter.

The year before the birth of Prophet Muhammad, the well '*Zum-Zum*' covered under mud was cleaned as a result of the dream shown to Prophet's grand father -*Abdul Muthalib*. After the victory of Mecca some of the believers who conducted Hajj and *Umra* shown disgust in running between *Safa* and *Marva*, since in their darkened period of life, these idols were worshiped and they argued that their idols were better than '*Isaf*' and '*Na-ila*' and turned their faces from *Safa* and *Marva*. That is why this verse was revealed and Allah teaches the believers that the running in between *Safa* and *Marva* is the part of *Hajj* and *Umra*. See the explanation 2: 52 and 152.

159. Indeed those who hide whatever be sent down as Explanations and Guidance, once We have explained it to mankind in the Book. Such are the one whom Allah cursed and the cursers entitled to curse.

160. Except for those who repent, reform and explain; from such I accept repentance from, for I am the receiver of the repentance, the Merciful!

161. Indeed those who hide the verses of Allah and die hiding all the verses of Allah will have Allah's curse upon them, as well as the Angels' and all mankind's.

162. To live with forever. Torment will not be lightened for them, nor will they be allowed to wait.

Today the Book means the Soul of Qur'an for entire mankind. Here it is mentioned the condition of men devil, hypocrites who lost the aim of life. They undeservingly boast as scholars and lead the life of satan instead of the life which

Allah satisfied. They do not follow the Soul of Qur'an knowingly It and not teach It to other people. Their similitude is that of a dog that changes not its attitude whether you attack or not, is told in the verse 7:176 and that of a Jew and donkey which carries the burdens without knowing what it carries as told in the verse 62:5. It is told in the verse 2:174 that these hypocrites, who hide the verses of Allah, are swallowing into their bellies nothing but fire. Allah will not address them on the Day of Judgment nor purify them; they will be thrown to the bottom of Hell without reckoning like the transgressed Pharaoh. Read together the verses 3: 86-91 and 4:145.

Such hypocrites who are twisting and distorting the verses of Qur'an during their speaking like in Friday sermons and the disbelievers who hear them blindly will be gathered together in the Hell, is told in the verse 4: 140. Read together the verses 6: 68 and 16:104-107. Both verses 9:73 and 66: 9 commands to the Prophet and believers to strive hard against the hiders of Qur'an verses and the hypocrites, and be wrath upon them; their abode is Hell-what an evil place to return! The verse 25:52 commands to the believer that obeys not these hypocrites who hide the Qur'an and strive hard against them with the Soul of Qur'an. Read together the verses 33: 1, 48 and 48: 6, 29. Allah has taught all living beings their own way of prayer and glorifying Him, is mentioned in the verses 17: 44, 24: 41. So by utilizing the Soul of Qur'an as the Balance to keep the Universe in its equilibrium, the believers should maintain the living things glorification of Allah. Then if the Earth is destroyed by hiding the Soul of Qur'an, the burden of that sin shall be carried by hypocrites in front of Allah. The verse 16: 61 says if Allah were to take mankind to task for their wrong doing, He would not leave even an animal up on the Earth; but He puts them off till an appointed deadline. Once their deadline comes they will not postpone it for an hour nor may they advance it. Both the verses 6: 47 and 46: 35 end with a question that so anyone will be destroyed except the people of wrongdoers or transgressors? The disbelievers mentioned in the verses 41:26-28 are the hypocrites who tell to the people do not hear the Soul of Qur'an and the disbelievers mentioned in the verses 41: 29 are the '*Fujjar*', who follow them blindly by hearing their words against the words of their Lord. These people shall go to Hell bearing the burden of others as told in the verse 6: 26. The verse 3: 91 says that certainly those who hide the verses of Qur'an and died rejecting all the verses will never have even all the Earth filled with gold accepted from anyone of them, even though they tried it to give as a ransom such will have painful torment while they will not have any helpers. Allah has promised hypocrites' men and women the fire of Hell, they shall dwell therein for ever, and for them is the curse of Allah and enduring punishment. See explanation 1:7 and 2: 140.

163. And your Deity is one Deity, there is no deity except Him, the Impartial, the Compassionate.

Prophet taught that this verse and also the verse 3: 2 belongs the most Glorious Names of Allah. For Deity, see explanation 2: 132.

164. Certainly in the creation of Heaven and Earth, the alternation between night and day, in the sailing of the ships through the sea for the benefits of mankind, and any water Allah sends down from the sky with which to revive the Earth following its death, and in the scattering of all kinds of beasts throughout it, in the changing of winds, and the clouds which are driven alone between the Sky and Earth, are indeed signs for the people who utilize their intelligence.

There are enough lessons for wise men in the creation of Heaven and Earth and in the alternation of night and day. They find the only Creator behind these creations. By utilizing the intelligence they will understand that the aim of creating all these creations is to investigate and find out the Creator. They praise and glorify Allah. They will seek refuge from the punishment of the Hell and they always keep remembrance of Allah as told in the verses 3: 190-191.

Allah taught mankind the knowledge and way to make the ship float and sail through the sea which is made out of iron. Even though the iron itself sink in the water, today men use ships made of iron, without sinking in water for transporting heavy loads, fishing and for war purpose. When rain is spray down to the dry and dead land it expands bloom and swell, seeds and weeds germinate, and thereby living beings like beetle, honeybee, ant and ant-eater. This phenomenon remembers wise men that Allah, the Wise will resurrect the dead men. Read together the verse 41: 39.

Our knowledge about living beings even in a room in houses is very limited. Allah created the living beings in a suitable bodily structure to live in several zone of universe in various climates. The chameleon in our country and that of Africa shows different bodily structure. The thinking wise men are those who find the Creator behind the creation of all these beasts, living and glorifying Allah. The verse 7: 185 says: "Have they not observed sovereignty over Heaven and Earth and whatever Allah has created any sort, that perhaps their deadline may be approaching? In what speech after these will they then believe"? The verse 88: 17 says: Do they not look at the camels how they are created? The reply to the question is Glory be to You Oh Lord! I have seen in my heart the Creator behind the creation of that camel. He is the one Who has no similitude and examples and He has the power over all things. The verse 42: 29 says "Among His signs is the creation of Heaven and Earth, as well as any animals scattered either of them. He is capable of gathering them whenever He wishes". This verse denotes that the living beings occupy in other planets also.

There are several kinds of winds. The breeze before coming of rain, the storm that makes disaster, whirlwind, sandstorm, dry fire wind, cold wind, etc. Pollination takes place through the wind as told in the verse 15:22. The wind is used to produce electricity. Thus it has several benefits to mankind. Allah has sent down Adam and Eve from Heaven to Earth by the rhythmic balance of the wind. Allah has risen up Prophet Jesus and Prophet *Idirees* to Heaven by whirlwind.

Having caused to die *Uzair* for hundred years he was resurrected to show how the dead is resurrected. Allah resurrected and gave life to his donkey, which was used as his vehicle by rhythmic wind, and which was adhered into the Earth as bones and thorns. The '*A'ad*', the people of Prophet *Hood* was destroyed by a dry and barren wind. That dry wind absorbed water content of their body completely and like wrinkled mango seed they fell and destroyed. That wind exceedingly violent blow over them seven nights and eight days. That people collapsed in it in the wind as if they were hollow palm trunks as told in the verses 69: 6-8. Read together the verses 41: 15-16. When the air circulation stopped, men and living beings become motionless like a wooden doll engraved. It is memorable that in the recent years, thousands of pilgrims died during the *Hajj* when the air circulation stopped due to the failure of electricity in the tunnel from *Mecca* to *Mina*.

There are mountains of clouds like that of on Earth, is told in the verse 24: 43. The verse 27: 88 says: "You will see the mountains, which you reckoned were solid, slip away just as the clouds slip away. Allah is the One who produced all things in a perfect order. He is acquainted with whatever you are doing." It is only in the recent years that the scientists found clouds like mountains which are mentioned in the Qur'an many years ago only after the invention of airplanes. These clouds are Allah's will are scattered to different place by winds and are sent down as rain. Read together the verses 45: 3-5. If we study about this universe and the phenomenon there with the Soul of Qur'an, we can find it is Allah -the One only the Creator and Lord and there is no equals, rivals, intercessors, middle men, partners or children to Him. There is not a living or non living thing like Him. See explanation 2: 28-29,152.

165. Yet there are some men who adopt instead of Allah, who they love just as they should love Allah. Those who believe have firmer in their love of Allah; if only those who are wrongdoers might see, when they face torment, indeed all strength belongs to Allah and Allah is severe with torment.

Those who make rivals, equals, and intercessors to Allah, the Creator of all and give offerings to satisfy them are wrongdoers. In a *Hadeeth Qudusi* it is taught to pray: "*Oh the self Surviving and the Supporter of all to survive, I seek help by Your Mercy*". Here the Mercy is the Soul of Qur'an. No deeds will be accepted and no prayers will be answered without the Soul of Qur'an is told in the Verse 2: 186. The believers don't have a state of being forgotten Allah. Those who have forgotten Allah, they become transgressors as told in the verse 59: 18. By utilizing the Insight-the Soul of Qur'an one has to understand the events going to happen in the Hereafter and have to correct their evils here itself. Otherwise they will be the wrongdoers and should enter to the Hell by confessing their sins in the Hereafter. It is told in the verse 3: 31 that if you do love Allah, follow me. Read together the verses 10: 17; 25: 27-30 and 32: 22. See explanation 2: 145.

166. When those who have been followed get free themselves from those who have been following, they would see the punishment and all the relation between them would be cut off.

167. And those who have been following will say: "If we only had another chance, then we would free ourselves from them just as they have freed themselves from us"! Thus Allah will show them their deeds as regrets on their parts. They will never come out of the Fire!

In several places the Qur'an describes the scenes in the Hereafter where these hypocritical leaders and their blind followers blame, argue, curse and abuse each other. (1). The verse 14: 21says: "They will all be unveiled without a screen before Allah on one Day. That Day those who were weaklings in this world will say to those who were the arrogant leaders: Verily in the material world we were following you. Therefore, is it possible for you to avert anything from the punishment of Allah for us? They will reply: If Allah had included us in the Guidance, we should have included you also in the Guidance. It is all the same for us whether we panic or be patient; in any way, nobody is there to save us. (2). The Paradise will be brought near to those who were following the Soul of Qur'an in this world, while Hades will be brought for those who were living aimless here and they will be asked, where is whatever you were serving instead of Allah? Will they help you or even help themselves? Thus they and the leaders straying in evil who prompted them to do so and the entire armies of '*Iblis*'-satan- together will be placed above one by one in the Hell. They will say while they quarrel away in it: By Allah, we were in obvious error when we held others as equals with Lord of the all worlds and none except the *mujrims* –madmen- have led us astray*. Now we have no intercessors or any bosom friend. Now if we only had a chance, we would be the believers. See the verses 26: 90-102

* Here the weaklings i.e. followers call their Hypocritical leaders as the *mujrims* -mad men.

(3). On the Day of Judgment Allah will call out them and ask: where are my associates whom you have been claiming? Then the ones against whom the charge will be pronounced will say: "Our Lord, these are the ones whom we misled as aimless! We misled them just as we ourselves were aimless. We absolve ourselves to you, it was not we whom they were worshiping*. It will be said to them: Call upon your associates. Then they will call them, yet they will not answer them and they will see the punishment. If only they had utilized the Guidance -Soul of Qur'an, they would not have strayed like this. See the verses 28: 62-64.

*The associates referred in this verse are those who are called upon besides Allah or the great souls among men, *Jinn* and Angels to whom offerings were given. The ones on whom the charge will be pronounced is the hypocrites who prompt the common man to do '*Shirk*' -associate others in the dominion of Allah.

(4). On that Day when their faces will be twisted by the Fire, they will say: "Woe to us, if we had only obeyed Allah and obeyed the messenger". They will also say: "Our Lord, indeed we have obeyed our superiors and our great men, they led us astray from the Straight path. Our Lord, give them double punishment and curse with a great curse. See the verses 33: 66- 68.

(5) And those disbelievers say: We shall neither believe by this Qur'an nor in the one which came before It. And if you could see the condition of these wrongdoers stationed before their Lord, they will toss the statement back and forth at one another. Those who had been despised as weaklings will tell those who acted as proud leaders. If it were not you we would have been believers. Those leaders will tell those who acted like weaklings: Did we block you from the Guidance after It reached to you. Nay, you were certainly mad men*. Weaklings will say to the leaders: Nay, there was a plotting by night and day when you ordered us to disbelieve in Allah and we setup rivals to Him. They will conceal their regret when they see the punishment; and We will place yokes around the necks of these disbelievers. Will they not be rewarded except for what they have been doing worldly life? See the verses 34: 31-33.

* Here the leaders say to the followers: You are mad men who don't try to understand the Soul of Qur'an. Both the leaders and their followers are included in the group of disbelievers and wrongdoers. A scene is warned in the verses 25: 27-29 that these kind of wrongdoers will bite their hands and say: Oh, woe to me, would that I had never taken such a one for an intimate friend, it was he who prevented me from the Soul of Qur'an after it had come to me. Satan had become a traitor to man.

(6) Nay, on that Day they are surrendered, some of them will step forth to question one another. The followers will ask: it was you who used to come at us from the right side. The hypocritical leaders will say: Nay, you were not believers; we had no authority or influence over you. Instead you had been such arrogant people. Our Lord's sentence (words) has been confirmed against us; we must indeed taste the punishment. Certainly we were of aimless people, so we led you too aimless. Thus verily they will become partners in punishment on that Day. Surely like that We deal with the madmen. The madmen referred here include both the hypocritical leaders and their followers *-fujjar* who read the Qur'an without understanding Its contents. See the verses 37: 26-34.

(7) It is memorable that they will quarrel with each other in the Fire. The weaklings will tell those who acted proudly as leaders: Certainly we were

following you, won't you then spare or prevent us from a portion of the Fire. The ones who acted proudly as leaders will say: Certainly we are all in it together. Truly Allah has judged between His servants with Justice. And those who are inside the Fire will tell to the keepers of Hell: Appeal to your Lord to reduce the punishment to us for at least a day. Then keepers will ask: Did there not come to you your Messengers with clear verses? They will say: "of course, they did come". Then the keepers will say: "well, and then make appeal by yourself". And the *prayer of disbelievers increases nothing except astray*. See the verses 40: 47-50. Disbelievers said here include both the proud leaders and the weakling followers among the Muslims who received the Soul of Qur'an but not utilized as safeguard from the Hell. Read together the verse 13: 14.

(8) The verses 41: 26-28 say: those who disbeliever will say: do not hear this Qur'an and you chatter away while It is being recited, so that you will succeed to down It. We will let those who disbelieve to taste severe punishment and will reward them for the worst, which they have been doing here. Such will be the reward for Allah's enemies, the Fire! They will find a home forever as a reward because they were repudiating Our verses. The verse 29 says, and the one who disbeliever will say: our Lord, show the Jinn and humans who misled us; so that we shall trample on both of them with our feet since we were the underdogs. Note that the disbelievers mentioned in the verse 26: 28 are the hypocritical leaders and those mentioned in the verse 29 are the despised weaklings.

(9) In the verses 43: 74-78 it is told that: Certainly, the madmen will remain in Hell's torment; it will not be seized or eased for them and they will feel confounded in It. We have not done any harm to them, but rather they had already harmed themselves. They will call the Angel *Malik*: Oh *Malik*! Would that your Lord put an end to us, *Malik* will reply: Nay, but you shall abide therein. We had come to you with the Truth. But most of you detested the Truth.

Therefore, the Soul of Qur'an should be used as the Insight which helps us to foresee the punishment coming in the Hereafter in order not to become one among them. There the screen will be unveiled and each and every moment of our life in this world will be seen in Record book which is set on our neck as told in the verses 17: 13-14. Read together the verse 45: 28-31and 50: 22. See explanation 1: 7.

168. Oh mankind, eat anything lawful, wholesome that exist on Earth, and you don't follow the footsteps of satan, certainly he is an open enemy of yours.

169. Certainly he commands you what is evil and shameful deeds, and to say what you do not know about Allah.

The verse 208 says, Oh you who believe, enter completely into Islam and do not follow the footsteps of satan, he is an open enemy of yours. Satan is mentioned about in ninety nine verses in Qur'an. So if we do not make our Jinn soul mate a believer with the Soul of Qur'an, we may follow his footsteps and become losers. Satan tempts men to have bad habits and observations like miserliness, lavishness, interest, theft, bribery, black money, reciting Qur'an to the dead, sorcery, magic, omen, zodiac, palmistry, prophecy by caged birds i.e. fortune telling by caged birds, horoscope, divination by observing the movement of lizard, dowry from women side, gambling, liquors, food items offered for other than Allah, and meaningless rhymes and songs moreover murdering, robbery, prostitution, sodomy, masturbation, sterilization, priesthood, communalism, nationalism, racialism, selfishness, partiality in ones own party, self conceit, arrogance, insolence, etc. The verses 36: 59-60 say on this Day: "Oh madmen! Get you apart, oh children of Adam, did I not make covenant that you should not serve satan, he is an open enemy of yours". It is told in the verse 12: 5 that certainly satan is an open enemy for men. It is told in the verse 28: 15: Verily he is enemy that manifestly misleads. Both the verses 6: 142 and 43: 62 end as: "Certainly satan is to you an open enemy". If anything saying about Allah without the Soul of Qur'an, it is satan making man to say so. That is why it is told to the believers in the verse 4: 43 that you should not approach '*swalath*' until you can understand what you say. It is told in the verse 61: 2: Oh you who believe, you shouldn't say which you didn't do, for it is grievously hateful before Allah. Prophet *Nooh* aggrieved before his Lord in the verse 71:21 that: Oh my Lord! Certainly they have disobeyed me. And follow whose wealth and children give them no increase except lose or they follow men devil, hypocrites. The verses 7: 27-28 say: Verily We made satan as friends to those without faith, when they commit indecency they say: "We found our forefathers doing so and Allah commanded us thus. You say: Nay, Allah never commands what is indecent. Do you say of Allah what you know not? The '*swalath*' without the Soul of Qur'an does not restrain from shameful and evil deeds and it will become the worship to satan. Read together the verse 29: 45. See explanation 2: 44, 152.

170. And when it is said to them: "Follow what Allah has sent down"; they say: "Rather, we will follow what we discovered our forefathers were doing", even though their forefathers didn't use their intelligence in any way nor were they guided (will they follow them).

The character of nine hundred and ninety nine persons out of each thousand is pictured here. When it is said to them follow the Soul of Qur'an, which Allah sent down, they blindly follow their forefathers and they are satisfied with their ways. The verse 5:104 says, whenever they are told: "Come to what Allah has sent down, and to the Messenger", they say: "We are satisfied with what we found our forefathers doing"; even though their forefathers did not know anything and were not guided! The disbelievers in every time say like this. About such disbelievers' activities, more explanations are given in the verses 43: 21-23 as: Or have We given them a book already which they try to hold It? Moreover they say, we found our forefathers following such a way and indeed we are nearly being guided along their footsteps. Just the same We have not sent any Warner into a country previous to you except the high livers said: "We found our forefathers with such a way, and we are merely being led along their tracks". These sayings of disbelievers are due to their soul mate being the disbeliever. The verse 31: 21 says, whenever they are told: "Follow whatever Allah sent down", they say: "Rather we follow what we found our forefathers doing"; Even though satan has been inviting them to the torment of the Blaze. Read together the verses 22: 3 and 4. See explanation 2: 6 and 7.

171. And the similitude of these disbelievers may be compared to that of a shepherd's cry and shouting to the cattle which listen to nothing except shout and cry: deaf, dumb, and blind, they do not use their intelligence.

The verses 25: 43-44 say, have you seen someone who has taken his own passion as his Deity? Would you act as a trustee or do you think that most of them do hear or even use their intelligence? They are just like cattle -indeed, they are farther strayed from the Straight path. Those who keep them distant from the Soul of Qur'an after receiving It, and those who try not to understand what, what for and why It, and the self respecting intellectuals who utilize the blessings of Allah only for the benefit of material world are included in this group. The verse 47:12 says; Allah will admit the ones who believe and do honorable deeds into Paradise beneath which rivers flow, while those who disbelieve will enjoy themselves and eat just as cattle eat, and the Fire will be lodging for them. Those who belie Our verses and reject It are deaf and dumb in the midst of darkness told in the verse 6: 39. The verse 10: 42 says, and some of them do listen to you carefully, yet can you make the deaf to hear even though they do not utilize their intelligence? The verse 10:43 says, and some of them look towards you. Yet will you guide the blind even though they do not utilize Insight? Through the verses 27: 80-81 and 30: 52-53 Allah says, you cannot make the dead hear nor even the deaf hear the appeal if they have turned their backs on it. You are no one to guide the blind out of their straying: Only you can hear someone who believes in Our verses and are submitted themselves to Us in peace. It is asked through the verse 43: 40: Can you then make the deaf hear or guide the blind as well as anyone else in manifest astray? The horrible scenes in the Hereafter for those who do not utilize their intelligence are described in the verses 67: 10 and 36: 62. See explanation 2:17-20, 24 and 99.

172. Oh you who believe, eat any wholesome things We have provided you with, and be grateful to Allah, if it is Him who you are serving.

Through the verse 7: 32 Allah says to ask the Prophet "who has forbidden Allah's amenities which He has provided for His devoted servants, and the wholesome things from His provision?" Say: "All these things are for the enjoyment of the believers in the life of this world though shared by others; but these shall be exclusively theirs on the Day of Resurrection. Thus do We make Our verses clear for the people who knowing. The verses 43: 33-35 say that if it were not that mankind has been a single nation, we would grant anyone who disbelieves the Impartial silver roofs for their houses and staircases to climb upon and doors for their houses and couches to recline on with precious gems; all that means nothing except enjoyment during worldly life while those who are heedful will be the Hereafter with your Lord. The believers live exclusively for Allah as His vicegerents in this world. To them shall have Paradise in the Hereafter while the rejecters are the representatives of satan. To them this material world is the Paradise and they will dwell in the Hell after the death. Read together the verses 14: 21-22.

The verse 23: 51 says, Oh Messengers! Eat wholesome things and do righteous deeds; surely I am Knower of anything you do. The worship will only be accepted from those who eat the things wholesome and lawful. The wholesome and lawful sustenance can only be identified by utilizing the Soul of Qur'an as Balance and Standard. See explanation 1: 4 and 2:147-148.

173. Certainly it is forbidden to you the dead meat, blood, flesh of swine and anything that has been set a parted for other than Allah as offerings. Yet any one who may be forced to do so without craving or transgressing due limits, will have no offence held against him; certainly Allah is Forgiving, Merciful.

The same verse is repeated in the verse 16:115. It is told in the verse 6: 145: that the flesh of swine and the things set a parted for other than Allah as offerings are so impious and filthy. Read together the verse 5: 3. Here the blood is included in the forbidden list. Whereas in the verse 6:145 it is mentioned only the flowing blood is forbidden. So the inner organs like liver, pancreas, hearts etc. even though contains congealed blood are permissible to eat.

If anyone is forced to eat these under compulsion of others without willful obedient and use it only to maintain life when it prevail non-availability of other food items, Allah will forgive it to them. As far as possible we should ensure whether the food is wholesome and lawful, when it is understood that the food items are forbidden, then stop eating it immediately and seek for forgiveness to Allah. The verse 6:121 says, do not eat anything on which Allah's name has not been remembered; and surely it is impiety! And the satan inspires their adherence to argue with you; and if you obeyed them, you would become among those who associates others in the dominion of Allah. Therefore, the meat of an animal will not become permissible only by mere pronouncing the name of Allah before it is slaughtered or before eating its meat. It is told in four places in Qur'an that all the food resources set a parted to other than Allah as offerings are forbidden. Dead fish and locusts are not included in forbidden, is taught by Prophet through the explanation of this verse. Read together the verse 5:100. See explanation 2: 168 and 169.

174. Certainly those who hide what Allah sent down in the Book and those who sell It for a petty price, they are not eating in to their bellies except fire, Allah will not speak to them on the Day of Judgment nor will He purify them; and they will have a painful torment.

Those who hide what Allah has revealed in the Book to the mankind are the hypocrites. They know the message of Qur'an but will not follow It or teach It to others. Read together the verse 2: 99. Some examples of selling the verses of Allah for petty price are: to receive remuneration by reading the Qur'an to the dead, neglecting the verses 6: 36 and 36:70, etc. standing as leader for *swalath* and get salary without learning or teaching the Soul of Qur'an, earning money by publishing books in the name of Islamic Publications in order to prevent the people from the Soul of Qur'an. To accept salary by teaching '*Hifz*'-byheart- and '*Thajveed*'-reading regulations- of the body of Qur'an neglecting Its soul. To write the verses of Qur'an on the dishes and metal pieces and tie it in threads and sell It in retail as well as wholesale etc. In brief, for what aim that Allah sent down the Qur'an, utilize It against that aim, and those who misuse It for material benefit included in this group. Those who sell the verse of Qur'an for a petty price are filling fire not only in their bellies but also their family members. 'Allah speaks them not' means, they shall go to Hell without reckoning on the Day of Judgment. Not purify them means, they shall not have chance for repentance in this world.

The verse 10:33 says, thus your Lord's Word proved true against the arrogant hypocrites that indeed they will not believe. The verse 40: 6 says, and thus your Lord's word proved true against the rejecters of faith who conceal the Qur'an; truly they are the inmates of the Fire. The verse 10: 94 says, surely Truth has come to you from your Lord, so you do not be among the doubters. The verse 95 says, and you should not be the one who reject Allah's verses; if so, you shall become among the losers. The verses 96-97 say, indeed those against whom the Word of your Lord has been proved true, that they would not believe even if whatever signs brought to them until they see painful torment. It is told in the verses 78: 21-22, truly Hellfire is waiting for those who live in accordance with their lusts, and their place of return is Hell. It is told in the verses 78: 27-28: they are the people who don't expect reckoning and repeatedly rejecting the verses of Qur'an. The verse 3:187 says, when Allah made an agreement with those who were given the Book: "You shall explain It to mankind and not conceal It, but they tossed It behind their backs and sold It for a petty price. What a bad bargain they made!" To put it brief the hypocrites who knowingly hide and their blind followers who reject the Soul of Qur'an are the wrongdoers, madmen and transgressors and they will have severe torment as per the verses such as 6: 21;

7: 37-40; 10: 17; 18: 57; 32: 22; 39: 22 etc. See explanation 2: 79, 159, 166 and167.

175. Such are the ones who have purchased astray instead of Guidance and torment instead of forgiveness. Then what a patience they are showing for the Fire.

The Guidance is the Soul of Qur'an. The verse 36: 11 says, indeed you will only warn someone who follows the Soul of Qur'an and fears the Impartial - Most Gracious even if He is unseen by seeing under the Light of Soul of Qur'an, inform glad tides of forgiveness and a generous reward to him. Read together the verse 67: 12. This verse also teaches that each one has to decide Paradise or Hell here utilizing the Soul of Qur'an as the Balance and Criterion. Read together the verse 4: 44. See explanation 2: 16, 38.

176. That is because Allah has sent the Book down with the Truth, while those who disagree in the Book go too far in schisms.

Today the Book for entire mankind is only the Qur'an. It is manifest, decisive and so should not take It as joke and evade. It is the criterion for trial on the Day of Judgment. It is sent down in order to decide each ones fate in this world by utilizing It as Balance as explained in the verse 16: 64. It is only the Qur'an, which will recommend without Allah's consent. Those who are taking some part of the book neglecting other part are gone far away from the Truth and their faith is incomplete. They, instead of holding the whole tree of Islam, hold a branch of it and thus became among associates in the dominion of Allah. Read together the verses 15: 90-92.

Allah by calling the believers through the verses 30: 31-32 says, you shouldn't become among those who associate in the dominion of Allah by splitting their '*Dheen*' and becoming different parties. Every party is rejoicing in what they have with them. The verses 23: 52-54 say, certainly this community of yours is a single community and I am your Lord, so you heed Me. But they cut off that agreement dividing into parties. And every party is rejoicing in what they have with them. Therefore leave them in their intoxication for a time. Allah says in the verses 21: 92-93: Certainly this community of yours is a single community, I am your Lord, therefore you live only for Me. But they cut off their affairs and covenants between them. They will all return to Us. It is told in the verse 6: 159:

Certainly as for those who divided in their '*Dheen*' and became different parties, you have no responsibility in their affairs i.e. you have no relation with them. Truly their affairs shall return to Allah and then He will tell them of all that they were doing in this world. Read together the verses 2: 213 and 3: 103-105. See explanation 2: 137 and 148.

177. Virtue does not consist in that you turn your faces towards the east and west, but virtue consists in one should believe in Allah, Last Day, Angels, the Book and Prophets; and no matter how he loves it, to give his wealth to nearest, orphans, the needy, the wayfarer and beggars, and towards freeing captives; and to keep up swalath and pay the welfare tax; and those who keep their word whenever they promise anything; and are patient under sufferings and hardship and in time of violence. Such are the ones who make the Qur'an true and they are the only heedful.

Allah is present everywhere. It is not virtue to turn faces towards *Qibla* bodily. But the belief and life style it should be molded under the Soul of Qur'an. In other words should live by seeing Allah through the Soul of Qur'an. Even though we are in need of money we should spend it seeking Allah's pleasure to His servants. The verse 3: 92 says you will never attain virtue until you spend something you are fond off; while Allah is aware of anything you may spend. About the virtuous it is described in the verses 76: 8-11 as, they offer food to the needy, orphans and captive out of love for Allah. That time their intention will be that we are only feeding you for Allah's sake, we want neither reward from you nor any thanks. We fear a gloomy, dismal day from our Lord, then Allah will shield them from that day's evil and they will meet Him with splendor and happiness. Allah says through the verses 92: 17-21 that the heedful will keep away from the fire. The one who spends money away and thereby purifies himself and who is not expecting any others reward except seeking the countenance of his Lord, the All Highest. Such a man shall be satisfied. The Virtue may be attained by giving wealth and help not only for Muslims but to any orphans, any indigent, and any wayfarer among the mankind. There may be murderers among the captives, while they are in jail; they are the vicegerents of Allah.

Allah created man in an independent nature i.e. the man has the right to select either ways -evil or right. By learning the Soul of Qur'an one can identify himself and the Creator, can mould the life depending upon his Lord and thus become self sufficient. Such a way freeing of captives can be achieved. So the virtuous people will utilize their all abilities and wealth for this purpose, and implement the teachings of Prophet that *the best among you is those who learn and teach the Soul of Qur'an.*

Certainly about all covenants shall be questioned, is told in the verse 17: 34. Anyone who enters to the path of Allah shall be subjected to trials. Whenever and wherever the Soul of Qur'an is explained shall be opposed by the hypocrites who forgot the covenant made with Allah. See explanation 2: 26-27. The virtuous people always remember Allah with the Soul of Qur'an in all their standing, sitting and laying. See explanation 2: 152. They will have firm consciousness and steadfastness that is the way of virtue. Such are the ones who make Qur'an true and only for them the Qur'an will witness and argue in favor. They are the one who bear Allah's vicegerents. The verse 49: 15 says, certainly those who believe in Allah and His Messenger and have never doubted that belief and have striven with their wealth and persons such are the only truthful. Today, the greatest strive is to learn and teach the Soul of Qur'an. It is commanded to the believers through the verse 25: 52 to do utmost strive against the disbelievers with the Soul of Qur'an. Read together the verses 9: 119; 33: 23 and 57: 19. See explanation 2: 5, 115, 156 and 157.

178. Oh you who believe, the equality has been prescribed for you in cases of murder: The free man for the free, the slave for the slave, and the female for the female. Anyone who is pardoned by in any way for it by his brother should follow this up appropriately, and handsomely make aments with him; that means a lightening as well a Mercy from your Lord. Then, anyone who exceeds the limit after that shall have painful punishment.

179. In the law of equality, there is life for you... Oh men of understanding; So that you may become heedful.

Whoever commits murder they are to be retaliated, i.e. if it is committed a freemen he has to be killed. If the murderer is a women, she has to be killed. If the murder occurred by mistake and the guardian of the slain forgives the retaliation, the murderer has to grant reasonable compensation. That should be given to the ancestors of the slain in the best manner.

'Anyone who exceeds the limits after that' means murder more people neglecting the concessions and Mercy from the Lord, implement the retaliation in a gruesome manner, not to give the compensation after deciding it or implement retaliation after accepting the compensation. They shall have a painful torment. It is told in the verse 17: 33 that you do not kill any soul that Allah has forbidden to you, except for just course means, except as retaliation. To conduct equality or to avoid it by accepting compensation has to be decided by the guardian or ancestors of the slain. A believer will never kill another believer except by mistake and whoever kills a believer by mistake, it is ordained that he has to free a believing slave and pay blood-money to the family of the murdered, unless they remit it freely, is told in the verse 4: 92. The verse 4:93 says, anyone who kills a believer deliberately will receive Hell as his reward to live in forever. And Allah will be angry with him and curse him and prepare dreadful torment for him. The son of Adam, *Qabeel* killed his brother *Habeel* deliberately and due to this he has to bear a part of the punishment of every murder takes place in the world, is taught by Prophet. It is told in the verse 5: 32 that if any one slew a person unless it for a retaliation or for spreading mischief on the land, it would be as if he slew the whole people, and if anyone saved a life it would be as if he saved the life of whole people. Each life is sacred in front of Allah since the '*Rooh*' -the soul plus life, is the part of Allah's *Rooh*. So committing the murder which separates *Rooh* from the body is equal to kill Allah.

If the retaliation is not implemented, the murders will increase without control. Bloodshed and mischief will expand throughout the world and that will result in the destruction of the Earth. Therefore it should be understood to the wise men that it is compulsory to retaliate for murder in order to keep the Earth in its equilibrium and to lead a natural life with tranquility and peace. That is why it is told that one should utilize the Soul of Qur'an as the Balance to keep the Universe in its equilibrium. These wise people are those who have identified the Creator, identified himself and aim of life. Today nobody is ready to put the do's and don'ts of the Qur'an into practice. Therefore there exist uncontrollable robbery, murder and mischief activities all over the world. See explanation 2: 2, 112, and 168.

180. It has been prescribed for you that whenever death faces one of you, if he leaves any property behind, that he has to make a bequest for parents and near relatives in a proper manner. This is a duty for the heedful.

This verse is revealed before the law of inheritance revealed in *surath An-nisa'*. It is ordained that those who die leaving any property should make a bequest to his parents, children and other relatives according to the proper manner. Then after the law of inheritance revealed in the *surath An-nisa'*, bequest prescribed in this verse is limited into one third of the total property and also ordered that there should not be any bequest to inheritors. The '*wasswiyath*' -bequest- is the ascertainment making by a man while he is alive and implement the inheritance after his death. Both the bequest and inheritance come into force after his death. This verse teaches that a believer knows the approach of his death. The verse 2: 241 also ends 'this is a duty of heedful'. Read together the verses 4:11-12 and 5:105-106. See explanation 2:106 and 107.

181. Then anyone who alters it once he had heard it, certainly the guilt shall be on those who alter it. Indeed Allah is all Hearing, all Knowing.

182. However there is no guilt to be charged who fears some alteration or any sin on the part of the bequest and so to make a smooth settlement among them. Indeed Allah is Forgiving, Merciful.

If a man made bequest against the do's and don'ts of Allah in wrong and partiality, there is no blame for those who heard the bequest to change it with more justice as according to the Soul of Qur'an. In other words, if the bequest is against the Soul of Qur'an, it should not be implemented.

183. Oh you who believe, fasting has been prescribed for you just as it was prescribed for those before you, so that you may become heedful.

184. On fixed number of days, then any of you who is ill or on a journey should make up the number of other days. For those who can afford fasting, but omit has to give food to poor man as ransom. Then if anyone gives voluntarily some more, it is better for him, although it is better yet for you to fast; if you only knew.

185. Ramadan is the month when the Qur'an was sent down, as Guidance for mankind, explaining clearly all the Guidance and as a criterion. Then any of you who witnesses that month should fast in it; while anyone who is ill or on a journey, the prescribed

days should be fulfilled in other days. Allah intends things to be easy for you and does not want any hardship for you. So complete the number and magnify Allah since He has guided you, so that you may become grateful.

The *swalath* and fasting are prescribed only for the believers, but Qur'an is revealed as the Guidance for entire mankind. Islam is the way of life satisfied by the Creator for all His creatures and there are fasting, *swalath, zakath*, etc. in all times. But in various "*Share'ath*" -cods of laws- their form, manner, number and character were different. It is prescribed fasting, *swalath* etc. in order to make the men self restrained and to become heedful. Here the numbered days mean the month of Ramadan which includes either 29 or 30 days. One can avoid fasting by giving food to a poor man, even if he is not ill or not on a journey. One day's food whichever he intakes have to be given as '*Fidiya*'-ransom. To give more food to more poor men is better. But to observe fasting is the best for those who know the Soul of Qur'an.

Since Qur'an is revealed in the month of *Ramadan* as the Guidance for entire mankind, the fasting is prescribed in that month. Read together the verse 2: 38. If it had been revealed in any other month, the fasting would have been prescribed in that month. Therefore, to learn and teach the Soul of Qur'an is the most important. The Soul of Qur'an and Prophet Muhammad are not only for the Muslims, but also for entire mankind, are told in the verses 7: 158; 21:107; 25: 1; 34: 28 etc. Those who follow the Soul of Qur'an are the heedful as explained in the verse 2: 2. Whatever the Guidance, It is included in the Qur'an which is the Words of Allah, The knower of all times -past, present, future, and all encompassed. That is why Prophet has taught that if anybody seeks Guidance other than in the Soul of Qur'an, Allah will let them free from the Guidance. Read together the verse 6: 38.

Furqan:- The Soul of Qur'an is the criterion and touchstone to identify truth and false, moral and immoral, light and darkness, justice and injustice, right and wrong, good and bad, the single way to the Paradise and various ways to Hell in all times and places of life. One should identify Allah and His party, satan and his party by utilizing the Soul of Qur'an as Criterion or Standard. Therefore those who do not accept the Soul of Qur'an as Criterion and Balance are associates in the dominion of Allah, and are included in the party of satan and losers in the Hereafter. The believers always keep remembrance of Allah with the Soul of Qur'an and ask all matters to Lord Allah by their hearts. By utilizing the Soul of Qur'an as Criterion they clear their all doubts and become firm believers. Then only they become grateful, otherwise they will be ungrateful disbelievers.

Allah commands through the verse 20:132 that Oh Prophet! Order your family for *swalath* and you be in constant of it, We do not ask you to provide sustenance; yet We will provide for you, and the blessed ending is for the heedful. Here, the meaning of saying 'Allah seeks not food' is that you should not observe fasting in difficulties by avoiding food, and the fasting should be by the soul for attaining the character of heedful. The verses 51: 56-57 say, I have not created Jinn and men except for serving Me, no sustenance do I require from them. Nor do I require that they should have to feed Me. Prophet taught as the explanation of this verse that how many fasting men become the victims of starvation by avoiding food and water since their fasting is not for Allah neglecting the Soul of Qur'an. See explanation 2: 121 and 152.

Oh Allah! Make us believers, always remembering You, Grateful and humble to You, fearing only You; make us learners, teachers and followers of the Soul Qur'an as It should be followed and enter us to the Paradise by taking the Soul of Qur'an as Ticket along with the fore-runners and virtuous. Oh, the Most Merciful One-among those who are Merciful.

186. Whenever My servants ask you about Me, (you say): I am indeed close to them. I answer for the appeal of the prayerful one whenever he appeals to Me. But let them respond to Me first and believe in Me as it should be believed, so they may become rightly be directed.

This verse revealed as a reply to the question of Prophet's companions whether Allah is near or far. It is told in the verse 50: 16 "We are nearer to him than his jugular vein and in the verse 57: 4 He is with you wherever you may be. The verse 89:14 says, indeed your Lord is ever watchful. The verse 40:19 says that He knows the treachery of the eyes and all that you hidden in chests. He knows the meaning of the breathing and heart beating is told, in the verse 84: 23. Through the verse 8: 24 by calling the believers Allah says: You respond to Allah and the messenger whenever He invites you to something that will give you life and you know that indeed Allah comes in between a person and his heart, and it is

He to whom you shall all be assembled altogether. As per the verse 59: 23 *Mu'min'* -the Believer- is mentioned as Allah's good name. So the believers are the ones who keep the Believer Allah in their hearts with the Soul of Qur'an. Both the verses 2: 34 and 38:74 end as he (satan) belongs among the disbelievers. The ones who do not make their soul mate believer with the Soul of Qur'an, they remain as disbelievers. See explanation 2: 152.

The verse 40: 60 says: your Lord has said, "Appeal to Me; I shall respond to you. The ones who are too proud to serve Me i.e. appeal to Me will enter Hell abused". But for getting answer to the appeal, there are two conditions mentioned in this verse. 1) They should respond to Allah's call first. 2) They have to believe in Allah as it should be believed. How can respond to Allah's call? When all mankind were sent down to the Earth from the Paradise, Allah said: "There will come to you the Guidance from Me, when it is received to you whoever follows the Guidance, on them there shall be no fear and for them will not be grieved". Today the Guidance for entire mankind is the Soul of Qur'an as told in the verse 185. 'To believe in Allah as it should be believed' means to understand Allah as revealed by 6236 verses. Therefore, only such believers will get the answer for their prayer. The *swalath*, fasting, *Zakath, hajj* etc. will be accepted only from them. As *hajj* is prescribed for mankind vide verse 3: 97, one can perform *hajj* without being a believer, but it will be accepted only after becoming a believer. Both the verses 13: 14 and 40: 50 end as the appeal of the disbelievers increase nothing except astray. As per the verses 7: 8-9 on the Day of Judgment the weight will be for Truth, Then those who increase their weight will prosper; while those who decrease their weight are the ones who have perished their souls because they had been darkening Our verses in this world. Those who do not utilize the Soul of Qur'an as the Balance in this world will not have any weight in the Hereafter. Read together the verses 40: 17, 57: 25. The Balance on which the deeds weigh on the Day of Judgment will be the Soul of Qur'an. See explanation 2: 147. Through the verses 18: 103-105 Allah says to ask the Prophet: "Shall We announce to you about those who have lost their deeds?" They are those whose aim of deeds was strayed during worldly life; while they reckoned that they were producing something fine. They are the ones who have hide the verses of their Lord and denied about meeting Him; so their deeds become lost and We shall setup no weighing for them on the Day of Judgment.

At least a part of a verse from the Qur'an is compulsory as the proof in order to accept any deeds. See explanation 2: 111. Those who do wrong and sins in the absence of the Soul of Qur'an, but repent after getting It, Allah forgive all sins at a time is told in the verse 39: 53 and a condition for that is prescribed in the verse 39: 55 as, to follow the Soul of Qur'an at the best. The verses 3: 21-22 say, certainly to those who hide the verses of Allah and slay the Prophets without justice and slay those people who learn and teach the Soul of Qur'an, pronounce the glad tidings to them a painful torment. They are those whose deeds will become futile in this world as well as in the Hereafter; nor will they have any helpers. The verses 4: 124; 16: 97; 20: 112; 21: 94 and 40: 40 say: No one enters to Paradise unless he is a believer. All the Prophets were believers and were included in the party of Allah, the only party which prospers. See explanation 1: 6.

No one become a believer without Allah's Permission-the Soul of Qur'an-as specified in the verses 10: 100 and 22: 65. The Hypocrites who hide the verses of Qur'an and the 'fujjar' who do not try to understand the Soul of Qur'an, but merely eat the body are the inmates of the Hell, and they abide therein forever as explained in the verse 2: 39. The verse 3: 4 says: Those who hide the verses of Qur'an shall have severe punishment, and Allah will revenge against them. It is told in the verses 6: 130; 7: 37 and 39: 59 that those who reject the Qur'an verses after receiving It and show arrogance as they have learned every thing will bear witness against themselves at the time of death as well as on the Day of Judgment that they were disbelievers.

It is told in the verse 7: 40 that Certainly for those who reject Our verses (*Fujjar*) and treat them with arrogance (Hypocrites), no opening will there be of the gates of Heaven, nor will they enter the Paradise until the camel can pass through the eye of the tailor's needle. Those who hide the verses of Qur'an are the losers of everything as explained in the verse 2: 121. It is told in the verse 35: 10 that the deeds shall not be accepted by Allah without the support of verses of Qur'an; nor the words of purity shall arise to Allah unless it is fulfilled by deeds.

It is told in the verse 13:18 that those who response to their Lord in the best manner are the successful and those who do not response, even if they had all that is in the Earth as much more would they offer for ransom from punishment on the Day of Judgment, will not be accepted. For them have a wicked reckoning, their abode will be Hell, what a worst cradles! See explanation 2: 159-161. It is told in the verse 39: 18, those who hear the Soul of Qur'an very attentively and then follow it in the best way are the ones whom Allah has guided and the ones endued with understanding. It is told in the verse 92: 5-7, then anyone who gives in the satisfaction of Allah, heedful and makes true the Best i.e. Qur'an, We will indeed make all the life way smooth and easy for him.

Those who live here without utilizing the Soul of Qur'an after receiving It are answering to the call of satan, and tomorrow the scene of how satan will say to them after the trial is warned in the verse 14: 22 as "blame not me for straying, but blame yourselves". It is told in the verse 67: 2 that death and life is made on you to test who among you works in this world in the best way as if seeing Allah. It is told in the verse 41: 31, who is better in speech than one who calls to Allah, does honorable deeds and proclaims that I am of those who submit whole to Allah. Then, to which Allah? The One who is presented by the Soul of Qur'an, call to Allah means call to Soul of Qur'an. Allah says in the verse 22: 24, you go ahead to the purest word and go ahead to His path Who is Self Worthy of all Praise. See explanation 2: 176.

Oh Allah! Make us fondness towards belief and aversion towards disbelief, hypocrisy and disobey. Oh Allah! Make us be guided with Soul of the Qur'an, make us leaders of guiding, make us one who commands righteousness; make us living as if seeing You. Make us all submitted to You by minds, words and deeds. Make us remembering you by heart and showing gratitude to You, make us courageous and forbearing persons, enlighten our heart with the Soul of Qur'an and decorate our conduct with Qur'an. Make us the followers of Qur'an as It should be followed. Make the Qur'an bear witness in favor of us, not against us; make the Qur'an argue in favor of us, not against us. Oh Allah! Enter us to the Paradise with the forerunners, and the victorious people by Your great Mercy, oh the Most Merciful among the merciful.

187. It is lawful for you to have intercourse with your wives on the night of the fast: they are the garments for you and you are the garments for them. Certainly Allah knows how you have been deceiving yourselves, so He has relented towards you and pardoned you. Therefore now onwards freely and frequently intercourse with them and seek what Allah has prescribed for you. And eat and drink until you can distinguish between the white and the black thread at day break. Then complete the fast till the

night appears, not mingle with women while you are secluded at your devotion in the Masjid. Such are Allah's limits, so you don't attempt to cross them. Thus Allah explains His verses to mankind in order that they may become heedful.

At the time of ignorant period men and women circle around *Ka'ba* in their naked state, but during the night in the bed they covered their body each one completely. And if the man wants to say something to his wife, they move their blanket a little and speak or touch, with fear that Allah is seeing them. This habit of them is mentioned in the verse 11: 5 as: "Indeed while they wrap their chest up to hide things from Him, whenever they attempt to cover themselves up with their clothing, does He know whatever they conceal, whatever they disclose? Indeed He knows the state of the chests". Read together the verse 10: 61. By revealing this verse Allah has permitted spouses to use single garment at their bed and allowed three occasions as their "*Ou'rath*" -nakedness-, as per the verse 24: 58. In the verse 7: 26 it is told that the heedful garment is the best i.e. the Soul of Qur'an.

'Certainly Allah knew what you have been deceiving yourselves' means before revealing this verse they were conducting intercourse in the nights of *Ramadan*, keeping a deformed understanding that Allah sees not in the darkness of nights. This verse teaches that during the nights of *Ramadan* drinking, eating and sexual intercourses are permitted like all other times, but they are only prohibited in the day time of *Ramadan* from dawn to dusk.

'Seek what Allah has prescribed for you with them' means sexual feeling is given to men by the Creator and it should be fulfilled in the satisfaction of Allah and witnessing Him. The great worship in Islam is the sexual intercourse where the two souls of man and woman become one and that is inducing the state as in Paradise. The verse 7: 189 says, He is the One Who created you from a single being and from that being He created his mate, so that he might find comfort with her. When he covers her, she conceives a light burden and walks around with it. When it grows heavy they both pray to Allah, their Lord saying: "If You will grant us an honorable child, we will be truly thankful". And the verse 30: 21 says: Among His signs is that He has created spouses for you from among yourselves so that you may console yourselves with them and He has planted love and kindness between you; in that there are signs for the people who think and reflect. Another meaning of saying: "Seek what Allah has prescribed for you with them" is you produce children by sexual intercourse. The verse 2:223 says: Your wives are your agricultural land; so go to your agricultural land as you like. Produce some thing for your souls and refrain from the displeasure of Allah. Bear in mind that you shall meet Him in the Hereafter, and give glad tidings to the believers. Prophet taught to pray at the time of intercourse "With the name of Allah, oh Allah! Keep away the despised satan from us and the child provided by this act for us".

Allah the Knower of all the Three Times, Knows that watches and clocks will come later in order to know the time, told here to eat and drink until the white thread can be distinguished by you from the black thread at day break. Therefore, on hearing the first call for *swalath*, there is no need to stop eating and drinking in order to enter the fasting. Prophet also taught that we can eat and drink until the second calling. But today just like deviated from teaching of Qur'an and Prophet in all life sectors, we can see majority of the Muslims will stop their eating and drinking by hearing the first call for *swalath* and enter in fast. This act of them is coming as Allah warned, some men serve Allah along the finches i.e. along the lines, and they are the losers in both worlds as told in the verse 22: 11.

During the last days of *Ramadan* while spending times in the *Masjid* as meditation should not approach with wives and even should not think about sexual intercourse. Since it is taught by Prophet that during the last days of the world the illiterates have to prevail biting the bottom of a tree and the literates have to prevail holding firmly the Soul of Qur'an with their molar teeth; today there is no 'meditation' in *Masjid*.

Allah told in the verse that He does make clear His verses for mankind in order that they may become heedful. Therefore it is the compulsory duty of Muslims who bear the Book to learn and teach the Soul of Qur'an to others in their own heart's languages. The verses 6: 51, 69; 7: 104; 20: 113 and 39: 28 also end as: 'In order that they may become heedful'.

188. Do not eat up one others wealth illegally, nor try to approach judges with it in order to attain a part of other people's wealth with sinfully while you realize.

The verse 4: 29 says, Oh you who believe! Don't consume others wealth illegally, unless it is for some business based on mutual consent among you. Do not kill yourselves by adopting illegal means. Indeed Allah is Merciful to you. If men covet others wealth illegally, there will grow up enmity, contempt and will cause increase murdering, bloodshed and destruction. This verse teaches that do not approach court with a forged case, give or accept bribery, tell lie, bear false witness in the court and eat up money earned through satanic activities like interest, gambling and liquor. The money earned through smuggling, hiding, black market, adulteration, black money and exploiting the ignorance of people are illegal. A believer should not feed his children by the money earned through all above mentioned illegal activities. Read together the verses 4:135; 22: 30 and 25:72. See explanation 2: 168 and169.

189. They will ask you about the phases of the moon (growth and decline of moon). Say: "They serve as date lines for mankind as well as the pilgrimage. It is not virtue for you entering in to houses through their back doors, but virtue is to keep Allah in your hearts; you get enter to the houses through their proper doors and heed Allah, so that you may prosper.

There were many superstitions existed in the ignorant period. For example, when the month of *hajj* comes, people were entering in their houses either on its back or by making a hole or through the windows for not seeing the moon. They did so for not seeing the phase of moon in order not to understand the time of *hajj* to escape from participating in it. Like that the Muslims in different part of the world today argue that they accept *Ka'ba* as *Qibla*, but they really do not accept It since they do not follow the fasting day, *Eid* day etc. as that of *Qibla* in *Mecca*. Not only that, they do not even know that the day is not varying in the world, but varies only in semi day. They do not have consciousness in such matters, but blindly follow their hypocritical leaders disobeying Allah and His messenger. Thus they obey the moon for fixing the fasting day and *Eid* day. They even consider the *Arafa* day, which is related to *Hajj* in different days. By doing so, they become the only people who prostrate to the moon denying the command of the verse 41: 37: "Among His signs are night and day light, the sun and the moon. Don't prostrate to sun nor to the moon; then you prostrate Allah alone who created them if you have been living only for the sake of Him". Read together the verses 6: 96 and 10: 5.

It is told in verses 10: 61; 12: 6; 22: 70; 34: 3 and 57: 22 etc. that whatever events occur in the Heaven, Earth and among you have been already decided by

Allah and that are recorded in the Book. It is told in the verse 55: 5 that an exact and limited route and law is determined for sun and moon. The meaning of what is told in the verse 55: 17: "The Lord of the two East and the Lord of two West" is both sun and moon rise from the east and set in the west, only day time or night changes anywhere in the world, and no change of full day. In which day the moon rises in Mecca where the Qibla is situated and is the center of the world, on that day itself all people in the world have to observe *Ramdan*, Fasting, *Arafa*, etc. if they are believers and then only they will become the acceptors of *Qibla*. Allah, the Knower of all Times who constructed all nations has constructed Mecca as the center of nations for not to see any divergent for people among believers except for the wrongdoers. It is told in the verses 9: 35-36 that the idolaters of Mecca shuffled days and months according to their likes, dislikes and whims. *Hajj* was not conducted in the real days before that of Prophet. Then *hajj* became performed in the real day only on the day of *Hajjathul-Vida*' onwards. Today, the Muslims by neglecting the Soul of Qur'an have deviated from the true Islam are observing fast, *Eid, Arafa, Hajj* etc. in different days all over the world. Thus they have become wrongdoers.

"To enter the houses through the proper doors" means to acknowledge open approach in all subjects without any twist, hide or reject and be conscious that Allah is acquainted of all things and observing. The verses 3: 130, 200; 5: 30, 90, 100; 7: 69; 8: 40; 22: 77; 24: 31 and 62: 10 also end as: " so that you may prosper." See explanation 2: 145,150 and 170.

190. Fight in the way of Allah to those who fight you, you do not be aggressors, certainly Allah does not love aggressors.

191. And kill them wherever you may catch them, and expel them from any where they have expelled you. Sedition is more serious than killing. Yet do not fight them at the sacred Masjid unless they fight you there. If they should fight you, then fight them back. Such is the reward for the disbelievers.

192. However, if they stop, indeed Allah will be forgiving, Merciful.

193. And fight them until there is no more sedition and the religion becomes exclusively for Allah. If they stop, let there be no hostility except towards wrongdoers.

Allah says in the verses 22: 39-40 by giving permission to the believers to fight, who were expelled from their own houses, from family members and from the country only because of that they believed in Allah and invited men to Him, "Certainly to those against whom war is made, permission is given to fight, Allah is the most powerful for their help. They are those who have been expelled from their homes for no cause except that they say our Lord is Allah. If Allah did not defend one sect of people by means of another, there would surely have been pulled down monasteries, synagogues, churches and *Masjids* in which the name of Allah commemorated in abundant measure! Allah will certainly help those who help Him". It is told in the verse 2: 216, "Fighting is prescribed upon you even if you dislike it. But it is possible that you dislike a thing, which is good for you and that you love a thing, which is bad for you. Allah knows and you know not". It is not allowed in the fight to kill women, children, old men, destruct animals, cultivations, etc. If anyone among the enemies heard not the words of Allah -the Soul of Qur'an, and if they ask asylum in front of the war should be granted it to him and escort him to reach the secure place, is told in the verse 9: 6.

By killing one his life ends, and no more persecution is thereafter. Whereas in sedition there is heavy torment not only to the body but also to the mind, it includes oppression and torture. That is why it is told 'the sedition is more serious than killing'. Islam means peace, tranquility and unity. The Soul of Qur'an is sent down in the language of Meccan associates. Almost all of them were literates, while Prophet and almost all his companions were illiterates. The Meccan associates were considered as disbelievers since they knowingly rejected and opposed the believers. Soul of Qur'an is the Balance and Trust to keep the Universe in its equilibrium. Then the hypocrites and their blind followers who associate others in the dominion of Allah neither utilize the Soul of Qur'an nor give It to other people to utilize are doing mischief and great sedition. That is why through the verses 4: 91; 9:123 and 33: 60-61 Allah commands the believers to kill them. But this command will be implemented only after the second coming of *Eisa*. See explanation 2: 99

"Fight them until there is no more sedition and the religion becomes exclusively for Allah" does not mean all men should become Muslims or believers, if it is so it will be against the verse 2: 256 that "there is no compulsion in religion". Read together the verses 10:99-100. No one can make anyone a

believer. It is Allah Who deputed mankind to Earth and also sent down the Soul of Qur'an as Guidance and Ticket to return to the Paradise. Islam is the only way of life satisfied by Allah for the entire mankind. Therefore it is ordained to the believers to fight to disbelievers until a circumstance prevails to observe their customs and belief not annoying by others.

In brief believers live exclusively for Allah, so they are fighting also for Allah. Allah says in the verse 8:17 to the believers who killed the enemies of faith in the battle of '*Badar*', "when you kill them, you killed them not; it was Allah who killed them". The battle of '*Badar*' is happened to identify in whose side the truth was. After the battle of '*Badar*', Allah asks through the verse 8:19 to the disbelievers, "if you asked the judgment, now has the judgment come to you; yet if you would only stop, it would be better for you; while if you aggress over again We shall too aggress. Your detachment will not give you any advantage. No matter how number it is. Allah stands always with believers". But next year in the 'Battle *Uh'd*, the final result was against Muslims. That was because no more Qur'an verses came to disbelievers of Mecca. And the Muslims in *Madeena* even though received Qur'an verses consequently, they did not increase their faith, instead they became more eager to achieve the 'booty of war', and they preferred the worldly life to the Hereafter. They forgot Allah and the aim of life and became transgressors. The battle of *Uh'd* at first glance was a failure to Muslims. Really the battle of *Uh'd* is happened to separate the believers from hypocrites, is told in the verse 3:166-167.

The enemies of Allah, the messenger and believers are the hypocritical transgressors, is told in the verse 64:4. And they have Hell fire as reward since they are repudiating Qur'an verses, is told both in the verses 7:51; 41:28. Today since there is not a group of believers anywhere in the world, there is no war or killing. Instead there is only Jihad with the Soul of Qur'an against the hypocritical disbelievers who hide It and the disbelievers who reject It, is told in the verse 25: 52. The disbelievers and wrongdoers are the same as explained in the verse 2: 254.

194. The prohibited month of battle matches with the prohibited month of battle, while sacred matters have the same compensation. Aggress anyone who aggresses you to the same extend as he has aggressed you, and heed Allah, and know that indeed Allah stands with the heedful.

As per the *Hijra* calendar the months *Dulka'd, Dulhajj* and *Muharam* are considered for *Hajj* and the month Rajab for *Um'ra*. Those months are considered as prohibited for battle from the time of Prophet *Ibrahim* itself. But gradually the idolaters of *Mecca* who were the strayed children of Prophet *Ibrahim* and *Isma'el* shuffled days and months according to their whims and fancies and fought against the believers during the prohibited months of battle, and they involved in the violence like robbery and theft. This verse is revealed ordering the believers to respond against such violence. Certainly the '*Nassee*" (shuffling the prohibited months of battle) is only an increase in disbelief. They made permissible what Allah prohibited and made prohibited what Allah permitted. Such wicked activities seem to be decorated to them by satan. Allah does not guide such disbelieving people as told in the verse 9: 37.

Now-a-days, when the day of *Arafa* comes on Friday, it is considered as *Hajjul-Akbar* -great *Hajj*, and so for convenience and in order to reduce the crowd, shifting it to another day, and observe fast and *Eid* in different days other than the day as in *Mecca* neglecting the *Qibla* are some of the examples for *Nasee'*. To postpone some important activities waiting to pass away the 10th *Muharam*, planetary evils, planetary conjunctures, looking of '*Nahs*' -ill omen day- for deciding marriage, house warming etc. all these non Islamic customs and rituals are coming as modern *Nasee'*. If the killings occur in the prohibited place, should be retaliated on the same place. The retaliation is described in the verse 5: 45 as: "Soul for soul, eye for eye, nose for nose, ear for ear, tooth for tooth and wounds for equal wounds". The verses 9: 36 and 123 also end as: know that indeed Allah stands wiith the heedful". It is told in the verse 16: 128: Certainly Allah is with those who is heedful and those who live seeing Him. See explanation 2: 179.

195. Spend in the way of Allah, and don't expose yourselves to ruin through your own hands. And live seeing Allah. Indeed Allah loves those who live seeing Him.

Through this verse Allah commands the believers to spend their sustenance for buying accessories of war such as weapons and vehicles. If they are niggardly, the enemies will succeed over them, thus may cause destroyed by their own hands. Those who are niggardly and bid others to be niggardly, hide the bounties which Allah has bestowed on them are the disbelievers. And Allah has prepared a heinous torment for such disbelievers, is told in the verse 4: 37. Read together the verses 9: 67-68. It is told in the verse 17: 29 that make not your hand tied to your neck, nor stretch it forth to its utmost reach, so that you become blames worthy and destitute. It is told in the verse 47: 38 that anyone who acts niggardly only so far as his own soul is concerned. Allah is transcendent while you are poor. If you should turn away He will replace you with some other people who then will not be like you at all!

Since there is no war in Islam today, to spend in the way of Allah means to spend money for learning and teaching the Soul of Qur'an to entire mankind irrespective of nation or religion. The believers who know the aim of life will spend all the bounties bestowed on them to learn and teach the Soul of Qur'an. Thus they help men to identify themselves, the Lord and the aim of life; thereby will try to stop bloodshed among mankind and to have human unity in whole world. By teaching the Soul of Qur'an they will make understand the men that they have fundamental right to observe any belief without hurting others, educate them to maintain water, air and environment without pollution to keep the Universe in its equilibrium. In brief being the vicegerents of Allah, believers' character and conduct will be that of Allah's i.e. to maintain peace and tranquility whereas the disbelievers being the representatives of satan will involve all evil activities to spread bloodshed such as a terrorism, racism, fascism, etc. The verse 5: 13 ends as: Indeed Allah loves those who live seeing Him. See explanation 2: 112.

196. Accomplish Hajj and Um'ra for Allah's sake. If you are prevented from doing so, offer a possible sacrifice. Don't shave your heads until after the offering has been reached its destination. For anyone of you who are ill or have an ailment on his head, (necessitating shaving) compensate either by fasting or feeding the poor or offering sacrifice. If any one wishes to make the Umra to the Hajj, he must make an offering such as he can afford. But if can't afford it, should fast three days during the Hajj and seven more days when you return home and thus complete ten days in all. That is for anyone whose family is not present at the sacred Masjid. Heed Allah and know that certainly Allah is firm in Retribution.

Umra: - For *Umra* from the appointed '*Meeqath*' -places scheduled for 'Ihram', one has to take bath and become fresh, after reaching *Mecca*, circle around seven times keeping the *Ka'ba* on the left, from '*Hajarul-Aswad*' (the

Black stone situated one of the corners of *Ka'ba*) to '*Hajarul-Aswad*' that is called '*Thwawaf*'. Then perform two *Raka'ath swalath* at '*Maqamu-Ibrahim*', reciting *Surath* '*Kafiroon*' in the first *Raka'ath* and *Surath* '*Ikhlas*' in the second *Raka'ath*; then walk to and fro starting from mount '*Safa*' and ending in the mount '*Marva*' for seven times. That is called '*Sa'ye*'. Then after that get release from Ihram after shaving or cutting the hair. '*Thwawaf*' and '*Sa'ye*' together is called *Umra*.

Hajj: - *Hajj* has three forms. (1) Thamathu' –In this form, after conducting '*Umra*' during the months of *Hajj* (from the first month *Showwal*), get free from Ihram. Then on the day of eighth *Dul-Hajj*, become fresh by taking bath, enter in to Ihram for Hajj at any place where he is and then go to Mina. Perform five times *swalath* there in the stipulated times shortening the *swalath* '*Dhuhur*' *As'r*, and *Esha'* in to two *Raka'ath* without *Jam'a*. On the day of ninth *Dul-Hajj* depart to *Arafa* after sunrise. Conduct the *swalath* of *Dhuhur* and *As'r* each in two *Raka'ath* jointly at the time of *Dhuhur*. Then stand in the Arafa excessively praying till sunset. After the sunset return to '*Musdalifa*' and conduct the *swalath Magh'rib* three and *Esha'* two *Raka'ath* jointly. Spend night at '*Musdalifa*', next day dawn after the prolonged prayer at the *Masjid Masharul Haram* till the sun rise; taking stones go to Mina, then throw seven times at *Jamrathul-Kubrah* (the pillar adjoining to Mecca). Then conduct sacrifice and shave the head, and after taking bath, go to *Ka'ba* and execute the *Thwawaf* and *Sa'ye* of *Hajj* and get release from Ihram. This is called first *Thahallul* (retirement). By this it is permissible what were prohibited in Ihram except intercourse. Here in this form the Umra is made joined to Hajj but retiring from Ihram after Umra, so it is ordained to offer a sacrifice for enjoying the things prohibited in Ihram. (2) Qiran:- In this form, make *Ihram* for *Hajj* and *Umra* jointly; i.e. after *Umra* not retiring from *Ihram*, stand in *Ihram* till *Hajj* ends. (3) Ifrad -In this form, makes Ihram exclusively for *Hajj* without *Umra* and goes to *Mina* directly. Those who have the sacrificial animal with them should take this form of *Hajj*.

The meaning of saying 'until after the offering has reached its destination' is to reach *Mina* where the sacrifice is conducted or till the animal be sacrificed on ailment condition. If anyone shaves his head before the sacrifice because of illness or has an ailment in his head shall give *Fidiya* –ransom as compensation. It may also have the meaning that if anyone is not in a position to cut his hair due to illness or shave his head before the sacrifice should give *Fidiya* and thus avoid from shaving the head. Prophet has prayed three times for those who shaved their head, after that only he prayed for those who cut their hair. Those who go to *Hajj* from India can accept the form of *Thamathu'*. But today in order to escape from sacrifice, some people after retiring from *Umra* go to *Madeena*. From there the adjoining days of *Hajj* by accepting the '*Qiran*' form they perform *Hajj* neglecting that Allah knows the states of mind. Those who conduct these kind of deeds have a severe retribution is warned through this verse. Read together the verse 22: 29. The verses 2: 211; 8: 13, 35 and 59: 4, 7 also end as "certainly Allah is firm in retribution". See explanation 2: 66 and 175.

197. The pilgrimage occurs during specific months. Anyone who decides to undertake pilgrimage during them shouldn't indulge in amorous intercourse, or any transgressing, or wrangling during the pilgrimage. Allah knows about any good you may do. So you increase provisions; yet the best of provision is to be heedful. So heed Me, oh men of understanding.

Amorous intercourse includes not only copulation but it includes kiss, glance, speech and behavior stimulating passion, embrace etc. The transgressing means to be in a state of forgetting Allah, and conduct deeds and speeches hiding from Allah which is not suitable for believers. See explanation 2: 6-7. Wrangling means dispute and counter dispute, that is to avoid the things which annoy other people like narrow-mindedness, to show proud in nationalism, language, color, speech and deeds like disturbing others for kissing the 'Black stone' etc. To increase provisions means to take some specific food items, clothes for Ihram, bed sheets in order to avoid begging, robbery, theft etc. In brief, the believers who are the guests and vicegerents of the Most Gracious should give preference to others in all matters than themselves. 'The best of provision is to be heedful means' one should become heedful by keeping Allah in their hearts. That is possible only with the Soul of Qur'an, which is the food, cloth and sight of the human souls as explained in the verse 7: 26. This is the only verse that ends as "so heed Me, oh men of understanding".

198. There is no blame on you if you seek the bounty from your Lord during the pilgrimage. When you return from Arafa (stay at Musdalifa), remember Allah near Masharul Haram. Remember Him as He has guided you, before that you were among the strayed.

'To seek the bounty of your Lord' means, during pilgrimage one can have trade of food items, clothes, chapels etc; that is beneficial to both the people and the trader himself. The *Quraishi* leaders did not go to *Arafa* as they were the preservers of *Ka'ba* and residents of there. Prophet taught that *Hajj* is *Arafa*. So everyone should stand in *Arafa*, otherwise *Hajj* will not be accepted. Standing in *Arafa* makes remembrance of the reckoning Day in the Hereafter. 'Remember Allah near *Masharul Haram*' means pray Allah by mind. 'Remember Allah as He has guided you' means follow the do's and don'ts of the Qur'an in order to be grateful to Allah and thus get ready to answer about each and every moment of the life after the age of fifteen. Read together the verses 7: 43. The verse 3: 90 says; indeed, those who disbelieve following their faith, then increase disbelief will never have their repentance accepted; such are the only strayed. See explanation 1: 7 and 2: 152.

199. Then stream forth from wherever the people stream forth and seek forgiveness from Allah. Certainly, Allah is Forgiving, Merciful.

200. Once you have performed your ceremonies, remember Allah just as you remember your forefathers, or even more fervently. There is the occasional men who says: "Our Lord give us (such and such) in this world", while he will have no share in the Hereafter.

201. And there is another kind of men who pray: "Our Lord! Give us fine in this world as well as fine in the Hereafter and shield us from the torment of Fire!"

202. Such will have a portion of any thing they have earned and Allah is swift in reckoning.

During the period of *Hajj* in ignorance, it was celebrated quoting the footprints and praises of forefathers. Therefore, from here onwards this is not permitted and ordained to remember and praise Allah alone, and should have the belief that each individual has to answer in front of their Lord about the life after the 15th age on the Day of Judgment. Therefore during *Hajj* each one has to confess before Allah every sin and should seek repentance. Today, to remember and celebrate the praises of Allah means to learn and teach the Soul of Qur'an. The hypocrites are the people who say: "Our Lord! Give us (such and such) in this world", while he will have no share in the Hereafter, as explained in the verse 2: 99. The believers, who know the aim of life, arrange the life of this world under the shadow of Qur'an aiming the victory of Hereafter. They themselves prevent Hell from here by utilizing the Soul of Qur'an as the Shield and Safeguard. This verse also teaches that everyone is earning Paradise or Hell in this world itself.

It is told in the verse 42: 20: 'for anyone who desires the harvest of the Hereafter, We give increase in his harvest, and for anyone who desires the harvest of this world We grant somewhat there of, but he has no share in the Hereafter. The verses 17: 18-19 say: Anyone who desires the transitory things of this life, We readily grant him such things as We please to whomsoever We wish, then We condemn Hell for him; he will roast in It, condemned and disgraced. Anyone who wants the Hereafter and makes a proper afford to achieve while he is a believer, will have their effort gratified. The verses 11: 15-16 say: Those who desire the life of this world and its splendors, they are given full reward of their deeds therein and shall not be diminished. They are the ones who will have nothing in the Hereafter except Hellfire. There they shall come to know that their deeds were futile and their actions were worthless. Being the explanation of these verses Prophet taught that this world is the harvest for the Hereafter. Therefore the believers do every deed aiming the victory for the Hereafter.

203. Remember Allah during the prescribed days. But if anyone hastens to leave within two days, there is no offence on him, while anyone who stays there is no offence either, but his aim should be bewaring Allah and then heed Allah, and know that you will be summoned to Him.

Here the prescribed days means three nights of staying at *Mina*. If anyone has indispensable matter, he can leave within two days, otherwise it is better to stay three nights, anyway he should keep Allah in hearts, i.e. he should remember every time that he has to answer about each moment of this life after the age of fifteen to his all seeing and all Knower Lord on the Day of Judgment. See explanation 2: 80 and157.

204. There is a certain man whose talks about worldly life dazzle you and he calls Allah to witness whatever is in his heart. He is extremely violent in quarreling.

These types of people are the hypocrites. They will say good words but they didn't do it. Through the verse 5: 41 Allah consoles the Prophet by saying:

Oh Messenger! Do not let those who rush off into disbelief worry you, such as those who say: "We believe" with their mouths, while their hearts do not believe. Through the verse 63: 1 Allah says: Whenever hypocrites come to you, they say: "We admit that you are Allah's Messenger. Allah already knows that you are His Messenger, while Allah testifies that the hypocrites are liars". They are the enemies of Allah, the Messenger and the believers, is told in the verse 63: 4. Read together the verses 48: 11-13. See explanation 2: 159-161.

205. Whenever he holds the upper hand, he rushes with his efforts towards Earth causing mischief, he destroys crops and breeding. Allah does not like mischief.

206. When he is told "heed Allah", arrogance will carry him to sin with strong. So Hell is enough for him, what an evil cradles!

Actually the aim of sending man to the Earth is to represent the Creator, to make the Earth as Paradise by cultivating crops and breeding, to do creative deeds for the benefit of all living things especially for mankind. But the hypocrites-vicegerents of satan- will encourage destroying the crops and breeding, bloodshed, ruining public properties etc, and thus they spread mischief which causes ruining of Earth.

But the deeds of the believer will be just opposite to the hypocrites. They will do creative activities for keeping air, water, etc. non-polluted and useful for living things. They know from the Soul of Qur'an that the mountains placed on Earth are nails to keep the Earth in its equilibrium. Therefore, they will not remove the mountains from their proper place. They will propagate the Soul of Qur'an in hearts language to entire mankind in order to establish the human unity. Wherever the bloodshed and mischief occur in Earth, the responsibility has to be born by the hypocrites since they know the remedy to stop it, but they not only utilize It but also not give others to utilize. See explanation 2: 11-12 and 99.

207. And among people there is one who sells his own soul seeking the pleasure of Allah. And Allah is full of kindness with His devotees.

The believers are those who follow the Soul of Qur'an and live only for Allah as His vicegerents on Earth. Their character is Qur'an -the words of Allah, which was the character of Prophet. It can be understood from the verse 9: 65

that Allah, the Qur'an and the Prophet are the same. Allah is full of kindness who values the activities of His servants. The verse 9: 111 says," Allah has bought up their persons and their property from believers, so they may have the Paradise instead. They fight for Allah's sake; they kill and are killed as a rightful promise from Him to be found in the old testaments, the Gospel and the Qur'an. Who is more trustworthy with His word than Allah? So rejoice in your bargain which you have reached with Him, that will be the supreme achievement

The verses 9: 71-72 say: The true believers, both men and women, are protectors of one another. They enjoin what is just and forbid what is evil; they establish regular *swalath*, pay welfare tax, as well as obey Allah and His Messenger. Such Allah will grant Mercy to; surely Allah is Powerful, Wise. Allah has promised to the believers, both men and women, Paradise beneath which rivers flow to live therein forever and they will have beautiful mansions in the Paradise of everlasting bliss. The pleasure of Allah is the greatest; that will be the supreme achievement. The verse 3: 30 also ends as Allah is full of kindness to His servants. See explanation 1:4 and 2: 195.

208. Oh, you who believe, enter absolutely in to Islam, do not follow satan's footsteps. He is an open enemy of yours.

See explanation 2: 168-169.

209. If you should lapse after explanations have come to you, then know that Allah is Powerful, Wise.

'Enter in to Islam absolutely' means accept Islam as the way of life wholeheartedly without any compulsion or hesitation. One should not have the evil thoughts like racialism, nationalism, communalism, selfishness, organizational partiality etc. and represent the impartial Allah in whole life, keep the remembrance of Allah in all walking, sittings, lying with the Soul of Qur'an. See explanation 2: 152. One can enter in to Islam wholeheartedly only after becoming a believer and followinf the total do's and don'ts of Qur'an. See explanation verse 2: 186. The verse 3: 102 says; "Oh, you who believe, heed Allah the way He should be heeded and should not die unless you are Muslims". You should not follow the footsteps of satan since it is come to you the Soul of Qur'an- the explanations- and Insight to see the ways of satan and Allah. If you follow the way of satan which is the way of nine hundred and ninety-nine out of every thousand men and Jinn, you will be the inmates of the Hell with satan. See explanation 2:132.

210. Are they only waiting for Allah to come along to them in the shadow of clouds as well as with the Angels, then the matters will be settled? Unto Allah do matters return!

The verse 6: 158 says: Are they waiting for the Angels or your Lord to come down to them or are they waiting to be given a certain sign of your Lord! On the Day when that certain sign of your Lord appears, the belief will not profit that soul which did not believe before, nor earned good through his profession of faith. Say: "You wait; we too are waiting". Allah asks this question to those who are not ready to follow the do's and don'ts of Qur'an? See explanation 2: 176. That is, do you wait for belief when death comes to you; are you waiting for death for doing goodness? In case of individual, death is the '*Qiyama*'. In that time the soul of believers look towards Allah with pleasure and soul of disbelievers look satan with sad as told in the verses 75: 22- 24. In the verse it is not mentioned that the disbelievers will see satan, if one is not seeing Allah through the Soul of Qur'an he will see the satan. The disbelievers will not see Allah in the Hereafter also. The verse 83: 15 says; indeed they will be screened off from their Lord on that Day. See explanation 1: 4 and 2: 175. The verses 25: 25-26 say: On that Day when the sky shall burst asunder with clouds and the Angels will be sent down ranks after ranks, the real Kingdom on that Day will belong only to the Impartial, it will be a hard Day for the disbelievers. Read together the verse 69: 17.

The verses 39: 55-59 say: Follow the best way that is revealed to you by your Lord before the death comes to you all of a sudden while you do not even perceive it. Lest someone should say: 'Alas! I neglected my duty towards Allah and I was one of those who mocked at His verses.' Or lest he should say: 'If Allah had guided me, I would have been one of the righteous.' Or lest he should say upon seeing the punishment: 'I wish I had another chance, I would certainly be among the one who live seeing Allah'. Then Allah will say to him: "Nay, My verses did come to you; but you rejected them, and were arrogant and were among the disbelievers". The verses 3: 109, 7: 44, 22: 76, 35: 4, and 57: 5 also end as "unto Allah do matters return". See explanation 1: 1-3.

211. Ask the children of Israel, how many clear signs We have given them, and anyone who changes Allah's favor once it has come to him, should know that Allah is severe in punishment.

See the verses 2: 40-60 for understanding the clear signs sent down to the children of Israel. The verse 22:16 says, "Thus have We sent down the clear verses and certainly Allah guides anyone He wants". The great Blessings and Mercy of Allah to entire mankind is the Soul of Qur'an. Those who hide It by not utilizing oneself and not giving It to other people, and thereby if the people who have not received the Qur'an misunderstand that this Qur'an only made these people the worst, and refuse to accept and understand It; the punishment should be borne by the non believing Muslims. Read together the verses 5: 67 and 6: 26. See explanation 2: 85, 176.

212. The worldly life has attracted to those who disbelieve. They ridicule those who believe! Yet those who are heedful will stand ahead of them on the Day of Judgment; Allah provides sustenance without measure to whom He wishes.

The verse 6:53 says: Even so do We try some of them by means of others so they may say: "Are those among us towards whom Allah has been Gracious? Is Allah not quite aware as to who are grateful?" The answer of the disbelievers to Prophet *Nooh* is mentioned in the verse 11: 27 as: "We see you as no more than merely a human being like ourselves; and we see that no one has followed you except the meanest among us, who are immature and without reflection; and we find nothing in you which gives you superiority over us: rather we think that you are lying". As per the verses 7: 88-89 the arrogant proud leaders of Prophet *Shuayb's* people said as: "Oh *Shuayb*! We will certainly run you as well as those who believe along with you out of our town or you should return back to our way of life. *Shuayb* replied: "Even though we detest it? We would invent a lie about Allah if we return to your way of life now after Allah has saved us from it. It is not possible for us to turn back unless Allah, our Lord, should wish us to. Our Lord has vast knowledge of everything. On Allah we have entrusted. Our Lord! Decide between us and our people with Truth, for you are the best among the deciders".

The disbelievers are the *mujrims* include both *fujjar*- who try not to learn the Soul of Qur'an and the hypocrites- who hide It. The Impartial Most Gracious gives more wealth, children and power in this world to these disbelievers, because they have Hell in the Hereafter. But the disbelievers misunderstand that Allah blessed them as they are in truth. The verse 9: 55 says: Let neither their wealth nor their children dazzle you: in reality Allah intends to punish them with these things in this life and that their souls may depart while they are still disbelievers. And they ridicule the believers who lead simple life aiming the permanent victory of life in the Hereafter. In the Hereafter the believers will be above them. The verse 6: 112 says: Oh Prophet! like that We had granted each Prophet his opponents - satans from among the mankind and *Jinns* - some of them inspire the others with seductive discourses of deception. If your Lord wanted, they would not have done so. Therefore, neglect them as well as what they invent. 'Human satans' mentioned here are the *mujrims* including hypocrites and *fujjar*. The verse 25: 31 says: That is how We made for every Prophet an enemy among the *mujrims*, but your Lord is sufficient for you as a Guide and Helper.

About a scene is warned through the verse 7: 48-51 that the disbelievers will ask for water and food to the believers in the Paradise. It is told in the verses 83: 29-34 that certainly, the *mujrims* used to laugh at the believers in this world and whenever they passed by them, they used to wink at each other in mockery, and they returned to their own family with jesting. And whenever they saw the believer they would say: Behold! These are the people truly astray. But they had not been sent as keepers over the believers. Therefore it is warned, in this Day (in the Day of Judgment) that the believers will laugh at *kuffar* - those who were repeatedly hiding the verses.

Then who has made this life attracted to the disbelievers? It is not the Impartial Allah, but the disbeliever satan. As per the verses 6: 43 and 19: 83 it is told: Why did they not humble themselves when the sufferings overtook them? On the contrary, their hearts became hardened and satan made their sinful acts seem fair to them. All the verses 6: 10; 9: 79; 11: 38 and 21: 41 say that the disbelievers will mock at believers and Prophets in this world, and tomorrow that mockery will turn against them. The verses 3: 27 and 24: 38 also end as, Allah provides sustenance without measure to whom He wishes.

213. Mankind was once a single community, then Allah deputed Prophets as heralds and warners. And He sent the Book down, along with them to bring the Truth, so as to decide among mankind concerning whatever they had been disagreeing about. None disagreed in it except those to whom It was given after the explanations had been brought them out of envy towards one another. Allah has guided those who believe from the matters

they have disagreed about the Truth with His permission. And Allah guides anyone He wishes to the Straight path.

The verse 10: 19 says: Once mankind was none except a single community; then they disagreed. If word had not come ahead from your Lord, what they have been disagreeing over would have been settled for them. All Prophets came in Islam to teach that "No Deity except Allah". The verse 21: 25 says: We didn't send any Messenger before you unless We inspired him with the fact "there is no Deity except Me, so serve and live for Me alone". The verse 16: 2 says: He sends down His Angels with inspiration from His Command to whom He wishes of His servants, saying: "warn mankind that there is no Deity except Me, so heed Me". Read together the verse 16: 36.

All Prophets were given only The Book, which is the Soul of Qur'an - the Truth. See explanation 2: 2, 147. In all times, only those who were given the Book divided in to schism. The verse 98: 4 says: Nor did those who were given the Book disagree about It, until after Explanations had come to them. Here the Explanation mentioned is the Soul of Qur'an. The verses 42: 13-14 say: He has ordained for you the same *Dheen* – way of life which He enjoined on Prophet *Nooh* - and which We have revealed to you, Oh *Muhammad* - and which We enjoined on *Ibrahim* and *Moosa* and Jesus: "Establish the *Dheen Al-Islam* and make no division in It". What you invite them to do seem intolerable for associates. Allah chooses anyone He wishes for Himself, and guides to Himself anyone who repents. They only separated after knowledge had come to them, because of envy towards one another. If word from your Lord had not already gone on ahead till a specific period, things would already have been determined among them. The fact is that those who were made to inherit the Book after them, are surely in never ending doubt concerning It. See explanation 2:176.

In the verses 45: 16-18 say: We already gave the children of Israel the Book, discretion and Prophethood, and We provided them with wholesome things and let them excel over everyone in the worlds. We gave them explanations from the Command. They only disagree after the knowledge- explanation- had come to them, out of envy towards one another. Your Lord will judge among them on the Day of Judgment concerning anything they have been differing over. Then We placed you on a *sharee'ath* -high way- from the Command, so follow along it and do not follow the whims of those who do not know. See explanation 2:120. Allah commands through the verse 3: 103 to believers to hold firm the rope of Allah which is the Soul of Qur'an and there by become one party i.e. the party of Allah as mentioned in the verses 5:56 and 58: 22. And the verse 16: 64 says: We have not sent down the Book to you except you may explain to them what they are differing over, and as a Guidance and Mercy for the people who believe. So the believers should confirm that their abode is Paradise from this world itself by utilizing the confirming Truth- Soul of Qur'an- as the Balance.

"Bi'idnihee" - by His permission - means the Soul of Qur'an. The verse 14:1 says that We have sent down this Book to you in order that you might lead mankind out of the depths of darkness in to the light by the Soul of Qur'an- towards the way of Exalted in power, Praise Worthy. Read together 24: 45-46. The verse 42: 52says: thus We have revealed a spirit (Qur'an) from Our command for you. You did not know what either the Book or faith was. But We have set It up a Light, **by means of which** We guide any of our servants whom We wishes. Verily you do guide the people to the Straight path. It is told in the verse 3: 101 that whoever holds fast Allah, already guided towards the Straight path. 'Hold fast Allah' means hold fast the Rope of Allah i.e. the Soul of Qur'an. See explanation 1:3, 6 and 2: 111.

Since the Impartial Allah has already given both ways (to the Paradise and Hell) i.e. the Soul of Qur'an to each individual, He will not lead any one to Paradise or Hell. So each soul should ask Allah individually for the Guidance by His permission - the Soul of Qur'an. Nobody including Prophet Muhammad can guide any one to Paradise. The verse 28: 56 which revealed in the case of *Abu-Thwalib*, the co-father and guardian of Prophet says: Indeed you do not guide someone you love, but Allah guides anyone He wishes. He is quite aware as to whom are to be guided. It is told in the verse 2: 272 that guiding them is not your duty, but Allah guides anyone He wishes to. See the explanation 1: 5 and 2:186.

214. Or did you reckon that you will enter Paradise when the same thing never happened to you such as happened to those who have passed away before you? They were afflicted with suffering and adversity assailed them, and were so violently shaken up until the Messenger and the believers with him cried out: "When will Allah's help come? Then they were comforted with the words: Be aware! Allah's help is ever close".

The verse 3: 146 says: "In the past many Prophets have fought in the way of Allah, with a large number of proud servants of Allah. They did not lose heart during the adversities that befell them in the path of Allah; they neither showed weaknesș nor bowed down their head to falsehood. Allah loves such patients". Mankind is sent down to Earth for trial. Only those who hold firm the Soul of Qur'an and seek refuge in Allah will be succeeded. It is taught to the believers through the verse 2:286 to pray as, "our Lord, Do not take us to task if we have forgotten or slipped up! Our Lord, do not lay any obligation upon us such as those You placed on those before us. Read together the verses 3: 142; 5: 65-66; 6: 42- 45; 7: 94-96 and 9: 16. See the explanation 2: 155- 157.

215. They ask you what they should spend in charity. Say: "Whatever you spend from the good should give it to parents, close relatives, orphans, the needy, and wayfarer. Allah is aware of any good you do.

This is the first verse revealed in the law of *Zakath*. It is commanded through the verse 26: 214 to warn the close relatives first with the Soul of Qur'an. The good mentioned in the verse is about the property. The verse 22: 77 says, "Oh, you who believe! Bow down your head, prostrate yourselves and serve only Allah and do good deeds in order that you may prosper. In this verse and generally "the good deed" means learning and teaching the Soul of Qur'an. It is told in the verse 25: 52 to strive strenuously with the Soul of Qur'an to the disbelievers who hide It. Read together the verse 4: 127. The verses 2: 273; 3: 93 also end as "Allah is Aware of any good you do". See explanation 2: 148.

216. Fighting is also prescribed for you, even though it may seem detestable to you. It may be you detest some thing which is good for you; while perhaps you love some thing even though it is bad for you. Allah knows, while you do not know.

Allah asks through the verse 4: 75, "what happened to you not to fight in the cause of Allah. Those who are being weak from men, women and children pray that our Lord! Rescue us from this country whose people are oppressors and raise one for us from You who will protect and help us". The believers believe that good and bad - everything - is from Allah. They fight in the cause of Allah, become martyrs and thus buy Paradise. See explanation 2:154. The verse 4: 74 says :Let it be known that only those people should fight in the cause of Allah who are willing to exchange the life of this world for the Hereafter; and whoever fights for the cause of Allah, whether he dies or is victorious, will soon be granted a mighty reward. Read together the verse 9: 111. It is told in the verse 4: 77 that have you not turned your attention to those who were told to hold back their hands and establish *swalath.* A section among them feared men as - or ever more than they should have feared Allah and they ask: "Our Lord! Why have ordered us to fight? Would you not grant us respite to our term". Say worldly enjoyment means little while the Hereafter is better for anyone who is heedful. You will not be wronged a bit. Read together the verse 4: 66. In the verse 8: 65 by calling the Prophet, Allah says: "Encourage the believers for the fight". It is told in the verse 47: 20: "When a *Surath* remembering about fighting is revealed, in whose heart there is a disease will be looking at you as if they were going to faint from fear of death". Read together the verses 2: 246; 33: 25. See explanation 2: 190-193.

The verses 2: 232; 3: 66 and 24: 19 also end as: Allah knows, while you do not know. The verse 16: 74 ends as: Surely Allah knows, while you do not know. But today there is no '*Qithal*' - fighting and slaying, on the other hand there is only '*Jihad*' - strenuous strive - with the Soul of Qur'an against the disbelievers who hide It. Read together the verse 9: 73. See explanation 2:195.

217. They ask you about fighting during the sacred month. Tell them: "Fighting in It is a serious; while obstructing Allah's way, disbelief in Him and the Sacred Masjid, and turning His people out of It are even more serious with Allah. Even sedition is more serious than killing". They will not stop fighting until they succeed in turning you back from your religion if they can manage to do so; and anyone of you who abandons his religion and dies while he is a disbeliever, will find their actions will miss carry in this world and the Hereafter. And such are the inmate of Fire; they shall remain in It forever.

Once Prophet deputed eight member team to *Naqla* - a valley between *Thaif* and *Mecca* – in order to observe the movement of *Meccan pagans*. They saw a group of pagan merchant returning to Mecca. They attacked and killed of them by thinking about the consequences after they reach *Mecca* and inform about them. As well as others were brought to *Madeena* as captives with their wealth. This event occurred either in the last days of the 6th month, *Jamadul Akhir* or in the beginning of 7th month, *Rajab*. Then the Meccan pagans and the

Jews as well as the hypocrites in *Madeena* started to spread allegation that Mohamed and his followers are fighting in the prohibited month, *Rajab*. As a result, the verse which commands for the fighting is revealed. This verse teaches that, if the believers after their faith turn back and die in hypocrisy, their deeds will become in vain and will fall into the Hell forever. Read together the verses 3: 91; 5: 36 and 10:54

It is told in the verse 5: 54 that Oh you who believe, if any among you turn back from his faith, soon will Allah replace a people whom He will love as they love Him, smooth with believers and harsh against rejecters and striving in the way of Allah, and not fear reproach from any critic. Such is Allah's bounty which He gives to anyone He wishes. Allah is Boundless, Aware. Read together the verses 9: 69; 33: 18- 19; 47 and 24- 25. See explanation 2: 105 and 191.

Oh, Allah make us not among the rejecters and losers, make us the followers of the Soul of Qur'an as It should be followed and enter the Paradise with Your righteous servants. Oh, the Most Merciful among those who are merciful!

218. Surely those who have believed, and who have migrated and striven for Allah's sake may expect to receive Allah's mercy; for Allah is Forgiving, Merciful.

Prophet taught that there is no migration after the victory of Mecca, but there is only strenuous strives with the Soul of Qur'an. The verses 8: 72- 75; 9: 16, 20, 71- 72, 88; 16: 110; 29: 6, 69; 49: 15 and 61: 11 stimulate for *Jihad* - strenuous strive - which means to utilize all abilities for the fulfillment of the aim of life. Today the greatest strive is to learn and teach the Soul of Qur'an to the entire mankind such that they may utilize It as the Balance and Trust to keep the Universe in its equilibrium as well as the Safeguard and Shield from the Hell and as a weapon against terrorism. See explanation 2: 145, 195.

219. They ask you about liquor and gambling. Say: "In each of them there lies serious sin as well as some benefit for mankind. Yet their sin is greater than the benefit". They ask you what they should spend; say: "As much as you can spare". Thus Allah explains His verses to you, so that you may think and reflect.

The verse 2: 266 also ends as "so that you may think and reflect".

220. Concerning this world and the Hereafter. They ask you about orphans. Say: "It is the best to deal with them justly; you may become co-partners with them, after all they are your brethren; Allah knows the mischief makers from the reformers. If Allah so wished, He might crush you. Surely Allah is Powerful, Wise."

The verse 2: 219 is revealed as the first stage of liquor eradication. Thereafter in the verse 4: 43 it is told to the believers, approach not *swalath* in a state of intoxication and until you know what you are saying. The *swalath* without the participation of soul will cause evil than good, and it is forbidden to recite the Qur'an without the participation of soul even in the *swalath* as taught by Prophet in the explanation of this verse. Prophet also taught to avoid *swalath* in the state when one is overcome by sleepiness, hunger and fatigue; and having urgency excretion or discharges. As the final stage, by calling the believers through the verses 5: 90-91 say: Certainly liquor, gambling, dedication to idols and division by arrows (lottery) are the filthy works of satan. Then get away from him, so that you may prosper. satan desires to stir up enmity and hatred between you with intoxicants and gambling and to prevent you from the remembrance of Allah and from *swalath* maintaining the Soul of Qur'an. Then will you not abstain?

Liquor includes all the opiates, ganja, cocaine, hashish, and all drugs abusing intoxications. All the things which make the intoxication are forbidden as taught by Prophet. Gambling includes playing cards, lottery etc by which earnings are made easily without effort. The verse 2: 215 is revealed as the first regulation about the welfare tax, explaining to whom it should be given. Then their question how much and what should they spend is replied through this verse, that spend the balance after the expenditure. Then in the verse 9:60 the list of deserved persons for paying welfare tax is revealed. Allah does make clear His verses in order that you may think and reflect. 'Concerning the life in this world as well as the Hereafter' means, mankind after their creation in the Paradise is deputed to Earth for constructing the Paradise here by using all the blessings that Allah bestowed upon them which they do not bring when they came and do not carry with them when they return, and he can inherit that Paradise after his death. The instrument for this is the Soul of Qur'an which is the greatest Bounty, but only the believers utilize It.

The verse 4:2 says: give orphans their property, do not substitute worthless things for good ones, nor swallow their wealth along with yours, indeed that is a great outrage. Then as per the verse 4: 10 those who unjustly eat up the property of orphans are filling fire in to their own bellies, they will eventually roast in a Blaze. Because of these verses, the believers in *Madeena* were worrying that if they mix their wealth with that of orphans will lead them to Hell unknowingly. At that time Allah advised them through this verse that, "It is the best to deal with the orphans justly; you may become co-partners with them, after all they are your brethren; Allah knows the mischief makers from the reformers. If Allah so wished, He might crush you. Surely Allah is Powerful, Wise". Really the believers will give preference to orphans than their own sons in all matters. Those who honor the orphans are the believers and the victorious as per the verse 89: 17.

Oh, Allah! Do not include us among the mischief makers, include us among the reformers. Oh, Allah! Show us the Truth as Truth and bless us to follow It, and show us the falsehood as falsehood and bless us to apart it.

221. Do not marry women who associate others with Allah, until they believe; a believing maid is better than a free associating woman, no matter how attractive she may seem to you. Do not let your daughters marry men who associates others with Allah until they believe; a believing slave is better than a free associator, no matter how attractive he may seem to you. Those people invite you to fire while Allah invites you to the Paradise and forgiveness by His Permission. He explains His verses to mankind in order that they may remember by hearts.

It is told in the verse 5: 5 that it is made lawful all wholesome things unto you, and so is the food of those who were given the Book lawful for you, while your food is lawful for them. And believing chaste woman is lawful to marry as well as chaste woman from among those who were given the Book before you, provided that you have to give them their due dowers and taken them in wedlock respectably, in order to avoid seeking any thrills and taking mistresses. It is told in the verse 4: 25 that if you do not have the wealth to wed free believing woman, let them marry believing maid from among those whom your right hand possess. As explained in the verse 2:186 only the believers shall enter in to the Paradise. So it is the duty of a believing man to save himself and his family members from the Hell. The verse 66: 6 says: Oh, you who believe! Save yourselves and your families from the Hellfire, whose fuel is men and stones; in the charge of fierce and mighty Angels who never disobey Allah's command and who promptly do what they are commanded to do. Men are the custodians of women as told in the verse 4: 34 that men are overseers over women since Allah has given some persons advantages over others, and because they should spend their wealth on them.

It is very easy to teach the woman from the people of the Book the faith- Soul of Qur'an - as they have the knowiedge of the Book. But it is not allowed to wed the believing women to the men of associates from the people of the Book as taught by Prophet, since men are custodians of women, she can't teach him the belief. Marriages are conducted by considering four matters like beauty, nobility, wealth and faith (*Dheen*). The meaning of the saying: 'No matter how attractive she/he may seem to you' in the verse is that the believing men and women give importance to Faith, and not for the other three matters. The marriage shall be conducted between men and women who know the Soul of Qur'an. Then only there will come good offspring and there by gathered together in the Paradise.

It is told in the verse 11:17 that anyone from the groups who disbelieve with the Witness-the Soul of Qur'an, then Fire is the promised abode to him. It is notable that here not mentioned "anyone from mankind" instead "anyone from the groups" who received the Soul of Qur'an. See explanation 2:121. Do not wed the believing woman to the hypocrite men who are killed by Allah as per the verse 63: 4. The verse 9: 68 says: Allah has promised the hypocrite men and the hypocrite women, and the hiders of Truth the fire of Hell to live therein forever, a sufficient recompense. Allah has cursed them and they shall have a never ending punishment. 'The hiders of Truth' mentioned here include both men and women who associate others with Allah after receiving Soul of Qur'an. The intention of revealing the Trust- the Soul of Qur'an is told in the verse 33: 73 as: To punish the hypocritical men, the hypocrite women, the men and the women who associate in the dominion of Allah, and that Allah will turn in Mercy to the believing men and the believing women: for Allah is Forgiving, Merciful. Since today there is no group of believers anywhere in the world marital life among believers is not possible. As per the verse 66: 11-12 Allah has made *Pharoh's* woman and *Maryam* –descendant of Imran- as fine models for both men and women believer. During these days it is advised by the prophet to stay by holding fast the Soul of

Qur'an with molar teeth individually. Therefore any men and women can only marry if they are ready to lead a life under the Soul of Qur'an. See explanation 2: 176.

"By His permission" means with the Soul of Qur'an i.e. each one should read the Soul of Qur'an by praying in mind "Oh my Lord! Increase my knowledge". As it says 'He explains His verses to mankind for remembering by hearts' means it is made easy to understand the Soul of Qur'an by hearts. So it is the extreme duty of Muslims, who have received the Soul of the Qur'an to propagate It to others. Read together the verses 18: 57; 32: 22 and 54: 17. The verses 14: 25; 28: 43- 46, 51; 39: 27 and 44: 58 also end as so that they may remember by hearts. See explanation 1: 6-7; 2: 170, 213.

222. They ask you about menstruation. Say: "It is a nuisance; so, keep away from women during their menstruation and do not approach them until they are cleansed. Once they cleanse themselves, and then go to them just as Allah has commanded to do. Surely Allah loves those who turn to Him in repentance and keep themselves clean.

Menstruation is a state of impure; so in that state one should not intercourse with women. The Jews were kept away from women in their menstrual period completely. But the Christians conducted sexual intercourse even during the menstrual period. Therefore the believers as taught by the Prophet have to take a moderate state during the menstrual period that all other bodily contacts are permissible except sexual intercourse. Here it is taught when the women are cleansed from menstruation, natural sexual actions are permitted by using the organs which Allah made for that purpose. The meaning of what satan told in the verse 4: 119 that I will shuffle the nature created by Allah, is I will order to conduct unnatural sexual actions.

Prophet taught that after the sexual intercourses if the situation permits take bath or at least take ablution before going to sleep. That will give vitality and increase interest for more sexual intercourses. Otherwise, the Angels '*Raqeeb*' and '*Atheed*' will not record the deeds of those who have '*Janabath*'- seminal ejaculation. As the customs of Prophet it is the habit of believers to take bath or take ablution before going to sleep as well as after the sexual intercourse.

Prophet also taught to pray when we wash our left leg in the last phase of ablution: *Oh Allah, forgive my sins and expand my home, give increase in my sustenance for life.* Also taught after testifying that "no Deity except Allah and Muhammad is His Messenger" to pray as *"Oh Allah, include me among those who turn to you in repentance more, and those who ordain others to attain purity more, and include me among the servants who are honorable".*

223. Your wives are your cultivation place; so go to your cultivation place whenever you wish. Send things on ahead for yourselves, and heed Allah; know that you will be meeting Him proclaim such to believers!

Every organs of body has its own duty. The genital organs of both men and women are to fulfill their sexual passions naturally as Allah satisfied. Therefore, one can approach their wives for sexual intercourse in anyway-from front, back, or sitting, lying- but it must be by using the genital organs witnessing Allah under the shadow of Qur'an. The life in the Paradise will be immortal and eternal. Intercourse should give the stature of the immortal and eternal life in the Paradise. Through this deed the spouses can be experienced the presence of the Creator. So in Islam it is the greatest form of serving Allah. See explanation 2: 187.

'Send things on ahead for yourselves' means the honorable offspring of the believers represent them on the Earth even after their death, so produce more children and teach them the Soul of Qur'an in order to identify the Creator, who is men, and the aim of life on Earth before their fifteenth age. Otherwise the horrible scene in the Hell is warned through the verse 7: 38 as: say: "Enter the Fire and join the community of *Jinns* and men who have gone before you". While each community will enter Hell, it will curse its predecessors till all are gathered there in a narrowed place, the offspring will say about the parents: "Our Lord! These have led us astray; therefore give them double punishment of the Fire". He will answer: "There will be double for all, although you may not know because of being predecessor or successor in sin and aggression". To fulfill the teaching of Prophet that this world is a cultivation place for the Hereafter, one has to arrange his entire life in accordance with the Soul of Qur'an.

The verse 9: 105 says: Tell them: "Do as you will. Allah will see your deeds, and so will His Messenger and believers. You will be brought back to Knower of the Unseen and the Visible, and He will notify you about how you have been working". As the explanation of this verse Prophet taught that the deeds of the offspring's of the believers will be shown to them in their tomb and if it is confirming the Soul of Qur'an, they will enjoy in it and if the deeds are against the Qur'an they will pray to Allah to rectify them. After one's death only three things will be beneficial to him. (1) Useful knowledge. (2) Existing charity. (3) The honorable children who pray for him. All the things may only become beneficial by learning and teaching the Soul of Qur'an which is the True Knowledge, Guidance and enlightening Book.

By the saying of 'Know that you will be meeting Him, proclaim such to believers!' it can be understood that only believers will see Allah at the time of death by the soul and with the eyes in the Paradise. The disbelievers- both the hypocrites and *fujjar* will not see Allah instead they will see only satan at the time of death as well as in the Hell. The verse 83: 15 says: 'indeed they will be screened off from their Lord on that Day'. The verses 9: 112; 10: 87 and 61: 13 also end as proclaims such to believers. This verse also teaches us that everyone has to construct Paradise in this world in order to inherit in the Hereafter. See the explanation 2: 177.

224. Do not use Allah as an excuse in your oaths, to keep yourselves from being virtuous, doing your duty and improving matters among mankind; Allah is all Hearing, all Knowing.

225. Allah does not take you to task for any idle talk in your oaths, but He does take you to task for whatever your hearts have earned. Allah is Forgiving, Forbearing.

This verse teaches that after taking an oath to do virtuous deeds, if break it for doing more virtuous deed which is beneficial for mankind is not unfavorable and make not Allah an excuse for doing such good deeds. Allah will not punish for idle oath, but will call to account the virtues and evils earned through confirming by the heart. The verse 53: 39 says that there shall be nothing for a man except what he intends for. Therefore, the *swalath* and recitation of Qur'an without linking to the heart will not only be accepted but also will be punished. Since Prophet taught that if anyone read Qur'an without participating the soul, he will be dart from the religion as the arrow darting from the bow. And the read Qur'an will argue and witness against him. The verse 5: 89 says, Allah will not take you to task for what you idle talk in your oath, but He does take you to task for anything you have sworn solemnly. Exoneration for it means feeding ten people with the average of what you would feed your own families, or clothing them or freeing a captive. Whoever does not find the wherewithal to do so, should fast for three days. This is what penance involves in order freeing yourselves from any oath you have sworn. Keep your oaths thus Allah explains His verses to you, so you may become grateful. Read together the verses 16: 91- 92, 94 and 63: 1-2. See explanation 2:186.

226. For those who fail to have intercourse with their wives, should wait for four month's longer. If they should then change their minds, well Allah is Forgiving, Merciful.

227. However if they insists on a divorce, surely Allah is all Hearing, all Knowing.

Conjugal relationship with their wives was a form of divorce existed during the time of ignorance. By revealing this verse Allah is ordering to annihilate that custom by saying the last limit to abstain from their wives is four months. Then when *Umar* asked his daughter *Hafsa* –one of Prophet's wives about the last limit of time that one can abstain from her husband, she replied as it is six months. On the basis of this, during the period of Islamic ruling all the troops were giving the facilities to meet their wives within six months. If the husband not comes after waiting four months, wife can divorce him and that is called '*Qulh*'. Nowadays, the gulf-life which separates the spouses makes evils not mere importance. It causes illegal and immoral activities like prostitution, fornication, divorce, illegitimate sons, sodomy etc. Since sodomy is against the natural way of life, Islam, Prophet taught to kill both of them who practice it. On the Day of Judgment when the skins and all the organs reflects the activities here in this world most of the men have to bear the sin of prostitution without participating in it, are some of the merits of the gulf-life!

Today, all these evil activities are seen more among Muslims who carry the Qur'an, perform *swalath*, observe fasting and *hajj* etc. is a sadden truth. The only reason for that is they are carrying the Book as a donkey like Jews during the period of Prophet mentioned in the verse 62: 5 without trying to learn Its soul. It is only this people who are compared to a dog which will never change the way of life whether you attack or not, is told in the verse 7: 176. It is against this bore people mentioned in the verse 25: 18 that Prophet will stand as a witness on the Day of Judgment bringing the Qur'an as told in the verse 25: 30. Read together the verses 25: 17-18. See explanation 1:7, 2: 66,170-172.

228. Divorced women should wait by themselves for three menstrual periods; it is not lawful for them to hide what Allah has created in their wombs if they believe with Allah and the Last Day. Their husbands aught to take them back meanwhile in case they want reconciliation. Women have the same (rights in relation to their husbands) as are expected in all decency from them; while men stand a step above them. Allah is Powerful, Wise.

Out of all things permitted by law, divorce is the matter which is most hateful in Islam, because marriage is a solemn agreement by witnessing Allah. See other verses explaining about the solemn agreement. About the marriage in the verse 4: 21 it is told that they have made a solemn agreement with you. With you mean husbands. The verse 33: 7 ends as we pledged a solemn agreement with them. 'With them' means the messenger having steadfast belief. Read together the verses 25: 54 and 30: 21. It is told in the verse 4: 34 that before the divorce, husbands should advise their wives, refuse to share their beds, beat them and even after all these stages, if the breach still exists appoint arbiters one from his side and other from her side and if the breach still remains after all these four stages, they can opt the divorce. Allah says to Prophet and believers through the verse 65: 1: Oh Prophet! When you divorce women, divorce them in to their '*Iddath*'-waiting period, and count accurately their waiting period, and heed Allah your Lord. Do not turn them out of their houses, nor should they be forced to leave except when they have committed some flagrant act of sexual misconduct. If the menstruation period of woman is clear, then the waiting period is three consecutive menstruations. The woman concerning about their menstruation you have doubt as well as with the ones who are still not menstruating, then their period is three months and the pregnant women their period is until they deliver as told in the verse 65: 4.

The waiting period of the widows is four months and ten days as told in the verse 2: 234. Since the man is the custodian of women, more encumbrance lays upon him to take back her. Read together the verse 4: 34. We can understand from this verse that divorce is not permitted during the menstrual period. See explanation 2: 187.

229. Divorce is only allowed twice: Then she should be allowed to stay with all decency or let go her in the best manner. It is not lawful for you to take anything back which they have given them

except when both parties fear they will not keep with in Allah's limits; then if you fear that they both will not be able to keep the limits of Allah, there is no blame on either of them, if by mutual agreement the wife compensates the husband to obtain divorce. These are the limits set by Allah; do not transgress the limits, and those who transgress the limits of Allah are the only wrongdoers.

In *Islam* giving dowry from man to the woman is compulsory but today on the contrary to the relevant dictum the most of the Muslims are following just opposite to the Qur'anic direction i.e. they receive dowry from woman side. Generally whatever given as the dowry should not be taken back. But man can demand his dowry back when she is involved in open sexual misconduct or she desires for another marriage and ask divorce by her. Since when a man is unable to fulfill the passion of the women and if she desires to marry another man, she can break the marriage relation by giving back the entire dowry, it is called '*Qulh*'. The verses 3: 94; 5: 45 and 9: 23 also end as: And those who transgress the limits of Allah are the only wrongdoers. Whoever not judge in their individual, family and social life with the Soul of Qur'an after receiving It such are the wrongdoers as per the verse 5: 45. The verse 24: 50 ends as: Nay! They are the only wrongdoers.

230. If he divorces her in the third time, it is not lawful for him to remarry her until after she has to be married with another man and get divorced from that man. In that case there is no blame on either of them if they return to on another provided they both think that they can keep with in Allah's limits. Such are Allah's limits; He explains them to the people who know.

Prophet cursed those who pronounce the words of divorce thrice at a time. So it is not an Islamic custom in to say three divorces at a time and consider it three and if he wants to marry her again, then make another man to stand as a middle husband, and he divorces without observing the stages of divorce prescribed by Allah in order to open way to the former husband for re-marriage. Actually the pronouncing of three time words of divorce is allowed if it is proved that the woman is involved in open sexual misconduct.

It is permissible to the former husband to marry her only after the new husband marry her naturally and divorce her considering all stages of divorce explained in the Qur'an. The children of Israel became monkeys since they disobeyed the command of Allah in the case of fishing on '*sabath*' day. Just like that the Muslims today forged many evil observances like standing as a middle husband for a re-marriage, say three words of divorce at a time and therefore they shall be entered into the Hell in the form of monkeys and swine. The burden of all these sins shall have to be carried by the transgressed hypocrites who do not teach the Soul of Qur'an after knowing It. See explanation 2: 66, 159-161 and 167.

231. Whenever you divorce women and they have reached the end of their waiting period either retain them in all decency or let part from them decently; do not retain them against their will in order to hurt. If anyone who does it merely hearts himself. And do not take Allah's verses aṣ a joke! Remember Allah's favor towards you and anything He has sent down to you out of the Book and Wisdom for your admonition. Heed Allah and know that surely Allah has knowledge of everything.

The heedful believers are those who live always remembering Allah with the Soul of Qur'an and follow its do's and don'ts. But today the Muslims who bear the Qur'an just like load bearing donkeys are gone astray far from the *Dheen*, Islam; not only in the matter of marriage but in all phases of life. They become forefronts of all evil deeds and far behind righteous deeds. They declined themselves for not having any rope to hold. Thus they became abused and disgraced everywhere in the world, because they hide the verses of Allah and witness the Prophet's life falsely. And they became such people about who mentioned the verse 6: 26 as: They themselves have turned away from the Truth and also forbidden It to other people. With such a behavior they harm none but their own souls though they do not perceive it. See explanation 2: 85 and 99.

The verse 65: 2 says: Then when their waiting period ends, either keep them honorably or part with them in an honorable way. Call to witness two honest persons among you, and Oh witnesses, bear witness equitably for the sake of Allah or witnessing Him. This advice is being given to all who believe in Allah and the Last Day. He who heeds Allah may be provided a way out by Him i.e. the way out of nine hundred and ninety in every thousand to the Paradise will be provided for the heedful. It is told in the verse 8: 29 to the believers: If you keep Allah in your hearts, Allah will grant you a Criterion, the honorable way. The way out mentioned in the verse 65: 2 and the criterion mentioned in the verse 8: 29 are the same, the Soul of Qur'an. You should not take the verses of Allah as a joke; certainly this Qur'an is the word which is serious, specific and not a joke as told in the verses 86: 13-14. The verse 18: 56 says: We send the Messenger only to proclaim good news and to give warnings, but with false arguments the disbelievers seek to defeat the Truth through mocking at My verses and My warnings. No one can consider Allah's verses as a joke except the disbelievers and wrongdoers. About the disbelievers through the verses 56: 81-82 Allah asks Is it such a word (Qur'an) that you would hold in light esteem. And are you making your food that you should reject the Qur'an.

It is told in the verse 18: 106 that since the disbelievers took Allah's verse and his Messengers by way of jest, their reward is Hell. Read together the verses 31: 6; 39: 55-59 and 45: 35. See explanation 2: 152, 176.

232. Whenever you divorce women and they have reached the end of their waiting period, do not prevent them from marrying their prospective husbands if they have agreed to do so with proper formalities among themselves. Whoever among you believes in Allah and the Last Day is instructed to act thus; that is purer for you as well as chaster. Allah knows while you do not know.

It is Allah who brought all mankind to Earth and granted a limited period of life with their sustenance. Therefore, no one owns to other whomsoever, everyone are independent and are dependent only to the Lord and live in such a conscious is the way of virtue and purity. It is Allah, the knower of all times, links his creatures by birth and through marriage. That is why it is told in the verse that does not prevent them from marrying their prospective husbands if they have agreed to do so with proper formalities among themselves'.

'That is prescribed for those who believe in Allah and the Last day' means Allah is the Owner of all worlds and He is ever observing whatever happening; and one Day is fixed for reckoning the whole creatures about their life in this world. See explanation 2: 216 and 222.

233. Mothers should breast-feed their children two full years, if the father wishes the breast-feeding to be completed. The reasonable cost of their maintenance and clothing will be the responsibility

of the child's father. Yet no person is charged with more than he can cop with. Neither a mother should be made to suffer on account of her child, nor a father on account of his child. An heir has the same duties in that respect. If they both prefer to wean the child when they have agreed on terms and consulted together, it should not be held against them; so if you decide to have a foster-mother for your children, it should not be held against you, provided you handover whatever you may have given in all decency. Heed Allah and know that Allah is observant of everything you do.

It is told in the verse 31: 14 that the mother bears him in her womb while suffering weakness upon weakness, while his weaning takes two years. It is told in the verse 46: 15 that bearing him and weaning him include thirty months. So if we read together the three verses 2: 233, 31: 14 and 46: 15, it can be understood that the short pregnancy period is six months. According to science generally those who deliver before seven months pregnancy period is considered as pre-mature delivery and the baby will not survive. But according to the Qur'an, in rare cases a baby born after six month's pregnancy shall survive and such child should be fed at least 24 months to complete 30 months. The baby born after ten month's pregnancy need at least 20 months breast feeding according to the verse 45: 15 to complete thirty months. If the mother is a divorcee, it is the duty of the father to give food and cloth during breast feeding period. In the absence of father, the duty lies on his heirs. Allah desires that no one shall carry the burden greater than it can bear and no child or mother or father and or heir become a burden to anyone. This verse also teaches that each individual has to construct Paradise in this world for the Hereafter.

'If they both prefer to wean the child when they have agreed on terms and consulted together, it should not be held against them'. Here by the saying 'if they both' means the mother and father's heir of the child in the absence of father.

234. And those of you who pass away and leave wives as widows behind, let hold themselves back four months and ten days. Once they reach the end of their term, you are not responsible for however they may dispose of themselves with due formality. Allah is well acquainted with what you do.

'You are not responsible for however they may dispose of themselves with due formality'- the word 'you' referred here is heirs of the deceased husband. If the widowed women are in their old age and having children, they can continue their life without another marriage. And if the women are young having children and they desire for another marriage they can. It is ordained through the verse 2: 240 to the husband about to pass away to bequest a year's maintenance to the widows without having them leave home, and if they go out of the house in their own will, there is no blame on the heirs. The aim of the bequest can be understood that to stimulate the widows for a marriage with the brothers of the diseased if they are young and both of them desire. Read together the verse 2: 275.

The verses 2: 271; 3: 180; 57: 10; 58: 3, 11 and 64: 8 also end as 'Allah is well acquainted with what you do'. That means Allah is the Knower of all times who encompasses whatever you do. The verse 31: 29 ends as 'certainly Allah is well acquainted with all that you do'. That means Allah knows about each soul where it should be born? Which parents? When and where? Which sex? What life? What food and cloth? Where to die? How much from their body reduced in the soil? Whether they go to Hell or Paradise? All these are already recorded in a book which is kept in preserved compact disc-'*Louhul mahfoodh*'. Read together the verses 85: 21-22. The verses 17: 13-14 say 'We have tied everyman's fate around his neck; and We shall produce it as a book for him on Resurrection Day that he will find spread open. It will be said to him read your Book; today it is enough yourself to make an account of you. The verse 15: says, who received the Guidance and utilize It, It is for his own benefit; who don't utilize It and goes astray does so to her own loss. No burdened soul shall bear another's burden. We have never acted as punishers until We have dispatched a Messenger. Read together the verses 6: 104, 39: 7, 41; 53: 38.

The verse 57: 22 says: 'No disaster ever happens on Earth nor to your selves unless it is recorded in a book even before We brought it in to existence. That is very easy for Allah. The verses 9: 51; 10: 64; 11: 6, 22: 70, 27: 75, 34: 3; 35: 11and 64: 11 are also with the same message.

The verse 35: 14 ends as 'no one can inform you a message like this except the Omniscient- '*Khabeer*'. The '*Khabeer*' mentioned in the verse 25: 58 is also Allah. The verse 59 ends as about the '*Khabeer*' –Allah- you ask to the '*Khabeer*'. Here the '*Khabeer*' is the one who knows explanation of the Soul of Qur'an -the '*Rooh*' and '*Kalimath*'-, in brief, Allah is Qur'an. When we know the Soul of Qur'an, we identify ourselves and Allah, and can lead a life as the vicegerents Impartial of Allah. The verses 3: 153; 9: 16; 58: 13 and 63: 11 end as 'Allah well acquaints all that you do'. The verses 24: 53 and 59: 18 end as 'Certainly Allah acquaints with all that you do'. The verse 17: 17 ends as sufficient is it for your Lord to be acquainted, observant of His servant's sins. The verses 17: 30 and 96 end as indeed He is acquainted, observant about His servant. Read together the verse 3: 7. See explanation 2: 106-107 and 146.

235. There is no blame on you if you make a proposal of marriage during their waiting period openly or keep it in your hearts. Allah knows that you will remember them in your hearts; however, be careful not to make any secret agreement, and if you wish to marry, speaks to them in an honorable manner. Do not confirm the marriage tie till the prescribed waiting period expires. You should know that Allah is Aware of what is in your hearts, so be careful with Him. And bear in mind that surely Allah is Forgiving, Forbearing.

The 'you' referred in the part of verse- 'there is no blame on you' is the brothers of the deceased husband. There is no blame on them if they desire to marry her, but shall wait four months and ten days. The meaning of what is told in the verse 'certainly Allah knows what is in your hearts' is that Allah created you from nothingness and He acquainted all that you do. In the verse 5: 116 Prophet Jesus will say on the Day of Judgment: You know the state of my soul though I know not the state of Your soul. Indeed You are the only knower of all unseen things. Read together the verse 31: 34. See explanation 2: 28 and 225.

236. There is no blame on you if you divorce women, when you have never touched with them or the dowry fixed is not settled. Provide for them, the well -to-do according to his means and the straitened according to his means; a reasonable amount in all fairness. This is an obligation up on who lives seeing Allah.

237. If you divorce women before you have had touched with them, but after the fixation of a dowry, give them half of their dowry unless they waive it, or the man in whose hand lies the marriage knot waive it. That you waive it is nearer to heedfulness. Do not

forget to be generous with one another. Surely Allah is observant of whatever you do.

There is no blame to divorce women before sexual intercourse and the fixation of dowry if there is a relevant reason. But has to be given them a reasonable gift, the wealthy according to his means and the poor according to his means. It is a duty to give a suitable gift to the divorced women for those who are heedful, is told in the verse 2: 241. If the divorce occur before sexual intercourse, but after the fixation of dowry, has to give half of the dowry unless she remits it or her guardian remits it.

It is better to divorce them giving whole dowry since the men have the special status (privilege) over them and not have sluggishness in the matter of marriage. And it is the character of righteous people who understand the aim of life and ever gratitude to their Lord for the blessing bestowed on them. The verse 4: 32 says: Do not envy that Allah has given some of you more than the others. Men will be rewarded according to their deeds and women will be rewarded according to theirs. So ask Allah for His grace. Surely Allah has perfect knowledge of everything. Therefore, every soul has to construct their Paradise Here in order to inherit in the Hereafter. Do not envy towards the blessing which Allah has bestowed on others and do not have grievances being men or women. But it is permissible to have envy and competition for learning and teaching the Soul of Qur'an. Read together the verses 3: 133; 57: 21 and 83: 26. See explanation 2: 112.

238. Guard your obligatory swalath, and keep up swalath in an excellent way and stand up devoutly to Allah.

239. If you are in a state of fear, pray on foot or while riding; and when you are safe, remembers Allah just He has taught you which you did not know before.

'*Muhsineens*' are those who live always seeing Allah under the Light-the Soul of Qur'an, in other words they always remember Allah in their standings, sittings and laying. See the verse 2: 152. But when we involve in various zones of life, there is a possibility for evil thinking, evil talking, evil doing etc. and *swalath* is prescribed for the confession of all these things to the Lord, Who does not affect slumber or sleep. The *swalath* with mere body without the participation of Soul will not only be accepted but also be punished. *Swalath* is prescribed only to the believers at stated times as told in the verse 4: 103. "*Thuma'neenath*" is one of thecompulsory observances of *swalath*. The *swalath* with "*Thuma'neenath*" is called '*Swalathul-wusthwa*'.

"*Thuma'neenath*" is the state of mind where exist peace and tranquility. That means to confess all things to the Lord with hearts during prostration and return only after getting the answer from the Lord by removing the burden of evil. "*Thuma'neenath*" for the mind will attain only with the remembrance of Allah by the Soul of Qur'an. It is told in the verse 13: 28: know that with the Soul of Qur'an do hearts find peace and tranquility. Only the '*Nafs-muthmainna*' -the soul which attained the "*Thuma'neenath*"- will return to the Paradise. Read together the verses 89: 27- 30. Those who are not able to perform such '*Wusthwa Swalath*' then, remember Allah in sitting, walking, laying or even traveling.

The *swalath* during the period of war is described in the verse 4: 103. But today, since the weapons of the war are guns, bombs, rockets and missiles the *swalath* described in the above verse is not applicable. As per the verse 29: 45, remembrance of Allah by The Soul of Qur'an is the most important. It is told in the verse 20: 14 to establish *swalath* for keeping remembrance of Allah. It is not possible to maintain the remembrance of Allah without the Soul of Qur'an. Therefore, today the teaching of Prophet during the '*Hajjathul vida*' that to hold fast the Soul of Qur'an by molar teeth should be adopted. In such a state one should have more nearness towards the Lord -Impartial.

Prophet taught that: *to learn a verse is more virtue than that of performing 1000 "Raka'ath" swalath and to teach a verse is more virtue than that of performing 100 "Raka'ath" of swalath.* One should not read the Qur'an even in *swalath*, unless he knows Its contents, if he does he will be dart out from '*Dheen*' as the arrows dart out from bow. First to recite the Qur'an with response, and then only perform *swalath* is commanded as per the verses 7: 170; 29: 45; 35: 29 and 87: 14-15. Believers always remember Allah with their hearts wherever they are, but in *swalath* their body is also involved in it and such *swalath* is called '*Swalathul wusthwa*'. See explanation 2: 46 and 186.

240. Fore those of you who pass away leaving widowed wives should bequest for them a year's provisions without causing them to leave their homes; if any woman should leave, then you does not

to blame for however they may dispose of themselves in all decency. Allah is Powerful, Wise.

241. Divorced women should have a reasonable amount in all fairness, an obligation up on the heedful.

242. Thus does Allah explain His verses to you in order that you may utilize your intelligence!

It is told in the verse 2: 236 that if you divorce a woman before consummation or fixation of dowry, give her a reasonable amount in all fairness as a gift and it is an obligation up on one who lives under the Light-the Soul of Qur'am. But as mentioned here, it is obligatory up on those who are heedful. It is told in the verse 16: 128 that certainly Allah is with those who keep Him in their hearts and who live seeing Him. It is told in the verse 4: 20 that if you decide to alter one wife in place of another even if you had given the latter a whole treasures of gold as dowry, take not the least bit of it back, and if you do thus it is a slander and manifest sin. If anyone divorces a woman after long time marriage life, has to give her a reasonable amount in all fairness in addition to the fixed dowry. And it is the duty of the husband to protect her until she marries another man unless she does not have a guardian. In Other words the reasonable amount - "*Matha'a*" in all fairness- should be enough to maintain her future life. Read together the verses 4: 128-130. See explanation 2: 73 and180.

243. Have you not seen those who have left their homes? There were thousands of them risking death. Allah told them: "Die". Then He revived them. Allah possesses Bounty for mankind, even though most men do not act grateful.

Here, Allah quotes an event which had taken place in the former generation and there by wake up believers and Prophet. Even though they were thousands in number, they abandoned their homes for fear of death. Then Allah told to them 'You die, and then only the rest of you can survive'. Those who do not prepare to fight and to be killed in the cause of Allah, they do not have right to live. Read together the verse 2: 206. Therefore the believers should prepare to fight in the cause of Allah submitting whole life to Him. This verse stimulates the believers to the battle of '*Badr*' and the battle thereafter. See explanation 2: 207.

The disbelievers fear death since they are living here without the aim of life. But the believers construct or buy the Paradise in order to inheriting It in the Hereafter. Prophet taught that: *those who were killed in the cause of Allah desire to come again to the Earth and become a martyr because of the sustenance that they enjoy in the Paradise.* Read together the verse 3: 145. On the basis of this teaching *Umar*, *Usman* and *Ali* were always praying to become a martyr. That is why they were killed by hypocrites. And today since the believer utilize the Soul of Qur'an as Shield and Safeguard there is no question of becoming a martyr. Thoşe who do not express the gratitude towards Allah are ungrateful disbelievers as per the verse 76: 3. The verse 8: 24 says; Oh you who believe, give your response to Allah and the messenger whenever he invites you to something that will make you live. And know that Allah slips in between a man and his heart, and to Him you be summoned. Read together the verses 9: 38- 42, 44- 45 and 24: 62- 64. The verses 12: 38 and 40: 61 also end as: Even though most men do not act grateful. The verses 10: 60 and 27: 73 end as, but most of them do not act grateful. Among the mankind nine hundred and ninety-nine out of every thousand go to Hell and only one shall enter the Paradise as explained in the verse 4: 118. See explanation 2: 152 and 154.

244. Fight in Allah's way and know that indeed Allah is All Hearing, All Knowing.

245. Who is there to offer Allah a handsome loan, so He may compound it many times over for him! Allah both withholds and bestows; to Him will you all be returned.

After revealing the verse giving permission for battle, Allah orders to spend their wealth to gather the necessities for battle such as food, weapons and vehicles etc. The verse 2: 261 says: The similitude of those who spend their wealth for Allah's sake may be compared to a grain which sprouts in to seven ears with a hundred grains in each ear. Allah multiplies things for anyone He wishes. Allah is Boundless, Aware. The verse 5: 64 revealed as a reply to the hypocrites and Jews in Madeena who said that Allah become bankrupt since He asked loan from men. The verse 36: 47 says: And when they are told to spend the bounties with which Allah has provided you, the disbelievers say for those who believe: Shall we then feed those whom if Allah had so willed, He would have fed. What happened to you, is it a deed against Allah?' Today there is no war, but only strenuous strive against those who hide Qur'an with the Soul of Qur'an. So, all the manpower and wealth should be utilized for learning and teaching the Soul of Qur'an. See explanation 2: 195 and 243.

246. Have you not seeing how the councilors for the children of Israel told a Prophet of theirs who came after Moosa? "Appoint us a king; we will fight for Allah's sake". He said: "Perhaps you will not fight even though fighting has been prescribed for you". They said: "What do we have to keep us from fighting for Allah's sake? We and our children have been driven out of our homes!" Yet whenever fighting was prescribed for them, all but a few of them turned away. Allah is well Knower with such wrongdoers.

The hypocritical policies of the children of Israel at the time of Prophet *Moosa* are described in several places in Qur'an. The verses 17: 4-5 says We decreed in the Book concerning the children of Israel "you will create mischief on Earth twice and display great haughtiness. When the first of both promises came, We dispatched servants of Ours to inflict severe violence up on you. They rampaged through your homes, and it served as a promise which was acted upon.

After the time of Prophet *Moosa* the children of Israel deviated from the truth, followed other people and became arrogant transgressors. They misunderstood that the majesty and splendor coming only through kingship. So they demanded a king for their leadership avoiding Allah's Prophets. Here it is teaching that the believers should not have such type of behaviors. The verses 2: 95; 9: 47 and 62: 7 also end as: Allah is well Knower with such wrongdoers.

247. Their Prophet told them: "Allah has appointed 'Twalooth' as a king for you". They said: "How could he hold control over us, since we are fitter to exercise control than he is? He has not been given ample wealth". He said: "Allah has chosen him out for you and added plenty to his knowledge and physique, Allah gives His control anyone He wishes; Allah is Boundless, Aware".

The thought of the people who have deviated from Truth is that the blessings are mere directly visible bodily prowess, material education, majesty, splendor and abundant wealth. But the knowledge about the Soul of Qur'an which is the food and cloth of the soul is the greatest blessing considered with Allah and believers. The verses 15: 87-88 say, we have brought you seven oft-repeated verses plus the mighty Qur'an. Do not straying your eyes towards what We let some types of them enjoy; do not feel sorrow up on them and lower your wings over believers. Read together the verses 62: 4and 63: 4. See explanation 2: 207and 218.

248. Their Prophet told them: "A sign of his control will be that the Ark shall come to you containing serenity from your Lord, as well as some relics which Moosa's house and Haroon's house have left behind 'carried by Angels'. In that there will be a sign for you if you are believers.

'The *Amaliks'* who defeated the children of Israel in the battle and took away the Ark which contained the discs of ten commandments which Allah gave to *Moosa*, the rode, the chapels of Prophet *Moosa* and samples of Manna and *Salva*. 'Carried by Angels' means the *Amaliks* could not open the Ark and utilize it, or even to understand what it contains. Therefore, to receive it back without any change was the clear sign to the believers. See explanation 2: 91- 93.

249. When Twalooth set out with the troops, he said: "Allah will test you at a river: Anyone who drinks from it will not be on my side; while anyone who does not taste it is with me, except for some one who scoops up only a palm full in his hand". Yet all but a few of them drank from it. When he and those who were along with him and believed had crossed over, they said: "We have no power to prevail over Jalooth (Goliath) and his troops"! Those who though they were going to meet Allah said: "How often has a small detachment defeated a larger detachment with Allah's Permission? Allah stands along side with the patient".

They suffered severe heat, tiredness and thirst. *Twalooth* had already told them that the real believers are those who drank not from the river but a mere sip with palm full in hand is excused. But when they crossed the Jordan River most of them except a few drank of it abundantly. When they reached on the next shore, all of them except the real believers said: This day we cannot fight with the forces of *Jalooth*.

These kinds of trial events occurred in the battle of *Bad'r* and *Uh'd* also. All the happenings which is occurring the world has already been recorded by Allah. Those who remember Allah with their hearts and submit whole life to Allah only attain victory both this world and the next world. It is only those who receive lesson from these trial events stand firmly in the way of Allah. These kinds of trials will be occurred in all times. See verses 29: 2- 4. The verse 8: 66 also ends as: And Allah stands along side with the patient. See explanation 2: 155-157.

250. When they marched forth to face Jalooth and his troops, they prayed: "Our Lord fill us full of patience and brace our feet and help us against such disbelieving people."

The disbelievers mentioned here are not only the *Jalooth* and his forces but also those who turned away after drinking the water and thus from the battle. Allah says in the verses 3: 146- 147 to the believers who lost the battle of *Uh'd*: "How many of the Prophets fought and with them large bands of mighty men. But they never lost heart, if they met with disaster in Allah's way, nor did they weaken or greave in. And Allah is with those who are firm and steadfast. Their statement was nothing except to say: Our Lord! Forgive us our sins and anything that excess in our duty, brace our feet, and help us against the disbelieving people. Read together the verse 2: 286. The magicians of Pharaoh failed in their competition with Prophet *Moosa* and believed in Allah. But Pharaoh was tried to deviate them from their belief. Then they prayed, "Our Lord! Pour out on us patience and constancy and take our souls unto you as Muslims." Read together the verse 7: 126.

251. They routed them with Allah's Permission. And Davood killed Jalooth, and Allah gave him kingship and wisdom and taught him whatever He wished. If Allah did not defend some men by means of another's the Earth would be ruined; but Allah possesses Bounty for everybody in the worlds.

During the time of Prophet *Shamveel* as mentioned in the Bible, under the leadership of king *Thwalooth*, believers went to fight with *Goliath -Jalooth-* the king of *Amaliks*. Prophet *Dawood* joined with the believers on their way to the battlefield. The youth *Dawood* killed the giant *Jalooth* in the duel fighting. Thus Allah gave kingship and wisdom (Prophet-hood) to *Dawood* and there by blessed that people. His son *Sulaiman* was also a Prophet and King blessed by wealth, prowess and splendor which were not given anyone in the world.

It is the way of Allah to defend one set of people by means of another. Read together the verse 22: 40. Believers are those who hold firmly the Soul of Qur'an and walk evenly on a Straight path anywhere in the world without fearing anyone depending only in Allah. Through the verse 67: 22 Allah asks: Who is rightly guided: he who walks with his face bent down, or he who walks properly on Straight path? It is told in the verse 25: 34 that, whoever turned away from the

Straight Path will be dragged upon their faces to the Hell and such are in the worst place as well as the strayed path.

It is told in the verse 6: 45 that, Thus We cut off the roots of the wrongdoers. All praises are due to Allah, the Lord of all worlds. Prophet *Nooh* prayed as per the verses 71: 26-28 as: Oh my Lord, leave not of the disbelievers, a single one on Earth. If you do live any of them they will mislead Your devotees and they will breed no one except the hypocrites and '*fujjar*'. My Lord, forgive me, my parents, as well as any one who enters on my house as a believer plus believing men and believing women. And don't increase wrongdoers in anything except destruction. See explanation 1: 1.

252. These are Allah's verses which We recite you for the Truth. Surely you are one of Our Messengers.

Allah, the Knower of all times, describe the events occurred in the past to the illiterate Messenger *Muhammad* through the Angel messenger *Jibreel*. After describing the history of *Zakariya, Yahya, Maryam and Eisa*, Allah says in the verse 3: 44: Such is some information about the unseen We have revealed to you by inspiration. The verse 35: 14 ends as: None can inform you this except the Knower of all times Who is all Aware. Allah says in the verses 28: 44-46: You were not on the western slope when We settled the matter for *Moosa* nor were you a witness; but We raised some generations, and their life time was prolonged for them. Nor were you a resident among the people of '*Madyan*', reciting Our verses to them, but We were to send emissaries. You were not on the slop of the mount '*Sinai*' when We called out, but as a mercy from your Lord so you might warn a people who no Warner had come to before you, so that they may remember by mind. The verse 93: 11 says: And declare the Bounty of your Lord. The 'Bounty' mentioned is the Soul of Qur'an. Allah chooses messengers from Angels as well as from men, is told in the verse 22: 75. *Muhammad* is the last Prophet and Messenger as told in the verse 33: 40. In the verse 21: 107 by calling Prophet, Allah says: We have not sent you except as a mercy for all the worlds. Read together the verses 7: 158; 11: 17; 34: 28 and 36: 3. See explanation 2: 119, 146 and 147.

253. These are the Messengers. We have preferred some above others, among them to some one Allah spoke directly; others He raised high in ranks; to Eisa the son of Maryam We gave clear signs and

endorsed him by means of the Holy Spirit. If Allah had wished, the people who came after them would not have fought against one another, once clear signs had come to them; however they disagreed. Some of them believed while others disbelieved. If Allah had wished, they would not have fought one another, but Allah does whatever He wants.

The history of Messengers mentioned in the Qur'an have revealed before this *Surath*. The verse 40: 78 says, We have send Messengers before you, some whom We have told you about, while We have not told you about others. No Messenger may bring any sign unless it is with Allah's permission. Once Allah's command comes matters will be decided with the Truth, and there the quibblers will loss out. It is told in the verse 4:164: Of some Messengers We have already told you the history, while of others We have not told you. And to *Moosa* Allah did speak direct. Read together the verse 7: 143.

Believers should pray the following prayer in the beginning of every day which Prophet taught: *Oh the Lord of Jibreel, Meechaeel, Israfeel, Azraeel, the Creator of Heaven and Earth, the only knower of seen and unseen matters, the glorious Lord of us and all creatures, and the dealer of its dominion, we seek refuge to you from the evils of all creatures, of whom You hold their forelocks. You will judge between the matters among your servants in which they have divided on the Day of Judgment, so lead us to the Straight path by means of Your Permission -Soul of the Qur'an, certainly none is there to guide except You.*

There are only two parties among the mankind, one is the believers' -Allah's party, and the other is disbelievers' -satan's party. Those who live only for Allah are included in the party of Allah and all others are included in the party of satan and are living for satan. It is told in the verse 64: 2: It is He Who has created you and among you some are disbelievers and some are believers, and Allah observes all that you do. Allah as a reply to the disbeliever's question in the verse 13: 27 says that, why is not a sign sent down to him from his Lord, truly Allah leaves to astray whom He wishes, but He guides to Himself those who turn to Him in repentance. The duty of men is to identify Allah and themselves through the Soul of Qur'an in which all matters are explained and there by construct Paradise here, to stop bloodshed on Earth and thereby keep peace and tranquility by establishing natural justice custom. For that Allah will never come down is told in the verse 2: 210. See explanation 2: 27-28 and 213.

254. Oh you who believe, spend out of what We have provided you with before a day comes alone in which there will be no bargaining, friendship, no any intercession. And the disbelievers are only the wrongdoers.

The believers will construct Paradise here by spending with what Allah has provided them. That is the aim of the life. But one should have to do so before the death comes to him. That time, there is no bargaining, friendship and no intercession will be availed. The day means death day for individual, and in the case of all mankind it is the Day of Judgment. Since the verse addresses by calling the believers instead of mankind we can understand that the disbelievers, wrongdoers and transgressors will come only from Muslims because they hide the Soul of Qur'an after receiving It. Read together the verse 2: 121. Those who do not judge in their individual, family and social life with what Allah has revealed- with the Soul of Qur'an- are disbelievers, wrongdoers and transgressors, is told in the verses 5: 44, 45 and 47 respectively.

It is commanded to the believers through the verses 10: 85-86 to pray as, "Oh our Lord, make not us a trial to the wrongdoers, save us with Your great Mercy from disbelievers". The great Mercy is the Soul of Qur'an. Hence include us those who utilize the Soul of Qur'an as '*Muhaimin*' -the Safeguard. Allah commanded through the verse 60: 5 to pray like this, "Oh our Lord, make not us a trial to the disbelievers, forgive us our Lord, surely You are Exalted in Might, the Wise". The verse 10: 17 says, who does more wrong than such as forge a lie against Allah by distorting the Qur'an verses or reject His verses after receiving It? Surely He never will prosper such '*mujrims*'. The verse 6: 21 also having same message. The verses 5: 51; 6:144; 28: 50 and 46:10 end as 'surely Allah does not guide the people who are wrongdoers'.

Therefore the disbelievers and wrongdoers are coming from Muslims who hide and reject the Soul of Qur'an after receiving It and live without the aim of life as told in the above all verses. The following verses are also describing about the disbelievers and wrongdoers in the same verses are 2: 258; 3: 86, 151; 4: 168; 5: 72; 7: 37; 14: 13, 34; 17: 99; 18: 29; 21:97; 29: 68; 34: 31; 39: 32. We can understand about disbelievers from the following verses 3: 10; 4: 150-

151; 5: 67; 7: 50, 151; 16:106; 18: 100-101; 29: 47; 39: 59, 71; 41: 26-29; 67: 6-11. More over, the disbelievers and the wrongdoers mentioned in continuous verses are the following 3: 56- 57, 116-117, 140-141, 149-150, 4: 167-168, 5: 44-45, 72-73, 6: 129-130, 7: 44-45, 8: 55-56, 10: 85-86, 11: 18-19, 67-68, 14: 27-28, 16: 27-28, 84-85, 18: 37-38, 21: 29-30, 22: 44-45, 71-72, 25: 26-27, 27: 43-44, 29: 46-47, 67-68, 30: 8-9, 35: 36-37, 39-40, 59: 16-17, 61: 7-8, 71: 27 and 28. See explanation 1:7; 2:166 and167.

255. Allah! There is no deity except Him, the Living, the Survivor and Sustainer of all! Slumber does not over take Him, nor does sleep. To Him belongs all that is in the Heavens and the Earth. Who is there to intercede with Him except by His permission? He knows what is before them and what is behind them, while they embrace nothing of His knowledge except whatever He may wish. His throne extends far over Heavens and the Earth; and preserving them both does not over burden Him. He is the Sublime, the Almighty.

This verse is known as '*Ayathul Kursiyye*' -'Verse of Throne' which is the glorious verse in the Qur'an or its message contains the quintessence of the Qur'an. Prophet recited this verse after each compulsory *swalath*, before going to sleep as '*Virdh*'. The verse from the Qur'an which is used for praying is called '*Virdh*'. *Those who hurrying to recite the verse of throne after the swalath will enter to the Paradise immediately after their death,* is also taught by Prophet.

'Ilah' -Deity: Whom one can call without being seen; to whom one can seek help; whom one can afraid of; whom one can entrust; to whom only one has to convince his accountability of life -He is *Ilah*'. He is Allah- the only Deity. '*Al Hayy*':- Self living, no origin, no death -eternal. '*Al Qayyoom*':- Keep surviving and maintaining all life.

Never will happen to Him sleep or slumber while all other beings have. Allah is ever watchful. Allah is the creator of all things on the Heaven and Earth and between them. He is the Lord of all things, and establishes and maintains them.No one is bold enough to recommend before Him except with His Permission-The Soul Qur'an. As per the verse 39: 44 "To Allah belong exclusively all intercession". Since the Soul Qur'an is Allah's Permission it will argue and intercede to one who follow It. Prophet taught: *You recite the Qur'an with Its Soul, certainly It will intercede for Its companion on the Day of Judgment.* But '*Qira'ath*' -reading- is only when heart linked with It, because Qur'an either argue in favor or against you.

'He knows what before, after or behind them' means, since Allah is Omniscient-the Knower of all times-, He knows everyone, when and where they to be born? What they earn? Their death, how much from their body adheres in the soil? In what form they are resurrected? Whether they go to Paradise or Hell? And Allah is well acquainted about all things, nothing hidden from Him. Read together the verses 3: 5; 14: 38 and 50: 4. Whatever happens on Earth or Heaven is already recorded in a Book as told in the verses 22: 70; 57: 22 and 64: 11. The verse 6: 59 says: "With Him are the keys of the unseen, the treasures that none knows but He. He knows whatever there is on the Earth and in the sea. Not a leaf does fall but with His knowledge. There is not a grain in the darkness of the Earth, nor any green leaf dry without His knowledge and to which plant such leaf become a manure are also already recorded in the Book. Read together the verses 10: 61; 11: 5-7 and 31: 16. This part-He knows what before, after or behind them- of the verse also present in the verses such as 20: 110; 21: 28 and 22: 76. No one can encompass the knowledge which Allah has bestowed except what He will. The verse 20: 110 have the same meaning. That is why Allah has commanded Prophet to pray through the verse 20: 114: "Oh my Lord increases me in knowledge". Prophet has prayed like this: *Oh Allah, benefit us what you taught, You may increase to us the knowledge which is beneficial, praise to You in all times except in the state of to Hell.*

His throne does extend over the Earth and Heaven means, His dominion exists in Heaven and Earth. It is told in the verses 39: 63 and 42: 12 that to Him belongs the seats of the Heaven and Earth. Allah needs no help from anyone to maintain the dominion of Heaven and Earth, no tiredness affect Him. Allah has no similitude, likeness, He is exalted in might, Unique, Despotic, Dictator and all are depended on Him, but He does not depend on anyone. Since the Qur'an is sent to introduce Allah, this verse fulfills that aim than any other verses. But disbelievers among the Muslims read this verse without Its soul. So the read Qur'an will argue and witness against them. See explanation 1: 3-4 and 2: 234.

256. There should be no compulsion in 'Dheen'. The right way has been made clear from the wrong way. Therefore, anyone whoever

rejects with the arrogant ones and believes in Allah has grasped the firmest handle which will never break. Allah is All Hearing, All Knowing.

The verses 10: 99-100 say: If your Lord had so whished, everyone on Earth would have believed, all of them together! So will you force mankind to become believers? It is not up to any soul to believe unless it with Allah's Permission; He places blight on those who do not use their intelligence. As per the verse 3: 145 it is told that no soul shall die except with Allah's Permission according to specific right. 'By the Permission' here mentioned means, by the Soul of Qur'an. The right way is the 'Truth' –the way of Allah to the Paradise; and the wrong way is the falsehood-the way of satan to the Hell. The Soul of Qur'an is the Criterion and Touchstone which differentiate the right and wrong. That is the Insight and unbreakable Rope to whole people. It is told in the verse 3: 103: holdfast together the rope of Allah and be not divided.

In the verse 3: 101 Allah says: Whoever holds fast with Allah, will indeed be guided towards the Straight path, and in the verse 22: 78 says: And hold fast with Allah. 'To holdfast with Allah' means to holdfast the Soul of Qur'an which is the firmest and unbreakable Rope. The verses 11: 118-119 say: If your Lord had so wished, would have made mankind in to one community, but they will not stop disagreeing, except for those to whom your Lord has shown Mercy. For that reason did He create them, and your Lord's Word is completed: "I shall fill Hell with *Jinns* and man kinds' altogether. Here mentioned 'Mercy' is the Soul of Qur'an. Read together the verses 7: 16-18; 15: 35, 43; 17: 62-65; 32: 13 and 38: 78-85. Therefore everyone should ask Guidance to Allah submitting everything he or she has and approving the fact that I am your servant, only You are my Lord and include me among the one to the Paradise and not among the 999 to the Hell.

Allah says in the verse 31: 22 that whoever submits his whole self to Allah and is a doer of good has grasped indeed the firmest handle and to Allah shall all to return. Prophet taught that: *the Soul Qur'an is the firm rope extended from Paradise to Earth. Therefore, let the Soul of Qur'an walk in front of you, not on the back, because It will make you return to Allah.* That means we should give more importance to the Soul of Qur'an in our life. The verse 7: 170 says: And those who hold firmly the Book and establish *swalath*; surely We never let the reward of such reformers go astray. See explanation 2: 185-186.

257. Allah is the Patron of those who believe, He brings them out of darkness into light, while who disbelieve have the arrogant ones for their patrons; they will lead them out of light into darkness. Such are inmates of the Fire; they shall remain therein forever.

It is told in the verse 14: 1 that the Book which We have revealed is to lead the mankind out of the darkness into light by the permission of their Lord to the way of Lord, the exalted in power, worthy of all praises. Allah is the light of the Heaven and Earth is told in the verse 24: 35. The Soul of Qur'an is the Straight path as well as the light as told in the verses 4: 174-175; 5: 15-16; 7: 157; 42: 52 and 64: 8. Since the light is referred in singular form and darkness in plural, we can understand that the only one way that Allah satisfied is the way of Qur'an and all other ways are the ways of satan. Those who lead the ways of satan are called as '*Thaghooth*' -the arrogant. All the evils like selfishness, partiality for ones own people, nationalism, communalism, rationalism, arrogance, the way of forefathers which is considered as the way of majority, loving parents, spouses, offspring's or other family members against the love of Allah are '*Thaghooth*'. Whatever that prevents men from the Soul of Qur'an are '*Thaghooth*'. In every thousand, nine hundred and ninety nine follow the way of '*Thaghooth*'. Only one from every thousand holds fast the Light -Soul of Qur'an and lives only for Allah as His vicegerent. Read together the verses 10: 62-63 and 58: 22. See explanation 2: 213.

258. Have you ever listened upon the one, to whom Allah had given the kingdom, who argued with Ibrahim about his Lord. When Ibrahim said: "My Lord is the One Who gives life and brings death". He replied: "I too give life and bring death". Ibrahim said: "Well, Allah brings the sun from the east, so you bring it from the west". The man who disbelieved was dumbfounded; Allah does not guide such wrongdoing people.

Prophet *Ibrahim* invited his father and the people to Allah who were idolaters. But they were not ready to accept the call of Prophet *Ibrahim* and follow him. They were not ready to believe in Allah. One day when they gone to participate a festival, *Ibrahim* destroyed all their idols except the big one. When they came back, they saw demolished idols and they informed about this to their king *Namrood*. Then *Ibrahim* was brought to the Durbar and was trialed by the king. This verse mentions about that event. *Namrood* asked to Prophet *Ibrahim*,

Oh *Ibrahim*, who is your Lord other than the Lord of your father and ours? *Ibrahim* said: "My Lord is the One Who gives life and brings death". Then *Namrood* brought two persons from the jail and he ordered to kill the one and let free the other and said I also give life and death. *Ibrahim* said My Lord brings the sun from the east; can you bring the sun from the west? *Namrood* had no reply. But they prepared hearth to burn *Ibrahim*. See the verses 21: 52-70.

This verse gives a reference one of the ten symptoms of the Last Day; i.e. Allah Who brings the sun from the east, will bring one day from the west. The verses 3: 86; 9: 19, 109; 61: 7 and 62: 5 also end as: 'And Allah does not guide such wrongdoing people'. Those who do not utilize the Soul of Qur'an after receiving It and hide It are the wrongdoers as told in the verses 18: 57 and 32: 22. See explanation 2: 254.

259. Or like the man who passed by a town which has fallen down with its roofs. He exclaimed: "How will Allah revive this following its death?" Thereupon Allah let him die for a hundred years, and then raised him up again. Allah asked: "How long have you been tarry?" He replied: "I have been tarrying a day or part of a day." Allah said: "Rather! You have tarried here for a hundred years. Yet look at your food and drink; they have not at even become stale! And look at your donkey. We will grant it as a Sign for mankind. Look how We set its bones together, then clothe them with flesh". When it was explained to him, he said: "I know that surely Allah is Capable of everything!"

The man referred here is *Uzair*, he happened to travel on his donkey through a country which was ruined. He thought in his mind that How Allah shall bring it ever to life. Then Allah caused him to die for 100 years. Then Allah raised him up and asked how long did you tarry? He said, a day or part of a day. Allah said to look his food -fig- and drink -grapes- which he had carried as food. They didn't show any sign of age that is remained without rotten. Then Allah asked to look his vehicle donkey, its bones were decayed due to hundred years. Then Allah in the presence of rhythmic wind re-coordinated all bones of that donkey and clothed with flesh and thus revived. So *Uzair* agreed that Allah has capable to bring to life the dead and has the power to keep immediately decaying food items to extend of decades without any decay. More over Allah is capable of everything. Because of this event the Jews considered *Uzair* as God's son.

The verse 9: 30 says, the Jews say: "*Uzair* is the son of Allah," and the Christians say: "*Masseeh* (Christ) is the son of Allah." That is what they say with their mouths, imitating the sayings of the former disbelievers. Allah has killed them! How perverted they are! The verses 2:20, 106, 109, 148; 3: 165; 16: 77; 24: 45; 29: 20 and 35: 1 also end as; surely Allah is capable of everything." See explanation 2: 255.

260. And remember that Ibrahim asked: "My Lord! Show me how you revive the dead"; He said: "Why do you not believe?" Ibrahim said: "Of course I do, but just to set my heart peace and tranquility". He said: "Take four kinds of birds, cut their bodies into pieces and mix them well then place a part of them on every mountain. Then call them; they will come to you at once. Know that Allah is Powerful, Wise."

Prophet *Ibrahim* asked Allah to show him How He revives the dead. Then Allah said to take four kinds of birds- cock, pigeon, peacock and crow- to slay cut them in to pieces and mix well. Then put a portion of it on every seven mountain, and then call to them. At once, the birds come to *Ibrahim* hastily by Allah's will. The Arabic word '*faswurhunna ilaika*' also has the meaning, to incline or tame unto you. In several places this kinds of pun words (having double meaning) are used in Qur'an. The purpose is to distinguish between the believers and hypocrites. Another example is the word '*muthawaffeeka*' is used in the verse 3: 55 in the case of Prophet *Eisa's* raising up to Allah. Only the believers will believe that Allah raised up *Eisa* bodily to the second Heaven as explain in the verse 4: 158 and the hypocrites during their life they will not believe in this, but at the time of death they will surely believe in this truth as told in the verse 4: 159. In the verse 75: 29 the word used '*walthaffathi ssaqu bissaqu*' means calamity will be joined to calamity for the departing soul and they will understand that their belief and understandings were false and they will be shown all their evils as a panorama which they have done after the age of fifteenth in their life. But the hypocrites who do not know the difference between the body and soul since they are killed by Allah as per the verse 63: 4 give the meaning as one leg will be joined with another instead of calamity will be joined to calamity. Read together the verse 3:59. See explanation 2: 79, 254.

261. The ones who spend their wealth for Allah's sake may be compared to a grain which sprouts into seven ears with a hundred grains

in each ear. Allah multiplies things for anyone He wishes. Allah is Boundless, Aware.

Here, we are getting seven hundred grains from a single seed. So the next year, we will get at least seventy grains as seeds, some years later, the crops of that area will be completely from that single seed. Hence, the believers have to do their all deeds with the intention that they have to get the crops and the reward in the hereafter multiplied. Allah says in the verse 36: 12, Surely We shall revive the dead, We are recording all that they are sending ahead and that their footprints, We have recorded everything in an open ledger. Everyone's evils and goodness which they did in their life and evils and goodness of the heritage which they left behind will be individually evaluated on the Day of Judgment. The verse 82: 5 says, and then each soul shall know what it has sent forth and what it left behind. The verse 75: 13 says, on that Day man will be informed with what he has sent ahead and left behind. The verse 24: 30 ends as 'certainly Allah is well acquainted with what they produce. The verse 29: 45 ends as; Allah knows what you are producing. In these two verses instead of saying "*ya'maloon*" -what they do- or "*tha'maloon*" -what you do- the word "*yaswnauon*" -what they produce- and "*thaswnauon*" -what you produce- are used. That means not only their deeds but also the credit and debit of the heritage which they leave behind for their followers will be reckoned.

The verse 4: 85 says, whoever recommends goodness; he will get a share from it and whoever recommends an evil causes a share in its burden. And Allah is capable of everything. Therefore, the believers should encourage others to do the deeds which are in accordance with the do's and don'ts of the Soul of Qur'an. When the deeds become against the do's and don'ts of Qur'an, they should prevent it by their hands. If not possible prevent it by their tongue. If that also is not possible at least hate it by mind. Prophet taught that: *If anyone does not express hatredness towards an evil by mind, he does not have belief as much as an atom.* The verse 6: 160 says, anyone who comes with a fine deed, will have ten more like it, while anyone who comes with an evil deed will only be rewarded its like; they will not be treated unjustly. The verse 28: 84 says, anyone who comes with a fine deed will have something even better than it, while anyone who comes with an evil deed will find that, those who perform evil deeds will not be rewarded except for whatever they have been doing. The verse 40: 40 says, the one who does evil shall be recompensed to the extent of the evil done; and the one who is a believer and does good deeds, whether man or woman, shall enter the Paradise and therein receive sustenance without measure. As the explanation of these verses Prophet taught that: *if anybody intends to do a good, but not done, then it will be recorded as a good, if he does it, he will be given at least ten times reward. If anyone intents to do an evil but not done, it will not be recorded as an evil. If he does it, he will be recompensed to the extent of that evil.* See explanation 2: 201-202.

The verse 29: 12 says, the hypocritical disbelievers say to the believers: "Follow us, and then we will bear the burden of your sins. But they will not bear any burden of their sins; they are surely lying". The verse 13 says, of course, they shall bear their own burdens as well as the burdens of others in addition to their own; and on the Day of Judgment they shall be questioned about their invented lies. The verse 16: 24 says, when the disbelievers are asked: "What is it that your Lord has revealed?" They say: "Fable stories of the ancients!" and the verse 25 says; in order to bear their own burdens in full and that of those whom they have misled without having any knowledge. What an evil burden they are bearing! Read together the verses 10: 26-27. See explanation 2: 166 and167.

262. Those who spend their wealth for Allah's sake, then do not follow up what they have spend with any reproach or scolding, shall receive their rewards from their Lord; upon them no fear and for them will not be grieved.

Allah deputed mankind to Earth in order to utilize all the blessings of Allah to construct Paradise Here for the Hereafter. Therefore, what we spend may not be for convincing others or getting certificate from others. The characters of virtuous men are described in the verse 2: 177. It is told in the verse 32: 19 that for those who believe and do righteous deeds have Paradise as a hospitable homes for they were doing here good deeds. It is told in the verses 7: 40- 43; 29: 7, 58; 39: 74; 41: 8 and 77: 44 that the Paradise should be constructed Here for Tomorrow by utilizing the Soul of Qur'an. See explanation 2: 207.

263. Kind words and forgiveness are better than any act of charity followed by a scolding. Allah is Self-sufficient, Forbearing.

Allah need not want men to do charity unwillingly or with difficulty. The verse 31: 12 says, We gave *Luqman* wisdom: "give thanks to Allah." Anyone who gives thanks, merely give thanks for his own sake; while anyone who is ungrateful then Allah is Self-sufficient, Praiseworthy. Allah will not accept any charity or service from the hypocrites. The verses 9: 53-54 Say: "Whether you give willingly or unwillingly, it will not be accepted from you; for you are the people who are transgressors." The reasons which prevent their contributions from being accepted are: That they disbelieve in Allah and His Messenger, and do not come to *swalath* except with laziness, nor do they spend anything except unwillingly. The verses 17: 26- 27 say, You shall give to your relatives their due and to the needy and to the wayfarers. You shall not be a spendthrift, as spendthrifts are the brothers of satan and satan is ever ungrateful towards His Lord. In the verse 28 says, yet if you have to avoid them, when they come seeking some bounty which you may expect from your Lord, then speak courteous words to them. Say that renders to kin, destitute and to wayfarers their due rights and if you do not have the money to give them, says them kind words. The believers always keep the remembrance of Allah and live in the conscious that Allah, the owner of all blessings, has the power to change the giver to the receiver. See explanation 1: 2; 2: 175 and 185.

264. Oh you who believe, do not cancel your acts of charity by any reproach or scolding like someone who spends his money simply for people to see it while he does not believe in Allah and the Last Day. He may be compared to a boulder covered with some soil which a rain storm strikes and leaves bare. They cannot do anything whatever they have earned. Allah does not guide such disbelieving people.

Those who do deeds without the conscious that Allah sees all, and do fearing men are included in associates. They are the people who neglect what is told in the verses 41: 19-24; 36: 65; 24: 24 and 99: 4 that on the Day of Judgment, their skins, hands, legs, hearings, sights, etc. will be witnessing against them. They expect gratefulness and certificate from people and believing not in Allah and the Last Day. No deeds will be accepted without being a believer. It is commanded that one should proud and be self sufficient with the Soul of Qur'an. Read together the verses 3: 79 and 47: 24. About all the blessings will be questioned on the Day of Judgment as told in the verse 102: 8. Therefore about whatever spent to learn and teach the Soul of Qur'an will not be questioned or can answer positively. Envy and arrogance are permissible in the matter of learning and teaching Soul of Qur'an. Prophet taught that: *if anyone has a mustard seed of arrogance in his heart, he will not enter the Paradise.* But the believers try to enter the Paradise by burning the arrogance with the Soul of Qur'an which is the Light.

Prophet taught: *Allah select family member from mankind. Somebody asked: Oh Prophet, who are they? They are the people of the Soul of Qur'an and they are particularly for Him.* The charity and *swalath* of hypocrites done with hatred or pretending piety (to be seen by others) will not be accepted; because they are the people who do not believe in Allah and His Messenger as told in the verse 9: 53-54. The verse 9: 37 also ends as: Allah does not guide such disbelieving people. See explanation 2: 186 and 254.

265. Those who spend their wealth seeking Allah's pleasure and to strengthen their souls may be compared to hill top; should a rain storm strike it, its produce is doubled, while if a rain storm does not strike it then drizzle does. Allah is observant of anything you do.

The example of how the believers spend their wealth is given in this verse. They spend their wealth with Allah's satisfaction and they will have strong intention to get the produce yield tomorrow in the real life or they know the aim of life that it is necessary to earn here for tomorrow. See explanation 2: 94-95 and 207.

266. Would any of you like to have a garden full of palms and grapes through which rivers flow? He would have all fruit in it yet old age will afflict him while he still has some helpless offsprings, and wind storm containing fire will strike it, so it is burned off. Thus Allah explains verses to you so that you may think and reflect.

Here, quotes an example of a man whose deeds are in vain and lost the life and there by make the men to think and learn lesson from it. A man had a garden in which there were all types of fruits, corns and other crops. To water the garden there were rivers around. One day while he was enjoying the life, a fiery whirlwind affected the garden and burned it. His children were weak and unable to do any job. Thus he become a loser in this world and aggrieved. In the Hereafter, he will have nothing. The life of those who live without the Soul of Qur'an and works without the intention to get the reward in the Hereafter will be in loss. Read together the verse 39: 63. Evaluate the condition of the Gardener mentioned in the verses 18: 32-44 and the condition of gardeners mentioned in the verses 68: 20- 31. See explanation 2: 121, 219 and 220.

267. Oh you, who believe, spends some of the wholesome things you may have acquired as well as anything We produced from the Earth for you. Do not choose the worthless parts of it for anything you spend which you yourselves would only accept disdainfully. And know that Allah is Self-Sufficient, Praiseworthy.

Whatever we earn and spend should be in the way that Allah has permitted; i.e. under the shadow of the Qur'an. Therefore it is in vain to earn and spend through interest, gambling, smuggling, bribery, dowry, robbery, adulteration, seizure, black money, dealing in fraud, since all these are prohibited. There is welfare tax for what we produce from Earth like fruits and corns. Read together the verse 6: 141. The wealth attained through prohibited ways and cheap quality things should not be given to others. Because if they are the receivers; they will not like to accept them. The verse 3: 92 says: You can never attain virtue unless you spend in the cause of Allah that which you dearly cherish; and whatever you spend, surely it is known to Allah. In brief, it is foolishness to think and attain virtue through prohibited ways. Allah is free of all creatures and self worthy of all praises. The verse 9: 34 says: Oh believers! Indeed most of the anchorites and priests will eat the wealth of people by prohibited way and obstruct them from the way of Allah -Soul of the Qur'an. The verse 5: 62 says: You will see many of them try to beat each other in sin and rancor, and they consume what is unlawful. Evil indeed is what they do. And in the verse 63 it is said that Why don't their anchorites and the priests forbid them from uttering sinful words and eating prohibited things? Evil are indeed their deeds. In the verse 5: 100, Allah commanded Prophet to say: Not equal are the things that are worthless and wholesome and the things that are good even though abundance of the worthless dazzle you, so fear Allah, oh you men of understanding -in order that you may be prosperous. See explanation 2: 177, 188 and 261.

268. Satan threatens you with poverty and commands you to commit what is indecent, while Allah promises you His forgiveness as well as bounties, and Allah is Boundless, Aware.

Satan threatens or orders about miserliness and poverty. Satan bids you the heinous and abominable things like prostitution, theft, sodomy, liquor, installation of idols, offerings other than to Allah, lottery etc. But Allah promises you forgiveness and enjoyable life in the Paradise. Satan prevents men from the Soul of Qur'an and thereby he prevents them from the way of Allah and lead to Hell with him. On the Day of Judgment satan will clear himself that his promises were false as told in the verse 14: 22. It is told in the verse 4: 120 that satan makes them promise and he creates in them false hopes. But satan's promises are nothing but deception. The verses 4: 37-38 say: Who are themselves niggards and enjoin others to be niggards, who hide the bounties which Allah has bestowed on them. For such disbelievers We have prepared a disgraceful punishment. Similarly, Allah does not like those who spend their wealth to show to the people, believing neither in Allah nor in the Last Day. In fact the one who chooses satan as his companion has chosen a very evil companion! The verse 43: 36 says: Who turns away from the Soul of Qur'an, We assign a satan for him, who becomes his intimate companion. Read together the verses 59: 16-17. See explanation 2: 99 and 166-170.

269. He gives wisdom to anyone He wishes; and anyone He gives wisdom to receive an abundant boon. Yet none will remember except people of understanding.

Wisdom means philosophy, discreteness, the ability to separate good and evil with the Soul of Qur'an as a criterion and the ability to join together the verses of Qur'an and there by confirm several subjects. The verse 8: 29 says, Oh you who believe, if you heed Allah, He will grant you a Criterion, absolve your evil deeds for you and forgive you. Allah possesses such splendid Bounty. The verse 39: 18 says, those who listen the verses of Qur'an attentively and follow It in the best way, such are the wise men. Read together the verse 3:7. The verse 36: 11 says: You can admonish such a one who follows the Soul of Qur'an and fears the Impartial unseen. Give such a one, therefore, good tidings of forgiveness and a reward most generous. See explanation 2: 231.

Prophet *Ibrahim* prayed to his Lord for wisdom as told in the verse 26: 83. Allah bestowed Wisdom on *Luqman* to show gratitude to Him as told in the verse 31: 12. Wisdom is the Soul of Qur'an. The verse 36: 2 says: By the Qur'an, full of Wisdom. We can make our whole life to Allah and keep His remembrance while walking, sitting and laying as His vicegerent. Those who received the Wisdom are the wise men. Read together the verses 3: 190- 191. The meaning of what is told in this verse 'whoever is granted wisdom is indeed given an abundant boon' and what is told by the Prophet: The best and noble one among you is who learns and teaches the Soul of Qur'an is the same. See explanation 2: 66 and 185.

270. Whatever you spend in charity or whatever vow you make, surely Allah knows it. The wrongdoers shall have no helpers.

Those who do not spend seeking the satisfaction of Allah- the Knower of all times, and those who expect the rewards and gratefulness from other than Allah and those who give offering to other than Allah are the wrongdoers and they do not get any aid or help. All the offerings should be for Allah only. And that is to spend to needy, poor, orphans and the captives. Read together the verses 76: 8-10. Today the noble deed is to spend wealth for learning and teaching the Soul of Qur'an. This is because any verse from Qur'an should support as proof in order the deed be to Allah. See explanation: 2: 111. Whatever offered for other than Allah is included in the prohibited flesh of swine as told in the verse 6: 145. Both of them are abomination and inducing hypocrisy. Read together the verses 6: 121and136- 140. The verses 3: 192 and 5:72 also end as: The wrongdoers shall have no helpers. See explanation 2: 173 and 254.

271. If you publicize any act of charity it is quite worthwhile; while if you conceal them and give to the poor it will be better for you, and will cancel out some of your evil deeds for you. Allah is well acquainted with what you are doing.

If anyone discloses his acts of charities before the public with the intension to stimulate others to do so, there is no blame on him. That will be accepted as according to the state of their hearts. But it is best for you to conceal the charity and make them reach to the poor men in secret. Allah will certainly accept it and there by blot out his evil deeds. Prophet, after the ceremony speech of *Eid*, went near to women and said: *"Oh women, I have seen many of you in the Hell than that of men, therefore you may increase your spending of charity.* As per the verse 9: 60 among the eight sects of people who deserve welfare tax, preference is given to the poor people. It is also told in coming verse 273 to give preference to the poor people. Read together the verses 39: 35; 48: 5 and 64: 9 See explanation 2: 234

272. Guiding them is not your duty, but Allah guides anyone He wishes to. Any money you may spend is for your own good and whatever you spend is craving to see Allah's face any money you spend will be repaid you, and you will not be wronged.

There was a belief among the believers that welfare tax and spending in charity will not be given to others except Muslims. Thus that doubt is annihilated through this verse. The Guidance is neither in the hand of Prophet nor in the hands of anybody else. Each individual has to ask the Guidance to the Lord by their soul. Therefore the believers will give welfare tax and spend in charity to any people irrespective of caste and religion seeking only Allah's pleasure. Those who spend their wealth to any people seeking only Allah's pleasure, Allah will renders back all their wealth and doubles it as told in the verse 2: 261.

Allah says in the verse 28: 56, certainly you will not be able to guide everyone whom you love but Allah guides whom He pleases and He knows best who receive Guidance. At the death time of Prophet's foster father *Abuthwalib*, Prophet told three times to him to say '*Shahadath*' (word of witness that there is no Deity except Allah) but he refused to say so. *Abuthwalib* asked: Oh Muhammad do you believe in the religion of forefather *Abdul Muthalib*? Prophet replied: 'No'. At that time this verse is revealed. As per the verses 9: 113 and 114 it is not permissible for the Prophet and the believers to seek forgiveness for those who associates others with in the dominion of Allah, even though they belong to near kin like mother and father after it is clear to them that they are the companions of Hell. This verse is revealed in the year of 9th *Hijra* during the last years of Prophet, pertaining to his mother. Prophet was prohibited to pray forgiveness for his mother since she had not followed the "Moosa's Shariath'- code of law of Moosa. Read together the verses 3: 128-129; 9: 23-24; 58: 22 and 63: 6. See explanation 2: 6 and 213.

A prostitute from the former people, when she saw a dog gulping mud to quench its thirst, she tore her cloth and tied it with her shoe and drew water from the well and gave the water to the dog and thereby entered in the Paradise. Another woman, she was very pious performed *swalath* and fasting but tied and killed a cat. She neither fed it nor untied to seek its own food and there by entered to the Hell taught by Prophet. The moral of these incidents are that, Allah sees to the heart while we are doing any deeds and the reward will be according to the intention. The believers should have mercy and love towards all creatures of Allah, and that is His character.

Today, the majority of Muslims have become merciless like that of a pretending pious woman who tied and killed the cat. They have become the party of satan. They belie Prophet in front of the public, who is sent as a Mercy to all worlds as per the verse 21: 107. They accept the name of Prophets, but their character and deeds are just opposite that of him. They are the people among the mankind who engaged more in bloodshed and mischief in Earth, and thus they worship or serve the satan and hide Allah and Prophets in the Soul of Qur'an. They are the '*Mujrims*' and fuel of Hell from mankind. Read together the verses 36: 59-62. This verse also teaches that each individual is earning Paradise or Hell for themselves. See explanation 1: 6.

Oh Allah! Make not us among the people who have forgotten You and the Day of Judgment. Make us among those who keep Your remembrance always with the Soul of Qur'an; and those who submit whole life to You by mind, words and deeds.

273. For the poor who being totally engaged in working for Allah's cause, cannot manage to travel around the Earth seeking their livelihood. An ignorant person might assure they are rich because of their modesty. Yet you will recognize them from their features: They do not make insistent demands on people. Anything good you spend yet Allah is Aware it.

Today, "totally engaged in Allah's way' means to spend time in learning, teaching and conveying the Soul of Qur'an. The poor men among these are given preference for welfare tax and charity because they are unable to engage in other activities like trade, commerce, cultivation etc. But they will not disclose their poverty to others; the ignorant men think, because of their modesty that they are free from want. But the believers shall identify them by their features. Prophet and his family do not deserve welfare tax and charity. But they deserve one fifth of the total booty. The verse 8: 41 says: And know that out of all the booty that you acquire in war, a fifth share is assigned to Allah and the Messenger and to near relatives, orphans, the needy and the way farer if you do believe in Allah and what We revealed to our servant on the day of discrimination and the meeting day of two forces, for Allah is capable of everything. Read together the verses 59: 7-9. See explanation 2: 215.

274. Those who spend their wealth in night and day, both privately and publicly, will receive their earnings from their Lord. On them have no fear and for them shall not be grieved.

The verse 13: 22 says: Those who patiently persevere seeking the countenance of their Lord, establish regular *swalath*, spend out of what We have bestowed for their sustenance secretly and openly and prevent evil with good, for such there is final attainment of eternal home. The verse 14: 31 says: Speak to My servants, who have believed, that they may establish regular *swalath* and spend out of the sustenance We have given them, secretly and openly, before the coming of a day in which there will be neither mutual bargaining nor befriending. The verse 35: 29 says that certainly those who recite the Book of Allah with Its Soul, establish regular *swalath* and spend out of what We have provided for them secretly and openly, hope for a commerce that will never loss. Read together the verse 16: 75. See explanation 2: 175 and 262.

275. The ones who are eating usury (earning by interest) will never stand up except like those who are knocked down by satan with a fit rise up again. That is because they say: Trading is just like usury, yet Allah has permitted trading and forbidden usury. Anyone who receives such an instruction from his Lord and stops doing so may keep previous gains; while his case rests with Allah. Those who do so over and over again will become inmates of the fire, to remain there forever.

Usury is from satan. Those who calculate the interest in the night go to sleep very late and in the morning he will find difficulties to awake and to continue his daily activities. Gradually, he will lose his sleepiness, his thinking ability and concentration and will lead a life that of a mad man. The trade and commerce in the condition of sharing only the profit without sharing the loss is also prohibited like usury. There is no prayer and excuse in usury. But there is prayer and excuse in the trade and commerce for seeking profit and it is also a service to people. Allah has permitted trade and commerce but prohibited usury and even to witness in transacting it.

Those who after receiving the instruction from their Lord if desist shall be pardoned the past and he has to teach the verses of Qur'an to other people for not involve in the usury and try to retreat them from usury. So Allah will pardon what he enjoyed in the past. But those who repeatedly receiving usury after receiving the do's and don'ts of Allah through the Soul of Qur'an, they are the inmates of Hell, they abide therein for ever. The verse 4: 29 says: Oh believers! Do not consume one another's wealth through unlawful. It means instead, do business with mutual consent; do not kill you by adopting unlawful means. Indeed Allah is Merciful to you. See explanation 2: 66 and 257.

276. Allah wipes out usury and nourishes acts of charity. Allah does not love any ungrateful sinner.

The verse 30: 39 says that which you give in usury increase through the property of people, will have no increase with Allah. But that which you give for charity seek in the countenance of Allah, it is these who will get a recompense multiplied. In the material vision usury will increase the wealth, and charity will decrease the wealth. But really, since Allah is satisfied with charity He will give increase the wealth and there by grant peace and tranquility. But, since satan is satisfied with usury, Allah has prohibited it, it will increase selfishness, niggardliness and hastiness to the material world, destroying peace and tranquility. But it will not be comprehensible to nine hundred and ninety-nine men out of every thousand since they have a veil on their eyes to the Soul of Qur'an. Allah will bring the Hell near to this sort of disbelievers on the Day of Judgment is told in the verse 18: 101. It is told in the verse 50: 22: Now We have removed your veil on eyes and sharp is your sight. It is only comprehensible to the believers since they utilize the Insight. But it will not be comprehensible to the sinners since they repeatedly reject and hide the verses of Qur'an. Read together the verse 6: 104.

277. Those who believe and perform honorable deeds, keep up swalath and pay the welfare tax, will receive their rewards from their Lord. On them have no fear and for them shall not be grieved.

Any deeds which justify at least a part of any verse from the Qur'an will only be accepted and become a good deed. Good deed means to make in practical life the do's and don'ts of the Qur'an. No deed will be accepted from hypocrites since they hide Allah and His Messenger in the Soul of Qur'an and they approach *swalath* unwillingly and with laziness and they give welfare tax with hatred as told in the verses 9: 53-54. From these verses we can understand that *swalath* and welfare tax are not sacred deeds but they are compulsory observances. Read together the verses 4: 142-143 and 107: 4. See explanation 2: 186.

278. Oh you who believe! Heed Allah and write off anything out standing gains from usury if you are true believers.

There are only two verses in Qur'an which begins as: 'Oh you who believe' and end as: 'if you are true believers'; the other verse is 5: 57. If we read together these two verses, we can understand that those who involve in usury are not believers, and the believers should not have relation with those who deal with usury. To heed Allah is possible only with the Soul of Qur'an. See explanation 2: 260-267.

279. If you don't do so, then be prepared to face war declared by Allah and His Messenger! If you repent, you may retain your capital, causing no wrong to others and you will not be wronged.

This verse is revealed on the day of '*Hajjathul Vida*' -'departing pilgrimage'- and the usury is completely prohibited. First usury relating to *Abbas*, younger brother of Prophet's father was prohibited. The verses 3: 130-131 say: Oh believers! Do not eat usury which is compounded over and over, and heed Allah so that you may prosper. Guard yourself against the Fire which is kept prepared for the disbelievers. And it was ordered to kill of those who involved in usury among the Muslims. That is the meaning of the saying in the verse: "Then be prepared to face war declared against you by Allah and His Messenger!" It is told in the verses 4: 160-161 that for the iniquity of Jews, We made unlawful for them certain good and wholesome foods which had been lawful for them. And they hindered many from Allah's way. That they took usury though they were forbidden and that they devoured men's wealth wrongfully. We have kept prepared for those among them who reject faith a grievous torment.

Today, as well as in all evil deeds Muslims is forefront in usury also. While other people demand and give moderate interest, the Muslims demand and give blade interest. By hiding and rejecting Soul of Qur'an which is the Light, most of them are following satanic footsteps such as smuggling, intoxicating drugs, black marketing, superstitions etc. The meaning of saying: "Causing no wrong to others and you will not be wronged" is you can take back the capital sum gradually without annoying the debtor and seek repentance to Allah about the usury you accepted in the past before receiving the Truth -Soul of Qur'an. See explanation 2: 188 and 261.

280. If the debtor is in a difficulty, grant him time till it is easy for him to repay; but if you waive the sum by way of charity, it will be better for you, if you only knew.

Believers are those who believe that real owner of all wealth are the Impartial and the most Merciful Allah. Since they are living as vicegerent of Allah, they will show sympathy to the debtors even by giving up the capital sum in order to reduce their brother's burden. Otherwise the believer will grant it as welfare tax, if he finds the debtor is unable to pay back the money. Prophet taught that *if anybody lightens the burden of his brother, Allah will also lighten his burden on the Day of Judgment; and if you show Mercy to those on Earth, He Who is in the Paradise will show mercy to you.* See explanation 2: 177 and 271.

281. Heed a Day when you will be brought back to Allah; when every soul will be paid in full according to whatever he has earned, and they will not be treated unjustly.

This verse is revealed nine days before the death of Prophet. This is the last revealed complete verse in the Qur'an. Those who have understood the aim of life and have constructed Paradise Here can return to that Paradise by their death. Allah warned through this verse that the real life begins after death and it will be eternal. So one shall has a conscious that he has to go back one Day. Only the believers shall have this conscious and reflect it by their mind, words and deeds. This verse also teaches that everyone is earning Paradise or Hell Here for Tomorrow. The verses 3: 25, 161; 6: 160; 10: 47, 54; 16: 111; 23: 62; 39: 69; 45: 25 and 46: 19 also end as: And they will not be treated unjustly. See explanation 2: 28, 254, and 274.

Oh Allah, show us the Truth and bless us to follow It, as It should be followed. Show us falsehood and bless us to avoid it, make us heedful who follow the Soul of Qur'an as It should be followed. Oh Allah, help us to remember our forgotten things and wash out it with the Soul of Qur'an -with full of Wisdom. Oh Allah, help us to die as innocent one as a new born baby submitting all before You in the time of our death. Oh Allah, enter us to Paradise with righteous and virtuous souls with the Ticket oh You Who sent down It! Oh the Most Merciful One among those Who are Merciful!

282. Oh you who believe! Whenever you contract a debt for a stated period, write it down. Let some literate person write between you properly; no literate person should refuse to write it down. And let the borrower dictate. May he heed Allah and not omit any part of it. If the borrower is feeble minted or incapacitated

or cannot manage to dictate himself, then let his guardian dictate it in all justice, and seek out two witnesses from among your men-folk to act as witnesses if there are not two men available, then one man and two women as witnesses from anyone you may approve of, so that if either of them should slip up, then the other woman may remind the other. Witnesses must not refuse to when they are called upon to do so, nor try to get out of writing anything down whether it is small or large, along with its due date. Such is more equitable, so far as Allah is concerned, because it facilitates the establishment of evidence and is the best way to remove all doubts; unless it is a common commercial transaction concluded on the spot among yourselves, there is no blame on you if you do not put it in writing. You should have witnesses whenever you engage in trade. Let no harm be done to the scribe or witnesses; and if you do so, you shall be guilty of transgression. Heed Allah; and Allah teaches you and Allah has knowledge of everything.

This verse is known as '*Ayathudhain*' -the verse of debt, which is the largest verse in the Qur'an. 'To write justly as Allah has taught' means, one should live in the conscious that all knowledge is from Allah and utilize that knowledge beneficial to other creatures and also have the conscious that Allah is watching all things, and one Day everyone has to answer in front of Allah about the blessings He bestowed upon them. The debtor who incurs the liability should tell the scriber to write all conditions without any loss or difficulty to the money lender.

Since it is told in the verse that if two men witnesses can't be found, then one man and two women you approve can be taken as witnesses, we can understand that it is not compulsory that the women might be believers. In the place of a man two women are prescribed to witness so that if one of them slip the other can remind her and generally the women are liable to enticement and menace and thereby they change their affidavit. Allah says in the verse 16: 97 that whoever put the do's and don'ts of the Soul of Qur'an in to practice, men or women, and has faith, certainly to them will We give a life that is good and pure in this world, and We will bestow on such their reward according to the best of their deeds, in the Hereafter". Read together the verses 3: 195; 4: 124 and 40: 40. From all these verses we can understand that the believing man and woman are equal and the believing woman never be deviated from the Straight path. Keeping the orders in the verses 4: 34; 24: 31 and 33: 59, the believers do not bring the believing woman before the public for witnessing and other purposes. That is why it is told in the verse to get two women such as you can approve as witnesses.

It is just and more suitable for evidence to write all dealings whether it is big or small for avoiding doubts in the future. There is no blame if not wrote on the spot transactions, but take witnesses in order to prevent the denial from the part of receiver without fearing Allah and not to loss the giver. Otherwise, the receiver some time may say that he received low quality items, or the low quality products that he bought from one shop will be returned to other shop and get the money cheating the shop owner. Those who keep not the conditions in the dealings and annoy the writer and witnesses are hypocrites who lost the aim of life are warned through this verse.

Today, the receipt, bill, cheque, etc. can be considered in place of witnesses. Prophet taught that the following persons' prayer will not be answered. (1) Those who maintain a wife with bad character not divorcing her. (2) Those who are not considering this verse by not writing the debt transactions, and (3) those who clear off the responsibility by giving back the property of orphans before they attain maturity. To put it brief, as there are guidelines in all sector of life, there are instructions in debt transaction also. Prophet taught that to pray always for giving back the debt.

Oh Allah, our Lord, make easy in our difficulties, make our matters without troublesome, keep away difficulties from us, bless us to repay our debts, cure our diseases, help us to fulfill all our good desires, Oh you, the Accomplisher who fulfill all demands.

Even though Prophet had not big debts, he used to pray as, "*In whose hands the dominion of all things, He who is Most Glorious. He gives refuge to all things but none give refuge to Him. He gives sustenance to all beings but no one give sustenance to Him, The forelock of all things in His hands. He lives by self and dies not. Oh Allah, no God except You, no Lord besides You. You are the first person and before You nothing, You are the last One and after You nothing (He has no beginning or end). You are the visible One and above You nothing, You are the innermost and nothing is in Your interior. Oh Allah, help to repay my debts and release me from poverty and make me among the one who prosper*"

If anyone dies in a state of debts, his debts and legacies should be paid before dividing his property to inheritors as explained in the verse 4: 12. See explanation 2: 245.

283. If you are on a journey and don't find a literate person to write down the transaction, then a deposit may be withheld as a lien. If one of you entrusts something to another, the one who has been entrusted with it should handover his security and he should heed Allah- his Lord and not hide any testimony. Anyone who hides it has a sinful heart. Allah is knower of anything you do.

The character of the believers is that they faithfully observe their trust and their covenants are told in both verses 23: 8 and 70: 32. The verse 4: 58 says: Certainly Allah commands you to give back the trusts to their rightful owners, and when you judge between people, you should judge with justice. Surely, excellent is the counsel which Allah gives you. Allah is He who hears and observes all. The character of Jews towards '*Amanath*'- trusts are shown in the verse 3: 75 as: If you entrusted some people of the Book with a heap of gold, they would hand It back to you. While if you entrusted with a gold coin, some of them would never hand it back to you unless you constantly keep on demanding. So the believers should not have that character since they are the representatives of Allah. As per the verse 44: 18 Prophet *Moosa* who was deputed to Pharaohs says: Hand over to me the servants of Allah. I am to you a Messenger, worthy of all trust. The verse 8: 27 says: Oh you who believe, betray not the trust of Allah and the Messenger, nor misappropriate knowingly the things entrusted to you. It is told in the verse 33: 72 that certainly Allah did indeed offer the trust to the Heaven, Earth and the mountains. But they refused to undertake It, being afraid their off. But the mankind undertook It. He was indeed wrongdoer as well as ignorant.

The '*Amanath*'- Trust means belief, responsibility, fearlessness etc. The Trust mentioned in the verse 33: 72 is the Soul of Qur'an that is the Balance to keep the Earth in its equilibrium. The Qur'an is the Guidance for all human beings. It is the responsibility of the believers to propagate Its soul to whole mankind irrespective of nation, religion, sex etc in order to avoid bloodshed, and there by make harmony of human unity. But the hypocritical men and women, who hide the Soul of Qur'an which is the Trust, divided into several parties and become

Mushrik. They do not give back any trust to its owner which they are assigned or they give back them making some changes. These people are the worst of beasts in all worlds. The purpose of sending down the Soul of Qur'an is told in the verse 33: 73 as: In order to punish the hypocritical men and women, *Mushrik* men and women; and to relent with believing men and believing women, Allah is Forgiving, Merciful. Read together the verse 59: 21. See the explanation 2: 99 and 140.

284. To Allah belongs whatever is in the Heavens and whatever is on Earth; whether you disclose what is in your minds or hide it, Allah will bring you to account for it. He forgives anyone He wishes to and punishes anyone He wishes; Allah is Capable of everything.

The verse 5: 120 says: To Allah belong the dominion of the Heaven and Earth and all that there in, and He is capable of everything. As per the verse 31: 16, the wise *Luqman* advised his son: Oh my son, if there be a thing related to you as small as a mustard seed and it was hidden in the layers of rock or anywhere in the Heaven or on Earth, Allah will bring it forth for reckoning. Certainly Allah is the most subtle, acquainted of all things. Prophet *Ibrahim* prays in the verse 14: 38 as: Oh our Lord, certainly You know what we conceal and what we reveal. For nothing whatever is hidden from Allah, whether on Earth or in Heaven. The verse 6: 103 says by introducing Allah: No vision can grasp Him, but His grasp is over all vision, He is subtle, acquainted of all things. In brief, any deed anywhere and whenever, which justifies not a part of verse in the Qur'an will be brought for trial. As per the verses 17: 13- 14 everyone's fate is fastened in their neck. The *Nafs-Muthmainna*- the soul which acquired peace and tranquility will only return to Paradise seeing Allah's face happily at the time of their death is told in the verses 75: 22-23. They were constructing Paradise here and have identified the Lord as well as themselves by utilizing the Soul of Qur'an as Insight. See the explanation 2: 106- 107 and 255.

285. The Messenger believed in what has been sent down to him from his Lord, and so do believers; everyone believed in Allah, His Angels, His books and His Messengers. We do not differentiate between any of His Messengers. And they say: "We have heard and obeyed. Grant us Your Pardon, Oh our Lord; to You we shall all return".

'To believe with Allah, His Prophets, His Angels' means to follow the life of Prophet by mind, words and deeds as it is seen from the verses of Qur'an. Allah says in the verse 4: 136 by calling the believers: Oh you, who believe, believe with Allah, His Messenger and the Book which He has sent to His Messenger and the Book which He sent to those before him. Any who disbelieves with Allah, His Angels, His books, His Messengers and the Day of Judgment has gone far astray. Here the word '*Kutub*'- books the plural form of '*Kithab*'- Book is used. To believe with books means not only to believe in four books and several booklets (written documents on leaves) but to believe that only 'one Book' is revealed and Its soul is the same while Its body is in different languages. See the explanation 2: 2. All the Prophets were given the Book, only those who received the Book are divided into schism. See the explanation 2: 176and 213.

But today, the men-devil hypocrites whom Allah has killed and ordered the believers to kill through three verses are hiding the Soul of Qur'an which is the greatest splendid book as told in the verses 41: 41-42. They are twisting the verses of Qur'an according to their whims and fancies. They make several superstitions and observances. By doing all these satanic activities they are destroying the Earth and Universe. As per the verse 4: 145 they will go to the deepest depth of Hell even without trial.

The saying of 'what We make no distinctions among the Messengers' is not against what is said in the verse 2: 253 that We gave special privilege to some Prophets than others. It is Allah who gives special privilege to Prophets. But what is told here is that the believers make no distinctions among any Prophets. They believe that all Prophets were deputed by Allah in order to declare that there is no Deity except Allah and all of them are believers and are included in the single party of Allah- which includes Allah, Prophets and believers as told in the verses 5: 56 and 58: 22. Read together the verses 37: 111, 122, 132 and 63: 8.

When we say: 'unto You is our return' we should pray by mind: Oh Allah, make our return to Paradise, and not to Hell with the Ticket. All mankind came from the Paradise. See explanation 2: 38. And those who desire to return back to the Paradise should take the Ticket which is the soul of the Qur'an as told in both the verses 73: 19 and 76: 29. See the explanation 2: 3- 5, 126 and 136-139.

286. Allah does not assign a soul except it cope with. It is credited with whatever it has earned, while it is debited with whatever it has brought upon itself. "Our Lord, do not take us to task if we have forgotten or slipped up! Our Lord, do not lay any obligation upon us, such as You placed on those before us. Our Lord, do not over burden us with more than we can bear! Pardon us, forgive us and show us mercy! You are our Protector, so help us against disbelieving people."

'it' referred in the verse, is the soul. The soul of men and women is the same whereas body is different. The 'soul' is usually used in feminine gender. The verse 39: 41 says 'indeed We have sent you down the Book with Truth for mankind, anyone who is guided, then it will be for his own sake, while anyone who goes astray will only stray because of it as well. You are not any setup as any guardian over them. Allah, the Impartial and Most Merciful, sends no one to Hell unless he bears witness against himself that he was a disbeliever. And it is told in the verse 36: 70 that the soul of Qur'an is sent down in order that they bear witness against themselves that they were disbelievers. As per both verses 6: 130 and 7: 37, those who do not utilize the Soul of Qur'an after receiving It will bear witness against themselves that they were disbelievers. The aim of life of mankind in the fourth phase on Earth is to prepare Paradise here in order to inherit it in the seventh phase.

Those who are literates should utilize their knowledge to learn the Soul of Qur'an and teach It to others. It is told in the verse 32: 22 that whoever turns away from the verses of their Lord after remembering It in their own heart's language, and lead their former way of life neglecting It are the wrongdoers. And Indeed We would revenge to such *Mujrims*. Even the time of Prophet a certain group of people, without participating in the war were deputed to learn the Soul of Qur'an and teach It to others as told in the verse 9: 122. It is told in the verse 9: 6 that if a pagan who has not heard the Soul of Qur'an ask asylum in front of war, grant it to him, so that he may hear the Words of Allah and should escort him to where he can be secure. But today, there is no war. In turn, only '*Jihad*' with the Soul of Qur'an against those who hide It as commanded through the verses 9: 73 and 25: 52.

The word '*Moulana*' is also used in the verse 9: 51. Both in the verses it is used for Allah only. Then, those who call '*Moulana*' for Prophet or others; saying that '*Moulana*' is the plural from of '*Moulavi*', '*Moula*', '*Moulaya*' etc. are the disbelievers and those who compel them to call are the men-devil hypocrites. Allah has warned through the verse 7: 180 to avoid such people. Likewise '*Moula*' and '*Mavaliya*' one can call the creatures '*Rabb*' as mentioned in the Qur'an. For e.g. Prophet *Yoosuf* mentioned about the king of Egypt by saying 'your rabb' to the youth who was released from the jail, as told in the verse 12: 42. But it is not permissible to any Prophet or believer, to call '*Rabbuna*' or '*Moulana*' except for Allah. See the explanation 1: 7, 2: 166 and167

Allah has commanded the believers to pray these verses always. These two verses 2: 285 and 286 are one of the two lights given to Prophet Muhammad from the Paradise which were not given to any other prophets. Prophet used to pray these verses after the *swalath* of '*Faj'r*' and '*Maghrib*' and before going to sleep.

Oh Allah, include us not among the disbelievers who hide, belie and reject the Truth. But include us among the believers, righteous people and with those who move seeing You and those who submit to You by mind, words and deeds. Oh Allah includes us with those who make the Qur'an truthful, with those to whom the Qur'an will bear witness and argue in favor. Oh Allah, enter us to the Paradise with the *Sabiqeens*- forerunners and virtuous with the Ticket, oh the One Who sent down the Ticket, Oh the Virtuous and the Merciful.

With the name of Allah, the Impartial, the compassionate.

3. Ali-Imran

The meaning of *Ali-Imran* is "*Imran's family*". This *Surath* is named *Ali-Imran* because the verse 33 refers about *Imran's* family. This *surath* contains the verses which explain about the battles between the believers and the disbelievers occurred in 2nd year of "*Hijra*" at "*Badr*", and 3rd year of '*Hijra*' at "*Uh'd*". It also contains the verses connected to the conversation of Prophet with a Christian group came from *Najran* on the 9th year of *Hijra*. After explaining the life histories of *Maryam, Eisa* - the son of *Maryam, Zakariya, Yahya*, etc. it invites the children of Israel and Christians - the people of Book- to the real belief and to their forefathers' way of life. As Qur'an is the one and only Book today for entire mankind, every verse which says about the "people of Book" is applicable to the Muslims, including hypocrites and disbelievers. This *Surath* teaches that the battle of *Uh'd* was made to separate the true believers and hypocrites from among the Muslims. Islam is the only way of life which the Creator well-pleased to all his creatures. This *Surath* also teaches that, it is not possible for anyone, even for prophet or any other creatures to admit or not to admit anybody in to this way of life.

This *Surath* contains so many verses which explain about the character of believers. Some of the people who had given Book earlier will announce their belief with tearful eyes by fearing Allah, whenever the Qur'an is recited to them. It commands to the believers to be a single party by holding the Soul of Qur'an firmly. This *Surath* is a component of '*Zaharavan*'-two flower gardens. It contains 200 verses. Prophet used to pray the verses 18, 26 and 27 daily as '*vird*' after '*Fajr*' and '*Magrib' swalath*. Prophet used to recite the verses 190 to 200 as soon as he wakes up from sleep.

With the name of Allah, the Impartial, the Compassionate

1. Alif- Laam- Meem.

The Book which is revealed from Allah through *Jibreel* to Prophet Muhammad. See the explanation 2: 1.

2. **Allah! There is no Deity except Him: The Ever living, the Survivor and Sustainer of all.**

This verse which contains the most glorious name of Allah has come as a part of the verse 2: 255. "The Ever living, The Survivor" belongs to the Supreme names of Allah.

3. **Step by step He has sent down to you this Book with Truth confirming whatever existed before It; and He sent down Thourat and Injeel.**

4. **In the past as Guidance for mankind; also sent down the Criterion. Surely those who hide the verses of Allah will have severe torment. Allah is Almighty, the capable of retribution.**

Allah has sent down only one Book in different periods to the Earth. The soul of the Book is the same even though they named differently as *Thourat* (Torah), *Injeel* (Gospel), *Zaboor* (Psalm) etc. The entire Book with single soul and different bodies were Guidance to the Truth for the people of relevant periods. The *Furqan* (criterion for judgment between right and wrong) of all periods was the quintessence of those books. But Qur'an is the only complete Book - *Al kithab* - which contains the Book and '*ummul kithab*'- the foundation of the Book or the opening *Surath*. It confirms and preserves all the books which revealed before It. It is the Criterion and Book which explains about all the necessary Guidance to the Truth for the entire mankind till the Dooms day. See the explanation 2:185. The verses 4:163 and 17:55 say that, We have given "*Zaboor*" to *Davood*. In the verse 26:196 says: Surely, this Qur'an is there in previous "*Zubur*" (previous *Psalms*). "*Kuthub*" (books) is the plural form of "Kithab" (Book); like that "*Zubur*" is the plural form of "*Zaboor*". See explanation 2:2, 121, 147 and 285.

The Soul of Qur'an is the only Balance to keep the Universe in its equilibrium and the only Ticket for mankind for returning to the Paradise. So, concealing It from others is the greatest sin. Surely, Allah will take revenge on them. In the verse 39: 63 it is told that, those who hide the verses of Allah are the losers; and as per the verse 32: 22 it is told that, they are the wrongdoers and

Mujrims, and indeed Allah will revenge on such *Mujrims*. The verses 4:17, 6: 54 and 16:119 say that: surely, Allah's forgiveness is only for those who do evils by ignorance. In verses 4:137 and 138 it is told to inform the "happy news" of painful punishment for the hypocrites who knowingly hide the message of Qur'an. The verse 5: 95 ends as; Allah is Almighty, Capable of retribution, and the verse14: 47 ends as; surely, Allah is Almighty, Capable of retribution. See explanation 2:161and 174-176.

5. Certainly Allah, nothing in the Earth or in the Heaven is hidden from Him.

The verse 14: 38 says "Our Lord! Certainly You know what we conceal and what we reveal. In fact, nothing on the Earth or in Heaven is hidden from Allah. The verse 40:16 says; nothing of them will be hidden from Allah, it will be asked in this Day (Day of Judgment) "whose is the Kingdom today?" It is Allah, the One, and the Almighty. The verse 41: 40 says that, surely those who distort and repudiate on our verses are not hidden from Us. Who is better, the One to be thrown to the Hell Fire or the one who comes safe and secured in the Day of Judgment? Do as you like; surely He is watching all your actions. See explanation 1:3, 2:255 and 284.

6. He it is Who shapes you in the wombs as He wishes. There is no Deity except Him, the Almighty, the Wise.

Allah has created the entire mankind (soul) in the Paradise itself at the same time when He created Adam. Allah asks in the verse 76:1 that: Has there not passed over man a countless period of time when he was nothing worth mentioning? He is the One Who shapes human body as male and female in the wombs, after passing various stages starting from "*Nuthfa*" (sperm of male and ovum of female). When the embryo having the life attains four months old, through an angel Allah blows the soul into it, which was kept on the nape of its father. See explanation 2: 28and 129.

7. He is the One Who sent you down the book, which contains decisive verses. They form the basis of the Book; while others are allegorical. Then those hearts are prone to falter follow whatever is allegorical in It, seeking to create dissension by giving their own interpretation of It. Yet only Allah knows its

interpretation, those who are versed in knowledge say: "We believe in It; It is all from our Lord". But none will grasp except the prudent persons who utilize their intelligence.

There are two types of verses in Qur'an. The verses which are having clear messages by themselves and well explained are called '*Muh'kamaat* verses'. They are the foundation of the Book. Previous Scriptures contained only such verses. The unique peculiarity of Qur'an is that; It contains '*Muthashabihath*' - verses. The unique peculiarity of Qur'an is that; allegorical. That is verses having comparable meaning also. In the verse 39:23 Allah says: Allah is the One Who has sent down this Book with best messages which contains both allegorical and repeating verses. By that, the skin of those who fears Allah will thrill; and their skin and heart will become soft; and they will deeply involve in the remembrance of "Allah", i.e., in the Soul of Qur'an. That is the Guidance of Allah, With It, He leads the One whom He wishes in the Straight path. Read together the verse 11:1.

The word "*Tha'veel*" in Arabic is translated as interpretation has different meanings like "news", "explanation", "prophesy" etc. The word "*Tha'veel*" mentioned in the verses 12: 6, 100 and 101 is about the interpretation (explanation) of *Yoosuf's* dream. "*Tha'veel*" mentioned in the verse 7:53 is about prophesies of Qur'an. But in this verse, "*tha'veel*" means the explanation of allegorical verses. This verse warns that, those persons who ask the explanation of allegorical verses are crook minded hypocrites. Prophet taught *"Do not recite Qur'an without knowing its content"*. Against this teaching, the above mentioned hypocrites only quote prophet's another teaching that *"no one recites Alif-Laam-Meem without recording ten virtues for each word (Alif-Laam-Meem)"*; and they say, though *Alif-Laam-Meem* do not have any meaning, reciting it is rewarded. By saying so, they mean that reciting Qur'an without knowing the content will be rewarded. Thus they prevent the common people from studying the Soul of Qur'an. They quarrel with the believers who inform the people that the Soul of Qur'an is made very easy to understand and to remember according to the verse 54:17. Quoting Prophet's teaching that *"reciting Qur'an without knowing Its content will make one to dart away from the Dheen like an arrow darts from its bow, and the recited Qur'an will argue and witness against him"*. Knowing the quintessence of complete Qur'an is worthless to such hypocrites. They will not follow or teach It to others. The verse 6: 26 says about them: they themselves have turned away from the Qur'an and obstruct other people from It. With such behavior they harm none, but themselves; but they do not perceive it. See explanation 2: 159-161, 166 and 167.

Prophet taught that those who recite Qur'an can be grouped into three. (1) *Fajir* – He eats Qur'an or eats using Qur'an, eating Qur'an means reading Qur'an's Arabic text from first to last without knowing its meaning or content by expecting reward from Allah. Eat using Qur'an means; earning and eating with It by reciting Qur'an near the dead body, teaching Qur'an's Arabic text, leading the *swalath* and writing Qur'an verses on paper, metallic sheet, plates etc and earn money by it. (2) *Kaffir* (hypocrites) - one who hides Qur'an after knowing Its content. (3) *Mu'min* (Believer) —One who understands and follows the message in his day to day life. From among these three groups who recite Qur'an, only the believer will get reward for reciting *Alif-Laam-Meem* and for other allegorical verses. Hypocrites will not get any reward though they know all its content. The verse 2: 174 says: hypocrites and *fujjar* are filling fire into their bellies. The verse 9: 125 says, by reciting Qur'an this people will add filth to their existing filth and will repel far. The verse 17: 82 says: Qur'an is healing and Mercy for the believers; while to the wrongdoers It increases nothing except loses. The verse 32: 22 says that, who could be the mad and the biggest wrongdoer than the one who turns away from the verses of his Lord after it is reminded in his heart's language. Prophet taught that *"the worst among the people is the one who reads Qur'an from first to last but gets nothing from It"*. Here it says '*fujjar*' (plural of '*fajir*') as the worst instead of saying about hypocrites, because Allah has killed the hypocrites and they will go to hell without even trial. Read together the verses 4: 145and 63: 4. '*fujjar*' are the *kafirs* - disbelievers- who go to hell after interrogation as told in the verse 39: 71. See explanation 2: 6, 7 and 254.

The verse 4: 162 also says about the people who have versed knowledge as the '*Rasikh*. They deeply research and find out the message of allegorical verses on the basis of the verses 16: 89 and 6: 38 which says that, Qur-an is the Book which explains about everything. The word "*Khabeer*" mentioned in the verse 25: 58 is Allah, Omniscient who knows about all the times-past, present and future. And in the verse 25: 59 says, about *Khabeer* Allah, you ask to *khabeer*- means the one who knows the spirit, soul and interpretation of Qur'an which is the knowledge about all the times- past, present and future. The "*Rasikh*" mentioned in this verse is the similar to that of "*Khabeer*" mentioned in verse 25: 59. In the verses 16: 43 and 21: 7 say that: Ask about the unknown facts to those who know the Soul of Qur'an. Based on this, Prophet taught: "*Such a person who has acquainted knowledge in the Soul of Qur'an is with noble virtuous angels.*" Read together the verses 80: 11-16. See explanation 2: 2, 152 and 269.

8. Our Lord! Do not deviate our hearts from the Truth after You have guided us. Grant us Your own Mercy generously. Indeed You are the Grantor of Bounties without measure.

Allah himself teaches that, this is the prayer of those who have well acquainted knowledge. They learn and teach the Soul of Qur'an by praying: "My Lord! Increase me in my knowledge" as taught through the verse 20: 114. Here the word "*Rahmath*" (Mercy) means the Soul of Qur'an itself. The word "generously" means without any measure, without any reason etc. In the verse 7, Allah has stated that the hypocrites are with doubtful mind; and here in this verse He says the prayer of those who are well acquainted in knowledge will be for not to make crookedness in our mind and not to include among the hypocrites. In the verse 38: 55, prophet *Sulaiman's* prayer also ends as: "Indeed, You are the Grantor of Bounties without measure". See explanation 1: 2 and 2: 105.

9. Our Lord! Indeed You will gather all mankind on a Day – about which there is no doubt. Surely Allah will never go back from His promise.

As told in the verse 64: 9: This is the Day on which selling and buying is not possible. The verse 13: 31 also ends as: Surely, Allah will never go back from His promise. The verse 3: 194 ends as: Surely, You never go back from Your promises. See explanation 1: 3 and 2: 281.

10. Certainly, for those who hide the Truth, neither their wealth nor their children will benefit them from Allah. And such are only the firewood for the fire.

The disbelievers mentioned here are the hypocrites who hide the Soul of Qur'an after knowing It, as told in the verses 2: 6-7. Both the verses 9: 55and 85 say that neither their wealth nor their children dazzle you; surely, Allah intends to punish them with these things in this worldly life, and that their souls may depart while they are still disbelievers. Prophet has prophesied about them at his Mecca period itself. Read together the verses 3: 116, 196 and 197. From Prophet's teaching reported by mother of *Ibnu Abbas*; she said: *One night when we were at Mecca, Prophet awoke and asked three times that "Oh Allah, didn't I convey?" At that time Umer awoke and replied that "yes, you did". Then in the morning Prophet said: Islam will spread all over the world, and then it will be replaced with refusals. The people of overseas (Europeans and Americans) will laugh at Islam. Then another period will come in which the people will study and recite Qur'an, and they will say and ask: We are reciting and teaching Qur-an, then who is better than us? Then Prophet asked: Is there any goodness in them? Then followers asked: Oh Prophet, who are they? Prophet replied: They are from among you; they themselves are the firewood of fire.* In this teaching Prophet said to the followers: "They are from among you" instead of saying: "They are you". From this we can realize that kafirs-disbelievers are coming only from the Muslim community. Instead of teaching the Soul of Qur'an, they teach Arabic text of Qur'an which is Its body, and the meaning which is Its life only.

Through the verses 4: 91; 9: 123 and 33: 61 Allah commands to the group of believers to kill such hypocrites. If there is a group of believers, Allah has promised ruling power on Earth to them in the verse 24: 55. As such a group of believers does not exist presently; this will be implemented only after the second coming of *Eisa*. Prophet taught that, *during the last days, a group of people who talk good words with a smiling face will come as the spokesmen of Islam. These people will say what they don't do, and will not do what they say. Such people will dart from Islam in the speed of an arrow dart from the bow;* and prophet also taught *to kill them whenever you meet with them.* See explanation 1: 7; 2: 39 and 254.

11. Like the family of Pharoah as well as those before them. They rejected Our verses. So Allah seized them on account of their offences. And Allah is severe in punishment.

The verses 8: 52 and 54 are also with the same contents. *Pharoah's* family means those who follow the footsteps of *Pharoah*. Like that "*Ali-Muhammad*"- family of Muhammad, includes the believers who follow his footsteps manners until the Last Day, let them be from his family or not. Allah punished *Pharoah* only when he became a transgressed hypocrite after realizing all the Truth. Read together the verse 9: 67. Like that, when there is not even a single *Mu'min* (believer) among Muslims; and whole Muslim multitude become hypocrites, Allah will put an end to this world. Read together the verses 46: 35. Their 5th phase "*Barsakh*" - the resting place after death- will be a pit from the Hell. There, the Hell will be exposed to them in its real appearance in every morning and evening. In the Day of Judgment, they will be thrown to the Hell without trial, is told in the verse 40: 46. See explanation 2: 99, 174-176.

12. Tell those who disbelieve: You will be defeated and summoned to Hell. What a horrible cradles!

The verses 2: 206; 3: 197; 13: 18 and 38: 56 also end as: "What a horrible cradles!" In this verse, the word cradle is used about the Hell, because the flames of the Hell fire will surround them like a cradle comfortably covers a child. In the verses 7: 40- 41 it is told that, for the mad wrongdoers, including *fujjar* who reject the Soul of Qur'an and hypocrites who are proud of their knowledge without the Soul of Qur'an, will have cradles in the Hell with its flame as their blankets. In the verse 2: 175 Allah asks: What a patience they are showing for the Fire. See explanation 2: 166 and167.

13. Indeed there was a sign for you in the two detachments that met in the battle field (of Badr), One detachment fighting in the way of Allah, the other disbelieving. With their own eyes they saw the others as twice their number. Allah strengthens with His own aid to whom He wishes. Surely there is a lesson for those who have Insight.

Here says about the battle of *Badr* occurred in 17th Ramdhan of *Hijra* 2nd year between *Islam* and *Kufr* -denial. One was Allah's party and other side was satan's party. Read together the verse 8: 48. Disbelievers were actually three times in number than the believers. But in the first sight believers felt that the disbelievers are only just double in number and thus Allah donated courage and stability for the believers. To get an easy victory for the believers, Allah gave laziness for the disbelievers by showing the believers as few in number. Thus Allah accomplishes what He determined earlier. In the verses 8: 43-44 Allah says: It is rememberable that in your dream Allah showed to you them as few in number, if He had shown to you them as many in number, you would surely have been discouraged and would have quarreled in your decisions. But Allah saved you. Surely He knows what is in the chest. And remember when you met in the battle, He showed to you them as few in number in your eyes and made you appear as few in number in their eyes, so that Allah might accomplish what He had decided: for all thing return to Allah for decision. Believers are those people who remember Allah always, entrust up on Him; and pray only to Him for protection at any situation. Read together the verses 8: 45-47. The disbelievers who came with great pride were well armed, more than thousand in number and had made battle as their life style. Against them on the other side, it was a small party of Allah with only 313 members, inexpert in war and without sufficient weapons. But Allah sent down angels to help them against the disbelievers.

Allah says in the verses 8: 17-19, it was not you who killed them, but it was Allah who killed them; it was not you who threw, but it was Allah who threw it, so that He might pass the believers successfully through this excellent trial. Surely, Allah is All-hearing, All-knowing. That is His dealing with you. Allah is He who weakens the evil plans of disbelievers. Allah says to the disbelievers, if you wanted for a decision, now it has indeed come to you. If you cease, it will be better for you. If you repeat your act, We also shall return. Your forces, however large in number they may be, shall benefit you nothing. Surely, Allah is with the believers. There are so many lessons in that event of the *Furqan* day -day of decision- for those intelligent believers who make use of the Soul of Qur'an as the Insight. Read together the verse 8: 41. Meaning of "there is a lesson for those who have Insight" is that Allah will help those believers who live as His representatives in an unseen way i.e. beyond reason and sense experience. See explanation 1: 4; 2: 102, 243 and 251.

14. The love of Passions from women and sons has made attracted for mankind, as well as accumulated gold and silver treasures, pedigreed horses, livestock and crops. That means enjoyment during worldly life, Allah holds the finest retreat.

15. Ask: Should I give you news of something even better than that? Those who are heedful will have Paradise beneath which rivers flow to live in forever with their Lord, plus purified spouses and good pleasure of Allah. Allah is observant of His servants.

For "nine hundred and ninety-nine" out of every "thousand" satan will make attractive the comforts of this world. But the believers, who are only "one" in each thousand, knowing the goal of life, will prepare the Paradise Here using the Soul of Qur'an. Allah created the entire mankind in Paradise and sent to earth to make Paradise Here. Keeping this aim in mind, they will utilize all the Bounties that Allah has bestowed to them in the light of Qur'an and will make the Paradise from Here itself utilizing this world as a farmland for the life of the Hereafter.

Read together the verses 8: 28 and 43: 32-35. In the verse 64: 15 Allah says: Surely, your wealth and your children are a temptation (destructive); whereas Allah, with Him is the greatest reward. And in verse 16 says: Therefore heed Allah as much as you can, listen attentively, obey and spend; that is better for your own souls. Those who are saved from their narrowness of soul; it is they, they are the only prosper. The following verses 16, 17 and 18 explain about the characters, prayers and deeds of such believers who are the most favorite servants of Allah. See explanation 2: 25 and 3: 10.

16. They are those who pray: "Oh our Lord, surely we sincerely believe. So please forgive us our offences and shield us from the torment of the Fire!

17. They are the patient ones, truthful, devotees, spenders and seek forgiveness in the late hours of night.

In the verses 25: 63-64, it is told that the servants who approved Allah as Impartial will spend their night for Him, by prostrating and standing. In the verses 51: 17-18 Allah describes about the character of heedful people, who entered to the Paradise as: They used to sleep but a little of the night, and were praying for forgiveness in the late hours of night. In the verse 33: 35 it is told that: Surely, the men and women who surrender to Allah, the men and women who believe, the men and women who devote, the men and women who make true the Soul of Qur'an, the men and women who are patient, the men and women who fear Allah, the men and women spending charity, the men and women who fast, the men and women who guard their chastity, the men and women who remember Allah always-for all such Allah has prepared and kept forgiveness and great reward. In the verse 32: 15 and 16 it is told that, surely those people who believe in Our verses are when remembered with It in their heart's language will fall down prostrating themselves in adoration and glorify the praises of their Lord; and they are not the one who turns with false pride. Their bodies do give up their beds of sleep and invoke their Lord with fear and hope and will always spend of what We have given them. In the verse 17 says: No one knows what delights have been kept hidden for them as a reward for their good deeds, which they were doing here. And the verse 18 asks that, can he who is a believer be like the one who is a transgressor? Of course they are not alike. The features of the believers further described in the verse 9: 112 as: Those who turn to Allah in repentance, serve Him, praise Him, move about in the land for His sake, bow down their heads prostrate in *swalath,* enjoin what is good and forbid what is evil, and observe the limits (permissions and prohibitions) set by Allah. Proclaim the good news to such believers (they are the ones who make such a bargain told in the verse 9: 111 with Allah). See explanation 1: 6; 2: 218 and 3: 7.

18. Allah witness: Certainly there is no Deity except Him. And the Angels and those who are well grounded in the Soul of Qur'an - standing with justice – also witness that there is no Deity except Him, the Almighty, the Wise.

In the verse 6: 19, after commanding to ask whose witness is the most reliable, Allah commands to the Prophet to say that witness between you and me is Allah and the Qur'an which has been revealed to me by Him; so that I may warn you there by and all those whomsoever It may reach. Then can you really witness that there are other deities besides Allah presented by Qur'an? Tell them: "I bear no such witness", again say: "Surely He is the one and only Deity. Surely I am absolutely innocent of that which you associate with Him". Allah, Angels and the believers who study and follow the Soul of Qur'an are in a single party- Allah's party. Read together the verses 5: 56 and 58: 22. Only such believers from among the mankind will recognize Allah as the One and Only Deity. The verse 35: 28 says about the scholars who know the Soul of Qur'an that, surely from mankind only the people who are well acquainted knowledge in the Soul of Qur'an will fear Allah. Both in the verses 8: 22 and 55 it is told that the hypocrites who knowingly hide the Soul of Qur'an and their blind followers who reject the Soul of Qur'an are the most evil creatures in the sight of Allah. As per the verse 98: 6 the hypocrites and their blind followers who associate others in the dominion of Allah are in the Hellfire and such are worst creatures in the land. Read together the verses 4: 145 and 6: 26. In the verse 29: 41 it is told that, those who take protectors other than Allah are like a spider, who builds a house for itself; surely the weakest of all houses is the spider's house. And in the verse 43 it is told: These are parables We make up for mankind, but none will grasp except those who are endowed with knowledge. In the verses 41: 30-31 say: As for those who say: "Our Lord is Allah, and then stay firm on it, the Angels will descend on them, saying: Let nothing fear or grieve you. Rejoice for the good news of Paradise that has been promised to you. We are your protectors in this life and in the Hereafter. There you shall find all that your soul's desire and all that you can ask for." Read together the verses 40: 7-9.

'Justice' means the Soul of Qur'an. So "standing with Justice" means always stand on the side of Justice by bearing true witness for the sake of Allah and become a commander for it, as specified in the verse 4: 135. Recognize that the Creator is only one and the Earth belongs to Him and He is the Lord of all creatures. Also recognize that, the Qur'an - the only Book - is for entire mankind, *Jinns* and all other creatures. And Muhammad is the Prophet for all worlds, and *Qibla* in Mecca is the centre of the world, and *Islam* is the only "way of life" which Allah has satisfied for the entire creatures, and the one and only party to the Paradise from entire mankind from Adam to the Last Day is Allah's party. And to recognize that since the day is not changing anywhere in the world; *Hajj*, *Eid*, Fasting etc. must be on the same day all over the world. See explanation 2: 234. Those people who recognize all these are the wise people who stand firm on Justice. See explanation 2: 140-144 and 255.

19. Surely, the only 'Dheen' -way of life- with Allah is Islam. Those who received the Book differed only after knowledge came to them, out of envy for one another. Whoever hides the verses of Allah after receiving It, and then surely Allah is prompt in reckoning.

"*Islam*" -the natural way of life is the only way of life satisfied by Allah for all his creatures. Then those who submit their will and power to Allah are called "*Muslimoon.*" In the verse 3: 85 Allah says that, if anyone is searching for a way of life other than Islam, it will never be accepted from him and he will be a loser in the Hereafter. Read together the verse 17: 44; 22: 18; 24: 41. This verse also teaches that only those who received the Book had divided into organizations and that was due to their selfishness, superiority complex, jealous, envy, competition etc. Today Qur'an is the only Book for the entire mankind. Those who split and fight each other after receiving that Qur'an are *Mushriks*- those who associate partners to Allah. They are belonging to satan's party and will have to live with him in the Hellfire. Today, the disbelievers, wrongdoers and transgressors are coming only from Muslims, since they hide and reject the Soul of Qur'an. See explanation 2: 159, 213 and 3:4.

20. If they should argue with you, then say: "I have submitted myself entirely to Allah, and so anyone who follows me". Then ask to those who have been given the Book as well as the illiterates: "Will you also submit yourselves to Allah?" If they submit themselves to Allah, surely they are rightly guided; and if they

turn away, then surely your responsibility is only to convey the Message. Allah is observant of His servants.

In the verse 12: 108 Allah commands the Prophet to say: This is my way, I am inviting you to Allah. I and my followers possess the same Insight; Glory is to Allah, and I never will associate others in the dominion of Allah. The verse 13: 14 says: To Him should go the appeal for Truth; those they appeal to instead of Him will never respond to them in any way, except as someone does who stretches out his hands to the water, and asks it to reach his mouth, it can not reach his mouth. The appeal of the disbelievers will not increase except astray. In the verse 28: 87 it is told: Let nothing turn you away from the verses of Allah after they have been sent down to you. Invite people to your Lord, and be not of those who associate partners in the dominion of Allah. In the verses 11: 61-62 when Prophet *Swalih* told to his people that my Lord is very close and ready to answer; the disbelievers replied that, till now you were the one on whom we had great expectations! Would you now advise us not to worship what our forefathers worshipped? Indeed we are in strong doubt about the One you are calling to. Read together the verse 14: 9

Islam means existing always in the remembrance of Allah by understanding that the whole universe belongs to Him and He is the One Who brings His creatures to the earth to a particular race, parents, period or nation of His choice; and also accepting that whole Bounties like intelligence, wealth, houses, children etc. are granted by Him only. That is to live for the sake of Allah as His representatives on Earth by understanding all His characters- i.e. following Soul of Qur'an, which is His words and character. Since Qur'an is the only Book today, the word "then ask to those who have been given the Book" means to ask the hypocrites who do not follow and teach the Soul of Qur'an. Illiterates means the common Muslims who are the *fujjar* who do not make use of the blessings like hearing, sight, intelligence etc. to understand the Soul of Qur'an, which is made very easy to understand as per the verse 54: 17. They also think that they will be rewarded by simply eating (reading) the body of Qur'an (Arabic text). See explanation 2: 78-79. Both of them are those who forgot the ultimate aim of the life. In the verse 7: 176, both of them are compared to a dog which would not change its behavior whether it is disturbed or not; and in the verse 62: 5, they are compared to Jews, and to a donkey which carries a burden without knowing what is inside. While we recite 1: 7 "Not the path upon whom Your wrath happened", we should keep in mind that "not in the way of hypocrites"; and when we say "And not who gone astray" should keep in mind "not to include among the *fujjar*." See explanation 2: 120-121, 166-167 and 174.

'To convey the message' means deliver the Soul of Qur'an to entire the mankind irrespective of nation or religion. Through the verse 5: 67 by calling the Messenger Allah says: "Deliver the Message which has been revealed to you from your Lord. If you do not do so, you will not have conveyed His Message - Letter. Allah is enough to protect you from the mankind. Surely, Allah will not guide the people who hide the Qur'an". As per the verse 7: 62, Prophet *Nooh* says to his people that, "I deliver to you the Message of my Lord and I am your well wisher; and I know from Allah something that you do not know". As per the verse 7: 68, Prophet *Hood* says to *Aa'd* – his community that "I deliver to you the message of my Lord, and I am an honest well wisher to you". Prophet *Swalih* was sent to the tribe of *Thamood*, and a camel was given to them as a sign. But when they arrogantly slaughtered the camel, they were wiped out after three days. As per the verse 7: 79 Prophet *Swalih* turned away from their ruins by saying in mind, "Oh my people, I delivered my Lord's Message to you and I was a well wisher to you. But you didn't love the well wishers". As per the verse 93, when Prophet *Shuaib* turns away from the *Mad'yan* people, he says in mind "Oh my people, I delivered my Lords Message to you and I was a well wisher to you, then why should I sorrow on a people who have denied the Truth".

The Soul of Qur'an is the Insight to fulfill the ultimate aim of this life Such as to identify Allah, oneself and to prepare Paradise here. This is the Message which Prophets and believers to convey entire mankind. But hypocrites and their followers-fujjar- by hiding the soul of Qur'an, the Balance and Trust to keep the Universe in its equilibrium teach and propagate the books written by creatures which explain about the religious customs and tales of forefather's. By their dress and customs they are with proud that they are following prophet and companion. But actually it is the dressing of Satan who came from *Najd* to the assembly of disbelievers who were in a conspiracy about killing Prophet. See explanation 2: 147-148 and 286.

21. Surely, as for those who hide the verses of Allah, and slay the Prophets without any justification, and kill those from among the people who teach Justice; then announce to them about the glad tiding of painful torment.

22. They are those whose deeds will become futile in this world as well as in the Hereafter and they will have no one to help.

Today "the verses of Allah" means the Soul of Qur'an. As per both verses 63: 4 and 80: 17 Allah has killed those who hide the Soul of Qur'an. Today "slay Prophets without any Justice" means leading a life against the do's and don'ts of Soul of Qur'an and teaching of prophet and thus make false prophets and Qur'an among public. Thus they torture the Prophets than slaying them at a time. "Kill those from among the people who teach Justice" means cause difficulties and harm to those who learn and teach the Soul of Qur'an. Today these three groups mentioned in this verse are coming from the disbelieving Muslim community only. This verse warns that all their deeds are in vain and will be disposed in this world as well as the Hereafter and will be thrown to the Hell, and there will be no one to help them. See explanation 2: 85 and 99.

23. Have you not ever seen of those who were given a portion from the Book? When they were invited to Allah's Book in order to judge between them; then a group of them turned away and this regarded.

24. That is because they say: "The fire will never touch us except for a few numbered days". The self invented delusions in their religions have betrayed them.

Since the Soul of Qur'an is the Book today, 'those who were given a portion from the Book' includes different organizations from Muslim community. If different organizations from Muslim community are invited to settle disputes according to the Soul of Qur'an, they will stand in their old way of life and organizational partiality by ignoring the message of the verses 18: 57, 30: 30-32, 32: 22 etc. Because of this character, in the verse 7: 176, Allah has compared them to a dog which does not change its behavior whether it is disturbed or not. As per the verse 76: 4 they will be resurrected as dogs in the Blaze. Through the verses 53: 29-30 Allah has commanded to Prophet and the believers to neglect those people who seek only the life of this world by ignoring the Soul of Qur'an. Like the Jews and Christians - the former people of Book, today's Muslims who are the carriers of Book are also in the same false belief that at any way they will not have to live in the Hell, except for a few days; and after that they will be entered to the Paradise by the recommendation of Prophet and great people. Through the verses 25: 27-29, Allah has warned about this people that they will mourn tomorrow in the Hereafter by biting their hands as: "These hypocritical leaders prevented us from the Soul of Qur'an after It is received to us. Ah! the satan was an ever betrayer of man". As per the verse 25: 18 the great people whom they were taking as patrons besides Allah and as per the verse 30 the messenger itself will witness against them that they were a boar people who were living by ignoring the Soul of Qur'an. To put it brief, by leading a life neglecting the Soul of Qur'an, this people has been declined to those who receive Hellfire as penalty for performing *swalath*, fasting, *hajj* etc. as told in the verses 25: 65-66. Read together the verses 9: 67-68 and 14: 28-30. See the explanation 2: 6-7, 80, 94 and 95.

25. Then, what will be their condition when We gather them on the Day -about which there is no doubt, and each Soul will be given what it has earned and they will not be treated unjustly.

This verse also teaches that Paradise or Hell is earned by oneself. Allah has decided a Day on which He will judge between His creatures with the Soul of Qur'an as specified in the verses 34: 26; 39: 69, 75 etc. Everyone will agree that, Allah - the Master of all Kingships- is the only owner of that Day. He is the most Impartial; the One Who will not show any injustice to any of His creatures, Monarch with justice, Sovereign, Dictator and Most Merciful. The judgment will be done by giving a computer spread open book to everyone as specified in the verses such as 17: 13-15; 18: 49; 45: 28-29 and 78: 27-29. See the explanation 2: 286 and 3: 9.

26. You pray: Oh Allah! Holder of control, You give the control to anyone You wish and snatch control from anyone You wish; You exalt anyone You wish and disgrace anyone You wish; good lies within Your hand; surely, You are capable of everything!

27. You cause the night to pass into the day and You cause the day to pass into the night; You bring living from the dead and You bring the dead from the living; and You provide sustenance to anyone You wish, without any measure.

After *Faj'r* and *Magh'rib swalath*, Prophet used to pray these two verses which contain the most glorious name of Allah as "*Vird*". Allah commands the Prophet and believers to pray like this: Oh Allah, oh the Master of all the kingship, oh the Controller of everything, oh the Owner of Straight path, oh the Donor of kingdom to whom You please and take away the kingdom from whom so ever You please, oh the One Who dissolves night on day and day on night, oh the One Who brings living from dead and dead from living, oh the One Who gives honor to whom You wish and disgrace to whom You wish, oh the One Who feeds anyone You wish beyond any reason and sense experience; all the good within Your hand. Surely, You are the Almighty Who able to do everything. So You guide the rulers to favor Your Book and the way of life you wished. Believers will teach the Soul of Qur'an to the entire mankind in their heart's language to aware them about their aim of life and thus will make them capable to elect the rulers who standing and judging with the Justice. That will be the nature of work of believers to implement the way of life of Islam which Allah pleased for entire mankind. In other words, believers are not supposed to satisfy the majority for getting concessions and ruling power. Also the believers should never search for any short cut to capture the ruling power or conduct any terrorist activities as Jews had done to create Israel. Believers will never think that ruling by Muslims can only implement the laws of Qur'an.

Those people who say that the fascist parties may come to power if the secular parties do not unite are neglecting these verses. Those who argue and try to get the power by assembling the parties of their own community without considering the entire mankind are hypocrites who hide these verses. They are giving wrong meaning to the verse 109: 6 as 'for you your way of life and for me my way of life' instead 'for me the True way of life-Islam'. They are the ones who welcome the *Maseeh-A-Ddajjal* and who consider this world as Paradise. As mentioned in both verses 41: 28 and 63: 4, hypocrites are the enemies of Allah and believers. So the believers will hate the hypocrites coming to power; and they will pray and work to keep the hypocrites away from power by spreading the Soul of Qur'an. Read together the verse 9: 73, 25: 52 and 66: 9. As per the verses 4: 91; 9: 123 and 33: 61 Allah commands to the party of believers if any to kill the hypocrites and *kuffar* who hide and reject the Soul of Qur'an. But it will be implemented only after the second coming of *Eisa.*

The meaning of the phrase" You cause the night to pass into the day and the day to the night" is the same that of the verse 39: 5, that "the One Who covers the day on night and night on day". The word "One who covers" gives evidence to the round shape of the earth. The verse 25: 61 also says that He is the One who succeeds day and night each other. The meaning of the phrase "You bring living from the dead and dead from the living" is that He is the One Who germinates mango tree from the mango nut and mango nut from the mango tree; and egg from the hen and hen from the egg; and the One Who blows the spirit to the four month old embryo and takes it back at the time of death; and brings believer from disbeliever and vice versa. See explanation 2: 258-260.

"He provides sustenance to anyone He wishes without any measure" means that wealth and resources of this worldly life is not given on the basis of any particular reason. Allah - the Most Gracious and Impartial, has given wealth and resources of this world mostly to the hypocrites. Thus He makes them to enjoy the life of Paradise least in this world and that is because they will be entered to the Hell by their death itself. But Allah- the Most Merciful, who gives the resources of the Hereafter only to the believers, gives His help and sustenance in this world without any particular reason only to the believers. In the verse 4: 139 Allah says: The hypocrites have selected the disbelievers as their friends instead of believers. Are they seeking honor and glory from the disbelievers? But surely, all honor and glory belongs to Allah alone. In the verse 63: 8 it is told that the honor belongs to Allah, to His messenger, and to the believers; but the hypocrites are not aware of this. In the verse 10: 65 it is told that let not their sayings grieve you, surely all honors and glory belongs to Allah alone. Read together the verse 37: 180. See the explanation of 1: 2; 3:14 and 15.

28. Let not the believers take disbelievers as their friends instead of the believers. Anyone who does so, will have nothing to do with Allah; except co-operating with them in conscious that Allah is observing. Allah warns you about Himself; and to Allah all of you return.

Through the verse 9: 23, Allah by calling the believers says: "Oh you who believe! Do not choose your fathers and your brothers as your protector and friends, if they prefer disbelief over belief. If anyone does so they are the wrongdoers". As per the verse 59: 23 Allah is the believer. Believers are the members of Allah's party. Allah is the protector and friend of believers. See the explanation 2: 257. And as per the verses both 2: 34 and 38: 74 Satan is the disbeliever. He is the protector and friend of disbelievers, wrongdoers, transgressors, hypocrites, repudiators, arrogant and mischief makers who hide and reject the Soul of Qur'an. They all belong to the Satan's party, and will abide with him in the Hell. Read together the verse 58: 19. Therefore the believers who follow the Soul of Qur'an as much as should not co-operate willingly with such disbelievers in this world (though they are their father, mother, spouse, brother, sister, guardian, leader, follower, who ever it may be). Read together the verses 16: 106-107. Otherwise they will have to regret in the Hereafter as specified in the verses 25: 29; 43: 67. Read together the verses 9: 24 and 58: 22. In brief, only the relations in the Light of Qur'an will be benefited in the Hereafter. All other relations will end in enmity and blaming each other. That is what the Prophet taught "*None among you will become a believer, until his wishes follow the one which I brought (Qur'an)*. See explanation 2: 254.

29. Say: Whether you hide what is in your hearts or reveal it, Allah knows it; and He knows whatever is in the heaven and whatever is on Earth; and Allah is capable of everything.

Allah commands to oppose and hate the satan and his party members by mentally, verbally and physically. He also commands, always be in conscious that Allah knows the state of chest and no one can hide anything from Him whenever and wherever he is. Through the verse 22: 70 Allah asks, "Do you not know that Allah knows whatever is in Heaven and Earth? That is contained in a Book; such thing is easy for Allah". As per the verses 10: 61; 34: 3 and 57: 21, that Book is the Soul of Qur'an. The verses 6: 103; 31: 16 and 67: 12 end as Allah is subtle, the acquainted. See explanation 2:255, 284 and 3:5.

30. On the Day when every soul will find whatever good he has done is presented as well as whatever bad he has done. On that Day they will wish there were a long distance between him and that. Allah cautions you about Himself. And Allah is full of kindness towards His servants.

Every soul - let it be of male or female - has to face a Day (Day of Judgment) on which they will find what it has earned, good or evil. This verse also teaches that Paradise or Hell is earned by one himself. "Between him and that" means "between the evil soul and its futile deeds" or it means "between him and the Day of Judgment." See how Allah is warning about this through the verse 78:40: On the day when each person shall see what it has sent on a head, the disbeliever will say "Oh, woe to me, if I were only dust." Read together the verse 4:42.

"Allah cautions you Himself" means that, as Allah has reminded about each and everything which is going to happen in the Hereafter by teaching the Soul of

Qur'an, one should has to decide his destiny either is in Paradise or in Hell. Nobody can blame Impartial Allah or as per the verse 14: 22 satan or as per the verses 7: 37-39 the parents or as per the verses 2: 166-167 the hypocritical leaders. "Allah is full of kindness towards His servants" means that, Allah has given the Soul of Qur'an- the Bounty and Mercy as 'weighing balance' by which each can weigh their deeds in this world, and thus one can realize from this world itself whether they are earning Paradise or Hell. Read together the verses 16: 64 and 39: 41. See explanation 2:207, 272 and 286.

31. Say: If you sincerely love Allah, then follow me; Allah will then love you and forgive you your offences. Allah is the Forgiving, the Merciful.

32. Say: Obey Allah and the Messenger. Yet if they should turn away, surely Allah does not love the disbelievers.

Those who wish to reach Allah should obey and follow His Messenger through out the life, that is from the head to foot. See the explanation 2: 143. In the verse 59: 7 Allah says: Accept whatever the Messenger gives you, and refrain from whatever he forbids you, remain conscious of Allah. Surely Allah is strict in punishment. In the verse 49: 14 Allah says: If you obey Allah and His Messenger, He will not make futile any of your deeds; surely Allah is the Forgiving, the Merciful. The verse 4: 80 says: Anyone who obeys the Messenger actually obeys Allah. If anyone turns away, We have not sent you as task master of them. *Aysha*- Wife of Prophet answered for a question about the character of Prophet Muhammad as: "Prophet's character is Qur'an". Allah says both in the verses 73:19 and 76: 29 that; surely, this Soul of the Qur'an is a Ticket for those who wish to reach to their Lord. In the verse 76: 30 says: "But you cannot will it unless Allah wills" means each and every soul should ask Guidance i.e. one should read the Soul of Qur'an by praying with heart that "My Lord, increase me in knowledge." Read together the verses 20: 114 and 81: 27-29. See explanation 2: 146.

33. Surely Allah did choose Adam, and Nooh and the family of Ibrahim, and the family of Imran above all the men of the worlds for His mission.

34. Some of their offsprings are descended from others. Allah is All-Hearing, All-Knowing.

After reminding about the Prophets- *Zakariya, Yahya, Eisa, Ibrahim, Is'haq, Ya'qoob, Moosa, Haroon, Isma'el and Idrees*; Allah says in the verse 19: 58 that, these are some of the Prophets on whom Allah bestowed His blessings from among the descendants of Adam, and those who carried with *Nooh,* and of the descendants of *Ibrahim* and Israel. In the verse 42: 13 Allah says: He has ordained for you the same way of life, which He enjoined to you, *Nooh, Ibrahim, Moosa and Eisa*. In the verse 49: 13 Allah says: Oh mankind! Surely, We created you all out of single male and female, and made you into nations and tribes that you might recognize one another. Surely, the most honored of you in the sight of Allah is the one who is most heedful. Surely, Allah Aware, acquainted. Here *Imran's* family refers to the Prophet *Eisa's* mother- *Maryam's* father's family. See the explanation 2: 132-133, 136, 213 and 3: 19.

35. Remember the occasion when the woman of Imran prayed: Oh my Lord, I avow to dedicate for Your service that is in my womb. Then please accept it from me. Surely You alone is All-Hearing, All-Knowing.

36. And when she gave birth, she said: Oh my Lord! Surely, I have given birth to a female child. Allah was quite aware of what she had given birth to, for a male is not like a female. And I have named her Maryam, and ask You to protect her and her offspring from Satan- the outcast.

Prophet taught: The temptation of satan will affect each and every child of Adam; i.e. entire mankind. But due this prayer, satan will not approach *Maryam* and her son *Eisa*. Prophet has taught to seek refuge in Allah from the outcaste satan at the time of intercourse as 'with the name of Allah, Oh Allah! Keep away the despised satan from us and the child provides by this act for us'. The meaning of saying "For a male is not like a female" is that a male can travel and stay alone anywhere at any midnight, but a female needs a guardian.

37. Then her Lord accepted her with all handsome manner and caused her to grow like a lovely plant, and entrusted her to the care of Zakariya. Every time Zakariya entered to the shrine to see her, he found she had already been supplied with food. He asked: Oh Maryam, from where did you get it? She replied: It comes from Allah. Surely Allah gives sustenance without measure to whom He wishes.

The shrine mentioned here is not the place in the *Masjid* where the '*Imam*'-leader of prayer-stands. Instead, it is a special chamber made in an ascended foundation with in a short distance from the *Masjid*, especially meant for meditation. As per the verse 19: 11, Prophet *Zakariya* also had separate shrine.

It was for the first time a female was appointed for the service of Allah in the *Masjid*. At that time a dispute occurred about her sponsorship, and they drew lots with arrows. Thus Prophet *Zakariya*, the old man with no children, got the sponsorship of *Maryam*. Read together the verse 3: 44. This verse teaches that, before sending the '*Maeda*'- food tray from Heaven- in reply to the prayer of *Eisa* as per the verse 5: 114, Allah had sent heavenly sustenance to his mother *Maryam* in an unseen way. This verse also teaches that, Allah is able to give sustenance to whom He wishes without any measures and reasons. When Prophet *Zakariya* saw *Maryam*, getting food from Allah without any reason, he had the expectation that Allah can give him a child. See the explanation 2: 260; 3: 26 and 27.

38. With that Zakariya appealed to his Lord; he said: My Lord! Grant me a goodly offspring as Your bounty. Surely You are the Hearer of appeals.

"With that" means, *Zakariya* who was in great sorrow without having a child, saw *Maryam* getting food from Allah without any reasons, he appealed for a child. "As Your bounty" means, beyond any reasons and sense experience. Incidents like this teach that the believers should fulfill their desires by praying with deep hearts to their Lord. Read together the verses 19: 2-6. In the verse 14: 39 it is mentioned the appealing of *Ibrahim* as: Praise be to Allah, Who has given me *Isma'el* and *Is'haq* in my old age as a bounty. Surely my Lord is the Hearer of prayers. Only believers' prayers will be responded as explained in the verse 2: 186.

39. The Angels call him while he was standing praying in his shrine: Surely, Allah gives you news of Yahya, who will confirm the word from Allah. He will be a leader with self-control, and Prophet from among honorable people.

40. He asked: "My Lord! How can I have a boy? Indeed old age has overtaken me, while my wife is barren?" He answered: "Even so does Allah do anything He wishes".

"The word from Allah" mentioned in the verse 39 is about the body of *Eisa*. In the verse 4: 171 Allah says: The *Maseeh Eisa*- the son of *Maryam*- was only a Messenger of Allah and 'His word' which He bestowed on *Maryam* and a spirit from Him. Not only for Prophet *Eisa*, but to all the creatures have the spirit of Allah. Read together the verse 4: 1. Confirming the word from Allah means that the miraculous birth of Prophet *Yahya* confirms the birth of Prophet *Eisa* without a father. 'Self control' mentioned in the verse has various meanings like without any relation with ladies, pious, chaste, unmarried etc. Read together the verses 19: 7-9 and 13. See the explanation 1: 6.

41. He asked: My Lord! Grant me a sign. He said: Your sign is that you will not speak to people for three days except through gestures. You should remember your Lord very much and glorify Him in the evening and in the early morning hours.

"In the evening and in the morning hours" means to remember Allah always and especially in between *swalath Magh'rib* and *swalath E'sha*, and *swalath Faj'r* up to sunrise. It should be noticed in this conversation that, Prophet *Zakariya* is asking to Allah directly, but the reply is getting through the Angels. Read together the verses 19: 10-11. The verse 42: 51 says: Allah should not speak to any human except through revelation or from behind a veil. This teaches that believers will ask directly to their Lord; whereas the disbelievers always will place mediators and intercedes in between them and their Lord. From the Hell, such madmen-disbelievers- will call the guard of Hell and will say: Oh *Malik*! Let your Lord put an end to us, he will reply "you must stay on here! We brought you the Truth even though most of you detest the Truth" as told in the verses 43: 74-78. As per the verses 40: 49-50, the people of Hell will say to the guards of Hell: Pray to your Lord to lighten us the punishment at least for one day. The Angels will ask: Did there not your messengers bring you Explanations? They will say: "Of course!" Angels will say: "Well, make appeal then! Yet the disbelievers' appeal will increase nothing except astray. " This verse warns that, those disbelievers who couldn't pray to Allah directly in this world cannot pray directly in the Hereafter also. Read together the verses 32: 4 and 39: 3.

42. Remember when the Angels said by calling: Oh Maryam, surely Allah has selected you and purified you and preferred you over all the women in the worlds.

43. Oh Maryam! Be obedient to your Lord; prostrate and bow down with those who bow down.

Prophet taught that, there are four women who are preferred over all the women of the worlds (1) *Maryam*-the daughter of *Imran* (2) *Khadeeja*- the daughter of *Khuvailid* (3) *Fathima*- the daughter of Muhammad (4) *Asya*- the woman of *Pharoah*. In the verses 66: 11-12, Allah has pointed the woman of *Pharoah* and *Maryam* as model for the believers both male and female. "Bow down with those who bow down" means, remember Allah always even on walking, sitting and laying down. See the explanation 2: 43, 152.

44. Such are some information about the unseen We have revealed to you. You were not in their presence as they drew lots with their pens (arrows) to decide which of them would be entrusted with Maryam, while they were so disputing.

The verse 12: 102 says: Such are some information about the unseen, We have inspire you with. You were not in their presence when they agreed on their affair and were plotting. Read together the verses 12: 3, 111. In the verse 7: 101, after explaining the history of Prophets *Nooh, Hood, Swalih, Shuaib, Looth* etc, Allah says: Such were the towns whose histories are explaining to you one by one. Certainly their messengers came to them with Explanations, but they persisted in their disbelief, thus Allah seal up the hearts of disbelievers. Read together the verses 29: 48-49 and 42: 52. See the explanation 2: 3 and 252.

45. Remember when the Angels said: Oh Maryam! Indeed Allah gives you the glad tidings with a word from Him, whose name is the Maseeh Eisa, the son of Maryam. He will be of great honor in this world and in the Hereafter, and one among of those nearer to Allah.

The verse 19: 17 says that, *Jibreel* who appeared in the shape of a human being informed this matter to *Maryam*, while she was lonely in her chamber far away from her people. Read together the verses 19: 18-20. The word "*Al-Maseeh*" means 'one who circum rotate' or 'one who wipe out'. Prophet *Eisa* used to heal the lepers and blind patients with the Permission of Allah by rubbing over them. While conveying the instructions by traveling around the world, the disbelieving enemies tried to crucify him. At that time Allah raised him up to the Paradise with his bodily. Read together the verses 3: 52-55 and 4: 157-159. During the Last Days, the '*Mos-E-Dayal*'- pronounce as '*Maseeh-A-Ddajjal*' in Arabic, will come to wipe out Islam. For that purpose, he will travel all around the world except *Hijas*- the provinces including Mecca and Madeena- At that time Allah will bring *Eisa* again to this world at same age of 33 years, to wipe out *Kufr*-refusal by killing *Ddajjal* and will establish Islam world widely. These are the reasons for getting the name '*Maseeh*' to *Eisa*. As *Ddajjal* wipes out Islam by traveling all around the world, the word '*Maseeh*' suits for him also. Prophet taught that the greatest misery which the children of Adam will have to face is *Maseeh-A-Ddajjal*. So Prophet also taught to pray against the evil deeds of *Maseeh-A-Ddajjal*, at the end of '*Athahiyyath*'-Lord's greetings- in every five time *swalath* per day. Read together the verse 4: 86.

46. And he will speak to people in the cradle and in maturity, and he will be one among honorable men.

The verses 19: 29-33 say: In response for the questions of the people *Maryam* merely pointed towards the baby. They said: "How can we talk to a babe in the cradle?" Whereupon the baby spoke out: "I am indeed a servant of Allah. He has given me the Book and made me a Prophet. His blessing is with me wherever I may be, and commisioned me to keep up *swalath* and pay the welfare tax as long as I live. He has exhorted me to honor my mother and has not made me authoritarian, hard to deal with. Peace be on the day I was born, and the day I shall die and the Day I shall be raised to life again".

47. She asked: "my Lord! How can I have a child – while no human being has ever touched me"? He said: "Thus it will be". Allah creates anything He wishes. When He decides a thing; He says to it "Be", and then it is.

The verse 36: 82 says: Certainly whenever He intends a thing, He needs only to say: "Be," then it is. Read together the verses19: 20-21. In the verse 54: 50 Allah says that, even the time for blinking of eye is not needed for coming to force Our commands.

48. He will teach him the Book and wisdom and the Thourath and the Injeel.

49. And will send him as a Messenger to the children of Israel. Surely, I have come to you with a sign (proof) from your Lord. I will make for you the shape of a bird from clay; I will breathe into it,

so that it will become a living bird by Allah's permission. I will heal the blind by birth or lepers and I will bring the dead back to life by Allah's Permission. And I will tell you what you have eaten and what you should stored in your houses. Surely in this, there is a sign for you – if you are believers.

Allah's Permission means the Soul of Qur'an. The verses 13: 38; 14: 11and 40: 78 are the three verses which teach us that, no Messenger can bring a sign (miracle) without Allah's permission. See explanation 2: 186 and 213.

Prophet *Eisa* brought the dead back to life by performing two *Rak'ath Swalath*, reciting *Surath Mulk* in the first *Rak'ath* and *Surath Sajada* in the second *Rak'ath*. After glorifying and praising Allah; he calls seven names from the 'best names of Allah'- 'Oh the One with out Beginning!', 'Oh the Unseen!', 'Oh Ever living!', 'Oh the Pair less!', 'Oh the One and Only!', 'Oh the Lonely!' and 'Oh the Absolute self dependant!'. And then he prays to Allah to bring the dead back to life. And in a situation when the dead do not come back to life; he again prays by calling other seven names of Allah, 'Oh Self living!', 'Oh the sustainer of all!', 'Oh Allah!', 'Oh the Most Gracious!', 'Oh Master of the kingship!', 'Oh the Light of heaven and Earth and the things between them!', 'Oh the Lord of Majesty and Glorious!'. After that he says: 'Stand up by the Permission of Allah'. Thus was he used to bring the dead back to life.

The verse 48 says that "Allah will teach him the Scripture". It means that Allah has taught the Soul of Qur'an to Prophet *Eisa*. See explanation 2: 2. In that Book, *Surath Mulk* was at first and *Surath Sajada* followed it. That is why Prophet Eisa recited *Surath Mulk* in the first *Rak'ath* and *Surath Sajada* in the second. The 'wisdom' mentioned in the verse 48 is the same that of signs (proof) mentioned in the verse 49. Allah taught the *Thourath* and the *Injeel* to Prophet *Eisa* in order to appoint him to the children of Israel; and taught the '*Al-Kithab*'- Soul of Qur'an-aiming his second coming to implement Islam all over the world and thus to fulfill the verses like 7: 157- 158, 21: 107, 4: 91, 9: 123, and 33: 61 which are not implemented during the time of prophet till today. See explanation 2: 269 and 3: 2-3.

Those who believe all these miracles as the ability of Prophet *Eisa* as well as those who say that these are clear sorcery without believing in Allah's miracles are disbelievers. Read together the verse 5: 110. The true believers will believe that Allah is the One who destines and applies it; and they will live only for Allah entrusting on Him, and as His representatives witnessing the Prophet's life truthfully. In the verse 10: 100 it is told that, it is not possible for any soul to believe except by the Permission of Allah i.e. without the Soul of Qur'an. See explanation 2: 213, 255 and 3: 7.

50. And confirming what I have already with me from the Thourath and to make lawful to you some of the things which were forbidden to you. I have brought you the clear signs from your Lord. Therefore heed Allah and obey me.

"To make lawful to you some of the forbidden things" is not about the things which Allah has forbidden; but it means about the things which were forbidden by the Jews themselves. Read together the verses 6: 146 and 16: 118.

51. Surely, Allah is my Lord and your Lord. So serve Him. That is the Straight path.

The verses 19: 36, 43: 64 also have the same message. "Serve Allah" means live in this world as a True believer by accepting Allah as the Owner Lord and all others as His servants; i.e. realize the character of Allah and be a true representative by pleasing other creatures only in Allah's please, show angry towards others only in Allah's anger, give to others only in Allah's pleasure, and not give to others in Allah's dislike. The verse 6: 153 says: And surely this is My Straight path; so you follow It; and you do not follow other ways which are diverged from this one and only way to Allah. Thus has He bequested you with It, so that you may become heedful. Read together the verses 36: 59-62 and 58: 22. See explanation 1: 4; 2: 21 and 3: 28

52. When Eisa sensed disbelief among them, he asked: who will be my helpers in the cause of Allah? The disciples said: We are Allah's helpers, we believe with Allah and you bear witness that we are Muslims.

When the children of Israel were not ready to believe, the disciples came forward to help Allah by conveying the Message of Allah to the mankind. They were only thirteen in number and one of them named *Sarjas* was even ready to be crucified instead of Prophet *Eisa*. The verse 61: 14 says: Oh you who believe! Be the helpers of Allah, just as *Eisa* the son of *Maryam* said to his disciples: "Who will be my helper in the cause of Allah?" And the disciples responded:

"We are the helpers of Allah." Then a group from the children of Israel believed and another group disbelieved. We aided the believers against their enemies, so they became victorious. Today to help Allah means to convey the Soul of Qur'an - His Message to entire mankind. Those who hide and reject His Message are the transgressors and disbelievers. Both they will witness against themselves that they were disbelievers at the time of death as per the verse 7: 37 and on the Day of Judgment as per the verse 6: 130.

Muslims mean those who submitted all to Allah in peace. From the saying of disciples that we are Muslims, we can understand that only the Islam was the way of life of believers in previous time also. In the verse 22: 78 Allah says that He named you Muslims before in prior scriptures and in this Qur'an, so that His Messenger may testify up on you and you yourselves may testify up on rest of the mankind. But today the Muslims all over the world are living by forgetting Allah, hiding Allah and the Prophet in the Soul of Qur'an and thus they become the transgressors and disbelievers. See explanation 2: 39, 99, 132 and 133.

53. Our Lord ! We believe in what You have sent down and thus we have followed the Messenger, so enroll us among the witnesses.

In the case of disciples "the Messenger" mentioned is Prophet *Eisa*. But this verse is also a declaration of a Christian gang who came to *Madeena* from *Najran* under the leadership of *Adiyy-ibnu-hathim* to see Prophet Muhammad. So in their case, "the Messenger" mentioned is about Prophet Muhammad. The verse 5: 83 says: When they (monks and priests) listen to that which is revealed to the messenger, you can see their eyes filled with tears, because of what they recognize from the Truth. They say: "Our Lord! We believe. Therefore write us down among the witnesses of Truth. The verse 57: 19 says: Those who believe in Allah and His Messenger (as revealed by the Soul of Qur'an) are the truthful and the true witnesses in the sight of their Lord; they shall have their reward and their light. But those who disbelieve and reject Our verses; they shall be the inmates of Hades. See explanation 2: 39 and 3: 10.

54. They plotted and Allah also plotted; and Allah is the best among plotters.

Here it is referred about the conspiracy of Jews to crucify Prophet *Eisa*. Like that, the Jews in *Madeena* also plotted to kill Prophet Muhammad. As per the verse 14: 46 it is told that the hypocrites have plotted against all Prophets at all time; and even though their plotting were such enough to move the mountains, they couldn't harm the Prophets and believers who entrust in Allah. The verse 13: 42 says that those who lived before them also plotted, but Allah is Masters of all plotters. He knows about what each soul earns and soon the disbelievers will come to know who will get the worst home as abode.

In the verses 27: 45-49 say: about the people of '*Thamood*', "We sent their brother Swalih; but they were not ready to accept him. And they said we consider you and your companions as a sign of bad luck. Prophet *Swalih* said: Your bad luck is with Allah. You are a people undergoing a trial. There were nine tribes who created mischief in the land and reformed nothing. They decided to attack and kill *Swalih* and his family by night, and to say to his guardian by swearing with Allah that we didn't witness the slaughter of his family. In the verse 27: 50 says: They plotted, We too plotted, while they did not perceive it; and in the verse 51 says: Then see what the end of the plotters was? We wiped out them completely together with all their people. In the verses 27: 68-69, Allah commands Prophet to say to the *Mecca* pagans, who denied Qur'an by saying it as the tale of ancient, "you travel through Earth and see what has been the end of the mad people". In the verse 70, Allah says to Prophet: Don't worry about them nor feel distress because of their plotting. In the verse 16: 127 Allah says to Prophet: Be patient, your patience is but from Allah. Don't worry and distress because of their plotting. In the verse 35: 10 says: As for those who plot for evil deeds, they shall have severe punishment; and they will be destructed themselves by their plotting. The believer should utilize the Soul of Qur'an as the shield and safeguard from all disasters as well as Hell and they will do '*Jihad*' with It to the disbelievers who hide and reject It. Read together the verses: 6: 123-124; 8: 30; 10: 21 and 12: 102 See explanation 2: 234-235, 3: 29 and 30..

55. Remember Allah said: Oh Eisa, Certainly I will take back you bodily and raise you up to Me and I will purify you from those who disbelieved, and I will place those who follow you above those who disbelieve until the Day of Judgment. Then to Me will you be return, then I shall decide among you concerning anything you have been disagreeing about.

56. As for those who disbelieve, I will punish them with severe torment in this world and in the Hereafter; they will have no helpers.

The disbelieving Jews priests influenced the Governor of Roman Emperor to crucify and kill Prophet *Eisa,* and at last they decided to do so. Allah informed Prophet *Eisa* about this conspiracy. In three different occasions Prophet *Eisa* asked 'who is ready to be crucified instead of me, he will be in Paradise with me.' Each occasions, *Sarjas* one among the disciples replied that he is ready for that. Thus when the Roman army came to catch Prophet *Eisa,* Allah changed the face of *Sarjas* as that of Prophet *Eisa*. The verse 76: 28 says: It is We Who created them and made their joints strong; but if We please We can make their shape changed with others, and raised Prophet Eisa bodily to Allah by means of a whirlwind. Read together the verse 4: 47. See explanation 2: 164. In the verses 4: 157-158 Allah says: Surely, they did not kill him. Allah raised him up to Himself. Allah is Almighty, Wise. The preposition '*Hu*' in the word '*Rafa'hu*' usually uses for males with their bodily form. In the case of soul alone (without body) uses '*Ha*' instead of '*Hu*'. The preposition '*Ka*' used in the word '*Muthavafeeka*', and '*Rafa'ka*' (raised up you) also usually used for male with bodily form. If for Soul alone, the preposition used will be '*Ki*'. See explanation 3: 43

In the verse 4: 159 Allah says: There is none of the people of the Book, who does not believe in him before his death, and on the Day of Judgment, he will bear witness against them. The meaning of "will bear witness against them" is against those people who neglected the teachings of the verse 3: 51 and became disbeliever by selecting Prophet *Eisa* and his mother *Maryam* as two deities besides Allah. In the verses 5: 116-117 say: Prophet *Eisa* will reply on the Day of Judgment: I never said to them anything other than what You commanded me to say, that is to live as the representatives of Allah, Who is my Lord as well as your Lord. I was a witness over them as long as I remained among them. After that Prophet *Eisa* will say to Allah: When You took me up completely (with bodily form), You were the Observer over them and You are the witness for everything. Here instead of saying "*Amathanee*" -when caused me to die, *Eisa* says: "*Thavaffaithanee*" -when took me up completely. That means Allah rose up Prophet *Eisa* with his bodily form. See explanation 2: 260.

As the part of the ten important signs of the last day Allah will bring again *Eisa* to Earth, on the same age of 33 years as mentioned in the verse 43: 61. And then he will kill *Maseeh-A-Ddajjal*- last form of satan- and will implement *Islam* the only way of life satisfied by Lord for entire mankind. By the killing of *Ddajjal* there will not be any testament for mankind on Earth. Mankind will lead a life of

Angels on Earth thus the verse 43: 60 will come in force. *Eisa* will rule on world as Mecca- the centre of earth- as the capital. On those days, there will be a single *Dheen* -way of life-and *Qib'la*. After ruling for seven years, *Eisa* will die peacefully at his age of 40 and will be buried in the grave near to Prophet *Muhammad*. It is told in the verse 19: 33 that the saying of Prophet *Eisa* in the cradle as: Peace is on me the day I was born, and the day I die, and the day I shall be raised again. From this one can realize that Prophet *Eisa* has not suffered and is not crucified, and also he will die with peace. Read together the verse 4: 159 See the explanation 3: 45.

By saying, "I will place those who follow you till the Day of Resurrection, above those who disbelieve", Allah does not mean that he will place Christians above Jews. Instead by this Allah announces that, He will place the True believers- who follow all the Prophets including *Eisa*- above the disbelievers in this world, and only they will be the real winners in this world as well as in the Hereafter. But today the disbelievers are coming only from Muslims who hide and reject the Soul of Qur'an which explains all these things. Due to this, worthless people are experiencing disgrace and ignorance all over the world. See explanation 2: 85 ; 3: 10. As per the verses 39: 69 and 75 the judgment will be based on the Soul of Qur'an on the Day of Judgment. So the believer in order to fulfill the aim of life should make his judgment on the basis of Soul of Qur'an in this world itself considering the verses 16: 64 and 39: 41. See explanation 2: 113 and 213

57. As for those who believe and do honorable deeds, will be granted their full reward. Allah does not love wrongdoers.

As for those who believe in Allah and realize themselves, and create Paradise in this world by realizing the ultimate aim of life from 6236 verses of Qur'an, Allah will grant the Paradise that they built here as an inherited property. Read together the verse 7: 43. See explanation 2: 38 and 186. The wrongdoers mentioned in this verse are the same disbelievers mentioned in the previous verse. The verse 3: 140 also ends as: "Allah doesn't love wrongdoers". The verse 42: 40 ends by saying: "Surely, He doesn't love wrongdoers". See explanation 2: 254.

58. That which We recite to you comes from the verses and wise reminder in heart's language.

The Soul of Qur'an is called "*Adhikr*". That is the explanation of Qur'an in the heart's language of mankind. In the verse 36: 69 says: This is nothing but a '*Dhikr*' - Reminder- and a clear Qur'an; and in verse 38: 1 says: Truth by the Qur'an which is the Reminder. In the *Surath Al-Qamar*, it has repeatedly told four times that "We have indeed made the soul of Qur'an easy to understand by ones heart". In the verse 36: 2, Qur'an is mentioned as '*Hakeem*' -Wise, whereas here '*Adhikr*' is mentioned as '*Hakeem*'. The verse 43: 44 says that, this is a Reminder for you and for your people, and both of you will be questioned about It. The verses 41: 41-44 say: Those who hide this Reminder when It comes to them should know that in fact it is a Mighty Book. No falsehood can approach It from before or after the codification. It is a revelation from the One Who is Wise and Praiseworthy. Nothing is said to you except that was said to the Messengers before you: That surely your Lord is the Lord of forgiveness, and at the same time the Lord of painful retribution. Had We revealed this Qur'an in a foreign language, they (same people) would have said: "Why have not its verses been made clear? Why in a foreign language, while the audience is Arabs?" Say : "To the believers, It is a Guide and a Healing; while the ones who do not believe are merely hard of hearing and it causes blindness on their part as well. Such are the people who act as they are being called to from a long distance off. Satan will forbid from '*Adhikr*' which is the Soul of Qur'an only, not from the body as well as the meaning of the Qur'an. For explanation, see the part both '*Adhikr*' of Introduction and the introduction of *Surath Al-Fathiha*.

Oh Allah! Make us follow the Soul of Qur'an as it should be followed and remind us what we have forgotten with the Wise Reminder- Oh the one sent down the Wise Reminder. And enter us with those who enter the Paradise without trial and with the virtuous people with the Ticket.

59. Surely in the sight of Allah, the example of Eisa is like the example of Adam. He created him from mud, and then He said to him: "Be" and then he was.

Adam is a creature of Allah without father and mother. After shaping Adam from the mud, Allah blew His spirit into it, thus Adam became a human-being. In the verse 4: 171 it is told that *Eisa's* body was a word "Be" and the Spirit was from the Lord. *Eisa* is an example for Allah's creation without father. All other human-beings are created by the mating of male and female. Read together the verses 4: 1; 7: 189; 32: 7-9 and 39: 6. In the verse 36: 82 says: Surely when He intends a thing He says "Be", and then it is. In the verse 16: 40 says: Surely when We intends to do anything, We say the word "Be", and then it is. See explanation 2: 28-29 and 3: 47

60. The Truth is from your Lord. So you don't be among the doubters.

See explanation 2: 147

61. If any one argue with you concerning It, after the knowledge has come to you; say: Come! Let us gather our sons and your sons, and our women and your women, and ourselves and yourselves; and let us pray against ourselves to invoke Allah's curse upon the liars.

'*Mubahala*' -prayer to invoke the curse- means that, gathering the people of different organizations who diverged by disputing on Allah, and praying against themselves by saying: "If we are saying the lie, may the curse of Allah upon us." From this verse it is clear that there is 'only *Mubahala* instead of dispute with those who come to argue after realizing the Truth. Today, Muslims- who became associates and disbelievers by forming different organizations after receiving the Qur'an- may be invited for *Mubahala*. But the believers should discuss using best words (the Soul of Quran) with the people of other religion to convey them the Truth. The verse 29: 46 says: Do not argue with the People of the Book except with the Soul of Qur'an- except with those who are wicked among them, and say: "We believe in that which is sent down to us and that which is sent down to you; Our *Deity* and your *Deity* is the same One *Deity* to Whom we submit as Muslims". See the explanation 2: 66

Knowledge means the Soul of Qur'an. Allah has mentioned Qur'an as the Knowledge, Guidance and Enlightening Book through both the verses 22: 8 and 31: 20 by saying: There are among the people who dispute about Allah without Knowledge, Guidance and Enlightening Book. The Soul of Qur'an is the knowledge of all times. See explanation 2: 169 and 3: 7.

62. Surely, this is the true explanation of incidents. There is no Deity except Allah. And surely, Allah- He alone- is the Powerful, Wise.

63. But if they turn away, then surely Allah is Well aware of the mischief makers.

In the verse 7: 35 Allah says by calling the children of Adam: Whenever the Messengers come to you from among you and recite to you My verses, then those who follow It and become righteous have nothing to fear or regret. See explanation 2: 38. Allah has warned about the scene of trial on the Day of Judgment in the verse 6: 130 that, Allah will ask: Did not come there Messengers from among you who explained to you My verses. In the verse 7: 176, a similitude of those who deny the Qur'anic verses are compared to a dog which doesn't change its attitude whether it is disturbed or not; and you explain the history to them- to meditate and reflect it by the listeners. In the verse 12: 3 Allah says: We will explain to you the best of the historic incidents by revealing this Qur'an. Before this you were heedless. The verse 12: 111 starts with the message that, there is a lesson in this historic incident for the people of understanding. See the explanation 2: 6, 11-12 and 3: 18.

64. Say : Oh people of the Book! Come to a common formula which we and you should agree. We shall not serve except Allah, and we shall not associate anything with Him, nor shall any of us take on others as Lords instead of Allah. So if they turn away then say: Bear witness that we are Muslims.

Today, Qur'an is the only Book. Allah has revealed 6236 Qur'anic verses to mention that there is no Deity except Him to seek help, to trust and to fear. Also, He sent more than hundred and twenty four thousand Prophets from Adam to Muhammad only to introduce Him. The verse 16: 2 says: He sends down His Angels with inspiration of His Command to whom He wishes of His servants, saying: "Warn the people that there is no Deity except Me, therefore heed Me." And the verse 21: 25 says: The fact is that to every Messenger whom We sent before you, We revealed the same Message: "There is no Deity except Me, so serve Me alone; i.e. live for me alone." Read together the verse 16: 36. The first question in the Tomb will be: "Who is your Lord?" Read together the verses 4: 1 and 9: 31-34. Those who didn't fulfill the aim of life that to find out Allah, will be unable to answer for this question. As per the verse 3: 103, Allah says believers to unite and form a single party by holding firmly the Rope of Allah- which is the Soul of Qur'an. And if different organizations of Muslims turn away from this, Allah commands the believers to say: "Witness that we are Muslims; i.e. we have fully submitted to Allah." Read together the verses 3: 101-102, 21: 52 and 53. See explanation 2: 132-137 and 176.

65. Oh people of the Book! Why do you argue about Ibrahim? Since the Thourath and Injeel were not sent down except after him. Will you not then think by using your intelligence?

The Jews and Christians- the people of the Book at the time of the Prophet argued that, they are following the path of *Ibrahim*. But the *Thourath* and *Injeel* were sent down to *Moosa* and *Eisa*, very long after him. And they are bound to follow that Book. Here it says that their talks without realizing the fact are very weak and they are deviated from the path of *Ibrahim, Moosa* and *Eisa* by not following the Book. Today, the question: Will you not then think using your intelligence? Is applicable only for the Muslims because they are the only people who accept Qur'an as the Book and carries It. Here Allah says to the Muslims that, *Ibrahim* and *Muhammad* lived by following the path of the Book- the Straight Path of Allah. But you turned away from It, following your forefathers blindly and become different parties, thus became the party of satan. And Allah asks: Will you not then think using your intelligence? In the verses 8: 22 and 55 it is told that the worst of creatures in the sight of Allah are the dumb and the deaf people who don't think using their intelligence, and they are the disbelievers. See explanation 2: 6-7, 170-171 and 3: 52.

66. Ah! You are the ones, who argued a lot in matters which is known to you. Then why do you argue about something which is unknown to you? Allah knows, while you don't know.

The meaning of "You argued a lot in matters which is known to you" is that, on those days Jews and Christians argued about *Ibrahim* and *Is'haq* according to the rumors they received from their forefathers. It was not based on the Soul of the Book which is the True knowledge. That is why in the previous verses it says that *Thourath* and *Injeel* were revealed till after *Ibrahim*. That means you should argue on the basis of *Thourath* and *Injeel.* The *Mou'idhath* (similar example) of this verse is that, one should realize Prophet *Ibrahim, Isma'el*, and *Muhammad* etc. only through the Soul of Qur'an. See the explanation 2: 146. And it should not be from the historic books like '*Qasasul Ambiya*' -history of Prophets- or any other books written by the creatures. See the explanations 2: 121, 254 and 3: 62.

67. Ibrahim was neither a Jew, nor a Christian; but he was a straight forward man fully submitted to Allah. And he was not of those who associate others with Allah.

Ibrahim was the one who submitted all the moments of his will and life to Allah and belongs to the single party of Allah specified in the verse 58: 22. See explanations 1: 4; 2: 135 and 136.

68. Surely the people nearest to Ibrahim are those who follow him, as well as this Prophet and those who believe; Allah is the believers' Patron.

Jews and Christians, who lived during the periods of Prophet in *Madeena* argued that they are the closest people with *Ibrahim, Is'haq* and *Ya'qoob*, and about Muhammad you have come with new ideas other than that of them. As a reply to their arguments, here in this verse Allah says: "Today this Prophet and those who believed with him are the closest people with *Ibrahim* who follow the Islam".

Though the Muslims are arguing that they are the followers of Prophet Muhammad and *Ibrahim* are not true followers, since they are not following the Soul of Qur'an. Instead they are falsifying and killing the Prophets by celebrating the death anniversary of Prophet as well as other non-Islamic customs like receiving dowry and ornaments from women's part making the marriage a burden to women side they are giving meat and other food materials as offering to the great people even though it is forbidden according to the verse 2: 173. On the Day of Judgment these great people and the Prophet itself will argue and witness against them with the Soul of Qur'an as told in the verses 25: 17-18 and 30 respectively. But it is the believers only who follow the life of Prophet and bear witness his life among the mankind by following the Soul of Qur'an. They are the only people who follow the path of *Ibrahim, Isma'el, Is'haq* and *Muhammad*. It is told in the verse 2: 257 that, Allah is the protector and friend of those who believe; and for the disbelievers, satan is the protector and friend. See the explanation 2: 146, 285 and 3: 21-22.

69. A faction from the people of the Book would like to lead you astray; yet they only lead themselves astray even though they don't perceive it.

Today Qur'an is the one and only Book, and Muslims are the carriers. The hypocrites, human devils will try to mislead the believers who are among the party of Allah into astray by deviating them from the Soul of Qur'an. In fact they themselves are in astray and they don't realize it. The verse 6: 26 says: They themselves have turned away from the Soul of Qur'an and also obstruct other people about It. With such a behavior they harm none except their own souls but they do not perceive it. Allah has killed such hypocrites. Allah has commanded to the group of the believers to kill them through the verses 4: 91; 9: 123; 33: 61. Since such a group of believers does not exist anywhere, it will be implemented only after the second coming of Eisa. See explanation 2: 6-9, 99 and 109.

70. Oh people of the Book! Why do you hide the verses of Allah? while to which you bear witness.

The Jews and Christians in *Madeena* concealed some parts of the previous Book which refers about Prophet Muhammad and Qur'an and behaved like unknown about it in front of Prophet. Moreover, they were asking one another while they were alone that "did you mention in your talks with believers about the part of the Book about the Prophet *Muhammad*, by which they may argue against you before Allah" as specified in the verses 2:76. Today the hypocrites among Muslims posses the same character of Jews. See explanation 2: 77-79, 140 and 3: 27

71. Oh people of the Book! Why do you dress Truth up with falsehood and hide the Truth while you have knowledge?

Since the Soul of Qur'an is the only Book today, this verse points towards the hypocrites - the satans from the mankind - who hide the verses of Allah from the mankind, and explain the verses according to their own will instead of Allah's wishes!. And explain the verses against the situation, and reveal only a part of the verse by concealing the other part in order to alter the original message of Qur'an. See explanation 2: 42 and 174-176.

72. And a faction from among the people of the Book says: Believe in what has been sent down to the believers in the morning and reject It in the evening, so that they may turn back from their faith.

In *Madeena*, at the time of Prophet itself, a faction of the Jews used to act as believers and participated in all the activities of believers from morning to the evening. But in the evening, they returned to their own camp and followed the rites and customs of their forefathers. Their intention was to mislead the common people by this activity. That is the common people should think that the wise people among us have studied well about the believers' way of life and find that there is no truth and modern in that, thus they have returned to their previous way of life. This was a trick to forbid the ordinary people even from thinking about Islam. When *Umer* told to Prophet that, one of my Jew friends taught me their Book, Prophet showed great anger and told: If *Moosa* is alive today, he is bound to follow me. In the verse 11: 17 it is told that any of the groups who reject the Soul of Qur'an, the Fire will be their promised abode. So you be not in doubt about It. It is the Truth from your Lord, yet many among men do not believe. See the explanation 2: 121.

To oppose such behaviors of Jews, and to teach believers that the rites and customs of *Islam* are against that of Jews in each and every sectors; Prophet told to some of his companions to enter into the Masjid by wearing chapels and shoes. But today, as foresighted by Prophet, the Muslims have become those who follow the rites and customs of Jews and Christians inch by inch and cubit by cubit. Not only this, the hypocritical leaders of Muslims are planning and practicing their schemes better than that of Jews to forbid the people from where the Soul of Qur'an is teaching as specified in the verses 41: 26-28. Due to the lack of True knowledge it can be seen today Muslims all over the world are forefront in all evil deeds than any other people. Dooms day will occur when all the people become transgressors as Muslims and there is not even a single believer on Earth. Prophet taught as a reply to the question of *Hudaifathul Yamani* that, in the absence of the believers' leader and single party of Muslims, one should go to the forest and stay by biting the bottom of a tree till death.

Two types of unities-the unity of mankind and the unity of believers are taught by the Qur'an. The communal unity is introduced by Jews and today the hypocrites are following and encouraging it. Read together the verse 4: 137. Allah ordered to give asylum to non-Muslims. The verse 9: 6 says: If anyone from the pagans ask you for asylum, grant it to him so that he may hear the Word of Allah, and then escort him to his place of safety: this should be done because these people do not know the Truth -the Soul of Qur'an; Whereas Allah has commanded the group of believers to kill the hypocrites and their blind followers through the verses 4: 91; 9: 123 and 33: 61. In the verse 41: 28 it is told that, the hypocrites are the enemies of Allah; where in the verse 63: 4 says: They are the enemies of believers and beware of them. In the verse 59: 13 it is told that, they fear the believers than Allah, and they are the enemies of Allah and messenger. In the verse 58: 8 says: They greet you in words which Allah does not greet you with, and ask themselves in mind: Why does not Allah punish us for what we say. Since today there is no group of believers anywhere in the world, believers here and there are demanded to do '*Jihad*' with Soul of Qur'an against hypocrites and their followers as told in the verses 9: 73 and 25: 52. See explanation 2: 6-7, 254 and 3: 28

73. And do not believe anyone except the one who follow your way of life. Say: Certainly, the Guidance is the guidance from Allah, lest one person should be given the same as what you have been given, or they should argue with you concerning your Lord. Say: Certainly, the Bounty is in Allah's hand and He grants It to anyone He wishes; Allah is Boundless, Aware.

74. He chooses anyone He wishes for His Mercy; Allah possesses splendid Bounty.

The Guidance, Mercy and The Bounty mentioned in the verses is Soul of Qur'an itself. Prophet taught that, *among you the best are those who learn and teach the Soul of Qur'an.* Allah has sent down the Qur'an as Guidance to the entire mankind and It justifies the previous books. But the Jews rejected the Qur'an only due to Prophet Muhammad was not a successor of Prophet *Is'haq*. They were not ready to accept the successor of Prophet *Isma'el*. The fact that only Allah has the right to select Prophets from His servants as He wishes, but the disbelievers will not accept it. As per the verse 2: 129, *Ibrahim* prayed: Our Lord! Send among them a messenger of their own who shall recite Your verses to them, and teach them the Book, and wisdom and purify them. Verily You are Exalted in Power, the Wise. But Allah fulfilled it after about 2500 years by appointing Prophet *Muhammad*. Allah Himself decides and practices everything. None of His creatures have the power, influence or right to interfere in His decisions. The verse 22: 75 says: Allah chooses His messengers from among the Angels and from among the mankind for surely Allah is All-Hearing, All-Seeing. The believers who live by observing Allah through the Soul of Qur'an, and serve Him alone by propagating and conveying His message to the entire mankind is only represent Him. Prophet taught that, to such one only the Soul of Qur'an will argue, witness and intercede in favor. Read together the verses 62: 2-4. See explanation 1: 2; 2: 105 and 135.

75. Among the people of the Book there are some who, if you trust them with a heap of treasure, will readily return it back. And there are others who, if you trust them with a single Dinar, will not return it back unless you keep on demanding. (The reason for this character is) they say: There is no question on us regarding these illiterates. They tell a lie about Allah knowingly.

Today, Muslims who carries Qur'an containing these types of verses possesses the same character of Jews and other people of the Book, especially the hypocrites. About them Prophet taught: *If they talk, will lie, cut the promise, and cheat people who put trust on them.* "There is no Question regarding these illiterates" means that, on that days the Jews and today the hypocrites deny the rights of common people by thinking that Allah will not ask any question about cheating the illiterates in the Hereafter; and in this world also they are unable to buy back the properties approaching the government or court. The meaning of "they speak lie about Allah knowingly" is that, they are rejecting the fact that, no one can step forward in the Day of Judgment without returning the rights of others. See the explanation 3: 30. The hypocrites having life only without soul neither follow nor teach the Soul of Qur-an which explains clearly about the Day of Judgment See explanation 1: 3; 2: 78-79, 159, 3:21 and 22.

76. Nay, any one who keep his covenant made with Allah, performs his duty and keeps Him in his hearts; then surely Allah loves such heedful.

One should understand the Soul of Qur'an - which is the Guidance, and should follow Its do's and don'ts throughout the life in order to be the heedful as specified in the verse 39: 33. In the verse 54: 17 it is told: The Soul of Qur'an is made very easy to understand with heart's language even for illiterates. It has warned in the verse 36: 59-62 that, those people who didn't keep their covenant made with Allah in this world by understanding it through the soul of Qur'an will be the *Mujrims* and should admit that they were serving the satan- the enemy of Allah and believers. As per the verses 6: 94; 18: 48; 19: 95 etc. each soul- male or female - has to appear individually in front of Allah. See the explanation 2: 26-28 and 3: 30.

77. Surely, those who sell the covenant made with Allah and their own pledges for a miserable price will have no share in the

Hereafter, nor will Allah ever speak to them, nor look at them on the day of Resurrection. He will not purify them while they will have painful torment.

• The meaning of "Allah will neither speak to them, nor look at them, nor purify them" is that, they will enter the Hell without even reckoning just like the people of *Pharoah*. Read together the verses 4: 145; 8: 50 and 51. It is because they lived here knowingly forgetting the aim of life and hide Allah and His Prophet in the Soul of Qur'an. See explanation 2: 174-176 and 3: 10-12.

78. Surely there is a group among them who twist their tongue around concerning the Book. So that you will reckon it is a part of the Book, while it is not from the Book. And they say: "It comes from Allah", while it is not from Allah. They knowingly tell a lie about Allah!

The examples of "twist their tongue around concerning the Book" is the activities like saying the words which are not told in the Book as if it is a verse in the Book in order to mislead the common people. Thus they make defect to the Book-without any crookedness- which is sent down by Allah. Activities like explaining the verse improperly in the occasions, and explaining the verses with different ideas that Allah intends not. By quoting only a part of the verse concealing other part to alter the original ideas is also a type of twisting the Book. It was the attitude of Jews and hypocrites in *Madeena* on those days. Today Qur'an is the only Book. Those who utilize Qur'an as Criterion can easily realize that, today the hypocrites are distorting Qur'anic verses than the Jews done with their Book. The verse 5: 13 also specify this behavior of Jews and today's hypocrites.

An example for twisting tongue is; in the assemblage of Prophet, instead of saying: "*Sami'na Va Atwah'na*" -we hear and we obey- they used to say: "*Sami'na Va Asway'na*" -we hear and we disobey. Read together the verse 4: 46. Today an example for twisting is saying "*La Thaqnathoo*" -not to be devoted- instead of "*La Thaqnathwoo*" -not to be desperate- by wrongly pronouncing "*thoo*" instead of "*thwoo*". Another example is to carry out '*Dhikr Halqa*' - celebrating *Dhikr*; i.e. saying: "No Deity except Allah", continuously in assembly by twisting the word "*Fad'kuroo'nee*"-then you always remember Me- in the verse 2: 152 to "*Fad'kuroo'lee*" -then you all say remember for Me. Infact it is told to remember Allah always, while standing, sitting and laying by hearts only as told in the verses 3: 190-191; 4:103, 62: 9-10 etc. The verse 7: 205 says: And remember your Lord deep in your soul with humility and in reverence without raising your voice, both in the mornings and in the evenings; and be not among the heedless. Today the leaders of all Muslim organizations wrongly explain the verses of Qur'an irrelevantly in improper occasions for satisfying their views and ideas. Read together the verses 4: 140 and 6: 68. See explanation 2: 79, 279; 3: 4 and 74.

In the verse 7:176 Allah has compared these hypocritical leaders, who don't follow or teach the Soul of Qur'an knowingly and the common man who do not even try to understand It, to a dog which doesn't change its attitude whether it is disturbed or not. Man is compared to a dog only in the verse 7: 176. Whereas the word about the 'dog' it is mentioned four times in the *Surath Al-kahf*, but some one while using the word dog in the *Surath Al-kahf*, they will use 'canine' in the verse 7:176 instead of dog in order not to understand by the ordinary people, is also another example for distortion.

When explaining the meaning of the word "*Dhik'ree*" in the verse 20: 124 they say: "My admonition" instead of saying: "The Soul of Qur'an in order to mislead the common people that, it is enough to read the books of admonition of various parties instead of the Soul of Qur'an; is also an example for the distortion. Whereas, mentioned in the verse 20: 126 it is told: "Our verses had come to you"- from this itself it is clear that the meaning of "*Dhik'ree*" mentioned in the verse 124 is the Soul of Qur'an. The word "*Dhik'ree*" told both in the verses 18: 101; 38: 8 is only about the Soul of Qur'an. While explaining the verse 3: 49, omitting the meaning "with Allah's Permission"; saying that Prophet *Eisa* has told "I will cure, I will bring the dead back to the life" to establish that the Prophets and saint people know about the unseen matters and they can show miracles; in order to deviate the faith of the common people about Allah, is also an example for distortion. Through the verses 13: 38; 14: 11 and 40: 78, it is told that no messenger can bring a miracle without Allah's Permission. Concealing these three verses when explaining the verse 45: 21, leaving its first part and saying that the life and death of saint people are alike, to establish the argument that they can help those people who call them after their death like they had helped while they were alive; is another example for distortion. Actually through this verse Allah asks: Do those who commit evil deeds think that -they and the heedful people's life and death shall be alike? What a bad judgment they make. See explanation 2: 66, 99 and 169.

79. It is not suitable for a man to whom Allah has given the Book, the Wisdom and the Prophethood that he should say to the people: "Be servants of me instead of Allah." On the contrary he should say: "Be proud representatives of your Lord as you have been taught by the Book and as you have been studying it.

80. He does not order you to adopt Angels and Prophets as Lords; would he order you to disbelieve after you have become Muslims?

Those people who pray, obey, fear and trust to anyone except Lord are disbelievers and they elect disbeliever satan as their protector. The verse 9: 30 says: The Jews say: "*Uzair* (*Azra*) is the son of Allah," and the Christians say: "*Maseeh* (Christ) is the son of Allah." That is what they say with their mouths, imitating the sayings of the former disbelievers. Allah has killed them! How perverted they are! Those who place mediators and intercede towards Allah are *mushriks* just like *Meccan mushriks*. Those who are not included in the single party of Believer- Allah- but have included in different parties and thus in disbeliever satan's party are *mushriks* and disbelievers. In the verse 4: 172 it is told that Prophet *Eisa* and Angels never feel shame or arrogance in being servants of Allah. Prophet *Muhammad* was one who lived depending upon Allah alone and he used to pray always: Oh Allah, I wish for Your Mercy. Oh my Lord, don't entrust me to care myself even the time for a single blink of eyes". Due to long night *swalath*, Prophet's legs became oedemate and about this the followers asked: "Oh Prophet, why are you struggling like this?" Prophet replied angrily: "Should I be a loyal servant?" Prophet taught that, you call me the servant and messenger of Allah. The verse 19: 80 says: We will inherit anything he says, and he will come to Us individually. The verse 93 says: every one who is in heaven and earth not comes to the Impartial except as a servant. See the explanation 2: 27.

"*Be Rabbaniyeen*-proud representatives of Allah- in accordance with the teachings of the Book" means that be proud always and live anywhere on Earth with raised head and without fearing anyone by holding the Soul of Qur'an as shield and safeguard firmly. Through the verse 67:22 Allah asks: Who is rightly guided? The one who walks with his face close to the Earth or he who walks upright? It is told in the verses 17: 97; 25: 34, those who forget Allah after receiving the Qur'an and live in this world by fearing and depending others are in astray; and they will be summoned to the Hell, prone on their faces. In the verse 25: 74 it is told that the most beloved servants of the Impartial who accept Him as the most Gracious will pray: Make us the leaders of the heedful who follow the Soul of Qur'an. In the verse 47: 24 Allah asks: Do they not proud about Qur'an, or are their hearts locked about it? In the verse 38: 25 it is told that We have sent down to you this blessed Book, so that men may ponder upon the verses, and the men of understanding may remember It by heart. The verse 4: 82 says: Will they not proud by the Qur'an. If it had been from other than Allah, they would have found many contradictions in It. So it is the duty of men to research any contradictions is there in the Soul of Qur'an. As the explanations of this verse Prophet taught that: *"Qur'an is the Prosperity, after It there is no poverty, and without It there is no prosperity"*. The meaning of saying 'to hold firmly Allah' in the verses 3:101 and 22:78 is 'to hold firmly the Soul of Qur'an', i.e. the Rope as per the verse 3:103 and that Rope will not break and it will lead to Allah-to the Paradise. Read together the verses 41: 41-43 and 76: 29. See explanation 2: 23-24 and 3: 58

Prophets and believers will say to the mankind to live depending only Allah by following the message of whole Qur'an. In brief, by studying and teaching the Soul of Qur'an, one is keeping Allah and messenger alive and driving the satan far away. Once Prophet told *Allah select family from mankind; Followers asked to the Prophet: who are they? Prophet replied: they are the people of Qur'an and they belong to His family and they are of Him alone.* In the verse 68: 37 Allah asks: Or do you have a Book other than this Qur'an which you read. It is told in the verse 34: 44 that, We have not given them the Book to study nor sent any Warner before you. Note that by reading the Arabic text-the body of Qur'an, as well as Its life-meaning, will not become "*Rabbaniyyeen*"-proud representatives of Lord- instead the Soul of Qur'an which is the food, cloth and sight of the human Soul, should learn and teach. See explanation 1: 4; 2:136 and 137.

81. And remember Allah took the agreement from Prophets: Have I not given you some of the Book and Wisdom? Then a Messenger came to you to confirm with what you already had, so you must believe with him and help him. Allah asked: 'have you

acknowledged and accepted that obligation of mine?' They said: "we so acknowledge It". He said: 'Then act as witnesses; I am one of those testifying along with you.

82. Then who so ever turns back after this- such are the one who are transgressors.

See the explanation 2:26. Only one Book- *Al-Kithab*- has come from Allah. All the Prophets have followed It and have advised the mankind to live by following It. Here Allah reminds about an agreement that He made with the Prophets at Paradise that all of you should help Prophet *Muhammad* and believe in the Book he brings- It is the last form of the Book *Al-Kithab*-which is kept safely with Allah. See explanation 2: 2. In the verse 33: 7 Allah says: Remember We took agreement from all Prophets- from you, *Nooh, Ibrahim, Moosa* and *Eisa*- the son of *Maryam*. We took a solemn agreement from all of them. In the verse 7: 156 says: Allah's Mercy overspreads to all things, therefore I ordain that Mercy for those who are heedful, pay charity and believe in Our verses. And in the verse 157 says: That is for who follow the Messenger, the illiterate Prophet whom they shall find described in the *Thourath* and *Injee*l with them, who enjoin them what is right and forbid them from what is wrong, and make lawful to them the good things and forbid them the bad things. He lifts from them the heavy burdens and chains that are upon them. Then those who believe with him, help him and follow the Light which is sent down with him will be successful. In the verse 7: 158 Allah commands the Prophet to say: Oh mankind! Surely I am sent to all of you as a Messenger of Allah to whom belongs the kingdom of Heavens and Earth. There is no Deity except Him. He brings to life and causes to death. Then believe in Allah and His words. Follow It so that you might be guided. Through the verse 3: 187 Allah reminds that He has took a solemn agreement from those who were given the Book to spread the teaching of the Book clearly to mankind and not to hide It.

Allah says in the verse 13: 43: The disbelievers say: "You are not Messenger". Say: Allah is enough for a witness between me and you, and those who have true knowledge of the Book. In the verse 29: 52 Allah commands the Prophet to say: Allah is enough for a witness between me and you. He knows all that is in the Heaven and Earth. Those who believe in falsehood and hide Allah in the Soul of Qur'an, it is they who shall be the losers. In the verse 11: 17 says that a "witness" is reciting to you; the "witness" mentioned here is about the Soul of

Qur'an. The verses 5: 47; 24: 4, 55 and 59: 19 also end as such are the ones who are transgressors. See the explanation 2: 140; 3: 18, 52 and 53.

Oh Allah! Do not make us the losers and hypocrites who hide the Soul of Qur'an. Make us the heedful and righteous who follow Qur'an; and include us with the successful who enter into the Paradise with the Ticket, mentioned in the verse 73: 19.

83. Are they seeking for a 'Dheen' -way of life- other than the Dheen of Allah, when all creatures in Heavens and on Earth submitted only to Him whether willingly or reluctantly? And to Him will they be returned.

As mentioned in the verse 3:19 *Islam* is the only *Dheen* -way of life- which Allah satisfied. All living and nonliving things submit and devote to Allah who created the Heaven, the Earth and every thing in between them from nothingness within six days and adopted all its control. Then, it is man who have blessed with intelligence and bound to live as representatives of Allah seeking for another way of life. So they are ungrateful and will admit in the Hell. It is told both in the verses 17: 44 and 24: 41 that, Allah has taught the way of prayer and glorifying Him to both living and nonliving things. The verse 16: 49 says that, all the living things prostrate to Allah. And they are not with false pride. The verse 13: 15 says that whatever beings in the Heavens and Earth do prostrate before Allah willingly or unwillingly, and so do their shadows in the morning and evenings. The verse 22: 18 says that all that are in the Heavens and the Earth prostrate to Allah- the sun, the moon, the stars, the mountains, the trees, the animals, a large number of people and a large number who deserve punishment (reluctantly). It is told in the verse 33: 72 that Allah offered the Qur'an, which is the Trust to keep the Universe in its equilibrium, to the Heavens, Earth and mountains, but they refused to undertake It and were afraid of It. But man undertook It. He was indeed wrong and foolish. The verse 19: 93 says: Every one who is in Heaven and Earth coming not to Impartial except as a servant. It is told in the verses 15: 23; 28: 58 and 19: 80 that, at last Allah will inherit everything of Heavens and Earth. And as per the verse 18: 8 Allah will remove every thing over the earth and will make it like a barren single marble covered floor. Read together the verses 20:105-109 and 51: 55-57. See explanations 2: 29.

84. Say: we believe in Allah, and what has been sent down to us, what was sent down to Ibrahim, Isma'el, Is'haq, Ya'qoob and the Tribes; and in what was given to Moosa, Eisa and the Prophets by their Lord; we do not differentiate between any one of them and to Him we submit ourselves.

See the explanation 2:136

85. If anyone is seeking for a way of life -Dheen- other than Islam, it will never be accepted from him; and he will be among the losers in the Hereafter.

The verse 21: 25 says: And We have not sent any messenger before you, except inspired to him that indeed there is no Deity except Me so you serve Me alone. Through the verse 43: 45, Allah demands Prophet to ask other Messengers in the night of *Isra'* and *Mihraj* after leading the *swalath* that "did We appoint any Deity other than the Impartial to be served?" Read together the verses 17:1 and 53: 1-18. In brief, Islam is the only way of life which Allah satisfied for all His creatures from Prophet Adam to the last day. All the Prophets have come to invite mankind to that way of life. All of them invited to the Lord of everything, and all the things in the universe are submitted to Him. Since Allah has appointed men as His representatives and blessed with Intelligence, they have more responsibility to submit themselves to Allah, to remember and glorify Allah than any other creatures of Heaven and Earth. See explanation 2:152. In other words men have to utilize the Soul of Qur'an as the Balance and Trust to keep the Universe in its equilibrium. Only the believers who learn and teach Soul of Qur'an bear the responsibility among the mankind. Those who hide and reject after receiving It are the disbelievers and representatives of Satan; and are worst beast in the sight of Allah. Read together the verses 41: 29; 84: 22-25 and 95: 4-6.

Prophet used to pray three times after '*Magrib*' and '*fajr*' Swalath like this: "I satisfied Allah as Lord, Islam as *Dheen*, and *Mohammad* as Prophet and messenger". In the verse 5: 3 it has told that, the way of life which Allah satisfied for all His creatures from Adam to the last day has completed and satisfied in the day of "*Hajjathul Vida*"-Departing Pilgrimage. The party of Allah - the one and only from first to last day - is the blessed party. It includes the Prophets and the believers. All other parties of Muslims are among the party of satan, and they live as the representatives of satan. In the verse 5:5 it is told that, anyone who hides belief -the Soul of Qur'an- will be losers in the Hereafter. See explanations 2:121, 213 and 3:19.

86. How should Allah guide a people who reject faith after they accepted it? And have testified that surely the Messenger is true, and evidence had come to them? Allah does not guide such a wrong doing people.

The evidence mentioned in this verse is the Proof that is the Soul of Qur'an. With which only one can become a believer as specified in the verse 10: 100. During Prophet's time the disbelieving people were the Jews while today, the disbelieving and wrongdoing people are Muslims only who hide and reject the Soul of Qur'an after receiving It. See the explanations 2: 111, 143 and 254.

87. The reward of such people is that, surely on them is the curse of Allah as well as the Angels and all mankinds.

88. They will remain in this state for ever. Neither their punishment will be lightened, nor will they be given any respite.

89. Except for those who repent after that and reform their deeds; then surely Allah is Forgiving, Merciful.

These verses mention about the hypocrites who know the Soul of Qur'an very well, but not follow It and hide It from mankind. It is told in the verse 63: 3 that Allah has sealed their hearts because they believed and then rejected the faith, therefore they will not understand the aim of life. See the explanations 2: 174 and 175. It commands the prophets to say through the verse 32: 29 as on the Day of Victory of believers, the disbelievers' acceptance of faith will not benefit for them, nor will be given them respite. The curse of Allah, Angels and all mankind fall on them because they are not learning and teaching the soul of Qur'an to mankind which is the only weapon to stop mischief, make harmony of human unity and the Balance to keep the Universe in its equilibrium. Read together the verses 4: 88-91 and 33: 60-61. But if anybody by reading the Soul of Qur'an then repent and reform their deeds in accordance of It, Allah will forgive their offences. See the explanations 2: 159-161 and 186.

90. Surely, those who disbelieve following their faith, then increase their disbelief; will never have their repentance accepted; and such are those who have gone astray.

'Those who have gone astray' mentioned here are the hypocrites who do not follow the Soul of Qur'an after receiving It , increase in their disbelief by hiding the Soul of Qur'an and leading a way of life against It, thus they falsify the Prophet as well as Qur'an. It is told in the verses 4: 137-138 that, surely for those who believe, then disbelieve and then again believe, then disbelieve and increase in disbelief, Allah will never forgive them nor guide them to the Straight path. To such hypocrites inform the glad tidings of painful torment. Therefore, today, the believer can't participate for *swalath* with these cursed and gone astray people either as Leader or Followers. Through the verses 95: 7-8 Allah asks that, then whoever falsify you (the Prophet) after getting the *Dheen* -way of life- the soul of Qur'an, is not Allah the best of all Judges? In other words, those hypocrites who disbelieve after receiving the way of life have painful torment; because Qur'an will bear witness and argue against them. A scene of the inmates in the Hell is described through the verses 23: 105-108 as "were My verses not recited to you then you were all rejecting them?" they will say: "Our Lord our misery has overwhelmed us and we were a people of gone astray. Our Lord, get us out of here! if we ever should return to disobedience we would indeed be wrongdoers" He will say sink down in to it and never speak to Me. See the explanations 1: 7; 2: 90-91,166 and 167.

91. Surely, as for those who disbelieve and die while they are 'Kuffar'- disbelievers, if they were ready to give Earth filled of gold as ransom (to escape from the punishment of Hell), that will not be accepted. There will be a painful punishment for them, and they will have no helpers.

"*Kuffar*" means the one who hide the message of all verses - not of one or two verses. "*Kuffar*" mentioned in this verse as well as in the verses 9: 123 and 48: 29 are hypocrites. In the verse 78: 28 it has told about them that, they falsified Our verses continuously. Since both in the verses 9: 73 and 66: 9, it is separately told as *Kuffar* and hypocrites- the *Kuffar* mentioned are the gone astray people. Hypocrites are the Muslim leaders who twist and hide the Soul of Qur'an knowingly, will enter the Hell without Trial as per the verse 4: 145. The gone astray people also disbelievers will be led to the Hell after Trial as specified in the verse 39: 71. To put it brief the losers' group such as *Kuffar, Fujjar*, Disbelievers, *Mujrims*, Wrong doers, Transgressors includes both hypocrites and gone astray people who hide and reject the Soul of Qur'an. Read together the verses 33: 72 -73 and 48: 6. See explanation 2: 39 and 99

The verse 39: 47 says: If the wrongdoers possessed all the treasures of the Earth and as much more besides it, they would gladly offer it as ransom themselves from the worst torment on the Day of Resurrection will not be accepted, and Allah will show them what they would have never imagined. The verses 5: 36; 10: 54 and 13: 18 are also with the same message. According to a *Hadeeth- 'Qudsi'* on the day of Judgment Allah will ask to the person of the Hell: if you had everything on the Earth, would you give it as a ransom to free yourself? He will say: Yes, Then Allah will say: I asked you much easier than this. I took a covenant from you while you were in the nape of Adam, that not to associate any thing to Me, but you lived by associating partners to Me. The covenant mentioned here is about the covenant referred in the verse 7: 172 that each Soul is made with Allah. See explanation 2: 27. In the verses 36: 60-61 say: Oh children of Adam did not take a covenant from you that you should not serve satan? Surely he is your open enemy. But you serve Me alone, this is the Straight path. The worship becomes for Allah, whenever one stay remembering Allah with the Reminder- the Soul of Qur'an. Whoever stays forgetting Allah by hiding and rejecting the Soul of Qur'an, then they are worshipping or serving the satan. The verse 47: 34 says surely for those who disbelieve and obstruct Allah's way, then die while they are "*kuffar*" Allah will never *pardon*. Read together the verses 9: 84-85; See the explanations 2: 28 and 3: 77.

92. You will never attain virtue until you spend something you are fond of; And whatever you spend, surely it is known to Allah.

One should give to others what he loves more for himself. Also he will not become a believer until he gives it for the sake of Allah. Prayers and deeds of the people other than the believers will not be accepted. Both the verse 13: 14 and 47: 50 end as the prayer of disbelievers increase nothing except astray. See the explanation 2: 186 and 267. The Soul of Qur'an is the most Mercy and Prosperity for the believers. So they will convey It to others in order to form the harmony of the mankind. That is the meaning of what Prophet taught: *The best one among you is the one who learn and teach the soul of Qur'an*. No one can become a believer without Allah's permission- the soul of Qur'an. The ultimate aim of the believers is to attain the Paradise by spending all the blessings that Allah given to them under the Light -Soul of Qur'an. See the explanation 2: 177; 3: 79.

93. Every kind of food was lawful to the children of Israel, except what Israel had banned for himself before the Thourath was

revealed. Say: Bring the Thourath and recite it, if you are so truthful.

As a criticism, Jews asked Prophet that the flesh and milk of Camel are forbidden in our law, but you are using it. As a reply Allah commands Prophet to say: You are bound to live according to the laws of *Thourath*, so you bring and read It to me. Prophet *Ya'qoob*-known in other name Israel-, while he was seriously ill, made a covenant that he will exclude his favorite food- camel's meat and milk. It means that Allah has not made it unlawful to them in the Book. See the explanation 2: 173.

94. Then whoever invent a lie and attribute it to Allah after that, such will be the wrongdoers.

Those who don't reveal what Allah sent down through the Book to the whole mankind, and attribute a lie to Allah are the utmost wrongdoers. The verse 5: 45 also end as those who do not judge with the Soul of Qur'an in their individual, family and social life such will be the wrong doers. Read together the verses 6: 21; 10: 14. See the explanations 2: 135, 239 and 254.

95. You say: Allah has spoken the Truth. Then you follow the straight forward way of Ibrahim; And he was not among those who associate others with Allah.

The verse 4: 122 ends as: Who can be more truthful than Allah in his words. In the verse 39: 33 it is told that who have received the Truth and make It true as it should be made are the heedful. The Truth means the Soul of Qur'an. After reciting Qur'an, one should pray that include me in the party of heedful- who make true-the Qur'an as it should be made and not among the rejecters and wrongdoers- who hide the Soul of Qur'an. Read together the verses 29: 68 and 39: 32. Instead of praying like this, today hypocrites are saying: 'Allah has told the Truth'- after reciting Qur'anic verses during admonition on Friday ceremony. But Prophet or believing scholars have not taught like this. In other words it is taught to pray according to the contents of each verse after reciting it. As per the verse 4:140 it is told that such hypocrites who gave certificate to Allah by saying 'Allah has told the truth;' in the 'Friday ceremony' and the audience disbelievers who listen this hypocrites will be gathered together the Hell. The verse 63:1 says about such hypocrites that, when the hypocrites come to you, they say: We bear witness that you are indeed the Messenger of Allah; But Allah knows that you are truly His Messenger, and He bear witness that the hypocrites are indeed liars.

Today Muslims lead a life opposite to the soul of Qur'an and argue that they are following the path of *Ibrahim, Is'haq, Ya'qoob*, *Muhammad* etc. Actually all Prophets' way of life was the Book. But as Jews of those days today's Muslims, lead a life which is away from the Soul of Book. Thus they not only serving the satan but also obstructing the way of Allah to other people. Read together the verses 25: 18 and 30. See the explanation 2: 44 and 3: 65-68.

96. Surely, the first House of worship set up for the mankind was the one at Mecca; it is a blessing and guidance for all the worlds.

97. In it are the clear signs such as Ibrahim's station. Anyone who enters it will be secure. Pilgrimage to the House is a duty imposed on mankind by Allah, for anyone who can afford a way to do so. If anyone who disbelieves this fact, then Allah is self Sufficient- beyond the need of anyone of the worlds.

Ka'ba is the first House for worship in this world, which is constructed at the time of Prophet Adam itself. It is demolished by the flood occurred at the period of Prophet *Nooh*. After that Prophet *Ibrahim* and *Isma'el* reconstructed it; Even though *Ka'ba* having this high dignity, Allah commanded to the Prophet and followers to face towards '*Baithul-Muqadhis*' as the Qib'la. Read together the verse 2: 143. Mecca is the centre of the Earth. Whole world will accept *Islam* by the second coming of *Eisa*, and he will rule the world keeping *Mecca* as the capital. 'For anyone who can afford a way to do so' means about, those who have wealth and health for performing pilgrimage. Allah has commanded to do *swalath*, charity and fasting only to the believers, but He commanded *Hajj* for mankind. In other words, even though one is not a true believer he can perform *Hajj* when the conditions are ready for that; and later when he becomes a True believer by learning and teaching the soul of Qur'an, he can change the *Hajj* that done earlier into an acceptable form. Without the soul of Qur'an- which is the Ticket to the Paradise- no one can become a believer and return to the Paradise. The verse 10: 100 says, it is not possible to any soul to become believer except with Allah's Permission; He places a blight for those who do not use their intelligence. Allah's permission means the Soul of Qur'an. Read together the verses14: 1, 22 and 76: 29. See explanation 3: 91.The meaning of "If anyone who disbelieves this fact, then Allah is self Sufficient- beyond the need of anyone of the worlds" is, if any one is thankful, then he does so for his own soul; and if any one denies, its consequence is for herself only. Read together the verse 31: 12. In brief, this verse also teaches that one should earn Paradise individually from this world itself. The Jews and Christians who argued that they are following the way of *Ibrahim* were not used to per-orm *Hajj* and Prophet taught that any one does not perform *Hajj*, let him die the death of a Jew or Christian as disbeliever. The verse 29: 6 also ends as: Allah is self Sufficient- beyond the need of anyone of the worlds. See the explanation 2: 125 and 286.

98. Ask: Oh, people of the Book! Why do you conceal the verses of Allah? While Allah is a Witness of anything you do.

The Soul of Qur'an is the only Book for entire mankind today. So the question is towards the Muslims who conceal Allah and His Messenger in the Qur'an and are immersed in deeds just opposite to the teachings of the Qur'an. They are living as if Allah is not seeing them, even though they read 'Slumber does not over take Him, nor does sleep' in the verse 2: 255 after every five times *swalath*. The similitude of this people is that of a donkey carrying load on its back which does not know what it carries as told in the verse 62: 5. See the explanation 2: 39, 99 and 3: 70.

99. You ask: Oh people of the Book! Why do you obstruct Allah's way for anyone who believes, seeking to make it crooked, while you are witness for that? And Allah is not heedless of what you are doing.

Today the hypocrites possess the same characters of the people of the Book- Jews during the time of Prophet. They are in false proud that they are the scholars and thus they lead the common people in a way of life just opposite to the Soul of Qur'an- Allah's way. Instead of teaching the Soul of Qur'an, they teach the books written by the people. Thus they prevent the entire community from the Qur'an and they became the satans among the mankind. About them Prophet foretold: The worst of all creatures beneath the sky will be their scholars. The verses 7: 44-45 say: In the Hereafter the residents of Paradise will say by calling the residents of Hell: We have found out that the promises of our Lord to be true. Have you too found the promises of your Lord to be true? At that time they will answer: Yes, we found out. At that time a herald will call and say in between them: The curse of Allah is on wrongdoers, who prevented himself and other people from the path of Allah and made the path crooked to follow It and they denied the Hereafter. The verse 6: 21 say: Who can be more wronged than a person who forges a lie against Allah or rejects His verses? Surely, such wrongdoers will never prosper. The verse 7: 50-51say: Then the inmates of the Hell will cry out to the residents of Paradise: "Give us some water or some of the food which Allah has provided you". The inmates of Paradise will reply: "Allah has prohibited both of these things to the disbelievers, who took their religion to be mere amusement and play and were deceived by their worldly life". Allah will say: "Today We will forget them as they forgot the meeting of this Day; and were repudiating with Our verses".

In the verse 18:1 Allah says: Praise be to Allah Who has sent the Book down to His servant in which there is nothing crooked or difficult to understand. In the verse 22: 78 it is told that, for you Allah has not imposed any difficulties in the '*Dheen*' which is the culture of your father *Ibrahim*. Those who utilize Qur'an as a weighing Balance can easily realize that, today the most difficult and hardship life is among the Muslims because of the rites and customs imposed by them. Everything like birth, marriage, death etc. is easy and justified in *Islam*- the natural way of life. But today Muslims have loaded so many artificial rites and customs in every field of life. Some examples are: Going to see the belly of ladies in their pregnant condition; giving ornaments to the new born babies- even though it is a boy; saying the words of marriage agreement by the scholars instead of recording it; making the '*Mahar*'- the rent to the women as a senseless thing, by giving and accepting the dowry as well as the compulsory fixed ornaments; feasts; fasting feasts; heavy expense to bury the dead one; conducting party and feast on the third, eighth, fortieth days and anniversary of death even by borrowing the money etc. All these are making the verse 9: 34 true, in which Allah has told by calling the believers by: Most of the scholars and anchorites will eat the wealth of people wrongly and will prevent them from the Straight path. See explanation 2: 74 and 3:78.

100. Oh you who believe! If you are obeying a group of those who have been given the Book, they would turn you back into disbelievers after your belief.

Through this verse Allah warns that, the hypocritical scholars who prevent people from the path of Qur'an will pull you to the house of satan- the Hell. In the verse 4: 59 Allah commands that: Oh believers! If you differ with the chief (authority) among you in any matter, refer it to Allah and the Messenger. The only one way to Paradise is the Soul of Qur'an; but to Hell there are nine hundred and ninety nine ways. Therefore today, the believer should holdfast the Soul of Qur'an with his molar teeth in order to stay in the Straight path. See the explanation 2: 109; 3: 28, 31 and 32.

101. And how can you disbelieve, while Allah's verses are being recited to you, and His messenger is among you? Anyone who clings with Allah, and then indeed he is guided to the Straight Path.

In the verse 4: 175 it is told that, whoever believes in Allah and hold firmly the Soul of Qur'an, then Allah will admit them to Mercy and Grace from Him and will guide them to the Straight path. The verse 4: 145 says that: Surely the hypocrites will be in the bottom of the Hellfire, and you will not find any helper for them. And in the verse 146 says: Except for those who repent, and live righteously, hold firmly with Allah, and make their whole life to Allah only-those are with the believers. Allah will grant immense reward to the believers. In the verse 22: 78 it is told to the believers: Therefore, establish *swalath*, pay welfare tax and holdfast with Allah; Who is your Protector - so what an excellent Protector and what a splendid Supporter! "To cling with Allah or holdfast Allah" means: Hold firmly to the rope of Allah-the Soul of Qur'an- which is the words and light of Allah- the Light as specified in the verse 24: 35. Satan prevents people from Allah by preventing from the Soul of Qur'an. Those people who teach others all the books except the Book of Allah, and who teach the meaning of Qur'an by leaving Its soul, and who inform the common people that by mere reciting Qur'an itself will be rewarded are hypocrites, and the human satans. Read together the verses 25: 29-30; 43: 36-39, 44 and 58: 19. See explanation 2: 6-7; 3: 10 and 86-91.

102. Oh you who believe! Keep Allah in your hearts as it should be kept. And you do not die except you are in a state of completely submitted to Allah.

No one will enter to the Paradise without being a believer. And no one can die as Muslim in the state of a new born baby without living as a believer. "Keep Allah in your hearts as it should be kept" means, if you are a True believer and keeping Allah in hearts with the Truth, you should not be gun-shouted by others. In other words, such a heedful is utilizing the Soul of Qur'an as shield and safeguard from all disasters and accidents and be '*Muhsins*'- who live seeing

Allah through the soul of Qur'an; and not be transgressors- who forgot Allah as well as themselves. Read together the explanation 2: 152 and 3: 58

Those people who do not possess any satanic habits like Communalism, Rationalism, selfishness, partiality towards ones own party and people, narrow mind ness etc. can return to Allah as pure as a new born baby by seeing Him in hearts with pleasure as he had seen Him from the Soul of Qur'an without fearing, worrying and sweating. They are the ones who are dying in a state of Muslims. Read together the verses 75: 22 and 23. All men are born as Muslims. Any one who died before the age of fifteenth can return to Paradise. After fifteenth, no one can return to the Paradise without taking the Ticket- the Soul of Qur'an as specified in the verse 73: 19. There for it is the duty of parents to give Ticket to their children. If not done so, Allah will gather both of them in the narrowed Hell, is warned about that scene in the verses 7: 37-39. The verse 49: 14 says: The desert Arabs say: "We have believed". Tell them: "You have not believed; rather say: "We have become Muslims"; for faith has not yet found its way into your hearts. If you obey Allah and His Messenger, He will not deny you the reward of your deeds; surely Allah is Forgiving, Merciful". In the case of desert Arabs Qur'an was not received as a text and all of them were illiterates. But today the Muslims are literates and proud of bearing the Qur'an, and lead a life just opposite to the Soul of Qur'an. So they are the people about whom Allah told that, surely Allah will not guide a people who hide the message of Allah as per the verse 5: 67. And at the time of death they will witness against themselves that they were disbelievers as per the verse 7: 37. See the explanation 3: 90 and 91.

The verse 3: 102 is the only verse that begins as: Oh you who believe! Keep Allah in your hearts as it should be kept. The verses 2: 278; 5: 35; 33: 70; 57: 28 and 59: 18 also begins as; Oh you who believe! Keep Allah in your hearts. Prophet has taught that no one will not become a believer except his wish follow what I have brought; i.e. the Soul of Qur'an. See the explanation 2: 121, 254.

103. All of you together, cling firmly the Rope of Allah and do not separate among yourselves. Remember Allah's favor towards you. When you were enemies; He united your hearts, so you became brothers because of His favor, you were on the brink of a fiery pit, and He saved you from it. Thus Allah makes His verses clear to you, so that you may be rightly guided.

The Rope of Allah is the soul of Qur'an. Prophet taught: Qur'an - the Book of Allah is the strongest and unbreakable Rope that stretched from the Paradise to Earth. Prophet also taught that Qur'an is the strongest Rope and the Straight path. See explanation 2: 256. Allah commands the believers to be the single party of Allah by holding firmly this Soul of Qur'an. In the verse 2: 176 it is told that, those who differed in the Book of Allah have gone far from the Truth by holding the branches instead of holding the whole tree. Except the party of Allah, all other parties belongs the party of satan. Read together the verses 58: 19 and 22.

As specified in the verses 2: 64, 105 and 10: 58 The Soul of Qur'an is the utmost favor. But only the believers will utilize It as a favor. Only by the Soul of Qur'an- the food, cloth and sight of the human soul, hearts can be united. Only by It-the Insight, one can realize that the soul of all creatures is same, and Allah has created entire mankind at the time of creation of Adam itself. Allah deputed entire mankind to Earth in order to live as His representatives and to construct Paradise here. But only believers become representatives of Allah by learning, teaching and conveying His message-the Soul of Qur'an. As per the verse 8: 63: By spending all that is in the Earth, Prophet could not have united their hearts. But Allah united their hearts by this Qur'an. In the verses 9: 71-72 it is told that the believing men and women are protecting friends of one another; and they enjoin what is right and forbid what is evil. The verse 62: 9 says oh you who believe, when the call to *swalath* on the day of congregation is proclaimed hasten to remember Allah and close your business that will be better for you, if you only realized it. To remember Allah' means here the "*Khuthuba*" -Friday ceremony- in which the Soul of Qur'an should be explained. Read together the verse 63: 9. Note that here the verse addresses the group of believers. As per the verse 24: 55 Allah has promised to appoint the believers performing honorable deeds as His representatives on Earth; just as He made those before them. So it is the duty of believers to teach the Soul of Qur'an entire mankind in order to form a party of believer. Who ever hide the Soul of Qur'an which is the Balance and Safeguard, such are the only transgressors. See explanation 2: 99, 272 and 3: 97.

104. And let there be a community among you who will invite others to the best, enjoin the just and forbid the evil; and only such will be the prosperous.

The community mentioned in this verse is the heedful people. 'Invite others to the best' means invite the people to the Soul of Qur'an and thus, towards Allah-the Lord. The verse 41: 33 says: Who is better in speech than the one who calls people towards Allah, does good deeds and says, "I am a Muslim?" To which Allah should call, to Allah revealing by 6236 verses. 'Enjoin the just and forbid the evil' means to command the do's and don'ts of the Qur'an. In the verse 16: 30 it is told that when the people who keep Allah in their hearts are asked: What is that your Lord has revealed? They say: The best. That is the meaning of what Prophet taught, the best one among you is those who learn and teach the Soul of Qur'an. In the verse 22: 77 it is told that, do good deeds, so that you can fulfill the aim of life and attain prosperity. Through the verse 5: 2 it is taught by calling the believers that co-operate with one another in deeds virtue and conscious; and don't co-operate in evil and enmity. Prophet taught: He who among you sees some thing evil should forbid it with his hands; and if he hasn't enough strength to do it, then he should do it with his tongue; if can't, then he should hate it with heart; and that is the least of faith. In another report it is taught that if anyone didn't hate the evil by heart, then he has no faith, even as such as a mustard seed. See explanation 2: 186.

Today there is no group of believers any where in the world. So the believer alone has to live by biting the Soul of Qur'an with his molar teeth as taught by Prophet during the *Hajjathul Vida'*-departing pilgrimage- itself. See explanation 2: 5-7, 148; 3: 81 and 82.

105. And be not like those who have split and disagreed after explanations had come to them; and such will have only awful torment!

Prophet taught: Jews fragmented into 71 groups and Christians to 72 groups. And my community will fragment into 73 groups and will be in the top in schism. All of them except one group will be in the Hell fire. They asked: Allah's Messenger, who belongs to that group? Prophet replied: It is the one who follow the way which I and my companions belong. That group is those who live by following the Soul of Qur'an and belong to the party of Allah from Adam to the last. All others are belong to the party of satan and will return to the house of satan -the Hell. Read together the verses 58: 19 and 22. 'After explanations had come to them' means the Soul of Qur'an has come to them. See the explanation 2: 176, 213; 3: 19-21 and 58.

106. One Day some faces will turn white, while some faces will turn black. Then those whose faces are blackened are the disbelievers after accepting the belief. It will be said to them that, taste the torment since you were concealing the Soul of Qur'an.

Here it is specified about the situations that have to be faced by hypocrites who lived according to their own whims by hiding the Soul of Qur'an after receiving It. In the verse 39: 60 it is told that, on the Day of Judgment you shall see the face of those disbelievers who concealed the Soul of Qur'an and fabricated lies concerning Allah as blackened. The same verse as well as the verse 72 ends as: Is there not a home in the Hell for such false prided persons? The verse 10: 26 says: For those who keep alive the Best-the Soul of Qur'an-shall have a good reward and even more besides. While neither soot nor any disgrace will line their faces; such will be the inhabitance of Paradise; they will live in it forever; and in the verse 27 it says: For those who earn evil deed without having the Soul of Qur'an, they have reward of like evil. Ignominy will be sealed on them. They will have none to protect them from Allah. Their faces will be black like the darkness of night. They will become the inmates of the Hellfire and will live therein forever. In the verses 80: 40-42 it is told that some faces will be covered with dust, and they will suffer by and ignominy. They are the disbelievers who hide the Soul of Qur'an and the *fujjar* who are not trying to understand It.

In the verse 18: 29 it is told that, this Qur'an is the Truth from your Lord. Then whosoever will let him believe, and whosoever will let him conceal. For the disbelievers We have prepared a Hell fire. Its flame have encircled them, whenever they ask for water, they will be given water like molten lead. That will melt their faces, what a useless drink, what a horrible resting place. Read together the verses 22: 72; 37: 62-71; 47: 15 and 48: 6. See explanation 2: 254; 3: 90 and 91.

107. And for those whose faces are whitened, will be in Allah's Mercy; and they will live there in forever.

These verses teach that people with blackened face and whitened face are from those who have received the Book. Those who concealed the Soul of Qur'an are the blackened faced hypocrites and those who followed It are the whitened faced believers. The verses 39: 17-18 say: As for those who refrain from worshipping *Thagooth* -Satanic forces- and turn to Allah in repentance, there are glad tidings. So you, give glad tidings to My servants who listen to the Soul of Qur'an and follow It in a best manner. Such are the ones whom Allah has guided and such are the ones who are endowed with understanding. Read together the verses 39: 55-61. In the verse 32: 18 Allah asks: Is then a man he who is a believer be like the one who is a transgressor? Of course they are not alike. Read together the verses 32: 19-20. In the verses 57: 12-19, Allah has explained the situations of these two groups in the Hereafter. In the verse 66: 8 it is told that the believers' prayer will be: Our Lord, perfect our light for us, and forgive us our sins. Surely You capable of everything. The Light mentioned is the Soul of Qur'an. 'Allah's Mercy' mentioned In the verse is the Paradise, and the Mercy Soul of Qur'an is the Ticket to the Paradise. See explanation 2: 38 and 39.

108. Those are Allah's verses, We recite to you with the Truth. Allah did not intend to show any injustice to the worlds.

Allah- the Knower of all times, have given the Soul of Qur'an to the mankind. Which explains about who is man? Where they were created at first? Why they were sent down to Earth? Etc. Those people who received the Soul of Qur'an can't say any excuse that we didn't see, we didn't hear etc. Moreover they have the responsibility to convey It to those who didn't received It. Thus each individual has to create the Paradise using the Soul of Qur'an. As per the verses 50: 27-29 and 14: 22 no one can blame Allah or satan for getting the Hell as abode. From the verses 55: 1-4 and 75: 14-15 it can be realized that, Allah has taught the Soul of Qur'an to the entire mankind at Paradise itself. See explanation 2: 38. As per the verses 3: 181, 8: 50 and 22: 9 it will be told to the hypocrites: "Taste the torment of burning", and as per the verses 3: 182; 8: 51 and 22: 10 say: "This is because of the deeds which your hands sent forth; for verily Allah is not unjust to His servants. The verse 21: 107 says: "We have not sent you except as a blessing for all the worlds. So on the occasion of the trial in the Hereafter, those who read these verses cannot say any excuse. In the verse 6: 26 it is told that those who don't utilize the Soul of Qur'an and don't give It others to utilize are destroying themselves but they perceive it not. Read together the verses 16: 24 and 25.

Therefore believers are those who are trying to extend the life span of Earth by learning and teaching the Soul of Qur'an. Hypocrites are the human satans who forbids the common people from the Soul of Qur'an and are hurrying for the destruction of Earth. As per the verses 17: 44 and 24: 41 to all the living creatures Allah has taught the mode of prayers and glorify Him with their souls. So the believers will try to keep the Universe in its equilibrium by conveying the Soul of Qur'an for entire mankind irrespective of religion or nation; Such that they will get a share of reward from the prayer and glorification of these creatures. But the '*mujrims*' who act mentally, verbally and physically to forbid the mankind from the Soul of Qur'an after receiving It, will have to bear the sins preventing the living things from their prayer and glorification. The verse 28: 59 says: Your Lord would never destroy the countries until He had sent in their centre (capital) a Messenger, proclaiming to them Our verses; and We would not destroy countries except when their dwellers had become wrongdoers. Mecca is the centre of the world and Muhammad is the Prophet for entire mankind as told in the verse 7: 158. Read together in the verse 42:7. See explanation 2: 261, 3: 96 and 97.

109. For Allah belongs whatever is in Heaven and whatever is on Earth, while every matters will be returned to Allah.

Allah- the Lord, created Heavens, Earth and everything in between them; and He controls the universe. One day He will gather everyone and judge between them. Since Impartial Allah taught men the Soul of Qur'an as per the verses 55: 1-4 from the Paradise itself, it is their duty to make the Jinn soul mates believers. On the Day of Judgment the Soul of Qur'an will be the Balance as per the verses 39: 69,75. Therefore the believers will utilize the Soul of Qur'an mentioned in the verses 42: 17 and 57: 25 as weighing Balance in this world. Read together the verses 16: 64 and 39: 41. They should represent and help Impartial Allah by conveying His message to entire mankind in order to maintain the Universe in its equilibrium. See explanation 2: 38, 152; 3: 7 and 58.

110. You are the best community that has been raised for mankind. You command with righteousness and forbid evil and you believe in Allah alone. If the people of the Book would only believe, it would be better for them; some of them are believers, while most of them are transgressors.

'The best community' mentioned in this verse is heedful people not the heedless people, who hide and reject the Soul of Qur'an after receiving It. Today this verse in Qur'an is reading Muslims only. They are in false proud that they are the People of the Book -Qur'an and best people. Actually it is their duty to convey the Message of Allah-the Soul of Qur'an- to entire mankind. Therefore they obliged to live according to the Soul of Qur'an in order to witness the Prophet's life among the mankind as told in both verses 2: 143 and 22: 78, that: The Messenger might bear witness on you the life of Qur'an and you might bear witness on mankind. In the verses 16: 25-26 and 29: 12-13 it is told: If not doing so, they will have to bear the burden of those whom they have misled.

Instead of following the Soul of Qur'an and become the best people of the community, today the Muslims become the worst people among the community by hiding and rejecting the Soul of Qur'an. Thus they become the people mentioned in the verse 6: 26 as: They forbid the people from the Soul of Qur'an and forbid themselves. Certainly, by doing so, they are not destroying except themselves, but they do not perceive it. The verse 5: 49 says: And you Judge among them with what Allah has sent down and don't follow their whims and beware of them lest they tempt you away from a part of that which Allah has sent down to you. And if they should turn away, then you know that Allah intends to afflict them with some of their own offences. And indeed Most of the people are transgressors. See explanation 1: 7; 2: 99; 3: 90 and 91.

111. They will never harm you except by annoying. If they should fight you, they will turn their backs; afterwards they will not be helped from anywhere.

This verse says about the character of Jews at the Prophet's period, and hypocrites of all times. In the verse 16: 99 it is told that satan has no influence over those who believe and put their trust in their Lord- the Knower of All times. Allah teaches here that, the hypocrites who are the human satans can't make any serious harm; but they may just nuisance the believers. In the verses 59: 11 and 12 it is told that hypocrites of *Madeena* offered their help to Jews against the believers. And when war occurred they didn't keep their offer, they turn back and fled; and then afterward they will not be given help. Read together the verses 9: 67-68; 48: 5 and 6. See explanation 2: 102-103; 3: 79 and 80.

112. Disgrace will be branded on them wherever they are overtaken except they have a bond to Allah and bond other men. Allah's anger has showered over them; disgrace and misery has been branded on them. That is because surely they have disbelieved in Allah's

verses and killed the Prophets without any just to; that is because they disobey and act so aggressive.

Jews of olden years were allowed to live in this world only by the Mercy of Allah that they are His creatures, and the mercy of the people that they are also from among the mankind. There was no goodness in them. On the contrary they selected misery by themselves, and were cruel and hard hearted. They were the most worst of the creatures. See explanation 2: 61. But today only the hypocrites are showing the same characters of Jews of olden years. Among Muslims, the hypocrites become majority but the True believers are very rare. That is why today, Muslims are experiencing more sufferings than that of Jews world widely. They are getting the curse and spit of others and are being dishonored. That is because they are living without the remembrance of Allah by neglecting the Soul of Qur'an; and not merciful towards the mankind and other creatures; instead they have become more cruel and hard hearted even than Jews. Today wherever terrorist activities occurred, they are behind it. Really they are responsible for ruing the Universe among mankind. Read together the verses 30: 41and 35: 41.

These hypocrites are being disgraced by copying the ideas of Jews for 'communal' unity among the Muslims instead of trying for the 'unity of entire mankind' by conveying the Message of Allah to them. The hypocrites are not only participating in any activities to convey the Soul of Qur'an to whole mankind but also obstructing the way. They have become the one who welcome *Maseeh-A-Ddajjal* by concealing the Soul of Qur'an and thus by hiding Allah and Prophet. By the second coming of *Eisa*, *Maseeh-A-Ddajjal* will be killed and the group of believers with him will kill 70,000 Jews -the agitators in *Madeena*- and other people who approve *Islam* as the way of life will kill the hypocrites and those whose hearts containing malice specified in the verse 33: 60 and thus the command of the verses 4: 91; 9: 123 and 33: 61 will be implemented. See explanation 2: 85; 3: 21-22 and 85-91.

113. All the people of the Book are not alike; among them there is a small group who spend the night by reciting the verses of Allah in standing and prostrating before Him.

114. They believe with Allah and the Last Day, enjoin the Best and forbid the evil, and rush compete in doing good deeds. And such are among the righteous.

115. And any good they do, its reward will not be denied to them. And Allah is well Aware of such heedful.

The above three verses explains about the character of honorable righteous people who will succeed, they will live by holding the Soul of Qur'an with their molar teeth; especially during this period as taught by Prophet. Read together the verse 3: 199. By forming the belief as revealed by the Soul of Qur'an, teaching others the belief and leading a life with family members without associating any partners to Allah itself is sufficient for non-Muslims to enter to the Paradise. There is no need to change their name, dressing etc. And no need to join with Muslims- who hide and reject the Soul of Qur'an and receive Hell as penalty for their *swalath*, fasting, charity and *Hajj* without being believers. See explanation 2: 62 and 186. In the verses 5: 83-85 say: If the Qur'an which is revealed to the Messenger is recited to them (previous people of the Book), you can see their eyes over flowing with tears because they recognize the Truth; and they say: Our Lord! We believe, so enroll us among the witnesses why should we not believe in Allah and any Truth that has come to us? When we desire that our Lord will admit us along with the honorable men. Then Allah will reward them with Gardens with rivers flowing beneath; wherein they will live forever. Such is the reward for those who live seeing Allah. Today we can see such characters remains comparatively among Hindus, Christians and other non-Muslim people than among Muslims. Hearts of Muslims have become hard like rocks, even though they read and hear such Qur'an verses; the Soul of Qur'an only increases filth over filth for them, since they become hypocrites. Read together the verses 9: 95 and 125.

In the verse 57: 19 it is told that those who believe in Allah and His messenger are the truthful and the true witnesses, and they shall have their reward and their light with Allah. But the hypocrites who hide the verses of Qur'an and '*Fujjar*' who reject It are the inmates of Hades. In the verse 2: 2 it is told that those who follow Qur'an, which is the Guidance, are the heedful. In the verse 43: 67 it is told that all the relations will become in enmity except which are under the Shadow of Qur'an. Read together the verses 25: 29; 9: 71 and 72. The character of heedful are mentioned in the verse 24: 37 as: By such people who neither business nor trading distract from the remembrance of Allah or from establishing *swalath* or from paying welfare tax. They fear a Day when their hearts and eyesight will feel upset. See explanation 2: 148, 257; 3: 52 and 53.

116. Certainly, for those who hide the Truth, neither their wealth nor their children will benefit them from Allah. And such are the inmates of fire and will live there in forever.

'Those who hide the Truth' mentioned here are the hypocrites who hide the Soul of Qur'an. They have become suitable for getting the curse and anger of Allah, due to hiding the utmost Mercy of Allah- the Soul of Qur'an, after receiving It. See explanation 2: 159-161. Since Allah has killed them, neither their wealth nor their children will benefit for them in the Hereafter. And they will go to Hell soon after their death even without trial. Read together the verses 9: 53-55. In the verses 45: 7-10 Allah says: Woe to each lying sinner, to whom the verses of Allah are explained and then he goes far away as if he had not heard them. Then inform him the "happy news" of painful torment. And if he learns something of Our verses, he takes them as a target for his mockery. For such people there is a shameful torment. And after death, Hell is there for them, and nothing of what they have earned in this world will be of any benefit to them, nor those whom they have taken as their protectors and helpers besides Allah. For them is a painful punishment. The verse 11 continues as: This is the Guidance. And those who conceal the verses of their Lord, for them have a painful filthy punishment. In the verse 9: 125 it is told that for the hypocrites, Qur'an will add nothing but filth over filth. In the verse 6: 145 it is told that the food items which are offered for others than Allah and the flesh of swine are filth and will induce excite hypocrisy. In the verse 47: 1 it is told that, the deeds of those who hide the Path of Allah- the Soul of Qur'an, and prevent others from It have gone astray. Read together the verses 59: 9 and 18. Whoever hides and reject The Splendid Book - the soul of Qur'an in ones heart's language after receiving It will be punished severely mentioned in the verses 41: 41 and 42. See explanation 2: 174-176 and 3: 10-15.

117. The comparison of what they spend in this life is to a freezing wind. It strikes the crop of people who have wronged against their own souls; and thus destroyed it. Allah has not wronged to them, but rather they wrong themselves.

Freezing wind will destroy the farm land as same as hot wind destroys. Deeds will be accepted only when it is for the sake of Allah by remembering Him with the Soul of Qur'an. The Soul of Qur'an is necessary to remember Allah always. The deeds, without the Soul of Qur'an will cause a negative effect instead of getting reward. In the verses 18: 103 and 104 Allah commands Prophet to ask: Shall We tells you who are the losers relating to their deeds? Those, whose all efforts in this worldly life have gone astray but them reckoning that they are producing well. In the verse 105 it is told that, they are those who conceal the verses of their Lord and forget the fact that they will meet Him. Therefore all their deeds are in vain; and on the Day of Judgment they will never get any weight. The verse 30: 41 says: Mischief has appeared in the land and the sea in consequence of man's own misdeeds. Through such mischievous Allah let people taste the fruit of their deeds, so that they may turn back into the aim of life that induces the Soul of Qur'an. Read together the verses 4: 78-79. The aim of life is to create Paradise from this world itself by spending all the bounties in Allah's please which is bestowed by Him. Believers will aim for the reward of Hereafter by all their deeds of this life. In other words, they will realize and practice the teaching of Prophet that "*forth phase worldly life is the farm land for the Hereafter*". Those who live only for the sustenance of this world are disbelievers and wrongdoers. They will be the losers in the Hereafter. Read together the verse 42: 20. See explanation 2: 57, 200-202 and 266.

118. Oh you who believe! Do not take for your superior authority other than your own fellows. They will not miss any opportunity to exploit you. They only desire you be distressed. Rank hatred has already revealed from their mouths; while what they conceal in their chests is even greater. Surely, We have explained Our verses clear to you, if you are utilizing your intelligence.

The believers-, who belong to the party of Allah, are brothers and sisters to each other. They will not obey the disbelievers, wrongdoers and hypocrites who belong to the satan's party. And will not take any one as their friends and authority except the people from among believers. The verse 4: 59 says: Oh you who believe! Obey Allah; obey the Messenger and those charged with authority from among you. If you have a dispute in anything, refer it to Allah and His Messenger, if you truly believe in Allah and the Last Day. That will be better and finer in the future also. Disbelievers will always desire for the failure of believers. They will magnify the simple mistakes of the believers and will publish in the public. Also the consequences of their activities will cause so many blind believes among mankind and this will make the life a burden. Disbelievers will encourage spreading the satanic footsteps like interest, smuggling, black market, black money, hoarding etc. In brief the believers invite the people towards Allah and Paradise; but the disbelievers are inviting towards satan and Hell. The verse 63: 4 says about such disbelieving hypocrites as: Whenever you see them, their physical appearance may attract you, while if they speak you will listen to what they say. They are like the pieces of logs stacked up on the wall. They reckon that every sound is against them. They are the real enemies of Allah and believers; so beware of them. Allah has killed them, how they are deluded. In the verse 9: 95 it is told that these hypocrites are filth, so avoid them.

The verse 48: 6 says: And that He may punish the hypocritical men and the hypocritical women and the men and women who are associating others with Allah, who entertained an evil thought about Allah. A turn of evil shall befall them, for Allah's wrath is upon them. He has laid His curse on them and kept prepared the Hellfire for them, a very evil abode. Today these hypocrites and associates are coming only from the Muslims, they received the Soul of Qur'an and are leading a life just opposite to the do's and don'ts of It. Read together the verses 33: 1, 48, 73; 9: 67-68 and 98: 6. See explanation 2: 14-16, 166-169 and 3: 28.

119. Ah! You yourselves are, loving such people while they do not love you. And you believe in whole Book. Whenever they meet you they say: "We believe"; while when they go off by themselves, they bite their finger tips in anger over you. Say to them: "Die with your rage". Certainly Allah is the Knower what is on your chests.

Believers didn't show any hesitation in living mingled with Jews and hypocrites who were living with them. Believers are those who believe that only one Book- with one Soul and different bodies has sent down to Earth in various periods; and It was Guidance for entire mankind of relevant periods. They also believe that, both Qur'an- the last form of the Book and the Prophet appointed by Allah is for entire mankind. The verse 7: 158 says: You say: "Oh mankind! I am the Messenger of Allah towards all of you from Him to who belongs the kingdom of the Heaven and Earth. There is no Deity except Him. He brings to life and causes to die. Therefore, believe in Allah and His Messenger, the unlettered Prophet who believes in Allah and His Words- Soul of Qur'an. Follow It so that you may be rightly guided". The verse 25:1 says: Blessed is the One Who has revealed the criterion to distinguish right from wrong i.e. the Soul of

Qur'an- to His servant, that he may be a Warner to all worlds. The verse 34: 28 says: We have not sent you except to the entire mankind, to give them glad tidings and warn them, but most men do not know.

The hypocrites show belief in front of the believers, and when they are alone they bite their fingers with anger against the believers. Their thoughts were only how to defeat Prophet and believers. Today also we can see that the hypocrites who are the enemies of Allah have great anger against the believers who follow the Soul of Qur'an. In the verses 25: 26-29 Allah has warned about the condition of such wrongdoers in the Hereafter that they will wail by biting their hands: Oh! Woe to me would that I had chosen the path of Messenger. Oh! Woe to me, would I had never chosen so and so as my friend. Indeed he forbids me from the Soul of Qur'an after It has reached to me. Satan is ever a betrayer of man. Read together the verses 5: 41 and 42. See explanation 2: 76, 85; 3: 111 and 112.

120. Whenever something good happens to you, it annoys them; while if any evil happens to you, they delight in it. But if you are patient and be heedful, their plotting will not harm you in any way. Surely Allah encompasses all that they do.

In the verse 89: 14 it is told that Allah is ever watchful; and in the verse 4: 78 says: Both good and evil is from Allah. Then in the verse 79 says: The good things are from Allah and evils are from you. Evil will not happen to the believers who remember Allah always. That is the meaning of 'if you are patient and be heedful, none will harm you.' See explanation 2: 152. In the verses 11: 56; 96: 15 and 16 it is told that, Allah is holding the forelock of all living creatures, and so none can harm the believers who have put their trust on Allah. Allah- the knower of all times, already decided and recorded everyone's fate around his neck which will be produced as a spread open book on the Day of judgment as told both in the verses 17: 13-14 and 45: 28-31.

Believers are those who pray always like this: "Oh Lord, who control forelock of all beings, I seek refuge from the evil that occurs from beings, of which fore lock is with you." Prophet has taught to pray like this seven times after *swalath Faj'r* and *Magh'rib*: *Allah is enough for me. There is no Deity except Him. On Him I have put my trust. He is the Lord of Supreme throne.* The verse 9: 50 explain the character of hypocrites as: If you gain a benefit, it will grieve them; but if an evil happen to you, they will delight and turn away by saying: We have already taken our precautions beforehand. In the verse 51, Allah commands Prophet to say: Nothing will happen except what Allah has written already for us. He is our Lord and on Him the believers trust their things. In the verse 4: 72 it is told that there is some one among you who would escape in participating war by giving preference to this life. And if any calamity falls on believers, they will say: Allah does favor to us in that we are not present with them. And in the verse 73 says: And if you are blessed with a Bounty from Allah, they will say as if there had been no relationship between you and them. Oh! Woe to me, I wish if I had been with them, then could I have participate in that great victory. The verse 22: 11 also specify such behaviors of hypocrites. In the verse 7: 176 the similitude of such hypocrites are compared to a dog, that doesn't change its behavior whether it is disturbed or not. See explanation 2: 255 and 3: 7.

121. And remember that morning when you left your household at an early hour in order to station believers at their battle-position. Allah is All Hearing, All Knowing.

The following verses are explaining about the battle of *Uh'd* which occurred in the tenth month- *Shawwal* in the third year of *Hij'ra*. In the previous year-ninth month- *Ramadhan*, the battle *Bad'r* had undergone and most of the leaders of Mecca *Mushriks* had been killed and about seventy persons were caught as captives in that war. As a revenge for that in the third year of *Hij'ra,* under leadership of *Abu Sufyaan* about three thousand soldiers with all weapons forced towards *Madeena*. In order not to turn back the soldiers and to encourage them, their women folks were also brought with them. Even Prophet and the prime companions decided to block them at centre of *Madeena* itself, some youths who were unable to participate in the battle of *Bad'r* and were desires for martyrdom, forced the Prophet to go to mount *Uh'd* with about thousand soldiers.

122. Remember when two of your fractions became worried as to whether they should both fall back, Allah acted as a patron for both of them. Then on Allah should the believers put their trust.

On the way three hundred soldiers under the leadership of the hypocrite leader *Abdullah Ibnu Ubbay Ibnu Alsulool* were turn back to *Madeena*. By seeing these two tribes '*Banoo-Salama*' and '*Banoo-Haris*'; are the two fractions worried. The verses 3: 160; 5: 11; 9: 51; 58: 10 and 64: 13 also end as: Then on Allah should the believers put their trust.

123. Surely Allah helped you at Bad'r where you were in disgrace, therefore heed Allah; so that you might become grateful.

In the battle of *Bad'r* three hundred and thirteen weak soldiers without having experience in battle as well as proper weapons were fought with thousand powered as well as properly weapon *Meccan pagans*. But Allah gave victory to His party. 'Therefore heed Allah; so that you might become grateful' means, remember Allah always keeping Trust on Him. As per the verses 76: 3 and 90: 10, the entire mankind has given either the way of grateful or ungrateful. So one can belongs to the grateful by following the path of Allah and avoiding the path of satan. Both ways included in the Soul of Qur'an. See explanation 2: 152, 3: 102 and 103.

124. Remember when you said to the believers: "Will it never be enough for you if your Lord furnishes you with three thousand Angels who have been sent down?"

125. Of course! If you remain patient and be heedful, Allah will send to your aid not three thousand but, five thousand specially marked angels in case of a sudden attack from the enemy.

126. Allah has not made this except a glad news for you, and that your hearts may feel peace and tranquility by it; and help not comes except from Allah, the Powerful, the Wise.

127. For that to cut off a flank from those who disbelieve or restrain them, so that they may return back disappointed (Allah offered this help).

Prophet had told them that if the disbelievers were three thousand in number, Allah will sent down three thousand Angels in order contradict them. Then Allah said: If you show patience and be heedful, He will send five thousand marked Angels to help you. This is to make your hearts peace and tranquility. Without conducting this battle, Allah can give you the victory. Actually this battle of *Uh'd* been to distinguish between the hypocrites and the believers as told in the verses 3: 166-167. After the battle the *Meccan pagans* returned disappointed without any gain.

128. You have no authority in taking the decision. Allah may accept their repentance or may punish them. Surely, they are wrongdoers.

129. And Allah possesses whatever is in Heaven and whatever is on Earth. He forgives anyone He wishes and punishes anyone He wishes. And Allah is the Forgiving, the Merciful.

In the beginning of the battle *Uh'd*, Muslims part had success and the enemies turned back. Read together the verse 3: 152. While most of the archers who were appointed on the top of the hill came down to collect the spoils of war, the cavalry soldiers of enemies led by *Khalid Ibnu Valeed* killed the remaining archers and came down to the battle field through the gap of mountain side. And other infantry of enemies under the leadership of *Aboo Sufyan* also surrounded the Muslims on other sides. Prophet was wounded in his head, lost his tooth and was proclaimed that "*Muhammad* has been killed." See the verse 3: 144. Muslims scattered and ran away without paying any attention to others, without observing even the call of Prophet again to the battle field. See explanation 3: 153. At that critical time Prophet had prayed against the enemies: "How those people could will be guided, who try to destroy the Messenger appointed to them?" Then as a reply these verses were revealed. The verse 39: 19 asks: Against whom the sentence of the torment been carried out, are you saving someone who is in the Fire? See explanation 2: 119 and 272.

As told, Allah brought *Khalid Ibnu Valeed* to Islam on the 6th year of *Hijra* in connection with the '*Udaibiya* Treaty.' And on 8th year, *Abu Sufyan*, his wife *Hind* and her slave *Wah'shi*- who killed Prophet's father's brother, *Hamza* in the '*Uh'd*' battle field- also came to Islam. In brief, Islam is not anyone's own property, but that is the only way of life accepted by Allah to His entire creatures. No one can bring others to this way of life. It is not possible even for Prophet to bring anyone into Islam even father's brother *Aboothwalib* or own mother. And for Prophet *Ibrahim*, own father and for Prophet *Nooh*, own wife and son; and for Prophet *Looth*, own wife. Read together the verses 9: 113-114; 11: 45-46 and 66: 10. In other words each and everyone should pray to their Lord and should utilize the Guidance -Soul of Qur'an- by oneself. Read together the verses 10:100 and 14: 1. See explanation 2: 213, 284; 3: 19 and 97.

130. Oh you who believe! Do not eat and accumulate usury by doubling and multiplying it, and heed Allah so that you may prosper.

131. And beware of the Fire, which has been kept prepared for the disbelievers.

132. And obey Allah and His Messenger so you may find mercy.

Dealing with usury are the habits of Jews and the hypocrites -human satan. Believers should try to eradicate the system of interest. They will spend all their blessings that Allah has given to them in order to unload the life burdens of the creatures and will inspire others to do so. They will give goodly loan to Allah by understanding the aim of life from the Soul of Qur'an. The verses 64: 15-17 say: Your wealth and your children are but a trial. It is Allah with who is the greatest reward. Therefore, heed Allah as much as you can, listen to His Message attentively, be obedient, and spend for your own good. Those who are saved from the covetousness of their own souls such are the only prospers. If you lend to Allah a goodly loan, He will pay you back manifold, and will forgive you your sins. Allah is Appreciative and Forbearing to those who are grateful. Not be the one who receives interest and not be miser who are not ready to spend and thus the hypocrites who return to Hell by living aimless and heedless. There is no war today. Instead, there is only *'Jihad'* against the disbelievers who hide the Soul of Qur'an using It as a weapon, as told in the verse 25: 52. So, today spending wealth and all blessings for learning and teaching the Soul of Qur'an is the only way to earn the Paradise. Also that is the only way to eradicate the usury system and miserliness. See explanation 2: 275 and 276.

Today "Obey Allah and His messenger" means follow the Message of the Soul of Qur'an. Prophet taught: *Whoever does a deed, which is not as per my command, will be rejected.* In the verse 4: 37 it is told that, those who are miser and enjoy miserliness on others and conceal the blessings that Allah has given to them, for such disbelievers we have kept prepared a shameful punishment. The verses 6: 155; 7: 63, 204; 24: 56; 27: 46; 36: 45 and 49: 10 also end as: "So you may find mercy." See explanation 2: 5, 24, 254 and 3: 30- 32.

133. Hasten towards the forgiveness from your Lord and to the Paradise as vast as the Heavens and Earth, which has been kept prepared for the heedful.

Here, the Impartial Allah teaches that He has kept prepared the Paradise and Hell earlier itself. The heedful people earn Paradise and the disbelievers earn Hell by themselves. Through the verses 89: 23- 24 it is warned that the Day, on which the Hell is brought near the man, he will remember: "I wasted my lifetime uselessly, if I were the one who utilized the Soul of Qur'an in the worldly life". It is also told that the Paradise will be brought near to the heedful, which will no longer be far away as told in the verses 50: 31-35. If the Paradise is as vast as the Universe, the Hell is very congested and narrowed. In the verse 50: 30 Allah says: On that Day We will ask Hell: 'Are you filled?' then Hell will ask: (As if it cannot afford more) 'are there more?' In the verses 7: 18; 11: 119; 15: 43; 32: 13 and 38: 85 it is told that Allah will fill the Hell with *Jinns* and human beings altogether. In the explanation of the verse 4: 118 Prophet has taught that in every thousand nine hundred and ninety nine human and their soul mates are to Hell, and one is to Paradise. In the verse 57: 21 it is told that be forerunners for the forgiveness from your Lord, and to the Paradise, which is as vast as the Heavens and Earth, which is kept prepared for those who believe in Allah and His messenger. That is the Bounty of Allah, which He grants to whom He wishes. And Allah is of limitless Bounties. By saying: "Grants to whom He wishes" means that, it will give to the one who asks to Allah. See explanation 2: 186. In the verses 83: 22- 27 it is told that surely, the virtuous are in bliss. In Paradise they will look each other by sitting on soft coaches. You will recognize a blissful splendor on their faces. They will be offered a sealed portion to drink whose seal will be musk. Then those who compete with others should compete for this Bliss of Paradise. Read together the verse 47: 15.

134. Those are who spend their blessings throughout happiness and hardship, and suppress their anger and pardon towards mankind. And Allah loves those who are living by seeing Him.

135. And those who, when commit to do an evil or made wrong to their own souls, will remember Allah soon by heart and seek forgiveness for their offences. And who will forgive to their offences, except Allah? And they will not persist knowingly in whatever they have been doing.

The heedful and virtuous people are those who give priority for the necessity of others than self in food, money etc., even though they are in need for them. See explanation 3: 92. They are those who spend secretly- as if the things that their right hand giving is unknown to left hand- by thinking that Allah is seeing and expecting His own pleasure. See explanation 2: 262- 264 and 274. The meaning of: "They are those who suppress their anger and pardon towards mankind" is that they will show anger to others in Allah's anger, and they will please others in Allah's please, and will keep anger towards the evildoers and hypocrites whom Allah has cursed, and will forgive to the people who are doing offence unknowingly. In the explanation of the verse 9: 80 Prophet taught that even though Allah give forgiveness to the ignorant people for seventy times, He will never give forgiveness to the hypocrites even for a single time. In the verse 9: 6 it is commanded that if anyone from ignorant people whom have not heard the words of Allah seek asylum in the battle field, then protect him and escort him to his place of safety. In the verse 7: 176 Allah compared the hypocrites who do not teach the Soul of Qur'an to others and not follow It, and the common Muslims who do not try to study It; to a dog which does not change its attitude whether it is disturbed or not. And in the same verse Allah says: Explain this news to them so that they may meditate and reflect It to others. Both through the verses 9: 73 and 66: 9 Allah orders by calling the Prophet that: do *Jihad* - strive hard- against the disbelievers and hypocrites, and behave harshly with them; their return is to Hell. Read together the verses 48: 29 and 25: 52. In the verses 4: 17-18, it is told that, Allah's forgiveness is only for those who do evil in ignorance and repent as soon as they realize the offences. Where as there is no repentance for those who do evil deeds until death approach, and then repent by saying: "Now I repent" while their '*Rooh*' -Spirit- reaches the throat; and for those who die as hypocrites. Read together the verses 39: 55- 60.

Those people, who are forerunners in doing good deeds by their own interest for the satisfaction of Allah, are those who are living seeing Allah through the Soul of Qur'an. In the verse 16: 90 it is told that Allah commands 'Justice and *Ihsan*' - doing good deeds only by expecting the please of Allah without any motivation of others. In the verse 7: 199- 202 it is told that, you show forgiveness, enjoy with Justice and avoid the ignorant. And if a part from satan touches you, then seek refuge in Allah- All Hearer, All Knower. Surely, those who are heedful, whenever a part from satan touches them- whereupon they will remember Allah by heart and they will become the insightful. As for satan's brothers, they take them to Hell by making them forgetting the aim of life and by dragging to errors. Read together the verses 43: 36-38 and 50: 27.

Prophet taught that evil deeds like prostitution, homosexuals, theft, robbery etc. will not happen from a believer. One will involve in major sins only after he becomes a '*mushrik*'-associating others with Allah. In other words one becomes a *mushrik* in a state he forgets Allah and when he is heedless that Allah is seeing and knowing everything. This happens because he has not made up the faith in Allah with the Soul of Qur'an. He can become the companion of the right side who goes to Paradise only if he reads the Soul of Qur'an and realizes all his sins and repents to Allah by hearts, and mould the rest of his life in accordance with the Soul of Qur'an. See explanation 1: 2; 2: 99 and 3: 15-17.

136. Such will have the forgiveness from their Lord as their reward plus Paradise beneath which rivers flow. Therein they will live forever. What a blissful reward will be for workers doing good deeds!

This verse also teaches that one should earn the Paradise by working in this world utilizing the Soul of Qur'an. The verses 29: 58 and 39: 74 also end as: "What a blissful reward will be for workers doing good deeds!" In the verse 32: 19 it is told that as for those who believe and do honorable deeds, will have '*Firdous Garden*' -the Paradise where Allah's throne is situated as hospitality for what they have been doing. In the Hereafter the believers residing in the Paradise will call out: "Praise be to Allah Who has guided us to this felicity. Never could be having found Guidance, had it not been for the Guidance of Allah. Indeed It was the Truth that the messengers of Lord brought to us. What a blissful reward will be for workers doing good deeds." Then they will be called out: "There is the Paradise which you may inherit as reward for your deeds in the world." See the verses 7: 42 and 43. The verses 43: 68- 71 say: "Oh My devotees! Today you have nothing to fear or regret" will be told to those who believed with Our verses and submitted all to Me: "Enter Paradise, you and your spouses; you will be made happy". There they shall be served with golden dishes and goblets, and they shall have everything that their souls can desire and all that their eyes can delight in- and it will be said to them: "Now you shall abide therein forever. Then the verses 72 say: You will be inherited that Paradise being the reward for your deeds in the world. In the verses 46: 13-14 it is told: "Indeed, those who say our Lord is Allah, and remain firmly there is nothing to fear about them or nothing to regret for them. They shall dwell in Paradise forever as reward for their deeds which done in the world. The verses 56: 10-23 explain about the blessings in the Paradise for those people who are forerunners into Paradise. After that in the verse 24 it is told: It is a reward for their deeds in the world. The verses 18: 107-108 say: However, those who believe and do honorable deeds, they will be entertained with the '*Firdous Garden*' to live therein for ever and they will never desire to go anywhere else.

Today 'to do honorable deeds' means to convey the Message of the Soul of Qur'an to entire mankind in order to utilize It as the Balance to keep the Universe in its equilibrium. And It is the only Mighty weapon against the mischief activities such as terrorism, bloodshed, riot etc. doing by forgetting the aim of life. Read together "The goal of life" in the Introduction and the verses 9: 100 and 35: 32. See explanation 2: 25, 218; 3: 58 and 97.

137. Surely, there have passed so many ways and practices before you. Therefore, you travel around the Earth and observe what the consequences of those who reject the Truth was.

Allah deputes the Messengers only when a multitude is on a stage about to be destroyed. From among them the hypocrites -who know the Soul of Qur'an oppose the Messengers. The people who believe the Prophet and the Book shall mostly be poor and weak. Upper-class people and chiefs of the community always oppose the believers. At last Allah delivers the Messenger and believers, and wipes out all the disbelievers due to their own deeds. Gradually, the successors of these believers go astray, split in to different organizations and falsify the Messenger as well as The Book. Then Allah appoints a new Messenger. The disbelievers who falsely proud that they are the true followers of former Messenger will be the forerunners to oppose the new Messenger.

Those believers who escaped in the ark of Prophet *Nooh* gradually deviated and became idol worshippers. And at the time, all of them became transgressors and be destroyed, Allah sent prophet *Ibrahim*. He called the people to the One and only Deity, and because of that the people including his father decided to kill him by burning in the fire. Read together the verse 21: 69. Prophet *Ibrahim* escaped from there. He settled his wife *Hajara* and son *Isma'el* in *Mecca*-depopulated and desert area. *Ibrahim* and *Isma'el* together reconstructed the *Ka'ba* for worshiping the only Deity -Allah. Gradually the children of *Isma'el* went astray and installed about 360 idols in *Ka'ba*, which included the idols of their forefathers, *Ibrahim* and *Isma'el*. These people who falsely proud that they were following the life way of Prophet *Ibrahim* and *Isma'el*, opposed Prophet Mohamed when he called them to the One Deity.

The *Zabur*, *Thourath* and Injeel have come to the lineage of Prophet *Is'haq* that is to the children of *Israel* who are the successors of Prophet *Ya'qoob*. The two Prophets, *Moosa* and *Eisa* who are among the '*Ulul-azm*' – who were stead fast in belief-, are also from the children of *Israel*. But the Jews tried to kill prophet *Eisa*, and the Christians went astray by introducing *Eisa* as the son of God. At *Mecca*, Prophet *Muhammad* gave the instructions of Allah to the people for 13 years. But when the *Meccan 'Mushriks'* planned to kill the Prophet, he migrated to *Madeena*. Jews and Christians of *Madeena* -the people of Book- were well aware about prophet from their Book. But they opposed the Prophet knowingly and encouraged the *Meccan 'mushriks'* to conduct war against Prophet.

Today, the Muslims are far away from the Soul of Qur'an and all the evil deeds of previous generations have been assembled in them. Since there is no Messenger to come, the decline of Muslim community will lead to the end of this world and to the Day of Judgment. When the *Islam* is going to diminish, Allah will bring *Eisa* second time to this world to make clear the Islam for all over the world. On that day, the Christians and Hindus will recognize and approve *Islam*. The hypocrites and '*fujjar*' from among the Muslims will accept '*Maseeh-A-Ddajjal*' -who comes before Eisa as the thirtieth pseudo Prophet and even Lord and thus they will become deserving to be killed as specified in the verses 33: 60-61; 48: 24 and 25.

The 'consequence' mentioned in the verse means results caused by their deeds, which were against the rules and commands of Allah. In the verse 91: 15 it is told that, they were not afraid about the consequence of it (consequence of falsifying prophet *swalih* by slaughtering the camel which had a sign from Allah). Today the Soul of Qur'an is the miraculous sign of Allah - the ways and practices of Allah. That is the character of the Prophet. But today's Muslims ignore the Splendid Book of the Lord and follow the books written by creatures. Ignoring Qur'an, the best speech they say about believers who follow the Soul of Qur'an that they are without '*Hadeeth*' and '*Sunnath*'. If a people do injustice to their Messenger, or reject Allah's Message they cannot continue in that place for a long time without Allah's punishment to destroy them, or any other people conquer them, or else the followers of Messenger survive them. It is the practice of Allah that if a people are not prepared to implement and sustain the Book, Allah will bring another people in their place who are ready for it. Read together the verses 4: 133; 6: 89 and 47: 38. The bearers of the Soul of Qur'an - the Balance and Trust to keep the Universe in its equilibrium-are not using It instead by hiding It from other people are forerunners to destroy the world. Therefore, each of them will have to bear the burden of destroying the world according to the proportion of their obstruction against the conveyance of the Soul of Qur'an by the believers. Read together the verses 9: 32-33 and 61: 8-9. The verses such as 6: 11; 12: 109; 16: 36; 27: 69; 30: 9; 35: 44; 40: 21, 82 and 47: 10 have the Message that 'have you or have they not traveled around the land and seen what was the consequence of rejecters, mad people, wrongdoers, mischief makers and transgressors. See the explanation 2: 159-161, 253; 3: 90 and 91.

138. This is an Explanation for mankind; as well as Guidance and a 'Mouidhath' -Good advice- for the heedful.

For the explanation, '*Bayan*' and '*Mouidhath*' see the Introduction. As per the verse 2: 185, Qur'an is the Guidance for entire mankind. But only the heedful who follow It will utilize it as the Guidance. The word '*Haqq*' told in the verse 25: 33 is mentioning about the '*Muhkamath*' as well as the '*Hikmath*' mentioned in the verse 16: 125. Whereas 'the best explanation' referred in the verse 25: 33 is '*Mouidhathul Hasanath*' of the verse 16: 125.

Mouidathul Hasanath-similar commands and examples- of some verses are given below:

1. Hikmath -direct meaning- of the verse 2: 113 is like this: "The Jews say the Christian have not to stand up on while the Christians say the Jews have not to stand up on, yet they quote and argue from the same Book" *Mouidhath* of this verse is like this; each organization of Muslims say about other organization that they are useless, while all of them are reciting the same Book- Qur'an. This is well suitable for the organization of Muslims like *Jamaath* and *Mujaid* who know the contents of the Qur'an. They themselves are the firewood for Hell as warned by Prophet through the explanation of the verse 3: 10. Through the verse 30: 31- 32, by calling the believers, Allah says: You should not become *Mushrik*- associate others with Allah- by dividing into different organizations and each organization are rejoicing with what they have. See explanation 2: 176 and 3: 101-103.

2. In the verse 9: 31 it is told that Jews and Christians selected their priests and anchorites and *Eisa*- the son of *Maryam*- as the lords besides Allah. But there is no Deity except the One Deity only. He is of limitless Glory and is above all that they associate. They were not commanded to serve, except for Him. *Mouidhath* of this verse is like this; today, Muslims who recite all these

verses are blindly following their anchorites and group leaders. Through the verse 9: 34 Allah has told by calling the believers: Surely, most of the priests and anchorites will eat the wealth of people falsely and will prevent them from the Path of Allah -Soul of Qur'an. Being deaf towards this verse, Muslims are following their religious and political leaders blindly than that of Jews and Christians today. See explanation 2: 166 and 167.

3. In the verse 5: 32 it is told: We decreed for the children of Israel that if any one kills a person except as a punishment for murder or mischief in the land, it is as if he had killed entire mankind; whereas if any one saves a life, it shall be as if he had saved the life of entire mankind. Surely, Our Messengers came to them with Evidence, even after that many of them committed mischief on Earth. As the *Mouidhath* of this verse Prophet taught that *Qabeel* -the son of Adam, who killed his brother *Habeel* will get the part of the punishment of each murder occurring in this world. But today the Muslims who carry this Qur'an just like a donkey carrying burden are dominant in all evil deeds like murder, robbery, smuggling, dealing with narcotics, defraud, diminishing the measurement, partiality, selfishness, communalism, rationalism, nationalism etc. throughout the world than others. In the verse 62: 5 Allah compares the Jews with donkeys that carry Book on its back. Since Qur'an is the only Book today, Muslims are most suitable for this comparison instead of Jews. Moreover the verse ends by saying: 'Allah does not guide such evil doing people, who reject the verses of Allah.' In the verse 7: 176 Allah has compared such people to a dog, which does not change its behavior whether it is disturbed or not. The verses 2: 85 and 5: 33 explain about the punishment for such people. This is the same people against whom Prophet will witness before of Allah in the Hereafter by bringing the Qur'an. See the verses 25: 27-30. According to this verse hypocrites who hide the Soul of Qur'an knowingly without following It; and the *fujjar* who are the heedless and are like animals, or even worse than them without using the faculties such as sight, hearing and heart to understand the Soul of Qur'an are the losers.

4. In the verse 5: 90 it is told that Oh, believers! Liquor, gambling, idols and division by arrows (lottery) are the filthy works of sathan. Get away from him, so that you may succeed. *Mouidhath* of this verse is like this; even though Qur'an has referred about liquor It has not said anything about ganja (marijuana) and other intoxicants (brown sugar, Hashish etc.) which are more fatal than it. All these become unlawful according to *Mouidhath* of this verse. Usury- which

exploits the people, card game, lottery, smuggling, black money, hawala etc. will come under the gambling. Offering towards saint people like *Mohiyadheen Sheikh*, *Bad'r* and other martyrs will come under paying tribute to idols. Offering cereals and vegetables to them are also come under it. The food items, which are offered to other than Allah included with the flesh of swine are filth and will induce hypocrisy as told in the verse 6: 145. See explanation 2: 173.

5. The verse 7: 40 says: Surely, the gates of Heaven will not be opened for those who reject Our verses and for those who treat them with arrogance (as if he has studied all), they will not be entered into the Heaven until the camel goes through the eye of a tailor's needle. That is how We shall reward for the *Mujrims*. *Mouidhath* of this verse is: Surely, the gates of Heaven will be kept opened for those who recite and convey Our verses and make It Truth. They will be entered into Paradise even without questioning. That is how We reward for those who live seeing Allah. See explanation 2: 112.

6. In the verse 34: 19 it is said: Allah made small towns between the natives of *Saba'* and the blessed city Palestine, so that they could travel between them safely both night and day. But they prayed: "Our Lord, lengthen the distance between our stops!" and they wronged themselves, so We turned them into legends; We scattered them into fragments and made them a part of history." Here, the meaning of "they prayed for lengthening the distance between their journeys" is that they started robbery and grabbing through out their journey became unsafe in the night, and thus the distance between the stops during their journey become longer. *Mouidhath* of this verse is like this; the Soul of Qur'an is the only instrument to stop the bloodshed and to keep Universe in its equilibrium by making the harmony of human unity. The Muslims are carrying the Qur'an without trying to understand Its contents. They neither utilize It, nor give It to others. By this activity they are like praying: Oh, our Lord! You bring soon the Day on which the sky asunder, the sun and moon meet together, oceans burn and the Earth submits its record. See explanation 3: 30.

7. The verse 7: 146 says: I will turn away from My verses those who are arrogant in the land without the Truth. Even if they see any verse they will not believe in It. If they see the Straight path in front of them, they will not follow It; but if they see a crooked path, they will follow it. That is because they reject Our verses and are heedless with them. *Mouidhath* of this verse is like this; Allah will turn away from the Truth-Soul of Qur'an- every swaggering boaster who

pretends as scholars without knowing the Real Knowledge. This is the very same conditions of the hypocritical leaders of the Muslim community today. Actually, they have not studied the Splendid Book- *Adhikr*- mentioned in the verses 41: 41-42. Instead of that, they studied all other books, which are written by the creatures. Qur'an and Prophet has taught us to be proud and self sufficient without depending others as taught by the Soul of Qur'an. See explanation 3: 79. In the explanation of the verse 2: 185 Prophet taught that those who seek the Guidance other than from the Soul of Qur'an will be turned away from It. Prophet also taught that Qur'an will lead those people who consider It as *Imam*-Leader- to the Light of Heaven and Earth, whereas It will push those who keep It behind, to the Hell- the camp of satan. And the verse 147 announces that all their deeds are futile and they are losers in the Hereafter. See explanation 2: 110, 186 and 3: 10

139. And you do not falter nor feel saddened, since you are superior if you are believers.

140. If some wound should afflict you, the other people also have been afflicted similar wound. We alternate these days of varying success and failure among mankind, so that Allah may know the true believers and take witnesses (grant martyrdom) from among you, and Allah does not love the wrongdoers.

141. And for Allah may purge those who believe and wipeout the disbelievers.

It seems as the Muslims received a defeat in the battle of *Uh'd*. The verses 166-167 say that battle of *Uh'd* been made happened by Allah's permission to distinguish the believers and hypocrites from among the Muslims. The thought of hypocrites was that if the Prophet and companions are the party of Allah and are standing for the Truth, how they were defeated? Through this verse Allah gives answer for that. Today, if you have received a wound and loss, the enemies also have received the same in *Bad'r*. Allah has fixed that days of battle to distinguish those who are in truth and who are in untruth; and also a chance for believers to become martyrs by seeing Allah and submitting whole to Him. Those who were killed in a way other than the way of Allah are wrongdoers, and Allah's anger has showered over them.

The disbelievers mentioned in the verse 141 are about the hypocrites from among the Muslims. In the verse 8: 19, which were revealed after the battle of

Bad'r, Allah asks to disbelieving *Meccan mushriks*: "If you demanded for a decision, now you have realized who are in truth and the victorious. And if you turn back, it is better for you. But if you repeat, We also shall react. Your force, however large in number they may be, will never benefit for you. Surely, Allah is with the believers". But because of the presence of hypocrites, Allah gave a victory to the *Meccan Mushriks* visually in the battle of *Uh'd.* The residents of Mecca have not received any verse after the battle of *Badr*. But the hypocrites from among the Muslims of *Madeena* who received the Qur'an verses continuously even after the battle explaining the behavior of disbelievers. Thus they became suitable for the punishment of Allah. This gives a lesson that Allah – the Supreme Judge- will punish only those who hide and reject Qur'an after receiving It. In the verse 4: 123 it is told that not the desire and guess of believers, nor those of the people of the Book (will prevail). Whoever does evil will be rewarded for it, he will not find any protecting friend or helper besides Allah. The verse 124 continues, if anyone does good works, whether male or female and he is a believer, will enter Paradise, then not the least injustice will be done to them. See explanation 2: 39, 111 and 3: 90-92.

142. Or did you reckon that you could enter Paradise easily while Allah still does not recognize those among you who strive nor does He know the patient ones?

See explanation 2: 214. This verse addresses the Muslim community. Allah- the knower of unseen is well Aware about the hypocrites and rejecters He does not need to make such battles in order to distinguish them. But by all these, Allah gives a chance for hypocrites to exhibit the hypocrisy hidden in their hearts and thus helps the believers to identify them. To distinguish between the party of Allah and satan and live with the party of Allah in order to return to the Paradise is the ultimate aim of this life. For that one should consider the Soul of Qur'an as the Ticket (76: 29), Criterion (2: 185) and Insight. (6: 104). See explanation 2: 155-157 and 3: 58.

143. And surely, you used to wish for death even before you met with it. Now you have seen it, and are looking it with your own eyes.

Some youngsters of Muslims, who were unable to participate in the battle of *Bad'r* in the last year, were in great enthusiasm to participate in the battle of

Uh'd and to become martyrs. But in the battle of *Uh'd* they scattered, turned back and ran because of the sudden attack of enemies.

"And are looking it with your own eyes" means that after the battle of *Uh'd,* Muslims will have to face so many other battles. But today there is no war since there is no group of believers. Instead only strive strenuous with the Soul of Qur'an to the disbelievers who hide It, is commanded through the verses 9:73 and 25: 52. Disbelievers will not digest the Soul of Qur'an when It is explained as Allah indented. The verse 68: 51 says, the one who disbelieves almost trip you up by glaring at you whenever they hear the Soul of Qur'an, and they say: Indeed he is possessed. Read together the verses 41: 26-29, 51:52-55. See explanation 2: 94-95and 216.

144. And Muhammad is no one except a Messenger. Surely, many Messengers have passed away before him. Then if he should die or be killed, will you turn back on your heels? Anyone who turns on his heels will never injure Allah in any way, and Allah will reward the grateful.

While the battle of *Uh'd* been going on, prophet was severely wounded on his head and lost a tooth. At that time satan proclaimed: "Muhammad has been killed". *Ibnu Qamee'a*, one among the enemy informed the *mushrik* leaders that he has killed Muhammad. By hearing this, Muslims who were weak in their faith were puzzled, scattered, turned back and ran away.

Eight years later when the prophet had a natural death, *Umar Khathab* denied the death of prophet and told holding the sword in his hand that "I will kill with this sword those who say prophet has died." At that time *Aboobacker Sidheeque* told: "Whoever has worshiped for Muhammad that Muhammad has died. But whoever worships for Allah, that Allah is Ever living and Eternal." Then he recited this verse also. Allah says in the verses 21: 34-35, we have not granted immortality to any human before you; then if you should die, would they live here permanently? Every soul should have the taste of death. We will test you with evil and good. And certainly all of you will return to Us. In the verses 39: 30- 31 Allah says: "Surely, you will die, and they also will die, then on the Day of Judgment, you will dispute in the presence of your Lord". The entire mankind is categorized in to two, the grateful and ungrateful as per the verse 76: 3. Those who serve only for Allah are the grateful. All others serving for satan are ungrateful. As per the verse 38: 82 satan has promised that: He will make all of the mankind aimless of life except the sincere innocent i.e. one in every thousand as taught by prophet the explanation of the verse 4: 118. See explanation 2: 152 and 252.

Oh Allah! Include us among those who are grateful to you and remember you with the Soul of Qur'an. Don't include us among the ungrateful disbelievers and losers who hide and reject the Soul of Qur'an.

145. And no soul shall die except with Allah's Permission. The time of death of every life is fixed by writing. And if anyone desires the rewards of this world, We shall give it to him. And if anyone desires the rewards of the Hereafter, We shall give it to him, and We will reward the grateful.

In the verse 4: 78 it is told: "Wherever you may be, death will catch you- even if you are in strong towers and castles. When they are blessed with some benefits they say, 'this is from Allah', whereas when an evil befalls them, they say, 'this is from you.' Oh Prophet! Tell them: 'Everything is from Allah', what happened to these people? They could not understand these speeches". In the verse 79 says: Whatever benefit comes to you is from Allah and whatever evil happens to you is from yourself, We have sent you as a Messenger to entire mankind. For that Allah is enough as a witness. Allah's Permission is the Soul of Qur'an. So, for those who are utilizing the Soul of Qur'an as the Shield and Safeguard they can decide their death. See explanation 3: 97 and 102. In the verse 10: 100 it is told that no soul can believe except by Allah's Permission, this Qur'an is made filth to those who will not utilize their intelligence. Whoever desires for the benefits of this world i.e. the wealth of booty and fame shall be given to him. And whoever desires the Hereafter and the martyrdom shall be given to him. The worldly life is a farmland towards the Hereafter for the believers who have realized the ultimate aim of life. So their all activities will be in the remembrance of Allah with the Soul of Qur'an, and they will desire only the reward from Allah. They are the grateful and will live as vicegerents of Allah. See explanation 2: 201-202 and 3: 136.

146. And how many from Prophets have fought along with many proud representative men of the Lord, they never faltered despite what had afflicted them in the Path of Allah; they neither showed

weakness nor surrendered to the falsehood, and Allah loves such men of patience.

See the explanation 2: 214 and 3: 79.

147. And their words were nothing except to pray: "Our Lord! Forgive us our offences and our excesses in our deeds and brace our footsteps and help us against the disbelieving people"!

148. Then Allah gave them reward in this world and also an excellent reward of the Hereafter. And Allah loves such ones who live by seeing Allah.

See explanation 2: 195, 250, 286 and 3: 133.

149. Oh you who believe! If you should obey those who disbelieve, they will turn you around on your heels and cause you return as losers.

150. Nay, Allah is your protector; and He is the best of all helpers.

Believers obey only Allah. And they obey all other creatures only under the Permission of Allah i.e. under the Light of Soul of Qur'an. Prophet taught, "There is no obeying to any of the creatures by disobeying the Creator" The verse 5: 30 ends with a message that then you will become one among the losers. See explanation 2: 6-7,121and 3: 122.

151. We will cast panic in to the hearts of those who disbelieve, because they have associated others with Allah, for which He has sent them no authority. Their refuge will be the Fire, what an evil lodging to such wrongdoers.

Even though disbelievers mentioned here is about the *Meccan Mushriks*, the disbelievers mentioned in the verse 8: 12 includes the hypocrites also. In the verse 59: 13 it is told that hypocrites are afraid of believers more than that of Allah. Read together the verses 59: 16 and 17. By saying 'associate others with Allah for which He has sent them no authority', does not mean that there is some proof (authority) for some other partners. In contrary, Allah has sent down all the verses of Qur'an in order to teach that there is no Deity except Allah. In the verse 14: 22 Allah has warned about the scene in the Hereafter that when the judgment is over, satan will say: I had no authority upon you. But just I called, and then you replied to me. So do not blame me, but blame yourselves. I reject what you did before, that you associated me with Allah. Certainly, wrongdoers have a painful punishment. Read together the verses 16: 2, 36 and 21: 25. See explanation 2: 254; 3: 77 and 85.

152. And surely, Allah fulfilled His promise to you when you grappled them with His Permission; until the moment you flinched, and fell to disputing about the command; you disobeyed the Prophet after He had shown you the thing, which you loved (booty of war). Among you who intended gain of this world and while others of you intended the Hereafter. After that He allowed you to be defeated in order to test you, and then pardoned to you, for Allah is gracious upon the believers.

In the beginning of the battle *Uh'd*, Muslims were victorious. When the enemies turned back, a fraction of the Muslims concentrated only in collecting the Booty-wealth of the war. Well skilled archers were posted by prophet on the top of the hill under the leadership of *Abdullah-ibn jubair*; and prophet had told them: "you should not come down even if you are seeing the birds swoop our heads." But except five of them thought that they will not get the Booty and so came down to collect it desiring the benefit of this world. By this occasion enemies killed the remaining archers and surrounded the battlefield. At that time Muslims scattered, turned back and ran away; and they disputed each other. A rumor such as "the Prophet has been killed" was spread. Thus they became weak and were allowed to be defeated in order to test them, as like their wings are broken (helpless). All these were happened to distinguish the hypocrites and believers from among Muslims.

153. When you fled without even looking back at anyone, the Messenger was calling you again from your rear, then, He gives you one distress after another. So you would not feel so sad because of what had eluded your grasp nor for what had afflicted you. And Allah is well acquainted with what you are doing.

Muslims retreated and ran by leaving the booty of war-which they desired a lot, and their weapons, companions and even their leader. Thus they affected sorrow after sorrow. This verse addresses the hypocrites who do not agree the fact that the control of all creatures is with Allah. Believers are always conscious that Allah is the One Who controls everything and they will live in the please of

Allah which is the Soul of Qur'an. Sorrows and losses will not befall on them. See explanation 2: 157. All the activities happening in the world -battles, victory, defeat etc. are pre-fixed by Allah and that is the meaning of saying 'Allah is well acquainted.' See explanation 2: 234 and 3: 145.

154. Then after this distress, He sent down a peaceful sleep on you, which overcame a faction of yours, while another faction, fretted themselves thinking something besides the Truth about Allah, guesswork from the ignorance. And they were asking: Did we have any power for taking any decisions in this matter? You say, surely, all power of decision and its implementation belongs to Allah. They do not reveal to you what they hide within their souls; they say: "If we had any power to do with the matter, we should not have been killed here so." Say, even though you were in your own homes, those for whom of death has been prescribed would have sown up on their death beds, on time. Allah made all this to reveal what is inside your chests and purge what is in your hearts and Allah is the well Knower of the state of the chests.

Thereupon in the night Uh'd battle, Allah granted a peaceful sleep to the believers and therefore they were in a non remembering situation about the pain of wounds and defeat. But the hypocrites were thinking that 'if we are Muslims why we get injury and defeat." Thus they were unsleeping, suffering sorrow and pain in its wholeness. As per the verse 8: 11 it can be seen that at the time of battle of *Bad'r* also a peaceful sleep overcame the believers, but it was on the previous night of battle. The hypocrites were in a false belief about Allah while thinking that all these are happening because of prophet; and they concealed enmity in their mind towards Prophet. They also told themselves: "If we had been in any power for taking decisions, we have been not killed like this." Allah says as a reply for that: Time and place of death of each and everyone is pre-fixed. When the time comes, everyone will drive towards his or her place of death. Read together the verse 9: 51 10: 61 and 63: 11.

The verse 31: 34 ends as: No one knows in when or where he will die. Surely, Allah is all knowing and all surrounding. All these made happened in the battle of *Uh'd* been to reveal what is inside the chest of hypocrites: And to make believers firm in their belief by washing out the doubts in their hearts. Both in this verse and the verse 48: 29, all the 28 letters of Arabic alphabet is included. See explanation, 3: 118-120.

155. Surely, those of you who turned away on the day when both troops met were only tripped up by satan because of something they had earned. Allah has pardoned them also. Indeed Allah is Forgiving, Forbearing.

This verse is discussing about the three hundred hypocrites specified in the verse 122, who didn't participate in the battle and turned back on the way to *Uh'd* under the leadership of *Abdullhibnu Ubayyubnu Sulool*; and also to the hypocrites who turned back and ran away during the battle. See explanation 3: 128.

156. Oh you who believe, do not be like those who disbelieve and tell their brothers while they are traveling on the Earth or while engaged in fighting as: If they had been with us, they would not have died nor been killed, so that Allah makes such things a cause of regret in their hearts. And Allah gives life and brings death; and Allah is the observant of anything you do.

On the death of relatives and friends during their travel on Earth or been killed during the war, the disbelieving hypocrites will mourn: "If they considered our advices and they had been with us, it would not have happened to them." In fact, they do not believe that life and death are occurring by Allah's will. This is the very same attitude of today's hypocrites also. If any danger or distress happens, they will seek for its reason. Also they will tell: "If they had done like that, it will not have happened like this. I had already warned they but they did not hear it, and that is why all these happened." They are those who do not consider Allah as Impartial and denying the verses such as 9: 51; 11: 5; 22: 70; 34: 3; 57: 22; 76: 3; 90: 10 ;91: 7-10 etc. Since they have earned Hell, they fear death; and consider the death as a loss. Read together the verses 9: 123-127. But the believers are those who do not fear death, and they believe that the real life starts after death. Also they consider this world as a farmland to the Hereafter. Read together the verses 8: 49; 9: 111; 48: 19 and 61: 10-13. See explanation 2: 96, 154; 3: 136, 144 and 145.

157. And if you should be killed for Allah's sake or die, the forgiveness and mercy from Allah are better than all that they are gathering.

158. Whether you should die or be killed, you will still be summoned before Allah.

Earning the Paradise by utilizing all the blessings bestowed by Allah is the aim of this life. Through Qur'an Allah has promised Paradise to the believers, if they spend their soul and their wealth in the way of Truth as per the verse 9: 111. If anyone is getting killed in the way of Allah, then he is entering into the Paradise directly. In the verses 36: 18-27 it can be seen that when a people stoned and tortured the Prophets appointed to their town, a believer named *Habeeb-Annajjar* came running from the hill far from the town and advised his people: "I have believed in your Lord, so listen to me." That people killed him. It was said to him: "Enter the Paradise." See explanation 2: 105.

159. Then it is from the Mercy of Allah that you are dealing gently with them. If you had been rough and cruel-hearted, they would have dispersed from around you. Then pardon them and seek forgiveness for them, and consult with them on the matters. Yet once you have reached a decision, then entrust on Allah; surely, Allah loves those who entrust upon Him.

Prophet behaved with the hypocrites after the battle of *Uh'd* in an excusing easy manner. It was due to the command of Allah since it was the first occasion. According to both verses 152 and 155 it is informed that Allah has pardoned to them. The victorious believers character has told in the verses 42: 36-40 as: Anything you are given is for enjoyment during worldly life; while what Allah possesses is better and more enduring for those who believe, and entrust on their Lord, avoid major sins and shameful deeds, forgive even when they are angry; and who respond to their Lord, establish *swalath*, conduct their affairs with mutual consultation, spend out of the sustenance which We have given them, and when they are oppressed, help and defend themselves. The recompense for an injury is an injury proportionate to it; but if a person forgives and makes reconciliation he shall be rewarded by Allah; He does not like the wrongdoers. In the verse 16: 127 it is told that your patience is only by the blessings of Allah. Do not grieve over the disbelievers and do not be distress yourself because of their plots. Verse 128 continues: Surely, Allah is with those who keep Him in their hearts and who live by seeing Him.

But the attitude of Allah and Messenger towards the hypocrites was not the same as above on all occasions. Prophet has implemented the command of both verses 9: 73 and 66: 9 that Oh Prophet! Do '*jihad*' -Strive against the disbelievers and the hypocrites more and more. Hate them and behave in rough manner with them. In the verse 48: 29 it is told that Muhammad, the Messenger of Allah, and those with him are strong against the disbelievers and compassionate to each other among themselves.

The command of Allah through both the verses 33:1 and 48 that Oh Prophet! Keep Allah in heart and do not obey the disbelievers and the hypocrites who reject the Truth had implemented by the Prophet. Through three verses 4: 91, 9: 123 and 33: 61 Allah has commanded to the party of believers to kill the hypocrites. This command, which has not been implemented up to this, will be practiced only after the second coming of *Eisa*. But the hypocrites today without considering the verses 9: 23-24, 71-72 and 58: 22, point out this verse (3:159) alone and make publicity that 'the anger is from satan.' They are not at all considering the teaching of Prophet that no one will become a believer till he shows anger towards others in Allah's wish. Verses 9: 67- 68 has told clearly about them. See explanation 2: 99 and 3: 27-28. They are those who denounce Prophet *Moosa* since he threw *Thourath* with anger as per the verses 7: 150, 20: 90- 97. They also quote the verse 20: 94 to affirm '*shirk*-' associating others in the dominion of Allah, is permissible to maintain the party spirit. They popularize that *Haroon* is the best to be followed than Prophet *Moosa* in this matter, and thus they distort the way of Allah. In the verse 4: 140 it is told that Allah will gather such hypocrites, and the disbelievers in the Hell. Allah never forgives to those people who knowingly hide and reject the Soul of Qur'an. They are not considering the warnings the verses such as 2: 159-161; 3: 90-91; 33: 72-73; 48: 6 and 63: 4 that the anger and curse of Allah be on them and Allah has killed them. It is commanded to the believer to tell such disbelievers through the verse 39: 8 "enjoy your disbelief for little while; you will be an inmate of the Fire" if they are in single and through the verse 14: 30 "enjoy yourselves even though surely your return will be to the Fire" if they are in group. Read together the verses 10: 15-16; 17: 73-75 and 18: 28-29. See the explanation 2: 6-7 and 3: 78.

160. If Allah helps you, there is no one who will overcome you; while if He should forsake you, then who is there to help you later on? Then upon Allah entrust believers.

The verses 8: 63-66 say: Allah has united believers' hearts: even though you spend everything on Earth, you could never unite their hearts; but Allah has united between them He is Powerful, Wise. Oh prophet, let Allah and the believers who follow you is enough to you. Oh prophet, urge believers on to fight! If there are twenty disciplined men among you, they will overcome two hundred, while if there are a hundred of you, they will defeat a thousand of those who disbelieve, since those are the people who do not understand the aim of life. Now Allah has lightened things for you; He knows how much weakness exists among you, if there are a hundred patient men among you, they will overcome two hundred, while if there are a thousand of you, and they will overcome two thousand with Allah's Permission. Allah stands with the disciplined. The verse 8: 74 says: and those who believe and emigrate and do '*Jihad*' for Allah's sake as well as those who grant them asylum and support, such are the True believers; they will have forgiveness and generous provision. Today '*Jihad*' is with the Soul of Qur'an only against the hypocrites who hide and disbelievers who reject It. To support Allah means to convey the messages of Allah for entire mankind in order to keep the Universe in its equilibrium. See explanation 3: 122, 139-140 and 152.

161. And no Prophet should hold back anything; and anyone who defrauds someone else will bring along whatever he has been withholding on the Day of Judgment. Then every soul will be repaid for whatever it has earned. And they shall not be dealt with wrongfully.

Hypocrites accused that Prophet cheated and made participate them in the battle by saying Allah has promised help by sending down Angels and that is why they got killed horrible like this. This verse is an answer to their accusation. This verse also teaches that Paradise or Hell is earning by oneself. Those who withhold anything as cheating and theft in this world will be presented in front of Allah with the cheated or stolen property on the Day of Judgment. Their skins, sight and hearing will be a witness against such disbelievers. See explanation 2: 286, and 3: 30.

162. Then is the one who always follows the pleasure of Allah like the one who incurs wrath from Allah? And his refuge will be Hell. What a bad abode to return!

163. They have different ranks with Allah. And Allah is observant of whatever they are doing.

Prophet and the believers are people who always seek and follow the pleasure of Allah. The hypocrites who hide the Truth knowingly and their blind followers who reject the Truth are the people upon whom Allah's curse and wrath happened as told in the verses 33: 60-61 and 48: 6. The verses 32: 18-20 says: Then the one who is a believer be like the one who is a transgressor? Of course, they are not alike. As for those who believe and do honorable deeds, they shall be awarded the gardens of Paradise as a reward for their works. But those who transgress shall be cast into the Fire. Whenever they try to escape from It, they shall be pushed back into It, and will be said to them: "Taste the punishment of the Fire which you were rejecting."

In the verse 10: 33 it is told that surely such transgressed people will not believe and the verses 80: 17 says: the one who hide the Soul of Qur'an is been killed. The verse 35: 36, says, as for the disbelievers, there shall be the fire of Hell, no term shall be determined for them so that they could not die nor shall its punishment be ever lightened for them. Thus shall We reward every disbeliever. The verses 39:17-18 say as for those who refrain from worshipping satanic forces and turn to Allah in repentance, there is good news. So you, give good news to My servants who listen to My verses and follow It in the best manner. Such are the ones whom Allah has guided and such are the ones who are endowed with understanding. The verse 40:35 says the ones repudiate the verses of Allah without any authority to do so having been brought them, incur the greatest disgust so far Allah is concerned and so far as those who believe are concerned thus Allah seals off every overbearing oppressor's heart. Read together the verses 39: 32-33. Prophet used to pray always: Oh Allah, I ask for your pleasure and Paradise and seek refuge to You from your wrath and Hell. See the explanation 2: 38-39.

164. Indeed, Allah has benefited believers whenever He sent them a messenger from among themselves, to recite His verses to them and purify them, and teach them the Book and wisdom whereas previously they had been in clear astray.

The verse 62: 2 says: He is the One who has risen among the illiterate people a Messenger of their own, who recites to them His verses, purifies them, and teaches them the Book and wisdom, whereas previously they had been in clear astray. Any people, who does not follow the Soul of Qur'an after receiving It is in clear astray. The verses 36: 2-6 say, by the wise Qur'an you are one among the Messengers along the Straight path with a revelation from the

Powerful, the Merciful, with that you may warned a people who have been not warned by their forefathers, so they are heedless. Today, it is well clear that the Muslims, who do not follow the Soul of Qur'an, are in great astray than any other people. It can be seen that they are in front in evil deeds and back in good deeds. Since they lost the aim of life they fear to die and wish for long life of this world; and leading the most luxurious life in the world. In the verse 62: 5 Allah has compared this people to the donkeys and Jews and has told what a worse similitude of the people who reject the verses of Allah, and Allah will not guide such wrong doing people. As per the verse 7: 176 it is compared them to the dog, which does not change its attitude whether it is disturbed or not. In the verse 25: 18 it is warned about the scene that on the Day of Judgment the great people whom they invoked besides Allah will tell about this people who lived forgetting the Soul of Qur'an, that they were a boar people; and as per the verse 25: 30 on the Day of Judgment, the Messenger will come with Qur'an and tell: My Lord, my own people of this neglected this Qur'an and flew away from It. That is the cause for this misfortune condition of them. In the verse 13: 11 says that Allah never changes the condition of a people until they intend to change it themselves. If Allah wants to afflict a people with misfortune, none can ward it off, nor can they find any protector besides Him.

As per the following verses 7: 40-41; 9: 19; 23: 24, 80; 25: 31; 32: 12, 22; 36: 59; 39: 59, 71; 41: 26, 29; 63: 6 and 67: 6-11; we can see that the disbelievers, wrongdoers, transgressors, mad people and those who lost the aim of life are those who hide and reject the Soul of Qur'an after they received It. See explanation 2: 269 and 3: 58.

165. Yet whenever some disaster strikes you, such as has struck you twice has heavy already, you have said: "What is this for?" Say: "This is from your own doing; Indeed Allah is capable of everything."

In the battle of *Bad'r* seventy warriors of enemies were killed and seventy were caught as refugees by Muslims. But in *Uh'd*, seventy from among Muslims have been killed. The hypocrites from Muslims were saying complaint on this disaster happened to them, because they guessed that the loss or defeat should never happened when one become Muslim, actually they are not submitted all to Allah in peace by mind.

Occurrence of evil things like failure or disaster from satan's side when one forgets Allah. By the remembrance of Allah with the Soul of Qur'an no evil things will happen, such believers utilize the Soul of Qur'an as Shield and Safeguard. The archers disobeyed the command of Prophet and came down to collect the booty of war. That was reason for the defeat in the battle of *Uh'd*. In the verse 41: 50, Allah explain the character of disbelievers like this; if he get a mercy from Ourself after a distress grasped him, he will say: Surely this is deserved to me. I don't think that the last hour will ever happen, and even if it happens I will get benefit there also. Through the verses 18: 32-43 about the conversation of a Gardner who wronged himself with his believing companion is specified as, he says: "I am wealthier than you, and have a bigger following" then while he entered his garden he said: "I do not think that this will ever disappear! I do not think the Hour is at hand; if I am ever sent back to my Lord, I shall find something better than this." Then his companion told him: "have you disbelieved in the One Who created you from the dust then from a drop of semen; then fashioned you into a man? However so far I am concerned, He is Allah my Lord, and I am do not associate anyone with my Lord! Why as you entered in to your garden, did you not say: 'whatever Allah may wish; there is no strength except with Allah alone'? Then later when his garden ruined he was saying: "It is too bad for me; I should never have associated anyone with my Lord! He had no party to support against Allah and he was not supported. Here the disbelieving Gardner did not associate anything with Allah except he did not consider the Impartial character of Allah. The verse 39: 65 and 66 says: surely there has been inspired in you as well as in those before you: 'If you associate anything with Allah your deed will collapse and you will be a loser'. Rather you should serve Allah alone and be act among grateful. See explanation 2: 152; 3: 114 and 152.

166. And what ever happened to you on the day when both troops clashed, occurred with Allah's Permission, so He might recognize believers.

167. And to recognize those who act hypocritically. When it was said to them: Come, fight in Allah's way or at least defend yourselves they replied: "If we knew how to fight we would have follow You." They were nearer to disbelief than to faith that day. They say with their mouths what is not in their hearts; and Allah is quite Aware of what they are concealing.

Battle of *Uh'd* been made happened to distinguish the believers and hypocrites from among the Muslims as told in the above verses. It was not for Allah to distinguish them, since He is the Omniscient-Knower of all times-hidden and revealed matters; but it was to distinguish for the Prophet and believers, Allah- the Supreme Judge and Impartial -will not put anyone in to the Hell until he admit himself that "he was a disbeliever." Both the verses 6: 130 and 7: 37 end as and they will witness against themselves indeed they were disbelievers. The death scene of those who did not utilize the Soul of Qur'an after receiving it is mentioned through the verse 39:59 says as, nay indeed My verses has come to you then you rejected and showed arrogance upon My verses and you were among the disbelievers. It was told by the people who turned back under the leadership of *Abdullah Ibnu Ubayy* that, "if we knew how to fight we would have follow you." They were nearer to disbelief than to faith that day." Actually they are saying according to their whims. In the verse 63:1 Allah says about the character of hypocrites: When the hypocrites comes to you, they say : we bear witness that you are indeed the Messenger of Allah. Allah knows that you are indeed His Messenger. Surely Allah bears witness that the hypocrites are liars. Even though Prophet and about 1400 companions went for "*Umra*" in the *Hijra* 6th year, the *Meccan idolators* blocked them on the way. Then as per '*Udaibiya Treaty*', Prophet and companions returned back to *Madeena*. At that time the hypocrites who has not went for '*Umra*' and remained at *Madeena* are saying to Prophet and companions followed as told in the verse 48:11 that we could not come with you since we have to look after our possessions and families. So please ask forgiveness for us. They speak with their tongue that which is not in their hearts. Oh Prophet, ask: If Allah wills to give you an evil or to give you a good, who is there to intervene it from Allah. Nay, Allah is omniscience who surrounds all you are doing. The verse 12 says, instead you thought that the Messenger and the believers would never come home to their families and that conduct seemed attractive to your hearts. While you thought such evil thoughts and were a worthless people. The character of the hypocrites that the saying: We believe with their mouth while their hearts do not believe is also mentioned in the verse 5: 41.

Today's the hypocrites also have the same character. They say any matter without confirming it with the Soul of Qur'an, which is the confirming Truth as per the verse 69: 51 it is the only remedy to annihilate any doubts or conjecture. The verse 15: 99 says that "serve your Lord until certainty comes to you". As per the verses 74: 39-47 when the inmates of the Paradise ask to the *mujrims* in the Hell that whatever induced you to be scorched? They will reply as "we were not among the prayerful nor did feed the needy we speculated along with speculators and kept denying the Day of repayment until certainty came home to us". The certainty mentioned both verses are death. That is each individual at the time of his death will see everything passed in his past time from 15th age up to death and one among every thousand will see his Lord cheerfully, the rest of nine hundred and ninety nine will see satan sadly as told in the verses 76: 22-24. See explanation 2: 111, 147 and 3: 95.

168. Those who tell their brothers while they remain behind: "If they had obeyed us, they would not have been killed. Say: "Avert death from yourselves if you are so truthful."

Since the hypocrites of all periods have the same misunderstanding about the aim of life, they consider the death as a loss. They will not remember that the distress occurs as a result of the deeds of their own hands, hiding the verses like 4: 78-79. All the verses such as 10: 61; 11: 6; 22: 70, 27: 75; 34: 3; 57: 22; 64:11 etc. say that all the things happens in Heaven and Earth are pre-fixed and recorded in the Book by Allah. Through the verse 9: 51 Allah commands Prophet and believers to say: Nothing will happen to us except what Allah has already written for us. The hypocrites does not believe not only these verses but also the verse saying that, any soul cannot believe with out the Permission of Allah as mentioned in the verse 10: 100. And the verse 3: 145 says that: No soul can die without the Permission of Allah. Those people killed by Allah, will try to find out a logical reason for any matters and will blame the believers for the disasters affected them. They are not grasping the message of the verses 7:174, 30:41 and 32: 21 that Allah explains these verses or taste them worldly small torment rather than severe torment in order that they may return to the aim of life and to the Soul of Qur'an. They are those who have not realized the way of Allah from the Soul of Qur'an. Hence they have not grasped that they will have to bear the sin of all the evils and blood-shed happening on the world by hiding the Soul of Qur'an knowingly. See explanation 2:10-12, 94-95 and 3:154.

169. Do not reckon those who are killed in the way of Allah are dead, but rather they are living with their sustenance in the presence of their Lord.

170. So happy will they be with whatever Allah has given them out of His bounty, and rejoicing with those left behind who have not yet joined with them, that on them there shall be no fear and for them will not be grieved.

See the explanation 2: 154. By the entrance in to the Paradise, believers will be satisfied to live in forever; they will never seek any transfer from there as told in the verse 18: 108. But those who become martyred in the way of Allah will wish to come again to the world and to get martyred again because of the splendid reward and enjoyments they have there, is taught by the Prophet. Based on this teaching *Khalifa Umar*, *Usman*, *Ali* etc. who participated in the battle of *Bad'r*, *Uh'd*, *Khandhaq*, *Thabook* and lead the battles after the Prophet also, used to pray for martyrdom. That is why they have been killed and become martyrs. Since there is no war and killing today, a believer should not pray to become a martyr, on the contrary they will implement the command of the verses 9:73 and 25:52 by making '*Jihad*' with the Soul of Qur'an against those who hide It and they are the one who utilize the Soul of Qur'an as Shield and Safeguard, Balance and Trust to keep Universe in its equilibrium. See the explanation 3:101 and 102.

171. They will rejoice with the favor and bounty from Allah and Allah does not deprive the reward of such believers.

The verse 7:170 says : those who hold firmly the Book and keep up the *swalath* surely, We do not deprive the reward of such reformers. Through the verse 10: 58 Allah commands the Prophet to say: Rejoice with the Bounty of Allah and His Favor; is better than all that you are collecting. The Soul of Qur'an itself is the Bounty and Favor mentioned in this verse. But It becomes the Bounty and Favor only for the believers who learn and convey Its message to entire mankind. For the hypocrites and disbelievers It adds nothing but loss, and will increase filth over filth; is mentioned in the verses 9:125 and 17:82. See explanation 2: 78-79, 3:74 and 79.

172. Those are the persons who respond to Allah and the Messenger even after some wound has afflicted them. For those who are living by seeing Allah and keep Him in their hearts from among them have great reward.

173. Those that people have told: "Indeed mankind has gathered against to you so fear them"; yet it increased their faith and they said: Allah is enough for us, what a best Bearer of Responsibility!

While returning after the battle of *Uh'd*, *Abu Sufiyan* asked by calling: Is there *Muhammad* among you? Is there *Aboobacker*? Is there *Umar*? By obeying the instruction of Prophet, none of them answered. But when he asked 'is there *Umar*' at the third times: *Umar* replied: yes, everybody is there. Then by saying that we shall meet again on *Bad'r* next year, they left. Then Prophet told to some companions to follow them. Thus about 70 believers followed them until the place '*Hamra-ul-Asad*', 8 mile far from *Uh'd*. It is told about this group of believers that "who respond to Allah and Messenger even after some wound has afflicted them."

Then in the next year -*Hijra* 4th year- situations did not allow the enemies of Mecca to march towards *Bad'r*. So they sent few propagators to *Madeena* in order to discourage the believers from marching towards *Bad'r* by spreading the news that: Abu *Sufyan* and his party are gathering a great army against you at Mecca, so afraid of them. But face this challenge some of the believers told: "Allah is enough for us, what a best Bearer of Responsibility!" and went to *Bad'r* along with the Prophet. About whom it is told for those who are living seeing Allah and are heedful from among them have great reward. See explanation 2: 177, 250 and 3: 15-17.

174. Then they returned home with favor and Bounty from Allah; no evil ever touched them. And they followed Allah's pleasure, and Allah possesses splendid bounty!

Prophet and companions stayed at *Bad'r* for eight days expecting the enemies. And there they involved in trade by the result they received good profit. The bounty mentioned in this verse is that profit. There they did not have to face any army. They successfully completed this trial of Allah. That is the meaning of saying "they followed the good pleasure of Allah." If the believers say that Allah is enough for us to put our trust; the disbelievers say that "our forefather's way of life is enough for us." See explanation 2:74,170-171 and 3: 89-91.

175. Surely, that was only satan who make fear his companion. So you do not fear them and instead fear Me, if you are believers.

Fear comes from satan. According to the verse 17: 64, it is given to satan the power to make fear men by means of his voice, by leading cavalry and infantry against them and to become a partner in their wealth and children. Through the Soul of Qur'an, Allah has given full information to men about the power of satan. Those believers who know well about satan from the Soul of Qur'an also can control him by using the Qur'an as '*Muhaimin*' -Safeguard. Believers fear only Allah and by means of that they will not fear satan or his companions. That is why in the verse 59:16 it is told that, satan says to man: "Deny Allah", and when he denies satan will say: I am leaving responsibility of you; I fear Allah, the Lord of the worlds. The verse 17 says that, thus the consequence for both men and his companion from *jinns*, will be partners in the Hell and remain there forever. Such is the reward for wrongdoers. The verses 8: 48 and 49 also describe the same message. The verse 43: 36 says that: The one who went apart from the remembrance of the Impartial with the Soul of Qur'an, We assign a satan to become a soul mate for him. In the verse 14:22 it is warned that, on the Day of Judgment after the trial satan himself will say: Do not blame me for getting Hell, blame yourselves. The verses 50: 27-29 say the man's *jinns* soul mate will say: "Our Lord! I did not mislead him. He himself had gone far astray." Allah will say: "Do not dispute with each other in My presence. I I had given you warning before ahead. My words cannot be changed, nor I am unjust to My servants. So it is the duty of man to make his soul mate believer with the Soul of Qur'an which is the food, cloth and sight of the human soul.

In the verse 5: 54 it is told that the believers, they will strive for Allah's sake and not fear reproach from any critic. The verse 33: 39 says the Prophets are those who transmit Allah's Messages and fear Him, while they do not fear anyone except Allah. Allah is enough as a Reckoner. The verses 50: 30-33 says Paradise shall be brought close to the heedful, which will be no more a thing distant, and it will be said: "This is what were promised, for every one who turns to Allah by praying the '*Sayyidul Isthigfar*' -the greatest prayer for forgiveness- constantly who fear the Impartial most Gracious without seeing Him and comes before Him with a repentant heart." The verse 67: 12 says, indeed those who fear their Lord by seeing through the Soul of Qur'an, shall have forgiveness and a great reward. The verse 98: 8 says, their reward with their Lord, shall be the gardens of eternity, beneath which the rivers flow, to dwell there in forever. Allah well pleased with them while they pleased with Him i.e. for anyone who fears his Lord. Read together the verses 23: 1-2, 32: 16 and 36: 11. Therefore, each individual has to identify the goal of life and to earn Paradise here by utilizing the Soul of Qur'an. See explanation 3: 136 and 139.

176. And let not those who hasten on to disbelief sadden you; surely they will never injure Allah in any way Allah intends to grant them no share in the Hereafter. And they shall have terrible torment.

177. Surely those who purchased disbelief instead of belief will cause no injure Allah in any way, and they shall have a painful torment.

Those who purchase disbelief instead of belief are the hypocrites. The verse 63:3 says about the hypocrites that this is because they believed and then renounced their faith. Their hearts are sealed; therefore, they are devoid of understanding. Even though they perform *swalath*, fasting and charity, it will not be accepted from them since they are without the remembrance of Allah. And as per the verse 63: 4 they have been killed by Allah, in the Hereafter they will enter the Hell without even Reckoning. Read together the verses 9: 53-55; 63: 9-11 and 64: 10. See explanation 2: 120-121; 3: 90-91, 111 and 112.

178. Let not those who disbelieve think that Our granting of respite to them is good for themselves. We grant them respite so that they may add more and more to their sins. They shall have a heinous torment.

Allah has granted each individual the ways to the Paradise as well as the Hell and they have given the freedom to choose either of the ways as per the verse 76: 3. Allah is Impartial but the hypocrites knowingly hide and deny this Truth and they just like the *Meccan mushriks* do not believe with Allah's Impartial character. The verse 25: 60 says when it is told to them, "prostrate you before the Most Gracious," they ask: "Who is that Most Gracious? Are we to prostrate just because you order us to?" It merely increases their disdain. Hence the Most Gracious Allah the knower of the Hereafter has given comparatively more enjoyments for disbelievers than believers, so that they may earn more and more sins and may go to the bottom of the Hell; proving the verse 4: 145 saying as surely the hypocrites will be in the bottom of Hell fire; and you will not find any helper for them. Read together the verses 43: 33-35

Both the verses 9: 55 and 85 says: let neither their wealth nor their children dazzle you: In reality Allah intends to punish them with these things in this life and that their souls may depart while they are still disbelievers. The Hell is earning by individuals here is told in the verses 8: 50-51; 22: 9-10 and 58:16-19. They are careless in their *swalath*, so that they will get the Hell as a penalty for performing *swalath* as told in the verses 25: 65-66. Their *swalath* and fasting are only some expressions to inform the people that they are great devotees. By that they will dart from the *Dheen-Islam* and will go to the depth of the Hell. Read together the verses 4: 142-143 and 9: 54. See the explanation 2: 166-167, 3:10-12.

179. Allah will not leave the believers in their present condition until He sorts out bad from good. And it is not Allah's role to disclose you with the unseen, but Allah chooses anyone He wishes from among His messengers, so you believe with Allah and his Messengers; and if you believe and be heedful, then you shall have a great reward.

In the verse 67: 2 it is told that death and life has created to test which of you is doing the best deeds by seeing Allah through the Soul of Qur'an. Both the verses 11: 7 and 18: 7 have the same message. Hence it is understood that Allah has made happened all these events in this world in order to separate the believers and disbelievers. After the completion of Qur'an, the message of complete Qur'an is the only Criterion to distinguish barbarians from virtuous. Believers are those people who spend their bounties and lifetime here to prepare and buy the Paradise by using the Soul of Qur'an as the Ticket and Guidance. But disbelievers are heedless about this aim. In the verse 42: 51 it is told that, Allah should not speak to any human except through inspiration or from behind a veil, or through sending a messenger anything He wishes to inspire with through His Permission. Believers are commanded to believe with Allah and His Messenger presented by 6236 verses of Qur'an. 'Be heedful' means keep Allah in hearts, and remember Him always even while walking, sitting and laying.

The believers have to maintain the relations in the pleasure of Allah that is in the Light of the Soul of Qur'an only. The verse 9: 23 says Oh you who believe! Do not take your fathers and your brothers as your friends if they prefer disbelief over belief. Anyone of you who take them as friends then such is the wrongdoers. The verse 43: 67 says On the Day of Judgment; even friends will become enemies to one another except those who were related under the Light of Qur'an. Through the verse 9: 84 it is commanded the Prophet and believers that never should perform '*death prayer*' for any hypocrites. Soul of Qur'an is the only Balance to distinguish the hypocrites from the heedful and It is the Insight and Criterion. See explanation 2: 2, 3, 285; 3: 58 and 79.

180. Let not those who act niggardly with any of His bounty Allah has given them consider it is better for them; rather it will be worse for them; All the wealth they hoarded with niggardly behavior will be hung around their necks like a collar on the Day of Resurrection. And Allah holds the inheritance of Heaven and Earth; Allah is acquainted what you are doing.

By utilizing all the blessings bestowed by the Lord which is neither brought at the time of birth nor will carry at the time of death; to construct the Paradise here is the ultimate aim of the life. Read together the verse 6: 93. Otherwise the death scene prescribed in the verse 6: 94 will be met. The verse says "and surely you have all come to Us individually, now, just as We created you in the first place you have left behind what We conferred on you, nor do We see your intercessors along side you whom you claimed were associated with you. They have been cut off from you all the relations, and what you have been claiming has merely led you astray."

The Soul of Qur'an is the utmost Blessings and Guidance from the Lord. Therefore, the believers will spend all their blessings to learn and teach the Soul of Qur'an by considering the verse 102: 8 that says: Then, on that day, you will be questioned about all the blessings. The verse 47: 38 says: Here you are those who are called upon to spend in Allah's way, even though some of you are miserly. Anyone who acts niggardly is miserly only so far as his own soul is concerned. Allah is Self worthy while you are poor. If you should turn away He will replace and substitute you by some other people, and they will not be like you at all. The verse 4: 37 says: those who are miserly and enjoin miserliness on others, and hide the bounties which Allah has bestowed upon them; for such disbelievers We have kept prepared a heinous torment. The verse 9:67-68 say: The hypocrite men and hypocrite women are alike. They enjoin what is evil and forbid what is good and close their hands (miserly). They forget Allah, and have forgotten by Allah, indeed the hypocrites are the transgressors, Allah promised the hypocrites, both men and women, and the disbelievers' fire of Hell for their abode. It will be sufficient for them. Allah cursed them, and theirs are lasting torment. The verse 9: 34 ends as those who hoard up gold and silver and spend it not in the way of

Allah, unto them give glad news of a painful torment. Then the verse 35 says: On the day when it will (all) be heated in the fire of Hell, and their foreheads, flanks and their backs will be branded therewith and it will be said unto them: Here is that which you hoarded for yourselves. Now taste of what you used to hoard. Both in the verses 28:58 and 57:10 it is told that, inheritance of Heaven and Earth belongs to Allah. See explanation 2: 234, 268 and 3: 7.

181. Surely, Allah has heard the saying of those who say : "Indeed Allah is poor and we are rich!" We will write down whatever they say and how they killed the Prophets without any just. And We shall say: "Taste the torment of burning."

182. That is because of what your hands send on ahead and indeed Allah is not unjust to His servants.

Through the verses 2: 245, 57:11; 64:17 etc. Allah asks: Who will give good loan to Allah. Then as joking about this, Jews and hypocrites said: "So Allah is poor and we are rich." In the verses 5:64 it is told that, those who become Jews say: Allah's hand is tied up. Nay, their own hands are tied up. Allah's both hands are widely stretched. He spends as He wills. It can be seen from the verse 9:67 that, the character of hypocrites also have the same as that of Jews. The verses 35: 15-17 say: Oh mankind! You are the poor in your relation to Allah. And Allah! He is the Absolute, the self Praiseworthy. If He so wished, He could take you away and bring some new creation. That would not be impossible for Allah to do. In the verse 36: 47 Allah has specified this character of disbelievers as when they are told: "Spend something Allah has provided you with", the ones who disbelieve tell those who believe: "Should we feed someone whom Allah would feed if He so wishes? You are in nothing except in manifest error.

The Jews have killed many Prophets physically. But the hypocrites are killing the Prophets both verbally and physically by falsifying the way of life other than that of the Soul of Qur'an. See explanation 3: 21-22. On the verses 63:1-5 and 58:8-10 it is told that such hypocrites are those who does not accept Prophet, and conduct conspiracy against Prophet in his absence. As per the verses 9:30 and 63:4 both Jews and hypocrites have been killed by Allah, whereas, as per the verses 4:91, 9:123 and 33:61 Allah has commanded the party of believers to kill the hypocrites. In the verse 2: 95 and 62: 7 it is told that, they will never wish for death because of they have sent ahead is the Hell. In the verse 9: 82

Allah says to the hypocrites who are involved in fun and jokes and live by losing the aim of life: Laugh a little and weep more - as a reward for what you have earned. In the verse 95 says: Surely, neglect them because they are filth. They will get Hell as refuge as a reward for what they earned. All these verses are teaching that each soul is earning Paradise or Hell by herself.

In the verse 8:50 Allah says: If you could see the death scene of disbelievers! The Angels will beat on their faces and their backs; and will say: Taste the burning torment. As per the verse 51, that is which your own hands sent on ahead; indeed, Allah is not unjust to His servants. In the verses 22: 8-9 It is told that, there are some among mankind who argue about Allah without the Soul of Qur'an. In order to lead others astray from the path of Allah, they always will move by beading their nape (by showing partiality). For him there is disgrace in this life, and on the Day of Judgment We shall make them taste the punishment of burning Fire. In the verse 10 says: That is which your own hands sent on ahead; indeed, Allah is not unjust to His servants. In the verse 59:18 says: Oh you who believe! Heed Allah! Let every soul watch out for whatever it has prepared for tomorrow, Heed Allah. Surely, Allah is acquainted with what you are doing. The verse 41:46 says: Who ever acts righteous does so for his soul's sake; while anyone who commits evil, does so for her on sake and your Lord is never unjust towards His servants. See the explanation 2: 6-7, 94-95; 3: 119 and 135.

183. Such as those who say: "Allah has made a covenant from us not to believe in any Messenger until he brings us some sacrifice which fire will consume", ask: "Messengers before me have already come to you with clear explanations and just what you have said; why did you kill them if you are so truthful?"

In ancient communities, there was a tradition of consuming (burning) the sacrifice by an unseen fire as a proof of acceptance. As explained in the verse 5:27 when the two sons of *Adam -Haabeel* and *Qaabeel* presented sacrifice, an unseen fire came and burned it; and thus its acceptance and non-acceptance was differentiated. Prophet *Ilyas*, who was appointed to the children of Israel, told to the priests who did worship the goddess '*Ba'l*': I am the only remaining Prophet of "*Yahova*!" And there are 450 Prophets of *Ba'l*. Give us two Bulls. You slay one Bull, make to pieces and place it over the fire woods without fire. I will also do the same with the other Bull. Then you call and pray your god and

I will pray in the name of *Yahova*. The sacrifice which answered by the fire can be considered as the god. They agreed the conditions. The unseen fire came and burned the Bull which is sacrificed by the Prophet *Ilyas*. But the queen of Israel, the worshipper of goddess *Ba'l* -become the enemy of Prophet *Ilyas*; and by her compelling her husband set out to kill Prophet *Ilyas*. At that time *Yahova* ordered: You begin your journey and return through the deserts of *Dammashakk*. (Refer the Bible the King lessons 18, 19).

Based on this incident, Allah is asking to that multitude -Jews of *Madeena* who lived with Prophet: Oh enemies of Truth, why you are demanding for a miracle? You were not kind enough to live the Prophet who shows the miracles by the Permission of Allah. The clear explanations mentioned in the verse are about the scripture and various miracles. But today, Jews are not demanding for such miracles. Hypocrites from among the Muslims have all the character of Jews. And that has taught by Prophet: "*You will follow the Jews and Christians foot by foot and step by step. If they are entering into the burrow of an iguana, you will also try to enter in it*" Prophet also taught that "*those who are living without holding the Soul of Qur'an firmly will go astray at that time.*" See explanation 2: 61, 66 and 3: 85-90

184. Then if they reject you; messengers before you have already been rejected when they came even with Explanations, the Psalms and the Enlightening Book.

The verse 35:25 is also with the same message. Here it is specified the character of disbelievers of every period. The explanations, the Psalms and the Enlightening Book are the Soul of Qur'an just like the Knowledge, Guidance, and the enlightening Book mentioned both in the verses 22: 8 and 31: 20. Here it is used "*Zubur*" which is the plural form of "*Zaboor*"-is about the *Psalm* given to Prophet *Davood*. In the verse 26: 196 it is told that; surely, Qur'an is found (present) in the ancient *Zubur*. Qur'an itself is the light-giving Book. Only one Book has sent down to Earth by Allah. Even though Its body are in different languages, Its Soul is the same. In all the verses like 4: 174; 5: 15; 7: 57; 64: 8 and 66: 8 it is told that Qur'an is the Light. In the verse 6: 33 it is told that surely they are not making you false, but the wrongdoers are repudiating towards the verses of Allah. Read together the verses 7: 50-51; 29: 47, 49; 41: 26-28 and 40-43. The disbelievers are the people of satan; and if anyone select satan as protecting friend, he will lead them to the Blaze as mentioned in the verses 22: 4 and 31: 21. The Explanations, Balance and the Book in the verse 57:25 also is the Soul of Qur'an. See explanation 2: 6-7, 285 and 3: 60-61.

185. Every soul will be tasting death: And you will be fully rewarded your earnings on the Day of Judgment. Then whoever is prevented him from the Fire and is admitted in to Paradise will have triumphed, and the worldly life is nothing except the enjoyment of illusion!

The part of the verse- "every soul will be tasting death" is also mentioned in the verses 21: 35 and 29: 57. In the verse 28: 88 it is told that "everything will perish except Allah's face." That means every living and non-living things will perish so from this it is understood that all living things have the soul. The difference of men from other living beings is that they have bestowed the intelligence.

Each individual himself has to prevent him from the Fire and admit into Paradise. See explanation 2:213 and 286. For the believers, Paradise is in the Hereafter and by utilizing the Soul of Qur'an and all other bounties they will construct and buy Paradise Here in order to inherit It in the Hereafter. And they will consider the worldly life as in the Hell. See explanation 3:136. But in the case of disbelievers will consider this worldly life is the only life and they will enjoy it at the maximum and after death they will be entered into the Hell. See explanation 3:182. In the verse 13:26 it is told that; when compared with the Hereafter, the life of this world is nothing but a single feast. The verse 57:20 also ends as and the worldly life is nothing except the enjoyment of illusion. Read together the verses 41: 26-29 and 35:5. See explanation 2: 254, 281 and 3:30.

186. You will certainly be tested by means of your wealth and through your own selves, and you will hear much abuse from those who were given the Book before you, as well as those associate others with Allah and if you are patient and heedful, then that is the way of firmness to fulfill all affairs.

Today, the believers will have to hear such words of stinging from the hypocrites and those who associates others with Allah from among the Muslims. Enemies of Allah and Messengers themselves are the enemies of believers. In the verse 25: 31 it is told that, thus for every Prophet We have made *mujrims*- both hypocrites and *fujjar*- as enemies. But for you Allah is enough as Guide and Helper. Read together the verses 10:17, 32:22, 36: 59-62 and 39:59. In the verse 98: 6 it is told that: surely, those who disbelieve from among the people of the Book and those who associate others with Allah will be in the Hell forever, they are the worst of all land creatures. They are the enemies of believers who are the best creatures of the land specified in the verse 98:7. The verse 8: 22 says indeed the worst animals in the sight of Allah are those deaf and dumb people who do not utilize their intelligence. The verse 8: 55 says the worst of animals in the sight of Allah are those who reject the Truth and do not become believers. In the verse 31:17, *Luqman* is giving advice to his son: Keep up regular *swalath*, enjoin good and forbid evil and be patient on obstructions which befalls you because of that. Surely, that is the way of firmness to fulfill all affairs. The verse 42: 43 also ends as then that is the only way of firmness to fulfill all affairs. Read together the verses 16: 99-100, 127-128; 18: 46; 64: 14-16 and 46: 35. See the explanation 2: 166-167 and 3: 10, 90 and 91.

Note that, today, the Book is Soul of Qur'an the people of the Book means the hypocrites who hide It and the associates who reject It coming only from Muslims. They are the boar people as mentioned both in the verses 25: 18 and 48: 12. The '*Kalimath*' -the *Rooh*- which includes both the Soul of Qur'an and meaning or includes the '*Hikmath*' and '*Mouidhath*' is the instrument to seek refuge from all evils and it is ordered to the believers to do *Jihad* with this weapon at the most to those who hide and reject It through the verses 9: 73 and 25: 52. Prophet taught to pray: "I seek refuge to Allah with the complete *Kalimath*, from all the evil whatever has created." All the Muslims in different parties except the party of Allah are belong to the satan's party and are *mushriks*. They are the enemies of believers who belong to Allah's party. Read together the verses 25: 29 and 43: 67. See explanation 2: 155-157; 3: 145, 166 and 167.

187. And remember when Allah made an agreement with those who were given the Book: "You shall explain It to mankind and not conceal It", but they threw it away behind their backs and sold it for a petty price. Then, what a bad bargain they made.

The Soul of Qur'an is the Splendid Book and It is the Guidance for the entire mankind as per the verses 2: 2, 185; 41: 41-42. Allah has taken pledge from the carriers of It, Especially from the scholars that they should explain Its message clearly to the mankind and should not conceal It. But today the bearers of Qur'an bearing It as donkeys bearing burdens as mentioned in the verse 62: 5, they neither utilize the Soul of Qur'an in heart's language nor give to others to utilize It. Thus they destroy themselves but they do not perceive It as told in the verse 6: 26. Thus they become the fuel of the Hell as taught by Prophet in the explanation of the verse 3:10. See the explanation 2:159-161 and 3:81-91.

Instead of giving priority for the Soul of Qur'an from the Self worthy and Praiseworthy they are teaching their children the books written by the creatures. By doing so, they have become exactly like what Prophet taught "*their scholars will be the worst creatures beneath the sky*." They not at all considering what Prophet taught that: "Best among you are those who learn and teach the Soul of Qur'an and not the body of Qur'an in other words Prophet taught the honorable among you are those who bear the Qur'an. And not told the honorable among you are those who by hearts It. They have forgotten the aim of life and are the human satans who hide Allah and prophet in the Soul of Qur'an and thus helping the satan for destroying the world. In the verses 28: 49-50 Allah commands Prophet to say: "Bring a book from Allah which gives better Guidance than the two- *Thourath* and Qur'an, I will follow It, if you are so truthful!" and if they do not answer you, then know that they follow their own whims. Who is more astray than one who follows his own whims without Guidance from Allah? Surely, Allah will not guide such wrongdoing people. Read together the verses 6: 112; 25: 18 and 30. See explanation 2: 79, 121 and 3: 77-78

188. Do not consider those who feel delighted about what they have been given and love to be praised for something they have not done, do not reckon they will found any means to triumph from the torment and they will have painful torment.

The Muslims, who believe Qur'an is the prominent "Miracles" given to Prophet, are delighting that they are the bearers of that Qur'an. But they are doing so without realizing what is, what for and why It is? They are satisfied in study to read It and are not interested to regulate their life according to Its Message. That is why they themselves have degraded world widely. If anyone says to them those who hide and reject the verses of Qur'an are the disbelievers, wrongdoers' transgressors, mad people and companion of Hell; they will not accept it or will not change their way of life. On the contrary they will say: the Soul of Qur'an is forged by someone other than Allah and should not tell like this, or say some more politely. As per the verses 10: 15-16 it can be seen that the *Meccan mushriks* also gave a same answer to Prophet at that period. If in this verse it has told as "you should not think that the disbelievers will escape from punishment" in the verse 39: 61 says "Allah will deliver heedful people from the Hell since they triumph by fulfilling the aim of life. No torment or sorrow will touch them there."

The verse 78: 31 says the heedful will have their scene of triumph. The heedful are those who make truthful the Truth when received It as told in the verse 39: 33. The verse 22: 72 says whenever Our clear verses are recited to them, you will recognize the disgust on the faces of those who disbelieve; They almost pounce upon those who recite our verses to them. Ask: "Shall I announce something even worse than that to you? The Fire! Allah has promised It to those who disbelieve, what a bad returning place!" See explanation 2: 44, 254; 3: 159 and 185.

189. And to Allah belongs the dominion of Heaven and Earth, and Allah is capable of everything.

The verse 67:1 says: "He in whose hands are the dominion is blessed, and He is capable of everything." In the verse 25: 26 it is told that, on the Day of Judgment the real dominion will belong to the Most Gracious, it will be a hard day for disbelievers. In the verse 40:16 it is told that, the Day on which everyone is brought in front of Allah with nothing hidden, it will be asked: Whose is the dominion today? And will be said: To Allah Alone, the Irresistible! The verse 17 says, today each soul will be rewarded for whatever it has earned. There will be no wrong done on that day; indeed Allah is swift and reckoning! He is the One Who created Heaven, Earth and all in between them from nothing, and He controls all. He has no beginning and end. He has deputed men to Earth as vicegerent i.e. to live here in His character -the Soul of Qur'an. But only the believers will take this Trust and the disbelievers represent satan, will return to Hell, without being taking the Ticket to the Paradise as told in the verses 73: 19 and 76: 29. In the verse 12: 103 it is told that, even if you try much, most men will not believe; and in the verse 106 says: Most of the men will not believe in Allah except by associating others with Him. Each one should ask themselves for Guidance to get it from the Soul of Qur'an to their Lord; but there is two conditions to get answer for the prayer and there get accepted the deeds as mentioned in the verse 2: 186. See the explanation 1: 3; 2: 255 and 284.

190. Surely, in the creation of Heaven and Earth, and the alternation between night and daylight, there are signs for the men of understanding.

191. Those who remember Allah while standing, sitting and laying on their sides; and meditate on the creation of Heaven and Earth. By saying "Our Lord, you have not created this in vain! Glory be to you! Then shield us from the torment of Fire!

Allah is the one who originated and arranged Heavens and Earth in a pattern that are seeing today, from joined condition by splitting it as explained in the verse 2:29. The aim of creation of Heaven and Earth is mentioned in the verse 45: 22 as: Allah has created Heaven and Earth with the true purpose, in order to reward every soul for whatever it has earned, and they will not be dealt unjust. The aim of creation of Jinn and mankind is told in the verses 51: 56-57 as I have never created *Jinn* -sprites- and man except for they should worship Me alone, I do not intend any sustenance from them nor do I need them to feed Me. So the aim of creating seven Heavens and Earths and all other things in between them is to identify the Originator and Creator of all things including men. It is told in the verse 4:1 that you heed Allah about whom you will be asked. The verse 25: 62 says and He is the One Who has caused the night and the day to succeed each other, for such who wish to remember their Lord or who wish to show their gratitude.

The most beloved servants of Most Gracious will live only for Allah as His representative. They will proclaim through the verse 1: 4 as We do live only for You and we do seek help only from You. They will keep Allah in their hearts and will remember Him always in their walking, sittings and laying to fulfill the command of the verses 2: 152, 4:103 and 62:10. They are those who think about Heaven, Earth and its creation. They will find out the Creator of all these, and will admit by mind that these are not created as a joke without any aim. Refer the verses 21: 16, 44: 38 and 39. Anyone after receiving the Soul of Qur'an is not found out this fact and not convey the Message to others will have to go to Hell. The men of understanding will always pray to save from the Hell. The verses 13: 3; 39: 42; 30: 21 and 45:13 end as, surely, in that are signs for the people who meditate (think and reflect). The following verses 7: 176; 16: 44 and 59: 21, end as let them meditate and reflect the Message. Read together the verses 25: 72-74; 32:15-16 and 39:9-10. See explanation 2:145-148. After reciting this verse, it should be prayed: "Oh Allah! Shield us from the torment of the Fire, and make us who remember and think always about you while walking, sitting and laying and be grateful to You and include us among those winners who enter the Paradise with the Soul of Qur'an.

192. Our Lord! Surely anyone You sentence to the Fire, then surely he has fallen in eternal shame, and there shall be no helper for such wrongdoers.

To realize who are the wrongdoers, refer the verses such as 2: 254; 5: 51; 6: 21, 47, 93; 7: 40-41; 9: 19, 23;10: 17, 85-86; 17: 82; 18: 57; 28: 50; 32: 22; 39: 62; 62: 5 and 76: 31.

Oh Allah! Not include us among the wrongdoers and shameful people who go to Hell. Make us heedful who follow the Soul of Qur'an as It has to be followed, and include us among the winners who enter the Paradise, Oh the Impartial, the compassionate!

193. Our Lord! Surely we heard a crier appealing for belief by calling out: "Believe in your Lord!" Then we have believed. "Our Lord! Forgive us our offences remove our evil deeds from us, and grant us a death with the Virtuous"

It is very clear that the crier mentioned in this verse is Prophet and today is the believer. Read together the verse 41: 33. After reciting this verse, pray like this: Oh Allah, You forgive us our offences, and shower Your mercy upon us, and remove our evil deeds from us, and grant us the death of Virtuous and enter to the Paradise with the Pioneers, Winners with the Ticket, Oh you who sent down the Ticket, Oh You Who the Virtuous, Merciful! . Prophet taught to pray: we believe with Allah and the Day of Judgment, and we are the ones who repent to Allah secretly and publicly. See explanation 3: 16 and 102-104.

194. Our Lord! Give us what you have promised us through Your Messengers and do not cause to fall us in eternal shame on the Day of Judgment. Surely, You never go back on any promise.

As per the verse 39: 74, the heedful who are entered the Paradise will praise Allah, who has truly fulfilled His promise to Us. According to the verses 7: 172-173 Allah has taken a covenant from every one by asking: "Am I not your

Lord? All they individually replied: yes, we bear witness to that". On the Day of Judgment, every one will be asked about It and that is the promise. No one can escape from Allah by blaming others even parents. Believers are those who remember and renew that pledge by praying "*Sayyidul Isthighfar*" at least two times a day, morning and evening. See explanation 2: 27. As per the verse 9: 68, Allah has promised Hellfire for the hypocritical men and women, and the men and women who associate others with Allah, and as per the verse 72 Allah has promised Gardens beneath which rivers flow for the believing men and women. Prayers of Prophet *Ibrahim* can see in the verses 26: 87 and 88 as: "do not put me in shame on the Day when everybody will be resurrected -the Day on which neither wealth nor children will be useful". Every one will have to answer about each and every moment of their worldly life after their 15th years old, in front of Allah-the Knower of all Times. On that Day, all secrets will be revealed.

As per the verses 50: 27-28, while the Jinn companion says: Our Lord! I did not compel him to the evil, but he himself had gone from the Truth far astray; then Allah will say: do not dispute each other in My presence. This promise (warning) had come to you earlier. Through the verses 91:7-10 Allah says: Each soul has given its wrong and right; and the soul who recognizes It, will be successful and she who did not recognize It will be failed. About this itself Allah says that the promise had come to you earlier. The verse 50: 45 ends as; with this Qur'an you remind the one who fear the promises. Through the verses 25:11-16 Allah asks: which is better, the Paradise which has been promised the heedful or the Blaze which is promised for the rejecters of Qur'an verses. It is also told, for the heedful there will be their reward and a good place to return. There they will live forever and will have all that they desire. It is a Promise that can be questioned in front of your Lord. Read together the verses 25: 27-30; 39:47-48 and 86: 9. See the explanations 2: 28; 3: 8 and 9.

195. So their Lord responded to them: "I shall never waste the work of any worker among you, whether it is a man or a woman. Some of you are from others. Then those who have migrated and were driven out from their homes and mistreated for My sake, and have fought and were killed; I shall remove their evil deeds and I shall admit them to Gardens below which rivers flow, as a Prize from Allah Himself, and Allah holds the finest Prize!"

Today there is no war and no migration in the way of Allah. But when one live in the way of Allah according to the rules and regulations of the Soul of Qur'an, and convey It to others, will have to face so many problems and sufferings especially from hypocrites and from those who associate others with Allah. In the verse 2:186 two conditions have told to get accept the deeds by Allah. (1) Give answer to the call of Allah (2) Believe in Allah as it has to be believed i.e. seeing Allah by heart from the Soul of Qur'an and obey His rules and regulations submitting through the Soul of Qur'an. Those people who do not keep these two conditions are answering to the call of satan and they are disbelievers. Both the verses 13:14 and 40: 50 end as the prayer of disbelievers are nothing except increase astray. According to the verse 14: 22 on the Day of Judgment satan will say to them : "You accepted my call". As per the verse 13:18 it has told that, there is an excellent reward for those who respond to the call of their Lord. For those who do not respond to Him have the worst inquisition on the Day of Judgment-even if they had all that on the Earth and twice as much to offer as a ransom in order to save themselves from punishment, it will not be accepted. And their abode is Hell.

Today, '*Jihad*' is only with the Soul of Qur'an to against the hypocrites and disbelievers from Muslims who hide and reject It. This is the period about which Prophet taught; '*on those days one should live by biting the Soul of Qur'an with molar teeth*'.

Each person-whether male or female-will have to answer individually about their life to Allah. The verse 16: 97 says whoever does honorable deeds, whether male or female, provided he is a believer, We shall surely grant him a wholesome life, and will reward them as per the finest deeds they have been doing. The verse 20:112 says while anyone who has performed honorable deeds and is a believer will need fear no harm, nor any injustice. The verse 33: 35 says Surely Muslim men and the Muslim women, believing men and the believing women, devout men and the devout women, truthful men and the truthful women, patient men and the patient women, the humble men and the humble women, charitable men and the charitable women, fasting men and the fasting women and men who safeguard their private parts and women who safeguard them, and men who remember Allah much and women who remember Allah much - for all them, Allah has prepared forgiveness and a great reward. Muslim men and women mean those men or women who are completely submitted to Allah. The verse 40: 40

says anyone who commits some evil deeds will merely be rewarded with something else like it, while someone who acts honorably, whether it is a man or a woman, provided he is a believer will enter the Garden. He or She will be provided for there without any reckoning. Read together the verses 18: 48 and 19: 95. Allah will forgive all the evil deeds of martyrs except their debts. Since there is no war today, no one can become martyrs. So the only way to get forgiveness from the Impartial Allah is realizing the sins by reading Soul of Qur'an and deeply repents by heart for the sins committed; and strenuously works to convey Soul of Qur'an to entire people in order to help them to realize their sins and they also shun their evil deeds. See the explanation 2:112, 218; 3:102 and 136.

196. Do not let to deceive you by the bustle of the disbelievers in the land.

197. Their enjoyment is brief; then their refuge will be Hell, and what a bad cradles!

The Soul of Qur'an is the Guidance and Ticket for entire mankind in order to return the Paradise. Those people who do not try to understand and follow Qur'an even after receiving It are the disbelievers. See explanation 3:10. They themselves do not utilize It, and forbid others from It. By that they harm none but themselves. But they do not perceive it as told in the verse 6: 26. In the verse 14: 30, it commands to say to the people who associate partners in the dominion of Allah to mislead people from His way that: you enjoy yourself for a while, surely your return is to Hell and in the verse 39: 8 says: when some trouble befalls man, he turns to his Lord completely and prays to Him. Then, when he get a boon from his Lord, he forgets about what he has prayed to Allah before and sets equals to Allah to mislead others from His way. Say to such people: you enjoy with your disbelief for a little while. Surely you are among the inmates of the Hell. In the verse 83: 7 it is told that, the record of the *fujjar* is in "*Sijjeen*" and in verse 82: 14 says: surely the *fujjar* will be in the Hades. Here in these two verses *fujjar* includes both the hypocrites and their blind followers i.e. gone astray people, who eat the body of Qur'an without Its Soul. What a bad cradles: here, for the Hell, the plural of the cradle is used. The cradle means the lying and resting place of babies. But here, for the disbelievers cradles mentioned as the Hell, means from all the sides the fire will surround the inmates of the Hell. See explanation 2: 6-7, 254; 3: 116 and 185.

198. However those who heed their Lord will have Gardens beneath which the rivers flow, to live in forever as a welcome from Allah; and what Allah possesses is the best for the virtuous.

The verse 32:19 says as for those who believe and do honorable deeds, they shall be awarded the gardens of Paradise as a gift and reward of their deeds in this world. The verse 18:102 says: Do the disbelievers think that they can take my servants as protectors, to save themselves from Hell, instead of Me? Certainly We have kept prepared the Hell as a gift for such disbelievers. In the verses 18: 100-101 say that the disbelievers are those who have a veil over their eyes towards the Soul of Qur'an and also they are unable to hear It. Read together the verses 18:103-106. And the verse 107 says that, for those who believe and do honorable deeds will get the "*Gardens of Firdouse*" as a feast (gift of welcome); and in the verse 76: 5 says the virtuous shall drink from a cup mixed with camphor. Both in the verses 82:13 and 83: 22 it is told that indeed virtuous will be in Bliss; and in the verse 83:18 says: the record of virtuous is in "*Illiyyeen*". The virtuous people mentioned here include both the Forerunners who enter the paradise without trial and the heedful who will be led to the Paradise after trial.

Oh Allah, do not make us the disbelievers and losers, and do not make our return to the Hell fire by leading a life of aimless and heedless people neglecting the Soul of Qur'an-the Guidance. Include us among the virtuous, heedful believing people who follow the Soul of Qur'an as it has to be followed; and enter us the Paradise with forerunners and heedful with Your Mercy, Oh the virtuous, the Merciful, See explanation 2: 38, 218 and 3: 58.

199. And indeed there are some among the people of the Book, who truly believe with Allah and what has been sent down to you, and what has been sent down to them, acting reverently towards Allah they do not sell Allah's verses for a miserable price: such will receive their reward from their Lord; surely Allah is very Swift in reckoning.

The verses 28: 51-55 say We have conveyed Our Word to them over and over again in order that they may take heed. Those to whom the Book were given before this (Jews and Christians), they do recognize the Truth and believe in It. When it is recited to them they say: "We believe in It, surely this is the Truth from our Lord: Indeed we were Muslims even before this." They are the ones who will be given their reward twice, because they have endured; they ward off evil with the best and spend some of what We have provided them. Whenever they hear any gossip, shun it and say: "We have our deeds and while you have your deeds." Peace be up on you: we do not desire the way of ignorance." Here it is mentioned about the characters of believers from among the people of previous Book -the Jews and Christians. In that group, Christians are the majority and the Jews are few in number. This can be realized from the verse 5: 82. Read together the verses 5: 83-85. Qur'an is the only Book today. Those people who hide and reject It by leading a way of life against the do's and don'ts of It are the inmates of Hell as explained in the verse 2: 39.

Acting reverently towards Allah means to fear Allah unseeingly i.e. always exist consciously that Allah is seeing us, or as if seeing Allah although one cannot see Him. In the verses 23:1-2 it is told that, the believers who fear Allah in their *swalath* are successful. In the verses 98: 7-8 it is told that, surely those who believe and do honorable deeds are best of all land creatures. Their reward with their Lord shall be gardens beneath which the rivers flow, where in they dwell forever. Allah is well-pleased with them and they are well-pleased with Him. That is which obtain for those who live by fearing Allah. In the verses 50:31-33 it is told that, on the Day of Judgment the Paradise will be brought close for those heedful people who fear the Most Gracious without seeing Him, repeatedly repent to Him, and pray the '*Sayyidul Isthighfar*', and remain with a conscious mind about to return back to Allah. Read together the verses 36: 11 and 67: 12.

Here, in this verse it says that "Allah is very Swift in reckoning." This can be easily understood for today's people who are well known about the computer and its application in their day today work. In the verses 17:13-14 says that, every human being carries his fate on his neck, and on the Day of Judgment he will get it as a open shining book to read; in other words, everyone carries his/her software on his neck. The verses 3: 19; 5: 4; 14:51 and 40: 17 end as, "Allah is very Swift in reckoning." Read together the verses 18: 49; 23: 62; 45: 28-29; 36: 12 and 39: 69. See the explanation 2: 45- 46, 79 and 3: 187.

200. Oh you who believe, act patient and be commanders with patient yourselves, and be tied up your hearts to be one and heed Allah so that you may prosper.

In the verse 22: 77 Allah says by calling the believers: Bow down, and prostrate yourselves, and serve Allah alone and do good deeds; so that you may prosper. Both in the verses 12: 18 and 83 Prophet *Ya'qoob* be quiet in the missing of his sons *Yoosuf* and *Binya-meen* by saying: Then patience is the best, and seek help to my Lord -All Knower, Wise is the only way. See explanation 2: 249. The verses 16: 41-42 say: Those who have migrated for Allah's sake after they were wronged, We shall settle them in something fine during this worldly life, while the reward in the Hereafter will be more greater, for those who act patient and entrust on their Lord. In the verse 50: 39 Allah says to Prophet that, therefore you bear with patience whatever these disbelievers say; and keep on praising and glorifying your Lord before sunrise and sunset. In the verse 30: 60 Allah says: Then be patient, surely the promise of Allah is True; and do not let to shake your firmness by those people who have no certainty of faith. The verse 76: 24 says: Therefore you wait with patience for the command of your Lord and do not obey hypocritical sinners or ungrateful disbelievers from among them. The verses 103: 1-3 say: By the time through the ages! Every man indeed is at loss except those who believe and do honorable deeds; and encourage with Truth and recommend with patience. Read together the verses 90: 17 and18. See the explanation 2: 5, 147-148.

After reciting this verse it should be prayed: Oh Allah! Make us among those who believe, honorable and be patient, and who are united with joined hearts, and who remember You always, and who are thankful to You. Oh Allah, keep our feet firm and help us against the disbelievers, make us those who follow the Soul of Qur'an as It has to be followed and join us with the heedful people who goes to Paradise, with Your Great Mercy. Oh, the Most Merciful among the Gracious.

With the name of Allah, the Impartial, the Compassionate.

4. Annisa

This *Surath* revealed in *Madeena* in between the last days of *Hijra* 3rd year and the beginning of *Hijra* 5th year. It is revealed after the battle of *Uh'd* in which 70 Muslim warriors were killed. It contains the laws pertaining to their widows and children, who became orphans, and the laws pertaining to indigents and the laws of inheritance. It was during the 'battle of *Dathurriqa*' after the *Hijra* 4th year that the verse pertaining to the *swalath* at the time of war was revealed. The verse pertaining to '*Thayammum*' -ablution by using dust in the absence of water was revealed during the battle of '*Banul Musthaliq*' after the *Hijra* 5th year.

This *Surath* contains 176 verses in which it is explained several stages of divorce, the list of woman by whom the marriage is prohibited, the list of real disbelievers, the laws of salutations, the code of conduct toward hypocrites, the real character of the people of Book, the severe torment for the rejecters of Qur'anic verses and the laws and ransom when a believer kills another believer by mistake. It contains the verses stimulating the believers for battle as self-defense and giving protection to women, children and the weaklings. It also contains the verses introducing satan, about Prophet *Jesus* raising up to the Heaven with bodily and his second coming to the Earth, and the verse which says that the Qur'an is sent down to entire mankind as the Proof and the Light.

With the name of Allah, the Impartial and the Compassionate,

1. **Oh mankind, heed your Lord who has created you from a single soul, and created its mate from it, and from them both scattered so many men and women. And heed Allah about whom you will be asked, and heed the wombs. Certainly Allah is ever watching over you.**

All humans (souls) are created in the Paradise. By saying six directly visible things in the verses 91: 1-6 - the sun and its heated light, the moon as it follows the sun and its glorious light, the day as it shows up its glory, the night as it conceals it, and the sky on which it establishes and the Earth as it rounded up as the egg of an ostrich; Allah says in the verses 91: 7-10: By the soul, the proportion and order given to it, given its wrong and its right. The one who identified the soul and purified it succeeds. The one who identified it not and corrupts it fails. The soul of man and woman is the same and is from a single one as told in the verses 7: 189 and in 39: 6 that: It is He Who created you from a single soul. Then *Awwa* is created from Adam's soul as the pair. As per the verse 15: 26 the body of Adam was created from 'sounding' 'pasty' and foul smelling black clay as a potter making a pot, then shaped him and breathed in to him from His *Rooh* (life + soul), as told in the verses 15: 29 and 38: 72. From 'her' created 'her's mate' means from the soul created its mate. The verse 30: 21 says: And among His signs that He created for you mates among yourselves for you may dwell in tranquility with them. And He has put love and mercy between yours.

Note that the soul of both men and women, and women with their body is mentioned in feminine gender; whereas men with body are used masculine gender. See the explanation 2: 286.

Allah says in the verses 32: 7-9, the creation of man began from clay and made his progeny from a quintessence of despised water. Then shaped him and breathed in to him His *Rooh*-the Spirit. The first father and mother ate the food material produces from the soil which contained the elements of soil. From this blood was formed. And from its essence the Creator fashioned '*Nuthfa*' -Sperm in case of male and Ovum in the case of female. Allah says in the verses 23: 12-13 certainly We created man from a quintessence of clay. Then We placed him as drop of semen in a secure resting place. When father and mother copulates as per the verse 7: 189, the sperm emits from father's '*Swulb*' (Ribs/testicles - early stage which was in the ribs) and Ovum from mother's '*Tharaa'ib*' (Loin-pelvis region of woman). Read together the verses 86: 6-7and 76: 2. Then the 'Embryo' (Sperm + Ovum) stays for forty days in mother's womb, then as '*Alaqa*' -clot a mass of congealed blood for forty days, and as '*Mudhuga*' -clinging mass of flesh for forty days. Then, the soul situated in father's nape is carried to the fetus in mothers womb during forth month. Read together the verses 22: 5; 23: 14; 35: 11; 40: 67 and 75: 37-40. Prophet taught as a reply to the question of Jews that the bones and nerves are formed from the '*Nuthfa*' of father, whereas blood and flesh are formed from the "*Nuthfa*" of mother.

Allah sent down Adam and *Awwa* from Paradise to Earth bodily by the rhythmic balance of wind. This fact is also included in what told in the verses 2: 164 and 45: 5 that there are signs in the change of winds for those who utilize their intelligence. Then, placed the children of Adam in to the nape of men who were saved from the flood at the time of prophet *Nooh*, as mentioned in the verses 17: 3; 19: 58, and 36: 41. Through the verse 76: 1 Allah asks: "Has not a long period passed for men, who was not even mentioned." See the explanation 2: 28 and 98.

Death is the departure of '*Rooh*' -the soul and life- from the body. Sleep is a minor death, where only the soul without the life is departing. Read together the verses 6: 60 and 39: 42.

'And heed Allah about whom you will be asked' also means fear Allah, through whom you demand your mutual rights and 'be heedful of the wombs' means that keep your ties of kinship. The first question in the tomb is about Allah. Therefore, the aim of the life in the forth phase is to find out Allah through the Soul of Qur'an. The Skins, Sights and Hearings, Hands and Legs, Tongues, Wombs and Earth will reflect their records on the Day of Judgment before their Lord by His command as told in the verses 24: 24; 36: 65; 41: 19-24 and 99: 4. The meaning of the saying that 'Allah ever watches over you' is that the believers shall live as He sees them even though they see not Him. They are the vicegerents of Allah. Those who live forgetting Allah are transgressors and the vicegerents of satan. See explanation 2: 255 and 3: 5-7.

2. And give orphans their property, And do not substitute something bad for something good nor swallow up their wealth along with your own wealth. Indeed, it would be a great outrage.

It is told in the verse 4: 6 that you may deal the orphan's property until they reach maturity. When they become matures, release their property to them in the presence of witnesses. And 'do not substitute something bad for something good' means you should not earn up the wealth through usury, gambling, smuggling, hording, black marketing etc. If anyone eats food earned through such forbidden ways then their body should burned in the Hell. The verse 4:10 says, that those who swallow orphans' property without having any right to do so will only suck up fire into their bellies and they will be roasted in a Blazing Fire. Those who hide the verses of Qur'an and purchase It for a miserable price are swallowing fire into their bellies, is told in the verse 2: 174. It is told in the verses 61: 2- 3, Oh you who believe, why say you that which you do not do? It is a great outrage with Allah that you say what you do not do. It is the behavior of hypocrites to say what they do not do. See explanation 2: 44. The verse 5: 100 commands the Prophet to say, evil and good are not equal, even though the abundance of the evil may dazzle you. So heed Allah, you prudent persons, so that you may prosper.

A good word may be compared to a good tree. Whose root is firm and whose branches soar up in to the Sky? It brings forth its fruits at all the season by its Lord's Permission. Allah composes parables for mankind so that they may make others be remembered as told in the verses 14: 24 and 25. The verse 14:26 says, and a bad word may be compared to a bad tree: it will be up rooted from the face of the Earth; it has no foothold. Just like that the believer and the hypocrites. It is told in the verse 35: 10 that the deeds which are stabled by the words of purity shall be raised up to Allah. Read together the verses 7: 40 and 28: 51-53. The word of purity is the Soul of Qur'an. See the explanation 2: 186, 188.

Today, those who construct orphanages as a shelter for orphans which is against the commands of Soul of Qur'an and falsely priding and interpret ting Prophet's teachings by showing the forefinger and the middle finger closer: "those who protect orphans and I, are just like this in the Paradise." They are not heedful about the inmates of orphanages. Most of them collect money in the name of orphans, accept commission and there by fill fire in their bellies neglecting what is said in the verse that you should not mix up their property with yours, and that is indeed a great outrage. They nourish anti-natural deeds and other evil deeds in orphanages. That is because they went far astray from the Soul of Qur'an. See the explanation 2: 220.

3. **And if you fear that you shall not be able to deal justly with the orphans, then marry off such women as may seem good to you in pairs, or three, or four. But if you fear that you shall not be able to deal justly, then one woman, Or someone your right hand controls. That is more suitable to prevent you from committing an injustice.**

There were more than ten wives to each one in the darkness period. By seeing the unjust dealing towards the females in their married life, the parents of female children had buried alive them as told in the verses 16: 58-59. This verse commands to reduce the number of wives into four and if unable to keep justice among them marry only one. Before revelation of Qur'an there was people who fostered the female orphans married them considering their wealth and beauty without giving their dower and dealt unjustly as if no one is there to question them. That custom is stopped by this verse. This verse also commands that if you are unable to keep justice towards female orphans, marry not them and in any way not marry more than four women. Read together the verse 4: 127. This verse also teaches that under which woman the orphans live, marry such woman and there by protect the orphans. Thus the orphans should live with their mothers in the absence of their fathers. It is the responsibility of the society to protect the orphans and the widows. But just opposite to this, people construct orphanages and prevent the love of their mothers by keeping apart from them and thus they become double orphaned. All evils and wickedness come out from such orphanages and cause it to spread in the society.

During the period of Prophet the captive women from the war were assigned to somebody else to protect them by the ruler. About such women are called 'your right hand controls.' It is specified in the verses 23: 5-6, the character of the succeeding believers that they guard their modesty except with their wives and captives whom their right hand controls. There from they are free from blame. It is told in the verses 24: 32-33, marry of any single persons among you, as well as your honorable servants and maids. If they are in poor, Allah will enrich them from His Bounty, Allah is Boundless, Aware. Let those who find not the wherewithal for marriage, keep themselves chased until Allah enriches them out of His Bounty. Should those whom your right hands control desire their freedom, and then draw up such a write for them if you know any good in them. Give them some of Allah's wealth which He has given to you. Do not force your girls whom you control in to prostitution so that you may seek the display of worldly life, if they want to preserve their chastity. Anyone you compels to do so, Allah is Oft Forgiving, Most Merciful even after forcing them to.

Today, there is no war and therefore no women of right hand controled also. There is only *Jihad* -strenuous strive with the Soul of Qur'an- against to those who hide and reject It as told in the verses 9:73 and 25: 52. See the explanation 2: 177 and 185.

Allah says in the verse 14: 1 that Allah sent down this Book in order to lead mankind out of depth of darkness into light by the Permission of their Lord. See the explanation 2: 213. But those who eat the body of Qur'an by merely reading It without giving face value what Prophet has taught, "they dart from the '*Dheen*' as the speed of arrows dart out from the bow." Since their deeds are against the do's and don'ts of Qur'an, what they recited from the Qur'an will argue and witness against them as per Prophet's teaching. This verse commands to mankind that they should not involve in the observances, customs and superstitions which will lead to destruction and darkness, and keep justice between wives, orphans and women in order to avoid practices of dark age again such as burying the female alive. Read together the verses 4: 128-130.

4. And give the women their dower as an obligation, but if they themselves waive some of it for you then consume it at leisure and with good cheer.

It is compulsory for men to give dower in the marriage. It is told in the verse 4:25 that when you marry women, give their rent even though they are the captives under your control. In any way in *Islam* it is forbidden to demand money from women's side directly or indirectly. But it is lawful to accept money from them if they give their own free will. Read together the verse 4: 34. See the explanation 2: 188, 229 and 236.

5. And do not give the feeble minded your property which Allah has granted you for their support; provide for them out of it and cloth them and address them with the words of kind and justice.

It is commanded in the verse that to deal with the wealth of women, children and people who are not heedful, witnessing Allah with responsibility as their own and to provide food and cloth from their wealth. And should behave to them in such a manner that the wealth of them is spending for their own benefit only. This verse also commands that one should not assign the wealth to feebleminded people who have no sense to deal with whether they are orphans or not. Wealth is the base for the existence of a society. Therefore, it is not suitable for the believers who consider the Qur'an as '*Amanath*'-Trust-, to allow any one to spend wastefully the wealth. The verses 17: 26-27 say and give your close relatives his due, as well as the indigents and the way farer, and do not squander your money extravagantly; indeed the squanderers are the brother of satan, and Satan is always been ungrateful towards his Lord. Read together the verse 4: 135.

6. And test orphans as soon as they reach a marriageable age. If you are sure of their maturity, then handover their property to them, and do not use it up extravagantly, over anxious lest they should grow up. Any guardian who is rich should restrain himself; while any guardian who is poor may eat off it for reasonable. Whenever you hand their property over to them, have it witnessed for them and Allah Suffices as a Reckoner.

When the orphans reach the age of marriage, it is necessary to make trial of them in several ways whether they are able to deal with their property with responsibility. If it is convinced that they are irresponsible, immature, spendthrift or foolish ones, guardian has to deal with their property for them as commanded in the previous verse. It is not permissible to spend the property of orphans in extravagantly or in haste manner, thinking that their property have to be handed over to them when they acquire maturity. If the guardian is a rich one, he is not allowed to accept anything from the property of orphans for dealing and shall be satisfied with what Allah has given to him. When the property is handed over to them, it should make witnesses for not having any ambiguity or doubt in future.

'And Allah Suffices as a Reckoner' means to take account that Allah is the Knower of all time, ever watchful, and has already decided every ones deeds and has fastened it to their neck. Read together the verses 17: 13-15. It is He Who has appointed you to deal the property of orphans. See explanation 2: 234, 282 and 3: 199.

7. For men shall have a portion of whatever parents and near relatives leave, while woman should have a portion of whatever parents and near relatives leave; no matter how small or how large it is, a portion is stipulated.

There was no right of inheritance for property to women during the darkness period. Moreover women were considered as a property for inheritance. Read together the verses 4:19 and 22. Therefore, in *Islam* there is a fixed portion for men and women in the property of parents and near relatives left whether it is few or many.

8. And when at the time of division, near relatives or orphans or indigents are present; feed them out of it and speak to them words of kind and justice.

9. And let anyone act cautiously just as themselves would fear to leave helpless offspring behind; so heed Allah and speak in a proper manner.

The dominion of all things in Heaven and Earth is to Allah Alone. He is the One Who decide orphans, indigents and rich from among mankind. Therefore if the orphans, indigents and poor are present at the time inherited property is dividing, behave to them as their own children fearing in mind that, what will be the situation if they had left a helpless offspring behind. And also do not show hatredness or curse on them. This verse also teaches that one should not spend extravagantly his wealth without considering his offspring behind. All the deeds should be done in witnessing Allah and in His satisfaction. See the explanation 2: 28, 266 and 267.

10. Certainly those who unjustly eat up the property of orphans will only suck up fire into their bellies, and they will be roasted in the Blaze.

Prophet taught that to eat up the property of orphans is one of the seven big sins. The character of the virtuous people who succeed is told in the verses 76: 8-11 as: Who feed the poor, the orphan and the captive for the love of Allah, saying in mind: "We feed you for the sake of Allah Alone; we seek from you neither reward nor thanks, and we fear from our Lord's torment of a very distressful Day." So Allah will deliver them from the evil of that Day, and bestow on them freshness and joy. Allah has criticized the deeds of disbelievers through the verses 89:17-20 as rather you are not generous with the orphan nor do you promote feeding the indigents, greedily you lay your hands on the inheritance of the weak, and you love wealth with all your hearts. Prophet himself was an orphan. The verse 93: 6 says: Did He not find you an orphan and give you shelter? Therefore you treat not the orphan with harshness. It is told in the verse 2: 174 that the hypocrites who hide the verses of Qur'an which contains the do's and don'ts such as how one should treat the orphans, indigents and poor, and the '*fujjar*' who sell It for a miserable price; suck up their bellies with fire. See the explanation 2: 159-161 and 4: 2.

11. Allah bequeaths you as concerning your children: a son should have a portion equivalent to that of two daughters. If the daughters left behind are more than two, then two-thirds of what ever he

leaves belong to them; yet if there is only one, then she has half. Both his parents shall each receive a sixth of whatever he may leave, if he had a son. If he had no son, and both his parents inherit from him, then his mother receives a third. If he has brothers, then his mother will have a sixth, after the bequeaths or any debt has been settled. You do not know whether your parents or your children are closer to you in usefulness, so consider as an obligation by Allah, indeed Allah is Aware, Wise.

Read together the verse 34. It is the responsibility of the male, whether he is husband or father, to meet the expenses of family. That is why it is given double portion of property to male than that of a female as inheritance. If the deceased left no children and if the father has other children as his brothers, the mother has a sixth portion since children's responsibility dues on father. Then the children get the inheritance only after the death of father. If the son dies before the death of father, son's children get no inheritance. But one third of the property may be bequeathed considering the conditions of the grand children.

The aim of life is to construct Paradise here with all the Bounties bestowed by Allah. But only the believers who live for Allah as His vicegerents can understand that all these do's and don'ts are justice. That is why it is told in the verse that Allah is All Knowing, All Wise and you know not whether your parents or your children are nearest to you.

In the verse, though bequeath is mentioned before the debts. Prophet has taught that debts should be repaid as early as possible before division of inheritance and if the debts still exist at the time of division, first preference should be given to repay it. Though one can make amendment in the bequest as per the verses 2: 180- 182, no excuse is allowed in the matter of debts. Prophet taught that even the debts of martyrs will not be excused. Debts are dues and trust among the creatures and Allah has nothing to do with it. But *swalath,* fastings and *hajj* are the duties of creatures to the Creator. Therefore Allah may excuse any laxity in the matter of *swalath*, fasting and *hajj* etc. if the creature asks Him. See the explanation 2: 186, 269, and 283.

12. And you will have half of anything your wives leave, provided they have no child. If they should leave a child, then you will have a forth of whatever they may leave, after the bequeaths has

been settled or any outstanding debt; while they will have a forth of anything you leave provided you have left no child. Should you have a child, then they will have an eighth of anything you leave, after settling any bequeaths or debt. If either a man or a woman inherit the 'Kalala' while he still has a brother or a sister, each one of them will have sixth. If there is more than that, then they should be partners in a third after settling any bequeaths or debt without causing any hardship. It is a bequeaths from Allah and Allah is Aware, Forbearing.

Even if the wives have children in their former marriage, the husband shall get only fourth as inheritance. If one has more than one wife, and having children - the eighth, and in the case of not having children -the forth; should divide equally in between the wives. If the deceased has no children or parents to inherit his property is called '*Kalala*'. There is difference in the *Kalala* mentioned in the verse 176 and here. The brother and sister of the *Kalala* mentioned here get equal share since their father is different but mother is same. But the brother who gets double portion that of sister of the *Kalala* mentioned in the verse 176 are from same fathers, just like that of what is mentioned in the previous verse that the brother gets double share that of sister.

'Bequeath or debt without causing any hardship' means, there should not be an occasion to have debt for the deceased person by squandering his wealth thinking that he has no direct inheritors or by making un justified bequeaths fearing his property goes to distant relatives. The unjustified bequeath may be amended considering the verse 2: 182, but the debt in any way should be repaid. To put in brief one should be conscious that all the Bounties are given by Allah, and utilizing it to prepare the Paradise here is the aim of life. See the explanation 3: 136 and 182.

13. These are Allah's limits. And anyone who obeys Allah and His Messenger will be admitted to Paradise beneath which rivers flow, to live there forever; and that will be the supreme achievement.

The verse 24: 62 says: Indeed the believers are those who believe in Allah and His Messenger. Whenever they are on some collective errand with the Messenger, they shouldn't leave until they have asked him the permission to do so. Those who do ask you for such permission are the ones who believe in Allah and His Messenger. Whenever they ask you for permission to some affair of their own, then give anyone of them you may wish, leave to do so, and seek forgiveness from Allah for them, Allah is Forgiving, Merciful. The one and only device for returning the Paradise is to utilize the Soul of Qur'an as the Guidance and Ticket. The verse 76: 29 says that, indeed the ticket for those who wants to select the way to his Lord. The verses 5: 119; 9: 89, 100; 61: 12 and 64: 9 also end as: "That will the supreme achievement". See the explanation 2: 38.

14. And any one who disobeys Allah and His Messenger and transgress His limits will be admitted in to a fire to live there in forever; and he will have humiliating torment.

See the explanation 2: 39, 3: 31 and 32.

15. And should any of your women commit some sexual offense, collect evidence about them from four persons among yourselves if they so witness, then confine the women to their houses until death claims them or Allah grants them some other way out.

16. If two of you should indulge in it, mistreat them both. If they repent and reform, make leave them alone. Indeed Allah is Relenting, Merciful.

If the woman engages in prostitution and four believing persons take witness for that, confine such women to the houses until death. 'Or until Allah ordain for them some other way' means that until the revelation of the verse for the punishment of prostitution in *Surath An-Noor* that beat them with 100 stripes whether woman or man. The saying if two of you should indulge in it in the verse 16 is about a woman and a man and not about two women or two men doing sodomy. More over if the word '*Ya'theehuma*' is used here that will be about two men, but here the word used is '*Ya'thiyaaniha*'- for both men and woman. Prophet taught to kill both those who engaged in doing the anti- natural sodomy.

In *Islam*, all the times the evils are annihilated stage by stage. The first stage of punishment for fornication is mentioned in this verse. The second stage is revealed in *Surath An-Noor* in which it is said that woman and man guilty of fornication flog each of them with a hundred stripes and let a party of believers witness their punishment. The third and final stage which Prophet had put into practice is to kill them by pelting stone, if both of them are married. That was the law in *Thourath* also, and Prophet *Eisa* had put it into practice. The word of

Prophet *Eisa*: 'Those who are free of sin pelt stone' indicate the punishment for fornication after marriage is the law in *Thourath*, and no one was there in that society of *Eisa* without doing sin.

Today, the second and third stage of punishment for fornication cannot be put into practice since there is no one free of sin in the society and there is no party of believers to witness the punishment. Hence, only the first stage may be put in practice. The one and only device to annihilate all evils including fornication and prostitution is to propagate the Soul of Qur'an and there by make the mankind heedful. See the explanation 2: 178 and 179.

17. **Certainly repentance holds with Allah only for those who do evil with ignorance, then repent shortly after; for such Allah turns up on them, And Allah is Aware, Wise.**

18. **And repentance is not for those who perform evil deeds until the death comes one of them says: "Indeed I have just now repented", and nor is it for those who die while they are disbelievers; for such We have kept prepared painful torment.**

'*Thouba*'- repentance- means to return to Allah. That means to return to the position from where he started to deviate. All are born in *Islam* i.e. submitting all to Allah in nature. Therefore repentance means to return that nature, to obedience and to the Creator, and to the way of Paradise. Evils come from mankind since they lost the aim of life in the absence of the Soul of Qur'an. That is because they did not identify themselves. Allah created all children of Adam till the Last Day in the Paradise and when He asked: "Am I not your Lord?" Everyone replied: "Yes our Lord, we do testify". This is because lest you should say on the Day of Judgment: 'Of this we were heedless' or lest you should say: 'our fathers before us made association in the dominion of Allah, and we were their descendants after them'. Will You then punish us because of the deeds of men who followed falsehood as told in the verses 7: 172 and173. And the verse 7: 174 says: Thus do We explain Our verses in order that they may return to that agreement. See the explanation 2: 27 and 28.

There is no repentance for those who involved in evils in whole life without any aim and when death reaches to him, he will say 'now I have repented'. And there is no repentance to '*kuffars*'- hypocrites- who hide the Soul of Qur'an. Prophet taught that Allah will accept repentance until the '*Rooh*' reaches to the throat for depart. It is told in the verse 33: 72 that, the man who undertaken the Trust which is the Soul of Qur'an to keep the Universe in its equilibrium was wrongdoer and foolish. It is told to the people of the Book in the verse 3: 187 that they should make It clear to mankind and not hide It. The scholars are only those who know the Soul of Qur'an. Among the servants such scholars will only fear Allah as told in the verse 35: 28. Therefore the one and only way to annihilate ignorance is to learn and teach the Soul of Qur'an which is the Light, Trust, Criterion, Insight, Guidance etc. The men devil hypocrites are the '*kuffars*' who hide knowingly the verses of Allah and hurrying for the destruction of the universe. Allah will never accept repentance from them. Read together the verses 9: 80 and 63: 6. Qur'an also warns that it is impossible to blame Impartial Allah, satan or parents for earning Hell if they do not utilize the blessings like intelligence, sight, hearing, knowledge of writing and reading which the Creator bestowed for learning the Soul of Qur'an. Read together the verses 54: 17. See the explanation 2: 6- 7; 3: 18; 90 and 91.

19. Oh you who believe, it is not lawful for you to inherit anything from women against their will; do not treat them with harshness, such that they may go away avoiding a part of what you have given them, except where they have been guilty of open lewdness, and treat them politely; even if you dislike them, perhaps you dislike something in which Allah has placed much good.

The widow of the deceased person had considered as an asset of inheritance in the pre-Islamic period. That convention is strictly prohibited through the revelation of this verse and also it is not permissible to prevent forcefully such woman from marriage with other persons if she likes to marry. See explanation 2: 232- 235 and 240. It is also ordained to the believers to avoid the non-Islamic customs like torturing women in order to give back their dower fully or partially. If you hate anything in them there may be some goodness which you do not know. See the explanation 2: 216. Therefore, it is commanded to lead a life which Allah satisfied under the Light of the Qur'an. Prophet taught that *one should not keep a woman who is guilty some open lewdness, if he does so Allah will not accept his prayers*.

Most of the Muslims in all parts of the world lead a life neglecting the do's and don'ts of Qur'an. They accept dowry from women's side, divorce them even for negligible things and not give back their dowry. Thus they made the marriage of women very difficult even more than that of the pre-Islamic pagans. It is against these peoples who do not believe with Allah and Last Day that the read Qur'an, without following its command, will witness and argue. The hypocrites who are arrogant as anchorites know the do's and don'ts of Qur'an but hiding It, they lead the common people to the Hell, thereby will go to Hell even without trial as told in the verse 4: 145. There are no other people in whole world except the Muslims who neglected this Qur'an such a lot. How meaningful is that Allah compared this people to dog as per the verse 7: 176 and to donkey as per the verse 62: 5. They declined to so cheap as if it is not applicable for them what Prophet taught: *The best one among you is one who deals with his woman in a best way*- i.e. under the Soul of Qur'an". See the explanation 3: 97.

Today the other people misunderstand that it is this Qur'an which has declined them so cheap. It is against these people that Prophet will argue with Qur'an on the Day of Judgment, is told in the verse 25: 30. About this people who reject the Soul of Qur'an is mentioned as a boar people in both verses 25: 18 and 48: 12. The verses 14: 28-30 say: Have you not seen those people who have responded to the favors of Allah with ingratitude and driving their people into the House of Perdition? That is Hell! Therein they shall burn, an evil place to live. They set up equals with Allah to mislead people from His Way. Tell them: "Well, you may enjoy yourself for a while, and indeed your final destination is the Fire". See the explanation 3: 112 and 167.

20. If you want to exchange one wife for another, and have given one of them a heap of gold as dowry, do not hold back any of it, would you withhold it through slander and open sin?

In *Islam* the dowry has to be given from men to women's side. Once in *Madeena* when *Umar* on the occasion of Friday speech, he wanted women to reduce their dowry to an extend in order to make easy men their marriage; hearing this a woman from *Quraish* tribe questioned him quoting this verse and asked who gave *Umar* such a right to say so which was not practiced during the time of Prophet or first *Khalifa Aboobacker Siddique*? Immediately *Umar* returned to the speech chamber and repealed what he had said and amended himself. To understand the habit and character of *Umar* see the explanation 3:144.

21. And how can you hold it back when you had enjoyed with each other and they have taken a solemn agreement from you?

The Creator ordains marriage. It is He Who created human from water. Then He has established relationships of both marriage and lineage, is told in the verse 25: 54. Therefore, marriage is a solemn agreement among the creatures testifying the Creator. So breaking such agreement is most hateful thing to Allah, even though He has permitted it. The Qur'an has put forward certain conditions for divorce which should be practiced stage by stage. Read together the verses 2: 226, 232; 4: 34- 35 and 65: 1- 2. If the couples find no compromise after observing all these stages they can divorce. But it is not permissible for men to take back the dower even if it is a large treasure. Only the relationship in the satisfaction of Allah is permitted to creatures. It is the responsibility of men to quench the sexual passion of women. Therefore, sexual intercourse is a great worship in *Islam*- the religion of nature. See the explanation 3: 81- 82 and 4: 1.

22. And do not marry any woman whom your father has already married- except what is past, certainly it is shameful, disgusting and the worst possible way.

In the pre-Islamic period when father died, their widows were married by their children and vice versa or accept them as their asset for inheritance. So Allah is teaching such deeds are shameful, disgusting and abominable. Therefore, such relationship should be broken after the revelation of this verse and the children born to them do not be considered as bastards. Prophet taught that if anyone makes sexual relationship with such women whom the marriage is prohibited should be killed.

23. Forbidden to you for marriage are your mothers, your daughters, your sisters, your aunts on your father's side as well as aunts on your mother's side, and your brother's and sister's daughters, your foster mothers and foster sisters, your mothers in law and your step daughters, who are under your guardianship, born of your wives to whom you have consummated marriage- however if you have not consummated with them, it will not be held against you, and the wives of your sons proceeding from your loins: nor may you bring two sisters together in wedlock except what is past. Certainly Allah is Forgiving, Merciful.

Here mentioned mother includes, mother, stepmother, father's mother and mother's mother. Grand daughters are also included in the list of daughters. In the list of sisters it is included the sisters in the same parents, sisters in the same father, sisters in the same mother or father. Just like that it is also prohibited to marry brothers and sisters of same parents or same father or same mother. It is prohibited for man to marry foster mothers, for women that mother's husband and also prohibited to marry their children since foster mothers who breast-feeder become mother and her husband become father and both their children become sisters and brothers to that fostered child. Prophet taught that whatever prohibits by the blood relation, will cause to prohibit with the breast-feeding. It is prohibited to marry the daughter of a woman to her husband; whether she is staying anywhere it is because Prophet taught that anyone who has seen a woman's vagina, her mother and daughter became prohibited to him. Through another report Prophet taught that Allah will not see any man who has seen vagina of both mother and daughter.

Since it is prohibited to marry the blood related son's wives, we can understand that there is no prohibition for marrying the widows of adopted sons or their divorced women. But it was considered as prohibited to marry the widows of adopted sons or the divorced women by the adopted son, and had considered permitted the widows of their own sons in the pre-Islamic period.

To annihilate this disgusting custom Allah first made marriage of Prophet's adopted son *Zaid* with *Zainaba*-Prophets aunt's daughter. Then Allah commanded *Zaid* to divorce and Prophet to marry her by giving dowry. Read together the verses 33: 4 and 5 which say that Allah has not put two hearts in a person's body: nor does He regard your wives whom you divorce through '*Dhihar*'- divorcing a wife by saying from now onwards you are as my mother, depriving her conjugal rights yet keeping her like a slave nor letting her marry anyone else- as your mothers: nor does He regard your adopted sons as your sons. These are mere words which you utter with your mouths; but Allah declares the Truth and guides you to the Straight path. Name your adopted sons with their fathers; that are more just in the sight of Allah, and if you don't know who their fathers are, then call them as your brothers in faith and your friends. There is no blame on you for an unintentional mistake, but you will be held responsible for what you do with the intention of your minds; Allah is Forgiving, Merciful. The verses 33: 36- 40 say: It is not suitable for a believing man or a believing woman to have an option in their affairs when a matter has been decided by Allah and His messenger; and whoever disobeys Allah and His messenger, he is indeed strayed into a clear wrong path. Oh Prophet, remember when you said to the one *Zaid*- Prophet's adopted son whom Allah as well as you had favored: "Keep your wife in wedlock and fear Allah". You sought to hide in your heart what Allah intended to reveal; you were afraid of the people whereas it would have been more appropriate to fear Allah. So, when *Zaid* divorced his wife, We gave her to you in marriage, so that there remains no restriction for the believers to wed the wives of their adopted sons if they divorced them. And Allah's Command had to be carried out. There can be no blame attached to the Prophet for doing what is sanctioned for him by Allah. Such has been the way of Allah with those who have gone before; and the decrees of Allah are preordained. Those who are charged with the mission of conveying the Message of Allah are to fear Him, they are supposed to fear none except Allah; for Allah is sufficient to settle their account. Muhammad is not the father of any of your men. He is the Messenger of Allah and the Seal of the Prophets. Allah has the knowledge of all things.

Grandson's wives are like the son's wives and it is prohibited for father's father or mother's father to marry them. As it is prohibited to maintain two sisters in wedlock at the same time, it is also prohibited to maintain in wedlock her mother's sister, father's sister, sister's daughter, brother's daughter at the same time, as taught by Prophet. In brief, suppose if it is a man among the two women, and marriage between them is prohibited, just like that to maintain in wedlock such two women at the same time is also prohibited.

24. And also prohibited any married woman except the ones under your control. Such is Allah's legislation prescribed to you and anything beyond, that is lawful for you, provided you court them by means of your wealth to bring them under your wedlock, rather than taking them on as mistresses and then if you have their by sought enjoyment with them, give them their marriage portions as is stipulated. And there is no blame up on you, if you agree mutually to vary it, after the dowry is stipulated, Indeed Allah is Aware, Wise.

The believers can marry the women who came as captives under their custody by giving their dowry. If a woman comes to the believers deserting her disbelieving husband and if convinced she is a real believer, and then sent her not back, it is not lawful to marry her until giving back the dowry of her former husband. And by giving her dowry, can marry her. If the woman deserts you to disbelievers, you have your turn to take back the dowry from them and if the women from disbelievers come to the believers give their dowry back, and if they do not give the same to you, you should not give the same to them as told in the verses 60: 10- 11. That means there is no compulsion in religion. And both believing men and women have the right to select the relationship in the satisfaction of Allah, but it should not be by neglecting the right of others.

'*Muth'a*' marriage was allowed in the first stage of *Islam*. It was a sort of marriage when anybody had to stay in a distant place for a long period; he was allowed to marry a woman temporarily from that place. The sexual intercourse was only allowed by giving the due dowry to women and if the woman gives some relaxation in the fixed dowry without any compulsion, there is no blame to accept it. But today the temporary marriage is not allowed. On the day of Meccan victory Prophet taught: 'Oh mankind it was permitted you the *Muth'a* marriage' but now indeed Allah has prohibited this marriage till the Last Day. If you have any such women desert them and take not back anything that you have given to them. But even today some Muslims in different parts of the world are in wedlock with more than four wives neglecting this saying of prophet. These are some examples of that they present Islamic culture in a deformed state. They are the arrogant rebellious. Since today there is convenience to carry the wives even to distant place and stay there, temporary marriage has little importance.

25. And any of you who cannot afford to marry noble believing matrons should then seek one of your believing maids under your control. And Allah is quite Aware as to what your faith consists of, each one of you has ties to others, so marry them off with their families consent and give them their rent decently as to keep matrons rather than taking them on as mistresses, nor having secret affairs with them as girl friend. Once they are so married off and should they then commit some sexual offence, they should have half the punishment that the ordinary matrons would receive. That goes for any of you who worry lest he may not control his sexual impulses; however it is better for you to be patient yourselves. And Allah is Forgiving, Merciful.

And any of you who cannot afford to marry matrons-chaste believing women; they may wed believing maids-captive women under their control with leave of their family members especially for those who fear illegal relationship without having self restrained. They may wed such women in the intention to make the captive women chaste and not having illegal sons in the society.

If such women commit indecency after they are taken into wedlock, their punishment is half of that for believing noble women. This is because the believing noble women get the protection from both her noble family and husband, whereas the slave women get protection only from their husband. The punishment for a deliberate sin should not be given to a sin which one does under the compulsion of circumstances and habit. Through the verse 33: 30 Allah says by calling the wives of Prophet that if any of you commit some flagrant act of misconduct, the punishment would be double to her. Read together the verses 33: 33 and 34. One should not be misunderstood from this verse that there won't be pelting stone to death for fornication of married men and women. The unmarried women and men guilty of fornication, their punishment is flogging each of them with a hundred stripes as per the verse 24: 2. But as per this verse if the women is a slave, her punishment is 50 stripes. Prophet taught that the punishment for the fornication of married women and men is to kill them by pelting stone. This is because they have understood the taste in sexual intercourse and then if they break the limits, the consequence in the society will be uncontrollable.

Today there are no slaves, but all are slaves. Therefore marriages shall be conducted between men and women who learn and follow the Soul of Qur'an. Prophet taught that it is the duty of parent to teach the Soul of Qur'an to their children before they attain the age of 15. If they do not do so, a scene in Hell is warned in the verse 7: 38 as the children will say about the parents: "Our Lord! These have led us astray; therefore, give them double punishment from the Fire." He will answer: "each shall have double, even though you do not realize it". Read together the verses 33: 35 and 49: 13. See the explanation 2: 221; 4: 3 and 15.

26. Allah wants to explain things to you all and to guide you in the customs of those who have preceded you and he turns to you, Allah is Aware, Wise.

There is only one way to reach the Paradise from Prophet Adam to the last Day. That system of life is called *Islam.* See the explanation 3:19. Today, it is only the Soul of Qur'an which is the Ticket to the one who wants to reach his Lord, is told in the verse 76: 29. By reading the Soul of Qur'an which is in their heart's language, one should identify his sins and seek forgiveness to Allah, then follow the Soul of Qur'an in his remaining life time can return to Paradise; and those who hide and reject the Soul of Qur'an after receiving It, their returning will be to the Hell. See the explanation 2: 38-39; 3:136 and185.

27. And Allah wants to turn to you; while those who follow their own passions want you drift far away from the Right path.

28. Allah wants to lighten things for you, since man was created weak!

The verse 90: 4 says, verily We have created man under stress. The verse 30:54 says Allah is the One Who created you out of weakness; then He has granted strength following your weakness; later on He has granted weakness and gray hairs in place of strength He creates whatever He wishes and He is the Aware, Capable. Allah says in the verses 35: 15-16 by calling mankind that you are all poor and always in need of Allah. It is Allah who is the One free of all wants, worthy of all praise. If He so pleased, He could blot you out and bring a new creation. But only the believers have this conscious and they live always with the remembrance of Allah; and those who forgot Allah and themselves are transgressors and they will lead you to astray. See the explanation 2: 99. Allah says in the verse 9: 115 it is not suitable for Allah to mislead a people after He has guided them until He teaches them what the do's and don'ts that they should keep. Certainly Allah has knowledge of all things. Since the Creator knows very well about His creatures, no burden is levied greater than they can bear. See the explanation 2: 286. It is told in the verse 54:17 that indeed We made the Soul of Qur'an very easy to understand and in the verse 17: 9 it is told that certainly this Qur'an does guide to that which is most right. And it is told in the verse 18:1 that praise be to Allah who has sent down to His servant the Qur'an without any crookedness. Read together the verse 22: 78. While the Qur'an which is the word of Allah, call the mankind to Allah and Paradise, the hypocrites and the strayed people who observe superstitions, conventions and their own lusts lead mankind to satan's house - the Hell.

The verses 95: 4-6 say verily We have created men with the finest stature, then reduced him to the dregs on the bottom, except for those who believe and perform honorable deeds – for them have never ending reward. The verses 92: 5-10 say for any one who gives generously and heed and made truthful with the best i.e. Qur'an, We shall facilitate an easy way for him. And anyone who acts miserly and consider himself independent of Allah and rejects with the best, We shall facilitate for him the hard way. See the explanation 1: 6; 2: 255- 257; 3: 101 and 102.

29. Oh you who believe, eat not up your wealth among yourselves illegal except some business on mutual consent among you and you do not kill yourselves, certainly Allah has been Merciful with you.

'Business by mutual consent' means the transaction should be with very frank and without any deception. It is not permissible adulteration, hoarding, black-market in trade. It is also not permissible to give duplicate things and demand the price of original. 'And do not kill yourselves', not only means to commit suicide but if you commit deception and be lying in trade, the person whom you deceived will not come again to you and there by may cause your trade become diminishing. And more over it will lead to hatredness and even to killing.

The '*Rooh*' is from Allah, the body is the vehicle for traveling the '*Rooh*'. The verses 51:55-56 say I have not created *Jinns* and men except then to serve Me; I do not want any sustenance from them nor do I need them to feed Me. The verse 15: 99 says serve your Lord until confirmation comes to you. The aim of living on Earth is to prepare the Paradise here. Killing is the separation of '*Rooh*' from the body. Therefore to commit suicide is just like declaring that I am not ready to live as your servant and representative. That is a great arrogance and abomination. See the explanation 4: 93. Those who consider Allah as Impartial will never kill any soul whom Allah has forbidden to kill except with the Truth as told in the verse 25: 68. Since the owner of the body is Allah, any activity which leads to killing of body like smoking, drinking, using other intoxicating drugs etc. are not allowed. To eat from the profit of these kinds of trade is also prohibited. The only way to lead a life with peace and tranquility is to follow the do's and don'ts of the Soul of Qur'an which is the food, cloth and sight of the human soul. See explanation 2: 188 and 3: 138.

30. And if any does that in enmity and wrongfully, We shall roast him in a Fire and that will be easy for Allah.

If anyone possessed the property of others by way of deception and exploitation deliberately, their body will be burnt in the Hellfire. The verses 9: 34-35 say: Oh you who believe! Indeed most of your scholars and priest misappropriate the wealth of people and hinder them from the way of Allah. To those who hoard gold and silver and do not spend it in the way of Allah, proclaim a painful punishment. The Day will surely come when their treasure will be heated up in the fire of Hell, and their foreheads, sides and backs branded with it. They will be told: "This is the treasure which you hoarded. Now taste what you were hoarding!" If anyone eats the forbidden things, their prayer shall not be accepted. The purification of soul is possible only by the Soul of Qur'an. One should utilize the Soul of Qur'an, which is the Balance to identify whether the food is lawful or not. Otherwise, it will cause for destruction of his body. For more explanation about 'Balance' see the verses 42: 17 and 57: 25. See the explanation 2: 168- 169, 186; 3: 97 and 187

31. If you will avoid the great sins which you are forbidden to commit, We will cancel out your evil deeds for you, and enter you through a noble entrance.

The seven most heinous sins are: associating others with Allah, engaging in the activities of sorcery, illegally killing a soul which Allah made sacred, eating interest, eating the property of orphans, retreat from the warfront, make scandals about innocent chaste believing women. Prophet taught to avoid those sins. It is told in the verses 25: 68- 70 that the servants who consider Allah as the Impartial, invoke not with Allah any other deities, not kill any Soul whom Allah has forbidden except for just cause, and nor commit fornication. After saying these three most heinous sins, it is said: Anyone who does so will incur a penalty. Punishment will be doubled for him on the Day of Judgment and he will remain disgraced forever in it except for someone who repents and believes, and acts in an honorable manner Allah will replace their evil deeds with fine ones, Since Allah is Forgiving, Merciful

If anyone does such most heinous sins, has to repent. The ransoms for these sins are to annihilate the circumstances for doing such sins from the people. For this, utilize the Soul of Qur'an as the Balance, identify errors as well as sins and confess before Allah. Then utilize his wealth and health to propagate the Soul of Qur'an among entire mankind. If there is a chance to commit indecency for not having the Soul of Qur'an, after receiving It they will keep away from the most heinous sins. Thus his sins will be changed into goodness, since others after having understood the Soul of Qur'an keep away from sins. The aim of life of men deputed on Earth is to construct Paradise Here by utilizing all blessings under the Light, the Soul of Qur'an and thus can be taken the constructed Paradise as inheritance in the Hereafter.

Everything in Heaven and Earth belongs to Allah alone. If any does evils will requite according to their deeds, but those who do goodness, he will be rewarded with more goodness. Such heedful people will never do most heinous sins and indecency, is told in the verses 53: 31 and 32. It is told in the verse 8: 29 that, Oh you who believe, if you keep Allah in your heart He will grant to you the Touchstone to identify Truth and false and wipe out your sins and forgive you. For Allah is the Lord of unbounded grace. Allah says in the verses 65: 2-3 that, if any who keeps Allah in their heart, will be given a way out and provides for him sustenance that he never could expect. And if anyone puts his trust in Allah, sufficient is Allah for him. Certainly Allah will accomplish His purpose (put into practice the desires of believers). Certainly for all things Allah has appointed order and due proportion. See the explanation 2: 38 and 3: 133- 136.

32. And do not envy the way that Allah has made some of you excel over others: men should have a portion of whatever they have earned, while women should have a portion of whatever they have earned. And you ask to Allah from His Bounties and indeed Allah is Aware of everything!

Here it is taught that one should not be envy to others for the blessing that Allah has bestowed upon them. But one can ask Allah of His Bounties. Prophet taught to pray like this: *"Oh Allah, no one can prevent what You have given, no one can give what You have prevented, no one can block what You have decreed and no one can decree what You have blocked. Autocracy of any autocrat is nothing before You"*. No man should have desire that if he were a woman, he would have sat in the house without participating in the war and no woman should desire that if she was a man she would have received inheritance doubled or she would have participated in war and become a martyr and there by get Paradise or free from menstruation. No one has the right to be born as man or woman, but the Creator- the Lord- decides all these. This verse also teaches that each individual is constructing either Paradise or Hell here, whether he is man or woman. The verse 59: 18 says: Oh you who believe! Heed Allah and let every soul see what it is sent ahead for tomorrow- Hereafter. Heed Allah; surely Allah is acquainted of all your deeds. As per the verse man shall not wear the cloth of woman and vice versa as disguising. Jealousy is permissible in the matter of learning and teaching of the Soul of Qur'an as taught by Prophet. The wealth, time and all other blessings spent for this purpose shall be recorded as a capital for tomorrow. See the explanation 2: 94- 95; 3: 73 and 74.

33. And for everyone We have placed executors for parents and close relatives may leave and give their share to those whom you have made contract; Certainly Allah is Witness for every things.

Inheritance is the share, which Allah has ordained among those who have blood relations. The verse 33: 6 says: Prophet is closer to the believers than their own selves and his wives are as their mothers. Blood relatives have a greater claim on one another in Allah's Book than the other believers and the emigrated refugees, except that you should act in a proper manner towards your friends that has been underlined in the Book. But Prophet taught that one can make bequeath one third of his total property for his adopted sons, grandsons, bosom friends etc. All of these should be done with equitable terms and conditions witnessing Allah. See the explanation 2: 180 and 3: 110-112.

34. Men are the protectors and maintainers of women, because Allah has given some persons advantages over others and because they should spend their wealth on them. Then the honorable women are devoutly obedient and guarding them unseeingly just as Allah has guarded it. As to those women on whose part you fear disloyalty and ill conduct admonish them and leave them alone in their beds and even beat them. If they obey you, do not seek any way against them. Certainly Allah is most Sublime, Great.

The physical structure of men is different from that of women. Men can travel lonely wherever and whenever they desire. But it is unsafe for women to travel lonely in the night as well as to distant place. Men spend their wealth for women. Prophet taught that if the youths have not the means to dowry, food and clothing for women, they should fast and live with self-restrained. Demanding dowry and ornaments from women is anti Islamic and that will lead the burial of female child alive as in the darkness age as mentioned in the verses 16: 57- 59. 'Then the honorable women are devoutly obedient and guarding themselves unseeingly just as Allah has guarded it' means to guard their chastity and the wealth of their husband, Or it means they will not go out without the permission of their husband or not contact with others whom their husband does not like or spend not in charity from his wealth without his permission.

There are three stages to be practiced before divorcing a disobedient woman. (1). Advise her with the Soul of Qur'an. See explanation 3: 138. (2).

Spend forty days in the same bed having no sexual intercourse. (3). Beat her by praying with hearts to Allah to convert her behavior to good. See explanation 2: 228 and 4: 25.

35. And if you fear a split between a man and his wives, appoint an arbiter from his family and an arbiter from her family. If both want to be reconciled, Allah will create a way of reconciliation between them. Certainly Allah has full knowledge, acquainted with all things.

'If both of them intend reconciliation' means either the couple or the arbiters. 'Allah, the Knower of all times' implies that both of them should sincerely pray to Allah and act with the belief that Allah has already recorded all things happening in the Book. See the explanation 2: 234, 255 and 3: 58

36. And you serve for Allah alone and do not associate anything with Him. And behave with parents in the best and with near relatives, orphans, the needy, the neighbor who is related to you as well as the neighbor who is a stranger, and your companion by your side, and the way-farer and anyone else under your control. Certainly Allah love not the arrogant, the boastful.

37. Nor those who are niggardly, enjoin with niggardliness upon mankind, and hide anything that Allah has given them out of His Bounty. And We have reserved such disbelievers a humiliating torment

The characters of hypocrites explained in the verses 9: 67- 68. To serve for Allah means to recognize the character of Allah from the Qur'an and live as His vicegerent. This verse command to behave in the best way towards parents, relatives, neighbors both related and strangers, the companions in your side, wayfarers etc. in the satisfaction of Allah i.e. under the Light-the Soul of Qur'an. One should angry with the anger of Allah, to give and give not with the satisfaction of Allah. 'And to anyone else under your control' means one should behave towards his subordinates, servants, domestic animals and other beings in the conscious that Allah will question about all these on the Day of Judgment.

Those who show niggardliness fearing to give the blessing to others which Allah has bestowed upon them and induce others niggardliness are ungrateful disbelievers and they are the one who lost the aim of life. Allah has kept prepared for them a heinous torment. Therefore, each one should pray by mind like this: 'Oh my Lord, make not lost me by being an ungrateful disbeliever'. Each one should construct Paradise Here by utilizing the blessings, which Allah has bestowed with the light- the Soul of Qur'an. Prophet taught that we should show the bounties of Allah bestowed in our food, cloth, vehicle, home etc. See the explanation 2: 264, 268; 3: 136 and 180- 182.

38. And for those who spend their wealth to be seen by other people and yet neither believe with Allah nor the last Day. Anyone who has satan an intimate, then he has an evil soul mate!

It is told in the verse 43: 36 that those who keep apart from the remembrance of Most Gracious i.e. from the Soul of Qur'an, We appoint for him a satan, to be an intimate soul mate to him. Such wicked companions hinder them from the Path of Allah, but they think that they are being guided aright as told in the verse 43: 37. Thus when they come to Us, they will say, "Alas! If the distance between the two Easts only lay between you and me! What an evil soul mate you are! is told in the verse 43: 38. "That Day, it will never benefit you today to have any partners in torment since you have already gone wrong, certainly they shall be partners in punishment", is told in the verse 43: 39. Read together the verses 50: 27- 29; 59: 17-19. See the explanation 2: 152.

No one can become a believer unless he makes his soul mate, Jinn comrade as a believer with the Soul of Qur'an. Prophet taught that those who spend wealth to be seen of others, they are commanded to ask their reward from them. If anybody spend their wealth for convincing others except Allah, that will become to satan. If anybody invokes other than Allah, they call upon but satan who is persistent rebel, cursed and making skeptic as told in the verse 4: 117. Through the verses 76: 5- 21 after explaining the bliss of Paradise for the virtuous people, as per the verse 22 say 'this is your reward, for your effort has been appreciated. See the explanation 2: 97, 168- 169 and 3: 90- 92.

39. And what does it matter for them if they have to believe in Allah and in the last Day and they spend out of what Allah has supplied them with. For Allah has full knowledge of them.

The believers who understand the aim of life construct Paradise Here by utilizing all the blessings, which they have not brought when they took birth on Earth and carry not when they depart from the Earth. Thus, they return to the constructed Paradise by their death, in a state that the Creator has satisfied with them as well as them with Him. They will have the conscious that each and every soul is constructing Paradise or Hell individually. Read together the verses 6: 94 and 32: 15- 17. See the explanation 2: 271; 3: 136 and 182.

40. Allah does not harm anything so much as an atom's weight: If a good deed exists multiplies it and adds a splendid reward from Himself besides.

Each soul is being given its evil and goodness. Then whoever work for the sake of Allah will increase the goodness, otherwise any deeds should support of a verse from the Qur'an as proof, will only become goodness. For more explanation about the Proof see the explanation 2: 111. All the deeds which do not have the support of any verses from the Qur'an become in vain, and on the Day of Judgment, they will have no weight in their Balance, is told in the verses 18: 103- 105 since they did not utilize the Soul of Qur'an as the Balance in worldly life. The verse 6: 160 says: anyone who comes with a fine deed will have ten more like it, while anyone who comes with an evil deed will only be rewarded with its like; they will not be treated unjustly. Prophet taught that *if any one desires to do a good deed shall have goodness in his credit, and then if he does a good shall have ten times as much to his credit. But any one desire to do an evil deed that will not be recorded as an evil in his credit, but if he does that evil, he shall only be recompensed according to that evil.* This verse also emphasis that the Impartial Allah will never make anyone to Paradise or to Hell lest they themselves have to decide their destiny. See the explanation 2: 186, 245, and 261.

41. How would it be if We were to bring a witness from every community, and bring you as a witness against these people?

The verse 16:89 says on the Day We shall raise up witness from every community against them from among themselves, and We shall even bring you as a witness against these people We have sent the book down to you to explain everything, a Guidance, a Mercy and as a good news for Muslims. The witness for each people is the Prophet deputed to them. Prophet Muhammad will witness against the people of his time as well as the Muslims all times as specified in the verses 25: 18 and 30. The verse 34: 28 says, We have not sent you except to the entire mankind, to give them good news and forewarn them, but most men do not knowing. The verse 21:107 says We have not sent you except as a blessing for all the worlds. But later to the prophet's time, the believers who witness prophet's life to the people will be the witnesses. The verse 39: 69 says the Earth will be shining with the light of her Lord, the Book of record will be laid open, the Prophets and other witnesses will be brought in, and the Judgment with the Truth shall be done among them: and they will not be wronged. Both in the verses 2: 143 and 22: 78 Allah says that the Prophet has deputed in order to witness for you, and you be witnesses for mankind. The life of Prophet may get from Qur'an as mentioned in the verses 2:146 and 6:20. The verse 4:115 says anyone who opposes the Messenger once Guidance has been explained to him and follows a path other than that of the believers, We shall leave him in the path he has chosen and cast him into Hell; which is an evil refuge. The verse 47:32 says the ones who disbelieve and obstruct Allah's way, and oppose the Messenger even after has been explained to them, will never injure Allah in any way while He will make their deeds in vain.

From the verses 37: 81, 111, 122 and 132 we can understand that all Prophets were believers. As per the verses 17:13 and 14 each man bear his fate in his nape and on the Day of Judgment We will put forward it as an open book, illuminated and will say you read your book and today it is enough you to reckon your account. On that Day each one's hands and legs will pronounce as per the verse 36: 65, skins, hearing and sight will stand witness as per the verses 41:19-24. Read together the verse 17:36. Also the Earth will reflect her record as per the verses 99: 4 and 5. Only the believer will make the Soul of Qur'an as witness and argue in favor, by learning and conveying It to others. See the explanation 3: 110-115.

42. On that Day those who have disbelieved and disobey the Messenger would like to have the Earth leveled of with them on it! And Allah will not hide a single word of them.

It is told in the verse 78: 40 that on the Day of Judgment when one will see what ever his own hands have sent on ahead and the disbeliever will say: woe to me if I were only dust. It is told in the verses 25: 27- 29 that the wrongdoer who neglected the Soul of Qur'an after getting It will bite at his hands and will say, 'Oh, would that I had taken the path of the Messenger. Ha! Woe to me would that I had never taken such a one for a friend; he did prevent me from the Soul of Qur'an after It had come to me. Ha, the satan was but a traitor to man. Then On that Day, he will agree himself that satan prevented men from the Soul of Qur'an and not from the body or life-meaning of Qur'an. See the explanation 2: 6-7. On that Day, as per the verse 25:30 the messenger will say upholding the Qur'an, "Oh my Lord, truly my people led a life neglecting this Qur'an that is why they fell in to such pathetic condition." Read together the verses 7: 176; 25:17 and 18. See the explanation 2: 66, 166-167 and 3: 30.

43. Oh you who believe, do not attempt for swalath in a state of intoxication, until you know what you are saying; nor after a seminal emission – except when you are passing by - until you take a full bath, if you are ill or on a journey or one of you has come from the toilet or has had sexual contact with women, and you do not find water then take some wholesome soil and wipe your faces and your hands with it. Certainly, Allah is Pardoning, Forgiving.

Read together the verse 5:6. This is the verse, which is revealed as a second stage for annihilating liquor. Allah warns through this verse that one should not approach '*swalath*' in a state of intoxication. And more over, one should not approach '*swalath*' when he overcomes by sleepiness or having excretory discharges, having severe hunger and thirst. Then approach '*swalath*' only after solving such conditions. Prophet taught that one should not recite Qur'an either in '*swalath*' or in other situation without knowing what he is saying i.e. when one's heart not participating in reading. Satan diverts the concentration of even those who know Its contents. Satan prevents one not from the text or meaning of Qur'an but from the Soul of Qur'an as explained the verses such as 5: 90- 91; 7: 175; 25: 29; 43: 36; 58: 19. Those who recite Qur'an without knowing Its contents, the recited Qur'an should argue and witness against them. Prophet taught *Qur'an is a testimony either in favor of you or against.* Prophet taught that one who eats the body of Qur'an is the '*fajir*' and he is the most worst among the mankind. Those who do not follow the Qur'an after knowing Its Messages and prevent others from It are the hypocrites. See the explanation 2: 24, 44 and 99.

Prophet taught: *a people will come in the last days whose swalath, fasting and other deeds will make little importance to that of swalath, fasting and other observances of the prophet's companions. They recite Qur'an but it will not come down under their throat to their hearts and there by they will be darted out from the 'Dheen' as the arrows dart from bow.* See the explanation 3: 10. Among the three groups who recite Qur'an, only the believers will get reward. It is only to these believers are ordained to perform *swalath, fasting, zakath, hajj* etc. Read together the verses 4: 103 and 9: 53- 55. The other two groups – '*fujjar*' and hypocrites belong to the '*mujrims*'. '*Mujrims*' are mentioned About 50 places in Qur'an. To establish regular *swalath* is for maintaining the Soul of Qur'an as told in the verse 20:14. It is understood from the verses 7: 170; 29: 45 and 35: 29. The first priority is given to recite and convey the Soul of Qur'an than that of any other deeds even *swalath*. Prophet taught that *to learn the contents of one verse is more virtue than that of performing 1000 rak'ath swalath and to teach one verse is more virtue than that of 100 rak'ath swalath.* No prayer or deed will be accepted without the Soul of Qur'an as explained in the verse 2: 186.

The Arabic word '*janabath*' means to keep apart or strangeness etc. which means to move away from the cleanliness of the body either by sexual intercourse or by ejaculation of semen. Prophet taught that those who having *janabath*, the Angels will not scribe until he clean and take ablution. But the computer, which is installed around the neck as mentioned in the verses 17: 13; 18: 49; 45: 28 and 29 will record all states. This verse teaches that those who have '*janabath*' should not stay in the mosque but can be passed by through. Those who are ill or on a journey, or in sexual contact with woman, find no water, they can clean themselves by rubbing with clean dry soil which is called '*thayammam*'. In the absence of water, dry sand or soil can be used for cleaning excretory discharges. Even if water is available and there prevails very cold condition one can adopt the method of cleaning by '*thayammam*'. To put it brief whatever the condition, the believers have to perform *swalath*. They are the wise men who remember Allah always in their moving, sitting and laying. See the explanation 2: 238- 239 and 3: 191.

44. Have you not watched those who were given a portion of the Book? They buy up astray and want you to astray from your Right path.

If this verse is revealed about the Jews and Christians at the time of Prophet, now it is about the different organizations among Muslims, since today the Book is only Qur'an. They neglect what Allah commanded in the verse 3: 103 that to holdfast the Soul of Qur'an – the rope of Allah, and become one party -Allah's party as told in the verses 5: 56 and 58: 22. They become '*mushriks*' by splitting different parties and each party rejoicing with what they have as told in the verses 2: 176; 6: 159; 23: 51-53; 30: 31 and 32. Thus they become the satan's party as mentioned in the verse 59:19. When the believers recite the verse 1: 7, "not the path upon whom Your wrath happened, "they have to pray with their heart not to include among the hypocritical leaders; when they recite, "and not on those who gone astray", they have to pray not include among the followers of different organizations of Muslims. See the explanation 2: 86, 109; 3: 90 and 91.

45. And Allah is quite Aware as to who your enemies are; Allah suffices as a Patron and Allah suffices as a Helper.

46. Of the Jews lift words out of their context and saying: "we have heard and disobeyed"; and you hear you without hearing and 'ra'ena', twisting their tongues around and stabbing at religion. If only they had said, 'we have heard and obeyed' hear and watch over us, it would be better for them and more straight forward; But Allah has cursed them for their disbelief, then no one will believe among them except a few.

This sort of hypocritical policy is clearly shown in the verses 5: 13, 41 and 42. See the explanation 2:93. 'Lift words out of their context' means to twist or change the structure of the words, to shuffle the words itself, to change the meaning by self interpretation, to quote a part of verse and hide the other part of verse in order not to understand the real meaning, to misinterpret and exaggerate what Prophet said, to make slander and prevent men from the real intention of the verses of Qur'an. These were the activities of Jews during the period of Prophet, who gone astray from *Islam*. See the explanation 3:72.

Today, the hypocrites who are the leaders of different organizations among the Muslims show this sort of approach towards Allah's Book and to believers. See the explanation 2:79 and 3: 78. Allah has cursed and killed them according to the verses 9:68 and 63:4 commanded to the group of believers to kill them as per the verses 4: 91, 9:123 and 33: 61. Allah ordained to the Prophet and believer not to seek forgiveness for them as per the verses 9: 80, 84; 63:6; and do 'jihad' against them with the Soul of Qur'an as per the verses 9:73 and 25:52. The world will end when even a single believer exists not and all the people become hypocritical transgressors. The verse 45: 35 ends with a question that 'any one will be wiped out except the people of transgressors?!' Really, these sorts of hypocrites are the enemies of *Islam* than that of Jews. One can understand by the Light of Qur'an that it is these hypocrites who scoff at the believers for teaching the Soul of Qur'an and this human satan plot against the class where the Soul of Qur'an is teaching and their number of such hypocrites are increasing day by day. That is why Prophet taught to the believers of today to holdfast the Soul of Qur'an by their molar teeth. See the explanation 2: 159- 161, 3: 195 and 196.

47. Oh you who have received the Book, believe in what We have sent down to you as a confirmation of what you already have, lest We dazzle your faces and set them on back wards or curse them just as We cursed the transgressors of the Sabbath. And Allah's command must be fulfilled.

Here it is addressed the Jews and the Christians who were given the Book before. See the explanation 2: 65-66. Those who caught fish transgressing the "*Sabbath*", Allah changed their bodily shape to monkeys and swine keeping their own faces in order to distinguish. Read together the verse 5: 60. Here it is warned the Jews in *Madeena*, that if they rebel, Allah will make their face ugly, eyes on the front of the face will be placed in the back, take away the faculties of hearing and sight. But today, this verse is warning the hypocrites among the Muslims who follow the ways of the Jews. It is only because of the prophet's prayer that their face shall not be changed to ugliness and their bodily shape into monkeys, dogs and swine. On the Day of Judgment, without trial, they will be entered in the Hell in such forms. Thus snakes and scorpions in the Hell will be from the men and *Jinns*. The snake and scorpion in this world will be turn to dust after the trial is over. See the explanation 4: 42. As per the verse 63: 4 Allah has killed this hypocrites, but they are given facilities and convenience in this material world because of Allah's Impartial character. The verses 43: 33- 35 say if it were not that mankind has been a single community of disbelievers, We would have given those who disbelieve the Impartial, such houses whose roofs, staircase to the upstairs all made with silver, and also the doors of their houses and couches to recline on and similar luxuries and all that means nothing but merely comforts of this worldly life, while Hereafter with your Lord is for the heedful. More over, if Allah changes the bodily shape of any hypocrites in this world, then the world will never end. Read together the verses 7: 175-176, 33: 72 and 73. See the explanation 2: 166- 167; 3: 30 and 138.

48. Allah does not forgive anyone for associating something with Him, while He does forgive whom ever He wishes to for anything besides that. Then anyone who associates anything with Allah has then invented such an awful sin.

The verse 4: 116 is also with the same Message. The verse 12: 103 says yet most men will not become believers, no matter how eager you may be, and in the verse 106 it is told that most of them do not believe in Allah unless they associate others with Him. The '*shirk*' – associating others in the dominion of Allah- comes from men since they understand not Allah as revealed by the 6236 verses of Qur'an. Those who do evil in ignorance and then repent, Allah forgive those sins as explained in the verses 4: 17 and18. The verse 31: 13 says, thus '*Luqman*' told his son as he was advising him: my dear son, do not associate anything with Allah, indeed the association is such a serious wrong. It is told in the verse 22: 31 that anyone associates partners to Allah, he is as if he had fallen from the sky and been snatched up by the birds or the wind had swooped and thrown him into a far distant place. That means such men will not reach to the destination. It is told in the verse 16: 100 that satan's authority is over those only who take him as patron and join partners with Allah. To join partners with Allah means to call upon His creatures seeking help when slipping, about fall and in other difficult situations. And those who are calling upon other than Allah, they call upon satan told in the verse 4: 117 and maintain middle men of recommendation or intercession in order to bring nearness to Allah without the conscious that it is Allah Who created him from nothingness and has full knowledge about him. The verse 32:4 says Allah is the One Who has created Heaven, the Earth and all that is between them in six days, and then firmly established Himself on the Throne of Authority. You have no guardian or intercessor besides Him. Will you not then make remembers others? The verses 39: 2-3 say: Certainly We have revealed to you the Book with the Truth: therefore worship Allah, offering Him your sincere obedience. Beware! Sincere true obedience is only to Allah! As for those, who take other patrons besides Him and justify their conduct, saying: "We worship them only that they may bring us nearer to Allah." Surely Allah will judge between them concerning all that in which they differ. Allah does not guide him who is a liar and a disbeliever. The verse 16: 74 says therefore, compare none with Allah. Surely Allah knows and you do not know. In the verse 36: 78 says He is making comparisons for Us forgetting his own creation, and through the verse 67: 14 would He not know,

Who has created them? He is the Knower of finest mysteries, and acquainted of everything. All other parties except the party of Allah are *'mushriks'* and belong to the Satan's party, as mentioned in the verses 58: 22 and 19 respectively. See the explanation 2: 176. Those who forgot Allah forget themselves and are transgressors as per the verse 59: 19 and are hypocrites as per the verse 9: 67 and are killed by Allah as per the verse 63: 4. They are human-devil who lead the common people to the Hell knowingly by hiding the Soul of Qur'an and therefore about them the verse 9: 68 says Allah has promised the hypocrite men, the hypocrite women, and 'the *kuffar*-who reject the verses of Qur'an after receiving It- the fire of Hell to live therein forever, a sufficient recompense. Allah has cursed them and they shall have a lasting punishment. They will be dragged to Hell prone on their faces as per the verses. 17: 97 and 25: 34. In brief, the believers living as the vicegerents of Allah here by understanding the character of Allah from the Soul of Qur'an and all other Muslims as mentioned in the verse 49: 14 are in the party of satan and included in 999 out of each 1000. Read together the verses 4: 118. See the explanation 3: 10, 79, and 160.

It is told in the verse 25: 29 that these '*mushriks*' will lament that, "I did not utilize the Soul of Qur'an after It had come to me." It is told in the verse 6: 26 that the hypocrites who do not follow the Soul of Qur'an after knowing It will have to bear the sins of those who do not received It. The verses16: 24- 25 say when they are asked about Qur'an: "What is it that your Lord has revealed?" They say: "fables of ancestors. In order to carry all their own burdens on the Day of Judgment as well as some burdens of those whom they have misled without having any knowledge. Surely what they bear is evil! As per the verses 29: 12-13 the disbelievers say to the believers: "Follow us, and we will bear the burden of your sins. But they will not bear any burden of their sins; they are surely lying. Of course, they shall bear their own burdens as well as the burdens of others in addition to their own; and on the Day of Resurrection they shall be questioned about their invented lies". The literates who do not utilize the Soul of Qur'an after receiving It neither become a believer nor enter the Paradise, as specified in the verses 32: 22; 40: 40 and 41: 41-43. As the verses 62: 2-3 say "He is the One who has dispatched the Messenger from the unlettered among themselves, to recite His verses to them and purify them and teach them the Book and Wisdom, even though previously they were obvious error; as well as others of them who have not at jointed them" it can be understood that the illiterates will understand the Soul of Qur'an than literates. Therefore the one who approve Allah as Impartial will ask Guidance by heart and by praying in mind, 'my Lord increase me my knowledge will read the splendid Book-Soul of Qur'an-' told in the verses 41: 41-42. It is forbidden as per the verse 7:33 that to associate partners to Allah, for which He has given no authority and saying about Allah without having knowledge from the Soul of Qur'an. The verse 22: 8 says there are some among people who wrangle about Allah without having the Knowledge, Guidance and Enlightening Book i.e. the Soul of Qur'an. It is told in the verses 41: 6- 7 that those who pay not welfare tax, deny the Hereafter and join partners with Allah have the 'wail' -severe torment part of Hell. See the explanation 1:4; 2: 169-170, 254 and 4: 38- 40.

49. Have you not seen those who purify themselves? Indeed Allah will purify any one He wishes to and they will not be harmed little bit.

50. Look how they invent a lie about Allah that is enough in itself as a clear sin.

These verse revealed as a reply to the Jews who claimed that they are purified men and offspring and followers of Prophet's and saint people and therefore we will not be entered the Hell. And even if we enter, we will stay there in only a fixed number of days in which we worshiped the cow. See the explanation 2: 80, 3: 70 and 183. But today, if consider the Soul of Qur'an as '*Mouidhath*' we can see all these are the characters of non-believing Muslims. They think that since they born as Muslims they will be entered in to the Paradise. They are not considering that all men take birth as Muslims, and they do not consider the admonition of Qur'an that each and every individual after the age of fifteenth shall be replied about every second of their life in front of Allah individually. They neglect what is told in the verse 49: 13 that no privilege is given by birth but privilege is only for heedful. They have the belief like that of Bedouin Arabs mentioned in the verse 49: 14 as the Bedouin Arabs say: "We have believed." Tell them: "You have not believed; rather say 'We are Muslims;' for faith has not yet found its way into your hearts. If you obey Allah and His Messenger, He will not deny you the reward of your deeds; surely Allah is Forgiving, Merciful". That is why Allah says in the verse 53: 32 that Allah knows you well when He planted you from the essence of the Earth and when you were hidden in your mother's wombs. Therefore, hold not yourselves purified. Allah, the Knower of the state of the hearts knows best that who is heedful. In otherwise the ancestors of today's Muslims were either '*mushriks*', Jews or Christians. See explanation 2: 136 and 285.

The meaning of saying that: you shall not purify yourselves is you shall not rejoice or boast about your period of birth, sex, nation, tribes, race, community and organization etc. But it is commanded to be purified each one individually by using the Soul of Qur'an that all these are given by Allah and thereby identify themselves and the aim of life. It is told in the verses 91: 9- 10 that he succeeds who purifies- identifies himself, and he fails who not purifies -not identifies herself. It is told in the verses 87: 14-15 that certainly those who identified-purified themselves, and remember the name of their Lord always and especially perform *swalath* for that have been succeeded. The verse 20: 14 says indeed I am Allah alone there is no Deity except Me, so serve Me and keep up *swalath* to remember Me- or to maintain the Soul of Qur'an. Allah has already decided everyone's destiny as per the verses 9: 51; 10: 61, 22: 70 and 57: 22 etc. Therefore the aim of life is to utilize all the blessings to learn and teach the Soul of Qur'an and there by construct Paradise here for tomorrow under Its Lights. Understanding this, we should pray by heart like this, "Oh Allah, I am your servant offended, loss me not owner Lord, my destiny has come, if it is to Hell, I am unable to amend it, therefore, my owner Lord, make me amend it myself". No soul will enter Paradise unless he become a believer told in the verse 40: 40 and to become a believer it is not necessary to change name, cloth etc. as told in the verses 2: 62 and 5: 69. Only the believers shall die peacefully like a newborn baby as Muslims – submitting whole self to Allah. See the explanation 3: 101- 103.

After receiving the Soul of Qur'an, if any Muslim cannot become believers they shall witness against themselves at the time of death that they were disbelievers, is told in the verse 7: 37. The disbelievers referred in the verses 41: 26- 28 are hypocrites and the disbelievers mentioned in the verse 29 are *fujjar*- common Muslims who are gone astray. Allah says in the verse 10: 17 who is the more wrongful than such as forge a lie against Allah or reject His verses? Certainly he will not prosper such *mujrims*- mad men. The verse 28-37 ends as he will not prosper such wrongdoers. Allah asks in the verse 29: 68 that who is more wrongful than the one who forges a lie against Allah or rejects His Truth when It reaches to him, is there not a home in Hell for such disbelievers. Those who forge lie against Allah mentioned in all the above verses are hypocritical disbelievers, and those who reject the verses of Qur'an after receiving It are *fujjar* disbelievers. Read together the verses 32: 3 and 39: 32. Prophet taught that *no one will become a believer unless his lusts follow what I have brought* i.e. no one can become a believer without utilizing the Soul of Qur'an. See the explanation 2:186, 213; 3: 185 and 4: 1.

51. Have you not watched those who were given a portion of the Book? They believe with the 'jibth' and 'thaghooth' and tell about those who disbelieve: are better guided to the Straight path than those who believe.

52. Those are the ones whom Allah has cursed; and anyone Allah has cursed, will never find a helper for himself.

Jibth – witchcraft- means falsehood, baseless, futile, in vain etc. The superstitions and conjectures like sorcery, sorcery against enemies, horoscope, omen, palmistry, astrology, fortune telling by observing the movement and sounding or falling of a house lizard, fortune telling by evaluating the card picked by the parrots, the first sight in the morning, planetary evils supposed to befall when Mars stands certain position of the zodiac, make an astrological calculation, seeking auspicious hour etc. come under *jibth*.

Thaghooth – arrogant- means to follow the self whims and fancies blindly follow the way of forefathers, to keep up organizational partiality, racialism, nationalism, selfishness, favoritism, communalism, sexual partiality etc. And all such ways are against the do's and don'ts of the Soul of Qur'an- the way of Allah- belongs to *thaghooth*, which is the way of satan. See the explanation 2: 257. Today, the Soul of Qur'an is the only complete Book, the Balance, Justice and Truth. But the Muslims, bearers of the Qur'an, are engaged and involved in all these superstitions. These people mentioned both in the verses 25: 18 and 48: 12 as boar people, without using the Soul of Qur'an-the Light, are living in darkness aimless and heedless. They are in forefront in doing all evils but back in doing any good. That is why they are become downtrodden and disgraced by the people like Jews upon whom Allah has cursed and His wrath happened. This is the punishment for them receiving in this world since they not only utilize the Soul of Qur'an but also prevent others from utilizing It. The Soul of Qur'an, the food, cloth and sight of human soul is the only device to stop bloodshed and make human unity among mankind. Otherwise they will have a severe punishment in the Hereafter as told in the verse 2: 85.

There are some Muslim organizations falsely priding that we are learning and teaching the Qur'an, then asking whoever is better than us. Such disbelieving hypocrites as explaining in the verse 3:10 are considering and saying that the disbelieving *fujjar* are better guided than the believers, even though *fujjar* eat the body of Qur'an or eat with It and maintain offerings other than Allah, believe in sorcery and magic, receiving dowry from women side, keeping up organizational partiality, self race partiality etc. They will not observe Fasting, Eid etc. on the real day of believers; but follow the way of majority by claiming the anti-Islamic communal harmony; they are not trying to form human harmony. They neglect what is told in the verse 6: 116 that if you obey majority of people on Earth, they will divert you from the way of Allah. And they not only accept the teaching of the Prophet that in every thousand, 999 go to Hell and only one is to Paradise, but also hide the fact from the people. They are the worst people who explain the Qur'an against Allah's intention. E.g. by neglecting the teaching of the verse 7:150, quoting the verse 20: 94 they teach the common people that even association in the dominion of Allah is permissible for maintaining the communal and organizational unity. They consider Prophet *Haroon* is more preferable to follow than the Messenger *Moosa*. Such hypocritical leaders say without any fear that we are inviters to organization and not to *Islam* and Paradise. Today, these men devil hypocrites try their maximum efforts to annihilate the classes where the Soul of Qur'an is being taught. The other people like Hindus, Jews or Christians never do it. Just like the Jews in olden days, today, the hypocritical leaders encourage even terrorism which causes the bloodshed of innocent people for having communal harmony among Muslims and to frighten other major community people. At a glance they are the Islamists opposing racialism and terrorism etc. But they take all these policies in order to get political power. They do not consider the Message of the verses 3: 26 and 27. Therefore, Allah has commanded the believer through the verse 25: 52 to strive strenuously with the Soul of Qur'an against these hypocrites. Read together the verses 9: 73 and 66: 9. See the explanation 2: 189; 3: 119 and 4: 48.

53. Or have they any share in control? If then they will not give speck to anybody.

The Jews as well as the hypocrites have not got the control of the world. If the Jews and hypocrites get the control of the world, there will not be any justice. See the explanation 2: 251. But when '*Maseeh-A-Ddajjal*' comes, they will rule all over the world except '*Hijaz*'-the provinces including *Mecca* and *Madeena*. That is the meaning of what Prophet taught, in the last days, *Islam* will retreat to '*Hijaz*' just like the snakes retreat to holes. That day, the hypocrites will join with Jews, and will approve the liar '*Maseeh-A-Ddajjal*' as the Prophet earlier and later as even their Lord as he argues. Prophet taught, such catastrophe like '*Maseeh-A-Ddajjal*' has never occurred to the children of Adam so far in the world. But, not too late, Allah will bring *Eisa* and he will kill *Maseeh-A-Ddajjal* and the leaders of Jews. On those days, the Hindus, Christians and the common people from Jews will be along with the *Eisa* and believers. Thus the believers who get the control of the world will implement the commands of the verses 4: 91, 9: 123 and 33: 60-61. See the explanation 2: 174- 176; 3: 166 and 167.

54. Or do they envy mankind for what Allah has given them out of His Bounty? Then certainly, We had already given Ibrahim's family the Book and Wisdom, and We gave them splendid control.

55. Then, some of them believed with It. While others of them averted from It and enough the Hell for such as to Blaze.

The Jews were arguing that Prophet Muhammad would come from the children of Israel. They did not accept Prophet Muhammad due to the envy that he came from the lineage of Prophet *Isma'el*- the first son of Prophet *Ibrahim*. Only one Book has been sent down to the Earth. Among the offspring of Prophet *Ibrahim* some of them believed with the Book and some obstructed themselves and others from It. For such disbelievers the Hell is enough to burn.

Among today's Muslims except the believers, even though they are learning and teaching the body and meaning of Qur'an to their own people, obstruct from learning the Soul for entire mankind. Thus they prevent others as well as themselves from It. The verses 6: 26- 27 say: They themselves have turned away from It and also forbid others from It. With such a behavior they harm none but their own souls but they do not perceive it. If you could have witness the scene, when they will be made to stand before the Hell fire! They will say: "We wish we could return to Earthly life again; then we would not deny the verses of our Lord, and we would join the believers!" The verses 32: 12; 35: 37 and 40: 11 are having the same message. Today, only the Soul of Qur'an is the Book for the entire mankind. Hence those who do not give It to others shall be thrown into Hell. This verse also teaches that each one constructs Paradise or Hell by himself.

Today the hypocrites are most envious towards the believers, who teach and follow the Soul of Qur'an. The Impartial Allah will never send any people to the Hell who does not receive the Soul of Qur'an, but the people who received the Soul of Qur'an if did not utilize, will go to the Hell. Allah, the Lord of all Worlds, may send those who didn't received the Soul of Qur'an to a World which is neither Paradise nor Hell. See the explanation 2: 169; 3: 74, 181 and 182.

56. Certainly, those who conceal Our verses, We will roast them in a Fire: each time their skins are toasted, We shall exchange them for some other skins, so they may taste the torment. Certainly Allah is Power, Wise.

It is told in the verse 20: 74 that the one who comes to his Lord as *mujrim*-mad man, for him is Hell there in shall he neither die nor live and in the verse 75 it is told that, the one who comes to his Lord as a believer, he has constructed Paradise, for them are ranks exalted. It is told in the verses 41: 20- 22 that, when the disbeliever's skins stand witness against them, they will ask to their own skins, why bear you witness against us- both you and me? Their skins will say: "The One Who gave the reflecting power to all things is reflecting also with me. It is He Who created you from nothingness. When you were in the state of sperm and ovum I was not there as a part of your body and unto Him as to you to return. You did never expect that your hearings, sights and skins stand witness against you. But you did think that Allah knew not many of the things, you used to do". The disbelievers who conceal the verses of Qur'an after getting It shall be burnt in the Hell. The modern science has found that if skin is removed from the body, there will not be any pain thereafter. It is told in the verse 87: 13 that then in the Hell will be neither death nor life. That means by adding fresh skins, they will not become nothingness by toasting skin. i.e. there is no death or birth in the Hell as well as in the Paradise as mentioned in the verse 37: 58-60.

The scene of disbelievers requesting for perish is warned in several places in Qur'an. The verses 40: 49 and 50 say: Those who are inside the Fire will tell the guards of Hell: Appeal to your Lord to reduce the torment for us by just a day. The guard will ask: "Did not your Messengers come to you with the Soul of Qur'an". They will say: "Of course!" They will say: "Well, then you make your own appeal; and the appeal of the disbelievers will increase nothing except astray." The verses 43: 77 and 78 say: The inmates of the Hell will cry out: "Oh *Malik*, have your Lord put an end to us". He will reply: "You must stay there. We had brought you the Truth even though most of you detest the Truth- Soul of Qur'an". The verses 84: 11 and 12 say: The disbelievers will appeal to be blotted out and will roast in the Blaze. See the explanation 2: 21; 3: 116 and 4: 42.

57. And those who believe and do honorable deeds shall certainly be admitted to Paradise with rivers flowing beneath. They shall abide there in forever and have spouses purified. We shall admit them to shades, cool and ever deepening.

In order to enter the Paradise we should form the belief with the Soul of Qur'an and follow Its do's and don'ts. No one shall be entered to Paradise with out being a believer. Those who do not get the opportunity to show the faith and to do honorable deeds after believing like the companions of cave or like the believer mentioned in *Surath Yaseen,* or like the sorcerers who failed in the competition with Prophet *Moosa* but believed shall also be entered in the Paradise. Read together the verses 4: 124; 16: 97; 20: 112 and 40: 40; See explanation 2: 25, 186 and 3: 133- 136.

58. Certainly, Allah command you to render back your trusts to those to whom they are due, and whenever you judge between people, you should judge with Justice, certainly, how excellent advice which Allah gives you. Certainly Allah is all Hearing, all Observing.

'Trusts' means the things, which some body are assigned to others in order to restore. Such trusts should be rendering back to its owner without any change or decrease. Allah says in the verses 16: 90 and 91 that, certainly Allah commands Justice, the doing of good and giving to kith and kin their rights, and forbids all indecent deeds, evils, rebellion. He instructs you for keeping remembrance by heart. And fulfill the covenant of Allah when you have entered into it, and break not your oaths after you have confirmed them. Indeed you have made Allah your surety. Certainly Allah knows all that you are doing. See the explanation 2: 283 and 3: 75.

59. Oh, you who believe, obey Allah and obey the Messenger and those from among you who hold command. If you differ in anything, refer it to Allah and the Messenger, if you do believe in Allah and the Last Day; that will be better and finest in the long run.

'The better and finest long run' means it is better not to differ between you and the leader, and live forward in unity in this world and for entering the Peaceful House in the Hereafter. See the explanation 3: 103. The verse 17: 35 says: Give full measure whenever you measure out anything, and weigh with the Balance that is straight- with the Soul of Qur'an; that is better and finest in the long run. See the explanation 3: 31 and 32. Prophet taught *no obedience to any creature by disobeying the Creator; and those who obey me, then he obeyed Allah and those who disobey me, then he disobeyed Allah.* It is told in the verse 59: 7 that accept what the Messenger gives you and refrain from what he prohibits you. Prophet taught *whoever does a deed which is not included in my command, shall not be accepted.* The verse 24: 52 says: Only those who obey Allah and His Messenger, have fear of Allah and do honorable deeds, are the ones who will be the winners. Read together the verses 4: 80 and 5: 67. The person who holds command means scholars, political leaders and religious leaders. Since it is told in the verse the person who holds command among yourselves, the believers shall only accept the commands from the believing leader. See the explanation 3: 28. No obedience to anybody by disobeying the do's and don'ts of Qur'an. Since it is told by calling the believers through the verses 30: 31-32, that all organizations among Muslims are *mushriks*, the believers should not obey any leaders of the Muslim parties. It is told both in the verses 16: 43, 21: 7 that, if you know not anything, you ask to those who know the Soul of Qur'an. Therefore, it is advised to the believers that, ask any doubts only to the scholars who knows the Soul of Qur'an, and not the anchorites who know knowledge of books other than The Book– Soul of Qur'an. About such anchorites, Allah says by calling the believers through the verse 9: 34 that, certainly there are many anchorites and priests who eat the wealth of men illegally and prevent men from the way of Allah- Soul of Qur'an. Read together the verse 9: 31.

Today, there is no scholars any where in the world who learn and teach the Soul of Qur'an . Lest there are anchorites who hide and sell the Qur'an for a miserable price and accept the wage for '*Imamath*' and there by filling fire into their bellies as well as to the bellies of their family members. See the explanation 2: 159- 161 and 174- 176. These are the days which prophet taught the believer to holdfast the Soul of Qur'an in all times and be away from all the parties among the Muslims, the boar people- as told both in the verses 25:18 and 48: 12. Today, the believer has the state of Prophet who went to the cave of '*Hira*'. Prophet has replied to the question of *Hudaifathul Yamani* that, in such condition the illiterates shall spend time by biting the bottom of any tree in the forest until death, but the literates shall live by biting the Soul of Qur'an with their molar teeth. Allah says in the verse 62: 9 by calling the believers: When the call is proclaimed for the Friday *swalath*, hasten earnestly to hear the admonition. That admonition should be with the Soul of Qur'an. Today, there is no party of believers and there is no sermon (Friday speech) in which the Soul of Qur'an is explained. Therefore, today there is neither Friday *swalath* nor other gathering *swalath*- just like in the first stage of Prophet in *Meccan* period. It is told in the verse 24: 55 that, if there is a party of believers, they shall be given the ruling power. And such group of believers shall put into practice the command in the verse 9: 123 i.e. to kill the hypocrites. But it will only be possible after the second coming of *Eisa*. See the explanation 2: 166-167 and 3: 7.

60. Have you not considered those who claim that they believe with what has been sent down to you and what was sent down before you. They want to seek judgment from "Thaghooth", where they are ordered to disbelieve with it. Satan wants to lead them far astray.

If anybody obeys any hypocritical leaders against the do's and don'ts of the Soul of Qur'an, it will become obeying the *Thaghooth*. It is told in the verses 5: 44- 45 and 47 that those who do not judge with the Soul of Qur'an in their individual, family and social life are disbelievers, wrongdoers and transgressors respectively. Prophet taught that *if anybody approaches thaghooth (Thangals, Musliars, Auliyas, Panickers, Mullas, Beevis, Shaiks, one who make astrological calculations, fortune tellers) and listen very attentively what they utter and do as according to what they said are not believed in what is sent down to Muhammad from his Lord,* that means they do not believe in the Soul of Qur'an. Only those who have identified the way of *Thaghooth* and the way of Allah by utilizing the Soul of Qur'an, as the Balance, Criterion and Insight, and live in the way of Allah can return to Paradise. See the explanation 1:7; 2:102; 3: 185 and 4: 51.

Allah brought everyone on Earth individually as per the verse 6: 94. The aim of life is to construct Paradise here by utilizing the Soul of Qur'an. So the believers one in every thousand live for Allah- The believer, and the cursed hypocrites and their blind followers gone astray people who are 999 in every thousand in number are living for *Thaghooth* and their return is to satan- the disbeliever. During the period of Prophet in *Madeena*, Jews and hypocrites were seeking judgment from *Thaghooth*; but today the *fujjar*- the gone astray people- mentioned in the verse 1: 7 seek judgment from their hypocritical leaders. The scene of quarrel, cursing and disgusting in between them in the Hell is described in the verses 2: 166 and 167. Both the Jinn and men satan prevents the men from the Soul of Qur'an as told in the verses 5: 90-91; 6: 112 and 58: 19. See the explanation 3: 10 and 4:48.

61. When it is told to them: Come to what Allah has sent down, and to the Messenger, you will see the hypocrites avert their faces from you in disgust.

This character of hypocrites is portrayed in the *Surath Al-Munafiqoon* especially in the verse 5 as: Whenever they are told: "Come, Allah's Messenger will seek forgiveness for you", they twist their heads around and you will see them trying to slip away while they act so haughty. These men devil hypocrites seize men to Hell as told in the verses 6: 112; 114: 6, and they are compared to that of donkeys and Jews in the verse 62: 5, and to that of a dog, which will not change its attitude whether you disturb it or not as per the verses 7: 175- 176. Even though they are assigned to teach the Soul of Qur'an, they are satisfied by teaching the body and meaning- life of Qur'an- and become the disbelievers as explained in the verse 3:10. Allah will never guide such wrongful and transgressed people as told in the verses 9: 19, 23-24; 61: 5 and 62: 5. See the explanation 2: 6-7, 99; 3: 90-91, 166 and 167.

62. How will it be when some disaster strikes them because of their hands have already prepared? Then they will come to you swearing by Allah: "We meant nothing except goodwill and conciliation.

The activities of hypocrites are mentioned in the verses 4: 88- 91. When they expect a favorable judgment, they come to Prophet and when they are in anxiety about getting favorable judgment they fear to come. The behavior of today's hypocrites can be seen as the same, if we see using the Insight- the Soul of Qur'an. The verses 24: 47-50 say: They will say: "We believe in Allah and the Messenger and we obey" Then a group of them will turn away even after that; those are not believers. Whenever they are invited to Allah and His Messenger, he may judge between them. Behold! A group of them decline to come. Yet, if they have the truth on their side, they come to him voluntarily. Does some malice lurk in their hearts? Either they act skeptical, or else they fear that Allah and His Messenger will cheat them. Nay such are the wrongdoers. The verse 32: 22 says: Who is more wrongful than the one who remembered his Lord's verses in his heart's language then decline about it? Certainly We will revenge with such *mujrims*. Read together the verses 33:60-61. These hypocrites who did not consider Allah as Impartial understand not that all disasters are occurring as a result of their own deeds which their hands have sent ahead, as told in the verses 7: 174; 30: 41 and 32: 21. Instead of teaching the people that everyone individually earns Paradise or Hell here; the aimless hypocrites are teaching Allah is only deciding people to Hell or Paradise neglecting the verses 2: 281, 286; 3: 30, 136, 182, 185 etc. See the explanation 4: 47

63. Allah does know what is in their hearts; so avoid them, but warn them and speak to them the words that penetrate to their inner hearts.

It is told in the verse 9: 95 that the hypocrites are filth, and Hell is their dwelling place being a suitable recompense for what they were earning, so avoid them. Allah does know the character of hypocrites, since He is the Knower of mental state. Allah says to the believers, not to waste their time by thinking about them, but abstain from them. In order to fulfill the believers responsibility, say words which penetrate to the inner heart of the hypocrites. It is told in the verse 25: 63 that when the ignorant one comes to argue with the beloved servants of Most Impartial, they will say: 'Peace to you i.e. you may go' and abstain from them. It is told in the verse 7: 198 that when the hypocrites are invited to the Soul of Qur'an they hear not but glare at you and they will not utilize 'Insight', and in the verse 199 it is told to give chance, command to utilize the Soul of Qur'an and turn away from the ignorant. It is told in the verse 10: 33 that these sorts of transgressors will never believe. And it is commanded to the believers in the verse 28: 55 that, if they witness vain talk or mocking, abstain from it and say to those who are involved in such matters: We have our deeds, and you have your deeds, you may go, and we seek not the way of ignorant. Read together the verse 39: 64. It is told in the verse 32: 30 to the Prophet to turn away from this sort of rejecters of faith and wait, they are also waiting. Allah has told both in the verses 15: 12 and 26: 200 that, We caused the Soul of Qur'an to enter the hearts of these sort of mad men- hypocrites and *fujjar*- as a blazing iron bar.

Some examples of the words that will penetrate into the hearts or the method of *Jihad*- Strenuous strive- with the Soul of Qur'an are as follows:

(1). When the foolish men ask whether the Qur'an is comprehensible to all, say to them: Allah has taught the Soul of Qur'an to everybody in the Paradise itself and the Soul of Qur'an reminds it through the verses 55: 1-5; 75: 14 and15.

(2). When the hypocrites say that, as per the verses 18: 109 and 31: 27 if the water of seven seas are utilized as ink to write the explanation of Qur'an, it will not be enough; then how it is possible to understand it to the common people. Say to them: It is repeatedly told four times in the *Surath Al-Qamar* that Allah has made very easy to understand the Soul of Qur'an by ones own heart's language. But who is ready to receive the admonition?

(3). When those who ask whether Prophet has called any man 'dog', say to them that, Prophet and believers never call anyone dog. Instead in the verse 7: 176, Allah, their Impartial Lord has compared the hypocrites who hide the verses of Qur'an and the laymen who follow them rejecting the verses of Qur'an to a dog; which will not change its attitude whether it is disturbed or not. That verse ends with a command to Prophet to memorize them their examples as donkeys vide verse 62: 5, as swine vide verse 5: 60, as monkey vide verse 2: 66 etc one by one in order that they may meditate and reflect i.e. those who heard it may propagate to others.

(4). Those who live with a belief that one who performs *swalath* and fasting will prosper, say to them that, *swalath* and fasting are only prescribed by calling believers and not to the disbelievers. The disbelievers will get Hell as a penalty for their *swalath* and Fasting as told in the verses 9: 53-54, 13: 14, 25: 65 and 107: 4 -5. And say to them that Prophet has taught those who recite Qur'an without knowing Its contents will depart from the *Dheen- Islam-* as the arrow darts from the bow.

(5). To those who say that the anchorites have said, it is virtuous to get reward by simply reciting Qur'an, even without knowing Its contents, say to them, Muhammad is deputed as the Prophet to the believers until Last Day. Therefore those who teach anything against the teaching of Prophet are killed by Allah and they are hypocrites- human satans. Read together the verses 4: 59 and 115. Hence, there is no virtue by the recitation of Qur'an even with knowing Its contents, but one should utilize It as a Balance, Criterion, Guidance and Ticket to the Paradise.

(6). To those who say that the scholars are the inheritors of Prophet, say them: Yes, that is only applicable to those who know the Soul of Qur'an. See the explanation 3: 7. But those who boast as scholars without the Soul of Qur'an as told in the verse 7: 146, are the worst of beasts under the sky. Read together the verses 8: 22, 55 and 98: 6. About such anchorites Prophet has taught that, their scholars will be worst creatures under the sky.

(7). To those who ask that whether the Prophet has made any one '*kafir*' or given right to make any one '*kafir*'. Say to them: Prophet has not made anyone *kafir*. But Allah has ordered the Prophet and believers that; one should himself decide whether he is a '*kafir*' or a believer by utilizing the Soul of Qur'an as the Balance. The verse 39: 8 commands the Prophet and believer to tell the person: Enjoy your disbelief for a little while; certainly you are the one of the inmates of Hell. As per the verse 14: 30 it is ordered to tell the group: Enjoy you all here; then indeed, all of your return is to Fire. See the explanation 2: 6-7, 254; 3: 86, 91, 119 and 159.

64. And We have not sent any Messenger except he was to be obeyed in accordance with Allah's Permission. If they had come to you and sought forgiveness from Allah whenever they wronged themselves, and the Messenger had prayed for forgiveness to them, they would have found that Allah is Ever-turning, Merciful.

It will never possible to happen that Allah comes to the Earth. As per the verse 6:103 instead He appointed Prophets as His Messengers. Allah sent down His Message- the Soul of Qur'an, which He satisfied for entire mankind the messengers from Angels to the Messengers from mankind. See the explanation 2: 1-2. 'In accordance with Allah's permission' means, without a verse or part of a verse as proof from Qur'an, therefore the saying of prophet will only be considered if it is justified by a verse or part of a verse from Qur'an. 'Those who do wrong against their soul' include those who associate others in the dominion of Allah, those who do not follow the Soul of Qur'an after receiving It and those who give offerings other than to Allah as per the verses 18: 57; 31: 13; 32: 22 and 39: 8. The verse does not contain the meaning that, if they go to Prophet and confess their sins to him, prophet will bear their sins. Lest it gives the meaning that, they will be very frank and take the advice of Prophet and they themselves seek forgiveness to Allah and then Prophet also seek forgiveness for them to Allah. The men devil hypocrites miss-quote this verse as a proof to seek help and forgiveness to Prophet and for rehearsing his praise and glory. If anybody trapped in their hands, their bad condition occurring in the Hell is explained in the verses 2: 166 and 167. See the explanation 2:213; 3: 128- 129, 185; 4: 17 and 18.

65. Yet by your Lord, they will never believe until they make you judge concerning what they are disputing over among themselves; and they find no inconvenience for themselves concerning what you have decided, and will accept it wholeheartedly.

This verse is applicable not only for the believers at the time of Prophet but also to the believers until the Last Day. It is told in the verse 33: 6 that, the believers should give importance to Prophet than their own selves. It is told in the verse 63: 8 that the Power and Honor belongs to Allah and His Messenger and to the believers, but the hypocrites know not. The people at the time of Prophet should completely follow his life. But the people of today's should see the Prophet from the Soul of Qur'an and evaluate themselves what way of life would Prophet accept if he is still living today and follow such life. See the explanation 2: 146. Read together the verse 4:115. That is why Prophet taught that, *among you no one becomes a believer unless and until his lusts follow what I have brought forth*. See the explanation 2: 121. It is warned in the verse 25: 30 that, Prophet will stand against his people who led a life treating the Qur'an neglected on the Day of Judgment. One should become a follower of Prophet only if he witnesses the Prophet's life among the people understanding from the Soul of Qur'an. See the explanation 2: 143, 176 and 4: 59.

66. Certainly, if We had prescribed for them: "Let yourselves be killed or expelled from your homes", only a few of them would have done so. If they had done what they were instructed to do, it would have been better for them as well as more stabilizing their soul.

The character of hypocrites is explained in the verses 9: 41-42 as when it is told to them strive strenuously in the cause of Allah lightly or heavily with your wealth and your persons, that is best for you, they would indeed swear by Allah that if we only could, should certainly have come out with you. They would destroy their ownselves, for Allah does know that they certainly are lying. If there had been immediate gain, or the enemies were weak or the journey is easy and in short, they would have followed you without doubt. The verse 76: 28 says: These disbelievers love the transitory life of this world and neglect the Heavy Day that is coming ahead. Today's Muslims who are reading these verses, are more attracted to the worldly life than any other people. See explanation 2: 96, 265-266; 3: 167 and 168.

67. If they done so, We should then have given them from Ourselves a great reward.

68. And would be guided them to the Straight path.

69. Anyone, who obeys Allah and the Messenger, he stands with those whom Allah has favored, such as Prophets, the truthful, the martyrs and the honorable men. And how fine are such companions.

70. That is the Bounty from Allah. And Allah is sufficient as Knower of all.

The believers and the Prophets are in the single party of Allah from Adam to the Last Day. All the Prophets are believers as told in the verses 7: 143; 10: 104; 37: 81, 111-112 and 132. It is told in the verse 57: 19 that, those who believe with Allah and His Messenger- they are the truthful and martyrs. In order to know the honorable men see the explanation 1: 6. When the believers recite the verse 1: 4 that, we serve only You, for that we seek help only to You, and when they recite the verse 1: 6 'the way of those on whom you have bestowed your grace', they have keep in mind the single party of Allah mentioned in the verse. All other parties from Muslims are belonging to the party of satan, and they will go to Hell. It is told in the verse 5: 56 that those who selected Allah, His Messenger and believers as friends, then the party of Allah certainly triumph. Allah, Prophet and believers are included in one single party and Allah's party are those who shall only be successful as told in the verse 58: 22.

Allah has told in the verse 30: 47 that, it is an incumbent duty upon Us to help believers. It is told in the verse 62: 4 that such is the Bounty of Allah, which He bestows on whom He wishes, and Allah is the Lord of the highest Bounty. In the verse 12: 38 Prophet *Yoosuf* says by advising his companions in the jail: It is the Grace of Allah to us and to mankind not to attribute any partners to Allah. Yet most men are not grateful. Here the Grace means to include in the party of

Allah. In order to include in the party of Allah, one should become a believer with Allah's Permission-the Soul of Qur'an. It is about this Grace that mentioned in the verse 10:58 as It is the Bounty and Mercy of Allah: there in let them rejoice, it is better than what they are collecting. Both the Bounty and Mercy mentioned in the verse is the Soul of Qur'an. That is the meaning of the Prophet's teaching: *Among you the best one is those who learn and teach the Soul of Qur'an.* It is told in the verse 5: 54 that, the believers will strive for Allah's sake and not fear reproach from any critic, such is Allah's Bounty which He gives to any one He wishes. Allah is Boundless, Aware. 'To anyone He wishes' means to one who ask Guidance by mind and go through the Soul of Qur'an by praying: 'my Lord increases me my knowledge' to Him. See the explanation 2: 213, 255 and 3: 173-175.

Prophet taught: When one is returning from the *Masjid* should pray after praying for Prophet: "Oh Allah, I seek Your Bounty" and when enters into the *Masjid* "Oh Allah, forgive me my offences and open the doors of Your Mercy to me". But as Prophet envisaged today's *Masjids* are concrete buildings and gone astray from the Guidance. Therefore, it is understood that the believers should not go to such *Masjid* for performing *swalath*. For the community of Prophet all places on Earth except graveyard and lavatories are '*Masajid*'- prostrating places. Therefore the believers should not enter these *Masjids* of hypocrites for performing *swalath*. See the explanation 2: 114, 152; 3: 73- 74 and 4: 49-51.

71. Oh you who believe, take your precautions and march off in detachment or march off all together.

72. And indeed among you there are some who procrastinate. If any disaster strikes to you, they say: Allah has favored me, for I was not a witness along with them.

73. And yet if some Bounty from Allah strikes to you, he will say, as if no affection had existed between you and him: "If I only had been with them, I should have achieved triumph splendid.

This character of hypocrites is portrayed in the verses such as 9: 50- 52; 33: 12- 20; 48: 6, 11- 12, 15 and 16. Today there is no war or killing, but only strenuous strive with the Soul of Qur'an against the hypocrites and disbelievers who hide and reject It. This hypocrites do not believe in the real destiny because, when a misfortune occur they charge the allegation to others and say: If it had done so, it would not have been happened so. When it is happened any annoyance or opposition to the people who learn the Soul of Qur'an, they will say: It will be better for us that we had not been among them. Otherwise we would also undergo pelting stone or being beaten. Consequently, they separate the link with the Qur'an. When it is happened some good thing to the believers who propagate the Soul of Qur'an, they will lament as: Oh I wish I had been with them, a fine thing should I then have made of it. These hypocrites, at the time of their death, will self-witness that they were disbelievers. Tomorrow, in the Hereafter, they will ask for the Light to the believers as mentioned in the verses 57: 13-16. See the explanation 2: 254- 257; 3: 161-162, 168; 4: 63.

74. Then those who fight in the way of Allah are barter worldly life for the Hereafter. And whoever fights in the way of Allah, and is either killed or is victorious, soon shall We give him great reward.

Allah says in the verse 9: 111 that, certainly We have purchased of the believers, their persons and their property instead of Paradise. They fight in the way of Allah and kill and are killed. This is a promised binding on Him in Truth, through the *Thourath, Injeel* and *Qur'an*. Therefore, those who fulfilled the covenant with Allah may rejoice in the trade with Allah, that is only the supreme triumph. Read together the verses 9: 71- 72. Allah asks in the verses 61: 10-11 by calling the believers, shall I lead you to a bargain that will save you from a painful torment. That you should believe with Allah and His Messenger and strive in Allah's way with your property and your persons; that will be better for you if you only knew. Read together the verses 61: 13 and 14.

'Jihad' means to strive by utilizing all capabilities to achieve the goal. The goal is to achieve Paradise in the Hereafter, to identify the Creator, and oneself from the Soul of Qur'an. One should identify himself, the Creator and satan from the Soul of Qur'an in order to maintain peace and tranquility on Earth and for avoiding the evils like racialism, partiality, favoritism, bloodshed etc. and there by mould the unity of mankind. See the explanation 2: 184, 186, 207- 208 and 3: 170-172.

75. And why should you not fight for Allah's sake when men, women and children who are considered weaklings say: "Our Lord! Lead

us out of this country whose people are so oppressive, and grant us a patron from Your presence and grant us a supporter from Your presence.

Today, the protection and support from Allah means the Soul of Qur'an, which is the Safeguard and Shield for body, wealth, and family from all disasters in this world as well as from Hell- in Hereafter- as explained in the verse 5: 48. Today there is no war or migration. Instead, Prophet taught on the day of Departing pilgrimage itself that, to lead a life by biting the Soul of Qur'an with molar teeth. The supporting authority mentioned in the verse 17: 80 is the Soul of Qur'an. The verse 17: 81 says: Truth has come, and false would be vanished; falsehood is so perishable. Truth mentioned in the verse is soul of Qur'an. Read together the verses 4: 82; 38: 24 and 47: 24. See the explanation 3: 79 and 101-103.

76. Those who believe, fight in Allah's way; while those who disbelieve fight in the way of the arrogant ones; therefore you fight satan's patrons, indeed satan's plot is weak.

This verse also teaches that basically mankind is divided into two groups, one is the party of believers which is the party of Allah and the other is the party of disbelievers which is the party of satan. Since 999 out of thousand will be followed the way of satan, it is mentioned as the party of arrogant ones. See the explanation 2: 257. Since today there is no believer's party anywhere in the world. After the second coming of *Eisa*, can only be executed the command of the verses such as 4: 91; 9: 123 and 33: 61 that to kill the men devil hypocrites and *fujjār* who are hastening for the destruction of the world by hiding and rejecting the Soul of Qur'an, the Balance and Trust. See the explanation 2: 176; 4: 51 and 63.

77. Have you not watched those who have been told: "Restrain your hands, keep up swalath, and pay the welfare tax?" Yet whenever any fighting is prescribed for them, then a group of them feel afraid of people just as they should be afraid of Allah, or they are even more afraid. They say: Our Lord, why have You prescribed fighting for us, if you would only postpone it for a little while longer!" Say: "Worldly enjoyment means little, while the Hereafter is better for anyone who is heedful and you will not be wronged a bit.

See the explanation 2: 216; 3: 143 and 154. In the early times, when it was commanded to the believers to perform *swalath* and spend in regular welfare tax, a section among them said, why should we bear all these oppressions and tortures if we are in truth? Why shall not we fight with disbelievers? But when it was given permission for fighting in the second year of *Hijra*, a section among them feared men as or even more than they should have feared Allah and become like the hypocrites who fear the death. By calling the believers the verse 63:10 says: And spend something from whatever We have provided you with before death comes to one of you as he says: "My Lord, if You would only delay things for me for a short while, then I will make the Qur'an Truth and become among the honorable men. See the explanation 3:18- 19 and 185.

Everyone has to construct Paradise or Hell here. Those who understand that the life in the material world is tilt for the Hereafter shall only be returned to the Paradise which they have constructed. Allah did not command fighting to the Muslims of today; in turn they are commanded to propagate the Message of Allah to entire mankind. That is the way of helping Allah as He demanded through the verse 61: 14. But they are not only ready for that but also keep apart from the Soul of Qur'an and lead a wicked life in the sense that none shall question them or shall not be answered before anybody. Though they are assigned to call entire mankind to Allah with the Soul of Qur'an, they have become the servant of satan hurrying for destroying the world by hiding the Soul of Qur'an which is the only device to form unity of human harmony. When it is told to them that today the only honorable deed is to propagate the Soul of Qur'an which is the Mighty weapon against the terrorist activities and blood-shed they will stare at those who say so as if it will remove the soil under the feet as told in the verses 22: 72 and 68: 51-52. It is told in the verse 48: 29 that, Muhammad is the Messenger of Allah and those who with him are strong against the hypocrites, compassionate among each other. See the explanation 1: 7; 2: 165 and 166.

78. Wherever you may be, death shall still over take you even though you are in well-built-towers. Yet if something fine happens to them, they say: "This is from Allah"; while if something bad happens to them, they say: "This is because of you". Say: "Everything comes from Allah. What happened to these people that they fail to understand this True speech".

79. Any good that happens to you comes from Allah, while anything bad that happens to you is through yourself. And We have sent you as a Messenger to mankind; and Allah is enough as a witness.

See the explanation 3: 145. Death is an inevitable fact to everybody as told in the verse 3:185. The believers, by their death, return to the Paradise which they have constructed Here itself. But the disbelievers, who fear death, shall go to Hell after their death because they lived Here without the aim of life. It is commanded the Prophet to say in the verse 62: 8 that, the death from which you flee will truly overtake you, then will you be sent back to the One Who is the Knower of unseen and seen and then you will be informed with you have been doing Here. It is told in the verse 50: 19 that, the stupor death comes in truth. This was the thing, which you were trying to escape. It is in vain to flee from death lest one should prepare to face it. See the explanation 2: 94 and 95. Allah says in the verses 74: 49-51 that, then what is wrong with them that they neglect about the ticket- the Soul of Qur'an- as if they were affrighted fleeing donkeys from a roaring lion. The verse 51: 50 says: Then flee to Allah, I am a plain Warner to you from Him. Flee to Allah means flee to the Soul of Qur'an. See the explanation 3: 101-103. Like the hypocrites in the early period, the hypocrites of today also make allegations on others whenever happen any evil thing. They do not believe that all things including good and evils come from Allah. Though it is mentioned as per the verse 78 that good and evil come from Allah, in the verse 79 it is told that good comes from Allah and bad comes through yourself. Really the bad comes from satan. So, no bad comes to anyone when he is in the remembrance of Allah with the Soul of Qur'an. In turn, those who forget Allah, they forget themselves and thereby become hypocrites. See the explanation 2: 99. The verse 30: 36 says whenever We let mankind taste Mercy, they are glad about it; yet if any evil should strike them because of what their hands have sent on ahead, then they become disappointed. Those who remain the remembrance of Allah with the Soul of Qur'an, will never happen any evils as explained in the verse 2: 152.

Maintaining the remembrance of Allah is possible only by the Soul of Qur'an. It is the only device to make the Jinn soul-mate a believer and to keep aloof satan. It is taught to pray through a '*Qudsee Hadeeth*': '*I seek refuge with all the words of Allah from all evils that has been created.* Here, the refuge is not sought with Qur'an, but with *Kalimath- Rooh*-spirit- which include the soul and meaning of Qur'an. Which will never be exhaust either by written or spoken as told in the verses 18: 109 and 31: 27. This verse also teaches that each one individually construct Hell or Paradise by himself. Only the believer who has identified himself and the Creator, utilizing the Soul of Qur'an as Insight and Criterion, will pray by mind: 'I am nothing, but a servant of You, You have neither origin nor end, self Sustainer, Immortal'. And he lives as His vicegerents on Earth. Another '*Qudsee Hadeeth*' teaches that *no evil occur either on Earth or in the sky with the remembrance of Allah and He is the all knowing, all Hearing.* See explanation 3: 191

'*Hadeeth*' - Speech- is the Soul of Qur'an as mentioned in the verse 4: 87. The speech mentioned in the verses 7: 185; 18: 6; 39: 23; 45: 6; 52: 34; 53: 59; 77: 50 etc. are the Soul of Qur'an Itself. Prophet taught the best talks is the Book of Allah. But the aimless hypocrites and heedless *fujjar* understand not, what is the Soul of Qur'an, Why and What for? they are the ones who lost the goal of life as told in the verses such as 7: 179; 8: 65; 9: 80- 81, 87, 127; 59: 13 and 63: 3- 7. Prophet is deputed with the Truth, both as a Herald and a Warner to mankind and is not deputed to make people either to Paradise or to Hell as specified in the verses 2: 119 and 39: 19. Read together the verses 29: 50- 52 and 34: 28. Both the verses 4: 166 and 48: 28 end as 'Allah is sufficient as a witness'. See the explanation 2: 272; 3: 128- 129, 136 and 182.

80. Any one who obeys the Messenger has obeyed Allah, while any one who turns away, then We have not sent you as a watcher over them.

By calling the believers Allah says through the verses 33: 70 - 71 who you believe heed Allah and speak straight forward words, He will improve your actions for you and forgive you your sins. Anyone who obeys Allah and His Messenger will achieve a splendid triumph. The only thing which makes the speech straight forward is the Soul of Qur'an. Those who make their speeches and deeds as according to the Qur'an become the doers of good. The Qur'an will bear witness in favor of them. Read together the verse 33: 66. See the explanation 2: 148. Those who follow the life of Prophet by seeing from the Soul of Qur'an can return to Paradise with him. All others will go to Hell with satan. It does not matter to reproach anyone or even satan for entering in the Hell as told in the verse 14: 22. The verses 53: 2-4 say about prophet that your companion has neither strayed nor has become aimless; he does not reflect from some whims it is nothing except the Inspiration revealed to him. The verse 17: 17 ends as: Sufficient is it for your Lord to be Acquainted, Observant of His servants' offences. Both the verses 17: 30 and 96 end as: 'Indeed He is Acquainted, Observant about His servants'. The verse 25: 58 ends as: 'Sufficient is it for Him to be acquainted about His servants' offences.' See the explanation 3: 31- 32; 4: 64 and 65.

81. And they will say that, they are obedient, yet when they show up somewhere else than with you, a fraction of them will spend the night at some thing quite different from what they told to you. But Allah writes down whatever they do at night. So avoid them and entrust on Allah. And Allah is enough as a Trustee.

The hypocrites were showing obedience in front of Prophet. But in the absence of Prophet and believers, they plotted against the Prophet and believers through the night in their houses. Their character is explained in the verses 58: 8- 10 as, have you not seen those who, even though they have been forbidden to hold secret counsels and persistently do what was forbidden? They hold secret counsels among themselves for sin, hostility and defiance to the Messenger. Yet when they come to you, they greet you in words which even Allah does not greet you with, and ask themselves: "Why does Allah not punish us for what we say?" Hell is enough for them; they shall be roasted in It, what an evil destination! Oh you who believe! Whenever you confer with one another in private, do not talk out of sin and hostility and defiance of the Messenger: confer with virtuously and heedfully, and fear Allah, before whom you shall be summoned together. Indeed confer comes only from satan, for he may sadden those who believe, yet he will not harm them in any way except with Allah's Permission; so on Allah let believers entrust. It is told in *Surath Munafiqoon* that when the hypocrites come to the Prophet, they say: We bear witness that you are indeed the Messenger of Allah, yes; Allah knows that you are indeed the messenger and Allah bear witness that the hypocrites are indeed liars. When they speak, you listen to their words, their bodies please you and they are as pieces of wood logs propped up. They think that every sound is against them. They are enemies of Prophet and believers. And they have been killed by Allah. They are transgressors who forgot Allah and themselves as per the verses 59: 19. Read together the verses 58: 16-19. Therefore, here it is commanded that fear not the hypocrites, keep away from them and put trust in Allah from all evils of them. It is told in the verse 59:

13 that, the hypocrites fear the believers than Allah since they are men devoid of understanding. The verse 9: 129 says if they should turn away, then say: "Allah is enough for me, there is no Deity except Him; on Him do I entrust, He is Lord of the mighty Throne. See explanation 3: 119-120 and 4: 60- 63.

82. Have they not pondered upon the Qur'an? If it had come from some other source than Allah, they would have found a great deal of contradiction in It.

See the explanation: 3: 79. The hypocrites are skeptic in the matter of Qur'an. They do not believe, or ponder or proud with the miraculous wonderful of Qur'an. They do not believe in the Prophesy of Qur'an. They do not earnestly seek to understand Qur'an so that they do not consider Allah, the way He should be considered. They did not accept the good name of Allah-'*Rahman*'-Impartial-just like the *Meccan mushriks*. And they do not believe the reality that each one individually constructs Paradise or Hell here. Though they teach the meaning of Qur'an, they do not ponder about Its Soul or *Rooh*. They do not confirm that there is no discrepancy in Qur'an. They are the disbelievers as explained in the verse 3:10. Those who treat the Qur'an with arrogant are these hypocrites as told in the verses 7: 40 and 39: 59. They are men devil who teach the laymen that there is virtue by mere recitation of Qur'an even without understanding Its content. They do not try to understand Prophet's sayings and the verses of Qur'an by linking them together. They shuffle the verses of Qur'an and misquote the verses in their Friday sermon. There will be contradiction in the beginning and conclusion of their talking even in the Friday sermons. Allah will gather together such hypocrites who conduct Friday sermons, and disbelievers who hear them in the Hell as told in the verse 4: 140. Allah asks in the verse 47: 24 that do they not proud and rejoice with this Qur'an? Or is that there are locks upon their hearts? And in the verse 47: 25 it is told that, those who turn back to disbelief after the Guidance has become clear are seduced by satan who gives them false hopes. So they shall have Hell. And in the verse 47: 26 it is told that, this is because they said to those- Jews who hate what Allah has revealed- Qur'an-: We will obey you in part of matter, but Allah knows all their inner secrets. Those who consider the Soul of Qur'an as the great Prosperity and Mercy will not have miseries, fearing or sorrows. That is why it is told in the verse 17: 82 that, Qur'an is a Healing and Mercy to those who believe whereas to the wrongdoers It will not increase except loss after loss. It is told in the verse 9: 124 that, Qur'an will increase the faith of the believers and in verse 125 it is told that, for the hypocrites it will increase filth over filth.

Qur'an will intercede and make others interceded for those who make It truthful. *Those who make It walk ahead in front, It will lead them to the Paradise and those who make It walk in the rear, It will pull them into the Hell.* If we read together the verses such as 3:101,103, 5:48; 7: 143, 59: 21, 59:23 etc. we can understand that, Qur'an and Allah is same. Qur'an is the speech of Allah. And indeed It is a Book of Splendid. The Soul of Qur'an indeed is a book of Splendid. No falsehood can approach It from front or behind is told in the verses 41: 41-42. See the explanation 2: 186; 3: 138 and 4: 75.

83. Whenever some order concerning safety or fear comes to them, they broadcast it. If they would only refer it to the Messenger and those among them who hold command, those of them who investigate matters would have known about. If it had not been for Allah's Bounty and Mercy towards you, all of you would have followed satan except a few.

The Bounty and Mercy mentioned in this verse is the Soul of Qur'an as well as that mentioned in the verse 10: 58. 'Among them who hold command' mentioned in this verse as well as that of 4: 59, are the '*Rasikheen*'- those who are deeply rooted in knowledge- mentioned in the verse 3: 7, and the '*Khabeer*'- the knower of all times mentioned in the verse 25: 59 are the same person who know the explanation of Qur'an. It is satan as well as hypocrites who will instigate men for spreading dreadful news and instigate miserliness as mentioned in the verses 4: 38- 39; 57: 23 and 24.

To publish articles like magazines, newspapers and books in order to prevent from the Soul of Qur'an are also belongs the ways of satan. When such hypocrites conduct Friday sermons, they quote the Prophet saying as: 'The best talk is the Book of Allah", and then as a scorn they will quote one or two verses from Qur'an. But they do not encourage people to study the Soul of Qur'an which should be the Friday sermon as told in the verse 62: 9. They do not confirm themselves that, there is not any contradiction in Qur'an by understanding Its contents as it is demanded by Allah through the verse 4: 82. Even though one should begin the day by reading the Soul of Qur'an which is the official newspaper of Allah, these hypocrites begin the day by reading mankir [illegible] official news papers, magazine etc. They do not consider what is told in the verse 29: 45 that, the remembrance of Allah with the Soul of Qur'an is the greatest thing, but in turn, they encourage common people to perform *swalath* without having the remembrance of Allah with the Soul of Qur'an neglecting command of the verse 20:14. Actually by performing such *swalath*, they are darted from *Dheen* as arrow dart from bow as taught by Prophet. Their *swalath* does not restrain them from shameful and evil deeds. They disorderly practice against what is told in the verse 29:45 that, recite what is sent down to you from the Book by inspiration first and then perform *swalath*. Those who perform *swalath* in such a way is in 'Wail'- a severe torment part in the Hell- is warned in the verses 107: 4-5. The prayers of these disbelievers will increase them nothing except astray are told both in the verses 13:14; 40: 50. Read together the verses 4: 142-143 and 9: 50-54. The believers only give greatest importance to the Soul of Qur'an.

In the hearts of each individual, there is a Jinn companion- soul mate. It is only possible to make the Jinn companion believer by the Soul of Qur'an- which is in one's own heart's language. No one can enter the Paradise unless he make her soul mate a believer, otherwise both of them shall be gathered in the Hell as mentioned in the verses 43: 36- 38; 50: 27-30; 59: 16 and 17. See the explanation 2: 105 and 3: 58.

84. Then fight in Allah's way, you are not responsible except for yourself and encourage believers; perhaps Allah will restrain the fury of those who disbelieve. And Allah is strongest in fury and sternest in punishment.

Everyone is responsible for himself. The verse 39: 41 says we have sent you down the Book with Truth for mankind, then anyone who is guided, will be so his own sake, while anyone who goes astray will only stray because of it as well. You are not set up as any guardian over them. But it is the responsibility of the believers to encourage men to do well without compulsion. Today there is no war, but only strive with the Soul of Qur'an against the disbelievers who hide It. See the explanation 2: 256 and 4: 63.

Since Allah is the controller of everything, He can easily annihilate the disbelievers and their strength is nothing with Allah. That is the meaning of what is said in the verse 'Allah is strongest in fury and sternest in punishment.' The verse 42:15 says as for the people of *Aa'd,* they acted proudly on Earth without the 'Truth'- Soul of Qur'an. They asked: "who is stronger than us?" Did they not see that Allah, who created them, is much stronger than them! They had repudiated Our verses. The mourning of disbelievers who didn't utilize the Soul of Qur'an here he warned through the verses 89: 24-26 as they say it is too bad for me what I sent on ahead during my life time on that day, no one will torment with the torment like His, and non can bind with bonds like His. See the explanation 3: 126 and 160.

85. Any one who intercedes in a fine manner shall have a share in it, while some one who intercedes in an evil way will be held liable for it. And Allah is overseeing everything.

The verse 6: 160 says: Anyone who comes with a fine deed will have ten more like it, while anyone who comes with an evil deed only be rewarded with its like; they will be not treated unjustly. The verse 36: 12 says: We revive the dead and write down what ever they have sent on ahead and the traces they left. We record everything in an open ledger i.e. on the compact disk placed on each individual's neck as told in the verses 17:13-14 and 45:29. That means they shall get not only the reward of the deeds, but also have a share in the deeds of their followers. Allah says in the verse 82: 5 that each soul will know what it sent on ahead and has left behind. The verse 75: 13 says: Man will be notified on that Day about anything he has sent on ahead or else held back. It is demanded through the verse 66: 6 that "Oh you who believe, save yourselves and your family members from Hell." The verse 42: 45 says that you will see them brought before awed and humiliated, looking at it with stealthy glances. The true believers will say: "The real losers indeed are those who have lost themselves and their families on the Day of Resurrection." Beware! Surely the wrongdoers shall suffer everlasting punishment. Believers are those who say what they do and do what they say. The verses 61: 2-3, say: Oh believers! Why do you say something that you don't do? It is very hateful in the sight of Allah that you say something that you don't do. Follow the do's and don'ts of Qur'an and earnestly instigate their followers for it. They do work as according to the Prophet's saying that the best and noble one among you are those who learn and teach the soul of Qur'an. Believers, by considering the verses 2: 159- 161, 174- 176 and 3: 187, will convey and propagate the Soul of Qur'an, which is the Message of Allah to entire mankind. It is told in the verse 16: 44 We have sent down this Message to you that you may explain clearly to men what is sent for them and that they may reflect to others. The believers utilize all their abilities for that. But the hypocrites utilize all their abilities to prevent the propagation of the Soul of Qur'an. See the explanation 2: 39 and 99. Whoever shed blood on Earth, its burden has to bear by these hypocrites. Read together the verses 6: 25- 27.

The hypocrites hide what Prophet has taught that the most wicked man is who recite the Qur'an without knowing Its Contents. But they only quote the Prophet's word, you recite not '*Alif- Lam- Meem*' from the Qur'an, unless it is recorded as ten times good for each alphabet and say to the laymen it is virtuous the recitation of Qur'an even without understanding the contents. Thus by bearing the burden of peoples' sins, they will go to the bottom of the Hell even without trial as told in the verse 4: 145. Among the three groups who recite the Qur'an, only the believers shall have virtue not only by '*Alif- Lam- Meem*' but also by whole Qur'an. There is no benefit with Qur'an to the '*fujjar*' who try not to understand Its contents and to the hypocrites who knowingly hide and do not follow. For them It will increase nothing but loss after loss as told in the verse 17: 82. And the recited Qur'an will argue and witness against them. That is the meaning of what Prophet taught those who recite the Qur'an without understanding Its contents dart from *Islam* as the arrows darts from the bow. It is told in the verses 8: 22 and 55 the worst of beasts are the dumb who knowingly hide the Soul of Qur'an but not convey to others and the deaf who hear not the Soul of Qur'an. They are decreed to be filled in the Hell as per the verse 7: 179.

It is warned in the verses 16: 24- 25 that those who say the Qur'an is the tales of ancients and prevent men from Its do's and don'ts having no knowledge about Its contents, shall bear a burden of those whom they misled. It is told in the verse 29: 12 that the disbelievers say to those who believe, follow our path then we will bear your sins. Never in the least will they bear their sins. In fact, they are liars. But they will bear their own burdens and a share in the burden of whom they misled as told in the verse 29: 13. The believers call mankind to the Soul of Qur'an and there by to a way of life which is easy and finally to Paradise. But the hypocrites call mankind to a life which is very difficult and thereby to Hell. The disbelievers mentioned in the verses 41: 26- 28 are the hypocritical leaders, and disbelievers mentioned in the verse 29 are their followers are the *fujjar* who are blindly following them. Read together the verses 17: 15; 27: 89-90 and 41: 40-44. See the explanation 2: 6- 7, 261 and 4: 49.

86. Whenever you are greeted with some greetings, then answer them back with some thing finer than it or at least return it. Verily, Allah is a Reckoner for everything.

The believers should enter any houses by greeting one another with a blessed and wholesome greeting from Allah as told in the verse 24: 61. On the day of *Isra'* and *Mihraj* when Prophet entered in '*Jannathul-ma'wa*'- garden of Paradise- and greeted Allah as: "All greetings to Allah and all prayers, all wholesome things. Allah greeted back saying: 'Oh Prophet! Let the peace up on you and His Mercy, His blessings. So, as 'greeting is done by Prophet first, start with '*Salam*' is voluntary. And as *Salam* returned back is by Allah, to return back the '*Salam*' is compulsory. Read together the verses 17:1, 43: 45 and 53: 1- 17. One man came to Prophet and said: 'Oh prophet, let the peace of Allah up on you'. Then by returning the *Salam*, Prophet said: ten. In another time that man came to Prophet and greeted as: 'Oh Prophet let the peace and Mercy of Allah up on you'. Prophet returned the *Salam* and said: 'Twenty'. In another time the same person came to Prophet and said: 'Oh Prophet, let the peace, Mercy and blessing of Allah up on you', Prophet returned the *Salam* and said: 'Thirty'. The indication of what Prophet taught is that the person who returns the *Salam* in the best way to the believers as told above shall get increasing virtue as ten times, twenty times, thirty times respectively.

Allah says to Prophet in the verse 58: 8 that, the hypocrites will greet you in a way that even Allah has not greeted you. And ask themselves, why Allah doesn't punish us for the tactics we make against Prophet. The Jews and hypocrites used to greet Prophet ironically and ridiculing as 'let the destruction up on you'. Then Prophet replied to them as: 'On you'. And if he had understood that what Jews and hypocrites saying are not the pray for curse, then he returns the greeting as: 'And on you'

It is taught by Prophet that no greeting should say to the hypocrites- who are killed by Allah, and commanded the believers for great *Jihad* with the Soul of Qur'an as per the verses 9: 73 and 25: 52. Read together the verses 4: 91; 9: 123; 33: 1, 61 and 48: 29. And if they greet you, then return the greeting to them in the deserving manner. As Allah has cursed and killed them, how the believers can pray as: 'Let Allah be with you' for such hypocrites? It is ordered by Allah to believers in the verse 9: 84 that, not to perform *swalath* on the dead body of the hypocrites, and not to stand near their grave. And as per the verse 9: 113 it is ordered by Allah to Prophet and the believers that, not to seek forgiveness for those who are doing '*shirk*', even if they are the father or mother. Read together the verse 58: 22. To know who are doing '*shirk*' see the explanation 2: 176, 4: 80 and 81.

87. Allah, there is no Deity except Him. Surely He will gather you all together on the Resurrection Day; there is no doubt about it. Who is more truthful than Allah- as a Narrator?

The verse 39: 32 says: Who is more in the wrong than someone who lies about Allah and rejects the Truth when It has come to him. Is there no place in the Hell for such disbelievers? The verse 33 says: Those who received the Truth and made It truthful such are the heedful. Read together the verse 29: 68. Here Truth implies the Soul of Qur'an. See the explanation 2: 2, 38 and 185. In the verses 7: 185 and 75: 50 Allah asks: Then in which speech you are going to believe after this? The verse 4: 122 ends as: 'Who could be more truthful in his words than Allah? In the verse 39: 22 Allah says: Then one whose chest Allah has widened to *Islam* and he is in a light from his Lord, will he be same as one whose heart has become hard and become astray, and there by entered in the street of the '*Wail*' in the Hell. In the verse 23 it is told that, Allah has sent down the best Speech and the Book that includes the verses in which similarities and examples are being referred repeatedly. By these verses the skins of those who are afraid of Allah will be thrilled. Then their skins and hearts will be vibrating humbly because of the remembrance of Allah, with the Soul of Qur'an. That is the true Guidance of Allah with which Allah makes into true Guidance whom He intends. And whom Allah made astray, there is no one to guide him. Read together the verse 35:14. "Oh Allah, make us heedful i.e. those who make the Truth truthful as It should be made truthful".

Prophet taught: The best Speech is the Book of Allah, and the best explanation is Prophet's sayings. All new narrations are evils. Newly formed customs and words are included in new narrations in Islam, and all new narrations are astray. All astray are into the Hell. Whom else is firm in that astray, he will go deep into the depth of the Hell. In the Qur'an everything is explained. The verses such as 16: 89, 17: 41, 89, 18: 54 and 39: 27- 28 denote that in the Soul of Qur'an everything is explained. Allah says in the verse 25: 33 that, they do not come to you with any questions, until the Truth of which is given to you and the best interpretation of which the people till Last Day will not get any chance to ask such questions. That means '*Ijithihad*'- to find out the Guidance- is to find out words of the Qur'an concerning any matter and to understand the idea of It through reading together the references given in the verses in different parts of the Qur'an. Really *Hadeeth* is the Soul of Qur'an, and *Hadiya* is the contribution of Prophet as the explanation of Qur'an specified in the verses 53: 1-4 and 75: 16-19. In brief, Qur'an is All times Knowledge of Allah- the Knower of All times. Prophet taught: The peculiarity of the Qur'an, the Speech of Allah above all other Speeches is the peculiarity of the Creator Allah above all His creatures. Therefore, Allah says in the verse 6: 155 that, this Book is a blessed One, We have sent down It, then you follow It and keep Allah in your heart so that you should be blessed. See the explanation 2: 78, 213; 3: 95, 138; 4: 78 and 82.

88. Then why should you take both sides concerning hypocrites. Allah has discarded them because of what they have earned. Do you want to guide someone whom Allah has let go astray; anyone whom Allah lets go astray, then you will never find a way back to Him.

Read together the verse 5: 49. It is told in the verse 2: 99 that, those who conceal the Soul of Qur'an are transgressors. The verse 59: 19 says: Those who forget Allah, forget themselves and are the transgressors. The verse 9: 67 ends as: Indeed the hypocrites are the transgressors. The verses 7: 175 and 176 say: As they ignore the Qur'an for a silly benefit of this material world after getting knowledge about It, the satan followed them and thus they lost the aim of life. According to the verse 58: 19 they are the party of satan who have forgotten Allah and the Soul of Qur'an. What Allah says in the above verse is that, the believers shouldn't have two opinions about the hypocrites. The Impartial Allah does not make anyone astray; instead they themselves select the way of astray. Through the verse 9: 95 Allah commands the believers neglect the hypocrites, since they are filthy. And their lodging will be the Hell as a consequence for what they have been earning. See the explanation 2: 26- 27, 159- 161; 3: 97 and 4: 47.

89. And they would love for you to disbelieve, just as they disbelieve. So you will be exactly like them. So do not take any of them as your friend till they migrate along the Path of Allah. If they should ever turn against you, then seize them and kill them

wherever you find them. And do not take any of them as your protectors or helpers.

The hypocrites referred in this verse are those who hide in their house for not participating in the battle with the believers. Today "till they migrate along the path of Allah" means, to stop the enmity towards propagating the Soul of Qur'an, to learn and follow It and to become ready to teach It to the entire people. The verse 25: 52 says: You don't obey the hypocrites who hide the Soul of Qur'an, instead you do strenuous strive against such hypocrites with It. In the verse 9: 23 Allah says by calling the believers: You don't consider and accept your parents and brothers as your friends and protectors if they are fond of disbelief than belief. If any of you do so, then such are the wrongdoers. Read together the verse 58:22. See the explanation 2: 109; 3: 28, 91 and 4: 60 - 63.

90. Except those who join a people with whom you have a treaty or who come to you because their chests shrink from fighting you or fighting with their own people. If Allah so wished, He would have given authority over you, so that they would have fought. Yet if they keep aloof from you, and do not fight you, and propose peace to you, Allah doesn't grant you any way against them.

91. You will find others who will try to make believe you as well as try to believe their own people; yet they every time come upon another chance for dissension, they plunge into it. If they neither keep aloof from you nor yet propose peace to you and hold back their hands, then seize them and slay wherever you may run across them. Over such persons We have given you clear authority.

If the hypocrites are living impartially without harming the believers or their own people, let them live in the Earth of Allah up to the period that Allah has fixed for them considering that they are the creatures of Allah. But when the believers are fighting with enemies, if the hypocrites indulge in it without keeping impartiality, then Allah orders to seize them and slay them wherever they are met with even after the battle. Both in the verses 41: 28 and 63: 4 it is told that the hypocrites are the enemies of Allah and the believers, and Allah has already killed them. Today there is no war, but only *Jihad* with the Soul of Qur'an against those who hide It. Both the verses 9: 73 and 66: 9 say: Oh Prophet! Make Jihad against the *kuffar* and the hypocrites and deal harshly with them. Hell shall be their home, and that is an evil abode! The verse 9: 68 says: Allah has promised the hypocritical men, the hypocritical women, and the *kuffar* the Hell Fire to live therein forever, a sufficient recompense. Allah has cursed them and they shall have an ever-lasting punishment. The *kuffar* mentioned in the verses are the gone astray people mentioned in the verse 1: 7. Allah orders believers not to behave harshly not to say greetings to the hypocrites who are involved in secret plots against propagating the Soul of Qur'an to entire mankind. Believers are also prohibited to take them as friends or helpers, even if they are their parents, brothers, sons, daughters etc as specified in the verses 9: 23-24 and 58: 22.

The command to seize the hypocrites and slay them wherever you met, through this verse as well as the verses 9: 123; 33: 61 is to the group of believes, not to the individual. Today, since there is no group of believers anywhere in the world, this order can't be implemented. If there is a group of believers, It is told in the verse 24: 55 that Allah will give them the power. But today a few believers are living individually here and there throughout the world. The *Maseeh-A-Ddajjal* will come as the Army General of Israel. Then all the hypocrites will accept him as prophet at first; later even as their lord. It is because he will fulfill the wishes and ambitions of hypocrites. Then *Eisa* will come and kill him. All the non-Muslim people will recognize and approve the *Islam* as their way of life. Then The hypocrites and their blind followers who falsify prophet and Soul of Qur'an can not find any shelter and hiding places. Even each trees and stones will proclaim that there is a disbeliever hiding behind It, so seize and kill him. Thus the orders of these three verses will be executed. The orders of these three verses mentioned in the Qur'an have not been implemented either by Prophet or any other Islamic rulers. No one has ruled the world keeping Mecca as the capital. The believers who are utilizing the Soul of Qur'an as Insight accept the day of Fasting, *Arafa* and *Eid* on the same day of *Mecca* where the '*Qibla*' is situated, considering the command of the verse "For any matter, wherever and whenever you may be, turn your faces towards it".

Today, what the believer to do on such hypocrites whom Allah has wanted to kill is to say them the words which penetrate to their inner hearts such as your similitude are like donkeys and Jews as told in the verse 62: 5; as dogs as per the verse 7: 176 and as pigs as per the verse 5: 60. Then warn them that they will be resurrected in the Hell in the shape of those ugly creatures. As per the verse 9: 120 these words which will cause to make the hypocrites anger will increase the weight in the Balance for believers. Otherwise, today using these words like donkeys, pigs, dogs, filth etc against hypocrites is more weight gaining than the weight gaining glorious words like 'Glory be to Allah and All Praises to Him, Glory be to Allah- the Great Glorious'. In brief, believers have to implement the teaching of Prophet that, when an evil is seen it is to be prevented by hand. If it is not possible, then prevent it by tongue. And even if it is not possible, then hate them by mind. If not do so, there is no belief even of an atom in him. See explanation 2: 254, 3: 119 and 4: 63.

92. And no believer should kill any other believer unless it happens by mistake. And anyone who kills a believer by mistake should free a believing slave and deliver blood money to his family, unless they forgive it as an act of charity. If he was from an enemy nation, which is at war with you and yet he was a believer, then free a believing slave; while if he was from a people with whom you have a treaty, then it means blood money should be delivered to his family and freeing a believing slave. Those who are impossible to free a slave should fast for two consecutive months as repentance from Allah. And Allah is Aware, Wise.

Blood money or deserving compensation has to be fixed by justice authority or ruler with justice. Read together the verse 5: 95. What Prophet fixed was either one hundred camels or two hundred cows or two thousand sheep or an amount equal to their cost as compensation. Even though the slavery system is not existed today, that command can be implemented by giving financial help to a person in order to seek his lively-hood himself. The preference in all aspects will be given to the believers. If the deceased believer belongs to the enemy people, no compensation is prescribed. But in any case to free a believing slave is compulsory as repentance is prescribed. Since instead of saying 'no slave was find to be freed' in the verse, it is told that 'those who are impossible to free a slave', it is enough to fast two months consecutively as a repentance from Allah. If the deceased believer belongs to a nation with which exist a mutual treaty, then rulers of that nation will decide the compensation amount with justice.

93. And anyone who kills a believer deliberately will receive as his reward of sentence to live in Hell forever. Allah will be angry with him and curse him, and kept prepare dreadful torment for him.

The first murder that took place in the world is the murder of '*Haabeel*' by '*Qaabeel*' - two sons of Adam. As it is told in the verse 5: 30 that his soul yielded for the murder, it can be understood that the murder was deliberately. Prophet has taught that he will get a portion of the punishment for every murder that take place in the world. See the explanation 4: 85. Allah has recorded in the Book for the children of Israel that if anyone kills a person except as punishment for killing a person or destructing the Earth, then it is equal to kill the entire mankind. And if anyone who spares life acts as he had granted life to entire mankind. Read together the verses 5: 32-33. Being the explanation of the verse 39: 53 Prophet taught a fact that Allah has accepted repentance of a person who made one hundred murders. We can understand that, the person did the murders not deliberately. The verses 39: 55- 59 say: Follow the best way revealed to you by your Lord- the Soul of Qur'an- before the death comes to you all of a sudden, while, you do not even perceive it. Lest someone should say: 'Alas! I neglected my duty towards Allah and I was one of those who mocked at His verses.' Or lest he should say: `If Allah had guided me, I would have been one of the heedful.' Or lest he should say upon seeing the punishment: `I wish I had another chance, I would certainly be among those who live seeing Allah through the Soul of Qur'an.' Then Allah will say to him: "Nay, My verses did come to you; but you rejected them, were arrogant and you were among the disbelievers."

Today only Muslims are reading all these verses. But ignoring the contents, they are involved in all mischievous deeds such as blood shed, and terrorism. Actually the read Qur'an will witness and argue against them. They would have to bear the sins of entire people for not utilizing the Soul of Qur'an, and they don't give others to utilize It as the Balance to keep the Universe in its equilibrium. See the explanation 2: 178- 179, 4: 29- 31 and 82.

94. Oh you who believe, whenever you get start in the way of Allah, discriminate carefully and do not tell someone who proffers a greeting: 'You are not a believer' seeking worldly gain, while with Allah has many booties. That is what you were like previously. Thus Allah bestowed His favors on you. So you discriminate very clearly. Verily, Allah is acquainted of what you are doing.

'Discriminate' means to express the belief in order to identify the real believers and the hypocrites. The verse 9: 6 says that If anyone from the *Meccan* associates ask you for protection, then grant him asylum, so that he may hear the Words of Allah, and then escort him to where he can find safety. That is because they are the people who do not know anything. Thus Allah says the believers that, if anyone seeks refuge to you in the battlefield or one declares belief saying salutation '*Salam*'- peace be upon you- then, the believers should not kill him wishing to take the gain of battle or forgetting their previous conditions and forgetting about Allah. Since the believers are the real vicegerents of Allah, how can they show enmity to a people who have even not heard or touch the Soul of Qur'an? How can the believers show communalism, racism, etc? How could they make bloodshed? Read together the verse 8: 17.

As there is no party of believers today, the believers have to live following the Soul of Qur'an, just like the life of Prophet in Meccan period, and they are not ordered for war or killing even as retaliation, implementing punishment for fornication, *swalath* of Friday- *Jum'a,* group *swalath- Jama'at* etc. Instead what they have to do is to implement strenuous strive with the Soul of Qur'an to those who hide It as commanded in the verses 9: 73 and 25: 52 and help Allah by conveying the 'Message' to entire mankind in order to keep Universe in Its equilibrium as told in the verses 61: 14. Those who kill the innocent people who have not even touch the Soul of Qur'an by acting as a self-bomb; have to bear the burden of sins of the entire human society. Actually what Allah's order to the party of believers is to kill the human dogs as told in the verse 7:176 who induce and encourage the common people that killing other people than the Muslim is the *Jihad.* See the explanation 4: 91. Those who are killing for the country, society, tribe, clans, community etc. are not believers, but they are the transgressors and belong to the party of satan.

There are two types of unities in *Islam*. One is the unity of believers. See the explanation 3: 103. And the second is the unity of entire mankind. See the explanation 2: 256; 4: 1. Communal unity is the creation of Jews. And today, the hypocrites implement it among the Muslims. Allah has already recorded all the deeds in this world. So the believers are aware of this and they will always remember Allah praying by hearts that, oh my Lord! Include me the one to the Paradise and not among the 999 to the Hell. See the explanation 2: 255; 3: 191; 4: 49-50 and 80.

95. Those believers who stay at home- without any physical disability- are not equal to those who strive in Allah's path with their

properties and persons. Allah has granted a higher rank to those who make strive with their property and their persons than to those who stay at home. For each, Allah has promised a good reward, yet Allah shows preference to strivers with a great reward over those who stay at home.

96. Such higher ranks from Him, as well as forgiveness and Mercy, Allah is Forgiving, Merciful.

'*Jihad*' means, to utilize all the will and power to fulfill the aim of life. The aim of life is to return to the Paradise. During the period of Prophet and later when there were believers in leadership fighting with body, weapons and property included in *Jihad*. The verse 9: 111 says: Indeed Allah has bought up from believers their persons and their property, instead they may have Paradise; they fight in the path of Allah and kill and are killed. As a rightful promise from Him, in the Old Testament- the *Thourath*, the Gospel and the Qur'an; and who is truer in fulfilling his covenant than Allah? So rejoice in your bargain that you have made with Him, and that will be the supreme achievement. The verses 61: 10-12 say: Oh you who believe! Should I tell you of a bargain that will save you from a painful punishment? You should believe in Allah and His Messenger and strive in Allah's path with your property and persons. That will be better for you, if you only knew. He will forgive you your offences and admit you to gardens beneath which rivers flow, and will lodge you in beautiful mansions in the gardens of eternal favors, that will be a supreme achievement. Since there is no party of believers today anywhere in the world the believer can do jihad with Soul of Qur'an to the hypocrites who hide and reject It. In the case of non-Muslims, there is no compulsion in religion or Jihad against them, since they didn't touch or hear or prevent the propagation of the Soul of Qur'an. Therefore, today the believers should utilize all favors like properties, persons, influences to learn and teach the Soul of Qur'an to entire world, in order to keep the Universe in its equilibrium. Allah has granted to him a higher grade than the one who live as believers without doing so. That is the only way for fulfilling the Prophet's teaching that, '*the best among you are those who learn and teach the Soul of Qur'an*'. So those believers who stay at home reading the Soul of Qur'an and performing *swalath* are not equal to those who strive strenuously to convey the Soul of Qur'an to entire world irrespective of nations or religions. Read together the verses 4: 77 and 5: 67.

But there are some organizations among Muslims who claim that they are doing '*Jihad*'. Actually they are *mushriks* and belong to the party of satan as explaining the verse 2: 176. The name suitable for them is not '*Mujahid*'- 'those who strive'- but '*Muja'ed*'- 'those who repudiate with the verses'. The verse 29: 47 ends as: 'No one will repudiate with Our verses except the disbelievers', and the verse 49 ends as: 'No one will repudiate with Our verses except the wrongdoers. And the verse 41: 28 ends as: 'The Fire is the reward for the enemies of Allah as they were repudiating with Our verses. See the explanation 2: 5, 39, 218 and 4: 85.

97. Verily, those whom the Angels gather up the soul in death will ask, as they are wrongful to themselves: 'What were you doing with?' they will say: 'We were living as weaklings on Earth'. They will ask: 'Was not Allah's Earth so vast; that you might migrate to else where on it?' Then their abode is Hell, what a bad returning place!

98. Except for those men, women and children, who are really weaklings and cannot find any other means, nor are they guided in any way.

99. For those Allah may eventually pardon. And Allah is Pardoning, Forgiving.

Those who are wrongful to themselves told in the above verses are about those who had means to come out for *jihad* in the path of Allah, but did not do so. Today the wrongful are those who did not utilize the Soul of Qur'an and not giving It to others in order to utilize It as the Balance to keep the Universe in its equilibrium. Read together the verses 6: 25-26. The verse 29: 56 says: Oh My servants who have believed! Surely My Earth is vast to migrate if needed, therefore serve Me and Me Alone i.e. if living only for Allah is impossible in a particular place, then migrate to another place where living only for Allah is possible. Read together the verses 29: 56-60. The verse 7: 37 says: Who is more wrong than someone who invents a lie about Allah or rejects His verses? Such will have their portion from the Book presented to them, so that when our Messengers from Angels come to gather their soul in death, they will ask: 'Where is whom you used to appeal instead of Allah?' They will say: 'They have left us in the lurch, and they shall witness against themselves that they have been disbelievers. The verse 31: 13 says that, it is very wrongdoing to ascribe partnership in Allah's Power and Right as explained in the verse 4: 48. Read together the verse 6: 130. See the explanation 2: 254; 3: 193 and 4: 75- 77.

To put it briefly, those who received the Soul Qur'an- the Ticket and Guidance to the Paradise for entire mankind- cannot say at the time of their death that we were minorities, weaklings and oppressors. The disbelievers, wrongdoers and the transgressors are those who do not make judgment with the Soul of Qur'an in their individual, family and social life, is told respectively in the verses 5: 44, 45 and 47. Today, the Muslims all over the world are living a life away from the Soul of Qur'an, so that they are seeing as oppressed, shamed, and humiliated. See the explanation 2: 85. Prophet taught this condition of Muslims who learn and teach the body and life of Qur'an without the Soul being the explanation of the verse 3: 10. Today, if we compare Muslims and non-Muslims people using the Soul of Qur'an, we can see that, the formers are very advance in all evils such as bloodshed, communalism, racism, hoarding, adulteration, drug abusing, usury, making deficiency in measure and weighing, thrift, robbery, theft, fornication, homosexuality etc; and they are in very back in all good and merciful activities. This aimless people who are very attractive to the worldly life and lead an extravagant life are compared by Allah through the verse 7: 176 to a dog that will not change its attitude whether it is attacked or not. Read together the verses 13: 14; 22: 72, 25: 17- 18, 27- 30 and 34.

Without saying: 'Allah will pardon to them', what is told in the verse is 'Allah may eventually pardon' means that, Allah may forgive to the actual weaklings from men, women, and children if they are hateful to disbelief, unjust, and hypocrisy by their mind and if they are wishing and praying to be seen established the Message of Qur'an which is the Light to all world. Allah will never forgive to those who are adjusted by mind with disbelief, unjust and hypocrisy. See the explanation 3: 79, 110-112 and 4: 91.

100. Anyone who migrates to Allah's path will find many places for asylum and accommodation on Earth. Whoever leaves his home as a refugee for Allah's and His Messenger's sake, then has death over take Him, his reward become due and sure up on Allah. And Allah is Forgiving, Merciful

Prophet taught, certainly, 'all deeds are according to the intention. Everyone has what he intends, therefore anyone starts migration to Allah and His Messenger, and then his migration is to Allah and to His Messenger. Anyone else starts migration intending the gain of any worldly life or to marry the woman whom he loved, then he has it'. Prophet taught about a person belongs to children of Israel who had killed ninety-nine persons. He enquired to a worshiper whether he has repentance. He answered that there is no repentance to him. Then he killed him also and completed hundred. Then he went to a scholar who knows the Soul of Qur'an and enquired about the repentance for him. The scholar answered, 'yes might have', and advised him to go to '*Baithul muqaddis*'-sanctified *Masjid* in Jerusalem. He started the migration soon, but in the way the Angels came to gather his *Rooh*, the Angels of mercy and punishment became arguing in his case. Allah ordered to measure the distance from his starting place and the distance to the destiny. It was seen that he had advanced one foot more to the destiny than to the starting place. And so the Angel of mercy gathered his *Rooh*. See the explanation verse 93.

The verse 53: 39 says that there shall be nothing for a man except what he intends for. That means Allah looks to the hearts while anyone do any deeds. The recitation of Qur'an even during five times *swalath* without participating the heart, not only receive any reward, but also it will cause for punishment. Since, the read Qur'an will witness and argue against him as taught by Prophet. That means the Soul of Qur'an is compulsory for any deed to be made as good and accepted. See the explanation the verse 2:186.

Prophet taught that there is no migration after Meccan triumph. Today there is no group or country of believers anywhere in the world. As Allah told in the verse 29: 56, Oh my believing servants! My Earth is enough vast to live if you are My real vicegerents living only for Me. i.e. the Earth is wide to live as believers and no need to migrate anywhere. Prophet replied to the question of one of his companion, *Hudaifath-al-Yamani* that in case there are not a group or '*Imam*'- leader- of believers, they have to go to forest and stay by biting the bottom of a tree till death. Prophet also taught in the day of *Hajjath-al-Vida*'- departing pilgrimage- itself the literate believers to stay by hold fasting the Soul of Qur'an with the molar teeth. As per the Indian constitution there is not any hindrance and difficult to live as a believer since it belongs to the fundamental rights to maintain any belief and do any religious customs which do not harmful to others. Today the non-Muslims like Hindus, Buddha's, Sikhs, Christians and even Jews have not any enmity towards the real believers. But the hypocrites and *kuffar* are the real enemies of the Believer-Allah, Prophets and the believers. They are only making different objection in propagating the Soul of Qur'an. This boar people have to bear the burden of sins for destroying the world. See the explanation 3: 101- 103 and 4: 85.

101. When you travel out on the Earth, there is no blame on you if you shorten from your swalath, especially when you fear those who disbelieve may harass you. Indeed the disbelievers are open enemies of yours.

Only the believers are ordered to perform *swalath*. It is told in the verse 25: 63 that the beloved servants of Impartial Allah will pray to Him to abstain from the Hell that will be given as penalty for Muslims who perform *swalath*, Fasting etc. without becoming believers. If there is possibility of passing the vehicle for his travel and afraid of things to be lost, so it is allowed to shorten the *swalath*. Considering the verse 2: 239, in journey it is allowed to postpone the *swalath* with the body while he has to remember Allah by heart. See the explanation 2: 152 and 239.

102. When you, are among them then stood up for swalath in front of them, then let a squad of them stand up along with you, and hold on to their weapons. After they finish their prostrations, let them withdraw to the rear and let the other squad who have not yet prayed come up to pray along with you; let them hold on to their precautions and their weapons. Those who disbelieve wish to see you neglect your arms and your baggage, so that they could suddenly attack to overpower you all in one stroke. However, there is no blame on you if you lay aside your arms because of heavy rain or because you are sick and you take precautions for yourselves. Verily Allah has prepared a humiliating torment for the disbelievers.

Through the verse Allah teaches method of performing *swalath* during the war when weapon like bows and arrows, sword etc. are used. Today, as there is no battle between believers and deniers, and the weapons like guns, bomb, rockets and missiles are used, this method of *swalath* is not applicable. Since this verse is applicable for all times, when the followers of Soul of Qur'an are performing '*Swalath-al-jumua*', *Eid* etc. isolate from the Muslim society this method can be adopted if the disbeliever, wrongdoer and hypocrites mentioned respectively in the verses 5: 44, 45 and 47 oppose it. In the *swalath* performed during the war, *Imam*-leader- will get two *Rak'ath* and each squad of followers will get one rak'ath. While one squad of followers is guarding against the enemies, the other group performs *swalath* with *Imam*. When they completed prostration they turn back without saying *Assalamu Alaikum wa rahmathullah*- the words pronouncing at the end of the *swalath* and takes duty of guard and the other squad who has not performed *swalath* come forward and perform *swalath* with Imam. During *swalath* they have to bear weapons and take precautions against the attack of enemies.

103. Once you have finished your swalath, remember Allah while standing, sitting and on your sides-laying. Then when you are in peace and tranquility keep up swalath in its complete form. Surely swalath is a timely prescribed duty for believers.

It is told in the verse 20: 14 that *swalath* is performed to maintain remembrance of Allah or the Soul of Qur'an. In the verse 29: 45 it is told that verily the acceptable *swalath* prevents one from the shameful and evil deeds, and the most important is Allah's remembrance with the Soul of Qur'an. As per the verse 11: 87 the disbelieving people of Prophet *Shua'b* asked him does your *swalath* command you that we must abandon what our forefathers worshipped, or that we should not do what we wish to with our property ; Yet you are only forbearing right minded one. The verse 63: 9 says, Oh you who believers, let not your wealth or children prevent you from the Soul of Qur'an, if anyone do so such are the only losers. It is told in verse 59: 19 that the believers should not have a condition of forgetting Allah. Those who forget Allah, they are the hypocrites who forget themselves. The verses 4:142-143, 9: 53-55, 67-68 say: as the hypocrites have no remembrance of Allah in their *swalath*, hence their *swalath*, charity, welfare tax etc. will not be accepted, upon them there are curses and anger of Allah. They have to stay constantly in the Hell by suffering the grievous punishment. Believers always exist in *swalath* by soul. In peace condition they will perform the '*Swalath-al-Wusthwa*' with 'peace and tranquility', as explained in the verse 2: 239 in which the body also participates. This verse also teaches that only the believers who follow the Soul of Qur'an need to perform *swalath*. The disbelievers, who hide or reject the Soul of Qur'an by performing *swalath* are thrown away from the '*Dheen*' just like the arrow dart away from bow as taught by Prophet. For those who perform mimicry *swalath* they will get the '*wail*' -the severe torment area of fire- as told in the verses 107: 4 and 5. For those who do any deeds in which the body stands witness but the soul does not, in the Day of Judgment their skins, hearings and sights will stand witness against them as warned through the verses 41:19-24. Read together the verses17: 36; 36: 65; 99: 4 and 5. See the explanation 2: 121, 3: 190-191 and 4: 43.

104. And yet you do not faint of heart in pursuit of people. If you have been suffering hardship, then they are suffering hardship just as you are suffering; while you expect something from Allah that they do not expect. And Allah is Aware, Wise.

This verse teaches the believers that they should not have any reluctance or laziness for joining to the battle, because disbelievers are also suffering difficulties and strains like the believers. Moreover, believers are expecting martyrdom, whereas the disbelievers are aiming the gains of worldly life and fear death. See the explanation 3: 146. The *Moui'dhath* of this verse teaches that since there is no war or killing today, the believers have to come forward without any reluctance, laziness, miserliness or fear to propagate the Soul of Qur'an to the entire people in their heart's language. The believers having the aim of life should not be like the disbelievers without the aim of life. Believers are living only for Allah and are helping Him by conveying His Message- the Soul of Qur'an. It is the mission of the believers to introduce Allah and His Messenger to all the creatures. It is ordered in the verse 25: 52 that does not obey the disbelievers who hide the Soul of Qur'an and do strenuous strive against them with It. See the explanation 1: 4; 2: 21 and 3: 139- 142.

105. Verily, We have sent the Book down to you with the Truth. So that you may judge with It among mankind as Allah intends. And you do not act as an advocate for traitors.

The verse 39: 41 says: 'Indeed! We have revealed to you the Book with the Truth, for the instruction of mankind. He who follows the Right Way shall follow it for his own good; and he who goes astray shall do so at his own perish. You are not set up as a guardian over them'. 'Sent the Book down with Truth'- means you have to exist according to the Book's commands and prohibitions and you have to invite the people to Allah according to the Book presents and you have to perform the duty of teaching the Book. It is told in the verses 34: 26; 39: 69 and 75 that in the Hereafter also the judgment will be made according to the Qur'an which is the 'Truth'. Read together the verse 10: 108. The verse 42: 17 says that it is Allah who has sent down the Soul of Qur'an which is Truth and Balance. So from this world itself everything should be weighed and should be decided according to the Soul of Qur'an. It is told in the verses 7: 8- 9 in the Day of Judgment there will be weight only to the 'Truth'. The verses 18: 103- 105 say: without Qur'an all deeds will be astray and there will be no weight in the Balance in the Day of Judgment. Not only among Muslims, but among mankind also Judgment should be made according to the Will and Desire of Allah which is the Soul of Qur'an as per the verse 16: 64. See the explanation 2: 146- 148, 213; 3: 128- 129 and 4: 78- 80.

106. You seek forgiveness to Allah. Surely, He is very Forgiving, Merciful.

107. You should not plead for those who betray themselves; Verily, Allah does not love anyone who has been a treacherous sinful.

108. They may try to hide from people while they can never hide from Allah; He stands along side them when they spend the night talking about something He does not approve off ; Allah encompasses anything they do.

In the verse 57: 4 it is told that He is with you wherever you are, and in the verse 58: 7 Allah says: three persons do not make secret talk except Allah is there as the fourth, and five persons do not make secret talk except Allah is there as the sixth. And decreasing or increasing persons do not make secret talk except Allah is not with them. It is told that Allah is The Micro Observer will inform them about all things. Read together the verses 10: 64; 11: 6 and 58: 8-10. 'Encompasses all things' means He has already determined and recorded everything not only the matters about each person but everything that will happen between the Heavens and Earth. See the explanation 2: 234, 255; 4: 81 and 88.

109. Ha! You, these persons argue for them in this world. Then who will be arguing with Allah for them in the Resurrection Day or who will take their responsibility.

The Resurrection Day is the day on which no one can do anything to others as explained in the verses 6: 164; 17: 15; 35: 18; 39: 7, and 52: 38- 42. Everyone has to answer individually before the Impartial and Justice Allah about every second after the fifteenth age of his worldly life. Read together the verses 6: 94; 18: 48 and 19: 95. On that Day the skins, hearings, sights, legs, hands and all parts of body of everyone will stand witness against them as per the verses 41: 19- 24; 24: 24; 36: 65 and 99: 4. As per the verse 6: 66 it is ordered the Prophet to say as I am not a responsible setup over you. The verse 10:108 ends as I am not a responsible set up over you. The verse 39: 41 ends as; you are not a responsible set up over them. The verse 39: 62 says Allah is the Creator of everything; He is the Custodian of everything. The verse 64: 13 says, Allah, there is no Deity except Him; so on Allah let believers entrust. Read together the verse 6: 102. Only the believers accept Allah as the Custodian and Guardian, whereas the disbelievers accept other creatures as custodians and guardians. Thus they actually accept satan as their custodian. Through the verse 14: 22; 43: 36-38 and 50: 27- 29 it is warned that on the Day of Judgment satan will clear out from the responsibility of misleading human by saying, 'you don't blame me, instead you blame yourselves'. See the explanation 2: 281; 3: 30, 122 and 4: 75.

110. And any one who commits evil or harms himself then seek forgiveness to Allah will find Allah is Forgiving, Merciful.

Read together the verse 39: 53- 55. See the explanation 4: 17- 18, 48 and 64.

111. While anyone who earns a sin, then earns it personally, Allah is Aware, Wise.

See the explanation 2: 286 and 4: 100.

112. Anyone who earns a blunder or a sin and then casts against some innocent person, will burden himself with slander and obvious sin.

See the explanation 4: 31. Through the verses 24: 11- 13 it is referred about the slander made upon *Ayisha*-one of Prophet's wives and *swafwan*- one of Prophet's companions by the hypocrites. Then in the verse 16 Allah asks the believers, "on hearing the slander why didn't you say: 'We ought not to talk about this. Glory be to You. This is serious slander! And as per the verse 17 it is advised as: not to repeat anything like it again if you are believers. See the explanation of the verses 2: 80- 81; 3: 97 and 4: 65.

113. If Allah's Bounty and Mercy were not lain upon you, a fraction of them would have aimed to plot about how to lead you astray; they only lead themselves astray and do not injure you in anyway. Allah has sent the Book and Wisdom down to you and taught you what you did not know. Allah's Bounty towards you has been splendid.

The verses 17: 73- 75 it is told about the disbelievers, they almost lure you away from what We have revealed to you, in order to invent something against Us; then they would adopt you as a bosom friend! If We had not braced you, you might have almost inclined a little bit towards them. Then We would have made you taste a double share of punishment in this life and a double one of dying; then you would not have found any supporter against Us. Read together the verses 10: 15- 16 and 22: 52- 55. See the explanation 2: 105 and 3: 186.

The verses 4: 105- 113 were revealed in connection with an event that happened in *Madeena* during the period of Prophet. One man named *Tha'math* who belongs to '*Banu safar*' tribe stole a war dress of an '*Ansari*' –helpers of migrated men from Mecca-. When the owner started enquiry about it, *Tha'math* gave it to keep near a Jew. The owner suited the case before Prophet and told his doubt about *Tha'math*. But *Tha'math* made conspiracy with his family, relatives and attributed it on that Jew. While the trial was undergone it was declared the Jew as innocent. But *Tha'math* and his family was pleading with partiality. They told: He is a Jew who rejects the Truth and Prophet. So, his argument is never believable and we are the believers and so our pleading is to be trusted. They wanted prophet to judge in favor of them. At the first look there was reason to keep doubt upon the Jew and to judge in favor of *Tha'math*. But by revealing the verses 105-113 and commanded to judge with the Truth among mankind as Allah's intention. The morality of this event is that the believers being the vicegerents of Allah should not have the bad characters such as selfishness, partiality of religion, cast, racism, communalism etc. Prophet taught; no one become believer till he satisfies others in the satisfaction of Allah, angers in the angry of Allah, gives to others in the satisfaction of Allah, and not to give to others in the dissatisfaction of Allah. Read together the verses 9: 113; 58: 22; 59: 9 and 64: 16.

The human devil hypocrites-the enemies of Allah- Prophet and believers aimed to plot against the Prophet and believers as told in the verses 5: 11 and 9:

74. The Bounty and Mercy, Book and Wisdom mentioned in the verse are the Soul of Qur'an. Therefore believers by utilizing the Soul of Qur'an as Safeguard and Shield can prevent the enmity from hypocrites and all other creatures. Then only the Soul of Qur'an becomes Bounty and Mercy and it will argue and witness in favor. See the explanation 2: 254; 3: 74, 101-103; 4: 88 and 97.

114. There is no good in most of their conspiracy except with someone who commands with charity, decency or reconciliation, among mankind. Whoever does so in pursuit of Allah's pleasure then We shall give him a splendid reward.

Through the verse 5: 2 Allah commands the believers "you co-operate and help each other in the matter of virtue and piety; and not to co-operate in transgression and enmity, but the hypocrites killed by Allah are plotting to obstruct the propagation of the Soul of Qur'an which is the Balance to keep the Universe in Its equilibrium and these human devils rushing in mischief making and communal unity among Muslims and thus destroying the world. As per the verses 9: 55, 84- 85, 95, 125 they are filth and Qur'an will increase for them filth over filth and they have to die as disbelievers and transgressors. See the explanation 2: 177; 3: 91; 4: 81 and 91.

115. Anyone who make schism from the Messenger once Guidance has been explained to him, and follows some path other than the believers', We shall turn him to wherever he has turned to, and roast him in the Hell. What an evil returning place!

Today the Soul of Qur'an is the Guidance for entire mankind as per the verse 2: 185. Its carriers are Muslims. But they neither utilize It nor giving others to utilize It. Thus they became the people upon whom the wrath and anger of Allah has happened and gone astray people. Thus they falsify the Prophet and the Soul of Qur'an. Among them the hypocritical leaders knowingly hide the Soul of Qur'an and the *fujjar* who eat the body of Qur'an without Soul, blindly follow the hypocrites. They are the fuel of Hell-fire as explained in the verse 3: 10. The life of Prophet was Qur'an. So the life of believers should also be codified under the Soul of Qur'an which is the Ticket to the Paradise and Safeguard, as well as Shield from the Hell. See the explanation 4:82. The verse 47: 32 says: The ones who disbelieve and obstruct Allah's way and show schism from the Messenger even after Guidance has been explained to them, will never injure

Allah in anyway while He will let their deeds futile. And in the verse 33 Allah says: Oh you who believe, obey Allah, obey His Messenger and do not leave your deeds useless. And as per the verse 34 it is told: "Allah will never pardon those who disbelieve and obstruct Allah's way, then die while they are disbelievers. See the explanation 3: 91

In the verses 8:13 and 59: 1-4 it is told that those who live apart from Allah and Messenger, they will be severely punished in the Hell. See the explanation 3: 101- 106; 4: 63- 65 and 80.

116. Allah does not forgive ones who associating others with Him; if forgive anyone He wishes for anything beyond that. Anyone who associates others with Allah then he strayed far away from the Truth.

See the explanation 1: 7; 2: 137, 166- 167; 3: 97 and 4: 48.

117. They appeal nothing instead of to Him except the female deities; and they are not call upon except some upstart satan.

Meccan pagans had considered Angels as Allah's daughters and *Jinns* as Allah's sons as explained in the verse 6:100. But as per the verses 34: 40- 42 on the Day when all His creatures will be summoned, Allah will be asking the Angels, 'where they invoking or serving you' they will reply, "Limitless Glory be to you! You are our Patron instead of them. They were invoking and praying to *Jinns* moreover most of them believing with *Jinns*." Allah will say; 'today none of you has any power to benefit or harm for others, We will tell those who have done wrong: "taste the torment which you have been rejecting". By invoking any of Allah's creatures including Prophets such as Muhammad, *Eisa*, *Moosa, Uzair* or any great person such as *Sheikh Mohiyuddeen*, *Ajmeer Kwaja*, etc. or Angels, *Jinns*, they are not invoking other than the upstart satan who prevents the human from Allah's Straight path- the Soul of Qur'an. The verses 25: 17- 18 warn that on the Day in which Allah will assemble His creatures and the persons to whom they were invoking other than to Allah, He will ask the great persons; were it you who led astray My servants? Or did they strayed themselves? Then those great person will answer; 'Glory be to You! We would never take on any Patron besides You! However You let them and their forefathers enjoy things until they forgot the Soul of Qur'an and became a worthless people. See the explanation 2: 154.

The verses 7:194- 195 say, indeed those you appeal to besides Allah are servants just like yourselves. Then appeal to them so they may respond to you if you are so truthful! Have they feet to walk with, or hands to grasp things with, or eyes to see with, or ears to hear with?" Say: "you call or your associates besides Allah; then plot away against me, and no need to give me any respite. Read together the verses 7: 190- 193, 196- 199. The verse 19: 93 says that everyone who is in the Heaven and Earth not coming to the Impartial except as servant. Fearing anyone other than Allah or obeying anyone by disobeying Allah is becoming the servants of satan-the disbeliever. As per the verses 19: 44- 45 Prophet *Ibrahim* says to his father; oh my father, you do not serve the satan. Certainly satan is disobedient to the Most Gracious. Oh my father! By selecting satan as patron, I fear that the punishment from the Most Gracious will afflict you. See the explanation 1:4, 3:154-155; 4: 51- 52, 75 and 76.

118. Allah cursed him. And he said: I will take a major portion of Your servants.

Allah cursed him means that, Allah has expelled him from His Mercy and broke the link. But Allah has cursed and killed the hypocrites who hide the Soul of Qur'an and ordered the group believers to kill them. Read together the verses 9: 67- 68, 80; 10: 33; 13: 25 and 63: 4-6. What satan said in the verse 'I will take a major portion of Your servants' is explained by Prophet as follows: From every thousand, one is to Paradise and nine hundred and ninety nine are to Hell, and this ratio is well-known, specific and fixed. Satan declared: Since you let me deviate now, I will live in ambush for mankind on Your Straight Path. I will come upon them from the front, from the rear, from the right, from the left and You will not find most of them to be grateful. Allah said: 'Get out of here, you despicable outcast; I will certainly fill Hell with you and all of them who follow you' is told in the verses 7: 16-18.

If your Lord has so willed, He could have made mankind one community, but they will not seize to differ except those on whom your Lord has bestowed His Mercy- means who utilize the Soul of Qur'an. And for this did He created them, and the word of your Lord shall be fulfilled 'I will fill Hell with *Jinns* and men altogether' as told in the verses 11: 118 and 119. Certainly, on you lay the curse until the Day for Repayment. Satan said: 'My Lord, let me wait till the Day when they are resurrected'. Allah said: "You will be among the one who are allowed a respite until the Day of known time". Satan said: My Lord, since You have let me go aimless astray, I shall make things on Earth seem attractive to them; and I will make aimless astray them all, except any of Your sincere servants who live only for You among them. Allah said: This is the Straight path up to Me. Surely you will not hold any authority over My servants except for some one who may follow you from among those who are aimless astray and the Hell is promised abode for them all, is told in the verses 15: 35 and 43

Satan asked: 'Tell me, and he is the one whom You have honored above me? If You will postpone things for me until the Resurrection Day, then I shall certainly uproot all except few of his offspring under my mastery.' Allah said: okay, you go, any of them who follow you will have Hell as his reward; it is such an ample reward! Entice any of them whom you can with your voice, set upon them with your cavalry and your manpower. Share wealth and children with them and promise them anything, and the promises of satan are nothing except deception. Surely, as for My servants you will have no authority over them; and your Lord suffixes as a trustee is told in the verses 17: 62-65

If We had so willed, We could certainly have brought every soul its true Guidance, but the word from Me will come true-promise is given to satan-certainly I will fill Hell with *Jinns* and men altogether. Now taste the reward for your forgetting the meeting of this Day, We too have forgotten you-taste the ever punishment as the reward for your deeds in the World. Read together the verses 32: 13-15. Certainly My curse shall be on you till the Day of Judgment. Satan said: Oh my Lord, give me respite till the Day when they are resurrected. Allah said: Respite then is granted to you till the Day the time of which is fixed. Satan said: By Your Power, I will lead them all astray except Your servants who live only for You. Then Allah said: This is the truth and the truth what I say that, I will certainly fill Hell with you and all of them who follow you, as told in the verses 38: 78-85.

The verses 16: 99-100 say: Certainly satan has no authority over those who believe on their Lord. His authority rests only on those who list him as a patron and who associate others with Allah. It is told in the verse 7: 27 that, satan and his tribe see you from a position where you cannot see them, We have made satan as friends and protectors to those who do not believe. The verses 10: 99-100 say: If your Lord had so wished, everyone on Earth would have believed, all of them together! So will you force mankind to become believers? It is not up to any soul to believe, except with Allah's Permission; He places blight on those who don't think utilizing their intelligence. Allah's Permission means the Soul of Qur'an. So nobody will become a believer without the Soul of Qur'an, which is the food and cloth of human soul as explained in the verse 7: 26.

Impartial Allah will not lead anyone to Paradise or Hell. But the believer will utilize the Soul of Qur'an as a Ticket to the Paradise and as a Safeguard and Shield against all disasters as well as Hell. Whereas satan will help the disbelievers in this World and lead them to the Hell by obstructing them from the Soul of Qur'an. The verse 19: 83 says: Don't you see that, We have sent satan to disbelievers to confirm their desires. The verse 6: 43 ends as: 'And satan whatever they were doing seem attractive to them!'

So what we have to do, to become the one in every thousand who enter Paradise is tell individually to Allah-the Lord- "I am Your servant, my destiny has come, I do not know whether it is to Hell or Paradise, if it is to Hell make me amend it by myself and include me the one to Paradise and not include me among the losers. Thus one should grasp the character of Allah from the Soul of Qur'an and follow It in this life and live as His vicegerent. See the explanation 2: 143, 146 and 152. As per the verse 2: 64 the *Rah'math*- Mercy- is the Soul of Qur'an. Those who live without the remembrance of Allah- without the *Rah'math*- worship satan and live for him. It is warned to such madmen in the verses 36: 59-61 that, on the Day of Judgment Allah will say: Did I not take covenant from you, Oh children of Adam! That you should not live for satan for that he was to you a manifest enemy? And did I not tell you that, you should live only for Me, which was the Straight path? See the explanation 2: 256-257; 3: 86-91 and 4: 91.

119. And surely, I will lead them astray, and conjecture them on. I will order them to slit the ears on life stock and order them to alter what Allah has created them. Anyone who adopts satan as patron instead of Allah has obviously lost out.

120. He promises them and conjectures them on; yet satan promises them nothing except delusion.

121. Such will have Hell as their refuge. And find no escape from it.

Satan tempted Adam and his wife to eat the forbidden fruit by creating false desires in them that, they can become Angels or immortal by eating it. He swears that he is their well-wisher and thus deludes both of them to expel from the Paradise as told in the verses 7: 19-22. Shortly Adam, who got the remembrance of Allah expressed the sorrow by his heart; and Allah Who knows about the states of heart put to him the words mentioned in the verse 7: 23. See the explanation 2: 37. In the verses 22: 3-4, Allah says: There are some among mankind who argue about Allah without any knowledge. They are following the satan who is deeply immersed in arrogance and commanding for it. It is recorded over him that whoever selects him as friend, surely will mislead him and will guide him to the Blazing Fire. In the verse 7: 201 it is told that: Surely, those who are heedful, whenever some impulse from satan touches them- whereupon they will remember Allah by heart- and then are granted insight. See the explanation 2: 122. The verse 202 says: As for satan's brothers, they drag them deeper into error and holds there firmly. Read together the verses 7: 175-176, 17: 27. In the verse 25: 29 it is told that, on the Day of Judgment man himself will confess that, satan forbid the man from the Soul of Qur'an. In the verse 43: 36 it is told that, We appoint a satan for those who turns away from the Soul of Qur'an, and he will become his intimate friend. In the verse 37 it is told that, satans will prevent them from the Path of Allah, and yet they think that they are in the Right path. In the verse 38 says: But in the end, when the man come to Us, he will mourn that: "Woe to me! How better it was, if there had been a distance of two East between you and me. What an evil soul mate you are"! The verse 50: 27 has explained about the scene on the Day of Judgment that, the satan - the companion from Jinn - will say: Our Lord! I did not mislead him compulsorily, but he himself was far away from the Truth. The verses 58: 16-19 has specified the condition of hypocrites- who are the human satans- on the Day of Judgment. Read together the verses 58: 16-19.

As per the verse 14: 22, satan will say when the matter is decided: Allah promised to you a true promise. I too promised you, but now I defy it. However, I had no authority over you, I just invited you and you replied to me. So do not blame me, but blame yourselves. I am not your protector and you are not my protector. Surely I reject what you did in the Worldly life that you associated me with Allah. Certainly there is a painful punishment for the wrongdoers. Both in the verses 6: 112 and 114:6 it is told that, there are satan's among men and Jinn. In the verse 59:16 it is told that, satan will quit the responsibility from those who became disbelievers by his command. And the verse 17 it is told that, thus the end of both- man and his soul-mate- will be that they will dwell in Hell forever; such shall be the reward for wrongdoers. In the verses 35: 5-6 Allah says by calling the mankind: Certainly the promise of Allah will come as true.

Therefore let not the life of this world deceives you, and let not the chief deceiver-satan- deceives you about Allah. Surely satan is your enemy, so treat him as enemy. Surely he is calling his followers to be burned with him in the Blazing Fire. See the explanation 2: 168-171 and 268.

In the verse 30: 30 it is told: So keep your face set upright towards the *Dheen*-the True religion-, Allah's natural handiwork, along which lines, He has patterned mankind. There is no way to alter Allah's creation. That is the upright way of life-*Dheen*, though most among mankind do not realize it. Prophet taught that all the creatures are being born in the nature as Muslims. Livestock are also being born in the natural way, i.e. without slitting the ears. The verse 5:103 refers about livestock with slighted ears that, they used to offer as *Baheerah, Sa'ibah, Wasweelah* or *Ha'm* by inventing lie against Allah. Prophet taught that satan only is commanding for such evil acts. In the verse 31: 21 it is told that, those who follow their forefathers blindly, satan is calling them to the punishment of Blazing Fire.

By saying "order them to alter what Allah has created them" means that, the body organs which are created by Allah will be misused against His wishes. In other words, for what purpose this Qur'an is revealed, satan will cause to deviate from that aim and will make them use the Soul of Book defectively as done by those who were given the Book before as explained in the verse 57: 16. Satan will command for evil deeds like lottery, gambling, usury, liquor, narcotics, omen, sorcery, theft, robbery, racism, bloodshed; and the anti-natural- non Islamic acts like homosexuality, fornication, family planning, monasticism etc. All the leaders from different Muslim organizations are human satan, cursed and killed by Allah and the *fujjar*, who follow them are the gone astray people. The scene of both of them blaming each other in the Hell can be seen in the explanation of 2: 166-167; 3:86 and 91. To such disbelievers, believers are commanded through the verse 109: 6 to tell 'for you your way of life, for me the True way of life-*Islam*'. See the explanation 4: 78 and 79.

122. And We will enter ones who believe and perform honorable deeds into gardens beneath which rivers flow, to live there forever. Allah's promise is true; who could be more truthful in his speaks than Allah.

See the explanation 4: 82 and 87.

123. Not your desires or those of the people of The Book. Anyone who commit an evil will be rewarded accordingly and not find any patron nor helper for himself besides Allah.

Each individual has to answer about each moment of his life which he spends after attaining the age of 15 years in front of Allah. The peculiarities of religion, caste, race, nation, family, or party will not get any consideration there. All these are not pleased by Allah. Any partialities based on such are the ways of satan. See the explanation 2: 120-121; 3: 195 and 4: 85.

124. And any one who performs honorable deeds, whether it is a man or a woman provided he is a believer, those will be entered the garden and not be harmed a speck.

Without being a believer, no one will be entered in to the Paradise. Both in the verses 13: 14 and 40: 50 it is told that, the deeds of disbelievers will not be accepted and their prayer will increase nothing except astray. The verse 16: 97 says anyone who acts honorably whether it is a man or woman provided he is a believer then We shall live a wholesome life and reward them with their earning for the finest deeds they have been doing here. The verse 40: 40 says anyone who commits some evil deeds will nearly be rewarded with something else like it, while some one who acts honorably, whether it is a man or woman, provided he is a believer will enter the garden. He will be provided for There without any reckoning. Read together the verses 39: 33-35 and 41: 46. See the explanation. 2: 186; 3: 97 and 4:115.

125. Who is better in Dheen than the one who submits himself completely to Allah, and live by seeing Allah, and follow the way of Ibrahim the upright and Allah adopted Ibrahim as a bosom friend.

It is the only verse that says: Allah adopted *Ibrahim* as a bosom friend. The verse 41:33 says: Who is better in speech than the one who calls people towards Allah, and performs honorable deeds, and says: "Surely, I am of those who completely submitted to Allah?" The verse 31: 22 is also with the same Message. See the explanation 2: 112, 257 and 3: 148.

126. All things those are in the Heavens and on Earth belong to Allah. He encompasses everything.

See the explanation 2: 234, 255; 3:128-129 and 4: 108.

127. And they will consult you concerning women. Say: Allah advices you about them, and what is recited to you from the Book concerning orphan-women whom you have not given what was assigned to them while you are disinclined to marry them; and minor children, and supporting orphans with fairness. Allah is Aware of any good you do.

Decision concerned with women are mentioning in the following verses. See the explanation 4: 2-6.

128. If some woman fears abuse or desertion by her husband, there is no blame if both of them agree to reconcile by means of a compromise. Coming to compromise is best, while greed is ever present in souls. If you are living by seeing Allah and keeping in hearts, then surely Allah is Acquainted anything you do.

When a man has two wives, and he feels a lack of affection towards one wife, they should compromise by discussing their problems each other with the Light of Qur'an and should lead a peaceful life. If one wife is unable to satisfy her husband in their married life, then the man can marry another woman by retaining the first wife. Husband and wife should lead a life only in the pleasure of Allah by leaving their selfishness and as per the nature demands realizing that Allah is the One Who unites the couples as told in the verses 25: 54 and 30: 21 and by with a conscious that, He has fastened the destiny of every human on His own neck as explained in the verses 17: 13 and 14. Both in the verses 59: 9 and 64:16 it is told that, only those who is saved from the selfishness of their own soul will only prosper. Allah has sent each person- whether male or female- to this Earth in order to prepare Paradise from here itself. That is the aim of this life; and everyone should live here without forgetting that aim and by remembering Allah always with the Soul of Qur'an. See the explanation 2: 177; 3: 136 and 4: 1.

129. And you will never manage to deal equitably with woman no matter how eager you may be to do so; yet do not turn completely aside from one so you leave another in suspense. If you reform good and you become heedful, then surely Allah is Forgiving, Most Merciful.

The Lord, Who knows the mental aspects of men, says: Even if you try your best, you cannot deal justly between your wives. But you should not incline completely towards one wife by suspending the other just like keeping the one waiting in vain. Man cannot deal equitably in all matters. Such situations, by considering the verse 128, they can discuss each for a compromise and come to harmony by giving her the protection and facilities completely and a term of once in a week or month for sexual intercourse. If one wife is too old and not interested in sex, then also according to the verse 4: 34 it is must for husband to give complete protection and comforts even if there is no sexual intercourse with her. *Sauda*- one of the wives of Prophet- was old. So she gave her term to another wife *Aysha* and remained as the wife of Prophet. See the explanation 2: 231-233.

130. Yet if they should separate, Allah will enrich each out of His abundance; Allah is Boundless, Wise.

Before creating each person itself, Allah has already determined and recorded their life-time, food and other resources. The verse 11: 6 says: No animal exist on Earth unless Allah provides for it. He knows its resting place and its go down; everything is in a clear Book. See the explanation 6: 38. In the verse 29: 60 it is told that, how many living creatures are there do not carry their sustenance with them! Allah feeds them and you. He is all Hearer, all Knower. In the verse 50: 4 it is told that, We know that where they will die and how much of their bodies will be consumed by Earth; and We have preserved a Book of everything recorded. Believers are living by accepting Allah as '*Asswamad*'- independent of others- and all others necessarily depend on Him. Read together the verses 112: 1- 4. Such are the ones who are living only for Allah as His vicegerents and will be entered into His house- the Paradise. Read together the verses 57: 22; 22: 70 and 31: 34. See the explanation 2: 236, 241-242; 4: 32 and 33.

131. And for Allah belongs whatever is in Heaven and whatever is on Earth. And indeed We have instructed those who were given the Book before you, and you as well, to heed Allah. And if you should disbelieve, Allah still owns whatever is in Heaven and whatever is on Earth. And Allah is Self-sufficient, Praise worthy.

132. For Allah belongs whatever is in Heaven and whatever is on Earth. And Allah is enough as a Trustee.

133. If He wished, He could remove you, Oh mankind; and bring others. For Allah has the Power to do so.

See the explanation 2: 2 and 29. Allah is the One Who created heaven, Earth and all the things in between them from nothingness in six days and He undertook its control. In the verses 14: 19-20 Allah says: Are you not aware that, Allah has created the Heaven and Earth with truth. If He wishes, He will remove you and appoint other as His vicegerents as He pleases, just as He brought you from the offspring of other people. See the explanation: 6: 133. In the verse 39: 7, Allah says: If you reject, then Allah is Self-sufficient and independent of you. He does not like ingratitude from His servants. If you are grateful, He will please with you. No bearer of burdens will bear the burden of another. Ultimately, all of you have to return to your Lord; and He will tell you what you were doing in this life. Surely He knows the state of the chests. In the verse 31: 12 it is told that; whoever shows gratitude, does so for the sake of him only; and if anyone is ungrateful, surely Allah is Self-sufficient Praise worthy. In the verse 35: 15 Allah says: Oh mankind you are poor who have the need of Allah; but Allah is self-sufficient, praise worthy. And in the verses 16- 17 say: If He wishes, He is able to remove you and replace you with a new creation. That is not at all difficult for Allah. In the verse 64: 6 it says that, when the people become denied and turned away, Allah adopted self-sufficiency. Allah is Self-sufficient, Praise worthy. Read together the verses 64: 1-9. See the explanation 3: 97.

The verse 47:38 says: Ha! You are those who are called upon to spend in Allah's way, even though some of you are miserly! Anyone who acts as niggardly is miserly only so far as his own soul is concerned, Allah is Self-sufficient while you are poor. If you should turn away He will replace you with some other people who then will not be like you at all. In brief, Allah commands to the human that, they should remember Allah always and should live only for Allah as His True vicegerents by keeping the covenant done with Him and by obeying the commands and prohibitions i.e. do's and don'ts of the Soul of Qur'an. But only the believers will consider this command and the transgressed persons will follow the ways of satan. And when there is not even a single believer on this Earth, the end of this word will occur. In the verse 9: 39 Allah says by calling the believers that if you are not ready to march forth in the way of Allah, He will punish you with a painful penalty; and He will replace you with another people who never cause any trouble to Him. Allah is able to do all things.

Allah is Self-sufficient or Prosperous as explained above. The Soul of Qur'an also is self-sufficient or prosperity as Prophet taught: "The Qur'an is prosperity there is no poverty after that and there is no prosperity without that". Today to spend in Allah's way means only to spend for learning and teaching the Soul of Qur'an. The Soul of Qur'an is the Balance and Trust to keep the Universe in its equilibrium and the instrument to make the unity of mankind by eradicating the bloodshed and enmity. The above verses are giving a warning that, Allah will replace those people who do not utilize the Soul of Qur'an and who hide It from others without giving It to them. In the verse 6: 89 it is told that, if this people – Muslims- hide the Qur'an, then We will entrust this to a people who will never hide. See the explanation 2: 157-161; 4: 47, 91 and 118.

134. Anyone who wants a Worldly prize; then should know near Allah has Worldly prize as well as in the Hereafter, Allah is all Hearing, Observant.

Mankind has been deputed as the fourth phase to the Earth in order to cultivate for the seventh phase of life. So the aim of life is to construct Paradise in this World by seeing the Paradise through the '*Baswaer*'- the Soul of Qur'an. For *Baswaer* see the verse 6: 104. If the eyesight is not utilized to see the 'Insight', they will be filled in the Hell as explained in the verse 2: 6-7. See the explanation 2:152, 200-202; 4: 43 and 100.

135. Oh you who believe! Command with justice keeping Allah as witnesses even though it is against yourselves, your own parents and near relatives; whether it concern a rich or a poor man, since Allah stands closer to them both. So you do not follow any whims so that you may deal unjustly. If you distort about or neglect, Allah is acquainted with whatever you do.

The verse 5:8 says Oh you who believe, be command for Allah as witnessing with justice and let not the hatred of people make you mad to do in justice. Do just, that is nearer to heedfulness. Keep Allah in your hearts. Surely Allah is well acquainted of all that you do. "Command with justice" means command with the Soul of Qur'an. The word *Qwisth*- Justice- mentioned in this verse as well as in all other verses such as 5: 8; 10: 4; 11: 85 and 57: 25 is the Soul of Qur'an. The verses 5: 42; 49: 9 and 60:8 end as: "Indeed Allah likes those who do justice with Qur'an". Both in the verses 17: 35 and 26: 182 it is told that you should weigh with '*Qisthasul Musthaqeem*', it means indeed you should weigh with the Balance of Justice which is '*Swirathul Musthaqeem*'- the Straight path- means the Soul of Qur'an. Believers will please others in the please of Allah; and will express anger in the anger of Allah; and will give to others in the please of Allah; and will not give in the unpleasantness of Allah. In the verse 58: 22 Allah says: You will never find any people who believe in Allah and the Last Day on friendly terms with those who oppose Allah and His Messenger- even though they be their fathers, or their sons, or their brothers, or their close relatives (or their leaders). It is they in whose hearts Allah has inscribed faith and has strengthened them with a "*Rooh*"- the spirit of Supreme from Him. He will admit them to the gardens beneath which rivers flow, wherein they will live forever. Allah is well pleased with them as well as they well pleased with Him. They are in the party of Allah. Know that, surely only the party of Allah will be prosperous. The verse 9: 23 says by calling the believers: Do not choose your fathers and brothers as your friends, if they prefer disbelief over belief. If anyone among you chooses them- then it is they, who are the wrongdoers. In the verse 25: 72 it is told that, the most beloved servants of most Gracious will not bear witness to falsehood. Each one should stand firm for justice and command to others for justice with a conscious mind that Allah is seeing everything and on the Day of Judgment the skins, arms, legs, sight, hearing, Earth etc. will reflect the real picture in front of Allah as told in the verses 17: 36; 36: 65; 41: 19-24 and 99: 4. So the believer should stands on the side of justice- even if it is against self, parents, relatives, friends etc. By forgetting Allah, do not show any partiality towards the rich people for getting petty benefits. Also do not show partiality towards the poor against the rich persons thinking that being rich such a small loss is not going to affect him. In brief, command for justice among people and children by existing within the boundaries of Allah. Do not try to deviate from justice by hiding the witness and distorting the words. Prophet taught that, "*The best witness is the one who produces his evidence before he is asked for it*".

This verse teaches that every one should lead the life in a conscious mind that everyone is carrying their actions whether are recorded and tied up on their neck by Allah as told in the verses 17: 13-14: We have tied every man's fate around his neck and We shall produce a book enlightening spread open for him on the Day of Judgment. And will Say: Read your book, today you yourself is enough to see your account. In the Heaven or Earth-nothing is hidden from Allah. Remain always by remembering Allah by thinking that, one Day everyone has to answer before Him about each moment of this Life after the age of fifteenth. See the explanation 2: 152. The verse 16: 90 says: Allah has commanded with 'Justice' and '*Ihsan*'- living by seeing Him. Fear Allah the One Who acquainted and encompassed all your actions. See the explanation 2:177, 255; 3: 5-7, 30; 4: 59 and133.

136. Oh you who believe! Believe with Allah and with His Messenger, and the Book which He revealed to His Messenger, and the Book which He revealed previously. Who denies Allah, and His Angels, and His Books, and His Messengers and the Last Day; then surely he has gone far astray from the Right Path.

In this verse by calling the believers, Allah again says to believe. It means that, claiming and saying that 'we are believers' is not enough, but should make assure in that belief by means of the Message of Qur'an. Here it is not told to believe "in Allah and in His Messenger" but is told to believe "with Allah and with His Messenger. It means to believe in Allah which the 6236 verses of Qur'an submit. In the verse 45: 20 it is told that, this Qur'an is a *Baswa'er*- Insight- for the mankind; and a Guidance and Mercy for a people who have assured faith. Insight is the one which clearly shows to each soul everything like Allah, satan, soul and body of each one, where is the first creation, why mankind were sent to Earth, what is the aim of life, what is death, what is sleeping, what is the difference between death and sleep, what is Qur'an, why Qur'an, what for Qur'an, why should one use Qur'an, what is the Hell and punishment in It, what is Paradise and what are the blessings and enjoyments there, Day of interrogation, life way of Prophets, Angels, *Jinns*, and seat of each soul whether it is in Hell or Paradise. In the verse 32: 12 it is told that, if you could see the scene when these mad people- hypocrites and *fujjar*- bend low there heads and surrender before their Lords! They will say: We have seen and we have heard, so send us back to the world to do good deeds, surely now we are assured in faith. Read together the verses: 6: 26-27; 7: 53 and 40: 11. Here Allah commands that, every one should make assurance from this world itself and making assurance after reaching the Hereafter is worthless.

In the verse 27: 82 it is told that, Allah will bring out from the Earth a monster before the Last Day and that will speak to the people: "Surely mankind have no assured faith in Our verses" In brief, saying "We have believed in Qur'an" is not enough, but should have assured faith. Read together the verses 27: 83-85.

In the verse 30: 60, Allah commands to the Prophet and believers: So have patience, surely the promise of Allah will come true, so let not those who have no assured faith, shake your firmness. Read together the verses 30: 56-59. In the verse 15: 99 it is told that, you live for your Lord until you get the assurance; i.e. death. Read together the verse 15: 91-98. And in the verse 69:51 is told that, surely this Qur'an is the Truth which gives the assurance. See the explanation 2: 208- 210, 285; 3: 102 and 4: 87.

137. Surely, as for those who believe, then disbelieve and again believe, and again disbelieve- increase in disbelieve; Allah will never forgive them nor will guide them to the Right way.

138. To such hypocrites, inform the happy news that, for them there is a painful punishment.

139. They are those who accept the disbelievers as their friends instead of the believers. Are they seeking honor and dignity at their hands? But surely all honor and dignity belongs to Allah.

In the verse 61: 5 it is told that, Allah will not guide a people who have become transgressors; and in the verse 9: 67 it is told that, hypocrites are the transgressors. In the verse 8: 2-4 it is told that, Soul of Qur'an is the instrument to increase the belief; whereas in the verse 9: 125 it is told that, for the hypocrites who hide the Soul of Qur'an knowingly, It will add filth to their existing filth. In the verse 9: 95 it is told that, hypocrites are filth. Their abode is Hell as the reward for what they earned. So believers should neglect them; and in the verse 96 it is told that, they will swear to you in the name of Allah that, they love you. But even if you love them, Allah will never love a people who have become transgressors. In the verses 78: 21-22 it is told that, the Blazing Fire has kept prepared as the home for those who have become the servants of *Thaghooth*- Satanic forces- by forgetting the aim of life. The verse 23 says: In it they will live for ever; and in the verses 24-25 say: In it they will taste neither coolness nor drink except boiling water and decaying filth; and in verse 26 says: All these are the full reward for what they earned; and in the verse 27 says: Surely they were not expecting the Reckoning; and in the verse 28 says that, they were rejecting and falsifying Our verses repeatedly; and in the verse 29 it says that, We shall not increase you nothing but punishment. In the verse 5: 57 it is told that, oh believers! Do not choose as friends, those from among the people who were given the Book before you and the disbelievers, who have made your religion a mockery and time pass, if you are true believers.

It can be seen that, today when the believers observe the *Eid*, Fasting etc. on real day, these hypocrites are neglecting that. They remain with those people who conceal the Soul of Qur'an and conduct "offering to devotees, instead of Allah" and thus become disbelievers. By doing so these hypocrites are expecting communal unity and thus seeking honor from them. In the verse 63: 8 Allah says that, the honor belongs to Allah, His Messenger and the believers; but surely the hypocrites are not aware of that. Believers always will seek refuge in Allah, but the hypocrites forgot Allah and are the human satans. In the verse 10: 65 it is told that, surely all honors and power belongs to Allah. He is all Hearing, all Knowing. Believes will seek honor and power in Allah; but the hypocrites will seek it in His creatures i.e. in majority. In the verse 35: 10 it is told that, if anyone is seeking honor, let him know that honor belongs to Allah alone. Read together the verses 9: 24, 53, 55, 80, 85; 63: 3 and 6. See the explanation 2: 26-27; 3: 28 and 4: 49-51

140. In the Book, He has revealed to you that when you hear Allah's verses disbelieved in and ridiculed, you should not sit with them until they change to some other topic. If you sit with them, then you would be just like them. Surely Allah will gather hypocrites and disbelievers all together into Hell.

Before this verse, Allah has revealed the verse 6: 68 which says: When you see those who are engaged in mocking our verses, turn away from them until they change their topic of discussion. And if satan causes you forget this, as soon as you recollect, withdraw from the company of evildoers. Based on these verses Prophet taught: "While reciting Qur'an, when satan deviate the heart from Its contents and interpretations, then you should stop reciting It. See the explanation 4: 43. Do not sit where the Qur'an is reciting to the dead, because it is against to the command of verses 6: 36; 30: 52-53; 36: 70 etc. The verse 17:36 says: Don't stand to hear something you have no knowledge about: your hearing, eyesight and intelligence will be questioned concerning it. Prophet taught that, body will stand witness against to those who do deeds without the participation of their soul. Read together the verses 41: 19-24. Here Allah commands to the believers that, while the hypocritical leaders who know the Soul of Qur'an deliver the Friday speech, or when they teach the Qur'an, or when they speak as the spokesmen of their organization; if they Quote the verses of Qur'an inappropriately, or if they twist the Message of verse by concealing the half part of it, then do not stand or sit there to hear it. Examples for twisting the verses are given in the explanation of the verses 3: 78 and 4: 63. This verse teaches that, those who twist the verse are hypocrites and the people who sit there to hear it are the disbelievers.

In the verses 33: 1-3 Allah says by calling the Prophet: Heed Allah and do not obey the disbelievers as well as hypocrites. And follow that which is revealed to you from your Lord. And entrust in Allah; for Allah is sufficient as Trustee. Allah is omniscient who encompassed all your actions. The disbelievers mentioned in verses 41:26-28 are the hypocrites and the disbelievers mentioned in the verse 29 are *fujjar*- who follows the hypocrites blindly. Both the hypocrites and *fujjar* collectively comes under the mad people- '*mujrims*'- . Hypocrites are those who twist the verses and do not follow the Soul of Qur'an even after knowing It. They are those who do not utilize their hearing, sight, and brain to understand the Soul of Qur'an. Read together the verses 7: 179; 18: 100-101; 20: 124-127. So the believers when reciting the verse 1: 7: "Not the path upon whom Your wrath happened", it should keep in mind that not among such hypocrites; and while reciting "And not on those who gone astray", it is not among those *fujjar* who accept such hypocrites as leaders". Way of believers is the way of Allah's single party which includes the truthful, martyrs, true witnesses and honorable men. See the explanation 2: 166-167, 254 and 3: 10.

141. Such are those who wait and watch about you. If you receive some victory from Allah, they say: "Were we not with you?" And if the victory is with the disbeliever, they say them: "Did we not help you and held off believers from you?" But Allah will judge between you on the Day of Judgment. And Allah has not granted the disbelievers any way to triumph over the believers.

Today, this is the very same attitude of the hypocritical leaders of different Muslim organizations and their followers who are the disbelievers. Each individual has the fundamental right to live according to his belief. Conveying the Soul of Qur'an is the only way to establish that right. Also that is the only way to help each one to identify him and to stop blood-shed and terrorism. When the believers convey the Soul of Qur'an, and if the impartial people come forward to accept Qur'an, then the hypocrites will say: "We are also saying Qur'an. In olden days, the disbelievers belonging to the Muslims majority who are offering to devotees instead to Allah had not allowed to say Qur'an here. But now, only because of our working everyone got the freedom to say Qur'an". Actually today the disbelievers are deeper in offering to devotees and invoking for dead at graveyards. Hypocrites are united with them in observing *Eid*, Fasting and have stopped criticizing their evil acts. These hypocrites say that even '*Shirk*'- associating partners in the dominion of Allah- is permitted for forming organizations and its unity. So the believers will not mingle with hypocrites and disbelievers- who don't lead a life under the shadow of Qur'an after receiving It- in any matter. And will do *Jihad* with the Soul of Qur'an against them. Also they will convey the Message of Qur'an to the entire mankind irrespective of nation or religion and will witness among them the life of Prophet. See the explanation 2: 113; 3: 119, 159-160 and 4: 73.

142. Indeed hypocrites try deceive Allah, while He is deceiving them. Whenever they standup for Swalath, they stand lazily to be seen by people. And not remembering Allah but a little.

143. Wavering in between, neither between these people nor those people. You will never find the straight way to some one whom Allah lets go astray.

The characters of hypocrites are portrayed in the verses 2: 6-16, 26-27, 99. They are wavering with doubt that where should they join- either to the believers or to the disbelievers. The verses 9: 53 and 54 Say: "Whether you give willingly or unwillingly, it will not be accepted from you; for you are the people who are transgressors". The reasons which prevent their contributions from being accepted are: they disbelieve with Allah and His messenger, and do not come to *swalath* except with laziness, nor do they spend anything except unwillingly. The verses 107: 4-5 it is told that, after entering the *swalath* by '*Thakbeerathul Ih'ram*', if there is no remembrance of Allah, then *swalath* will become for the satan. The *Wail*- severe torment part of Hell is for those who perform *swalath* with absent mind. It is told in the verse 20:14 that the five times *swalath* is prescribed to maintain the remembrance of Allah or to keep up the Soul of Qur'an. Without becoming a believer by the Soul of Qur'an, nobody's prayer will be responded or deeds will not be accepted as explained in the verse 2: 186. Allah commands Prophet and the believers first to recite the Qur'an and then to perform *swalath* through the verses 7: 170; 29: 45 and 35:29 etc. But the hypocrites will give first preference for *swalath* by neglecting the Soul of Qur'an. Actually they are mocking Allah, His verses and Prophet just like that of hypocrites in *Madeena* mentioned in the verse 9: 65. So they will get Hellfire as a penalty for performing *swalath*, fasting etc as told in the verse 25: 65. See the explanation 4: 56; 88: 90; 3: 90 and 91.

144. Oh you who believe! Do not choose disbelievers as your friends instead cf believers. Would you like to give Allah a clear authority against you?

This verse says to the believers who are among the party of Allah not to select the hypocrites who are the disbelievers and the disbelieving *fujjar* who do not try to learn the Soul of Qur'an, as your friends. Both of them are among the party of satan. And if anyone selects them as friends, who are against the command of Allah, then He will punish them severely. Read together the verses 61: 2- 3. In the verse 43: 67 it is told that, on the Day of Judgment all the relations will be in enmity except under the shadow of Qur'an. In the verses 25: 26- 29 it is warned that those who did not utilize the Soul of Qur'an in this world after receiving It will mourn in the Hereafter: 'Woe to me! Would I had never chosen so and so as my friend. He was the one who prevented me from the Soul of Qur'an after It had reached to me. Satan is ever a betrayer of man'. From the introduction of *Surath Alfathiha*, it is understood that satan will prevent human only from the Soul of Qur'an. Read together the verses 9: 17- 19, 24, 70 and 72. In the verses 31: 14- 15 it is told that, show gratitude to Me and to your parents. And if they compel you to commit '*Shirk*'-to associate partners to Me- about which you have no knowledge, then do not obey them. Still treat them according to the commands of Qur'an, but you follow the way of the one who has turned to Me. See the explanation 4: 59, 63 and 135- 140.

145. Surely, the hypocrites will go to the lowest depth of Hellfire; and you will not find any helper for them.

146. Except for those who repent and reform, holdfast to Allah, and dedicate their way of life purely to Allah only, such are with the believers, Allah will give believers a splendid reward.

147. What does Allah gain accomplish through your torment provided you act grateful and believe. Allah is Appreciative, Aware.

The Soul of Qur'an has explained about all the incidents which happened in the past, happening in the present, and going to happen in future. Also It is the Criterion to entire mankind to distinguish the way of Allah as well as the ways of satan, and the Balance to keep the Universe in its equilibrium. The hypocrites knowingly hide this fact from the mankind and because of that; they will go to the Hell without trial. See the explanation 2: 99 and 174- 176. As per the verses 42: 17 this Qur'an is actually a Balance for each individual to weigh their deeds from this World itself. Read together the verse 57: 25. As per the verse 17: 13-14 since each individual has fastened his fate around the neck as computer software, they have to reckon themselves their earnings in this World using the Soul of Qur'an as Balance. The verse 16: 64 says: We have not revealed this Qur'an to you except that you may explain to them in those things in which they differ, a Guidance and Mercy for the people who believe. These hypocrites, even after knowing the Truth are standing one step ahead in arrogance than the satan- the outcast one. They are falsifying and distorting Allah's way of life. In the verse 41: 26- 28 it is told that, they are enemies of Allah and Hell is their eternal home that is because they were repudiating against the verses of Allah. Read together the verses 7: 50- 51.

Fujjar are the disbelievers who do not utilize the faculties of hearing, sight, intelligence etc. which are given by Allah to understand the Soul of Qur'an and thereby fulfill the aim of life. Read together the verses 39: 32 and 7: 179. As per the verse 39: 71, they will be driven to Hell in troops only after trial. In the Hell, the hypocrites will be in the deepest bottom, then wrongdoers will be above that, and the common Muslims- *Fujjar*- will be on the top. These *fujjar*, who are the disbelievers, may be entered into the Paradise by the recommendation of believers who are residing in the Paradise after completing their punishment period concerned. Read together the verses 34: 23 and 50: 25. But the wrong doers and hypocrites have to reside in the Hell for ever. One day in the Hell is equal to fifty thousand years of Worldly life as specified in the verse 70: 4. Paradise or Hell is earning by each individual from this World itself. See the explanation 3: 136 and 182. Those people who go to Paradise without trial are called '*Sabiqeen*'- foremost people as specified in the verses 9: 100; 35: 32. Those who will be driven to the Paradise after trial are called the 'Right hand side'. For them, Prophet has to come and open the door of Paradise. See the verses 39: 73- 74. But for the disbelievers, the doors of Hell will be opened as soon as they reached near it as told in the verse 39: 71. In the verse 38: 50 it is told that, the doors of Paradise are already kept opened for those who go to Paradise without trial. The hypocrites will not try to understand their sins and will not repent on it. The verse 63: 4 says that, the hypocrites are the enemies of Allah and believers, and Allah has killed them. And the verse 10: 33 says that they will never believe. Through the verses 4: 91; 9: 123 and 33: 61 Allah commanded the party of believers to kill these hypocrites. But it will take place only after second coming of '*Eisa*'. As per the verses 9: 73 and 25: 52 it is commanded to the single believers to strive hard against these hypocrites and *kuffar*- who hide the Soul of Qur'an. Believers should tell them openly that, they will go to the deep of the Hell before the Jinn-satan. By hearing this, if they realize their faults, repent all to Allah, propagate the Soul of Qur'an to mankind which they were hiding earlier, and thus follow the way of believers who are foremost to the Paradise. Then they can enter the Paradise after undergoing Reckoning. See the explanation 3: 77- 78, 81- 82, 91 and 187.

Holdfast Allah means, remain always in the remembrance of Allah by the Splendid the Soul of Qur'an specified in the verses 41: 41-42 and follow the do's and don'ts of It. See the explanation 3: 101- 103. 'Allah is Appreciative' means for each person Allah has given the freedom to choose either the way of grateful or ungrateful as specified in the verse 76: 3. See the explanation 4: 1 and 132. If the creatures believe with the Creator by identifying Him and show gratitude, then Allah Appreciative and well Acquainted.

148. Allah does not love the evil talk in public, unless it is someone who has been injured thereby. Allah is all Hearing, all Knowing.

Believers should be always with a well conscious mind that, all the incidents occurring in this world is planned and recorded by Allah earlier itself. But they should not deal gently with hypocrites and wrongdoers, because it will lead them to more hypocrisy and evils. Therefore their character should be announced to the public openly and clearly. For example:- If one person borrowed money and did not giving it back even when he is able to return it, then it should be announced to the public so as to prevent others from falling in his trap. Read together the verses 9: 73; 16: 126- 128 and 48: 29. See the explanation 2: 254; 3: 74-75 and 4: 63.

149. If you do a virtue openly or keep it secret or forgive an evil, then surely Allah is Forgiving, Capable.

This verse inspires to do good deeds openly and secretly. One should not propagate the sins of others, but should forgive it. Qur'an is the greatest virtue. In the verse 32: 22 it is told that, Allah will revenge with those who do not utilize It or not give It to others after receiving It. See the explanation 2: 284, 3: 133-136 and 4: 131- 133.

150. Surely, those who deny Allah and His messengers; and those who make a separation between Allah and His messengers; and those who say: "We believe in some and disbelieve in others"; wanting to adopt a course in between.

151. Such are the disbelievers in Truth and We have reserved humiliating torment for disbelievers.

Disbelievers are those who hide and reject the Truth after knowing It. In other words those who hide Qur'an after receiving It. That is disbelievers are: (1) Those who do not realize Allah and His messengers from the Soul of Qur'an; (2) Those who make a distinction between Allah and His messengers; and those who believe in Allah and disbelieve in messengers; and those who believe in Qur'an and disbelieve in Prophet's teachings which are Its explanation; (3) Those who believe in some messengers of Allah and disbelieve in others. Read together the verses 2: 136, 285 and 3: 84. (4) Those that accept some verses of Qur'an and reject other verses. See the explanation 2: 85 and 121. (5) Those that are not included in the one and only party of Allah from the Adam to the Last Day, and became '*mushrik*' by joining in different Muslim organizations. See the explanation 2: 166-167; 3: 10 and 4: 136- 140.

Among these disbelievers, those who hide more verses are called '*kuffar*'. In the verses 9: 123, 5: 36, 39: 47 and 10: 54 it is told that, for such *kuffar*, if they have everything in the Earth and twice as much to offer as ransom to escape from the torment, it will not be accepted. In a verse, if it says only about '*kuffar*', then it includes both wrongdoers and hypocrites. If it is says only about '*dwalim*'- wrong doer- like in the verse 39: 47, then it also includes hypocrites. The verse 9: 73; 66: 9 has mentioned about both '*kuffar* and hypocrites. In such verses the '*kuffar*' are wrongdoers. In the verse 46: 35 ends as: 'Then shall any be destroyed except the transgressors?' And the verse 6: 47 ends as: 'Shall any be destroyed except the wrongdoers?' Then the end of this World will happen only when there is not even a single believer among the mankind and when all of them become wrongdoer or transgressor. Read together the verse 46: 35. In Qur'an, this is the only verse which starts as 'such are the disbelievers in Truth'. But in both in verses 8: 4 and 74 it is told that 'such are the believers in Truth'.

152. And for those who believe in Allah and His messengers, and make no distinction between them, for such We will give their due rewards. And Allah is Forgiving, Merciful.

"Make no distinction between them" means make no distinction between the messengers i.e. all massagers were in the same *Dheen*- Islam- and were propagating the same and are included in the single party of Allah-the only party of believers-. "Their due rewards" means the Paradise which they are constructing here. See the explanation 2: 132-136, 285; 3:136 and 4: 136.

153. If the people of Book ask you to bring down a book for them from heaven, surely they have asked Moosa much greater things than this afore time. They asked him: "Show us Allah in public". As a result of their wickedness, suddenly a thunderbolt seized them and they fell down unconsciously. Then they adopted the calf even after explanations had come to them. And We still pardoned them that; and We gave Moosa a clear authority.

In the verse 17: 93 it is told that, the Meccan pagans told the Prophet that, we will not believe in *Mihraj*- ascending to Paradise to meet Allah- until you bring down a Book for us that we can read. Read together the verses 17:90-94. The verse 25: 32 says that, the disbelievers used to ask that, 'why is not the Qur'an revealed to Prophet at a once as a single Book?" Read together the verses 17: 105-106. To Prophet *Moosa*, Allah gave a clear signs like "changing his staff to snake" and "shining the hand when it is put on to arm-pit and taken out. Read together the verses 7:133 and 28:31-36. Besides these clear signs, Allah commanded Prophet *Moosa* to strike the sea with his staff and the sea cleft aside as each part appeared like mountain as told in the verse 26: 63, and made a dry path along a sea as told in the verse 20: 77; and thus delivered the children of Israel. After they crossed the sea, Allah drowns the *Pharoah* and his party in front of their eyes as told in the verses 10: 90-92. Also for the children of Israel Allah gave the shadow of clouds, as an umbrella at the deserts of '*Seena*'; and gave 'Manna' and '*Salwa*' as their food; and divided them into12 tribes. And when the people asked for water, Allah commanded Prophet *Moosa* to strike the rock with his staff and there upon 12 springs gushed out from the rock, so that each tribe has its drinking place. Even after seeing all these signs and proofs, in the absence of *Moosa*, when he went to receive *Thourath*, they made a calf out of their ornaments under the leader ship of '*Samiryy*' and started to worship it. Read together the verse 7:148. Allah still pardoned them that, Allah gave the *Thourath* to *Moosa* as written on the stone discs as specified in the verses 7: 145, 150 and 154. But even after receiving It, they demanded that, they want to see Allah with their own eyes, Then *Moosa* went to "Mount *Thwoor*" with seventy selected persons to meet Allah. Then a thunder like quake seized them and they fell down unconsciously. Then Allah brought them back to life as specified in the verses 7:155-158 and 25: 21-23.

The authority which was given to Prophet *Moosa* includes all these signs, and *Thourath*, and Its explanation- which is the '*Furqan*'- Criterion. Jews and disbelievers who lived at the time of Prophet also demanded for a codified complete book. Even though, today that Book is present in the houses of Muslims in dozens and dozens, they are neglecting the verses such as 25: 18; 28: 48-50; 32: 12; 45: 31; 59: 19 etc.; flee from It like the wild donkeys flee by hearing lion's roaring as specified in the verses 74: 49-51 than any other people from their Book. The verse 25:30 says about the scene of Prophet saying complaint to Allah in the Hereafter against this people, on the Day of Judgment. As The Soul of Qur'an is the Splendid Book without entering any falsehood from before or behind for the entire mankind, those who do not utilize It and hide It from others are the most worst creatures as mentioned in the verses 8:22 and 55 and who will accept 30th pseudo prophet *Maseeh-A-Ddajjal* will be killed by the second coming of *Eisa*. They are the fuel of Hellfire from mankind. Read together the verse 33: 60-61 and 48: 6. See the explanation 2: 110-111; 3: 183 and 4: 91.

154. We raised the Mount Thwoor over them to take the solemn pledge from them. And We commanded them to enter the gates of that land prostrating in humility, and told to them that "do not break the law of Sabbath day". Thus We took a solemn pledge from them.

In the verse 7:171 it is told that, We suspended the Mount *Thwoor* over them as an umbrella to take a solemn pledge from them that "they will hold fast the *Thourath* and remember Its content with heart". And they thought that the Mount was going to fall upon them. Here it reminds about the incident that Allah told them to enter the Palestine through its real entrance and by saying "peace" to its residents. Read together the verses 5: 21-26; 7: 161 and162. In the verses 2: 65-66 and 7:163-166 it is explained about the matter of saying "do not break the law of Sabbath day". See the explanation 2:58, 63; 3:81; 4: 21, 46 and 47.

155. Because of their breaking the pledge repeatedly, their disbelief in Allah's verses, their killing the Prophets without any right to do so, and their saying: "Our hearts are covered over" instead, Allah has stamped them with their disbelief. Then they will not believe except a few.

156. And because of their disbelief, and their talking such terrible slander about Maryam.

157. Also for their saying: "Surely, we killed Maseeh, son of Maryam, Allah's messenger. In fact they neither killed nor crucified him, even though it seemed so to them. Surely, those who differ in his matter are also in a never-ending doubt; they have no real knowledge about him except by following conjecture. And they did not kill him confirm.

158. Rather Allah lifted him up towards Himself. Allah is Powerful, Wise.

See the explanation 2: 88 and 3: 21-22. These verses portrait the repeated arrogance and haughtiness of Jews. They accused the terrible slander of prostitution about *Maryam*. They boasted that they have killed the messenger of Allah, *Eisa Maseeh* the son of *Maryam*. As per the verse 9: 30 it is told that, they said that "*Uzair* is the son of Allah". Because of all these Allah cursed the Jews as well as the hypocrites, and He sealed their hearts and ears, and killed them. See the explanation 2: 99. Even though Allah has not commanded the believers to kill such Jews, but commanded to kill the hypocrites- who hide and twist the Soul of Qur'an and thereby introduce falsely the Qur'an and Prophet to the public by leading a life just against It. That is because they are one step ahead in arrogance, haughtiness and miserliness than the Jews. See the explanation 4: 37 and 38. In the verse 9: 84 it is told that believers should never pray for any of them who dies, nor stand at their grave by praying for them. Read together the verses 6: 25-26; 9: 55, 67-68 and 22: 6-10. If the Jews spread a slander about *Maryam*, the hypocrites of *Madeena* spread slander about *Aysha*- wife of

Prophet. For those people who utilize Qur'an as Insight can see that, today all the character of the Jews of that period is present in today's hypocrites all over the world. Allah has commanded to make the unity of mankind by conveying the Soul of Qur'an-food, cloth and sight of human soul- but the hypocrites are doing against It by arguing and trying to make the communal unity of Muslims. In the verse 3:103 Allah commanded by calling the believers: "Be a single party of Allah by holding fast His rope -the soul of Qur'an and do not differ". Neglecting such verses like 2: 176; 6: 159, 21: 51-53; 30: 30-32 etc. hypocrites form different groups and each groups rejoice what they possess with them. Hellfire is promised them as per the verse 11: 17.

'Even though it seemed so to them' or 'they are made fools' means when the Roman soldiers came in the supervision of Jews to catch and crucify Prophet *Eisa*, Allah- the Unquestionable, Powerful, The One Who do as He likes, the Almighty, the Wise- gave the face cut of *Eisa* to one of disciples named *Sarjas*, and lifted *Eisa* up to Him in his bodily form itself by a rhythmic whirlwind as explained in the verse 2: 164. Soldiers caught *Sarjas* who had the resemblance of *Eisa* and crucified him. In the verse 76: 28 Allah says: It is We Who created man, and We knows their frames and secrets. If We wishes, We will change their appearance. See the explanation 2: 158.

"Those who differ in his matter are also in a never-ending doubt" implies about the Christians, and Muslims who have no real knowledge. Some of the Christians believe that Christ got crucified by bearing all the sins of entire mankind. Among them there are those who believe that he has not crucified. Some others believe that Christ got crucified, resurrected and raised up on the third day. Today, none of the Christians have real belief about Prophet *Eisa*. In every thousand, 999 Muslims are also having the same belief of Christians about Prophet *Eisa.* Some of them claim that Prophet *Eisa* was crucified and only his soul was risen up to the Paradise. But here in this verse Allah has told "Allah lifted him up towards Himself". The preposition '*hu*' in the word '*Rafa'hu*' uses only when raise up the man in his bodily form. If it is the soul alone, then the preposition used will be '*ha*' instead of "*hu*". Both the soul of male and female are usually mentioned as feminine gender, and that can be realized from so many Qur'an verses like 2: 286; 6: 104, 164; 17: 15; 39: 42; 59: 18; 75: 22-23; 89: 27 etc. Soul of all believers will be raised to the Paradise up on their death. If only the soul of *Eisa* was raised to Paradise, then here it was not necessary to say the noble abilities of Allah- Powerful, Wise. One in thousand who utilizes the Soul of Qur'an as Insight alone can believe that Irresistible, Exalted Allah has raised his messenger *Eisa* up to Him in his bodily form. See the explanation 3: 45, 54 and 56.

He is the One Who changed the nature of fire to cool and peaceful for Prophet *Ibrahim*. Read together the verses 21: 68-70. He also showed *Ibrahim* that, how He gives life to dead, as explained in the verse 2: 260. While passing through a township which was fallen down up on its roof, *Uzair* soliloquized that, "who is there to bring this dead town back to life?" or "How could Allah bring this dead town back to life?" Then He is the One who caused *Uzair* to die and resurrected after 100 years, and resurrected the donkey which he used as his vehicle by bringing its bone together and covering it with flesh, as explained in the verse 2: 259. Naturally, the snakes getting birth by means of evolving of egg or by means of delivery, but He is the One Who changed the staff of *Moosa* to a snake against the natural laws. He is the One Who has given a camel- which is not begot nor begotten- as a sign for the people of *Thamood*. When the seven youngsters of the cave announced that, they will not call and pray anyone except their Owner Lord; He is the One Who led them to a cave behind a dog which not begets nor begotten, and caused them to sleep there for about 300 years. Read together the verse 18: 18. He is the One Who inspired Prophet *Moosa* to strike the sea with his staff and made the sea cleft to two part as if the water of each part appeared like mountain, and thus made a dry path in the sea for *Moosa* and his followers, as told in the verses 20: 77 amd 26: 63. He is the One Who brought *Pharaoh* and his troops to that dry path and caused the two parts of sea to join and drowned them in the sea. He is the One Who kept the dead body of *Pharaoh* safely in the sea for about 2800 years and then in Egyptian Museum as specified in the verses 10: 90-92. He is the One who inspired *Moosa* to strike on the rock with his staff and caused to gush out 12 springs from it when *Moosa* asked for water for the children of Israel.

He is the One Who delivered Prophet *Nooh*, and the believers, and a pair of each livings species of the World in an ark and drowned all disbelievers in the flood. He is the one who send the birds '*Ababeel*' which pelt the stones to destruct the army of '*Abrahath*' with elephants who came to demolish *Ka'ba* and thus left them just like chewed-up chaff; even though there were 360 idols inside the *Ka'ba*. Read together the verses 105: 1-5. He is the One who taught that, He will deliver believers from sufferings by delivering Prophet *Yoonus* when he prayed in the belly of whale that "there is no Deity but You, You are the Glorious One without happening any sin. Surely, I have become among the wrongdoers". He is the One Who gave food to *Maryam* in an unseen way. When Prophet *Zakariya* prayed by seeing this incident, He is the One Who gave him Prophet *Yahya*, as the son beyond any cause and reason. He is the One Who created Adam without a father and mother. He is the One who created *Eisa* without a father, and made *Eisa* talk with the People while he was in the cradle as per the verses 19: 28-34. He is the One who gave *Eisa* the ability to heal blind and lepers, and even to bring the dead back to life. See the explanation 3: 49, 5: 110. He is the One Who sent down "*Ma'eda*"- heavenly food tray- by making *Eisa* to pray for that as per the verses 5: 114-115; and He is the One Who transformed those Jews in to swine who are eaten from the feast then became suspicious about it was from the heaven or from here and thus defied the sign of Allah, as explained in the verse 5: 60. He is the One Who transformed those Jews-who transgressed the law of Sabbath and caught fish- into apes as a lesson for succeeding generations as explained in the verses 2: 65 and 66. He is the One Who made *Jinns* and satans obedient to Prophet *Sulaiman*. He is the One Who caused to bring the throne of Queen *Sheba*- which was about 1500 km far- in front of Prophet *Sulaiman* with in 'twinkling of an eye' by making pray the person using the 'Glorious names' who had the knowledge of Book. He is the One Who taught the language of birds and beasts to Prophet *Sulaiman*. Read together the verses 27: 18-19. As per the verses 38: 41-44 satan afflicted on Prophet *Ayyoob* and he boar distress and suffering for long as 15 years. At last he prayed as per the verse 21: 83 that, "adversity has afflicted me, You are Most Merciful of the Merciful". Then He is the One Who told him to stamp with his foot on the ground, and caused to have a cool spring, and told to drink and take bath with that and thus made cure all his diseases. He restored him, his family and gave doubled of His wealth and offspring.

He is the One Who unites the sperm from the semen of father and ovum from the semen of mother and cultivates it in the womb of mother in three darkness- chambers, and when it attains 4 months growth, He causes to takes the soul which is kept on the neck of father by Angel and blown into the "embryo" which has undergone various stages in the womb of mother. Thus He creates and moulds. See the explanation 4: 1. He is the One Who survive the life in the body by keeping the spirit which is the life + soul; and He is the One Who causes to die by taking the spirit from the body as told in the verses 6: 60 and 39: 42. He is the One Who developed the heart- which does the work for about 4 millions' rupees in a second; and brain- its nature of work is unknown and mysterious; and flesh, skin, hair, eye, nose etc, from a part of a single drop of semen. He is the One without having the beginning and end; Incomparable, Dictator, One and only Dominion of every thing Who acts as He wishes. Nothing is there unable for Allah, the Lord of the Worlds. Through the verses 82: 6-8 Allah asks: Oh man, what has lured you in the matter of your Lord; Who created you from nothing, then fashioned you, proportioned you, molded you and numbered you in whatever form He pleased? He is the One Who traveled Prophet Muhammad bodily from Mecca to *Baithul-Mugaddis* and from there to *Jannathul-Ma'wa*- which is situated above 7 Heavens and the border of Cosmos- and brought back in a single night as specified in the verses 17: 1 and 53: 1-17. He is in the One Who raised Prophet *Idrees* bodily to Heaven, as per the verses 19: 56 and 57. See the explanation 2: 28-33 and 4: 133.

159. And indeed there is nobody from the People of the Book except who will believe with him before his death, while on Resurrection Day he will act as witness against them.

The people of the Book includes all the people who has received a portion of the Book- particularly all Muslims. Read together the verse 7: 37. They will believe with him before his death also means they will believe with him before their own death. Appearance of *Maseeh-A-Ddajjal* and coming of Prophet *Eisa* are among the ten major signs of Dooms Day as taught by Prophet. As per the verses 43: 61-62 indeed he is the information for the coming of the Doom Hour. Therefore, have no doubt about it and follow me, this is the Straight path. Let not satan obstructs you; indeed he is an open enemy to you. As per the verses 43: 57-58 Allah says when the son of *Maryam* is quoted as an example, why, your people resist him! And they ask: "Are our deities better or is he?" They not quote him to you except for the sake of argument; indeed they are such quarrelsome people. Therefore before the actual death of *Eisa*, all the people will believe with him. Read together the verses 43: 57-65. See the explanation 3: 45 and102.

The people of Book including Jews, Christians and Muslims each will believe with the real stature of *Eisa* before the death of themselves. But with that belief they will not be benefited. In the verse 6: 158 Allah says, on the Day when some of your Lord's signs arrive, belief in them will not benefit any person who has not believed in them already, nor earned some good through his faith. See the explanation 4: 17 and 18. The death scene is prescribed in the verses 75: 22-30 as, on that Day, the believers' faces will be bright, looking towards their Lord by their souls; while the faces of disbelievers will be gloomy on that Day-looking satan- *Maseeh-A-Ddajjal*- with their souls- thinking that some backbreaking calamity is about to be inflicted on them. Indeed, when a man's spirit is about to leave and reaches to the throat, and someone says: "Is there any enchanter to help?" Read together the verses 56: 83-87. Then man will conclude that, it was the time of departure from this world, while agony will heap on agony; towards your Lord will be driven on that Day. 'Agony will heap on agony' means that he will distinguish that his belief was false and he will see all his evil deeds one by one that done during his lifetime after the age of fifteen. At that time all the people of the Book will believe with the actual position of *Eisa*. As per the verse 7: 37 the hypocrites who twist the verses of Allah and the *fujjar* who reject the Soul of Qur'an are more in wrong and they will witness against themselves at the time of death that "indeed we were disbelievers" and as per the verse 38 they will be told that "enter to the Fire along with the communities of *Jinns* and mankind who passed away before you. The believers by utilizing the Insight- Soul of Qur'an- will realize ahead the scene of coming during their worldly life, and they will codify their belief and deeds according to It. Read together the verses 39: 18, 33 and 53-60. See explanation 2: 186.

As per the verse 3: 49 and 43: 59 *Eisa* was appointed as a Messenger only to the children of Israel. 'While on Resurrection Day he will bear witness against them' mentioned in the verse means that he will bear witness which is against the Jews who tried to kill and boasted as explained the verse 157, and the Christians who became disbelievers by adopting *Eisa* and his mother as two deities besides Allah which is against the teaching of *Eisa* explained in the verse 3: 51. Read together the verses 5: 116-118. And by the second coming, he will bear witness against the Muslims since they made Prophet Muhammad and Islam false. Read together the verses 7: 157-158. The second coming of *Eisa* is not as a Messenger, but only to introduce Prophet Muhammad as the Mercy for all the worlds as told in the verse 21: 107. That is why *Eisa* is not leading the *swalath* but performs *swalath* behind the believer. Since today, Qur'an is the only Book for entire Worlds, the believer who learns and teaches the Soul of Qur'an will witness against the Muslims who hide and reject It. See the explanation 4: 115. The '*Ummath*'-community of Prophet Muhammad includes entire mankind since he is appointed to the Last Day, whereas his '*Quom*'- people includes the Mecca *mushriks* of that period and the Muslims later on. The verse 43: 44 says: Indeed it is a Reminder for you and your people and both of you will be questioned about It. If the Prophet who prayed for the favor of the community, will witness against the people on the Day of Judgment as told in the verse 25: 30. Read together the verses 25: 17-18 and 7: 175-176. See the explanation 3: 19, 55-56; 4: 150 and151.

The Maseeh-A-Ddajjal and the second coming of Eisa:-

Prophet taught that, "The children of Adam will not afflict more subversion than that of *Maseeh-A-Ddajjal*. All the Prophets have warned their people about the subversion caused by *Ddajjal*. I am the last Prophet and so *Ddajjal* will appear on you. Therefore teach your children about *Ddajjal*".

He will appear as a famous general of Israel army in the name of 'Mose-Dayal', *Maseeh-A-Ddajjal*. Prophet taught "thirty false Prophets will come forth from on words *Musailimath-al-Kaddhab* who came at the time of Prophet itself". Among them, *Ddajjal* will be the last and final false Prophet. He will pervade all over the world and will bring the world under his ruling power except '*Hijas*'- the provinces including Mecca and *Madeena*. Prophet taught that, "3 year before his appearance, the rainfall and agriculture will become less by one by third; in the second year, will become less by two by third; and in the last year, there will not be agriculture and rainfall. At that time he will appear". Prophet also taught, "On that period, the believers will live by *Thahleel*- announcing His solitary- and *Thakbeer*- announce His greatness- and *Thasbeeh*-make Him Glorified- and *Thahmeed*- praise Him". He is the tallest creature among human, and the greatest abilities of satan will be expressed through him. First he will argue that he is a Prophet, and will cause rainfall, germinate agriculture and give food for people. Later he will argue that he is the Lord. He will ask a village resident that "will you accept me as Lord, if I resurrect and bring your dead father and mother back to life?" And he will resurrect his father and mother by means of cloning or by any other methods. Prophet taught that: satan will form as his father and mother, and then the father and mother will tell him that he is your lord, so you accept him". The verse 23: 14 ends as: So blessed be Allah the best of all creators", it means that there are creators besides Allah- satan in the form of *Maseeh-A-Ddajjal* is given the power to create, and Qur'an is not against for that argument. "Allah is the Best creator of all creators" means that, only

Allah is able to create anything out of nothingness. Others can create the body alone -that itself from developing the cell. Anyway, Allah is the One Who gives spirit- life plus Soul.

We-the companions asked to Prophet: "how long will *Ddajjal* stay on Earth?" Prophet said: Forty days. The first day will be as long as a year, the second day as long as a month, the third day will be as long as a week, and the rest of the days will be like your ordinary days. We asked: Oh Prophet is it be enough five times prayer on such year long day? Prophet answered: No, but you have to calculate (i.e. 5 X 354) the times of *swalath*. We asked: "Oh Prophet! How he quickly will be reached around the earth? Prophet replied: Like clouds driven by the wind, he will reach all the places wherever mankind resides.

A believer from *Madeena* will come to *Ddajjal* who will be in outside *Madeena* to confirm about his appearance and will tell to him: "Surely, you are the same *Ddajjal* whose description was given us by Allah's Messenger. Then *Ddajjal* will say to the people: "If I kill this man and bring him back to life again, then will you believe that I am the Lord?" The believer will say: "No". Then *Ddajjal* will split him into two equal longitudinal parts and will keep a distance of a spear. Then by joining two parts he will resurrect him. The believer will say: "I was unable to see and distinguish you before in deep Insight as today". By hearing this, *Ddajjal* will try again to kill him but he cannot do so.

Oh the servants of Allah! Your Lord is not blind; you will see Him only after death. Read together the verse 6: 103. But the *Maseeh-A-Ddajjal* is having one eye. Prophet taught his right eye will be like a dry- sucked grape. Even for the illiterate believers who utilize the Soul of Qur'an as Insight could recognize him as disbeliever. But the hypocrites who hide the Soul of Qur'an will welcome and help him, and the common Muslims will be entrapped by him, because he will fulfill the ambitions of hypocrites and disbelievers. All the hypocritical men and women who live in *Hijas* will shift to other places where *Ddajjal* rules. By splitting a believer and resurrecting him, *Ddajjal* will ask: Am I the one who created you, and therefore could you recognize me as the Lord? Then that believer will reply: Nay, you are the fraud, *Maseeh-A-Ddajjal*; today, I came to know your reality than before. There will be hell and paradise with him. But his hell will be the paradise for believers; and his paradise will be paradise for hypocrites and hell for believers. Prophet taught, this World be like a hell for the believers, and they will get Paradise only after the death; but for the hypocrites this World is like the paradise and they will get Hell by death. See the explanation 3: 10, 136 and 182. Prophet taught, believers should recite the opening verses of *Surath Al- ka'hf*, so that the hell of *Ddajjal* will become cool and peaceful as that of the fire became cool and peace to Prophet *Ibrahim*. Read together the verse 21: 69. By reading the opening verses of that *Surath*, it is helpful for the believers to get the firmness belief of "the dwellers of the cave". Read together the verse 13: 28.

'*Hijas*' will get freed from the ruling power of hypocrites and will come under the leadership of "*Imam Mahdi*". Then the believers will assemble at the white minaret *Masjid* of Damascus under the leadership of *Mahdi* for the last fight against *Maseeh-A-Ddajjal*. While standing for the *swalath*, will hear a buzzing sound, the believers will look at the sky. They will see *Eisa* descending by placing his hands on the wings of two angels as like sitting in the armed chair. He will be on dress with saffron colored cloths as in 'Ihram'. When he will be called to lead the *swalath*, he will say that, the believers are leaders to one another, and hence perform *swalath* in the leadership of the one to whom for "*Iqamath*" called; and he will perform *swalath* behind the *Imam*. After the *swalath* the doors of the *Masjid* will be opened as per the command of *Eisa*, and there will be the *Maseeh- A-Ddajjal* and his 70,000 Jew soldiers ready to fight against believers. On seeing *Eisa, Ddajjal* will start to melt just as salt dissolve in water. Then *Eisa* and believers will follow him and will catch him at the place of '*Babu-ludh*' (Lyda airport). And *Eisa* will kill him with his spear and will show the blood to the people. Then the believers will kill 70,000 Jews soldiers of *Ddajjal*, the agitators in *Madeena* specified in the verse 33: 60. The non-Muslim people in the entire world will recognize and approve the *Islam* as their way of life. Then the hypocrites and those who have a disease in their hearts specified in the verse 33: 60 who hide and reject the Soul of Qur'an as well as falsify prophet and Islam will not find any shelter or hiding places anywhere in the world. Even each trees and stones will proclaim that there is a disbeliever hiding behind it, so seize and kill him. Thus the orders of three verses 4: 91; 9: 123 and 33: 61 will be executed. Thus the ruling power of world will come in to the hands of *Eisa* from the *Maseeh-A-Ddajjal,* and he will rule the World centralizing Mecca- the centre of the Earth- as capital. On that day all World will become like one country, and there will be one way of life- Islam, one Deity and one *Qibla*. On realizing the real faith, the Christians themselves will break the crosses and kill the swine; and Hindus will remove idols from all the temples. On that day Peace and freedom will come on Earth, so that anyone- even for women- can travel anywhere in anytime in the world without fearing others. After ruling the world for 7 years, *Eisa* will die at the age of forty, and will be buried in a grave near to Prophet Muhammad which is kept vacant now.

160. Because of the wrongdoing of those who became Jews, We have forbidden them certain wholesome things which had been permitted to them; due to their obstruction of so many people from Allah's path.

161. Taking of usury although they had been forbidden to, and eating other people's property in futile, We kept reserved painful torment for those among them who are disbelievers.

The verse 6: 146 says: We have forbidden to those who became Jews everything having a claw, and in the case of ox, sheep and goat, We have forbidden them their fat, unless it is located in their backs or entrails or that is mingled with their bones. That is how We have rewarded them because of their insolents and indeed We are Truthful. See the explanation 3: 93. As per the verse 16: 118, Allah says: We forbade those who became Jews what We have already told you; We did not wrong with them, but they were doing wrong to themselves. The Jews gradually made forbade some wholesome and lawful things themselves.

Today it can be seen that, the hypocrites are in the forefront than any other People even the Jews in all satanic foot steps like usury, smuggling, hoarding, narcotics dealing etc. by neglecting the verses 2: 188, 279. Even though in Islam- the natural way of life- the birth, marriage, and death are very easy, they make false, rites and customs against the teaching of the verse 7: 157; and there by add more load to the life burden of mankind in every sector. Thus they falsify Prophet and *Islam*. They speedup the coming of *Maseeh-A-Ddajjal* through falsification of *Islam* and the hypocrites will be the helpers of him. Read together the verse 7: 169. See the explanation 2: 275, 281; 4: 138 and 145.

162. Yet those of them who are well versed in knowledge as well as believers, believe in what is sent down to you and what has been sent down before you; and keep up swalath, pay the welfare tax and believe with Allah and the Last Day, for such ones We shall give a splendid reward.

Through the verse 26: 197 Allah asks: Do they not have a sign since the scholars from the children of Israel knew about this Qur'an. Today those who are well versed in knowledge and the scholars who fear Allah are those who know the Soul of Qur'an. See the explanation 2: 3-4; 3: 7, 79; 4: 82 and 136.

163. Indeed, We have inspired you just as We inspired Nooh and the Prophets who came after him; and as We inspired Ibrahim, Isma'el, Is'haq, Ya'qoob and the tribes, and Eisa, Ayyoob, Yoonus, Haroon and Sulaiman; and to Dawood We gave the Zaboor.

By saying that We gave the *Zaboor* - Psalm- to *Dawood*, it does not mean that only to *Dawood* has given the Book. Only one Book has been revealed from the Paradise to all messengers- whereas the soul is same and the body is in different languages. The name of the Book given to *Dawood* is *Zaboor*, the plural of it is '*Zubur*'. The verse 26: 196 says: Indeed, this Qur'an can be found in the *Zubur*- Psalms- of earlier. The verse 21: 105 says: We have written in the Psalm following the reminder: "Indeed, My honorable servants shall inherit the earth". The Psalm mentioned in this verse is The Book-Qur'an- as mentioned in the verse 15: 91. If it is the question that, why *Zaboor* is mentioned in the Place of the Book, then the answer is the *Zaboor* was in Poetical form. Read together the verse 24: 55. See the explanation 2: 2, 136; 3: 33 and 34.

164. And some Messengers about whom We have told you previously, while other Messengers We have not yet told to you about; and Allah spoke directly to Moosa.

As per the verse 40: 78 Allah says: We have sent Messengers before you some of whom We have told you about, while We have not told you about others. No Messenger can bring any sign unless it is with Allah's permission. Once Allah's commands come, the matters will be decided with Truth, and thereby the futile men will be the losers. See the explanation 2: 253; 3: 84 and 85.

165. Messengers conveying good news plus a warning, so that mankind would have no argument against Allah after the Messengers had come. Allah is Powerful, Wise.

Allah deputed all the Messengers for the same mission that to inform glad news to the believers who follow the Message that the Messengers brought, and as a warning to the whole mankind. As per the verse 21: 25 Allah says: We did not send any Messenger before you unless We inspired him with the fact that there is no Deity except Me, so serve Me alone! The verse 16: 2 says: He sends down Angels with the spirit of His command on any of His servants He may wish: "Warn mankind that certainly, there is no Deity except Me; so heed Me alone". The verse 16: 36 says that, We have dispatched a Messenger to every community who said: "Serve Allah alone and turn away from the arrogant ones". Then some of the communities, Allah has guided, while others there are for whom astray has been confirmed. Travel around the Earth and see how the consequences for those who reject the Soul of Qur'an. Messengers have been sent in order to witness the life which Allah satisfied among whole mankind, as told in the verses 33: 45 and 48: 8. And they will produce their witness in front of Allah on the Day of Judgment, as explained in the verse 4: 41, 159. As per the verses 17: 13 and 14, each individual is bearing his fate around his neck as a software and on the Day of Judgment it will be taken out as a spread open book to him and will tell: You read your own book, and today it is enough you to settle your account. And as per the verse 15, anyone who utilizes the Guidance will be guided for him concerned, while anyone who strays away only strays by itself. No burdent soul shall bear another burden. And We have never acted as punishers until We have dispatch a Messenger. Read together the verses 28: 48-50. See the explanation 2: 143, 150; 3: 128-129 and 4: 80.

166. Nevertheless Allah bears witness with what He has sent down to you; He sent It down with His full Knowledge, and the Angels testify too; though Allah suffices as a Witness.

The verse 7: 52 says: We have brought them the Book, We have spelled It out knowingly and as a Guidance and Mercy for the people who believe. The verse 6: 155 says: this is a blessed Book We have sent down, so follow It and be heedful. So you may be among those who receive Mercy. See the explanation 3: 18, 81 and 187.

167. Surely, those who hide and obstruct Allah's way have strayed far away from the Path.

The verse 6: 26 says: They obstruct others from It- the Soul of Qur'an- and remain aloof from It; by that they destroy none except themselves but they do not perceive it. During the time of Mecca *mushriks* the Qur'an was not available in the book-form due to that as per the verse 17: 93 they say to Prophet that we will never believe in your ascending up to the Paradise until you bring down a book for us to read. The Muslims of todays have many copies of It, but they do not utilize themselves and do not giving to others to utilize It as the Balance to keep the Universe in its equilibrium; so they should have to bear the burden of the destruction of the World since they hide the Trust which is the Soul of Qur'an. As per the verse 25: 18 the great people will blame them as they were a boar people who forgotten the Soul of Qur'an and as per the verse 30, Prophet himself by bringing the Qur'an will claim against them on the Day of Judgment that, my people neglected this Qur'an. Through the verses 9: 73 and 25: 52 Allah by calling Prophet, commanded not to obey such disbelievers who hide and reject the Soul of Qur'an and do great Jihad- strenuous strive- against them with It. See the explanation 1: 7; 2: 166-167 and 4: 63.

168. Surely, those who disbelieve and act wrongfully will not find that Allah will forgive them nor guide them along the Road.

169. Except the road to hell, to remain therein forever and that will be so easy for Allah.

Allah, the Impartial does not send anyone to the Paradise or Hell. He has taught the Soul of Qur'an containing both the ways to the Hell as well as to the Paradise to every mankind as told in the verse 55: 1-4. Then He sent down the reminder as the Messengers for every community. The Soul of Qur'an is the Guidance and Ticket for entire mankind, as per the verses 2: 185; 7: 158 and 76: 29. And It is the Straight Path as well the Balance to keep the Universe in its equilibrium as explained in the verse 6: 157. So anyone who did not utilize and not giving others to utilize are helping the satan to destroy the Universe. Therefore they will be led to the Hell, the home of satan. Read together the verses 7: 40-41; 32: 22 and 39: 55-59. See the explanation 2: 121; 3: 90-91 and 4: 140-145.

170. Oh mankind, the Messenger has brought you the Truth from your Lord, so believe, since It is best for you. If you should disbelieve, Allah still holds whatever is in Heaven and Earth; Allah is Aware, Wise.

In the verse 10: 57 Allah says by calling the mankind: There has come to you an Advice- the Soul of Qur'an, from your Lord, and Healing for whatever is in your chests and a Guidance and Mercy for believers. That is the Soul of Qur'an, which is the remedy to clear all doubts in one's heart. See the explanation 2:

147. Through the verse 10: 108 Allah commands to the Prophet to say: Oh mankind! The Truth from your Lord has come to you. So whoever guided him utilizing It, does so for his own good; and whosoever goes astray without utilizing It, does so for her own hurt. And I am not a custodian over you.

From these 3 verses, it can be realized that the Truth- Qur'an and Prophet are for the entire mankind; the Prophet has deputed in order to convey the Message of Allah- the soul of Qur'an; and those who live by utilizing It as Criterion, Guidance and Ticket should not have to fear or sorrow. See the explanation 2: 38. Those who hide and reject It after receiving It are the inmates of Hell, as explained in the verse 2: 39. Mankind is deputed to the Earth in order to prepare Paradise from Here, utilizing the Soul of Qur'an. Each and everything in the Heavens and Earth Glorify His Praise, as explained in the verse 2:33. See explanation 2: 136, 3: 136 and 4: 133.

171. Oh People of the Book, do not exaggerate in your religion and tell nothing about Allah except the Truth. The Maseeh, the son of Maryam is merely Allah's messenger and His Word which He cast in to Maryam, and a Spirit proceeded from Him. So believe in Allah and His Messengers and do not say: "Three!" Stop saying it will be better for you. Allah is only One Deity; Glory be to Him, beyond His having any son! He owns whatever is in Heaven and whatever is on Earth; and Allah Suffices as a Trustee.

Both in the verses 5: 17 and 72 it is told that, indeed those who say that "Allah is the *Maseeh*- son of *Maryam*" had become the disbeliever. The verse 5: 73 says: Certainly those who say that "Allah is the third of three, have disbelieved that there is no deity except Allah alone. If they do not stop saying what they say, painful torment will afflict those among them who disbelieve. The people of Book mentioned here are the Christians. The Soul of Qur'an which is the Truth submits Allah justly and true manner. In order to understand about the creation of Prophet *Eisa,* See the explanation 3: 39-40 and 4:1. All Prophets including *Eisa* are deputed for a same mission. Therefore those who deny any of the Prophets are the true disbelievers as told in the verses 4: 150-151. The verses 112: 1-4 introduce Allah as: He is Allah, the One only. He is independent and all are depending on Him. He begets not, nor is He begotten. And there is none comparable to Him. The verse 42: 11 says that, there is nothing like Him. Read together the verses 34: 46; 39: 3, 6, 36, 42, 45-46, 75; 57: 1-6; 58: 7; 59: 19-24 and 64: 1-3.

Today Qur'an is the only Book for entire mankind. Since, the bearers of It neither utilize nor give others to utilize It, became most arrogant people and they are the worst among all beasts. Thus, what Prophet foresighted is coming true that 'the ignorance' will come in its complete form during the Last Period? See the explanation 2: 90, 116-117 and 4: 155-159.

172. The Maseeh is never disdained to be Allah's servant, nor is the Angels who are closes to Allah. Whoever disdains to serve Him and acts too proud, He will summon all together to Him.

The verse 19: 92 says that, it is not suitable for the Most Gracious that He should choose a son; and the verse 93 says: There is none in Heavens and on Earth but must come to the Most Gracious as a servant. As per the verses 94-95 it is told that, He numbers them and counts them up. Each of them is coming to Him on Resurrection Day Individually. Read together the verse 22: 18. See the explanation 3: 51, 83. Through the verse 40: 60 Allah, your Lord has said: "Appeal to Me; I shall respond to you. The ones who are too proud to serve Me will enter Hell abjectly". By saying; 'He will summon all together to Him' means that, not only those who turn back by arrogance will be gathered, but all the creatures also. See the explanation 2: 186; 3: 30 and 4: 42.

173. As for those who believe and perform honorable deeds, He will pay them their earnings full and had even more for them out of His Bounty. And those who act disdain and proud with, He will punish with painful torment; and they will not find any patron for them nor any helper besides Allah.

It is told in the verse 50: 35 that, they will have anything they wish in the Paradise, and have more reward from Us. Read together the verses 50: 31-35. More reward means, they will get the permission in order to recommend for the heedless after their deserved torment from the Hell; except the transgressed hypocrites. Read together the verse 34: 23. Those who express disdain arrogance and proud just like satan, they will be punished with heinous painful torment. They will not find any patron, any intercessors and any supporters there. Read together the verses 6: 94; 7: 146 and 147. As per the verse 50: 32, the heedful will be told that, this Paradise is what you have been promised for everyone who repeatedly repents and observe the prayer, '*Sayyidul Isthigfar*', as explained in the verse 2: 27.

Believers are those who pray always especially in their prostrations as follows: Oh Allah! Make us humble and fear You always, and the One Who express gratitude to You. Do not include us among those who forgotten you, and who associate partners to You, and who have become losers. See the explanation 2: 120; 3: 185; 4: 118.

174. Oh mankind! Proof has come to you from your Lord; We have sent a Clear Light down to you.

175. Then those who believe with Allah and hold firmly It, Allah will soon enter them into Mercy and Bounty from Himself, and guide them along a Straight path towards Him.

The Proof, the Clear Light mentioned in the verse 174 and, the Mercy, the Bounty and the Straight path mentioned in the verse 175 is the Soul of Qur'an, as explained in the verses 2: 111 and 4: 113. It is for the entire mankind. The verse 3: 101 ends as: Anyone who hold firm to Allah is already guided to the Straight path. 'Hold firmly to Allah' means, hold firmly to the rope from Allah which is the Soul of Qur'an, as explained in the verse 3: 103. Only for those who can quote a word from Qur'an as a proof for any matter, Qur'an will argue in favor and will stand as a Witness. The verse 28: 75 says that We shall drag a witness out of every community and We shall say: "Bring on your proof"! Then they will realize that indeed the Truth belongs to Allah while whatever they were inventing has left them in the lurch. In the verse 21: 24, three names of Soul of Qur'an such as *Burhan, Haq* and *Dikhr* is used. Therefore, each individual should have a proof from the Soul of Qur'an to clear their deeds in front of His Impartial Lord on the Day of Judgment.

In the verse 24: 35 it is told that, Allah is the Light of the Heaven and Earth. Through the verses 5: 16 and 17 it is told that, indeed a Light and Clear Book have been brought to you from Allah with which He will guide any one who seeks His approval along path ways of peace; He leads them out of darkness into the Light by His Permission, and guides them to the Straight path. The verse 7: 157 ends as: Those who follow the Light which is sent down with him, such will be the only prosperous. The verse 64: 8 says: Believe in Allah and His Messenger and the Light which We have sent down; Allah is acquainted about anything you do. The verse 42: 52 says: Thus We have revealed a Spirit from Our command for you. You did not know what either the Book or Faith was, but We have set It up as a Light by means of which We guide any of Our servants whom We wishes. And indeed You are guiding towards the Straight path. The Spirit, the Light and the Straight path mentioned in the verse is the Soul of Qur'an. Both in the verses 22: 8 and 31: 20 Allah says that someone are there who argue about Allah without having any knowledge, Guidance and any Enlightening Book. Here the Knowledge, Guidance and Enlightening Book mean the Soul of Qur'an. Hence without the Soul of Qur'an none has the right to talk about Allah. As per the verse 66: 8, the believers' prayer will be always that, Our Lord, perfect our Light for us, and grant us forgiveness; indeed You are capable of everything.

Our goal of life is to return to Allah in the Paradise by burning all the satanic habit and characters such as arrogance, envy and pride utilizing the Soul of Qur'an- the Light. Both the verses 9: 32; 61: 8 it is told that, hypocrites try to extinguish the Light by blowing with their mouth; but Allah will indeed perfect His Light. Read together the verses 9: 95 and 125. It is told in the verse 57:13 that, on the Day of Judgment the hypocrites- men and women will say to the believers: 'Wait for us! Let us borrow some light from your light. It is told in the verse 57: 19 that, those who believe with Allah and His Messengers, they are the sincere lovers of the Truth and the witnesses in the sight of their Lord, will have their reward and Light. And those who hide and reject Our verses are the inmates of Hades.

Through the verses 55: 33-34 Allah asks: Oh company of *Jinns* and mankind, if you can manage to penetrate beyond the boundary of Heaven and Earth, then pass beyond them! Yet you will not penetrate them except with some authority. So which of your Lord's Bounty will both of you deny? As per the verse 17: 80, Allah commanded to pray: "My Lord let me enter through a truthful entrance and leave me by a truthful exit. And grant Me a supporting authority from Your presence. The Authority, Truth and Bounty mentioned in these verses are the Soul of Qur'an. If anyone utilizes the Soul of Qur'an as Proof, Authority and Light they can enter the Paradise. And those who show arrogance and reject the Soul of Qur'an after receiving It, the gates of the Heaven will not be opened to them, nor will they be enter the Paradise until a camel can pass through the eye of a tailor's needle. Thus We reward *mujrims*, who do not utilize their intelligence as told in the verse 7: 40. Read together the verse 14: 22. See the explanation 1: 6; 2: 166-167 and 4: 170.

176. They will ask you for your verdict Say: "Allah advices you concerning the 'Kalalath'. If some man should pass away and has no son while he leaves a sister, then she shall have half of anything he may leave; while he inherits from her if she has no child if they are two women (who are sisters), they shall both heir two thirds of whatever he may leave. If there are more than two men and women, then each brother shall have the same share as two sisters would have". Allah explains things to you lest you go astray. And Allah is Aware of everything.

Read together the explanation 4: 12. The heirs of 'Kalalath' mentioned here is the brother or sister of the same father. They will get a share of heirs that is equal to the children have from own father, as explained in the verse 4: 11. If the '*Kalalath*' has more than two brothers and sisters, then each brother shall have the same share as two sisters would have, as like for the brothers and sisters from their own father as explained in the verse 4: 11. If the deceased '*Kalalath*' is a woman having husband as the direct heir, then the brother will get balance after husband's share is given. Allah instructs like this guidance to men in order not to go astray from Allah's path to the path of satan. But today satan obstructs men from the Soul of Qur'an, so most of the people are not following these instructions from their Lord. When the believers recite the verse 1: 7: "Not in the path who go astray", they have to keep in mind that not the path of those who did not follow these instruction of Qur'an. See the explanation 3: 90; 4: 13-14 and 167.

Oh Allah, make our hearts light with The Light, and decorate our character with the Soul of Qur'an, makes us depart away from the Hell with the Soul of Qur'an, and enter us the Paradise with the Soul of Qur'an, Oh the Gracious One Who revealed the Soul of Qur'an. Oh Allah, makes the Qur'an a blossom to our hearts, and makes our chests Enlightened with It, extinguish our sorrows with It, help us to remove all our sufferings and disasters with It. And help us to utilize It as Evidence and Proof to You and the Paradise with splendid Bounties, oh the Best Merciful among the Merciful!

With the name of Allah, the Impartial, the Compassionate.

5. Al-Maeda

This *Surath* includes the verses revealed at the end of *Hijra* 6th and at the beginning of *Hijra* 7th years. This *Surath* contains 120 verses. When disciples asked Prophet *Eisa* as mentioned in the 112th verse that "can your Lord send down a food tray on us?" Then *Eisa* prayed for a food tray as mentioned in the verse 114. Thus the food tray was sent down and the people including Jews ate from it. But when some of the Jews who ate from it become suspicious about it, Allah transformed them into swine. It is from this, the name of the *Surath* '*Maeda*' - the Heavenly food tray- originated.

In *Hijra* 6th year Prophet and about 1400 followers set out for *Umra*. At *Hudaibiya* they were detained by *Meccan mushriks* and made an agreement with them. By this agreement they were allowed to do *Umra* in the next year. The verses teach some manners and regulations to be obeyed while going for *Umra*, the courtesies to be kept while in *Ihram*, the verses advising to fulfill all obligations, to be heedful were revealed. The part of the third verse, "Today I have perfected your *Dheen* for you completed My blessing on you and I have chosen Islam as your *Dheen*" is the last part of the verse revealed. The 6th verse discourses about ablution and *Thayamum*-ablution with soil. Reminding the murder of *Habeel* by *Qabeel*- the sons of Adam, Allah gives judgments for such crimes. It is declared that those who do not judge by what Allah has revealed are indeed disbelievers, wrongdoers and transgressors. It is explained that the food and women of those who were given the Book before are lawful to the believers. The expiation of broken oath, the form of how to do last bequest when death approaches, the interrogation of the Messengers by Allah on the Day of Judgment, the complete prohibition of intoxicants, gambling and the eradication of some Ignorant system such as '*Baheerah*', '*Saaebah*', '*Wasweelah*', '*Haam*' etc. are also discussed in this *Surath*.

With the name of Allah, the Impartial, the Compassionate

1. Oh you who believe, fulfill all contracts you may make. You are permitted all beasts of cattle except those which are hunted while you are in Ihram and those already have been explained to you. Indeed Allah judges anything He wishes.

By calling the believers, Allah commands to fulfill not only the *Hudaibiya* agreement but all other agreements also. In the verse 23: 8, while explaining the characters of believers Allah says, they will fulfill the trusts and agreements. As Prophet taught one of the three signs of hypocrites is that they will not keep their promises. All domestic animals such as goat, camels, cow, buffalo etc. are known as '*An-Aam*'-cattle- whereas the '*Bahimath-ul -An-Aam*' also include all edible animals such as Rabbits, deer, wild buffalo etc. 'Those which are already have been explained to you' means those which are explained in the verse 5:3. The carnivorous animals and the birds with long nail are not permitted to eat. Hunting is forbidden while in *Ihram*- prohibited dress- as well as in the boundary of '*Haram*'-prohibited area. See the explanation 2: 173.

2. Oh you who believe, do not disrespect the symbols of Allah and the war in prohibited months. Keep away from attacking the animals brought for sacrifice. Do not violate the animals with garlands as the mark of sacrifice. Do not prevent the people from visiting the Ka'ba seeking the grace and satisfaction of their Lord, hunt after your Ihram. Let not the hatred of some people- who once hindered you from the Sacred Masjid- incite you to commit transgression. Co-operate with one another in virtue and heedfulness. Do not co-operate in enmity and aggression. Heed Allah alone. Certainly Allah is severe in punishment.

The marks or symbols of Allah denote everything such as His boundaries, rights, laws etc. Avoidance of stitched dresses by men during *Umra* is also a symbol of Allah. Considering the words of Allah "There is no compulsion in Religion", it is the duty of a believer not to disrespect the worshiping symbols of other religions. The national flag should not be disrespected by the believers. It has been taught in the verse 6: 108: "Those whom they call upon besides Allah should not be insulted". The verse 49: 11 says: "Oh believers let not some among you call each other your nick names; and those who do not repent after doing these it is they who are wrongdoers". The mocking of or laughing at other's dress, walking, cultures etc. are considered as disrespecting Allah's symbols. As per the verses such as 3: 119; 4: 63; 9: 120-121 it is permitted to use tough and harsh words penetrating the inner hearts of hypocrites. Believers follow the same policy of Allah towards the hypocrites. To maintain nationalism, racism, communalism etc. are included disrespecting the symbols of Allah.

Believers should keep respect towards the war-forbidden months. Allah reminds the believers not to harm or rob the animals which are to be sacrificed, and not to disrespect the garlands hung around their neck as a distinguishing mark. Meccan pagans prevented the Prophet and the followers entering Mecca on pilgrimage. But they would not prevent others. So the Muslims are advised not to retaliate other '*mushriks*' when they pass through the Muslim country to Mecca. The words and deeds that destroy the calm and peace of *Masjidul Haram*- Sacred *masjid*- should not come out from any of the believers. The word "hunt after *Ihram*" does not mean that, you should hunt when you are free from Ihram, but remember Allah always, while you are in *Ihram* avoiding all other physical profits. In the verse 94 Allah says: "Allah will surely make a trial of you by sending animals which to be hunted within the reach of your hands and your spears in order to know who fear Allah though He is unseen". The verse 58: 8 says that, even though the hypocrites of *Madeena* were forbidden conspiracy, they would hold their conspiracy for crime and wrongdoing, and in the verse 9, by calling the believers Allah says: "Oh believers, when you hold secret counsel, don't do it for sin and hostility disobeying the Prophet, but do it for virtue and heedfulness", and in the verse 10 it is said that "secret counsel or conspiracy is only from satan in order to make grief to the believers, but without Allah's Permission he cannot do any harm to the believers, so let the believers put their trust in Allah". The verse 16: 99 says that satan has no power over those who believe and put trust in their Lord. See the explanation 2: 102, 177; 3: 4, 90 and 4: 167-169.

3. **Forbidden to you anything that dies by itself, blood, flesh of swine and that which has been dedicated to any other than Allah, whatever has been strangled, beaten to death, trapped in a pit, killed by goring, eaten by wild animals- unless you are able to slay it before its death, sacrificed on idols and divided by raffling of arrows. All those are hypocritical sinful acts. Today the disbelievers have lost all their hope of your Dheen. Do not have fear of them. And fear Me alone. Today I have perfected your**

Dheen for you. Completed My blessing towards you and I have satisfied Islam as your Dheen. Anyone who is compelled by hunger eat anything from these not intending to do sin, will find Allah, as the Forgiving, Merciful.

It is forbidden to eat the flesh of any animal killed by an accident. But it is permitted to eat the flesh after removing the blood by slaying before its death. The blood of the animal killed by beating or falling etc. clings to the flesh, but when we slay an animal its blood will flow out and its flesh will become free from blood. As blood is forbidden, flesh should be free from blood.

Altars are places on which the animals are used to be sacrificed to idols. Anything that has been dedicated to any other than Allah may be sacrificed on altars or not are forbidden. Meccan pagans used arrows as a sort of lottery by giving them numbers to know the good and bad in the future, to foretell the future, to divide among them the goods, foods etc. It has been commanded in the verses 90-91: Oh believers, intoxicants, gambling, paying tribute to idols, divination by arrows are filthy works of satan, so leave him aside. See the explanation 4: 51.

The word 'Today' does not mean a particular day, but it is a period in which the verses were revealed. It is the last part of the verse revealed on the day of *HajjathulVida*'-departing pilgrimage- in 10th year of *Hijra*. Thus *Islam* became a perfect system of life. See the explanation 3: 19 and 85. Gradually *Islam* began to deviate from its original path. As per Prophet teaching there will be three groups who recite Qur'an-hypocrite, blind follower and, in which only believer will get reward since they follow what they said. Prophet also taught: *There will come a group of people, they will recite Qur'an, but It does not reach below their throat, by that act they will be darted out from Islam as if an arrow darted out of its bow*. Today, the majority of Muslims including the hypocrites and their blind followers have fallen in every iniquities and wrong deeds. They eat and drink the forbidden foods. They do not try to understand the Soul of Qur'an. Because of their wrong deeds, *Islam* itself is ridiculed by other people. Read together the verses 7: 176; 13: 11; 62: 5; 25: 17-18 and 30. See the explanation of 3: 28, 72 and 4: 165.

4. They will ask you what has been made lawful to them; say: All wholesome things are lawful for you, and all the things that your

trained animals- trained by you with the knowledge given to you by Allah- catch for you. Eat what they catch and bring for you. But you have to make remember the name of Allah over it. Heed Allah; surely Allah is swift in reckoning.

The things caught by trained animals or birds such as dogs, tigers, falcons, cheetah, eagles etc are lawful since they catch prey for their masters, not for them. But when a trained animal is sent, it is compulsory to remember the name of Allah. The word '*Alaihi*' indicates that the name of Allah should be remembered before prey's death. If it were '*Alaiha*' then it would be a justification for the argument that "it is enough to pronounce the name of Allah at the time of eating". The verse 6: 121 says: "Do not eat of that on which Allah's name has not been remembered. That is indeed a sinful act. Satan's do inspire their friends to argue with you. If you obey them, you will surely be among associates". The verse 6: 119 says: "Why should you not eat that on which Allah's name has been remembered. He has clearly explained what is forbidden to you, except under compulsion, surely many will mislead you by their errant views without knowledge. Verily your Lord knows best who the transgressors are". See the explanation 2: 120, 145; 3: 190- 191 and 199.

5. **This Day, all good and wholesome things have been made lawful for you, and so is the food of those who were given the Book lawful for you, while your food is lawful for them. The marriage with chaste woman from the believers and the chaste woman from the people of the Book who were given the Book before you are lawful for you, if you bring them in your marriage protection desiring not to enter in fornication and not have unlawful children, intending chastity and giving them their dowries. Anyone who rejects faith, all his good deeds will be in vain and in Hereafter, he will be one among the losers.**

Every human being should use good and lawful food. But only the believers obey this. The flesh of the killed animals is only being lawful to eat. The income from business is only lawful, if the business is occurred by satisfying each other. See the explanation 2: 188 and 4: 29-32. Intermarriage with the people of the Book is permitted. A believer can marry a believing woman or a chaste woman from among the people of the Book by giving them their dowries. But the intention or motivation should be good. It should be to give them protection and shelter.

As per the verse 66: 6 it is the duty of a true believer to save his wife and his family from Hell-fire. That is why it said in 4: 34 that men are protectors of women. It is the duty of men to quench the sexual emotion of women. Thus a man can transform his wife to a true believer. As a disbelieving man may lead his family to the Hell, due to this the marriage between a non believing man and a believing lady is not permitted. See the explanation 4: 25 and 165. If any one ignores the laws and orders of Allah after he received it, all his deeds will be in vain. The verse 39: 65 says: "It has already been revealed to you and to those before you that if you commit '*Shirk*'- associate others with Allah- all your deeds will certainly be in vain". As it is said in the verse 8: 2 that the faith will be increased only by the Soul of Qur'an, then those who hide It, will become one among the losers. See the explanation 2: 121, 176 and 221.

6. **Oh you who believe, whenever you stand up for Swalath wash your faces and hands including elbow, wipe of your heads and your feet up to the ankles. If you are in a state of unclean because of emission of semen, purify by taking full bath. If you are ill or on a journey or one had defecate and urinate or you have been in intercourse with the woman and you don't find any water, then resort to pure soil and wipe your faces and hands with some of it. Allah does not want to make any inconvenience on you, but He does wants to make you pure and to complete His blessings upon you so that you may be grateful.**

This verse explains the method of ablution. The whole face from ear to ear and from hair of the head to the last part of the jaw including forehead should be washed. The arms including elbow should be cleaned. The whole head including inside and out side of the ears should be rubbed. The feet including the ankles should be either washed or rubbed. Wiping is enough if it is difficult to wash because of ill or severe cold. There is no need to remove the socks before ablution. A rub over it is enough. But ablution should be taken before wearing the socks. The duration of this is three days for travelers and one day for settlers. See the explanation 4: 43.

When 'Thayammum'- ablution with soil- is done, as it is recommended to "rub the hands and face", it is enough to rub the hands to the wrist and no need to rub the elbow. Tissue paper (toilet paper) can be used in toilet, when water is not available. Here 'cleaning with soil' Allah does not mean the cleanliness of physical body, but the cleanliness and purity of soul. Only those who attain purity of soul can enter into the Paradise. Read together the verses 87: 14; 91: 9-10. The Soul of Qur'an is the only instrument to purify the soul. See the explanation 2: 186. Prophet taught to pray at the end of ablution as: "Oh Allah, Forgive me my sins, widen me my house and give me increment in my sustenance (and then after saying words of witness), oh Allah, include me one among those who repent, those who command others to be purify and among those servants who do honorable deeds." Prophet taught us that purity belongs to belief. But today, as the Muslims have deviated from the Soul of Qur'an they have become filthy, far behind in virtue and far advanced in evils. See the explanation 2: 152, 254; 4: 49 and 91.

7. **Remember Allah's favor towards you and the oath which He ratified with you, when you said: "We hear and obey." Heed Allah; Allah knows the state of your chests.**

The verse 2: 285 says: "Prophet and the believers believe in Allah, His Angels, His Books and His Messengers and they make no discrimination between any of His Messengers, and they say: "We hear and we obey". It has been reminded in the verses7: 172-173 that, when Allah created Adam, He created every human soul till the Last Day in Paradise and asked them: "Am I not your Lord?" They replied: "Yes, we bear witness". But it is only the true believers who will keep this oath. Similarly in the verse 3: 187 it is told that Allah has accepted a solemn oath from those who were given the Book to make it known and clear to mankind and not to hide It. By deputing a Prophet, Allah saved the believers from the edge of Hell and transformed them to the best people who lead to the Paradise. This is the favor that Allah asked to remember. Allah knows the state of the chests and nothing can be concealed from Him. On the Day of Judgment, every one has to answer about each and every moment of his worldly life after the fifteenth age. Hence every one is asked to be conscious of Allah. The only instrument to get this is to utilize the Soul of Qur'an as the Ticket. Read together the verse 76: 29. See the explanation 3: 102; 4: 21 and 113.

8. **Oh you who believe, be command for Allah as witnessing with justice and let not the hatred of people make you mad to do injustice. Do just, that is nearer to heedfulness. Keep Allah in your hearts. Surely Allah is well acquainted of all that you do.**

See the explanation 4: 135. The verse 68: 8 says about Prophet that, you are of the highest noble character. The word 'noble' has been used for Qur'an also. The character of Prophet was the Qur'an itself. The character of Prophet was the character of Allah. The believers, the representatives of Allah should have the same character. Prophet taught the believers to pray as: "Oh Allah, make this Noble Qur'an the blossom of our heart and the Light of our chest." In another prayer it is taught that, "Oh Allah enlightens our heart and adorns our heart with the Soul of Qur'an." See the explanation 2: 177, 234; 3: 97 and 4: 2.

9. And Allah has promised those who believe and perform honorable deeds that they have forgiveness and splendid rewards.

The verse 24: 55 says: Allah has promised to those among you who believe and do honorable deeds that, He will surely make them representatives on the earth as He made the ancestors before them and that He will give opportunity to establish their own *Dheen* and after their present state of fear, they will be given peace and security. So serve only for Me and don't associate any others with Me. If any one who deny the Truth after this, it is they who are the transgressors. In the verse 36: 11 Allah informs the glad tidings of forgiveness and noblest reward to those who follow Allah's Message and fear the Impartial, unseen. See the explanation 2: 186; 3: 136, 194 and 4: 95.

10. Those who hide and reject Our verses will become inmates of Hades.

This verse is repeated in the verse 5: 86. The verse 57: 19 also ends as: Those who hide and reject Our verses will become inmates of Hades. See the explanation 2: 38- 39; 3: 10 and 4: 140.

11. Oh you who believe, remember Allah's favor towards you when some people indented stretched their hands against you to harm you, but He withheld their hands from you. Heed Allah and Let the believers entrust on Allah.

This verse points out an incident reported by *Ibnu Abbas*. In *Madeena* some of the Jews had planned to invite the Prophet and believers to a party for to killing him and thus to vanish *Islam* forever. But Allah informed the Prophet about this and thus he did not participate in the party. From here onwards the direction of the speech turns towards the children of Israel. The believers should avoid the policy that was accepted by the people of Book. That is, the believers should not break their oath as the people of *Moosa* and *Eisa* broke their pledges taken from them by Allah. See the explanation 4: 72. The believers should not do the mistakes as the people of the Book did. Today, Allah invites the disbelieving Muslims of different organization to the real way of *Islam*. Thus they have to show the Straight Path -the way of Qur'an- the only way of salvation to entire mankind. But we can see the Muslims who are not the actual believers are going deep in wrong deeds such as arrogance, sin, iniquity etc, when we compare them with other people. It is because of they eat the body of Qur'an without trying to learn Its soul. When the thirtieth pseudo prophet *Maseeh-A-Ddajjal* comes, their disbelief will attain in maximum and they will fall in the trap of *Maseeh-A-Ddajjal.* By the second coming of *Eisa*, the all other peoples will accept *Eisa and Islam*. Then the hypocrites and those whose hearts is malice mentioned in the verse 33: 60 will be killed and thus the command of the verses 4: 91; 9: 123 and 33: 61 will be executed. See the explanation 3: 102-103 and 4: 159

12. And Allah has taken a covenant from the children of Israel and He has appointed twelve captains from them for their Guidance. Allah said: "Certainly I am with you keep up swalath and pay the welfare tax, and believe in My messengers, and strengthen them and lend Allah a handsome loan. I will certainly cover your evil deeds and enter you in to the Gardens beneath which rivers flow. Anyone of you who disbelieves following that will have strayed from the Right Path".

"Lend Allah a handsome loan" means spend money in the way of Allah. Today it means utilize money, time, intelligence, eyesight etc. to learn, teach and propagate the Soul of Qur'an. In the verse 7:156, Allah says: "My punishment affects whom I please, but My Mercy embraces all things. I shall ordain it for those who keep Me in their hearts, pay welfare tax, and believe in Our verses"; and the verse 157 says: "To those who follow the Messenger, the Prophet illiterate who can neither read nor write whom they find described in the *Thourath* and the *Injeel* with them. He commands them with what is good and forbids them what is evil, allows them as lawful what is good and prohibits them what is bad, releases them from their heavy burdens and from the chains that are upon them. Therefore it is those who believe in him, strengthen him, help him and follow the Light, which is sent down with him. It is they who will be successful". Read together the verse 67: 12. See the explanation 2: 245, 3: 81; 4: 31 and 136.

13. Then, since they broke their oath, We have cursed them and made their hearts hard, they change the words from their places. They forgot a good part of what they had been told to bear in mind, in the coming days you will not cease to discover one by one from their deceits except from a few of them. So retrain from them and wait; verily, Allah loves those who live seeing Him.

See explanation 2: 74-75. Today the 'Speech' of Allah is the Soul of Qur'an only. The hypocrites from this community have to bear the guilty of the sin whoever distort or repudiate with the Qur'an verses and not the present Jews anywhere in the world. Today, it is these hypocrites who break the pledge mentioned in the verse 3: 187. It is this group whom Allah has cursed, killed and commanded group of believers to kill. See the explanation 2: 159-161; 4: 91 and 105.

In the verse 32: 24 Allah says: "When the children of Israel showed patience and had sure faith in Our verses, We appointed from among them the leaders giving Guidance under Our command". Today, the phrases such as: "Allah cursed the Jews" or "Allah killed the Jews" or "Allah made the hearts of the Jews hard" etc. are more suitable to the hypocrites from Muslims if consider the Soul of Qur'an as '*Mouidhath*'. See the explanation 2: 26 and 27.

The verse 5: 78-81 say: The hypocrites from among the children of Israel were cursed by the tongue of the Prophet *Davood* and *Eisa*. It is because they disobeyed and transgressed and they would not prevent the people from doing inequities; and they made friendship with the disbelievers. So they fell in Allah's curse and they will abide in the punishment. See explanation 3: 28.

14. We accepted their agreement from those who say: "We are Christians"; then they forgot a portion of what they had been reminded of, so We have stirred up enmity and jealousy among them until Resurrection Day. And Allah will certainly inform them what they had been producing.

The verse 3: 52 says: When *Eisa* saw disbelief in the people; he asked them: Who will help me in the cause of Allah? The disciples replied: We are helpers of Allah, we believed in Allah, bear witness that we are Muslims. Read together the verse 61: 14. It is from this the word '*Nasara*'- Helpers of Allah-originated. Prophet *Eisa* or Muslims had never given the names like '*Eisa'ee*'- Christ's- or '*Maseeh*'- Christians- to his disciples. He did not form any organizations; he did not give his disciples new names. They followed the '*Shari-at*'- the way of life- of Prophet *Moosa*. They did their religious observances with Jews in the house of *Baithul Muquadhis*. Gradually the difference in opinions originated. See the explanation 2: 176 and 213.

15. Oh People of the Book, of course Our messenger has come to you, to explain much of what you have been concealing out of the Book, and to excusing with much of It. Light and a clear Book have been brought to you from Allah.

16. With that Book Allah guides those who seek His pleasure to the ways of peace and safety; He leads them out of darkness into Light by His permission and guides them along a Straight path.

The only Book that comes from Allah is '*Adhikr*'- The Soul of Qur'an. When the people of the Book made many changes in It, Allah deputed Muhammad as a Messenger with Qur'an- the latest form of the Book- to reveal them many things which they hide. Today, the Soul of Qur'an is the only Book to lead the people out of darkness to Light. It is the Ticket to reach Paradise by crossing the bridge over the Hell. Read together the verses 41: 41-42; 43: 52 and 76: 29. 'Allah's Permission' means the Soul of Qur'an. In the verse 10: 25 Allah says: "Allah calls to the Home of peace and safety. He leads whom He pleases to the Straight path". See the explanation 1: 6; 2: 185; 4: 174 and 175.

17. Indeed those who say "Allah is the Christ- the son of Maryam", disbelieve. You ask them: "Who has the power to prevent Allah from His decision, if He decides to destroy the Christ, the son of Maryam, his mother and every one who is on Earth?" Allah holds the dominion over Heaven and Earth as well as anything in between them. He creates anything He wishes. Allah is capable of everything.

Allah is the One who created Heaven and Earth from nothingness. The creation of *Eisa* has been explained in the verse 4: 171. The creation of the mother of *Eisa* and how she brought up *Eisa* has been explained in the verses 3: 34-37. It is told in the verses 4: 157-159 that, Allah raised *Eisa* up to Him with his physical body and he will come back to Earth after the appearance of *Maseeh*-

A- Ddajjal; and will wipe out *Maseeh-A-Ddajjal* and '*Kufr*'- disbelief- and will implement *Islam* all over the world. See the explanation 3: 55; 4: 131-133 and 172.

18. And the Jews and Christians say: "We are Allah's children and His favorites". Ask them: "Then why does He punish you for your offences? Rather, you are human beings just like anyone else He has created. He forgives anyone He wishes and He punishes anyone He wishes. Allah holds the dominion over the Heaven and Earth, and whatever lies between them. And towards Him is the final destination".

The Jews and Christians during the period of Prophet had an attitude that, they were the children of Allah as well as His favorites. See the explanation 2: 94-95, 111, 113 and 283. But today this argument is with the Muslims. As per the verse 2: 186, any deeds without the Soul of Qur'an will not be accepted. Today we can see the Muslims are being punished all over the world. It is because of their disgust towards the Soul of Qur'an. The verse 32:21 says: We shall certainly make them taste the lighter torment in this life before the greater punishment of the Hereafter, so that they may return to the Right Way. They are not ready to learn lessons from the punishments and are not trying to learn and teach the Soul of Qur'an to others. It has been warned in the verses 25: 17-18 that, the great people to whom they were invoking besides Allah will complain against this people that, this people were a people of worthless; since they forgot the Soul of Qur'an. The verse 29 warns that, this people will say themselves in despair that satan had prevented man from the Soul of Qur'an and he is a cheater to the mankind. The verse 30 says: Prophet will complain that my people of discarded the Qur'an and that is the reason of their wretchedness. In the verse 62:5, Allah compares the people who discarded His verses to donkeys and Jews and says that He will not guide such wrongdoing people. The verse 7: 176 says: The people and their leaders who reject and hide the verses of Allah have been compared to dogs that do not change its attitude if it is disturbed or not. Read together 7:174 and 30: 41. See the explanation 2: 91, 284 and 4: 165-167.

19. Oh people of the Book, Our Messenger has come to explain things to you after an interval between in the Messengers, lest you say: "No Herald or no any Warner has ever come to us". So the Herald and Warner have indeed come to you! Allah is capable of everything.

The deputation of Muhammad was about 570 years after the Prophet *Eisa* is lifted up. No Prophets from the *Isma'el* lineage had been appointed for about 2000 years. The *Sharee'at* of *Mossa* was the way of life Allah satisfied for whole world during that time. But when the children of *Isma'el* as well as the Jews and Christians deviated from that way of life, Allah appointed Prophet Muhammad, as the answer for *Ibrahim's* prayer as per the verse 2: 129. Allah deputes Messengers as heralds to the believers and Warner's to the transgressors. See the explanation 2: 213.

Allah says in the verses 6: 155-157 to the Meccan *mushriks* who say and argue that they follow the way of *Ibrahim*: "We have revealed a blessed Book, lest you should say that, the Book was revealed only to two parties -Jews and Christians- before us and we could not learn It. Or lest you say: If the Book had been revealed to us, We could have followed Its Guidance better than them. It has now come to you from your Lord as a Guidance and Mercy. Those who deny the verses of Allah and turns away from them will face dreadful punishment". The verses 35: 42 and 43 say that, they swear strongly by Allah, if a Warner came to them they would be better guided than any other communities; but when a Warner came to them it has increased nothing but aversion. They behaved arrogantly in the land and they indulged in plotting evils. The evil plot will recoil none but its authors. The verse 28: 48 says: When the Truth has come to them from Me, they asked: "Why is he not given like those which were given to *Moosa*?" But they had rejected those, which were given to *Moosa*. They said both the Qur'an and *Thourath* are two magic assisting each other, certainly we are the ones who disbelieve both. The verse 49 Allah asks the Prophet to say: "Bring a book from Allah better guide than these two; I shall follow It, if you are so truthful".

Today Soul of Qur'an is the only Book for entire mankind which is the Balance and Trust to keep the Universe in its equilibrium, But Muslims who bear and read these verses. Then if they hide and reject the verses of Qur'an, they will have to bear the penalty of all sins of mankind, and they will be sent to the deepest depth of the Hellfire. See the explanation 4: 133-134 and 145. The Soul of Qur'an is the Laws of Allah. When the World deviates from It and becomes in darkness, *Maseeh-A-Ddajjal* comes. Then *Eisa* will come and by teaching the Soul of Qur'an will rule the whole World capitalizing Mecca, the centre of the World. After his death the World once again comes in darkness; *Ya'jooj* and

Ma'jooj will come out, the *Ka'ba* will be demolished, and thus the Dooms Day will happen.

Allah, who originated the Heavens and Earth from nothingness, turns them back to their old nature as specified in the verses 21: 103-104. Prophets are informers of heralds and Warners. They can't guide anyone to the Straight path. See the explanation 2: 272; 3: 128 and 129. Every soul has been given the Right way and the wrong way according to the verses 76: 3; 90: 10 and 91: 8-10. Those who hide the Soul of Qur'an and show blindness against It will be the dwellers of Hell. A Warner is the one who reminds all these. Those who identify and purify themselves by utilizing the Soul of Qur'an will be succeeded. To those who devote everything to Allah, Qur'an will be a Guide, a Blessing and a Herald as told in the verses 16: 89 and 102. A Herald is the one who informs all these good news. It is told in the verse 17: 9 that, surely this Qur'an guides to the way, which is most right and gives glad news to the believers who do honorable deeds. From all these it can be seen that, the life of Prophets were the Qur'an Itself. See explanation 2: 90; 4: 1 and 5: 8-10.

20. Remember when Moosa told his people: 'Oh my people, remember Allah's favor towards you when He appointed Prophets among you and set you up as kings; and gave you what He had not given to any one in the Worlds.

Here Allah reminds the favored upon the children of Israel. For their good Guidance Allah has appointed more than one Prophets at a time. It is in them the father and the son were appointed as the Prophets. *Yoosuf*- the son of *Ya'qoob* was appointed as the king of Egypt. Allah gave them the blessing. Allah saved them from Pharaoh through *Moosa*, gave them '*Manna*' and '*Salva*' as food; when they asked drinking water, 12 springheads were given to them. All these are some of the favors that He had bestowed upon them. In the verse 61: 5 Allah says: Remember when *Moosa* said to his people: Why do you trouble me, knowing that I am the Messenger of Allah to you. But when they wavered Allah let their hearts waver too. Allah will not guide such people who are transgressors. Read together the verses 63: 5-6. See the explanation 2: 6-7, 122 and 211.

21. Oh my people, enter the holy land which Allah has assigned to you. Do not turn your back on it, lest you be sent away as losers.

This speech was made by *Moosa* when they camped in the desert of *Pharan* close to northern borders of Arabia and southern borders of Palestine. The holy land mentioned here is the Palestine. In verse 17: 1 Allah says: 'Glory to Him, who took His servant by night from *Masjidul Haram* to *Masjidul Aqsa*, the environs of which have blessed, to show him some of Our signs. Surely He is all Hearing, all Seeing. Read together the verse 7:137.

22. They said: "Oh Moosa, indeed in it there are people of exceeding strength. We will not enter it until they leave it. If they go out, then we will enter.

23. Two men from among those, who fear-Allah favored them both-said: "Enter into them through the gate. Once you have entered it, You will surely be victorious. You should rely on Allah, if you are believers".

24. They said: "Oh Moosa, as long as they remain in it, we will never enter there. So go both you and your Lord and fight. Indeed we are sitting here".

Prophet *Moosa* selected 12 captains one from each of the twelve tribes of the Israel's children and sent them from the desert of *Pharan* to know about the situation of Palestine. After forty days they returned to *Pharan* and said to Prophet *Moosa* at the assembly: "We went to the country, it is indeed a rich country, but its inhabitants are strong and powerful. We can't go against them. We seemed ourselves as locusts" when the children of Isra'el heard all these, they cried the whole night. They said that they wished they had died at Egypt. Why does Moosa take us to that country as to be killed by the enemy? They said to each other that they are going to return Egypt. Among the twelve spies sent out to explore Palestine, there was *Joshua*- the son of *Noone* and *Caleb*- the son of *Yafunna* slit their garments and said: "The country we explored is a good country, if *Jehovah* deigns, He will give the country to us. Don't fear them; we must entrust in *Jehovah*". But the crowd rejected all these instructions. They turned against them and prepared to stone them. There flamed the anger of *Jehovah*. He decided not to give them the inheritance of the land. But He decided to give the land to their children and to those who were below 20. But they can enter only after wandering 40 years; that is, after the death of those who were above 20 years except *Joshua* and *Caleb*. By this decision of *Jehova* they took 38 years to reach Jordan from the desert *Pharan*. But within these 38 years all those youths who were sent to explore Palestine and those who rejected the advice of *Caleb* and *Joshua* had died. But *Caleb* and *Joshua* were still alive. After the victory of Jordan, *Moosa* also died. It was under the leadership of *Joshua* that Israelis got victory over Palestine. See the explanation 2: 58 and 59.

25. Then Moosa prayed: "My Lord! I have no control except myself and my brother, so distinguish between us and this transgressed people".

The verses 7: 150-151 say that, when *Moosa* returned to his people, he saw his people worshipping a calf made up of their ornaments and he became extremely angry. He threw down the Stone disc- *Thourath*- and seized his brother's hair. *Haroon* said: "Son of my mother, the people made me weak and about to kill me and let not make my enemies rejoice over me and do not count me among the wrong doing people". Thus realizing the truth *Moosa* prayed: "Oh, my Lord forgives me and my brother and admit us into Your Mercy. You are the Most Merciful of those who show Mercy".

26. He said: It will be proscribed them for forty years. They will wander around the Earth. So do not worry over this transgressed people.

Allah reminds the Jews not to disobey the Prophet as their ancestors did the Prophet *Moosa*, and if they do, the punishment will be severe. But most of them continued their disobedience and transgressions. So they wandered on the Earth until 1948 up to the Nation Israel formed. Today this Jewish country controls even America. As Muslims are living in great boast and disobedience to the Book as well as Prophet, they are being punished in all over the World. See explanation 2: 99 and 254.

Maseeh-A-Ddajjal will come as the chief of Israel army. The hypocritical leaders all over the world from Muslims will welcome him. But after *Eisa* comes, he will kill *Ddajjal*. Then by killing the hypocrites, *Eisa* will implement the orders of the verses 4: 91; 9: 123 and 33: 61. Surely, the hypocrites, they are the transgressors is told in the verse 9: 67. See the explanation 2: 26-27 and 5: 19.

27. Recite information to them about the Truth concerning Adam's two sons. When they both presented sacrifices, it was accepted from one on them and not accepted from the other. He said: "I

will surely kill you" the other said: Surely Allah accepts from the Heedful".

28. Even if you stretch your hand towards me in order to kill me, I will never stretch my hand against you to kill you. I fear Allah, the Lord of the Worlds.

29. Indeed I want you to bear my sins as well as your own sins, you will become an inmate of Fire. And that is the reward for the wrongdoers.

30. His soul yielded him to kill his brother. Thus he killed his brother and he became one among the losers.

In each delivery Adam couple would get twins, one man and one woman. The man in the first delivery would marry the woman in the second delivery and the man in the second delivery would marry the woman in the first delivery. The woman born with *Qabeel* was beautiful but the woman born with *Habeel* was not beautiful. So *Qabeel* persisted to marry the sister born with him. It was against the *Sharee'at* on that time. Therefore, to get a resolution they decided to offer a sacrifice. *Habeel* decided to offer a good goat but *Qabeel* who was a farmer offered some bad and good mixed corn. The fire from Heaven burned the sacrifice of *Habeel* and thus proved to be accepted. *Qabeel* threatened *Habeel* that he will kill him. But *Habeel* said that, Allah accepts the sacrifice of the heedful only. Read together the verse 2: 186. But the soul of *Qabeel* led him to kill his brother; thus he murdered him and became one among the losers. Prophet taught that *Qabeel* who did the first murder would get a part of the punishment of each murder happens in the world. See the explanation 3: 183 and 4: 85.

31. Then Allah sent a raven, which scratch the Earth in order to show him how to dispose his brother's corpse. He said: "Alas! It is too bad for me, have I failed to be like this raven and dispose of my brother's corpse". Thus he became One among the regrets.

32. On account of that, We prescribed for the children of Israel that, anyone who kills any person except as a punishment for murder or for causing mischief in the land, it will be as if he had killed all mankind; and if any one who spares life, acts as if he had granted life to whole mankind. Our Messengers have brought

them explanations. Then afterward many of them committed excesses on Earth.

33. The reward of those who make war on Allah and His Messenger and spread havoc through the land, is to be slaughtered or crucified, or have their hands and feet cutoff on opposite sides or to be banished from the land. That will mean their disgrace in this World, while they will have serious torment in the Hereafter.

34. Except for those who come to repent before you overpower them. Know that indeed Allah is Forgiving, Merciful.

Today, if we utilize the Soul of Qur'an as Insight, we can see that these kinds of habits are with the hypocrites. Concealing Allah and His Prophet in the Soul of Qur'an; and knowingly doing and encourage laymen to do mischief and flow bloodshed on the land in order to maintain their leadership and power, thus they are declaring war against Allah and His Prophet. Really they are responsible for destroying the earth by causing bloodshed, and spreading communalism, nationalism, racism, selfishness, narrow mindedness, partiality etc. along the Earth by hiding the Soul of Qur'an. They have dispelled peace, happiness, communal harmony etc. from the Earth by making different organizations. See the explanation 2: 85; 3: 21-22 and 4: 91.

35. Oh you who believe, heed Allah aspire for contact with Him; strive hard in His way in order that you may prosper.

'Aspire for contact with Him' does not mean to maintain intercessors. It can understand from the following verses 25: 59; 32: 4; 36: 78; 39: 3, 36, 44 etc. that Allah doesn't need any intercessors, helpers and He is enough for His servant as Protector and Helper and if any invoke except Allah will be the enemies on the Day of Judgment. See the explanation 4: 117. The verses 17: 56 and 57 say: "Say to them: Pray to those whom you assume besides Him. They have no power to relieve or to change your troubles. Those to whom they pray themselves aspire the way of approach to their Lord and they try to be those who are the nearest to Him; they hope for His Mercy and fear His punishment. Indeed, the punishment of your Lord is terrible". The verse 7: 194 says: "Surely those whom you call besides Allah are servants like you. So call them and let them answer you, if you are so truthful". The Qur'an no doubt declares that the Paradise and the Hell is earning by individual Here. No one can give Guidance to anybody.

Abstain from sins whenever one gets an opportunity to do it and spend time, money etc. to convey the Message of the Soul of Qur'an in order to familiarize Allah and Prophet. The significance of the following words of Prophet is also the same, "*I can't promise Paradise to those who keep constant 'swalath' and to those who stead fasting; but it will be said to enter the Paradise to those who abstain, fearing Allah, from committing fornication or adultery when a noble woman inviting him to do so*".

Jihad- Strive hard in the way of Allah- include participating in wars and spend money to buy weapons and other things, during the period of Prophet and later. But *Jihad* of today is only learning and teaching the Soul of Qur'an, since there is no party of believers anywhere in the World. The verse 25: 52 say "therefore, do not obey the disbelievers, and make a Strenuous strive with this Qur'an against them". The verse 54: 17 says that "Allah made the Soul of Qur'an easy to understand by hearts. The verses 5: 91; 7: 17; 25: 29; 43: 36; 58:19 etc. say that satan prevents man from the Soul of Qur'an only and not from Its body or life- meaning. It has been explained in the verse 2: 186 that without the Soul of Qur'an the '*swalath*', charity, fasting, *hajj* etc. will not be accepted. But today no one is ready to learn and teach the Soul of Qur'an. Read together the verses 39: 17-18, 32-33 and 41: 30-32. See the explanation 2: 286; 3: 136 and 4: 172-175.

36. Certainly for those who are disbelievers owned whatever is on Earth plus its like besides, in order to redeem themselves from torment by means of it on Resurrection Day, it will not be accepted from them and they shall have a painful torment.

Those who hide and reject the Soul of Qur'an which is the Balance and Trust to keep the Universe in its equilibrium, if they owned whatever is on Earth plus its like beside in order to redeem themselves from the torment by means of it on Resurrection Day, it would not be accepted from them, they will have painful torment. The verses 20: 99-100 say we have brought you a reminder from our very presence anyone who neglect it will bear a burden on Resurrection Day. In the verse 33: 72 it is told that the Soul of Qur'an- the Trust- is revealed in order to punish the hypocritical men and women as well as the associates men and women who associate others with Allah. Today, all these verses are reading and hearing only the hypocrites and their blind followers gone astray people among mankind but they are carrying Qur'an as burden carrying donkeys as specified in the verse 62: 5 they are not ready to change their attitude. Hence they are the boar people who receive the Hell as the penalty for performing the *swalath,* fasting, *hajj* etc. as specified in the verses 14: 28-30. They are the only aimless and heedless people. See the explanation 2: 186; 3: 90-91 and 4:56.

37. They will wish to get out of the Fire, yet they will not get out of it; for them have constant torment.

The verse 32: 20 warns as: "The hypocrites will be cast into the Fire. Whenever they try to come out of it, they will be thrown back into it saying: Taste the punishment which you have been denying". In the verse 9: 68 Allah has promised the hypocrites and the '*Kuffar*'-rejecters of the truth one over one-the Hellfire. They have to live therein forever. It is sufficient for them. Allah has cursed them and for them have constant torment. Read together the verses 22: 19-22 and 48: 6. See the explanation 4: 136-140 and 145.

38. Whoever is guilty of theft, Man or Woman shall have cut off his and her hands with a penalty for whatever he or she has earned, as an example set by Allah, Allah is Powerful, Wise.

It is the right hand, which should be cut off for the first theft. Prophet taught that the hands of a cheater should not be cut off. This law affects only those who steals others property deliberately. The hands of those who stole fruits, vegetables and such eating materials should not be cut off as punishment.

Today this law also cannot be executed as the laws in the case of fornication, adultery, liquor etc. All these laws can be executed only in an Islamic society when there is a group of believers. Since these verses are revealed by addressing the believers. Through the verse 24: 55 Allah promised to the believers who do honorable deeds that, He will grant them the ruling power on Earth. Today we can see it is the Muslims, the people of Qur'an are in the forefront of all evils such as robbery, drug traffic, stealth, murder, looting etc. all these because they bear Qur'an without trying to understand its contents. Therefore in order to reduce such evil things of disbelieving satanic footsteps the laws and regulations of Qur'an has to be implemented, especially among Muslims. When Prophet reached *Madeena* he made an agreement with the Jews. According to this agreement, the Jews can Judge among themselves using their Book- *Thourath-*

and the Muslims using Qur'an. Before giving a judgment among the Jews, Prophet had asked them to bring and read the *Thourath*.

Here in the verse 'man' is mentioned first as a truth we can see that in the case of theft, men comes forefront of women. Whereas in the verse 24: 2, the 'fornicating women' is mentioned first, so as a truth, we can see that the women take initiation in fornication or adulteration. All these are the proofs for the words mentioned in the verse 41: 42, which says about the Soul of Qur'an: "No falsehood can come to it from before or from behind of Its codification and It is a revelation from the Wise, Self Praiseworthy". See the explanation 4: 82. In the verse 60: 12 Allah says to Prophet, when the believing women come to you to take the oath, take their pledge with the condition that they will not commit '*shirk*'-associate others with Allah-, they will not steal, they will not commit adultery and they will not kill their children and they will not give a cause for scandal and they will not disobey you in any just matter and pray to Allah for their forgiveness. Allah is Forgiving, Merciful. See the explanation 2: 66.

39. Anyone who repents following his wrongdoing, and reforms; then surely Allah relent towards him; surely Allah is Forgiving, Merciful.

This does not mean not to be cut off the hand when someone repents after his wrongdoing and reforms, but it advices to repent and reform his conduct after executing the punishment. This verse teaches one thing that whoever repents after his crime, he can save himself from the anger of Allah. If anyone who does not repent after his hand was cut off it means that, the sin of theft still remains in him. Allah will not give him forgiveness. Prophet taught that one person as a believer can't do fornication, theft etc. So one can do theft only if he forgets Allah and become transgressor as mentioned in the verse 59: 19. With Allah's Permission -the Soul of Qur'an- only a literate become a believer. And one can reform his activities by propagating the Soul of Qur'an- the food, cloth and sight of human Soul- among entire mankind with an intention to help them to become the believers and reform their deeds as accordance with the Soul of Qur'an. The deeds of a disbeliever will not be accepted and he can't enter into the Paradise. Read together the verses 25: 68-70. See the explanation 3: 116 and 4: 48.

40. Do you not know that surely Allah holds control over Heavens and Earth? He punishes anyone He wants, and forgives anyone He wants. And Allah is Capable of everything.

Everything in Heaven and on Earth has already been recorded in a Book as per the verses such as 9: 51; 10: 61; 11: 6; 22: 70; 34: 3; 57: 22 etc. That Book is the Soul of Qur'an which is explained each and everything as specified in the verse 16: 89. See the explanation 2: 2, 284 and 4: 131-132

Who will do theft, whose hands will be cut off, who will be killed, who will seek Allah's forgiveness, to whom the forgiveness will be given, who will be rewarded Paradise, who will be given Hell etc. have already been recorded in this Book. Whoever use this Book as the Balance to identify themselves, to identify the way of Allah and the way of satan; whoever pray Allah by heart that if their fate is to Hell let them give opportunities to do good deeds; and whoever try to learn and teach the Soul of Qur'an, then such people can enter the Paradise, the house of Allah. See the explanation 3: 136, 185 and 4: 118.

41. Oh Messenger, be not let those who rush off into disbelieve worry you, such as those who say: "We believe" with their mouths, while their hearts do not believe and of the Jews. They are the listeners of lies and listeners for those people who have not come to you. They lift words out of their context knowingly. They say: "If you are given this, then take it, while if you are not given it beware!" If Allah intends to put any one for trial, you can do nothing to save him from Allah. Allah has not intended to purify their hearts. They will have disgrace in this World, while in the Hereafter they will have terrible punishment".

'The men' mentioned here who say with their mouth that they believed, while their heart being disbelieved is the hypocrites. They have the same habits of Jews. They will try to execute or inspire others for doing evils such as communalism, nationalism, racism etc. They will not do anything to make the unity of mankind. They hear and learn Qur'an only to distort It and to spread lies. They come to hear the classes explaining the Soul of Qur'an as Allah intends for their leaders. Whenever any point mentioned from Qur'an against them, against their organization, they deliberately turn away from the assemblies as specified in the verse 9:127. When they returned to their centre they say others: "There he distort Qur'an, he says all organization among Muslims are disbelievers and associate others with Allah etc. Thus they try to prevent others from the Soul of Qur'an. These hypocrites not only talk insolently to the verses but also prevent the common people from hearing It by telling them not to go to that particular class. Just like the disbelievers specified in the verses 41: 26-28. And the verse 41: 29 says: "The common people who obeyed the words of these hypocrites blindly will say on the Day of Judgment: "Our Lord! Show us those among *Jinns* and men, who misled us, we shall crush them beneath our feet, since we were the underdog". Read together the verses 25: 27-29; 36: 62 and 67: 10. See the explanation 1: 7; 2: 166-167; 4: 140 and 5: 13.

42. They are listeners for lying, and eaters of forbidden things. Hence if they should come to you, you may judge between them or ignore them. If you ignore them they will never harm you in any way. While if you judge among them, then judge with Justice. Surely Allah loves who judge with Justice.

They hear Qur'an only to distort It and for the sake of falsehood. 'They are eaters of forbidden things' means that they make false statements for the sake of people taking bribe from them; they will argue to maintain the non-Islamic dowry system in marriage and receive a percentage of it. they will argue to maintain the forbidden things such as offerings, profane things concealing the verses 5:3 and 6: 145, in which it has been told that all offerings other than to Allah and the flesh of swine are forbidden or are filthy things; they feed the common men the forbidden things. Today it is a fact that, all over the World; the hypocrites from this community are forefront of devouring the substance or wealth of the mankind when we compare the rabbis and the priests of other people. Calling the believers Allah says in the verse 9: 34: Indeed, most of the rabbis and the priests devour the wealth of the mankind wrongfully and hinder them from the way of Allah- the Soul of Qur'an. Using Qur'an as Criterion, the believers should identify and desert such rabbis and priests. Otherwise, theirs wretchedness in the Hereafter will be as explained in the verses 2: 166-167.

This verse reminds an incident which happened at the time of Prophet. The Jews used to come to Prophet to get Judgment. Prophet gave them Judgment according the laws of *Thourath*. A noble woman and a man from a Jewish family in *Madeena* adulterated. The punishment for this crime in *Thourath* was stone to death. The Jews did not like this law to be carried out. They brought this case to Prophet. They wanted a favorable decision. Prophet judged them to stone to death. The Jews were not ready to accept it. Then Prophet asked them: "What is the punishment of this crime in *Thourath*?" They replied: "Beating with lash and riding on the donkey as the face being rubbed over with carbon". Keeping as

Allah witness Prophet asked the Jews priests: "Is it the real punishment for this crime of adultery in *Thourath*?" They once again lied. Calling *Ibnu Suriya*, the well-known scholar of *Thourath*, Prophet said: "Keeping Allah witness, who saved you from *Pharoah* and who gave you *Thourath* at Mount *Sina*, I ask you the same question". He said: "If you had not mentioned those words, I would not have disclosed the real fact; the punishment of adultery in *Thourath* also is stoning to death; but when this crime increased in our society, our arbiters made a submissiveness, and thus when a case of adultery comes in front of them, they freed the people of higher position and they execute this law of *Thourath* among the common people. When this submissiveness made the common people dissatisfactory, we brought this new system, changing the law of *Thourath*". Thus the Judgment of the Prophet was carried out.

'If you judge between them, judge with Justice' means judge with the Soul of Qur'an as the order of Allah. Those who judge by what Allah has revealed are believers and those who do not judge by what Allah has revealed are disbelievers, wrongdoers and transgressors as told respectively in the verses 5: 44, 45 and 47. Read together the verse 16: 64 and 49: 41. See the explanation 4: 133-135, 155-156; 5: 18 and 19.

43. How can they choose you as a judge when they have the Thourath, which contains Allah's Judgments? Yet even then they will turn away, and such persons are not believers.

Only one Book was revealed by Allah. Since some of the law of *Thourath* were against the selfish, interest and the wishes of Jews; ignoring *Thourath* they accepted the laws written by their priest and rabbis and considered them as from the Lord. Read together the verses 9: 31-32. Then Allah deputed Muhammad as His Prophet. The Jews were not ready to accept him. See the explanation 2: 41 and 42. Even though they would bring the cases in front of the Prophet expecting they may get favorable judgment from him. See the explanation 2: 78-79 and 3: 78.

Today the only Book for entire mankind is the Qur'an. The character of the hypocrites who bear It today has become worse than that of Jews and hypocrites of those days. Thus all over the world Muslims have become a people of scoundrels and execrated. It is because of their belief just opposite of the belief presenting the Soul of Qur'an. See the explanation 2: 120-121; 3: 79, 91; 4: 61-65 and 91.

44. Indeed, We have sent down the Thourath, containing Guidance and Light. The Prophets who were committed to live in peace judged among the Jews. The rabbis and priests were those who were entrusted the protection of Allah's Book and they were witness for It. So you do not fear mankind, fear Me and do not sell My verses for a miserable price. Those who do not judge by what Allah has sent down then such are the only disbelievers.

All Prophets were those who dedicated everything to Allah and were judged in accordance with the Book of Allah. At first, the priests and rabbis judged in accordance with the Book among the Jewish people. The verse 32: 24 says: "We appointed from among them the leaders giving Guidance under Our command when they were patients and were having firm belief in Our verses. But gradually by fearing the people rather than Allah they began to give the Judgment in favor of people and thus they sold Allah's verses for miserable prices. Today the hypocrites of Muslims have the worst character than the rabbis and priests. When the believers remind them with the verses they will oppose them and will not be ready to rectify; since they fear the people rather than Allah. They by dividing in different organizations they have become the associate others with Allah and thus become the party of satan. Today Qur'an is the only Book that Allah satisfied for entire mankind. Hence after receiving the Soul of Qur'an, those who do not judge in their personal, family and social life with It are the only disbelievers. See explanation 2: 140; 3: 157; 4: 150-151.

45. We had prescribed in Thourath for them a life for a life, an eye for an eye, a nose for a nose, an ear for an ear, a tooth for a tooth and a Similar retribution for every wounds. If any one remits the retribution, then there will be an act of atonement for him. Those who do not judge by what Allah has sent down then such are the only wrongdoers.

Atonement is the ransom giving as compensation to someone who pardoned him the retribution for a wrong deed. The ransom specified in the verse 2: 183 is for not observing an obligatory deed such as fasting without any serious reason. So the difference between the atonement and ransom may be understood that the atonement is liable to a person whereas ransom is liable to the Lord.

Today those who not utilize the Soul of Qur'an themselves and not give others to utilize It are the only wrongdoers as told in the verses 6: 21, 33, 47,

93; 9: 23; 10: 17; 18: 57; 29: 49; 32: 22; 62: 5 etc. They are the *mujrims* and inmates of Hell. See the explanation 2: 254; 3: 192 and 5: 19.

46. We appointed Eisa, the son of Maryam, to follow in their footsteps in order to confirm what had come before him from Thourath, and we gave him the Injeel - Gospel- which contains Guidance and Light, to confirm what the Truth of what ever there still remained in Thourath and as Guidance and an Admonition for the heedful.

In the verse 3: 49, it is mentioned that *Eisa* was appointed to the children of Israel as a Messenger. In this verse it is told that '*Eisa* is appointed to follow their foot steps' i.e. *Eisa* followed the foot steps of Prophets before him so that a share of *Eisa's* deeds will be given to the Prophets who were appointed before among the children of Israel. Read together the verse 36: 12. See the explanation 2: 213; 3:138 and 4: 85.

47. And let the people of Injeel judge by what Allah has sent down in It; Those who do not judge by what Allah has sent down then such are the only transgressors.

The verse 9:67 ends as the hypocrites are indeed transgressors. Today, what Allah has sent down is only the Soul of Qur'an. Therefore the hypocrites who hide the Soul of Qur'an and their blind followers who reject the Soul of Qur'an are the transgressors. Read together the verses 9: 24, 80; 24: 55; 61: 5 and 63: 6. See the explanation 2: 26-27, 99; 3: 81 and 82.

48. And We have sent you down the Book with Truth, to confirm what was already from the previous Book and as a Safeguard upon It. So judge between them by whatever Allah has sent down, do not follow their whims concerning any Truth that has been given to you. We have given each of you a code of law and a program. If Allah had wished, He might have made you into one community. But He wants to test you in what He has given to you. So you rush to the best deeds. To Allah is your return entirely. He will then inform you the reality of the matters in which you were disagreeing.

To confirm that only one Book has been sent down, see the explanation 2:2. And today that is the Soul of Qur'an which is confirming all the Books previously revealed. The Safeguard means such a thing which protects and support. Here the Soul of Qur'an mentioned as Safeguard. That is why It contains each and every law of all other Books that came before. The verse 15: 9 says, "Surely We have revealed the Soul of Qur'an; and We will surely preserve It Ourself. Note the point that here it is not told We have revealed the Qur'an and preserve it, instead we will surely preserve the Soul of Qur'an. As per the verses 41: 41-42 the Soul of Qur'an is the Splendid Book revealed from someone Wise, Praiseworthy in which no falsehood shall approach It from either in front of It or behind It. The verse 43 says anything that has been told you is merely what was told Messengers before you, your Lord is the Master of Forgiveness as well as the Wielder of painful punishment. Therefore the hypocrites who hide the Safeguard- Soul of Qur'an- after receiving It will be punished severely in this world as well as in the Hereafter. As long as in the Soul of Qur'an exists, the contents of all other Books, which were not distorted or changed, will also exist, in this way Qur'an act as safeguard to other Books. As per the verse 98:3 the straight parts of all books contains in Soul of Qur'an. The Safeguard is mentioned in the verse 59: 23 as one of the good name of Allah. Then the Soul of Qur'an as well as Allah is not only a Safeguard and Shield against the Hell but also it will protect the person, his family members and his wealth and property from all type of disasters and calamities. It is the permission of Allah to become believer. See explanation 3: 58, 101-103 and 4:174-175.

Since it is told in this verse that 'do not follow their whims concerning any Truth that has been given to you' prophet and the believers can not follow or give preference to anything other than the Safeguard-the Soul of Qur'an. Read together the explanation 2:120 and 147. The code of law and the program mentioned in this verse known in Arabic as '*Dheen*' and '*Shariath*'. '*Dheen*'-the religion- is the same every time as explained in the verses 3: 19, 85 whereas the '*Shariath*'-practical deeds- is differ time to time. Even early period and the later period of prophet Muhammed, '*Shariath*'-practical deeds- is different. *Dheen*'-the religion- is related to the individual whereas *'Shariath'* is demanded to the group of believers. Today, since there is no group of believers anywhere in the world, there is no '*Islamic shariath*'. During this time it is taught by the prophet to the believer here and there to remain by holding fast the Soul of Qur'an with his molar teeth. Without forming the belief with the Soul of Qur'an no '*Shariath*'-

practical deeds- will be accepted as explained in the verse 2: 186. See explanation 2:148 and 4:1.

'If Allah had wished, He might have made you in to one community' This part of verse teaches that the almighty Allah is capable of everything as like make the mankind a single community like angel without disobeying. Therefore prophet and believer should not grieve about the astray of disbelievers. As per the verse 76: 3 Allah has given freedom to accept men either the way of grateful or ungrateful. The verse 16: 37 says even if you are eager upon their guidance then Allah still does not Guide the one who misleads himself and they will have no supporters. So it is the responsibility of each individual bestowed with the faculty of intelligence to utilize the Soul of Qur'an which is the Guidance, Mercy, Bounty, Safeguard, Shield etc. No man can blame Allah, the Impartial or anybody else even his soulmate satan companion for his astray. See the explanation 2:213, 256 and 4:118. But He wants to test you in what He has given to you, mankind created in the Paradise has been deputed on earth in order to undergo test that who will select the way of Allah to the Paradise and the way of satan to the Hell. See explanation 2: 155-157 and 'Goal of life' in the introduction.

Today the 'forerunner' who will enter the Paradise without trial is the one who help the Impartial Allah by propagating and conveying the Soul of Qur'an- the Balance and Trust- to entire mankind. The believers one in every thousand to the Paradise will not postpone their trial to the Day of Judgment instead they will utilize the Soul of Qur'an as the Balance and Truth in this world in order to differentiate their way of life from 999 in every thousand to the Hell. Aimless hypocrites and heedless gone astray people will not utilize their intelligence and faculty of thinking, sight and hearing in this world and they will lead a life more astray than cattles. They are the worst people in the sight of Allah as per the verses 8: 22 and 98: 6. Read together the verses 35: 32 and 61: 14.

Even though the verse ends as 'He will then inform you the reality of the matters in which you were disagreeing', the Impartial Allah will not inform or judge anything instead each individual will be given the book fastened around his neck and will say read your book, today it is enough yourself to see your account as specified in the verses 17: 13-14; 18: 49; 45: 25-32 etc. The disbelievers who are living here forgetting the aim of life will not see their Lord. Indeed between them and their Lord a screen will be formed on that Day is told in the verse 83: 15. See explanation 2:113.

49. And you judge among them with what Allah has sent down and do not follow their whims and beware of them lest they tempt you away from a part of that what Allah has sent down to you. And if they should turn away, then you know that Allah only wants to afflict them with some of their own offences. And indeed most of the people are transgressors.

The verses 17:73-75 say they almost lure you away from what We have revealed to you, in order to invent something else against Us; then they would adopt you as a bosom friend and if We had not braced you, you might have almost inclined a little bit towards them. Then We would have made you to taste double share of punishment in this life as well as in the Hereafter; then you would have found no helper against Us. Those who hide the Soul of Qur'an after received It are the transgressed hypocrites-arrogant human devils. They are the one who have made their trial here itself and the one who have to go to the bottom of the Hellfire without any reckoning on the Day of Judgment. Read together the verses 10: 15-17; 57: 16 and 27. See the explanation 2:99, 145; 3:97; 4: 88 and 145.

50. Do they seek the judgment from the time of ignorance? Yet who is finest in judgment than Allah for any people who have convinced belief?

The Soul of Qur'an is Insight for mankind, a Guidance and Mercy to the people with convinced belief, is told in the verse 45:20. Read together the verses 39:17-18 and 55-59. The verses 41: 33-34 say, "Who is better in speech than the one who calls people towards Allah submitted by the whole Qur'an, does good deeds and says: " Indeed I am one among who wholly submitted to Allah?" The good things - the deeds under the shade of Qur'an are not equal to the evil things. Repel others' evil deeds with the best - the Soul of Qur'an, then you can see that he, with whom you had enmity, will become your close friend. The verse 29:46 says: "Do not argue with the people of the Book except with what is good – with the Soul of Qur'an - except with those who are wicked among them" and say: "We believe in that which is sent down to us and that which is sent down to you; Our Deity and your Deity is the same One Allah to Whom we submit as Muslims."

In the verse 33:72 Allah says "When We offered the Trust-the Soul of Qur'an- to the Heavens, to the Earth and to the mountains, they refused to undertake It and they were afraid to bear It, but man bore It. He was indeed wrongdoer and fool". To put it briefly, those who reject the Soul of Qur'an after they received It, are foolish, wrongdoers, transgressors and losers. See the explanation 3: 110; 4: 78, 82 and 87.

51. Oh you who believe, do not take Jews and Christians as your patrons. Some of them are acting as patrons for one another. Any of you who make friends with them becomes one of them. Surely Allah does not guide such wrongdoing people.

The verse 9: 23 says: "Oh you who believe, Do not take your fathers and your brothers as your protector if they prefer disbelief to belief; anyone of you who took them as protector, then such are the wrongdoers". As the Book of today is the Soul of Qur'an only, believer can not take hypocrites and their blind followers as protectors and friends as specified in the verse 58: 22. Instead, '*Jihad*' with the Soul of Qur'an should be done against them who made different parties disputing in Allah's Book. This verse says: 'Some of the Jews and Christians are friends to one another'. The verses 9: 71 says that the believers, both men and women are protecting friends of one another; and the verse 8:73 says: 'The disbelievers are friends and helpers to each other. But the verse 9: 67 says: 'the hypocrites both men and women are of one kind'. Note that, the words 'helpers to one another' has not been used in the case of hypocrites. The verses 6: 144; 28: 50 and 46: 10 also end as 'surely Allah does not guide such wrongdoing people'. See the explanation 3: 28, 186-187 and 4: 144-147.

52. You may see those who have disease in their hearts dashing among them saying: "We fear some disaster will affect us", perhaps Allah will bring some victory or command from Himself, so some morning they will awaken regretfully about what they have concealed within themselves.

The hypocrites of *Madeena* had run seeking help from the Jews and Christians. But whenever the believers received any profit or victory, then the hypocrites did regret for not having joined with them. See the explanation 4: 73. In the verse 59: 11 Allah says: "Have you not turned your attention to those who are hypocrites, they say to their fellow disbelievers among the people of the Book: If you are driven out, we too will go out with you. We will never obey any one in your affair. If they fight against you, we will certainly help you". Then in the verse 13 Allah says: "In the hearts of hypocrites there is a greater fear about believers than Allah. That is because they are the people not understanding the aim of life". See the explanation 3: 119 and 4: 89-91.

53. And those who believe will ask: "Are these the ones who swore by Allah with their most solemn oath that they stood along with you? Their deeds have failed and they have turned out among the losers.

The hypocrites solemnly swore by Allah that, they were with the believers. But in some situations such as deportation of a Jew tribe-'*Banu-Nadheer*'-, as they could not get the share of financial profit, they would regret for not having joined with the believers. Allah says that the works of hypocrites are in vain. Read together the verses 63: 1- 4. The prayer of such disbelievers will increase nothing except astray is told in the verses 13: 14 and 40: 50.

The verses 9: 75-77 say: There are some among them, who made covenant with Allah, saying: If He grants out of His Bounty, we will spend in charity and will certainly be among the honorable men. But when He gives them out of His bounty they become stingy and turn back from their covenant averse. So He planted hypocrisy in their hearts till the Day on which they shall meet Him. Because they broke their covenant with Allah which they had promised Him and for how they had been lying. If we utilize the Soul of Qur'an as the Insight and Standard the activities of today's hypocrites are same as those of earlier; even though the hypocrites know that the '*Eid*' comes next to the day of *Arafa*, they celebrate the '*Eid*' with majority of Muslims next to the original day of '*Eid*'. See the explanation 2: 189; 3: 77, 120 and 4: 142-144.

54. Oh you who believe, if any of you turn back from his 'Dheen', and then Allah will bring a people whom He will love just as they love Him. They will be humble towards the believers, stern towards the disbelievers, they will do 'Jihad' in the way of Allah, and they do not fear the blame of any critic. That is the grace of Allah, which He gives to any one He wishes, Allah is Boundless, Aware.

The verse 48: 29 says: "Muhammad is the messenger of Allah and those with him are hard against the hypocrites and compassionate to each other among themselves. Calling Prophet, through the verses 9: 73 and 66: 9: Allah says in

"Make *Jihad* against the Kuffar and the hypocrites, be wrath with them. Their ultimate abode is Hell, what a worst returning place". The believers represent Believer Allah whereas the hypocrites represent disbeliever satan. Read together the verses 58: 19, 22. Today the only *Jihad* is with the Soul of Qur'an. In the verse 25: 52 Allah orders the believers: "Don't obey the disbelievers, who hide and reject the Soul of Qur'an and do *Jihad* against them with It. The mode of *Jihad* with the Qur'an can understand from the explanation of the verses 2: 66 and 4: 63. In the verses 33:1, 48 Allah by calling Prophet says: "Don't obey the disbelievers and hypocrites". To get a clear idea about disbeliever, see the explanation of the verses 2: 166-167, 254; 3: 90-91; 4: 150- 151 and 5: 36

55. Indeed your patron is Allah as well as His messenger and those who believe who keep up swalath, pay the welfare tax and bow down their heads in service of Allah.

56. Whoever selects Allah, His messenger and those who believe as his close friends, it is then the party of Allah will certainly be victorious.

It is the party of Allah- the only party from Adam till the Last Day to enter the Paradise- which includes the Prophets and the believers. All other parties are satan's party to enter the Hell as specified in the verse 58: 19. In the verse 63: 8 Allah says: "Might and Honor belongs to Allah, to His messenger and to the believers, but the hypocrites do not know". The verse 8: 64 says: "Oh Prophet! Allah is sufficient for you and for the believers who follow you. See the explanation 2: 257; 3: 18; 4: 59 and 136-139.

57. Oh you who believe, do not take those who treat your 'Dheen' as a mockery and sport from among the ones who were given the Book before you and the 'Kuffar' as protecting friends, and heed Allah if you are believers.

58. When you call them for swalath they take it as a mockery and sport. That is because they are the people who don't use their intelligence.

. By this verse Allah teaches the believers not to take the hypocrites who hide the Soul of Qur'an and the 'Kuffars' who reject to learn the Soul of Qur'an, they make the '*Dheen*' mockery and fun and are living without having the aim of life, as their leaders and friends. The verse 29: 64 says: The life of this World is nothing but amusement and sport, yet the final home will mean real living, if they only realized it". The verses 7: 50-51 say: When the inmates of Fire will call out to the inmates of Paradise, "Give us some water and some of the food which Allah has provided to you", they will reply: "Allah has forbidden both of these things to the disbelievers who took the life as amusement and sport". Therefore the believers keep Allah in their heart with the Soul of Qur'an and they will not waste their time in amusement and fun. They are the vicegerents of Allah on Earth and will return back to His house, the Paradise by utilizing the Ticket specified in the verse 78: 29.

The verse 51: 55 says: "And keep on admonishing them with the Soul of Qur'an, certainly the Soul of Qur'an is beneficial to the true believers. The verse 56 says: We have not created *Jinns* and men except to serve Me alone. The verse 57 says: I require no sustenance from them nor do I ask that they should feed Me. Allah appointed entire mankind on Earth to live as His vicegerents. But it is only believers who know the Soul of Qur'an will live as vicegerents of Him and prepare Paradise Here in order to fulfill the aim of life by teaching entire mankind the Soul of Qur'an - the Balance to keep the Universe in its equilibrium. See the explanation 1: 4 and 3: 136.

In *Madeena* the Jews and hypocrites were disbelievers, and when they heard the calling for *swalath*, they had mocked at it. But today the hypocrites are the leaders for *swalath* and their charity and *swalath* are futile since they are not having the Soul of Qur'an as told in the verses 9: 53-55. Then the believers shouldn't follow these hypocrites who have been killed by Allah as specified in the verse 63: 4. Today there are no believers to lead the *swalath*, believers can't go to *Masjid* to perform *swalath* with hypocrites and gone astray people. So disbelievers and hypocrites mock at the believers. Today, if the Prophet, Qur'an, the *swalath* and the believers are mocked by other non-Muslim people, then punishment will be for the hypocrites and the disbelievers from the Muslims who do not follow the do's and don'ts of the Qur'an. Their *swalath* do not prevent them from sinful life and evil deeds as mentioned in the verse 29: 45. Their *swalath* is only with their body without the participation of soul. See the explanation 4: 142-144."The scene on the Day of Judgment is warned in the verse 36:62 as: satan has led astray a great among you, could you not then use your intelligence?" As per the verse 67: 10: On that Day, they will mourn: "if we had heard the Soul of Qur'an or used our intelligence, we would have not been among the inmates of the Blazing fire. Read together the verse 8: 35. See the explanation 2: 91; 3: 102; 4: 135 and 5: 48

59. Say: "Oh people of the Book, what makes you retribution with us except we believe with Allah and what have been sent down to us, and what was sent down previously? And indeed most of you are transgressors".

Today the Soul of Qur'an is the only Book for entire mankind. So the believer has to ask the same question to the Muslims forgetting Allah and His Book. It is mentioned in the verses 85: 8-9 about those who witness the trench of fire in which the believers were burnt. For which they have no reason for retribution except they believe in Allah, the Almighty, the Praiseworthy to whom belongs the kingdom of the Heavens and Earth, and Allah is witness for everything.

In brief, the believers have always been faced persecution and oppositions from their own people that is from the hypocrites. It is told that the hypocrites are the real enemies of Allah and believers in the verse 63: 4. Allah orders to the Prophet and the believer to do *Jihad* individually against the hypocrites who hide the Soul of Qur'an and *Kuffar* who reject the Soul of Qur'an through the verse 9: 73; and to the party of believers in order to kill them as explained the verse 4: 159. The end of the world will occur when there exist no such believers who do *Jihad* to the hypocrites and all the people become transgressors and wrongdoers. See the explanation 2: 99; 4: 63 and 5: 49.

60. Say: "Shall I announce to you something worse than this, as recompense from Allah?" They are those whom Allah has cursed, to whom His wrath has fallen, those of whom He transformed into monkeys and swine and those who worshiped 'Thaghooth'; such are worse in position and more far astray from the Straight path".

Allah tells Prophet to ask the Jews who are in front of him: Do you hate us because we believe on Allah and the Book that has come to us? Is there any other reason that makes you retribution upon us? Most of you are transgressors.

But it is to your forefathers, whom Allah has cursed and condemned, whom He transformed into monkeys and swine and to those who worshiped the 'Thaghooth' had more worst retribution or recompense from Allah. It has been mentioned in the explanation of the verses 2: 26 and 65-66 that, they who fished breaking the prohibition of the *Sabbath* day, breaking the laws and commands of Allah deliberately were transformed into monkeys. Read together the verse 7: 166.

When *Eisa* prayed as mentioned in the verse 5: 114: "Sent down for us a food tray from Heaven as a sign from You and as a feast for the first and last of us". Allah answered as per the verse 5: 115: "I will send it down to you; but any of you disbelieve after that, I shall punish him with a punishment which I have never punished anyone in the World". Thus Allah sent it down from the Heaven and more than four thousand people ate from it. Then some of the Jews who ate from the feast became suspicious about it, whether it was from the Heaven or not and thus defied the sign of Allah and due to their deliberate transgression they were transformed into swine.

Today, the hypocrite's deeds like hiding and distorting the Qur'anic verses are more transgressed actions than that of Jews. In the verse 7: 176 they are compared to the dogs, which do not make any change whether it is disturbed or not. In the verse 62: 5, comparing these hypocrites to the donkeys, Allah says that He will not guide such wrong doing people. See the explanation 5: 51. The hypocrites and their blind followers-gone astray people- are mentions as the worst beasts who do not utilize their intelligence as per the verse 8: 22 and they are the worst one in the land creatures as per the verse 98: 6. Read together the verses 9: 67-68; 33: 60-61, 72-73 and 48: 6

It is mentioned in the verses 2: 6; 9: 80 and 63: 6 that whether the Prophet seeks forgiveness for them or not, Allah will neither forgive nor guide such transgressors. The verse 2: 174 says: "Those who hide Qur'an, the Book which Allah has revealed and those who sell Its verses for miserable prices, fill nothing in their bellies except the Fire, and on the Day of Judgment Allah will neither speak to them nor purify them". The verse 4: 145 declares that, such hypocritical people will be thrown into the bottom of Hell without any trial. They will be resurrected in the Hell with their own face and the body of execrable animals such as swine, dogs, donkeys, monkeys etc. See the explanation 2: 159-161; 3: 79, 90-91; 4: 47 and 91.

It is told in the verse 42: 16 that, those who argue concerning Allah without giving answer to His calling, their disputes or arguments have no effect or weight with their Lord, on them is His wrath and for them there will be a severe punishment. All those who do not serve Allah as His representatives are representatives of satan and they are serving 'Thaghooth' See the explanation 2: 257 and 4: 48-52. There is only one party as well as one path to Paradise, and all other parties and ways are to Hell. Prophet taught that one out of every thousand is to Paradise and nine hundred and ninety nine are to Hell in the explanation of the verse 4: 118.

61. And when they come to you, they say: "We believe", while they have entered with disbelief and they leave with it. Allah knows the best with what they have been hiding.

The Qur'an has explained this habit of Jews and the hypocrites in various places. See the explanation 2: 6-20, 79 and 4: 141-145. Today if we utilize the Soul of Qur'an as the Insight, we can see this habit is having mainly with the hypocrites through out the world. They observe *swalath* and *fasting* with their body without participation of the soul, in order to show the people. They will not keep the command mentioned through the verses 7:204 and 205. The verse 47:16 says that among them there are some who listen to you and when they go out from you they ask to those who have knowledge "what was it that he said just now". Such are the men whose heart Allah has sealed and who follow their own desires. And in the verse 17 Allah says for those who follow the Guidance, their guidance will be increased to them and they will be given their heedfulness. Calling the believers Allah says in the verse 8: 21, Oh you who believe, obey Allah and His Messenger, and do not turn away him when you hear from him and do not be like those who say 'We have heard' while they not even listening. Read together the verses 8: 2-4; 39: 23 and 42: 52. See explanation 2: 38; 4: 174 and 175.

The verses 9:124 and 125 say: whenever a *Surath* is revealed; the hypocrites will ask "whose faith from among you is increased by this? Certainly the faith of the believers has increased and they do rejoice with it. For those whose hearts are in disease, it will add filth over filth and they will die in a state of disbelief. The verse 127 says whenever a *Surath* is revealed, the hypocrites look at each other to see whether anyone is watching them and then they slip away. Allah has slipped away their hearts because they are the people who do not comprehend. Read together the verses 6: 155-157 and 9: 63-65. See explanation 4: 46; 5: 41-42 and 49.

62. You will see many of them hastening in sins and enmity and eating forbidden things. What they have been doing is so wretched.

The things prohibited by Allah and His messenger are forbidden things. It includes eating and taking of other's property or trust, by making new observances or customs against the law of Allah and His Messenger. Today this habit of Jews of that period exists only with the hypocrites. By exploiting the belief of the people and by making new observances and superstitions they eat the forbidden things. These hypocrites do conduct an artificial prayer for those who earned money by smuggling, hoarding, accepting interest and thus eating a portion of it. They insist recitation of Qur'an for the dead against the command of verses 6:36 and 36: 70 and make judgment unjustly in favor of the people who give them money. They encourage the dowry system and accept a share of it by quoting the artificial words of '*Nikah*'. They collect money from others in the name of orphans and accept commission from it. They feed their family members with this money and thus they fill their bellies with fire as explained in the verse 4:10. They are not ready to teach the Soul of Qur'an. Instead they fill their bellies with fire by receiving money to lead the *swalath* as *Imam.* In brief, all their deeds are sinful and against the belief of Islam. It is told in the verses 41:19-24 that their hearing, sight, skin etc. will bear witness against them on the Day of Judgment. Allah asks through the verse 2: 175 that what a tolerance these hypocrites show to Fire. It is told in the verses 52: 25-26 that when the inmates of Paradise ask each other in their conversation how they reached in the Paradise, they will reply: we were full of fear about our family members burning in Hellfire if they were fed with the forbidden things during our Worldly life. See explanation 2: 188; 3: 92; 4: 50-51and 5: 42.

63. Why not their rabbis and priests prohibited them from speaking sinful words and eating forbidden things? What they have been producing is so wretched.

It is the duty of rabbis and the priests to prevent the people from uttering sinful words and eating forbidden things. Through the verse 9:34 Allah says calling the believers "Most of the rabbis and the priests devour the wealth of the mankind wrongly and hinder them from the way of Allah, i.e. the Soul of Qur'an. Since the verse starts calling the believers, such hypocritical leaders will come only from Muslims. Therefore those who accept them as the leader and feed them will be among the disbelievers. When we say the verse 1:7: "Not upon whom

Your wrath happened", we have to keep in mind these hypocritical leaders; and when we say "not of those who gone astray", we have to keep the common Muslims who accept and feed these hypocritical leaders.

"What they have been producing is so wretched" means not only the deeds of hypocrites but also their footsteps leaving to the off springs are so worst and leading to the Hell; while the believers' deeds and footsteps leaving to the off springs must be under the Light-the Soul of Qur'an- and thus to the Paradise. See explanation 2:166-167; 4: 29 and 85.

64. And the Jews say "Allah's hand is tied up"; it is their own hands that are tied up and they cursed because of what they have said! Nay, both His hands are widely outstretched. He dispenses things as He wishes. Any revelations sent down to you from your Lord increase many of them in arrogation and disbelief. We have tossed enmity and wrath between them until the Day of Judgment. Every time they kindle a fire for war, Allah extinguishes it out. They rush to spread mischief on earth. And Allah does not love those who do mischief.

'The hand is tied up' mentioned in the verse means 'showing miserliness'. The verse 17:29 says; you should neither tie your hands to your neck nor stretch them; lest you sit back blame, worthy destitute. This means not to be so lavish and not to show miserliness. It is said in the verse 25: 67 that the true servants of the Most Gracious are those who, when they spend are neither extravagant nor stingy, but keep a mid-way in between. It is told about the hypocrites in the verse 9: 67 that they will withhold their hands from spending wealth as well as knowledge. See explanation 2: 195. The Jews of *Madeena* could not see any possibilities to regain their old prestige. More over the Prophet Muhammad was from *Isma'el* lineage. So they were not ready to accept the Book revealed to Prophet. In order to express their anger and disbelief they used the words such as "Allah's hands are tied up", "He has nothing to give us except distress and destruction."

These habits of Jews can be seen in Muslims of today who have no faith. They are not ready to get dignity by using the Soul of Qur'an. Instead they get hatred and indignity or humiliation. In the verse 17:30 Allah says "Surely your Lord give sustenance in abundance for whom He pleases and He provides in a just measure for whom He pleases. Certainly He is fully Aware of His servants. He observes them closely". The verse 36: 74 says "Forgetting their own creations they are making comparisons for Us". The verse 16: 74 says "Don't make up any similitude for Allah, surely Allah knows and you do not know." In the verse 16: 71 Allah says "Allah has made some of you above others in sustenance. So will you give away your sustenance to your servants so as to make you both equals? Is it then about the blessing of Allah that you are arguing?" Read together the verses 16: 75-76, 83. In the verse 16: 96 Allah says "All that is with you will come to an end, but what is with Allah is everlasting. We will certainly reward to those who are patient according to the best of theirs deeds". The best action or deed is to learn and teach the Soul of Qur'an. The worst action is reciting Qur'an without trying to understand its contents and without considering the Prophet's words. Those who recite Qur'an without knowing Its contents will be darted away from the '*Dheen*' as if an arrow darted away from a bow. They are called *fujjar*. The *fujjar* will certainly be in the Hellfire as told in the verse 82: 14.

When we use the Soul of Qur'an as the Balance, we can see that the enmity and wrath exist between the Muslims of today all over the world. The enmity and wrath cannot be seen in any other community as much as in the Muslim community. It is because they hide and reject the Soul of Qur'an- the only instrument to make peace and harmony among mankind. They have become a people suppressed by all other community. Their prayers are not accepted. They will get Hell-'*Jahannam*'-as a penalty for their *swalath*, *Fasting* and *Hajj* etc. as told in the verses 25: 65 and 66. Today Muslims involved in terrorism; communalism and racism etc. throughout the world. In the verse 9:32 Allah says "The hypocrites try to extinguish Allah's Light with their mouth. But Allah will not allow it to happen. He wants to perfect His Light even though the disbelievers may dislike it". The verse 61:8 has the same message. As per the verse 66: 8 "The believers pray always, Our Lord, perfect our Light for us, and forgive us our offences; indeed You are capable of everything" and will go through the Soul of Qur'an- The Light. See the explanation 4:49, 174 and 5:54.

65. If the people of the Book would only believe and follow the do's and don'ts of It, We should certainly have remove their evil deeds for them and enter them to the gardens full of Bliss.

66. If they had only kept up the Thourath and Injeel, and whatever was sent down to them from their Lord, they would have certainly

been nourished from above them and from beneath their feet. Some of them form a moderate community, while most of them are doing evil deeds.

Any people who believe and follow the do's and don'ts of the concerned Book their evil deeds, will be forgiven and they will be entered in the garden full of Bliss. "Keep up *Thourath, Injeel* and that which was revealed to them" means identify Allah and themselves, recognize the aim of life and follow the Soul of the Book. In the verse 31:17 says; enjoin what is good and forbid what is wrong, and endure with patience whatever befalls; that is the way of determination. The verse 35:32 says: then We have given the Book as inheritance to those of Our servants whom We have chosen. Among them there are some who did wrong to their own souls (the companions of the Left Hand as per the verse 90:19) and someone who follow a moderate life (companions of Right Hand as per the verse 90:18) and someone among them are foremost in good deeds by Allah's Permission i.e. the Soul of Qur'an (Forerunners are those who enter the Paradise without Trial as told in the verse 9:100); that is the highest grace. Read together the verses 56:7-11. See explanation 5:48-49.

The verse 7:96 says: if the people of the country believed and followed the do's and don'ts of the Book, We would indeed open out to them blessings from Heaven and Earth. But they rejected the Soul of Qur'an. So We seized them on account of their earnings. Read together the verses 6:42-47; 7:94-95. The destruction of the Universe occurs in consequences of man's own misdeeds as told in the verses 16:61 and 30:41. The World will come to an end when all the mankind of the Earth becomes wrong doers and transgressors as Muslims of today, who live with vanities more badly than Meccan pagans. Those who hide and reject the Soul of Qur'an after receiving It, which is the splendid Book revealed from the Mighty Praiseworthy will have severe torment. No falsehood would enter either in front of It or behind It as told in the verse 41:41-42. Read together the verses 7:169 and 170. See explanation 2:2-5; 5:51 and 59.

67. Oh Messenger, deliver whatever has been sent down to you from your Lord. If you do not do so, you will not have conveyed His message. Allah is enough to protect you from mankind. Surely Allah does not guide such disbelieving people.

The duty of Prophet is only to deliver the Message to entire mankind. In other words the Messenger is the one who is deputed by Allah from the mankind itself to show them how to live in this world as Allah's vicegerent. The Soul of Qur'an is the only message - the letter, that Allah revealed to all Messengers from the beginning to the end as explained in the verse 2: 213. Therefore whoever hides Soul of Qur'an the Balance and Trust to keep the Universe in its equilibrium without conveying to entire mankind are the disbelievers, wrongdoers and transgressors. The believer utilizes the Soul of Qur'an as Safeguard and Shield from all disasters as well as from the Hell. In Qur'an, two verses end as 'Surely Allah does not guide such disbelieving people' i.e. 16:107. See the explanation 3:10, 79-80; 5:48 and 51.

68. Say: "Oh the people of the Book, you have no ground to stand until you keep up the Thourath and Injeel as well as anything that has been sent down to you from your Lord. What has been sent down to you from your Lord increases many of them in arrogation and disbelief. Yet do not despair about disbelieving people!

The saying of anything that has been sent down to you from your Lord and what has been sent down to you from your Lord, denote the Soul of Qur'an. And that is the only Book today for all mankind. The verse revealed addressing the Jews of *Madeena* is now only applicable to the Muslims. They are only reading and hearing the Qur'an verses carrying the book as that of burden bearing donkeys and leading just opposite life of Qur'an and prophet. If a believer try to remind them with the Soul of Qur'an they even not ready to hear it and their approach to the believer just like the approach of disbelievers of prophet's time as mentioned both in the verses 22: 72 and 68: 51-52. Actually the read and heard Qur'an will argue and witness against this boar people as mentioned both in the verses 25: 18 and 48: 12. Through this verse Allah says to them: You cannot be proud of or be the leaders of the people until you follow the Book and advise others to follow It without concealing Its Message. Otherwise you will get curse, disgrace and anger in this world and severe punishment in the Hereafter. See the explanation 2: 85.

Prophet and believers shouldn't have sympathy to the people who hide and reject the Soul of Qur'an and shouldn't fear about their plotting against the Truth. The verse 16:127 says: "Be patient- for your patience is not but with the help of Allah- do not grieve over them and do not distress yourself because of their plots". See the explanation 2: 159-161; 3: 72 and 5: 60.

69. Certainly those who believe and those who are Jews, the Sabeans and the Christians anyone who believes with Allah and the Last Day and acts honorably, on them there shall be no fear and for them will not be grieved.

See the explanation 2: 62. Today, all Muslims are wearing only the garments of body and not wearing the garments of the soul. Without wearing the garment of the soul which is the Soul of Qur'an mentioned in the verse 7: 26, after receiving It, will not become a real believer. Today, the common Muslims through out the world are in the state of Bedouin Arabs- as mentioned in the verse 49: 14: "The Bedouin Arabs say: "We have believed". Tell them: "You have not believed; rather say: 'We have become Muslims'; for faith has not yet found its way into your hearts. If you obey Allah and His messenger, He will not deny you the reward of your deeds; surely Allah is Forgiving, Merciful". The prayer and deeds of disbelievers who hide and reject the Soul of Qur'an will not be accepted. See the explanation 2: 186.

Note the point that, the non-Muslims will not become the disbelievers, wrong doers, transgressors, *mujrims* and the inmates of Hell until they hide and reject the Soul of Qur'an specified in the verses 41: 41-44 which are the Guidance and Ticket to the Paradise. Then the hypocrites will ask where will be the dwelling place of idolaters from non-Muslims? The answer is that their burden of sins should be borne by the hypocrites and disbelievers from among Muslims as per the verse 6: 26. There are not only two worlds- the Paradise and the Hell- with the Lord of the Worlds, so those who didn't receive the Guidance or Ticket may send to any other Worlds besides the Hell. Whoever likes to return the Paradise from where entire mankind are sent down to Earth should utilize the Ticket mentioned in the verse 76: 29 as: "Indeed this is the Ticket for those who likes to adopt the way to his Lord. See the explanation 2: 26-27 and 3: 58.

70. We made an agreement with the children of Israel and sent them the messengers. Whenever there come them messenger with the message that was against to their desires, some of them were rejecting and others are being slaying.

See explanation 3: 81 for the solemn agreement. Today these habits of Jews; i.e. rejecting and killing of the messengers are seen among the hypocrites and disbelievers from Muslims all over the world. They are actually rejecting and killing the messengers by concealing their life style in the Soul of Qur'an. See explanation 2: 146 and 3: 21. They are only bearing Prophets' names and garments. It is told in the verse 10: 33 that, such transgressed people indeed will not be believed, they are human satans. The similitude of those who live carelessly even after they are reminded with the Soul of Qur'an and the hypocrites who hide the Soul of Qur'an is that of a dog mentioned in the verses 7: 175 and 176. The despised satan prevents man from the soul of Qur'an as specified in the verses such as 25: 29; 43: 36-38; 50: 27-29; 58: 19; 59: 16-17etc.

Note the point that, it is told in the verse in present continuous tense: others are being slaying i.e. today the Muslims having names of prophets by selecting other way of life than *Islam* are actually falsifying and killing the prophets as well as Jews and hypocrites in *Madeena* were trying to kill Prophet. See explanation 4: 91 and 5: 11.

71. They reckoned that there would be no testing. Thus they acted blind and deaf. Yet Allah accepted their repentance; but again many of them acted blind and deaf. And Allah is Observant with whatever they are doing.

Just like the hypocrites and the Jews in *Madeena*, today Muslims all over the World are pretending blindness and deafness, leading the same life as mentioned in this verse forgetting the aim of life. Today the Jews are considered learned people, they control the World themselves and even they are leading indirectly the Muslim countries. They are being recognized by all other countries. It is from them, *Maseeh-A-Ddajjal* will come. He will rule whole World except *Hijaz*- the provinces including *Mecca* and *Madeena*. *Eisa* will kill him with his spear and will show the blood to the people. Then the believers will kill 70,000 Jews soldiers of *Ddajjal*, the agitators in *Madeena* specified in the verse 33: 60. The non-Muslim people in the entire world will recognize and approve the *Islam* as their way of life. Then the hypocrites and those who have a disease in their hearts specified in the verse 33: 60 who hide and reject the Soul of Qur'an as well as falsify prophet and *Islam* will not find any shelter or hiding places anywhere in the world. Even each trees and stones will proclaim that there is a disbeliever hiding behind it, so seize and kill him. Thus the orders of three verses 4: 91; 9: 123 and 33: 61 will be executed. Thus the ruling power of world will come in to the hands of *Eisa* from the *Maseeh-A-Ddajjal*, and he will rule the World centralizing Mecca- the centre of the Earth- as capital.

The verse 25: 73 says: "The true servants of the most Impartial Gracious will not fall deaf and blind when they are remembered in their hearts language with the verses of their Lord. Read together the verses 8: 2-4, 22; 17: 72; 39: 23 and 41: 44. See explanation 4: 158-159 and 5: 36

72. Certainly those who say: "Indeed Allah is Maseeh, the son of Maryam" have disbelieved. But Maseeh said: "Oh children of Israel, you serve Allah alone; He is my Lord as well as your Lord". Certainly anyone who associates others with Allah; then already forbidden the Paradise and his lodging will be the Fire. And for such wrongdoers will not have any helpers.

See the explanation 5: 17. According to this verse the Christians in *Madeena* during the time of Prophet were disbelievers, because the Book had with them whereas the Qur'an was not yet codified. Moreover the Prophet was witnessing the life of all other Prophets before including *Eisa* upon them. See explanation 2: 143. But after the codification of Qur'an, It is the only Book for entire mankind. And whoever after receiving It, hide and reject Its belief and not follow the do's and don'ts will only become the disbelievers, wrongdoers and transgressors.

Note the saying 'certainly anyone who associates others with Allah' in the verse i.e. whoever can utter the word 'Allah' in Arabic if associates others in his dominion of Allah are only coming under the associates whose lodging will be the fire. They are mentioned as associates in the verses 33: 73; 48: 6 and 98: 6. They are denoted as the ones whose hearts have a disease in the verses 22: 53; 33: 60 and 74: 31; as disbelievers in the verses 4: 145; 41: 29; 57: 15; as *kuffar* in the verses 9: 68, 73 and 66: 9; as rejecters in the verse 2: 39; 5: 10, 89; 57: 19; 64: 10. To put it brief they are the gone astray people who blindly follow the hypocrites mentioned in the verse 1: 7. See the explanation 2: 254; 3: 51; 4: 48 and 5: 48.

73. Those who say: "Surely Allah is third of the three", have disbelieved. There is no deity except one Deity. If they do not stop saying what they say, a painful torment will afflict those among them who disbelieve.

For the argument of trinity, see the explanation 4: 171-173. For the explanation about the Deity, see the explanation 1:4 and 2: 133. And whoever knowingly denying the Truth whether the Muslims or the people of the Book will get a painful torment is told in the explanation of the verse 2: 113. See the explanation 3: 52-55, 83-91 and 5: 60.

74. Why do they not turn towards Allah and seek His forgiveness? And Allah is Forgiving, Merciful.

Allah command Prophet to say through the verses 39: 53-55: "Oh My servants who have transgressed against their souls, do not despair of Allah's mercy, for Allah forgives all the sins at a time. It is He Who is the Forgiving, Merciful. Turn in repentance to your Lord, and submit to Him before there comes to you the death: for then, there shall be none to help you. And follow the best way that is sent down to you from your Lord before the death comes to you all of a sudden while you do not even perceive it. The verses 39: 56-59 say: "Lest someone should say: 'Alas! I neglected my duty towards Allah's way and I was one of those who mocked at His verses.' Or lest he should say: `If Allah had guided me, I would have been one of the heedful.' Or lest he should say upon seeing the punishment: `I wish I had another chance, I would certainly be among the one who live seeing Allah". Then Allah will say to him: "Nay Indeed My verses did come to you; but you denied them, you were arrogant and you were among the disbelievers."

It is explained in the verses 4: 17-18 that, when death approaches, there is no effect in saying the readiness of repentance and to give some more time. Today these verses are reading only by the Muslims, and they are only able to pronounce the word 'Allah', but ignoring the Soul of Qur'an they have become the transgressed hypocrites who forgotten Him by mind. See the explanation 2: 99. They are in forefront of all evils making Allah asleep hiding the most honorable verse 2: 255. They lead a practical life, which is worse than the life of Christians- who believe the God is third of the three or *Eisa* is God- and that of the worshippers of idols. Hiding Allah and Prophet in Qur'an, they have accepted the satanic hypocrites and the priests as their Lords; i.e. against the verse 9: 31. They are the liars by saying: '*Hadeeth*' is not Qur'an but the words of Prophet, which against the verses 4: 78, 87; 7: 185 etc. They are not ready to agree the words and deeds of Prophet as the explanation of Qur'an and thus act against the verse 4: 82. They have become associates by accepting different groups against the only way of life-*Islam*- and their party leaders as their *Imams*- leaders-ignoring the Soul of Qur'an, the real *Imam*. See explanation 2: 159-161; 4: 135-140 and 5: 67.

75. Maseeh, the son of Maryam is none except a messenger. Many messengers have already passed away before him. His mother was a truthful woman. They both ate food, look how clearly We explain Our verses to them, yet see how they turn away from It.

The verse 6: 46 says "Ask them: "Have you ever think, if Allah takes away your hearing and your sight and seals up your hearts, is there any deity other than Allah who could restore them to you?" Look how We display Our verses again and again and yet they turn away. The verses 17:45 and 46 say "When you recite the Qur'an We put an invisible barrier between you and those who do not believe in the Hereafter. We have put coverings over their hearts to prevent them from grasping the Qur'an and a block in their ears. When you mention your Lord alone in Qur'an they turn back in aversion". The verse 47 says "We know best what they hear when you are listened by them and when they say in their private conversation "the man you follow is none but a man bewitched." The verse 48 says "See what sort of examples they make up about you! They have surely gone astray and cannot find the Right Way. Read together the verses 25: 4-10.

Today even though the Muslims have got more acquaintance with Allah and His messenger from the Qur'anic verses their deviation from the Truth is more than that of the followers of *Eisa*. That is due to their arrogance and rejection of the Soul of Qur'an. They hide Allah and His messenger in the Soul of Qur'an, and make alive arrogant satan by accepting and following their hypocritical leaders. Thus they have become aimless and heedless. They didn't consider the Prophet's teaching that "Those who recite Qur'an without trying to understand its contents will be thrown out of *Dheen* as if an arrow darted away from a bow". It is against these people only the recited, seen, heard and touched Qur'an will bear witness and argue. Read together the verses 17: 36; 41:19-24 and 36: 65. See explanation 1: 7; 2: 166-167; 4: 63, 170 and 171.

76. Ask, Do you worship something instead of Allah that doesn't have power to make any harm or any benefit for you? While Allah alone is the all Hearing, Knowing.

The verse 25: 53 says: "He is the one who combined the two seas, one is sweet and fresh, and the other is salt and bitter. He has made an invisible barrier and separation between them". The verse 54 says: "He is the One Who has created man from water, then made for them blood relationship and matrimonial relationship, your Lord is indeed Powerful". The verse 55 says: "Yet they are serving others besides Allah which can neither help nor harm them. The 'disbeliever' has become a clear helper against his Lord i.e. those who call for help or fear other than Allah is the disbelievers and they are the helpers of the satan-the disbeliever- as per the verse 2: 34. The verse 7: 188 says: "I have no power to acquire benefit or avert any harm from myself except whatever Allah may wish. If I had known the unseen, I would have tried to increase good things for me, while no evil would ever touch me. I am none except a Warner and Herald for the people who believe". See the explanation 4: 78-79.

Muslims who are reading these verses become '*mushrik*' and '*kafir*' by associating others in the dominion of Allah and by forming different organizations. But the believers who live only for Allah and while reciting the verse 1:4, "We do live only for You and we do seek help only from You", they will pray by mind to include the one to the Paradise in every thousand and not to include among nine hundred and ninety nine to the Hell and not belong to the satan's party. See the explanation 4:118. In the verse 39: 64 Allah commands the Prophet to ask "Oh Ignorant people, do you order me to serve some one other than Allah?" In the verse 65 Allah says: "It has already been revealed to you and to those before you, if you commit shirk, all your deeds become futile and you will surely be among the losers". The verse 66 says: "Nay, but you live for Allah only and be among the grateful". The verse 10:18 says that "they worship others besides Allah who can neither harm nor benefit them. And they say: "These are our intercessors with Allah. Are you informing Allah of something He does not know in the Heavens or Earth? He is limitless in His glory and far above anything to which men may ascribe share". Read together the verses 6: 53, 60, 114, 117 and 41: 37. See the explanation 2: 152, 255 and 4: 48.

77. Say: "Oh People of the Book do not exceed the bounds in your Dheen beyond the truth. And don't follow the whims of people who have already gone astray before and misled many as they stray from the Level Path".

See the explanation 4:170-171. The people of the Book mentioned here is Christians. And the people who have already gone astray before and misled many as they stray about the Level Path is Jews. The Christians of *Madeena* are advised not to follow the vain desires of Jews. See the explanation 1: 7. And But today those who gone astray are the transgressed hypocrites who hide these verses of Qur'an and follow the Jews. The common people of the Book are advised not to follow them. The believers only take the Soul of Qur'an as the '*Mouidhath*'. See the explanation 3: 90-91; 4: 91; 5: 60 and 72.

78. Those who deny the Truth from among the children of Israel were cursed by the tongue of Davood and Eisa, the son of Maryam. That was because they disobeyed and they had acted defiantly.

Because of their disobedience and aggression, Allah Himself cursed them and converted them as monkeys and pigs. At the time of Prophet *Moosa* itself, as they behaved arrogantly, disobeyed and transgressed the laws and commands, the land of Palestine was prohibited to them as explained in the verses 5: 21-26. These Jews not only themselves went astray but led many others to astray. So the Christians are advised not to follow the vain desires of these Jews who were cursed by the tongue of the Prophets *Davood* and *Eisa*. See the explanation 2: 61 and 66.

Since the Book of today is Qur'an for entire mankind, the followers of Qur'an are advised not to follow these Jews and Christians who had gone astray. Forgetting all advises of Allah and His messenger, today they follow the similar path of those Jews and Christians. While Jews and Christians celebrate the birthday of their Prophet's, the strayed Muslims celebrate the death day of the Prophet Muhammad. Prophet's Birth and Death was on the same date. At the time of birth, he was not a Prophet, but at the time of death, he was a Prophet. So the Muslims are celebrating his death day. Read together the verses 25: 18 and 30. See the explanation 2: 6-7; 3: 97 and 4: 118-121.

79. They would not prevent one another the iniquities that they committed. How evil is they had been doing!

This habit of Jews has been explained in the verses 7: 163-167. When they gave up the act of enjoying what is right and forbidding what is wrong, Allah appointed Prophet *Eisa* to them. But they tried to kill him. See the explanation 3: 52-55 and 4: 158-161.

But today it is the Muslims who indulged in evil deeds throughout the world. Instead of trying to make the unity of mankind they argue for the communal unity. They strive hard to keep their erroneous observances. Even if they are advised in the verses 3: 104, 110 to enjoin what is right and to forbid what is wrong, they enjoin what is wrong and forbid what is right- the deeds of transgressed hypocritical men and women as mentioned in the verse 9: 67. They do not take the habit of the believers into account as mentioned in the verses 9: 71-72 and 111-114. Prophet taught: If an evil thing is seen, it should be prevented by hand; if it is not possible it should be prevented by tongue; and if it is also not possible, then hate the evils by mind. Otherwise he has no faith even the weight of an atom. Today by accepting the hypocrite human satan as scholars and by making different organizations that fighting each other, the Muslim community has deteriorated and become worst astray than any other people. They neither learn nor teach the Soul of Qur'an- the Standard or the Guidance to mankind in order to identify right and wrong as explained in the verse 2: 185. They become the disbelievers as explained in the verse 3:10. So, what the non-Muslims are to be advised is that, the Soul of Qur'an is the only instrument to keep the Universe in its equilibrium. By teaching It to entire mankind for identifying themselves and aim of life, the blood shed, terrorism, selfishness etc. can be avoided. The hypocrites and disbelievers of this Muslim community of today will never do it. They have become a people for arguing communalism, nationalism, racism, terrorism etc. They have indulged in robbery, loot, killing innocent people, sodomy, drug abuse, smuggling etc. The Muslim rulers of today in all over the world are the cruel and extravagant dictators. They are leading luxurious life. Their scholars stand in front of them like the dog as mentioned in the verse 7: 176, which loads its tongue whether it is disturbed or not. The community itself destroys when its squires and scholars become worse. Prophet taught that, *the World will no longer exist when there comes a time in which iniquity is not forbidden.* See the explanation 2: 256; 3: 86-89; 5: 59 and 62-64.

80. You will see many of them making friends with those who disbelieve. How wretched is, what their souls have sent on ahead for them. As Allah's wrath is on them, they will abide in punishment forever.

Avoiding Prophet and the believers the Jews and the hypocrites made friendship with each other as specified in the verses 33.: 12- 15 26-27 and 59: 11-12. Allah says in the verses 47: 25-26: "Those who turn their back after the

Guidance was clearly shown to them, evil one has instigated them, to them is the loss, that is because they said to those who showed aversion to what Allah has revealed- the Soul of Qur'an; we will comply you in some matters". Allah knows their secrets. The verses 26-28 say: At the time of their death, the Angels will strike on their faces and their backs. That is because they followed those whom Allah has condemned and they hated Allah's good pleasure; therefore all their deeds became in vain. See the explanation 2: 186.

But today, this habit is found only with the hypocrites. They avoid the believers who follow and advise others to be united holding the Soul of Qur'an as explained in the verse 3: 103. While the believers say that all organizations among Muslims except the party of Allah are '*mushriks*' and belongs to satan's party, according to the verses 2: 176; 6: 158-159; 23: 51-53; 30: 31 and 32, they mock at and turn away arrogantly from the believers. Avoiding the believers they make friendship with the *fujjar*- disbelievers- who observe superstitions in religion. They together are called *mujrims* and wrongdoers as mentioned in the verses 7: 35-36, 40-41; 32: 22; 39: 59 etc. They will blame and curse one another when they are thrown into the Hell as explained in the verses 2: 166- 167.

The individual himself is earning the Hell or Paradise. Read the 'Goal of life' in the Introduction. The Impartial Allah directs no one either to Hell or Paradise. Calling the believers Allah says in the verse 59: 18 that, to look what every soul has earned on ahead for Tomorrow. The verse 62: 7 says that the Jews in previous period and the hypocrites of today will never long for death as their hands have send on ahead for them is Hell. See the explanation 2: 94 and 95. The verse 18: 57 asks: Who is more wrongdoer than the one who turns away from the verses of his Lord when he is remembered in his hearts language and forgets what his hands may have sent ahead for him? The verse 8: 49 says: The hypocrites and those in whose heart has a disease were saying: "Their faith has deceived the believers" and in the verses 50-51 it is told that at the time of their death the Angels will strike their faces and their back saying: taste the punishment of the Blazing fire. This is for what your hands have sent on ahead for you. Allah will never show any unjust to His servants. And the verses 8: 52-53 say: This is because they concealed verses of Allah and He will never change the blessings, which He has bestowed on a people until they themselves change. Read together the verses 7: 37-38 and 13: 11. The believers who spend their money, time and all other blessings to learn and convey the Message of Allah will not have any fear to die. It is because they have already taken the Ticket to the Paradise. They are well pleased by Allah and are well pleasing with Him. Read together the verses 5: 119; 9: 100; 13: 28; 58: 22; 89: 23-24, 27-30 and 98: 8. See the explanation 3: 182; 4: 137-140 and 5: 51. Prophet taught to pray: "*Oh, Allah, we ask You Your pleasure and the Paradise and we seek You refuge from Your wrath and Hell*".

81. If they had believed with Allah, Prophet and with what was sent down to him, they would not have adopted them as their friends and helpers. But most of them are transgressors.

Believers are those whose whims follow the Soul of Qur'an. So they would not adopt the hypocrites and the gone astray people who hide and reject the Soul of Qur'an as friends or protectors. Read together the verses 9: 23-24. See the explanation 3: 28, 110; 4: 59; 5: 47-49 and 55-59.

82. You will certainly find the most violent in enmity to the believers among the people are the Jews and those who associate others with Allah. And you will find most affectionate of them towards those who believe, are those who say: "We are Helpers". That is because among them there are men devoted for learning and men who have renounced the world and they do not behave so proudly.

Today, those who show enmity to the believers are the hypocrites- the enemies of Allah and the members of different Muslim organizations. And those who show affection or sympathy to the believers- the members of Allah's party are Christians and Hindus especially their priests and hermits. It is because they are those who have deserted or renounced the life of this world, who remembers Allah with their hearts and who show no proud or arrogance. At the same time it can be seen that the members of different Muslim organizations love for long life, they fear death and live luxuriously. They are the heedless people. See the explanation 2: 95. Today it can also be seen that the hypocrites show more avidity to this world than the Jews as mentioned in the verse 2: 96. In the verse 7: 176 both the hypocrites and their blind followers are compared to a dog, which does not change its attitude whether it is attacked or not. This transgressed people will be the receptionists of *Maseeh-A-Ddajjal* when he comes intending to annihilate *Islam*. Prophet taught that his arrival will be a great calamity to the children of Adam. Then after *Eisa* comes, he will kill *Maseeh-A-Ddajjal*. Then the Christians, Hindus and all other non-Muslims will accept real *Islam*- the True way of life. Thus the hypocrites and the associates of others with Allah will be killed and the verses 4: 91; 9: 123 and 33: 60- 61 will be executed. Therefore the believer when reciting the verse 109: 6 'For you your way of life and for me the Real way of life-*Islam*' should remind both hypocrites and those who associate others with Allah. See explanation 5: 72.

In the verses 7: 146-147 say that I shall turn away from My verses those who behave as scholars arrogantly on Earth without having the Soul of Qur'an; if they see the clear Guidance, they will not believe in It, but if they see a crooked way they will accept it; this is because they denied the verses of Allah and are being heedless of them. And those who deny the verses of Allah and the Hereafter, their deeds are in vain. It can be seen that the disbelievers mentioned in the verse 41: 26 are the hypocrites- the enemies of Allah and that in the verse 29 are the common people who accept and follow them as scholars and who will be gathered in the Hell together as told in the verse 4: 140. So the believers who know the Soul of Qur'an should not make friendship with both of them or ask help from them. It is told in the explanation of the verses 3: 79-80 that, those who received the Soul of Qur'an should be proud with It.

'Among them there are some men who have renounced the World' does not mean that Islam encourages Monasticism. It is told in the verse 57: 27 that Allah did not enjoin the monasticism upon the followers of *Eisa*, the son of *Maryam*, but they invented it for themselves, seeking good pleasure of Allah, but they did not observe it as it should have been observed. Yet Allah will give the reward to those who attained faith. But most of them are transgressors. Giving the answer to a question of *Hudaifathul Yamani*, Prophet has taught: When there came a time with no *Imam* of believer and a single group of Muslims; spend time until death keeping everything away, even if it is by biting the bottom of a tree in a forest. See the explanation 3: 200; 4: 82 and 172.

Pray: "Oh Lord, do not make us transgressors and losers; make us those who fear You, always remember You, show gratefulness to You, stand for Truth firmly to do honorable deeds and live only for You following the Soul Qur'an as It should be followed, and make us one among those who enter the Paradise with Your Mercy. Oh, the Most Merciful among those who show Mercy.

83. And When they listen to what has been sent down to the messenger you will see their eyes overflow with tears, because of the Truth

they recognize, they pray: "Our Lord, We do believe, then enroll us among the witnesses".

84. Why should not we believe with Allah and the Truth that has come to us? As we wish for our Lord to admit us along with the honorable people.

As explained in the verses 3: 52-55; 4: 159 that when *Eisa* comes in the second time and slays the anti-Christ *Maseeh-A-Dajjal*, they will believe *Eisa* and will follow the real way of life- *Islam*- submitting by the Soul of Qur'an, and they will say to *Eisa*: You bear witness that we are Muslims, who have surrendered everything to Allah; and they will pray: Our Lord, we believe in what You have revealed and we follow Your messenger, so enroll us among those who bear witnesses. Especially during prostrate, the believers will pray: Oh Allah enters us to the honorable servants with the Mercy-The Soul of Qur'an. Read together the verse 7: 196; 57: 16 and 19. See the explanation 1: 6; 2: 146-148; 3: 199 and 5: 69.

85. And for their sincere prayer, Allah will reward them with Paradise beneath which rivers flow and there they live in forever. Such is the reward for those who live seeing Allah.

Prophet taught: '*Ihsan*' means live just like you see Allah even if you don't see Him, He is seeing you. That means live under the Light-the Soul of Qur'an. See the explanation 2: 112; 3: 191; 4: 174 and 175. The verse 36: 11 says: You can only warn those who follow the Soul of Qur'an and fear the most Impartial seeing Him through the Soul of Qur'an. So, give such one the good news of forgiveness and honorable reward. The verse 67: 12 says: Indeed as for those who fear their Lord though they have not seen Him, shall have forgiveness and a great reward. The verses 39: 17-18 say to those who give up living for *Thaghooth* and turn to Allah in repentance, give good news to them: They are those who listen to the word of Allah and follow It in the best way; and it is they who are in the Guidance of Allah and are the ones who utilize the intelligence. Read together the verses 63: 9-10. See the explanation 2: 38, 218; 3: 148; 5: 65 and 66.

86. And those who hide and reject Our verses, such are the inmates of Hades.

The verses such as 22: 57; 48: 6; 57: 19; 64: 10 and 98: 6 are having the same message that the hypocrites who hide, and the associates of others with

Allah who reject the Qur'an verses are the fuel of Hellfire from mankind and upon them afflict Allah's curse and wrath. And they have painful punishment. See the explanation 2: 39; 3: 106; 4: 56 and 5: 10.

87. Oh you who believe, do not make forbidden the wholesome things, which Allah has made lawful for you. And do not exceed the limits; certainly Allah does not love the defiant.

88. And eat any lawful, wholesome things which Allah has provided you with. And heed Allah with whom you believe.

The verses 16: 114 says then eat any lawful wholesome things Allah has provides you, and be thankful for Allah's favor if you have been serving Him. The believers who are living as the vicegerents of Allah will eat and use only lawful and wholesome food and sustenance. Since Allah is wholesome He will accept only the wholesome things. Those who utilize the Soul's food and cloth -Soul of Qur'an -as the Balance to distinguish between lawful wholesome sustenance from the impure and eat only wholesome things, would only be understood the Soul of Qur'an. The verse 56: 79 says that no one grasp the Soul of Qur'an except the purified ones. Read together the verses 80: 11-17. The hypocrites and the gone astray people are eating impure and forbidden food and without objecting others from eating such food as specified in the verses 9: 34 should never understand the Soul of Qur'an. They are filling only Fire in their bellies as explained in the verse 2: 174. Any sustenance achieved through the footsteps of satan is impure and forbidden. See explanation 2: 168 and 5: 63.

The verses 23: 51-52 say 'Oh messengers, eat wholesome things and act honorably; I am Aware of anything You do, this nation forms a community while I am your Lord, so heed Me.' Man has no authority to decide lawful and forbidden things but Allah the Lord decides. Any things if approved either lawful or forbidden against the do's and dont's of the Soul of Qur'an which has been made allowed by the priest and hypocrites, then that is as much approve them as Lord vide verse 9: 31. Through the verse 45: 13 Allah is the one who subjected whatever is in Heaven and whatever is on Earth to you; it all comes from Him, certainly in that are signs for the people who meditate and reflect. That means the Impartial Allah taught man the great Bounty and Mercy- the constitution of Universe-, which explains each and everything. Therefore it is the inevitable duty of the heedful to utilize and convey the Soul of Qur'an- the Balance and Trust- to keep the Universe in its equilibrium irrespective of religions or nations. See explanation 2: 172; 4: 50-51; and 5: 77.

89. **Allah will not hold you for your unintentional oaths. But He will hold you for your deliberate oaths. Then the penalty for a broken oath is to feed ten needy persons with such food you normally provide to your own family or to cloth ten needy people or to free one slave. The one who cannot afford any of these must fast three days. That is the expiation for the oath you have sworn. And keep up your oaths. Thus Allah does make clear to you His verses in order that you may act grateful.**

For the saying: 'Keep the oath' has many meanings. Oaths should not be used sweepingly and unnecessarily. When an oath is made, it should not be ignored; it should always be remembered. Forgetfulness should not be a cause for the breaking of oath. If it was broken, the expiation should be given. Through the verses 18: 23-24, Prophet and believers are advised: Never say anything "I will certainly do it tomorrow" without adding "if Allah so wills" and if you forget to say this, then say so when you are aware of it later. The heedful who is living under the Light of soul of Qur'an is the one who is conscious every moment of its life and he will not break any oath or pledge. See explanation 2: 225; 3: 99 and 5: 36.

90. **Oh you who believe, certainly the liquor, gambling, idols and arrows are the filthy works of satan. Hence you shunt aside him; so that you may prosper.**

91. **Satan only intends to make enmity and hatred among you with means of liquors and gambling; and to prevent you from the remembrance of Allah and from the swalath. Will you not then abstain?**

In the verse 90 instead of saying '*Fajthaniboohunna*' -you shunt aside them-, '*Fajthaniboohu*'- you shunt aside him- is told; hence not only shunt aside the evil things mentioned in the verse, but also all the evil things caused by the satan should be shunted aside. See the explanation 2: 208 and 4: 118. This verse revealed as the third stage of the liquor prohibition. The believers in *Madeena* devastated the vessels of liquor declaring: "Our Lord, we are retiring from this". A stream of liquor was flowed there. Thus there came the order: Liquor is 'filth' and the cloths and body should be cleaned when the liquor happened to be on them. Prophet taught that liquor is the key of all inequities. Then the most intoxicating and dangerous things like marihuana, opium, brown sugar etc. are not mentioned in the Qur'an, comes under the *Mouidhath* of this verse and all modern things harmful to the body and life and society are included in this forbidden group. Gambling with money or not, is prohibited. It will not only waste the time but also lead to the enmity, murder, robbery, theft etc.

Idols are considered as the statue of God, which is against the glory of Allah. The verse 112: 4 says: "There is none comparable to Him" and it is told in the verse 42: 11 that "there is nothing like Him". Therefore giving comparison for Allah to any thing or person against His Permission-The Soul of Qur'an is a great sin induced by the satan. See the explanation 2: 255; 4: 48. In ancient times to divide the things as lottery, arrows were used. Therefore any thing utilizing as lottery may be considered as '*mouidhath*' may come under the filthy matters of satan which will prevent from the remembrance of Allah.

This verse just like the verses 7: 175, 25: 29, 43: 36-38, 58: 19, 63: 9 also teaches that the satan prevents mankind from the Soul of Qur'an with which remembrance of Allah can only maintain. As per the verse 20: 14, the *swalath* is maintained to keep the remembrance of Allah with the Soul of Qur'an. So satan prevents from the *swalath* having the remembrance of Allah with the Soul of Qur'an. Such *swalath* surely will keep away from shameful and forbidden things as told in the verse 29:45. Satan will not prevent the *swalath* of those who do *swalath* without participation of the Soul. Such peoples are '*mujirim*' and their life and deeds are for satan. See the explanation 4: 142-143. On the Day of Judgment these *mujirims* should have to admit that they were worshipping the satan as specified in the verses 36: 59-60. Read together the verses 14: 22. It is told in the verses 41: 19-24 that, the hearing, sight and the skin of those who do *swalath* without the participation of soul will bear witness against them, and they will get the Hell as the penalty. So the servant of Impartial Allah will always pray: "Abstain the punishment of Hell from us, for its punishment is a penalty for performing *swalath, Fasting, Hajj*, Charity etc. without the Soul of Qur'an. Certainly Hell is an evil abode and resting place" as told in the verses 25: 65-66. See explanation 2: 152.

It is told in the verse 6: 145 that the flesh of swine and the offerings made other than Allah are filth and will induce hypocrisy. In the verse 9: 95 it is told that the hypocrites are filth, so that you should shunt aside them. Their abode shall be the Hell as the reward they have been earned here. The verse 9: 125 says: For the hypocrites in whose heart is disease, the Qur'an will only add filth over filth and they will die as disbelievers. Therefore the hypocrites-the human devils- will prevent the people from the Soul of Qur'an. See explanation 1:7; 2: 275; 4: 43 and 5: 60.

92. Obey Allah and obey the messenger, and beware about the satan. If you should ever turn away, know that Our messenger's duty is only to deliver the message clearly.

The verse 64:12 says: Obey Allah and obey His messenger, but if you turn away, the duty of Our messenger is only to convey the message. The verses 64: 16-17 say "therefore, heed Allah as much as you can, listen to His message carefully, be obedient, and spend for your own good. Those who are saved from the covetousness of their own souls, it is they who are truly successful. If you lend to Allah a best loan, He will pay you back manifold, and will forgive you your evil deeds. Allah is Appreciative, Forbearing to those who are grateful. The verse 9: 65 ends with a question that have you been joking with Allah, His verses and His messenger. From this we can understand that if anyone follows the Soul of Qur'an, obeys Allah and His messenger. And if anyone turns away from the Soul of Qur'an he has adopted satan as his friend and protector. Therefore to beware satan means to holdfast the Soul of Qur'an-the unbreakable rope. It says in the verse 7:201 whenever an impulse from satan is tempted to those who are heedful, they have but remember Allah with their hearts and then they shall become insightful. Read together the verse 6: 104. See explanation 3: 25-33; 4: 59, 80 and 5: 67.

93. There is no blame on those who believe and do honorable deeds for what they ate in the past, provided they abstain from the unlawful things, remain steadfast in their belief and continue their honorable deeds and again (abstain from unlawful things) ensure the faith and belief, and keep Allah in their hearts and live under the Light-the Soul of Qur'an, and Allah likes the one who live under the Light.

The contents of this verse are similar to the verse 4:136 and against the habit of hypocrites mentioned in the verses 4:137-138. See the explanation 3:

133-136. Heedfulness means a deed about which there is any doubt whether it is right or wrong, then not to do it fearing that if it is wrong it cannot be rectified on the Day of Judgment; and doing a deed not considering other's objections, if it is just and right as per the Qur'an verses.

'To ensure the faith and belief and do honorable deeds' means learn and teach the Soul of Qur'an to others in order to the help them abstain from the disbelief, evil doings, hypocrisy etc. and convert them to those who repent. The only way to avoid all evil deeds is to understand the Soul of Qur'an in one's heart's language. The evil deeds of such people will be transformed into good deeds as told in the verses 25:69 and 70. The verses 18: 57, 32:22 say that those who turn away from the verses of their Lord after they reminded them in their heart's language are the most wrong doers and Allah will take retribution to such '*mujrims*'. Read together the verses 7: 40 and 41. See the explanation 2: 157; 4: 174-175 and 5: 85.

94. Oh you who believe, Allah will surely test you by means of some of the game within the reach of your hands and your spears, in order to know Allah who fears Him unseen. So anyone who aggresses after this for him has a painful punishment.

Through the verse 29: 2 Allah asks "do men reckon that they will be left alone on saying 'we believe', without being tested'. The verse 29: 3 says those who lived before have also been tested in order to identify who are the truthful and who are the liars. The verse 76: 2 says that 'certainly we created man from mingled sperm and ovum in order We might test him, so we gave him hearing and sight'. It is told in the verse 3: 166 and 167 that the battle of the "*Uh'd*" happened in order to identify the believers from the hypocrites. All men have been taught the Soul of Qur'an-the Insight- from the Paradise itself. That is why it is told in the verses 75: 14 and 15 that "Indeed, man shall bear witness against himself, even though he shall plead with excuses". Therefore it is the duty of individual to confirm that he is a believer by utilizing the Insight-the Soul of Qur'an. See the explanation 2: 28; 3: 4.

This Qur'an is revealed in order to warn those who are alive and to establish the charge against the disbelievers as told in the verses 36: 69-70. The Impartial Allah will not enter anyone to Hell without bearing witness against themselves that they were disbelievers who hide and reject the Soul of Qur'an after receiving It. Read together the verses 7: 37 and 39:59.

Adam couples ate the fruit of the forbidden tree. Then Allah-the Knower of state of hearts- saw the repentance in their heart. He inspired them the words of repentance specified in the verse 7: 23. See explanation 2: 37. Then He deputed mankind from Adam to the last Day to the Earth in order to test them. He said to all of them that His Guidance would come to them and who ever follows It can return to the Paradise itself. See the explanation 2: 38. Those who received the Guidance should clearly deliver It to entire mankind in order to fulfill the agreement made with Allah specified in the verse 3: 187. Whoever hides the Guidance- the Soul of Qur'an upon them falls the cursing of Allah, Angels and entire mankind as explained in the verses 2:159-161 and 3: 86-88. The ones who keep away others from the Soul of Qur'an-Allah's Permission to become a believer- and keep themselves away from It destroy themselves, but they do not perceive it as told in the verse 6: 26. See the explanation 2: 121,186; 3: 97; 5: 15 and 16. 'In order to know Allah who fears Him unseen' does not mean the subtle and well acquainted Allah does not know about His creatures, but it is to identify the real believers and hypocrites to his vicegerent believers

Then there must be a question such as why today such testament not undergo as that of occurred in the early period? The answer is only believers will be undergone the test in order to form a group of believers. Since these last days there will not be formed a group of believers but only can expect the possibility of human harmony. Today most of the predictions of the Qur'an verses can be seen occurred by the naked eyes fulfilling the verse 41: 53. As per the verses 17: 13 and 14 everyman's fate has tied around his neck; and it will be produced as a spread open Book for him on Resurrection Day and will say "Read your Book; today yourself is enough to call your account". From these verses as well as the verses 18: 49 and 45: 28-31, one can easily understand in this cyber era that each individual's fate is tied up around his own neck. Therefore by teaching the Soul of Qur'an to entire mankind everyone may make awareness about his aim of life and thus human harmony can be formed. See the explanation 3: 7; 4: 133 and 5: 8.

95. Oh you who believe, do not kill hunting animals while you are in the state and area of forbidden. If anyone of you who kills hunting animals deliberately may make compensation through the same from cattle equivalent to what he has killed, as judged by two just men from among you. This offering has to be reached to Ka'ba;

or else expiation may mean either feed a few poor people or fast their equivalent days. It is to taste himself the consequences of his deeds. Allah pardons whatever is a thing of the past. If anyone repeats this, Allah will take retribution to him. And Allah is Powerful, the Wielder of Retribution.

'while you are in the state and area of forbidden' means when you are wore the cloth of pilgrimage and while you are in the forbidden area-sacred *Masjid* area and the surroundings- is specially prohibited from killing any soul or even picking up the leaves of a tree. Both self-hunting and helping others to hunt are forbidden. The hunting animals caught by others for the sake of one who have worn the pilgrimage cloth are also forbidden. But it is lawful to eat the flesh from a part of animal, which was caught by others by hunting for their food and not for the person who is in forbidden state. Then the killing of a harmful or dangerous being just like snake, scorpion, mad dog etc. is permitted even in the state and area of forbidden.

If the person on forbidden state and area has deliberately killed the hunting animal should make compensation through the same from cattle the price and size of the wild animal which has been killed, should be determined by two just men. The cattle should be brought to the Ka'ba for slaying and the meat should be distributed among the people there and he shouldn't eat from it. The number of poor to be fed and number of days of fasting as expiation in the case of such and such animals are also determined by the two just men. But if anyone does kill again, Allah will take revenge. Allah has Power to do anything on His servants. Allah gives rewards in accordance with the intention of the deeds. He will not do any injustice to anyone. It is told in the verse 32: 22 that those who live ignoring the verses of Allah when it is reminded in his heart's language are '*mujrims*' and wrongdoers and Allah will take revenge on them. Read together the verses 7: 40 and 18:57. See explanation 4: 140 and 5: 49.

96. Hunting in the sea is lawful for you. The food from it has been made sustenance for you as well as for travelers. Hunting from land is forbidden you so long as you are under the forbidden state and area. And you heed Allah, the One to whom you will be summoned.

See the explanation 5: 3. The fishes and locusts, even though dead are lawful for eating as taught by the Prophet. This verse teaches all edible animals in the sea are lawful to catch and eat whether it is dead or alive. The one in forbidden state as well as all other travelers can eat the fish and other animals of sea. They can take the fish and other animals of sea with them on their journey even if they are in forbidden state. 'Heed Allah' means consider Allah as all Knowing and Seeing, who is watching closely and on the Day of Judgment each individual has to answer about each and every moment of his life after the age of fifteen. See the explanation: 2: 177; 3:185 and 5: 5

97. Allah has placed the Ka'ba, the sacred house to be maintained for mankind; as well as the sacred months and the animals for offering and the garlands that mark them. That is to make you know that indeed Allah knows whatever is in Heavens and whatever is on Earth and that Allah is Knower of everything.

The verse 9:36 says Allah has ordained on the Day He created the Heavens and the Earth that the number of the months in His Book is twelve and four of them are sacred -war prohibited months- that is the Straight way of 'Dheen', so do not do wrong against yourselves in these months. On the same Day itself Allah has ordained the days of *Eid*, *Fasting*, *Hajj* etc. up to the end of world. The verse 22:70 says "don't you know that Allah does know all that is in the Heaven and on Earth and all these recorded in a Book and that is easy for Allah. Qur'an is the Record or the Book in which everything has recorded. But only those who know about the Soul of Qur'an and the one about whom told as '*khabeer*' in the verse 25:59- observe *Fasting, Eid, Hajj* etc. on its real day approving *Ka'ba* as '*Qibla*'. All others-999 in every thousand-are deviated from the Book and become '*mushriks*' and disbelievers just like 'Meccan *Mushriks*' who do not follow the real '*Dheen*'. It is told in the verse that Allah placed *Ka'ba*, the sacred house to be maintained for all mankind. This peculiarity of *Ka'ba* will be approved only after the second coming of *Eisa*. See the explanation 2:189; 3:96-97; 4:125-126 and 5: 82.

98. Know that indeed Allah is severe in punishment and surely Allah is Forgiving, Merciful.

Allah will not forgive to those who do sins deliberately, but He forgives to those who do sins accidentally and unknowingly. Since the hypocrites are knowingly transgressing, Allah will never give forgiveness or Guidance for them. In the verse 41:43 Allah says "Nothing is told to you except that had not told to the messengers before you. Your Lord is indeed full of forgiveness as well as the Wielder of painful punishment. To the hypocrites who hide the Soul of Qur'an knowingly, Allah will give severe and painful punishment as per the verse 4:138. To those who commit sins and ask forgiveness after receiving and understanding the Soul of Qur'an, Allah will give forgiveness as told in the verses 4: 17 and 18. But indeed those who rejected the Soul of Qur'an when they received will not have forgiveness instead they will have painful punishment as told in the verse 41:41. Both the verses 29:68 and 39:32 say and who is more wrongful than the one who forges a lie against Allah by distorting the verses of Allah or rejects the Truth when It reaches him? Is not the Hell a fitting abode for such disbelievers? In the verses 15:49-50 Allah says "Tell My servants that I am indeed most Forgiving, Most Merciful but My punishment is the most painful one. See the explanation 1:2; 2: 166-167 and 4:145.

99. The duty of the messenger is nothing except to convey the message, Allah knows whatever you show and whatever you hide.

The Impartial Allah has taught all the human souls, the Soul of Qur'an from the Paradise itself as per the verses 55:1-2. The Soul of Qur'an contains the way to the Paradise as well as the way to the Hell. Read together the verses 76: 3; 90: 10 and 91:7-10. See the explanation 4:1. Allah created the men in a nature of forgetting and remembering. Allah sent down the Reminder to make remember i.e. Soul of Qur'an with the messengers. See explanation 2: 213; 5: 48 and 67.

100. Say: "Evil and good are not equal even though the abundance of the evil may fascinate you; so heed Allah oh you People of understanding, so that you may prosper".

It is the duty of each individual to purify its soul and body in order to save it from the Hell fire. The Soul of Qur'an is the food and cloth of the soul according to the verse 7: 26 and It is the Standard and Balance in order to distinguish between the evil and good things. See explanation 2: 185. Good things and honorable deeds are to Allah in the Paradise whereas the evil things and evil deeds are to the satan in the Hell. It is explained in the verse 2:186 that without the Soul of Qur'an- the Permission of Allah- no one can become a believer and no response will be there for their prayers. Soul of Qur'an- the words of Allah- is pure and good. See the explanation 4: 29, 5: 90 and 91. Impure women are for impure men and impure men are for impure women; good women are for good men and good men are for good women; and they -good and pure people- are free from the impure people's accusations as told in the verses 24: 26. See the explanation 2: 221 and 5:5.

It is told both in the verse 25: 18 and 48: 12 that the hypocrites who hide the Soul of Qur'an and '*fujjar*' who reject It belongs to the worthless boar people. As per the verse 9: 95 it is told that hypocrites are filthy and so leave them alone. They will ask you to be pleased with them; but even if you please with them, Allah will never be pleased with these transgressors as told in the verse 9: 96. The verse 17: 82 says: the Soul of Qur'an is Healing and Mercy for the believers, while it will increase nothing but loss to the wrongdoers. See the explanation 2: 121; 3: 196-197; 4: 78-79 and 5: 19.

101. Oh you who believe, do not ask about such things as would worry you if they were revealed to you, yet if you should ask about them while the Qur'an is being sent down, they will be revealed to you, Allah pardons about it. And Allah is Forgiving, Forbearing.

102. Indeed people before you asked such things; then they became disbelievers because of it.

See the explanation 5:41. The Jews and hypocrites in *Madeena* were asking strange, foolish and meaningless questions to the Prophet. Once a man asked, 'Who was his original father?' Similarly when the verse 'you are ordained to do *Hajj*' is revealed, one of them asked the Prophet 'Should it be done every year?' Prophet did not answer. When the man repeated the question three times, Prophet answered; 'If my answer is 'Yes', then it will be so, but you can't do it every year and thus the order will be disobeyed'. The verse 25:33 says, and they do not bring any question to you except without Our conveying to you with the Truth and the best explanation to every one at all times.

Here the expression 'Indeed people before you asked such things' is about the Jews. When they were asked to sacrifice a cow, they asked many questions. At last they did it unwillingly. See the explanation 2: 71-73 and 108. The verse 33: 69 says; 'Oh believers! Be not like those who slandered *Moosa*, but Allah cleared him of what they said - for he was honorable in the sight of Allah. See the explanation 2: 55; 3:7 and 5: 20-26. But today, instead of Jews, the hypocrites and their blind followers are those who hide and distort the Truth. See the explanation 3: 78 and 4: 46. It is ordered to the Group of believers to kill these hypocrites. This order will only be implemented by the second coming of the '*Eisa*'. See the explanation 2: 118, 4: 63 and 91.

The verses 61:2-3 say: Oh you who believe! Why do you say something which you don't do? It is very hateful in the sight of Allah that you say something which you don't do. So the believers will practice what they read from the Qur'an. Since the Soul of Qur'an is the Balance to keep the Universe in its equilibrium, believers not only read the Soul of Qur'an but will convey It to others in order to utilize It as the Balance and Ticket to the Paradise. See explanation 3: 10 and 5: 67. Prophet taught: *The one who has deep knowledge in the Soul of Qur'an is with the honorable Angels.* But these hypocrites distort and mislead the Prophet's words by saying that those who read the Qur'an perfectly is with the honorable people. And they ask, has not the Prophet taught that those who read the Qur'an with strain and without flow has two rewards? Actually the two rewards is for those who learns to read after learning the contents, then only he become the believer. Only the believer has virtue and reward by reading of Qur'an. Knowing to read Qur'an fluently one expresses stammer and strain in reading It, he will get painful torment instead of reward. The common people who know the reading of Qur'ans' body fluently they read the Soul of Qur'an in their hearts language by taking strain, will get two rewards. That is the meaning of what Prophet taught. The hypocrites reject stupidly the teaching of Prophet that you only read Qur'an when the reading complies with your hearts. The '*Thilavath'* is only possible to those who know the Soul of Qur'an. But according to the verse 2: 44 the hypocrites will conduct *'Thilavath'*, but the enemies of Allah who is killed by Him will not get reward since they have to enter the Hell by death without trial. See explanation 4: 145.

Satan will only obstruct the mankind from the Soul of Qur'an and *swalath* with the remembrance of Allah by the Soul of Qur'an as told in the verses 5: 90-91; 7: 175-176; 25: 29 and 58: 19. The remedy to make the Soul mate a believer is only the Soul of Qur'an. Otherwise the consequences in the Hereafter are warned in following verses 43: 36-38; 50: 27-29; 59: 16 and 17. The Soul of Qur'an is a must to accept and reply for prayer is taught through the verse 2: 186, but almost Muslims by ignoring this verse conduct *swalath, Fasting* and *Hajj* with their body. Thus they should have to receive the Hell as penalty as told in the verses 25: 65-66. These people who are strayed than the cattle, heedless and living without utilizing the intelligence are to be filled in the Hell as told in the verse 7: 179. The party of Allah includes only the believers from the Adam to the last man of the world as told in the verses 5: 56 and 58: 22. All other parties among the Muslims are associates in the dominion of Allah as per the explanation of the verse 2: 176. And all of them belong to the party of satan as mentioned in the verse 58:19. Therefore, when the believer says: all the Muslims should omit all their different parties and should hold together the rope of Allah- the Soul of Qur'an as per the verse 3:103 and should become the single party of Allah; these hypocrites will ask: Is there no need of any organizations? Is not told that the hands of Allah are with the '*Jama'th*' -party of majority-? Has not the Prophet taught that those who turn away from the *Jama'th* will become separated alone? By saying such disagreement words, they will try to make the believers dart from the *Dheen*. They do not proclaim the teaching of the Prophet that in every thousand only one goes to Paradise and nine hundred and ninety nine to the Hell in the explanation of the verse 4: 118. They are not heedful in the teaching of Prophet as a reply to the question of *Hudaifathul Yamani* that in the absence of the single party of Muslims one should go to the forest and may stand by biting the bottom of a tree till death. The other questions of them are: then is there no need of *Masjids*? No need of *Jama'th* prayer? No need of *Jumua*? They are heedless that the group of believers is not present anywhere in the world. And if the group exists, the command of the verses 4: 91; 9: 123 and 33: 61 that the hypocrites must be killed should be implemented. And in the verse 24: 55, it is told: If there is the group of believers, they will get the power on earth to implement Islamic rule. They are not thinking about the teaching of Prophet that, the *Masjids* of theirs will be big concrete building, but there will be no Guidance- the Soul of Qur'an. Today, *Masjids* all over the world have become such *Masjids* as that of the '*Masjid-Al-Dhirar*' made by the hypocrites in *Madeena*, which was demolished by the believers. And the Imams –leaders- who guide the *swalath* are by receiving salary and thereby filling fire in their bellies as told in the verses 2: 174-176. If the believers remind them the consequence of selling the *Qur'anic verses* for miserable price, then their questions will be: How can they live without money? How can they nourish their children? They will not follow the Prophet's way of life by cultivating crops, cattle and doing business. Thus they falsify and kill the Prophets and survive the devil satan.

Today, the Soul of Qur'an is not learned, taught or permitted to teach in *Masjids* any where in the world. So, all the *Masjids* have become the house of satan, instead being the house of Allah. The type of *swalath* and worship mentioned in the verse 8: 35 being conducted in all these *Masjids*. Read together the verses 9: 17-19. Since today, there are only odd believers present in all over the world, there arise no question of *Jumua'* or *Jama'th swalath*. Instead to sit by biting the Soul of Qur'an by the molar teeth as taught by the Prophet on the day of *Hajjathul Vida'*-departing pilgrimage- is only applicable. Some of the hypocrites ask: Is Qur'an enough? But they don't think about the question through the verse 39: 36 that is not Allah enough for His servants? One can understand that Allah and the Soul of Qur'an is the same, if they read together the verses 7: 143 and 59: 21; 5: 48 and 59: 23; 3: 101 and 22: 78. The belief in Allah and Prophets may only be formed by the Soul of Qur'an only. See the explanation 2: 146. Actually the '*Hadeeth*' and '*Sunnath*' itself is the Qur'an as explained in the verses 4: 78, 87. But these hypocrites say falsely that '*Hadeeth*' is the words of Prophet. That is why the verse 63: 1: When the hypocrites come to you, they say: "We bear witness that you are indeed the Messenger of Allah. Allah knows that you are indeed His Messenger, and Allah bears witness that the hypocrites are liars," has become true.

103. Allah has not setup any 'Baheerah' or 'Saaebah' or 'Wasweelah' or 'Haam'. But those who deny the Truth invented (all these) lies about Allah. Most of them do not use their intelligence.

'Baheerah':- When a she camel gave birth to her fifth and if it is a male, the she camel would be dedicated to God as her ear slit, such camels were free from work, their milk would not be used, they were prohibited from slaughter, and they could eat and drink from any field and pool. Such camels were called *Baheerah*.

'Saaebah':- On returning safely from a journey or on recovery from an illness, a camel was dedicated to the intercessors of God showing the gratitude. Or when a she camel gave birth to a sequence of 10 female offspring, then they were let to pasture freely. Such camels were called *Saaebah*.

'Wasweelah':- If the first offspring of a goat is a male, it would be slaughtered as a sacrifice for the intercessors of God and if it is a female it would be allowed to live. But if it is a twin birth with a male and a female, the male was dedicated to God, which is called *Wasweelah*.

'Haam':- When a camel's grandbaby attained capable of riding, its stallion camels were made free from work. Such camels were called *Haam*. When a male camel reproduces ten babies was also freed. That is called *Haam*. See explanation 4:118-122. "Most of them do not use their intelligence" means they will never lead a life different from the cattle utilizing Qur'an as the Light and Proof as mentioned in the verses 4: 174-175. The verse 36: 62 warns, on the Day of Judgment, this '*mujrims*' will be told that the satan has led a great number of you astray, had you not utilized your intelligence? See explanation 2:166-167, 171, 3:91, 5: 59 and 60.

104. Whenever they are told: "Come to what Allah has sent down, and to the messenger," they say: "Enough for us the ways on which we found our forefathers", even though their forefathers didn't know anything and were not guided.

See explanation 2:170; 4: 59,135 and 5: 8.

105. Oh you who believe, you are responsible for your own selves. No one who goes astray will harm you, provided you are guided. Towards Allah will you all return together? Then He will notify you about whatever you have been doing.

This verse also teaches that each and every soul has to answer in the court of Allah individually. It is told in the verse 9:71 that the believers, the men and women are protecting friends of one another; 'they enjoin what is just and forbid what is evil, they observe regular *swalath*, they pay the welfare tax as well as obey Allah and His messenger. To understand the character of believers see the verses 9: 23-24, 100, 113-114, 23: 1-11, 58: 22 and 63: 9. The aim of deputation of men created in the Paradise in to Earth is in order to earn either Paradise or Hell here. See explanation 2: 286 and 3: 185. The verses 6: 94, 104; 39:41; 18:48; 19:80, 95 etc. also teach us that every soul has to answer individually in the court of Allah. The verse 62: 8 says; (Oh Prophet) say; the death from which you flee will surely meet you; then you will be sent back to Him who knows the unseen as well as the seen, He will inform you about whatever you have been doing. See explanation 6: 60. The verse 31: 15 says; If your parents force you to commit '*shirk*' -associate others in the dominion of Allah- of which you have no knowledge, then do not obey them, but treat them under the shadow of Qur'an in this world, and you follow the path of those who turn towards Me. Then to Me all will you return, and He will notify you about whatever you have been doing.

"He will notify you about whatever you have been doing" means He will bring out from each one's neck the book of his deeds as a spread open illuminating one, and will be said to him: Read your book, today you yourself is enough to call your own account, as told in the verses 17:13 and 14.

The verse 16:125 says, you call to the way of your Lord with '*Hikmath*' and with good '*Mouidhath*', and argue them with the Best -the Soul of Qur'an. Your Lord knows best who have strayed from His path and who is rightly guided. The verse 16:128 says; Surely, Allah is with those who keep Him in their hearts and who live by seeing Him as revealed by the Soul of Qur'an.

This verse does not mean that each individual has his own buried pit, and so no need to see other's matters. Read together the verses 7:163-166. Correcting this misunderstanding *Aboobacker Sidheeq* said; Oh, people, Are you giving misinterpretation for this verse by reading it. I have heard Allah's Prophet saying; "When a time comes in which the evil doings are not prevented deliberately, Allah will subject every one to His punishment. By Allah, you should enjoin what is good and forbid what is wrong; otherwise Allah will appoint transgressors as your rulers. They will subject you with great troubles and misery. Then some of you may pray to Allah, but He will not respond it." Prophet taught that *among you the best one is who learns and teaches the Soul of Qur'an.* Note that Prophet not stopped only by saying; the best among you is the one who learns the Soul of Qur'an. The verse 8: 25 says, "Heed you lest dissension strike those of you especially who do wrong. Know that indeed Allah is severe in punishment." The verse 33 says, "Allah would not punish them while you were present in their midst, nor does Allah punish people while they are asking His forgiveness." Today, Prophet is not living. So anyone who lives by hold fasting the Soul of Qur'an and teaching It to others, Allah will not destroy the nations. See explanation 3: 110-112, 156, 160; 4: 123-126 and 5: 78-80.

106. Oh you who believe, testimony should be taken by you whenever death appears for one of you; at the time for drawing up any bequest, two of you who are just minded or two others besides yourselves if you are traveling around the Earth and the calamity of death should strike you. Detain them both after swalath so they may swear by Allah if you have any doubt: "We will not sell it for any price even to a near relative, nor will we hide Allah's testimony: If do so surely we will be among the sinners."

The command of this verse has to implement only once in one's life. When a man appears the death and if he is making the bequest, the two just men among the believers have to witness for it. If death approaches during journey while he is making the bequest should be witnessed by two just men from any people. If the heirs have any doubt about witnesses, then the witnesses should be reminded about Allah and the Day of Judgment. And after the *swalath*, they should swear by Allah saying; "We have not made any change in the bequest for our relatives or for our own interest. If we do so, we shall be surely among the sinners." See explanation 2:282 and 283.

107. If it becomes clear that either of them has been accused of any sin then let two others than the first two from among those who deserve to be standup in their stead. Let them both swear by Allah: "Our testimony is indeed more truthful than the testimony by either of them; we have never aggressed if so indeed we would be among the wrongdoers.

108. It is most appropriate for you in order to secure testimony at its face value, or for them to fear you check back by means of fresh oaths following their own oaths. And heed Allah and listen; Allah doesn't guide the people of transgressors.

One gets peace and tranquility when the law and order of Allah prescribed in entire Soul of Qur'an are observed in individual, family and social life. Read together the verses 13: 28. The believers are those who implement them in their individual life and try their best to implement them in the family and society. The verse 64: 16 says, Keep Allah in hearts as much as you can; listen to His words and obey them by following it, and spend wealth and time for the best future of yourselves; and those who saved from the greediness and selfishness of their own souls, such are the ones who prosper. The following verses such as 9: 24, 80; 24: 55; 61:5 etc. also end as 'Allah will not guide such transgressing people.' See the explanation 2: 99. The verse 63: 6 also ends as: Surely Allah will not guide such transgressing people. The verse 9: 67 ends as: Surely the hypocrites are the transgressors. The verse 10: 33 says, thus The word of your Lord has proved about the transgressors that indeed they will not believe. See the explanation 2: 26-27, 254; 3: 136, 182 and 4: 159

Oh Allah, do not make us among the transgressors and losers of life, make us among those who live seeing You under 'the Light', and with those who keep

You in their hearts, and those who surrendered by mind, words and deeds to You who follow the Soul of Qur'an as it should be followed and enter us in to Your Paradise with those who are prosperous with Your Grace; Oh, the Most Merciful among those who are merciful.

109. One day, Allah will assemble all the messengers and ask: "What response have you received?" They will say: "We possess no knowledge; indeed You are the Knower of all unseen things."

On the Day of Judgment when Allah assembles all creatures together, the scene of questioning especially the Messengers is informed here. We can understand from their reply that the Messengers have no knowledge about anything after their departure of the worldly life. But only the heedful will utilize their intelligence. The verse 7:6 says: Then indeed We will question the people to whom We have sent and the Messengers We sent. See the explanation 1: 3; 4: 41 and 42.

110. Allah will say: "Oh Eisa, son of Maryam, remember My favor upon you and upon your mother when I strengthened you with the Holy spirit, you could speak to people from the cradle and as an adult, when I taught you the Book and wisdom, the Thourath and the Injeel. And you created something out of clay looking like a bird with My Permission; then you breathed into it, and by My Permission it became a bird! You cured anyone born blind and leper with My Permission, and when you brought forth the dead by My Permission, and when I protected you from the children of Israel when you came to them with clear signs and those who deny the Truth said: "This is nothing except the evident magic (sorcery)."

111. And remember when I inspired the disciples: "To believe in Me and in My messenger", they said "we believe, so You bear witness that we are Muslims."

See the explanation 3: 49-52. With these verses Allah reminds *Eisa* his favors bestowed upon him. In the saying of the favor upon you and upon your mother includes the creation of *Eisa* from his mother without a father. See explanation of the verses 4:1 and 171. To understand the favors of Allah bestowed upon *Maryam* see explanation of the verses 3: 42-45. The incidents how Allah saved *Eisa* and declaration of disciples that they were Muslims have been explained in the verses 3: 52-55. See the explanation 5: 82-85.

112. Remember the disciples asked: "Oh Eisa, son of Maryam, can your Lord send a food tray down from Heaven for us?" He said: "Heed Allah if you are believers!"

The question they asked to *Eisa* was whether Allah-the Lord of the worlds could send down a food tray from the Heaven for them. *Eisa* said, "Don't ask such questions if you are believers. When He intends a thing, He needs only to say "Be" and it is done or made, i.e. the thing comes to existence." Here, note the point that the disciples not asked to *Eisa* that could he send down a food tray from Heaven for them. So the disciples were believers because they know that *Eisa* can't bring a food tray from the Heaven without the Permission of Allah. But from the reply of *Eisa* that don't ask such question if you are believers, we can understand that the disciples' belief was not firm. The belief can only be firmed with the Soul of Qur'an specified in the verse 69: 51. Read together the verse 36: 82. See the explanation 3: 59-60; 4: 174 and 175.

'*Ma'eda*' means the gut -abdomen, so the tray which contains the things to fill the gut is called '*Maeda*'. In the Hell the hypocrites will be given the scalding water which will cut their guts into pieces as told in the verse 47:15.

113. They said: "We intend to eat from it and to get satisfaction for our hearts, and to know that indeed you have told us the Truth, and to belong among the witnesses for It."

See the explanation 2: 238-239, 260; 4: 103p; 5: 83 and 84.

114. Eisa, the son of Maryam prayed: "Oh, Allah, our Lord, send us down a food tray from Heaven. As it may be a recurring feast for both the first of us and last of us and as a sign from You! Provide for us, since You are the best of all sustenance providers."

The verses 22: 58; 23:72; 34:39 and 62:11 also end as; Allah is the Best of all sustenance providers. See the explanation 3: 27 and 37.

115. Allah said: "Indeed I will send it down to you; then any of you who disbelieve after that, I will punish him with such a torment which I have never punished any one in the world".

The Omniscient Allah made *Eisa* to request for '*Ma'eda*' -food tray- by praying as, Oh, Allah our Lord, feed us, You are the best among the sustenance providers was in order to send down the food tray from the Heaven itself. And moreover in the next verse Allah told as the reply for *Eisa's* prayer, indeed I will send down it. Then the food tray containing different food articles was sent down from the Heaven and they ate from it. Hearing about the food tray of the Heaven, people including disbelievers came, and about four thousand people ate from it. Then the food tray was raised up to the Heaven in the state of getting down without reducing anything from it. Then some of the Jews who ate from the feast became suspicious about it whether it was from the Heaven, and thus defied the sign of Allah and due to their deliberate transgression they were transformed into swine. See explanation 5:60. Today those having doubt about the '*Ma'eda*' whether it was sent down or not are the ones who are not utilizing the convinced knowledge-the Soul of Qur'an. Read together the explanation 4:82. Before all these occurred, when *Ibrahim* asked Allah "How You give life to the dead? Allah showed *Ibrahim* how He gives life to dead as per the verse 2: 260. Before the food tray was sent down to *Eisa*, Allah had given food without reason and measure to his mother *Maryam* as told in the verse 3:37.

The disciples asked food tray to be sent down in order to get their heart peace and certainty. Only the soul attained the certainty and peace can enter into the Paradise. In order to get the certainty after the revelation of the Qur'an, the entire Soul of Qur'an is a must. The verse 13: 28 says "Know that with the Soul of Qur'an you will get hearts peace and tranquility." Calling the souls which got peace and certainty Allah says through the verses 89: 27-30, "return to your Lord as your Lord is well pleased with you and you are well pleased with Him, so live only for Me and enter in to My Paradise." Calling Prophet Allah says through the verse 15: 99, serve for your Lord until you get the certainty (death). About Qur'an it is told in the verse 69:51 that surely it is the Truth of certainty. See the explanation 2:147-148 and 5: 48.

116. And remember when Allah will ask: "Oh Eisa, son of Maryam, have you told people: "Accept me and my mother as two deities besides Allah?" He will answer "Glory is to You, it was not possible for me to say what I had no right to say. If I had said so, You would have certainly known it: You know what is on my mind, while I do not know anything that is on Yours. Indeed You are the Knower of all unseen things.

Christians maintain different beliefs such as *Eisa* is the God itself, God is the one in three-the son, father and the Holy Spirit, God is three in one etc. See explanation 5:72. Besides, they consider *Maryam*-the mother of *Eisa* as the mother of God. For Deity see the explanation 1:4. Allah criticizes all these belief through this verse. Qur'an contains all the things that happened in the past, that which is happening in the present and that which is going to happen in the future. One third of the total verses warn about the coming Day of Judgment. So everyone should mould his life by seeing the Day of Judgment from the Soul of Qur'an. While the reply 'indeed You are the Knower of all unseen things' told in the verse 109 is by all Messengers, whereas in this verse it is the reply of *Eisa* himself. That means You are the One and only who does not depend on others while all creatures and servants depend You. For the explanation of the phrase "Glory is to You", see the explanation 2: 32-33. Also see the explanation 2: 27-28, 255; 3:3-7 and 5:105.

117. I have never told them anything except what You have ordered me to: "Serve only for Allah who is my Lord and your Lord. I was a witness for them so long as I remained among them, but when You gathered me back, You became the watcher over them and You are a witness for everything.

See the explanation 2: 283-284; 3: 51-56; 4: 1 and 155-159.

118. If You should punish them, they are still Your servants. And if You should forgive them, surely You are the Powerful, Wise.

One day in Prophet's night prayer, as he could not complete this verse, he spent the whole night with bowing and prostrating. When being asked about this, Prophet said to *Abu Durr*: "I asked my Lord's Permission to intercede for my community; Allah gave me it, '*Insha-Allah*', any one who does not associate others with Allah will be given it." But on the Day of Judgment, the Prophet, who prayed for his community will witness against his own people. "As oh my Lord, surely, my own folk considered this Qur'an as outdated", is told in the verse 25:30. So those who did not utilize the Soul of Qur'an after receiving It are the real disbelievers. The verse 43: 44 says: "This is a Reminder for you and for your people; and both of you will be questioned about It. Today Muslims only come under the people of Prophet; whereas entire mankind from his appointed time to the Last Day include in his community. See the explanation 2: 185, 213; 4: 4 and 116-120.

119. Allah will say: "This is the day when their truthfulness will benefit the truthful: They shall have Gardens with rivers flowing beneath. There they live in forever. Allah is well pleased with them and they are well pleased with Him. That is the great triumph.

The verse 39:33 says, anyone who confirms the Truth when It comes to him is the heedful, and the verse 32 says, those who reject the Truth when it comes to him are wrongdoers and disbelievers. Prophet taught that the most truthful words (Sayings) are the 'Book of Allah'. See explanation the verses 4: 78, 82 and 87. In the verse 9:119 Allah says: oh believers, keep Allah in your heart and be with those who are truthful. The verses 54: 54 and 55 say, indeed the heedful are in midst of gardens and rivers in the seat of Truth near the Almighty Sovereign. Read together the verses 33: 35; 59: 8; 63: 9-10 and 75: 31-32. It is told in the verses 9:100, 58:22 and 98:6 that Allah is pleased with them and they are pleased with Him. Besides, the verses 89: 27-30 say, oh fully convinced peaceful soul, return to your Lord well pleased with Him and well pleasing to Him. See the explanation 2: 140; 3: 95, 4: 13 and 5: 48.

120. Only to Allah belongs the sovereignty of Heaven and Earth and all that is there in. And He is capable of everything.

See the explanation 2: 28-29, 284-286 and 4:131-133.

Oh Allah, Include us among those who make true Your Book, who follow Your Book as It should be followed; and give us opportunity to do honorable deeds, make us among those who enjoin good and forbid evil, make us among those who die as Muslims, count us among those who are righteous and enter us to the Paradise with Your mercy, i.e., the Soul of Qur'an. Oh the Most Merciful among those who are merciful, Oh the Lord of all that is in Heaven and Earth, and the One Who is capable of everything.

With the name of Allah, the Impartial, the Compasssionate.

6. Al-An'am

In the verses 138- 139, 143- 144 of the *Surath* some cattle are categorized as prohibited and permitted for their use without any criteria by the Meccan pagans. From these verses, this *Surath* has got the name *An'aam* -livestock. Allah's favors are also referred throughout this *Surath* so the name *An'aam*-favors- is also meaningful. This *Surath* containing165 verses were revealed as a whole in Prophet's last period of Meccan life at a time. This is the first Meccan *Surath* in serial order of codification. *Asma* stated: *Surath An'aam* was revealed when Prophet was riding on a camel and I was holding the rein of the camel. Because of the heaviness of the contents of this *Surath*, the camel tired and I thought its bones would be broken. Prophet wanted to write this *Surath* on the day itself it was revealed.

Some of the believers had already gone '*Hijra*' to Ethiopia because of intolerable torture from *Quraish* in Mecca. The condition of Prophet became the worst after the death of his wife *Khadeeja* and father's brother *Aboo-thwalib* who were giving the support and consolation to him, so all the physical dependents were lost. '*Quraish*' continued preventing the people from hearing the Qur'an. They succeeded to extend in their attempt. It was in this condition some people belonged to '*Ous*' and '*Khasraj*' tribes from *Madeena* came to Mecca, and after speaking with Prophet they accepted *Islam* as the way of life. Then by reaching back at *Madeena*, they began to propagate *Islam* there.

The theme of this *Surath* is mostly to counter the '*shirk*' - associating others in the dominion of Allah- and to establish '*Thouheed*' -dominion of Allah. This *Surath* discusses the necessity of belief in the Hereafter, establish that this World is a cultivation land to the Hereafter, sweeping out superstitions to build a society of believers having morality and also a reply to allegations about Prophet and the Qur'an. It also deals with the consolation for the unhappy condition of the companions of Prophet due to default of the preaching effectively, advice to haughtiness of the rivals and also warning and threat to them.

This *Surath* has the peculiarity that it is mentioned about the great favors- the Soul of Qur'an- than any other *Suras*'. It is said in verse 19 that Allah and the Qur'an, which is revealed to warn the entire World are the great two witnesses. The verse 6: 26 says: Those who do not utilize Qur'an and not allow others to utilize, have to bear the punishment of others too. The verse 33 says: They do not reject you, but these wrongdoers repudiate to Allah's verses. The verse 36 says: Those who hear the Qur'an will only reply to you, and Allah will resurrect the dead and will assemble them to Him. As per the verse 38, there is nothing without being recorded in the Qur'an. In the verse 90, after mentioning about 18 Prophets by their names, it is told that the Guidance given to all these Prophets are the same and that is the Soul of Qur'an which is the Reminder to the entire World. In the verse 104, it is reminded that the Soul of Qur'an is the Insight to the mankind from their Lord. The verse 112 says: There are satans in both mankind and *Jinns* and they are enemies to all Prophets. The verse 116 says: If you obey the majority of the people on Earth, verily they will make you astray from the Straight path. As per the verse 122 the people having life are only those who follow the Light which is the Soul of Qur'an and the others are wandering in the darkness. As per the verse 126 it is told that, the Soul of Qur'an is the bridge to your Lord in the Paradise and in the verse 130, those who do not follow the Soul of Qur'an after they received It, then on the Day of Judgment they will do witness against themselves that they were disbelievers. In the verse 145 it is told that, all things which are devoted as offer other than to Allah and the swine flesh are filthy and will induce transgression. In the verse 149 it is told: If Allah had intended, would have given only the True Guidance to all. Those who utilize the Soul of Qur'an, which is the only True Guidance from Allah, in a way as arguing in favor of them can only succeed, and others on whom the Qur'an argue against will fail. As per the verse 155 Qur'an is the blessed Book. And as per the verse 157 those who reject It will be given evil punishment; and as per the verse 159 Prophet and believers have not any relation with those who have divided in their '*Dheen*'- *Islam*- into different organizations. The verse 164 says that every soul has to earn for her, and no bearer of burden shall bear the burden of another.

With the name of Allah, the Impartial, the compassionate,

1. **Praise be to Allah, Who created Heaven and Earth, He granted darkness and Light, yet those who disbelieve make other things equal to their Lord.**

This is one among five '*Suras*' which begin with "praise be to Allah." *Al-fathiha* '*Al-Kahf*', "*Saba*'" and '*Fathwir*' are the other four. In the verse darkness is used in plural form, whereas Light is used singular form. That is, the way of Allah-the Light- is the one, whereas the ways of satan-darkness- are many. As per the verse 24: 35, *An-Noor* -the Light- is Allah and as per the verses 5: 15-16 *An-Noor* is the Qur'an. The verse 6: 153 says: Verily this is My Straight Path, follow It, and not follow other ways, for they will lead you away from Me. This is what He satisfied on you, so that you may guard yourselves against evil. Those who sought other ways instead of Allah's way are the disbelievers. It is told in the verse I4: 1that 'the Book' is sent down in order to release mankind from the utter 'darkness' to the Light with the Permission of their Lord to the path of Powerful, Self praiseworthy. Permission means the Soul of Qur'an. 'With the permission of their Lord' means each individual must acquire It by asking to his Lord. The verse 64: 2 says: It is He Who has created you all, among you there is disbeliever, and there is believer, and Allah is observing all that you are doing. Even after all these explanations, disbelievers ascribe substitutes to Allah and are doing injustice. See the explanation 1: 1; 2: 213; 4: 174 and 175.

Oh Allah! Make us among '*Muvahhids*' who recognize You as the One and only Deity, and remembering You always and showing gratitude only to You with the Soul of Qur'an.

2. He is the One Who has created you from clay, then decreed a fixed term of life, and a deadline have been set by Him; yet you go on doubting!

Human body contains soil factors. Allah created the first man 'Adam' with clay and then made his progeny from the quintessence of the despised water. Read together the verses 32: 7-9. Father and mother eat food from soil; from which sperms and ovum are formed. Human body contains both the sperms of father and ovum of mother. The verses 86: 5-7 say: Human body is created by ejaculated water from *Swulb* (testicles) of father and '*Tharaa'ib*' -pelvis region of mother. The verse 76: 2 says: We have created human out of a drop of mingled sperm and ovum. Really this body is the vehicle to travel for the soul. According to Allah's order Angel takes Soul from the nape of father and it is blown to the foetus which has already having the life and passed different stages in the womb of mother. Then he or she gets the ability to move. Withdrawal of this life and soul together (spirit) from the body is called death that is the fixed term of life mentioned in the verse.

In the verse 31: 34, it is told that no one knows in which land he will die and certainly Allah has already decided it and He is well acquainted of everything. In the verse 10: 49 it is told that every community has an appointed term; when the term is reached, they neither are delayed nor are advanced. The verse 17: 58 say no town exists except we shall act as its destroyers before the Day of Judgment or as its punishers by means of severe torment that has been recorded in the Book line to line. "There is another fixed term" mentioned in the verse is the deadline of the World to gather all creatures of Allah from the beginning to the last of the World and for the trial of the mankind and *Jinns*. The verses 7: 14-15; 15: 37 and 38 say: Satan is given respite until the Day of Judgment.

In the verse 43: 61, it is told that coming of *Eisa* is the sign of the Day of Doom and so you do not have doubt about Its happening. Truth is from your Lord, which is the Soul of Qur'an. You do not have doubt in what It presents. According to the verse 69: 51, the Soul of Qur'an is the only confirming Truth to clear all doubts which explains each and everything. Read together the verse 16: 89. Then if anyone goes on doubt without utilizing the Soul of Qur'an will become hypocrites and disbelievers. Read together the verses 6: 60-61; 39:41 and 42. See the explanation 2: 28, 147-148; 4: 78-79; 5: 114 and 115.

3. He is Allah in Heaven and Earth. He knows both your secret and anything you publish. And He knows whatever you are earning.

In the verse 43: 84 Allah says: He Himself is the 'Deity' on Earth and He is the Deity in Heavens. He is the all Knower and the Wise. The verse 36: 76 says: And then let not their words grieve you; surely, We know what they hide and what they reveal. And in the verse 27: 70 says: But grieve not over them nor distress yourselves because of their plots. Then in the verse 74 Allah says: Indeed your Lord knows what is there hidden in the chest and what they reveal. In the verse 75 it is told that there is nothing in the Heaven or in the Earth hidden except it is recorded in a clear Book. This verse teaches that the fate of everyone has come, and everyone should try to change his fate to Paradise by utilizing the Impartial Allah's Permission -the Soul of Qur'an. See the explanation 2: 255; 3: 185 and 4: 118.

4. And not one of their Lord's verses ever reaches them except they shun It.

This verse is repeated in 36: 46. In the verses 20: 99-100 Allah says: We have given you Our '*Dhikra*'- Soul of Qur'an- in one's hearts language, then one who neglects It, verily will bear a burden on the Day of Judgment and in the verse 101 says that a grievous is the burden he bears. The verse 20: 124 says: One who neglects the Soul of Qur'an in the heart's language, surely have a narrow life in this World, and on the Day of Judgment he will be resurrected as a blind. And in the verse 72: 17 says that those who neglect their Lord's verses will be pushed out into severe punishments. In the verse 18: 28 it is told that you do not obey one who has made his heart neglected from the Soul of Qur'an. In the verse 68: 8 says: So you don't obey those who reject the Soul of Qur'an. The verses 7: 40-41; 18: 57 and 32: 22 say that those who neglect the verses of Qur'an even after getting It are wrongdoers, mad men and Allah will cover their hearts with a veil, so that they cannot understand the Soul of Qur'an. The verse 25:52 says: Therefore, do not obey the disbelievers, and strive- *Jihad*- against them with It, a mighty *Jihad*- strenuous striving. See the explanation 2: 121; 4: 63 and 5: 57.

5. They already rejected the Truth, whenever It came to them, yet more news will reach them concerning what they have been making fun of.

The Truth mentioned in the verse means the Soul of Qur'an. All the verses revealed through the previous Books before are also from the Qur'an. See the explanation 2: 2 and 5: 48. Utilize the Soul of Qur'an as a Balance in all sector of the life and that is the only Criterion to check himself whether his earnings will lead him to Paradise or Hell. Everyone has to decide his fate by utilizing the Soul of Qur'an in this World itself. The verse 16: 64 says: We have not revealed to you the Book except to explain them the reality of those things in which they differ. And It is a Guidance and Mercy for those people who believe. Both in the verses 39: 69 and 75 it is told that, on the Day of Judgment trial will be executed with the 'the Truth'- the Soul of Qur'an. See the explanation 2: 147 and 185.

This verse intimates the Prophet and his companions the time of migration to *Madeena*. This verse also teaches that the believers would hear mockery in this World by the disbelievers. But in the Hereafter, they would be the winners and will be mocking at the deniers. See the explanation 2: 212.

6. Have they not seen how many generations We wiped out whom We had established on Earth before them in a way We didn't

establish you? We showered for them abundant rain from the sky, We made rivers flow beneath them; and yet because of their sins We wiped out them all, and raised up other generations to succeed them.

In the verse 'have they not seen' means have they not understood by their hearts. The verse 32: 26 says: Do they not learn a lesson from the historical events of so many generations We have wiped out before them in whose dwelling-places they move about? Surely there are signs in this. Then do they not listen? The verse 50: 36 says: How many generations have We wiped out before them? They were much braver than they are and stormed through the land. Yet have they escaped? And the verse 41: 15 says: As for '*Aa'd*' people, they acted proudly on Earth without justice, and they asked: "Who is stronger than we are?" Did they not see that Allah who created them, is much stronger than they were? They had repudiated Our verses. Read together the verses 11: 42-44; 30: 9; 44: 25-26 and 57: 20. The verse 22: 46 says that have not they traveled on Earth or not they have heart to think? Or ears to hear? But verily the blindness is not for their eyes, but is for the hearts in their chests. From this verse it is understood that heart is participated for the sight and hearing.

Allah orders us to travel through the countries which were destroyed in different periods and to seek morals from their debris and there by think and learn about their conditions. When examining the remaining of ancestors, it can be understood that they were with more power and strength than we are. We could see that people '*Thamood*' bored the rocks to make rooms and halls for residence. It is found that the people who lived in Mohanjedaro and Harappa B.C. 5000 had made bathrooms, drainage systems etc. Moreover, even today we can see in America and some other countries, sixty or seventy feet height buildings with stones about thousands of tones, made by the people lived B.C. 2000. Who made such constructions in a period when there were no cranes or other such facilities to raise the stones and other materials! Because of the incapability of the modern world to make such buildings, Taj Mahal remains as one of the Seven Wonders of the World even today. Through this verse, Allah teaches the modern World not to be pride boast in their scientific progress, but be humble in front of Allah and be pride only with the Soul of Qur'an. The verse 7: 146 says: Allah will turn away from the Soul of Qur'an those who pride on the Earth without the Truth. See the explanation 3: 79; 4: 82 and 5: 65-66.

7. **Even though We sent you down something written on a papyrus scroll; so they might touch It with their own hands, those who disbelieve would still say: This is surely nothing, except clear magic.**

In the verse 17: 93 the disbelievers in Mecca are saying to Prophet: 'We shall not even believe in your ascendance or your meeting with Allah until you bring us an open Book for reading'. As per the verse 25: 32, the disbelievers ask: 'Why has not the Qur'an been sent down to him as a single Book? Through the verse 6: 91 Allah wants Prophet to ask them: 'Who then sent down the Book which *Moosa* brought, It teaches you the knowledge which you and your forefathers had not received before, and It is a Light and Guidance for all mankind, which you made in paper, revealed a few and concealed the majority of It. You also say them: Certainly it is Allah, and then let them free to go on with their mockery'. That means disbelievers of that period had demanded Prophet a codified Book. But the Knower of past, present and future- Allah- says: If they are given such a Book, they would not utilize or believe in It.

Even though all the disbelievers of todays have received such a Book, they are eating Its body and thus become '*fujjar*'. The verse 82: 14 says: And surely the *fujjar* are in the Hades. We can see them as inferiors in all respects than the Jews who are compared to a donkey which carries bundle of books as per the verse 62: 5. Those who do not have received the Soul of Qur'an, misunderstand that the Qur'an is responsible for Muslims worst conditions of life and thereby they do not try to learn It. In the verse 28: 48 says: When the Truth from Us came to them, the disbelievers asked Prophet: Why are not signs of Allah sent to him as if the signs sent to *Moosa*? Did not they deny what was *Moosa* given? Moreover, they said the Qur'an and *Thourath* are the two kinds of sorcery each assisting the other, and they declared that we deny all Books. Through the verse 49 Allah wants Prophet to say them: If you are saying only truth, bring a Book that contains more Guidance than these two, and then I will follow It. In the verse 50, it is told that if they are not giving reply, you know that they follow their whims. Then who is more astray than those who follow his whims without Guidance from Allah; surely, Allah does not guide such a wrongdoing people. Disbelievers say: The Qur'an is nothing except sorcery, but believers utilize It as clear Remembrance, Grace, Insight, Balance and Remedy for everything. Read together the verses 16: 25 and 26. In the verse 17: 47 Allah says: Certainly We know the best what they are hearing when they listen to you and what they murmur in their secret conversation and those wrongdoers say to the believers: You follow none other than a man bewitched. See the explanation 2: 120-121; 3: 138 and 5: 51.

8. **And they say: Why is not an Angel sent down to him? If We had sent an Angel down, the matter would be settled; then would no longer be allowed to wait.**

9. **Even if We made him into an Angel, We would have made him a man as well, to confuse them just as they confuse themselves.**

The views of foolish people of every period are that those who are appointed as Prophets must be beyond the behavior of man and must be in the behavior of the Angel. They misunderstood that people should not be throwing stone or abusing at him and they should not affect any human feelings such as thirst, hunger, anger, diseases, or any other sufferings. If we take the Soul of Qur'an as the Insight, we can see today's Muslims also have such a belief about Prophets and saint peoples. The Soul of Qur'an is compulsory to avoid '*shirk*' in belief. It is the Criterion to identify believer and disbelievers among the people. Angels are sent down either to withdraw spirits of the individual or to wipe out the people of a region. The verse 32: 11 says: "The Angel of death assigned for you will carry off your souls and bring you back to your Lord". The verses 25: 21 and 22 say: Those who do not expect to meet Us on the Day of Judgment will ask: "Why are not the Angels sent down to us or why do we not see our Lord?" Certainly they are too haughty of themselves, and have revolted in a great revolt. On the Day when they see the Angels at their time of death, it will not be a Day of rejoicing for such *mujrims*; rather they will cry: "May there is a stone barrier between us and the Angels of punishment". Read together the verses 7: 37; 16: 28; 25: 7-9 and 20.

What *Thamood* people told about their Prophet *Swalih* is mentioned in the verse 54: 24 as: Are we to follow one man from among ourselves? If so, certainly we will be in gross error and stupid. In the verses 17: 94 and 95 say: 'whenever Guidance- the Soul of Qur'an- came to them, nothing has ever kept people from believing in It except their argument: What! Has Allah sent a man like us to be a Messenger? Allah wants Prophet to say: If there were the Angels living on Earth peacefully in all respect, then Allah would have sent down Angels as Prophet from the Heaven. In the verse 39: 71, the condition of the disbelievers who will be driven to the Hell after the trial is explained as: When they reach near the Hell and the door is already opened, then Its keepers will ask them: "Have there not come to you Messengers of Allah from among you explaining Allah's verses and warning you to have to meet this Day?" They answer: "Yes, there did come, but the decree of punishment has been fallen due upon the disbelievers".

'Angels living peacefully' means all Angels are believers and obedient. The verse 66: 6 says: The Angels never disobey whatever Allah has commanded, but they do whatever they are commanded. To achieve the character of the Angel, men have to lead a life according to the Soul of Qur'an. Prophet taught us: *Those who have versed knowledge in the Soul of Qur'an are with the noble, virtuous Angels*. The verse 13: 28 says: Know that with the Soul of Qur'an the soul will get peace and tranquility. The men who are created independently can acquire the higher position than the Angels by living as the vicegerents of Allah by learning and teaching the Soul of Qur'an. The verse 22: 75 says: Allah chooses His Messengers from among the Angels as well as from the human beings, for surely Allah is all Hearing, all Seeing. There is no Prophet chosen other than from males. Both the verses 16: 43 and 21: 7 say: "And We sent not as Our Messengers before you other than male whom We inspired. Ask the knower of the Soul of Qur'an if you know not!" In the verse 19: 17 it is told that the Angel *Jib'reel* went to *Maryam* in the form of a man to inform her glad news about *Eisa*. The Angels who were appointed to destroy the people of Prophet *Looth* appeared before *Ibrahim* and *Looth* as handsome men. Read together the verses 11: 69-81 and 51: 24-34. "*Khidh'r*", who was appointed to teach special knowledge to *Moosa* was also an Angel as understood from the verse 18: 80 which says: And as for the boy (killed by "*Khidh'r*"), his parents were believers and ***We*** feared lest he should oppress them by rebellion and disbelief. Here *Khidh'r* says: ***We*** feared', instead of 'I feared'. And in the verse 19: 64 *Jib'reel* says to Prophet: ***We*** descend not except by the command of Your Lord". The Angels do work only under the command of Lord. So they even in single are talking for the sake of Allah only. See the explanation 2: 30-33, 210; 4: 97 and 136.

10. And surely, Messengers have been ridiculed before you; then about which reality they were ridiculing the Messengers, such reality itself affected on them.

The verse 21: 41 is the same verse. In the verses 16: 33-34 Allah asks: What are these disbelievers waiting for other than the Angel should come directly to them or Allah's command should happen. The people before them also had done so. Allah has not done any unjust on them, but they were doing unjust to themselves. The evil result of their activities was affected on them. The punishment about what they ridiculed itself affected on them. The verse 45: 33 says: Then the evil of their deeds will become manifest to them, and they will be completely encircled by that which they used to ridicule at. Allah saved *Nooh*, believers of his family, and other believers in a ship, and drowned all the disbelievers including his wife and a son who ridiculed when *Nooh* made the ship. Read together the verses 11:36-49.

The '*Aa'd*' people made very big houses and became pride. They asked themselves: Who is mightier than us, made false the Prophet Hood, rejected despicably the warning of Hood. They were swept away from the Earth by a furious storm blew for seven nights and eight days. At last they with their huge houses became nominal just like the palm trees fallen uprooted. Read together the verses 11: 60 and 69: 7. A camel was given to *Thamood* people as a sign of Allah. However, the people who rejected and made false Prophet *Swalih*, killed the camel defiantly and challenged that we have done that task, and then you bring the penalty that you are warned. Then Prophet *Swalih* said: Live you in your houses for three days. That is the promise which not to be belied. Read together the verse 11: 65. According to the verse 11: 67, those people were destroyed in their houses by a mighty blast as if they had not lived there.

The verses 11: 80-83 say: Allah destroyed *Looth's* people with their residence who involved in sodomy- anti-natural sexual activities-, by turning the land upside down and by raining brimstone of baked clay. The people of Prophet '*Shu'ayb*' ridiculed him when he advised them to weigh and measure correctly, and not to shorten measurement in their commodities and thereby not to make destruction on Earth. Read together the verses 11: 87-91. According to the verses 11: 94 and 95, Allah destroyed them by a mighty blast. As per the verses 10: 88-92, Allah drowned *Pharaoh* and his hosts who oppressed *Moosa* and children of Israel in the sea. In the verse 36: 30, Allah says: Alas! For my servants, whenever any Messenger come to them, except they were never ridiculing him. And the verse 51: 52 says: No Messenger ever came to those who preceded them, except they said: "He is a sorcerer or a madman". See the explanation 2: 14, 212 and 4: 140.

11. Say: Travel around the Earth and then see how was the consequence of those who rejected the Truth.

According to the verses 42: 11-15, *Thamood* people denied Prophet *Swalih* and arrogantly killed the camel. Thus with their own hand they deserved for the punishment, and they were not afraid of its consequence. This verse demands us to travel around the Earth and to learned morals from the ruins and historical events by hearing, seeing and thinking; such as the places where people of *Looth* had lived- that place exists as the Dead Sea still today. As the water in it is with high density, there is no chance to be drowned. The Dead Sea brings to mind us about the people who ejaculated the semen through homosexuality. The Almighty Allah, Who kept *Pharaoh's* body in the ocean about two thousand eight hundred years, was being shifted to a museum in Egypt. It remains as morality to the coming generations after him as explained in the verses 10: 91and 92. The verse 10: 39 says about the rejecters of Truth of all times as: Nay! They do not believe that which they cannot grasp, for they have not yet seen its prophecy fulfilled. The same way of those who passed before them disbelieved. But see what the end of the wrongdoers was! In the verse 30: 42 Allah orders Prophet to say the people: You travel along the Earth and see how the consequence of those who lived before you was. Most of them were associating others in Allah's dominion and became wrongdoers. See the explanation 2: 38 and 39.

12. Ask them: Who owns whatever is in the Heavens and Earth? You say: 'To Allah does'. He has prescribed Mercy for Himself. So He gathers you on the Resurrection Day, concerning which there is no doubt. Yet those who have lost their souls will never believe.

If it is asked to the disbelievers: Who owns whatever is in the Heavens and Earth? They will keep quiet. That is why it is ordered to say by the questioner: "To Allah does"- that means, you also belong to Him. As Allah had made decree Mercy as His character, He does not destroy you for your denial and disobedience. Those who fail to understand and recognize the Soul will never become believers. The verse 42: 45 says: You will see them solemnly trying to avoid it because of the disgrace they steal furtive glances at it. The one who believe will say: "the losers are the ones who have lost their own souls and their families' on Resurrection Day. Beware! Surely the wrongdoers shall suffer everlasting torment. The verse 39: 15 says: As for yourselves, I have conveyed to you the Truth and if you do not believe, then worship what you want besides Him". Say:

"The real losers are those who will lose their souls as well as families on the Day of Resurrection. Ah! That will indeed be an open loss". And the verse 66: 6 says: Oh believers! Save yourselves and your families from Hellfire, whose fuel is men and stones; in the charge of fierce and mighty Angels who never disobey Allah's command and who promptly do what they are commanded. See the explanation "The goal of life"- in the 'Introduction'.

These verses teach that who do not recognize themselves will not become the believers. Allah says in the verses 91: 9-10 that, those who have recognized them succeeded, and those who have not recognized them failed. No one can enter the Paradise without being a believer. To become a believer he has to keep Allah in his heart with the Soul of Qur'an. See the explanation 2: 28 and 152. The Impartial Allah allows the deniers to enjoy the life in this World itself. It is just because of His character- the Most Merciful. A day is determined for the said Judgment. Therefore, it is the duty of everyone to save him or her to fulfill the aim of life on Earth. Those who have lost their souls are the hypocrites. See the explanation 1: 3; 2: 99, 121 and 3: 9.

13. To Him belong all things that rest in night and daylight. And He is the all Hearing, all Knowing.

Allah, for Whom sleepiness or drowsiness do not affect see anything you do at any place irrespective of day and night. There is nothing hidden from Him in anywhere in Heavens or Earth. See the explanation 3: 5. Allah- Knower of all times has encompassed all the happenings in Heavens or on Earth is already recorded in this Book- the Soul of Qur'an as told in the verses such as 9: 51; 10: 61; 11: 5; 22: 70; 28: 75; 34: 3; 57: 22 and 64: 11. Therefore who ever live under the Light- the Soul of Qur'an is '*muhsin*'- the one who is living by seeing Allah. See the explanation 2: 255 and 284

14. Ask them: Shall I adopt someone as a patron besides Allah- the Deviser of the Heaven and Earth? He feeds everybody, yet is not fed, say: Certainly I have been ordered to be the first who has submitted himself to Allah, and not to be among those who associate others with Allah's dominion.

The verse 39: 64 says: You ask to the '*mushrik*': "Oh ignorant! Do you bid me to worship someone other than Allah?" In the verse 39: 65 it is told that certainly it has been inspired to you as well as in those before you: 'if you do associate anything with Allah, all your deeds will collapse; and you will become surely among the losers. In the verses 23: 88-89 Allah commands Prophet to ask: In whose hand has the dominion of all things, He gives refuge to all, no one gives refuge to Him; give answer if you have knowledge. Then they will say: 'To Allah'. Again ask: 'Then how are you deluded?'

In the verse 39: 12 it is told: I am ordered to be first among the devotees to Allah. In the verse 6: 164, Allah commands Prophet to ask: 'Am I enquire a Lord besides Allah, as He is the Owner of everything?' The verse 27: 91 says: Say: Certainly I have only been ordered to serve the Lord of this country, which He has made sacred, He possesses everything. And I have been ordered to be among the Muslims. The verse 10: 104 ends as: And I am ordered to be among the believers. And the verse 105 also ends as: And not to be among those who associate others with Allah's dominion. See the explanation 2: 113, 135; 3: 83-85 and 4:116.

15. Say: Certainly I fear the torment of an awful day if I should disobey Lord.

This verse is repeated in the verse 39: 13.

16. Whoever is averted the torment of that Day, then certainly, he is bestowed mercy and that will be the clear triumph.

See the explanation 2: 213, 286; 3: 185 and 5: 119.

17. If Allah should let any harm touch you, no one would remove it except He Himself; while if He should let some good touch you, then He is capable of everything.

The verse 39: 38 says: If you should ask them: "Who created Heaven and Earth?" They will surely say: "Allah". Ask them: "Do you think then that if Allah intends to harm me, can they- to whom you invoke besides Allah-, save me from His harm or if He wants some Mercy for me, can they withhold His Mercy?" Tell them: "Allah is all-sufficient for me. On Him do the reliant rely". In the verse 10: 107 says: If Allah afflicts you with a calamity, none can remove it except Him; and if He intends to bestow a Favor, none can withhold His Bounty. He bestows it on whomsoever of His servants He pleases; He is the Forgiving, the Merciful. The verse 7:188 says: You tell them: "I have no power to acquire benefit or avert any harm from myself, only that happening which Allah wants. Had I possessed the knowledge of the unseen, I would have acquired many benefits to myself; and no harm would have touched me. I am no more than a warner and herald for the believers". Prophet taught to pray: *"Oh Allah no one is to ban that what you have given, no one is to give what you have banned. No one is to cancel what you have judged and none's proud or dignity will benefit upon You.* See the explanation 2: 147-148; 3: 74 and 5: 76.

18. And He holds supreme authority over His servants. And He is the Wise, Acquainted of all things.

All goods and evils are from Allah. Evils are not affected when one remains with Allah's remembrance. See explanation 2: 234; 4: 78 and 79.

19. Ask: Whose witness is the biggest? Say: Allah is the witness between you and me. And the Qur'an which is revealed to me as divine Message in order to warn you with It as well as anyone It may reach, then do you testify that there are other deities along with Allah? Say: I will not witness so! Say: He is the Deity alone, and surely I am innocent of whatever you associate with Him.

They keep silent when they are asked: Whose is the biggest witness? Then Allah orders to say: Allah's is the biggest Witness. He is also enough as Witness between you and me, and this Qur'an which is revealed to me to warn you and to those who have reached It, also is a Witness. In the verse 16: 44 Allah says: We bestowed you this Soul of Qur'an to explain what is revealed from their Lord to the people in order to meditate and reflect. Prophet taught that the Soul of Qur'an will witness either in favor of you or against you. It gives witness favorably for those who make It true, while for those who hide and reject It will witness against them. In the verse 11: 17 it is told that Prophet is recited a witness from Allah, and before It there is the Book given to *Moosa* as Guide and Mercy. See the explanation 2: 121 and 140.

The verse 17: 96 says: Say them: Sufficient is Allah as a Witness between you and me. He is the One who is well acquainted and Observant of His servants. In the verse 29: 52, Allah commands Prophet to say: Allah is suffices as a Witness between you and me. He knows all that in Heaven and on Earth. Then those who believe in falsehood and hide Allah, such are the only losers. Hide Allah means hide the witness-the Soul of Qur'an. In the verse 16: 2 it is told that Angels are descended with inspiration from His commands on to whom He wishes. There is no Deity to you except Me to worship, and so you keep Me in your hearts. The verse 21: 25 says: I have not sent any Messengers without giving divine Message that there is no Deity except Me, then you live only for Me. The verse 18: 110 says: I am but a human being like you; the revelation is sent to me to declare that your Deity is One Deity; therefore, whoever hopes to meet his Lord, let him do good deeds and not associate others in the serving of his Lord. As all Prophets have come to introduce Allah, after getting this Qur'an if anyone takes others as Deity or Lord instead of Allah, they are the '*mushriks*' and inmates of Hell. Read together the verses 23: 51-53; 30: 31 and 32 See the explanation 1: 4 and 2: 176.

20. Those to whom We have given the Book know Him just as they recognize their own sons, yet those who have lost their souls will never believe.

See the explanation 2: 146.

21. Then who is the more wrongdoer than one who invents a lie about Allah or one who has rejected His verses? Surely He will never lead such wrongdoers towards prosperity.

The verse 10: 17 says: Then who is the more wrongdoing than one who invents a lie about Allah or one who has rejected His verses? Surely, He will never lead such *mujrims* towards prosperity. Both through the verses 29: 68 and 39: 32 Allah asks: Who is the more wrongdoing than one who invents a lie about Allah or denies the Truth when It comes unto him? Is not there a home in the Hell for such disbelievers? In the verse 6: 93 Allah asks: Who is the more wrong doing than he who invents a lie about Allah or he who without getting revelation says: I get revelation or I can reveal like what Allah presents. The verse 32: 22 asks: Who is more wrongdoing than one who is remembered his Lords verses in his heart's language, then neglect It; indeed We will revenge with such *mujrims*.

"The more wrongdoing than one who invents a lie about Allah" means if this Qur'an is not from Allah, Prophet is the biggest wrongdoing man, if it is from Allah, then the more wrongdoing are the one who does not follow It. Today, the more wrongdoing are the hypocrites who knowingly hide the Soul of the Qur'an as well as twist and distort against Allah's wishes, and the common people who reject or neglect the Soul of Qur'an after receiving It. Both are coming from Muslims who are proud without Justice that they are the people of Qur'an. Actually they are the disbelievers, wrongdoers and mad men. In the verses 10:

69-70 Allah commands Prophet to say: Certainly those who invent a lie about Allah will never succeed. The life of this World is momentary sustenance, then their return is to Us, and then We will taste them severe torment as reward for their hiding of the soul of Qur'an. The verses 6: 135; 12: 23 and 28: 37 also end as: 'Surely He will never lead such wrongdoers towards prosperity.' See explanation 2: 254; 4: 56; 5: 51, 59 and 67.

22. And on one Day We shall summon them all together; then We shall ask those who have associated others with Us: "Where are your associates which you have been claiming to have?"

23. Then there will be no trouble for them except they say: By Allah, our Lord, we have not been associates.

24. Look! How they lie even about themselves, whatever they have invented has misled them.

In the verses 23: 69-76 Allah asks: Or is it they deny him because they do not recognize their Messenger, who is a member of their own community? Or are they really convinced that he is a mad man? Nay! In fact he has brought them the Truth and most of them dislike the Truth. Had the Truth followed their whims, Heavens, Earth and everything therein would have been disrupted. Nay! We have given them their Reminder -Soul of Qur'an, but they are heedless towards It. Or is it that you are asking them for some recompense? But the recompense of your Lord is the best, for He is the best provider of sustenance. As a matter of fact, you are calling them to the Straight Path; and surely those who do not believe in the Hereafter will ever stray from the Straight path. If We show them Mercy and relieve them from their affliction, they would obstinately persist in their transgress, blindly wandering to and fro; for even now, when We have inflicted the punishment on them, they have neither submitted to their Lord nor humbled themselves towards Him.

'The death scene of such disbelievers' is warned in the verses 39: 59-60 as: Then Allah will say to him: Nay! My verses did come to you; but you rejected them, were false proud and you were among the disbelievers. On the Day of Judgment you shall see that the faces of those who uttered falsehood against Allah shall be blackened. Is there not an abode in Hell for such arrogant? And after the Judgment they will be led to the Hell is mentioned in the verses 71-72 as: The disbelievers will be driven to Hell in groups. When they reached there, its gates automatically be opened and Its keepers will ask: Did there not come to you Messengers from among yourselves reciting the verses of your Lord and warning you about the meeting of this Day? Yes, they will answer. But the sentence of punishment has been already decreed against the disbelievers. And they will be told: Enter the gates of Hell to live therein forever. What an evil abode for the arrogant!

When the associates see their patrons whom they associated with Allah, they will say: Our Lord! Whom we called and prayed without You are they. Then those patrons will answer: You are certainly telling lies. On that Day they will surrender completely before Allah and all that they sandaled on Allah will become astray from them. Those who hide the Soul of Qur'an and prevent others from the Straight path will be given added punishment for the mischief they had done in this World. Read together the verses 10: 28-30. In the verse 25: 27-30 it is warned the conditions of the wrongdoers very clearly. They will say: It was very better if I had accepted Prophet's way and if I had not accepted human satan as friend, who prevented me from the Soul of Qur'an after I had received It. Moreover, Prophet will come with the Qur'an and will say: This misfortune came to them because they were neglecting the Soul of Qur'an. The verse 7: 53 ends as: 'Whatever they have invented has misled them'. See the explanation 2: 24; 6: 1 and 94.

25. Some is there who pretend that they listen to you, but We have laid a lid on their hearts and a veil in their ears lest they should understand It. Even if they saw every sign they still would not believe in them; so whenever they come to you, they argue with you, those who disbelieve say: Certainly this is nothing except the fables of ancestors.

In the verse 17: 45 Allah says: When you recite Qur'an We will make an invisible veil between you and those who disbelieve in the Hereafter. And the verse 46 says: We have made a lid on their hearts for not to understand It and a veil in their ears. The verse 18: 57 says: Who is more wrongdoing than the one who, when reminded with the verses of his Lord, turns away from them and forgets what his own hands sent ahead? In regards to such people, We have cast lid over their hearts, so they do not understand this Qur'an, and have become hard of hearing. Call them as you may towards the Guidance, they will never be guided. The verse about the hypocrites 63:3 says: that is because they have believed, then disbelieved so their hearts are sealed off such that they do not understand a thing. Read together the verse 7: 179. The saying of disbelievers about Qur'an is told in the verse 25: 5 as: It is fables of the ancestors, which is written and are dictated to him every early morning and evening. The verses 16: 24-25 say: If they are asked what their Lord has sent down, they will say: Fables of ancestors. They are doing so to bear on the Day of Judgment the burden of sins of their own and a share of the burden of those whom without knowledge they have misled. What a bad burden they bear! The verses 8: 31; 23: 83 and 27: 68 also end as: 'Certainly this is nothing except fables of ancestors'. The verse 46: 17 ends as: 'This is nothing but fables of ancestors.

If we utilize the Soul of Qur'an as Insight, we can see that the activities of today's Muslims who are the bearers of Qur'an are also the same as the disbelievers of all times. When they are reminded by quoting the Qur'anic verses that you have to avoid the bad customs which is anti-Islamic, they will reply: Those verses are applicable to Meccan *mushriks*, Jews and Christians, and are not applicable for Muslims who are fasting and performing *swalath*. Moreover, according to the verse 2: 143 if they are reminded that we have to bear witness the Prophet's life in the society, they will answer: It is impossible to lead the Prophet's life which is the Soul of Qur'an. For example, if it is told according to the verse 9: 84 which was presented at *Madeena* in *Hijra* 9th year that do not perform funeral *swalath* if any hypocrite dies, some of theirs reply will be that this verse is told about '*Meccan Mushriks*' and some of them even ask that how can we recognize the hypocrites? Those human satans, whom Allah has killed, do not consider the Soul of the Qur'an as Balance, Insight and Criterion. See explanation 2: 99, 171; 4: 63, 78 and 6: 7.

26. And they forbid the mankind about It and forbid themselves about It. Certainly, by doing so, they are not destroying except themselves; but they do not perceive it.

'About It' means, about the Soul of Qur'an, that they didn't give It to others which is the Guidance for entire mankind. The hypocrites are not allowing learning the Soul of Qur'an even for common Muslims, thus they forbid them from It. Since Meccan mushrik did not have the codified Qur'an, 'they' mean the Muslims of today, especially the hypocrites. The Soul of Qur'an is the Balance and Trust to keep the Universe in its equilibrium. So by hiding It the disbelieving hypocrites not only destroy them but also the Universe. So the burden of the destruction of the Universe should be born by these human satans- hypocrites- in front of Impartial Lord of the Worlds. Read together the verses 20: 100-101

The Meccan mushrik's saying is quoted in the verse 17: 93 as: 'We shall not believe your ascendance to the Paradise and your meeting with Allah until you brings us an open Book for reading. See the explanation 6: 7. The Soul of Qur'an is the food, cloth and sight of the human soul as specified in the verse 7: 26. It is the Ticket to the Paradise as specified in the verses 20: 3; 69: 48 and 76: 29, Criterion to distinguish the truth and falsehood as per the verses 3: 4 and 25: 1, Proof and Light as per the verse 4: 174, Balance to weigh all things as per the verses 42: 17 and 57: 25, and a Weapon to do Jihad against the disbelievers who hide It as per the verses 25: 52 and 9: 73. Allah's curse as well as mankind' and Angels are upon those who hide the Soul of Qur'an is told in the verses 2: 159-161. The verse 4: 145 says: The hypocrites who conceal the Soul of Qur'an after knowing It will go directly to the deepest of the Hell without even trial. Those who do not use the faculties of ears, eyes and power of intelligence to understand what is, what for and why Qur'an, and thereby lead a heedless bad life than the cattle, will be driven to Hell after reckoning. Read together the verse 7: 179. See the explanation 3: 58, 187; 4: 91 and 5: 48

27. If you could see when they are set before the Fire and say: Alas! If we might only be sent back, and had not rejected our Lord's verses and we had been believers.

By pointing the scene of rejecters in the Hereafter, Allah is consoling Prophet and believers. The verse 7: 53 says: Now are these people waiting for its prediction? The Day of Prediction comes along, those who already forgotten It, will say: "Our Messengers did come with the Truth. Have we any intercessors to intercede for us? Or should we be sent back, then we would have act so differently from the way we have been acting". Indeed they have lost their souls, and what they have been inventing has left them in the lurch. In the verse 40: 11, it is warned the scene that the disbelievers will say: Our Lord! you have made us die twice and have revived us twice, we have identified our sins, and then is there any way out from here. The verse 32: 12 says: If only you could visualize when the *mujrims* will hang their heads before their Lord saying: "Our Lord! We have sighted and we have heard (the crying and roaring of the Hell); then send us back to the World, so we can do good deeds; surely we are now convinced". The verse 35: 37 says: Therein they shall cry for help in the Hell: "Our Lord! Take us out;

from now on we will act honorably, so differently from the way we have been acting. The response will be: "Did We not give you long enough life so that you would be the one who bears things in mind might remember during its course? And the warner came to you. Then you taste the torment". Wrongdoers will have no helpers. The verses 89: 23-24 say: Hell shall be brought in sight. On that Day man will remember that how better was it if he had utilized the Soul of Qur'an? He will say: "Alas! Would that I had sent forth some good deeds for this Life".

The verses 45: 31-35 say: But as to those who disbelieve, it will be told: "Were not Our verses recited to you, and yet you acted proudly and were *mujrims*". And when it was said that the promise of Allah was true and that the Hour there was no doubt about it, you used to say: `We do not know what the Hour is: we are only making a conjecture and we are not convinced'. Then will appear to them the evil of what they did and they will be completely encircled by that which they used to mock at! It will also be today: "This Day We shall forget you just as you forgot a meeting on this Day of yours! And your abode is the Fire and you have no helpers! "This is because you used to take the verses of Allah as joke and the Worldly life has deceived you". On this Day neither they shall be taken out of Hell, nor shall they be given a chance for compensation. Read together the verses 14: 44-45 and 39: 56-60. See the explanation 2: 28; 3: 91 and 6: 11-15.

28. Rather what they have been hiding previously in the Worldly life will be appeared to them; even though they were sent back, they would still return to what they have been forbidden. And certainly they are only liars.

The verses 39: 47-48 say: If the wrongdoers possessed all the treasure of the Earth and as much more besides it, they would gladly offer as ransom themselves from the painful torment on the Day of Resurrection will not be accepted. And Allah will show them what they would have never imagined. The evils result of their deeds will become manifest to them and they will be completely encircled by the very thing they used to ridicule. The hearings, sights and even skins of such enemies of Allah will witness against themselves is mentioned in verses 41: 19-24 as: the Day when the enemies of Allah will be brought together and led to the Hellfire in groups. Finally when they reach there, their ears, their eyes, and their skins will testify to their misdeeds. And they will ask their skins: "Why did you testify against us?" Their skins will reply: "Allah Who gives the faculty of reflecting power to everything, has made us reflected.

He is the One Who created you at first time, and now to Him you are being brought back. During your Worldly life you used to hide yourselves while committing crimes, you never thought that your own ears, your own eyes and your own skins would ever testify against you. Rather you thought that even Allah does not know many things that you do. This thought of yours which you entertained concerning your Lord, has brought you to destruction and now you have become of those who are utterly lost". Then, whether they have patience or not, the Fire will still be their home, and even if they beg for repentance, it shall not be granted to them.

The verses 18: 100-101 say: We shall place the Hell on the Day of Judgment near to the disbelievers, whose eyes had a lid about the Soul of Qur'an and they had not been able to hear It. And the verse 50: 22 says: It will be said: "You were heedless of It, but now We have removed your lid, so your eyesight is sharp Today!" The verses 23: 99-100 say: These people will never refrain from wrongdoing until when death comes to anyone of them, then he will say: "Oh Lord! Send me back, so that I may do good deeds in the World that I have left behind". Never! This is just a statement which carries no value, it will be too late because there will be a barrier between them and the World they have just left till the Day they are raised to life again. By calling the believers through the verse 63: 10 Allah says: And spend what We have given the sustenance before when death comes to anyone of you, then he shall say: "Oh my Lord! If only you would delay for a short, then I would make the Soul of Qur'an truth, spend Charity and be among the honorable".

'And certainly they are only liars' means; the hypocrites are those who are killed by Allah, because they knowingly hide Allah and Prophet in the Soul of Qur'an. Their character is that if they open the mouth they will say lies only. See the explanation 4: 85, 150-151; 5: 36 and 67.

29. And they say: Surely the life is nothing except our Worldly life; we will not be raised up again.

In the verse 17: 49 the asking of these deniers is referred as: Shall we be resurrected newly even if we become bones and ant-hill. Allah orders Prophet to say them: Even if you become rock or iron or anything that you think in your heart as difficult to be resurrected, you will certainly be resurrected! The verse 36: 78 says: The denier attributes similitude for Us forgetting about his creation and he even ask: Who will revive our bones once they have rotted away. In the verse 79 Allah orders to say: The One Who raised them up in the first time will revive them, and He alone is the Knower of all creations. The verses 50: 3-4 say: "After we are dead and have become dust we shall be raised to life again, such a return is far from reason". We know all that the Earth consumes from their bodies, and We have a Book which keeps records of everything. The 'Book' mentioned here is the Book mentioned in the verses 10: 61; 11: 6; 22: 70; 34: 3; 57: 22; 85: 21 and 22 i.e. the soul of Qur'an Itself.

The verses 10: 52-53 say: Then it will be said to the wrongdoers: "Taste the everlasting punishment! Should you not be rewarded according to your deeds?" They ask you: "Is what you say really true?" Tell them: "Yes! By my Lord, it is absolutely true! And you will not be able to avert it". The verses 23: 83 and 84 say: We were already promised this, we and our forefathers. Lo! This is nothing but fables of the ancestors. Even the disbelievers recognize the existence of Allah. Ask: To whom belongs the Earth and whosoever is therein, if you have knowledge? The verse 64: 7 says: The disbelievers claim that they shall not be raised to life again. Tell them: "Indeed, by my Lord, you shall surely be raised to life again! Then you shall be told of all that you have done, and that is easy for Allah". See the explanation 5: 57-60 and 64-68.

30. If you could only see as they are made stand before their Lord, He will ask: "Is not this is the Truth?" They will say: "Of course by our Lord!" He will say: "Taste the torment, since you have been disbelieving".

The verse 46: 34 says: On the Day when the disbelievers will be brought before the Fire, Allah will ask: "Is not this is the Truth?" They will reply: "Yes, by our Lord!" Allah will say: "Well, then taste the torment now, since you were hiding the Soul of Qur'an". As per the verses 67: 10-11 the disbelievers will say: "Had we only heard the Soul of Qur'an or used our intelligence, we would have not been among the inmates of the Blaze". Thus shall they confess their sin; so away from the Mercy of Allah will be the dwellers of Hell. Read together the verses 32: 20; 39: 60 and 42: 26-29. See the explanation 2: 39; 3: 106 and 5:19.

31. Certainly, those who reject 'the meeting with Allah' have already lost out, so when the Hour comes suddenly upon them, they will cry: Alas! We have been neglecting about this Hour". And they

will be carrying the burden on their backs. Know that, they are carrying evil burdens.

The verses 20: 99-100 say: Thus do We relate to you, some information of the past events; and indeed We have sent you the Soul of Qur'an from Our self. Those who reject It, shall bear a heavy burden on the Day of Resurrection. In the verses 10: 7-8 it is told: Certainly, those who do not believe the meeting with Us are satisfied with the life of this World and will find satisfaction in it. Those who are heedless about Our verses, they will be fallen in the Blaze which they had been earning in this World. And the verse 15 says: If this Qur'an is explained to those who do not expect the meeting with Us will demand to bring a Qur'an not like this, or to make some changes in It. In the verse 45, it is told: Those who rejected the meeting with Allah, and who denied it, and who did not utilize Guidance after he had received It are indeed the losers. Those who lead a life without having the consciousness about the fact that they will have to give reply in front of Allah about the life after his 15th age are deniers of Hereafter, and their life is completely lost. In the verses 18: 103-105 Allah orders Prophet to ask: Shall we tell who will be the greatest losers of all deeds are? All their deeds in this World are astray, but they think that what they are producing are good deeds. Such are the hiders of the Qur'anic verses and the meeting with Allah. Thus, all their deeds became in vain. And they will not have weight in the balance on the Day of Judgment since they didn't utilize the Soul of Qur'an as the Balance in this World. In the verse 84: 6, it is told that 'Oh mankind, you are running strive to your Lord. Thus, you will verily meet Him'. Read together the verses 18: 110 and 25: 21-23.

'About this Hour', in case of individual it is the death time, whereas for whole mankind, it is the Last Day- Dooms day. The verses 17: 13-15 say: And every man's fate We have fastened to his own neck, and We shall bring forth for him on the Day of Resurrection a Book which he will find wide open. And it will be said unto him: "Read the book. Today you yourself are sufficient to take your own account". He the one, who utilize Guidance, shall be guided to his own sake, and he who goes astray does so to her own loss. No bearer shall bear the burden of another on the Day of Judgment. We do not inflict punishment until We send forth a Messenger. In the verse 29: 23 Allah says: Those who hide Allah's verses and deny the meeting with Him, such are the hopeless about My Mercy and for them have severe torment. Read together the verses 29: 12 and 13. See explanation 2: 186; 4: 85; 6: 4-5 and 24.

32. This Worldly life is nothing but some sport and amusement, house of Hereafter is the best for those who lead heedful life, Will you not then think by using your intelligence?

The verse 29: 64 says: The life of this World is nothing but sport and amusement! It is the life of the Hereafter, which is the true life, if they knew. In the verse 57: 20 it is told that certainly, the life of this World is nothing except sport and amusement, boasting among you, competing in lavishness and competing to gather abundance of wealth and children. See the explanation 3: 14- 17, 185, 196-197; 5: 57-58 and 6: 6.

33. We well know that indeed what they say saddens you, yet they are not rejecting you, but these wrongdoers are repudiating with Allah's verses.

In the verse 17: 82 it is told that the Soul of Qur'an is Healing and Mercy for the believers, and for the wrongdoers It will increase nothing except losses. In the verse 41: 40 it is told that those who pervert the Soul of Qur'an are not hidden from Us. Who is better the one who is cast into the Fire or the one who emerges safely on the Day of Resurrection? Do as you like; surely He is watching all your actions. See explanation 5: 45 and 6: 21.

Prophet taught us that *none of you will become a believer until his whims follow what I brought;* i.e. the Soul of Qur'an. In the verse 42: 26 says: Permanent residence of Allah's enemies is Fire and it is given to them as a reward because they were repudiating with Our verses. It is told in the verses 29: 47 and 29:49 that no one will repudiate with Our verses except the disbelievers and the wrongdoers. The verse 40: 35 says the ones who repudiate about Allah's verses without any authority to do so having been bought them, incur the greatest disgust so far Allah is concerned and so far as those who believe are concerned. Thus Allah seals off every over bearing oppressors' heart. The verse 40: 56 says: those who repudiate about Allah's verses without having any authority to do so, only feel pride within their breasts; they shall never achieving anything so take refugee with Allah He is All hearing, the Observant. Read together the verses 7: 50-51; 40: 4 and 5

The verse 68: 52 says: The one who disbelieves almost trip you up by glaring at you whenever they hear the Soul of Qur'an, and they say: "Surely he is affected with Jinn". Read together the verse 22: 72. The transgressors, wrongdoers and disbelievers are not rejecting and making false Prophet and the believers, but they are rejecting and making false the verses of Allah. The Meccan mushriks who considered Muhammad as 'Al-Ameen'- the Honest- changed their view as 'useless', when he was began to say the Qur'an. In case of believers the opposition will come from the disbelievers when the Soul of Qur'an is told to them as Allah intends. It is told in the verse 63: 4 that the hypocrites are enemies of believers and Allah, so keep them away. See explanation 2: 99. It is reported that once *Aboojahil* said to Prophet in a conversation between them that: We are not rejecting you, but we reject what you have brought with. See the explanation 2: 24; 4: 56; 5: 67; 6: 25 and 26

Oh Allah, do not include us among the repudiators with the Truth-Soul of Qur'an, allow us to do jihad against the wrongdoers who are repudiating with Your verses!

34. And surely Messengers before you have been rejected, yet they held patiently on being rejected and abused, until Our support came to them. And there is no way to change Allah's words. News of other Messengers has already come to you.

In the verse 7: 64 it is told that Prophet *Nooh* was rejected by his people and as per the verse 72 the wiping out of *A'ad* people happened when they rejected Allah's verses. As per the verse 92 it is told that those who rejected Prophet *Shua'yb* were the losers. The verses 91: 11-14 say: The people of *Thamood* rejected the Truth with their arrogant transgression, when the great wicked man among them was deputed to kill the she-camel. The Messenger of Allah warned them as: "This is Allah's She-camel. Let her drink on her turn". They rejected him and slew her. Therefore, for that crime, their Lord let loose His torment upon them and leveled them. In the verse 36: 15 it is told: The people of a country to whom three Messengers were appointed, and they rejected Prophets, sayings that you are only human like us and the Most Gracious has sent down nothing, you are none except liars. The verse 21: 77 says: We helped Prophet *Nooh* against those people who had rejected Our verses; surely they were an evil people, so We drowned them all in a great flood. The verse 23: 90 says: The fact of the matter is that We have brought them the Truth, and undoubtedly these people are liars. The verse 34: 45 says; those who lived before them denied It and did not achieve a tenth of what We gave them. They even rejected My Messengers, so how was My disgust. The verse 35:4 says; if they should reject you, well,

Messengers before you have already been rejected, to Allah are matters referred. Read together verses 67: 6-10.

'There is no way to change Allah's words' means, Allah- the knower of all times has already recorded in His Book what will happen in the World as specified in the verses 22: 70; 27: 75; 35: 11; 57: 22; 64: 11 etc. so none can change the words of Allah. The verse 15: 9 says: Surely We have revealed the Soul of Qur'an; and We will surely preserve It Our self. And every human's fate had been recorded earlier as told in the verses 9: 51 and 17: 13-15. And no power can change it except by the individuals themselves utilizing Allah's Permission-the Soul of Qur'an. 'There is no way to change Allah's creation' is also told in the verse 30: 30. So by understanding all these matters from the Soul of Qur'an, Prophet and believers should be ready to face trials, entrusting all things in Allah, considering that He is observing everything. And to remain patiently seeking Allah's help always; and should change their habits and character as that of the Lord by utilizing the Soul of Qur'an which is the ways and practice of the Lord. See the explanation 2: 214; 3: 195; 4: 78-79; 6: 10 and 11.

35. And if their reluctance bear so heavily upon you, then how would it be if you managed to bore a tunnel through the Earth or to climb a ladder up to Heaven and brought a sign to them? If Allah so wished, He would gather them together upon Guidance. Then you should not be among the ignorant ones.

Even though the people of Mecca were awakened for a long period, they did not come to the Truth. Seeing this condition, the believers often wished that if any sign or evidence to prove the honesty of the believers and to destroy the denial of the disbelievers may be sent down. This verse is the reply for their wishes. In the verses 26: 3-4 it is said that you may be spoiling yourself by following them, for they do not become the believers, but if We had wished We may send down any sign to deniers and thus make them obedient on It by bowing their necks. If Allah had wished He would be able to make gather all the people in the Truth. But Allah has not intended so. Allah has given to every human soul both Allah's and satan's path, and also has given freedom to select either path. See the explanation 4:1. Everyone is appointed to Earth to identify the Creator, to purify himself and to make Paradise here by utilizing the Soul of Qur'an. That is the aim of life. This verse teaches that the believers must lead a life by conceiving Allah's specialty as '*Rahman*'-Impartial- and must submit will and power mentally and physically to Allah and thus become innocent, asking the Straight path always to Allah only. Read together the verses 6: 111 and 13:31.

The verses 22: 15-16 say: If anyone thinks that Allah will not help His Messenger in this World as well as in the Hereafter, let him stretch out a tent rope to the sky if he can, then cut it off. Let him see for himself whether his scheme will take away whatever is irritating him. Thus We have sent It down as clear verses; and verily Allah guides whom He wishes. See the explanation 3: 128-129; 4: 17-18, 82 and 118.

36. Verily, those who listen to you will respond; and as far as the dead, Allah will resurrect them and unto to Him they will be all returned.

'Who listen to you' means those whose conscience is active that means their wisdom and thinking power are not frozen. See the explanation 2: 7, 18 and 171. Their hearts are not locked with padlock by partiality and they are proud with the Soul of Qur'an. The verses 47: 23-25 say: Such are those whom Allah has cursed and made them deaf and blind. Will they not ponder upon the Soul of Qur'an? Are there locks upon their hearts? Those who turn back to disbelief after the Guidance has become clear are seduced by satan who gives them false hopes. In the verses 36: 69 it is told that this is nothing but a Reminder and a manifest Qur'an. Then the verse 70 says: To warn with it those who are alive and to establish the charge against the disbelievers. i.e. the individual should say "I was a disbeliever" in order to punish him for the Lord-Impartial. Read together the verses 6: 130 and 7: 37. The verse 35: 22 says: Allah makes listen whom He intends, and verily you will not make listen those in grave; and in the verse 14 says: "The saint man in the grave will not hear the invoke make to him, and even if they could hear their invoke, they would not respond, and on the Day of Judgment they will deny their attribution of association to Allah. The verses 30: 52-53 say: You cannot make the dead hear, nor can you make the deaf hear your call especially when they have turned their backs and are running away; nor can you guide the blind out of their error. None will hear you except those who believe in Our verses and submit themselves to Me as Muslims. Read together the verses 7: 194-195; 10: 42 and 43. See explanation 6:25.

The Meccan mushriks were not reading the Qur'an to the dead, or on the grave. But today the bearers of Qur'an as they bear It like the burden bearing donkeys; even though reading these verses, read It to the dead - which is against Allah's teaching. And the human Satans knowingly and silently are encouraging this. So 'the dead' mentioned in this verse also includes living hypocrites' i.e. who hide the Soul of Qur'an knowingly. Thus they are in the state of sleeping without having the soul. The common Muslims who blindly follow these hypocrites as scholars without utilizing sights, hearings and intelligence to understand what is, what for and why Qur'an? Are also heedless and will be the inmates of the Hell. They follow the way of satan- the way of majority of forefathers- without any thought with their intelligence. Read together the verses 18: 100-101; 36: 62; 89: 23 and 24. See the explanation 2: 166-167; 4: 135, 150-151 and 5: 48.

37. And they say: "If a sign were only sent down to him from his Lord ! " You say: "Certainly, Allah is able to send down a sign, even though most of them do not know it".

The disbelievers were asking Prophet to bring a 'Miraculous sign' which is supernatural event, like Prophet *Moosa's* staff changed into snake and some events such as Prophet *Eisa* cured the disease of vitiligo, leprosy, and even gave life to the dead with Allah's Permission. As per the verses 29: 50-51 they ask: "Why have the signs not been sent down to him from his Lord?" Tell them: "The signs are in the hands of Allah. I am only a plain warner. "Is It not enough for them that We have sent down to you this Book, Al-Qur'an, which is recited to them, surely It is a Blessing and a Reminder for those who believe". The verse 17: 59 says: We refrain from sending miraculous signs only because the men of former generations had treated them as false. For example, We sent the she-camel to the people of *Thamood* - a manifest sign - but they laid violent hands on her. We send the signs only by way of warning, and if people reject the sign after receiving it, they are doomed. We do not send the miraculous sign for not other than making fear the people. The verse 10: 20 says: In regards to their saying: "Why has not a sign been sent down to him from his Lord?" Tell them: "Allah Alone has the knowledge of the unseen. Wait if you will: I too shall wait with you." In the Verses 13: 38, 14: 11 and 40: 78 say, no one can bring a miraculous sign from Allah except with the Permission of Allah.

Qur'an is the biggest miracle which explains all signs revealed before. It is the True Guidance to the entire mankind and Remedy for all diseases and Mercy for the believers. But today, Muslims all over the World do not utilize the Soul of Qur'an and thus they have become the worst of mankind in all sectors. In the verse 13: 11 says: the fact is that Allah never changes the condition of a people until they change it themselves. See the explanation 6: 26. By seeing the worst living condition of Muslims, non-Muslim people hate even to hear the word Qur'an and the name of Prophet *Muhammad*. In their sight *Muhammad* is a terrorist and cruel man. When the believers say that the Soul of Qur'an is the only instrument in order to form human unity to avoid bloodshed, they laugh and will ask, then why the bearers of the Qur'an are being hatred throughout the World, spited by others and are the contemptible? This condition will be continued until the arrival of *Maseeh-A-Ddajjal*. He will complete this darkness to the maximum. By the second coming *Eisa*, the non-Muslims will recognize *Islam* which is the only way of life satisfied by Allah. See explanation 2: 177, 211, 3: 49-50, 6: 4 and 5.

38. And no animals on Earth, nor any bird flying with its wings unless they exist communities like yourselves. We have not neglected anything in the Book; then to their Lord they will all be summoned.

All creatures belong to different communities like human and Jinn; and on the Day of Judgment all of them will be gathered together in front of Allah. Men have been provided with intelligence, and that is the difference of men from other creatures. Prophet taught that there are six hundred communities in the ocean whereas in the land there are four hundred communities. It is told in the verses 17: 44; 24: 41 and 22: 18 all these creatures are praising and glorifying Allah with their souls. But humans and *Jinns* are independent creatures provided with intelligence. Among them believers always remember Allah by learning and teaching the Soul of Qur'an in order to keep the Universe in its equilibrium. Thus they help to maintain other creatures praise and glorification. The believers- vicegerents of Allah- cultivate and provide food for other creatures also. In the verse 16: 89 it is told that We have sent down to you this Book which has explained everything- a Guide, a Mercy and Herald to Muslims- those who submit all to Allah. 'The Book' mentioned in the verses 10: 61; 11: 6; 22: 70; 28: 75; 34: 3; 35: 11; 57: 22; 64: 11 is also the Soul of Qur'an which is the complete form of

'*Al-Kithab*'. The verse 18: 54 says: We have given all kinds of examples in this Qur'an to make the people understand this Message, but man is exceedingly repudiating. The verse 30: 58 says: The fact is that We have set forth every kind of example for men in this Qur'an, but whatever verses you may bring, the disbelievers are sure to say: "You are preaching falsehood". The verse 39: 27 says: We have cited for mankind every kind of parables in this Qur'an, so that they may learn a lesson. And in the verse 17: 89 says: In this Qur'an We have used different methods to make the people understand the Message, yet the majority of them persist in disbelief.

In brief, the Soul of Qur'an is the knowledge of the Knower of all times. On the Day of Judgment every creatures will be gathered as witnesses, and will give them a chance to say complaints about all cruelties they were subjected to suffer from humans and *Jinns* and then they will be turned into dust. As per the verse 78: 40, on that Day the disbeliever who lived neglecting the Soul of Qur'an- which explains all these forthcoming facts will cry, saying: "I wish! I could remain merely dust" i.e. be were a dog, donkey, pig etc. See the explanation 2: 255; 3: 7-9; 5: 60 and 105.

39. And those who reject our verses, they are deaf and dumb in darkness, Allah lets anyone He wishes go astray, while He sets anyone He wishes upon the Straight path.

See the explanation 2: 170-171. The verse 8: 22 says: the worst 'living being' in the sight of Allah are the deaf and dumb people, those who do not utilize their intelligence. In the verse 7: 176 it is told that those who reject the Soul of Qur'an are compared to dogs which will not change its attitude whether it is disturbed or not. Then the verse ends as you explain one by one so that they may meditate and reflect. Read together the verses 8: 55, 33:73; 48: 6 and 98:6

Impartial Allah has given each soul the good way as well as the evil way. Therefore each individual should ask Guidance always to Allah by learning and teaching the Soul of Qur'an. In the verse 14: 22 it is told that there will be no excuse by blaming the satan for one's astray. The verse 16: 37 says: No matter how eager you may be for their Guidance, you should know that Allah does not guide those who go astray by themselves and such people will have no helpers. The verse 12: 103 says: Even though you try much, most of the people will not become believers. The verse 106 says: And most of them believe not in Allah except that they attribute partners. The verse 39: 41 says certainly we have sent down the Book with Truth for mankind then, anyone who is guided will be for his own sake while anyone who goes astray will only stray because of the Soul as well, you are not set up as any guardian over them. Read together the verse 16: 64. See explanation 4: 118; 5: 10, 15-16 and 6: 1.

40. Ask them: Have you ever thought whether, once Allah's torment comes to you or the Hour comes to you, will you appeal to someone instead of Allah if you are so truthful?

41. Rather it is to Him you will appeal and if He wishes, He will remove whatever you have appealed to Him about, and then you will forget what you have associated with Him.

The verses 10: 22-23 say: He is the One Who sends you traveling along on land and at sea until when you are on board a ship and sailing alone under a fair wind and they feel happy about it, a stormy wind comes upon them and waves reach at them from all sides and they think they are being surrounded by them. They appeal to Allah sincerely, submitting all life to Him: "If You save us from this, indeed we will be among grateful". Yet once He has saved them, behold! They rebel in the Earth without any Justice. Oh mankind! Your rebellion falls only against yourselves to be enjoyed during Worldly life; then to Us will be your return, and We will notify you about whatever you have been doing.

The verses 29: 65 and 66 say: If they embark on a ship, and the ship gets into trouble, they call upon Allah, being sincerely obedient to Him; but when He brings them safely to land, they start committing '*shirk*'. Such that they may become ungrateful for the blessing that We have bestowed on them and enjoy the life of this World! They will soon come to know the result of this behavior. The verse 31:32 says: When any giant wave covers them like a canopy, they pray to Allah with all devotion making their faith pure for Him. But when He delivers them safely to land, some of them falter between belief and unbelief. None reject Our verses except the treacherous and the ungrateful. The verse 39:59 says: Rather surely My verses came to you, but you rejected and you were arrogant against the verses and you were among the disbelievers. See explanation 6: 14.

42. And verily, We have sent to communities before you and seized with suffering and hardship, so that they might act submissively.

The verse 7: 205 says: And remember your Lord submissively in your soul and in reverence without raising your voice, both in the mornings and evenings; and be not of those who are heedless. The verse 32: 21 says: We shall certainly make them taste the lighter torments before the greater punishments, so that they may return to the Straight Path. The verse 30: 41 says: Mischief has appeared on the land and at the sea in consequence of men's own misdeeds. Through such, Allah let people to taste the fruit of their deeds, so that they may turn back from evil to the aim of life. Read together the verses 7: 172- 174. See explanation 5: 65 and 66.

43. Then why did they not act submissive when Our sufferings came to them, but instead their hearts were hardened. And satan made attractive to them whatever they were doing.

See the explanation 2: 61 and 99. In the verse 27: 24 it is told about Queen *Sheeba* and her people that satan has made their actions attractive to them and obstructed them from the proper way, so they were not the people who utilize the Guidance- the Soul of Qur'an. The verse 19: 83 says: Don't you see that We have sent satan to the disbelievers for fulfilling their whims? See the explanation 4: 78-79; 5: 90, 91 and 94.

44. Then, when they forgot what they had been reminded with, We opened up the doors of everything for them, until just when they were happiest with what they had been given, We caught them suddenly. Then they were becoming despair.

The Soul of Qur'an reminds us about Allah, about the actions what Allah had taken on ancestors, and what is going to happen in the future. The verses 43: 74 and 75 say: Surely the *mujrims* will abide in the punishment of Hell. Their punishment will never be lightened, and they shall remain despair therein. The satan prevents from the Soul of Qur'an. At last the Last Hour comes when there won't be even a single believer who utilizes the Soul of Qur'an, and thus everyone becomes hopeless transgressor or wrongdoer. Read together the verses 21: 46 and 45: 35. See the explanation 5: 49, 51, 67; 6: 25 and 36

45. Then the root of the people who had been doing wrong was cut off. And praise is to Allah, Lord of the Worlds.

The verses 21: 11-14 say: How many nations We have destroyed because of their wrong deeds and have replaced them by other nations! When they felt that Our punishment was coming, they took to their heels and fled. They were told: "Do not run away. Return to your luxuries of life and to your homes, so that you may be asked". They told: "Woe to us! Indeed we were wrongdoers". The verse 46 says: If a breath from your Lord's torment should ever touch them, they will say: "Woe to us! Indeed we were wrongdoers". The verses 4: 160-161 say: Because of the iniquity of those who call themselves Jews, their hindering of many people from the way of Allah taking of usury in spite of its prohibition, and cheating others of their properties- We made many wholesome things unlawful which were formerly lawful for them. We have prepared a painful punishment for those among them who reject faith. The verse 11: 117 says: It is not possible that your Lord would destroy the towns wrongfully while their habitants were trying to reform. See explanation 2: 57, 254; 3: 192 and 6: 21.

46. Ask them, have you ever considered whether, if Allah should snatch away your hearing and your eye sight, and sealed off your hearts, who is the deity besides Allah who can give them back to you. Look! How We explain Our verses, yet they still turn away.

The verse 36: 66 says: Had it been Our will, We could surely have blotted out their eyes; and let them run about groping for the way, then how could they see? The verses 23: 78; 32: 9 and 67: 23 say: He is the One Who has given you hearing, sight and intelligence- yet seldom you show gratitude. The verse 76: 2 says: Indeed, We have created man from the sperm drop containing both sexes, so that We have to test him. Therefore, We gave him the faculties of hearing and sight. So the aim of life is to identify the Creator and himself. Whoever utilizes faculties of hearing, sight and intelligence to identify the Creator submitting through the Soul of Qur'an are the grateful. See explanation 2: 18; 5: 19 and 6: 24.

47. Ask them: "Have you yourself considered whether, if Allah's torment should come to you suddenly or openly, any except wrongdoing people would be wiped out?

The verse 45:35 ends as, 'then any except transgressing people would be wiped out. The verses 5: 45 and 47 say, those who do not judge with the Soul of Qur'an in their individual, family and social life are the wrongdoers and transgressors respectively. It is told in the verse 17: 82, there is Mercy and Healing for believers in Qur'an, while for the wrongdoers it will increase nothing except losses. In the verse 9: 125 it is told that for the hypocrites the Qur'an will not increase other than filth over filth, and they will die as disbelievers. The verse 8: 33 says, Allah is not apt to punish them while you are among them, nor will Allah be their tormenter so long as they seek forgiveness. Here, 'while you are there among them' means while a believer who testifies the Prophet's life is remains on Earth will not be destroyed. See explanation 2:143; 5: 51; 6: 26-28 and 45.

48. And We do not send any Messengers except as heralds and warners. Then any one who believes and reforms, on them there shall be no fear and for them will not be grieved.

49. And those who reject Our verses the punishment will affect them because of they have been transgressing.

All Prophets are deputed for giving glad tidings to the believers and warning to disbelievers. No Prophet can bring anyone to the Guidance. See the verses 3:128 and 129. So everyone has to acquire the Guidance from their Lord through repeatedly asking by hearts as specified in the verse 20: 114 and going through the Guidance-the Soul of Qur'an. See explanation 1:7; 2: 213, 272; 5: 59 and 6: 21-26.

50. You say: 'I do not tell you that Allah's treasures lie with me nor do I know the unseen, nor do I even tell you I am an Angel. I merely follow what has been inspired to me. Then ask: Are the blind and sighted man equal? Will you not think and reflect?

The verse 11: 31 says: I do not say Allah's treasures lie with me, nor do I say I know the unseen, nor I do not say I am an Angel, nor do I tell those about whom your eyes are contempt that Allah will not give them anything good. Allah is quite Knower of what lies in their souls .If I say so, I will be certainly one among the wrongdoers. In the verse 39: 9 Allah commands to ask the prophet and the believer to the disbelievers, "are those who know the Soul of Qur'an, to be considered equal to those who do not know! Only the men of understanding can be reminded". The verse 40: 58 says, the blind and sighted person are not equal, nor are those who believe and do honorable deeds, and an evildoer, seldom do you remember in mind. In the verse 35: 19 it is told that blind and sighted will not be equal, and the verse 20 says that nor are the darkness and light, and the verse 21 says that nor the shadow and the sun's full heat, and the verse 22 says, the living and dead are not alike. Certainly, Allah lets to hear any one He wishes, while you will not make hear those in their graves. See the explanation 6: 36.

The question 'Will you not think and reflect' is not actually applicable to any other people except the Muslims who are reading these verses. In the verse 32: 18 by asking: 'Are the believers and hypocrites equal', Allah replies: 'No, they are not alike'. In the verse 11: 24 it is told that both groups can be compared to blind and a dumb man along side a sighted and hearing one. Are they alike for the purpose of comparison? Will you not remember with the hearts? So each individual should ask Guidance to their Lord continuously. All Prophets including *Muhammad* are the Messengers appointed by Allah from among the humans to introduce this fact to the people. Read together the verse 18: 110. In the verses 17: 90-94 it is told that the disbelievers will say: We will never believe in you unless you cause a spring to gush forth from the Earth for us, or have a garden full of date palms, grape vines and make rivers gush forth plentifully through the midst of them, or you cause the sky to fall in pieces upon us just as you claim, or bring Allah and His Angels to vouch for you, or you have a luxurious house built, or ascending up there; we will never believe in your climbing up there until you bring down a open Book for us to read. You say: "Glory is to my Lord, I am none except a human Messenger?" Read together the verses 7: 158, 203 and 10: 49. See the explanation 5: 109, 6: 7-9 and 17-19.

51. By the Soul of Qur'an warn those who fear that they will be summoned to their Lord; they will have no patron, nor any intercessor besides Him, so that they might be heedful.

The warning 'by the Soul of Qur'an' will be useful only to those who have understood the fact that everyone should have to answer before Allah about the life of every second after the 15th age of this World. The verse 32: 4 says: Allah is the One Who created the Heaven and the Earth, and that which is between them in six Days. Then He established himself the throne. You have no a protecting friend or intercessor besides Him. Will you then make others remembering with their hearts?. 'Heedful' are those who follow the Truth-the Soul of Qur'an as it should be followed vide verse 39: 33. The verses 10: 9-10 say: It is also a fact that those who believe sincerely in the Truth which is revealed in this Book and perform honorable deeds, their Lord will guide them because of their faith, and rivers will flow beneath their feet in the Gardens of bliss. Their slogan therein will be: "Glory be to You Oh Allah!" And their greetings therein will be "Peace be upon you!" And their closing remarks will be: "Indeed praises be to Allah, the Lord of the Worlds!" The verses 25: 56 and 57 say: And We has not sent you except as a bearer of glad tidings and a warner. Say: I ask you no reward for this, except that whosoever may choose a way unto his Lord. But whoever likes to return to His Lord, the Ticket mentioned in the verse 76: 29 should have to be taken. The verse 10: 3 says, your Lord is Allah, the one who has created heaven and Earth in six days. Then He ascended the Throne to regulate the matter, there is no intercessors except after His Permission. Such is Allah, your Lord. So you worship Him, will you not reflect. Read together the verses 9: 115. See explanation 2: 2 and 5: 48.

52. **Do not drive away those who appeal to their Lord wanting His presence in the early morning and evening. You have nothing to do with their reckoning, while they have nothing to do with your reckoning. Then if you drive them off, you would become one among the wrongdoers.**

The verse 18: 28 says: Restrain yourself concerning those who appeal to their Lord in the morning and evening wanting His presence; and yet do not let your eyes wander too far from them desiring the attraction of Worldly life; do not obey anyone whose heart is heedless about Our Reminder and follows his own whim, thus his case results in dissipation. In the verses 76: 23-25 it is told that: Verily, We are sending down this Qur'an stage by stage, so you show patience for the Judgment (the complete Qur'an) of your Lord and you don't obey any of them who are sinful hypocrites and ungrateful disbelievers. You keep remembrance of your Lord in the dawn and dusk. In the verses 33: 1 and 48 say: You keep Allah in hearts and don't obey disbelievers and hypocrites. Verily, Allah is the All Knowing, Wise.

In the verse 10: 104, Allah commands Prophet to say: Oh mankind, are you in doubt about my '*Dheen*'-way of life- surely, I am not living for other than Allah for whom you do live , but I live only for One Who makes you die, and I am ordered to be included among the true believers. The verse 105 says: And set your face steadfastly towards the *Dheen*, you will never be among those who associate partners to Allah. And in the verse 106 it is told that you don't invoke other than Allah who does not make either benefit or harm. If you do, then indeed, you will be among the wrongdoers. In the verses 26: 214-216 say: You warn the nearest of your family and lower your wings to the believers who follow you;

and if they are defying you, say: Indeed, I am not responsible for what you do. Read together the verses 17: 73-75; 32: 22 and 48: 29.This verse also teaches us the fact that everyone has to do his reckoning and no one can involve in others reckoning. See the explanation 2: 286; 3: 30; 5: 105 and 6: 159

The believers in all periods were the common people including slaves and poor. During Prophet's period the believers were from the slaves, dependants of the *Quraishi* rich people. Because of that they refused to sit with believers. They ridiculed Prophet and believers saying: Could Allah get only these poor and slaves from us. They blamed holding the sins of these poor and slaves committed before Islam and they said humiliatingly that these believers had been doing sins till yesterday and now they become great and good. This verse is revealed as the reply for such types of blaming. The verses 10: 40-41 say: Of these people there are some who will believe in It and some will not: and your Lord best knows the troublemakers. If they do not believe you, say: "I am responsible for my actions and you are for yours! You are not accountable for my actions, nor am I responsible for what you do".

Through the verses 39: 39 and 40 Allah command Prophet to say: "My people act according to your choice, I am so acting, then you shall know who will be given such torment as will disgrace Him, and on whom lasting torment will settled down". The verses 11: 27-30 say: In answer to this, the chiefs of the disbelievers among his people said: "We see you as no more than merely a human being like ourselves, and we see that no one has followed you except the meanest among us, whose judgment abilities are immature, and we find nothing in you which gives you superiority over us, in fact we think that you are a liar". Prophet Hood said: "Oh my people look! If I am given clear Evidence from my Lord, and He has bestowed on me His Grace, then you are blinded about It, shall We compel you to accept it while you dislike It? Oh my people! I do not ask you any wealth for this work; my reward comes only from Allah. Nor am I driving away those who believe; for they will be meeting their Lord. Yet I do see you are a people act out of ignorance. And Oh my people! Who will save me from Allah, if I drive them away? Will you not bear this in mind? Read together the verses 10: 71; 11: 53-56 and 91-95. See the explanation 2: 212; 3: 75-77 and 4: 1.

53. Even so We test some of them by means of others, so they may say: Are those the ones among us towards whom Allah has been gracious? Is Allah not quite Knower as to who are grateful?

The rich and arrogant people of all periods are not accepting Allah's good name '*Rahman*'- the Impartial- and they are with a wrong belief that they are given wealth and dignity as they are in Truth. And about the believers, as they are not in Truth are not bestowed with these wealth, and in the Hereafter also their condition will be the same. They thought so firmly and proudly forgetting that the mankind is deputed to Earth to undergo trial. See the explanation 2: 157. That is why Allah called them transgressors. They were ridiculing Prophet and the believers saying: Has Allah selected these people for leadership who have no power, status and wealth. The example of their joking towards prophet and believers and its reply can be read through the verses 43: 31-32 as: "Why is this Qur'an not revealed to a man of great importance from either town (*Mecca and Ta'if*)? Are they dividing up your Lord's Mercy? We divide up their livelihood among them during worldly life, and raise some of them higher in rank than others, so that some of them may take others for a laughing stock. Your Lord's Mercy is better than what they are collecting. The ridiculing question of hypocritical disbelievers to the Prophet as well as believer can be seen in the verse 38: 8 as, "has the Reminder been revealed just to him among us". Allah replies, "Indeed they are in doubt about My Reminder-the Soul of Qur'an, rather they have not yet tasted any torment". Through the verse 38: 9 Allah asks, or do they have treasures from the Mercy of your Lord, the Powerful and Bountiful. The verses 15: 87 and 88 say: We have given you seven oft repeated verses and the Glorious Qur'an. Do not strain your eyes towards what We let types of them enjoy to different people among them, nor grieve at their condition. Leave them alone; do not feel saddened upon them, and lower your sheltering wings for believers. The verse 25: 20 says: We have never sent any Messenger before you unless they ate food and walked around the market. We have placed some of them as a trial for others. Will you be patient while your Lord is observant? See the explanation 3: 196-197; 4: 113 and 5: 94.

54. And whenever those who believe in Our verses come to you, then you say to them: "Peace be up on you". Your Lord has prescribed Mercy for Himself. So any of you who commit evils out of

ignorance, then repents later on and reforms, then indeed your Lord will be Forgiving, Merciful.

55. And thus We explain Our verses, in order to manifest the way of mujrims.

See the explanation 4: 17-18. Allah is Merciful. He will forgive all the evil deeds done because of ignorance. For that one should read the Soul of Qur'an and by realizing the evils should repeatedly repent for it. And for great sins he should pay proper ransom also. This verse also teaches that those who teach the Soul of Qur'an have to greet those who are coming to learn; because the hypocrites will come as audience to hear the Soul of Qur'an. See the explanation 5: 41 and 42. Hypocrites had also come as audience near Prophet. Since to start greeting is optional, while reply is compulsory, the teacher can greet to those who are believers. As it is ordered to strive hard against the hypocritical disbelievers, it is not advisable to greet them. If they greet you, you return greetings only in the manner they have greeted you. See the explanation 4: 86.

Hypocrites hide the Soul of Qur'an knowingly. Therefore, Allah will never forgive them. Allah will only forgive to those who do wrong due to ignorance. Read together the verses 10: 33, 95 and 96. In the verses 36: 55-58, after explaining conditions of the companions of Paradise, it is told in the verses 59-60 that oh *mujrims*! You stand separately today; didn't I make a covenant from you that you don't serve satan? We cannot see such a covenant anywhere in the Qur'an; instead, the *mujrims* are those who do not keep the covenant made with Allah as per the verse 7: 172 and they are serving satan. See the explanation 2: 26-28. *Mujrims* are the hypocrites and '*fujjar*' who perform *swalath* and fasting without the remembrance of Allah. See the explanation 4: 142 and 143. The purpose of revealing the Trust-Soul of Qur'an- is to punish the hypocritical men and women and the associating men and women, and also to turn Allah upon believing men and women, Allah is forgiving, Merciful as told in the verse 33: 73. See the explanation of 2: 254; 6: 21 and 5:101.

Behavior of *mujrims*, wrongdoers and disbelievers differ from that of believers in all aspects. They will neither down their heads nor be humble or confess the sins nor spend money as ransom to make repentance. In the Qur'an *mujrims* are mentioned about 50 places. Prophet taught that they are the hypocrites and *fujjar* of Muslims. In the verses 15: 12 and 26: 200, it is told that We are piercing this Qur'an to the heart of the *mujrims* as a burned metal rod, but they will not believe. The verse 25: 31 says: Thus, We made *mujrim* as enemies to all Prophets; Allah is enough to guide and help you from them. On the Day of Judgment, as per the verse 34: 31, the *fujjar* who are included in *mujrims* will say: If it were not you, we should have been believers. And as per the verse 32 the hypocritical leaders will reply as: "Did we prevent you from the Guidance after It is come to you? Rather you yourselves were *mujrims*". On the Day of Judgment as per the verse 26: 99 the *fujjar* will say about the hypocritical leaders: None has obstructed us from the Guidance except the *mujrims*. As per the verse 37: 32, hypocrites will say to *fujjar* on the Day of Judgment that we misled you, for we ourselves were astray; and in the verse 33, on that Day both the leaders and followers will be partners in the punishment. In the verse 34, it is told that thus shall We deal with the *mujrims*. From all these verses we can understand that the *mujrims* include the hypocritical leaders of Muslims and the *fujjar* who follow them blindly. See the explanation 1: 7; 2: 166 and 167.

Oh Allah, do not include us among the mujrims. Make us to live by seeing You and make us living to you submissive by mind, words, actions by utilizing the Soul of Qur'an which is Your permission. Enter us the Paradise with the virtuous and victorious with the Mercy of You; Oh, the best among the Merciful. If one pray like this, he brings in practice at least hundred verses of the Qur'an.

56. Say them: Verily I am forbidden to serve those whom you appeal to instead of to Allah. Say: I do not follow your whims: In that case I would go astray, and not to be Guided.

Allah is the only Lord of all of you and me. And He is the one who decides death, life, birth etc. So the believers should not live according to their whims. Instead they will be the vicegerent of Allah having His character by the Soul of Qur'an and helping Him by conveying His Message to entire mankind. They are the one who rightly guided. See the explanation 1: 4; 2: 120, 145 and 6: 50-52.

57. Say: Indeed I am upon an evidence from my Lord, while you have rejected It. I do not have what you are trying to hurry up; certainly the judgment belongs none except to Allah. He relates the Truth, and He is the best among Deciders.

58. Say: If I had what you seek to hurry up, the matter would have been settled between you and me. And Allah is quite knower with the wrongdoers.

'*Bayyina*'- Evidence- and Truth mentioned in the verse is, the Soul of Qur'an. But in the verses 57: 25; 23: 28, '*Bayyinath*' means various signs and divine miracles. The verse 98: 1 says, the disbelievers from the people of the Book and the *mushriks* doing *shirk* will not be released from their doubt until they receive the *Bayyina*. And in the verse: 98:2 the '*Bayyina*' is explained as the Messenger from Allah who makes '*Thilavath*'-recite- the holy Qur'an upon them. The verse: 4 says, those who given the Book were not divided except after they received the *Bayyina*. Here *Bayyina* means the only Book i.e. the Soul of Qur'an. See explanation 2: 2 and 121. Muslims boast and pride saying that the biggest Miraculous sign given to Prophet is Qur'an, but they hide and reject It and thus they are more deviated than that of any other people even than 'Meccan Mushriks', Jews and Christians during the period of Prophet in *Madeena*. The disbelievers of all the time are hurrying up for the Day of Judgment promised by the Qur'an. The disbelievers' asking to the believers 'when this promise will be fulfilled, if you are so truthful' is mentioned in the verses such as 10: 48; 21: 38; 27: 71; 32: 28; 34: 29; 36: 48 and 67: 25. The verse 10:11says: If Allah were to hasten up evil for mankind just as they seek to hasten good, then their deadline would have been decreed for them. We leave those who do not hope to meet Us, blundering aimlessly in their arrogance. The verse 19 says: And mankind was none except one community; then they disagreed. If word had not come on ahead from your Lord, what they had been disagreeing over would have been settled for them.

The verse 35:45 says: If Allah should take mankind to task for whatever they have been earning, He would not leave any creature on its surface; but He puts them off for a specific period. Once their dead line comes, Allah will indeed be observant with His servants. Read together the verses 16: 61, 22: 47, 33: 63 and 41: 47. See explanation 2: 213; 6: 3 and 21.

59. He holds the keys of the unseen; none knows the unseen except He; and He knows whatever exist on land and at sea. And no leaf falls down except He knows it, nor any seed lies in the darkness of the Earth, or anything wet or dry except recorded in a Clear Book.

The clear Book means the Soul of Qur'an which is the knowledge of three times -past, present and future- from the Knower of all times. 'By the clear Book' mentioned both the verses 43: 2 and 44: 2 is the Soul of Qur'an. In the verse 36: 69 it is told that this is nothing except the Reminder and a clear reading. See explanation 2: 2,107; 4: 108 and 6:38.

The verse 10: 61 says: No matter what affairs you may be engaged in, what portion from the Qur'an you may be reciting, and whatever deeds you may be doing; We are a Witnesses thereof when you are deeply occupied with it: for there is not even an atom of anything in Earth or in Heaven that is hidden from your Lord, neither anything smaller than that nor larger, but is recorded in a Clear Book. See explanation 2: 255, 284; 3: 58 and 79.

60. And He is the One Who takes your souls at night and He knows what you have accomplished during the day, then next day raises you up again to complete your allotted span of life. To Him you shall all return, and then He will notify you about whatever you have been doing."

The verse 39: 42 says: Allah takes back the souls of men upon their death and of the living during their sleep. He withholds the souls of those on whom He has passed the decree of death, and restores the rest till an appointed term. Surely there are signs in this for those who meditate and reflect. So Allah takes back soul both during the sleep and death. Then, what is the difference between the sleep and death? In sleep only the soul departs from the body whereas in death '*Rooh*'- spirit- together the soul and life is departed. The '*Rooh*' blown to the foetus in the fourth month of the pregnancy as mentioned in the verse 32: 9 is separated from the body is called the death. In the verse 32: 11 says: In order to gather that '*Rooh*', an Angel is appointed and then all of you will be returned to your Lord. See the explanation 2: 28, 4: 1 and 5: 105.

Prophet taught to pray when approach to sleep "Oh Allah, with the name of You I die and live, if you catch my soul there, You bless her, if You are sending her back, You keep her with the soul of Your honorable servants". And while awaking from sleepiness "The praise is to Allah Who brought us to live after had our death, and to Him we will be resurrected and gathered in the last". Even though he or she is single person, says 'we' since his or her 'soul mate'-Jinn companion- is also included. Read together the sub title '*Rooh*' in the introduction.

61. He has Irresistible Supreme power over His servants. He sends guardian Angels over you, so that whenever the death approaches

for any of you, Our messengers will gather him, and they are not negligent in performing their duty.

62. Then they will be sent back to Allah, their true Patron. Surely, the Judgment belongs to Him; He is the Swiftest Reckoner.

The verse 13:11says: Each person has been assigned guardian Angels before him and behind him, who watch him by the command of Allah. The fact is that Allah never changes the condition of a people until they intend to change it themselves. If Allah wants to afflict a people with misfortune, none can ward it off, nor can they find any Patron besides Him. The verse 82: 10 says: You should know that guardian Angels have indeed been appointed over you. The verse 11 says: They are honorable writers and in the verse 12 says: They know what you are doing. In the verse 86: 4 says: over each soul there is an appointed guardian Angel. In the verse 50: 18 says: Not a single word does he utter but there is a vigilant guard ready to note it down. These guards and recorders are Angels. When the term determined for them is completed, the Angel of death put in charge of him comes with more Angels and gather the *Rooh*-spirit- as mentioned in verse 32: 11.

'And they are not negligent in performing their duty' means all Angels are believers and they perform their duty promptly. The verse 66: 6 says: O believers! Save yourselves and your families from Hellfire, whose fuel is men and stones; in the charge of fierce and mighty Angels who never disobey Allah's command and who promptly do what they are commanded. The verse 40: 7 says: Those Angels who bear the Throne of Allah and those who stand around It glorify their Lord with His praises, believe in Him and implore forgiveness for the believers, saying: "Our Lord! You embrace all things with Your mercy and knowledge. Forgive those who repent and follow Your Way-the Soul of Qur'an-, and save them from the punishment of the Blaze. Prophet taught, everyone is connected ten Angels in the day and ten in the night. There will be Angels as guards when he is in the remembrance of Allah with the Soul of Qur'an. While one is in the state of forgetting Allah only the satanic *Jinn* companion will be with him and then the evil and distress happens. See the explanation 4: 78 and 79. The verses 41: 30-31 say: Certainly, those who say: "Our Lord is Allah," and then stay firm on it, the Angels will descend on them, saying: "Let nothing fear or grieve you. Rejoice for the good news of Paradise that has been promised to you. We are your protectors in this life and in the Hereafter. There you shall find all that your soul's desire and all that you ask for:

Only with the Soul of Qur'an one can acquire tranquility and peace condition as told in the verse 13: 28. Read together the verses 89: 27-30. Allah is only real Ever living Master, Patron and Owner of you. From Him everyone comes here, and to Him everyone will be returned. But, only the believers who live only for Allah recognize this fact. That is why the believers even if he is in single, says through the verse in 1: 4 as, "we do live only to you, and for this we seek help only from You". The verse 35: 39 says: He's the one Who has made you vicegerent on the Earth. Then, whoever disbelieves bears the burden of his disbelief; and for the disbelievers their disbelief does not increase anything except the loathing near their Lord and the disbelievers do not gain anything except an increase in their loss. Read together the verse 39: 7. See the explanation 3: 199; 5: 48; 6: 7 and 19.

63. Ask them: "Who saves you from the darkness on land and at sea?" you appeal to Him humbly, politely and fearfully in inner mind" if He will rescue from this, we will be among the grateful.

64. Say them: "Allah will rescue you from it, and from all distress. Yet you still associate others with Him!"

Allah saves you when you are aimless in the darkness of the wide desert and he is the only one who saves you when you are aimless without knowing the route in the wide sea. In these occasions everyone pray to Allah entrusting to Him completely with fear in his inner and devoting complete life to Him. Through both the verses 7: 55 and 205 Allah orders the believers to pray with their soul humbly and politely fear Him with their hearts and without pronouncing 'Allah' with their tongue irrespective of dawn or dusk. The verses 16: 15-17 say: "He has set up mountains as head lands on Earth lest it away with you and rivers and paths so that you may be guided; as well as land marks, and also by the stars they guided. Then the One Who Creates is like the one who does not create anything? Will you not remember this with hearts?" The verses 30: 33-34 say: 'When an affliction befalls the people, they turn in prayer to their Lord in repentance. But when He let them taste a blessing from Him, lo! Some of them associate patrons in their Lord, showing no gratitude for what We have given them. Enjoy yourselves; soon you will find out your folly. See explanation 3: 190 and 191.

'Distress' includes difficult, danger, trouble, dilemma, confusion, disaster etc. The verse 21: 87-88 say: "We blessed *Yoonus* when he departed in anger, thinking We would not take him to task for this, but later he prayed to Us from the depths of darkness, "There is no Deity but You, Glory be to You! Indeed I was the one who committed wrong." We accepted his prayer and delivered him from the distress; thus do We save the believers". Before all of them Prophet *Nooh* had prayed to Us, then We replied to his prayer and We saved him from the serious disaster. We saved him from the people who rejected our verses. Verily, they were evil people. Thus We drowned them. Read together the verses 21: 76-77; 37: 76 and 115. The verse 21: 90 says, all these Prophets were quick in emulating for good deeds and they were praying to Us sacrificing all they had and fearing in their inner with expectation. See explanation 2: 152 and 6: 40-44.

65. Say: "He is able to send torment from above upon you or from underneath your feet, or to divide you to different groups and there by to attack one with others". See, how We explain our verses to them so that they may understand the aim of the life.

This verse teaches that Allah is capable of punishing us by natural calamities like flood, storm, earthquake, famine, and drought or divides us into different groups to punish us by clashing with one group to other. The verses are explained like this so as to understand the aim of life and not to be divided and be among the single party of Allah by holding steadfastly the Soul of Qur'an. See explanation 3: 101-103. In *Islam* from the beginning to the last, only one party is in Truth. Read together the verses 5: 56 and 58: 22. And all other parties belong to satan's party as told in the verse 58: 19. See explanation 2: 113 and 176.

Once Prophet at his night *swalath* prayed for three things, but Allah answered only for two. That is not to destroy my community with natural disasters like floods, storms etc. just like you destroyed the previous communities and not to be suppressed my people by other people. But, Allah did not answer the third prayer that not to divide the Muslims in to groups. Today, we can see that the Muslims are divided in to more groups than that of any other people and each group attack one another. And by hiding the Soul of Qur'an they encourage the coming of '*Maseeh-A-Ddajjal*' who will implement false hood all over the World except in *Hijaz*- the province including *Mecca* and *Madeena*. Thus the principle of not answering to the third prayer of Prophet will be fulfilled by this. In the verses 7: 50- 51; 41: 26- 28 and 63: 4 it is told that the hypocrites who repudiate or hide the verses of Qur'an are the enemies of Allah, Prophet and believers. With the second coming of *Eisa*, all other people of the World will recognize and accept *Islam* as the only true way of life and then the party of believers under the leadership of *Eisa* will implement the command of the verses 4: 91, 9: 123, and 33: 61 by killing the hypocrites and their blind followers who accept *Maseeh-A-Ddajjal* as Prophet at first, and even as Lord later. See explanation 2: 6-7, 251; 4: 159 and 6: 26.

The soul of Qur'an teaches the aim of life i.e. to identify the Lord, ourselves and to prepare the Paradise here in this World in order to inherit It in the Hereafter. See the explanation 3: 136. The hypocrites killed by Allah have lost this aim. The verse 63: 3 says: 'that is because they believed, then disbelieved, therefore their hearts are sealed so that they understand not the aim of life'. The verse 7: 179 says: 'Certainly, We have destined many *Jinns* and human beings for Hell; those are the ones who have hearts with which they do not understand the aim of life, they have eyes with which they do not see the Soul of Qur'an, they have ears with which they do not hear the Soul of Qur'an. They are like cattle - or even worse than them, because they are those who are heedless'. The verse 9:87 says about the hypocrites who didn't participate with the Prophet in the *Thabook* expedition: 'They preferred to be with those who remain behind; as a result, a seal was set upon their hearts so that they do not understand the aim of life'. The verse 9:127 says about the hypocrites: 'Whenever a *Surath* is revealed they look at each other as if to ask, "Is anyone watching?" Then they silently slip away. Allah has slipped their hearts from the Guidance, for they are a people who do not want to understand the aim of life'. See the explanation 2: 99; 4: 118 and 6: 25.

66. And your people rejected it although It is the Truth. Say them I am not your 'Vakeel'-bearer of responsibility.

See the explanation 2: 147. In the verse 39: 41 says: 'O Prophet, surely We have revealed to you the Book with the Truth, for the instruction of Mankind. He who follows the Right Way shall follow It for his own good; and he who goes astray shall do so at his own peril. You are not set up as any guardian over them. The verse 62 says: 'Allah is the Creator of all things and for all things He is the Guardian'. In the verse 64: 13 says: 'Allah! There is no Deity except Him; therefore, in Allah Alone let the believers put their trust'. The verse 43: 44 says: 'This Qur'an is a Reminder for you and your people; and both of you shall soon be questioned about It'. Therefore it is the duty of the Muslims to propagate the Message of Allah to all His creators irrespective of nation or religion. Otherwise they have to bear the evil burden of other people and admit to the bottom of Hell even without trial. See the explanation 5: 67. Both in the verses 39: 69 and 75 it is told that the Balance of the Judgment will be the Truth-the Soul of Qur'an. Those who belie or reject after receiving It are the wrongdoers as well as disbelievers as per the verses 29: 68, 39: 32. As per the verse 25: 18 the honorable people on the Day of Judgment will say against the people who lived here forgetting the Soul of Qur'an that they were a worthless people. As per the verse 25: 30 on the Day of Judgment Prophet will come with the Qur'an and complain to Allah against this people that my people of this were living neglecting this Qur'an. The verse 38: 26 says: 'Oh Dawood! Indeed We have made you vicegerent in the Earth, so judge among the people with the Truth and do not follow your own desires which will lead you away from Allah's path. Indeed for those who go astray from Allah's path will have a severe punishment because of forgetting the Day of Reckoning'. In the verse 47: 38 says, if this people are not ready to spend their wealth to learn and teach the Soul of Qur'an, then Allah will bring another people in the place of them. Prophet taught, those who live hold fasting the Soul of Qur'an, their enemies can't make any disturbance to them. See explanation 2: 186; 3: 122; 4: 133 7and 5: 48.

67. For every prophecy there is an appointed time, and soon you will come to know.

68. And whenever you see those who ridicule Our verses, avoid them till they speculate about some other topic of conversation. And even if satan ever makes you to forget to do so, then do not sit around with such wrong doing people once you become remembered.

The 'wrong doing people' mentioned in this verse include both the hypocrites who say the Qur'an verses falsely and the disbelievers who hear it. The verse 17: 82 says: 'This Qur'an will not increase other than losses for the wrong doing people'. See the explanation 2: 254; 3: 78 and 4: 140.

69. And those who keep Allah in their heart are not accountable for them in any way, but to remind them so that they may become more heedful.

The heedful people have no responsibility to lead others in to Truth, but to remind others with the Soul of Qur'an in order that they become more heedful, and have to witness to others the Qur'anic life. They should not have chance to say excuse tomorrow, the day on which the skins, hearings, sights, hands and legs will reflect. Moreover, they have to be reminded with the Soul of Qur'an in order to have peaceful life in this World. The verse 7: 164 teaches about the heedful people who command with the righteous and forbid the evils as 'Also remind them about the conversation among some of them, when they asked: "Why do you admonish a people whom Allah will destroy or sternly punish?" They replied: "To be able to offer an excuse before our Lord, that we did discharge our duty, and also in the hope that they may refrain from His disobedience and become heedful". See explanation 2: 143; 4: 89- 91; 5: 60 and 105.

70. And leave those people alone, who take their religion as mere play and amusement and are deceived by the life of this World. However, keep on admonishing them with the Soul of Qur'an, lest any soul become reckless with what he has earned; he will have no patron nor any their intercessor besides Allah, and if he seeks to offer every imaginable ransom, it shall not be accepted from them. Such are those who are reckless with what he has earned. For them have boiling water to drink and painful torment because of their hiding the verses of Qur'an.

This verse also teaches that each individual is earning the Paradise here. The Soul of Qur'an should be utilized here as the Balance and Insight in order not to become despair in the punishment of hereafter. The verses 25: 27-29 say: 'on that Day the wrongdoer will bite his hands saying: "Oh, would that I had only taken the pathway alongside the Messenger!" Woe to me, Would that I had never chosen so and so for my companion. He was the one who led me astray from the Soul of Qur'an even after It had reached me. Satan is ever treacherous to man". Therefore in order to include Allah's party one must holdfast the Soul of Qur'an which is the Rope of Allah stretched from the Paradise to Earth. See explanation of 3: 90-91; 4: 77; 5: 57-58 and 6: 44.

71. Ask them: "Should we appeal to something that can neither benefit us nor harm us, instead of Allah? Shall we turn on our heels after Allah has guided us, like the one whom satan has enticed away on

Earth, while his companions are calling him to the Guidance: "Come this way!" Tell them: "Allah's Guidance is the only Guidance. We have been ordered to submit ourselves peacefully to the Lord of Worlds.

The verse 7: 175 says: 'Recite them the history of the person to whom We gave our verses but he turned away from them, as a result Satan persuaded him until he became aimless of life'. The verse 25: 55 says: 'Yet they worship those deities besides Allah who can neither help nor harm them, the disbeliever has become a helper of every rebel against his own Lord. Through this verse the believers, the party of Allah, are ordered to ask to the disbelievers, who are the party of the satan Shall we turn on our heels after Allah has guided us, like the one whom satan has enticed away on Earth, while his companions are calling him to the Guidance: "Come this way!" Tell them: "Allah's Guidance is the only Guidance. We have been ordered to submit ourselves peacefully to the Lord of Worlds. In addition the believers are commanded to tell through the verse 109: 6 to the disbeliever 'for you your way of life, and for me the True way of life.' See explanation 1: 4; 4: 116, 120 and 5: 72.

72. And to keep up swalath and heed Him; and He is the One to Whom you will be summoned.

Believers are ordered to be vicegerent of Allah, who lives and serve only for Him, for this the Soul of Qur'an is to be followed. In the verse 20: 14, it is ordered to perform *swalath* in order to maintain the remembrance of Allah with the Soul of Qur'an. In the verse 29:45 says: the utmost importance is the remembrance of Allah with the Soul of Qur'an. The verse 35: 29 says, indeed the ones who recite Allah's Book, keep up *swalath* and spend something both secretly and publicly from whatever He has provided for them, can hope for a business which will never slacken. The verses 8: 2-4 say: 'The true believers are those whose hearts tremble with fear when Allah is remembered, and whose faith increase as they listen to His verses and they put their Trust in their Lord, who establish *swalath* and spend in charity out of the sustenance which We have given them. Such are the true believers; they hold ranks with their Lord as well as forgiveness and generous provisions. The verses 39:22 and 23 say: 'Is the one whose hearts Allah has opened to *Islam* and is walking with the Light -Soul of Qur'an- from his Lord like the one who has learned no lesson and is still a disbeliever. So woe to those whose hearts are hardened against the remembrance of Allah! They are clearly in error. Allah has sent down the finest beautiful speech-a Book consists in Its verses yet repeating its teachings in different ways. The skins of those who dread their Lord tingle with it; then their skins and their hearts are softened up for remembering Allah. That is Allah's Guidance: He guides anyone He wishes with It, while anyone whom Allah lets go astray will have no one to guide him. Read together the verse 7: 170 and 38: 8. See the explanation 2: 238-239; 3: 79; 4: 82 and 103.

73. And He is the One Who really created the Heavens and the Earth with the Truth. And any Day He says: 'Be!' then it is! "His speech is the Truth. And He will hold the control on the Day when the Trumpet will be sounded. He is the knower of the unseen and Visible, and He is the Wise, well acquainted"

It is told in Qur'an in several places that Allah has created the Heavens and the Earth only with the Truth. That means there is a great aim behind that creation. Man is deputed to Earth on the fourth phase is in order to testify whether he fulfils the aim of life or not. The verse 45: 22 says: Allah created Heaven and Earth with the True purpose, and every soul may be rewarded for whatever it has been earned and they will not be harmed. The verses 44: 38-39 say: We have not created the Heavens, Earth and all between them playfully. And We have not created them except with Truth, even though most of them don't realize It. The verse 23: 115 says: Did you think that We had created you without any purpose and that you would never return to Us for accountability?" The verse 38: 27 says: We didn't create Heaven and Earth, and whatever in between them as falsehood. That is the guess of those who disbelieve, so those who disbelieve should have '*wail*' from the Fire. The verse 15: 85 says: We have not created the Heavens and the Earth, and all that between them except with the Truth. The Last Hour will surely come, so overlook their misbehavior in a gracious manner. The verses 21: 30-31 say: Have not the disbelievers ever considered that the Heavens and Earth were once one mass, then We split them asunder? And We made water to survive all living things. Will they still not believe? And We have planted mountains on Earth lest it should tilt to one side with them and We left between them open passages so that they may find the right direction.

'His speech' means, the Soul of Qur'an. The verse 21: 47 says: On the Day of Judgment We shall set up scales of Justice i.e. the Soul of Qur'an, so that no one will be dealt with unjustly in any way; even if someone has an act as small as a grain of a mustard seed, We will bring it to account, and sufficient are We to settle the accounts. The verse 41:53 says: Soon shall We show them Our verses in the universe and in their own souls, until it becomes clear to them that this Qur'an is indeed the Truth. Is it not enough that your Lord is a witness over everything? On the Day of Judgment when the trumpet is blown for the first time with the command of Allah; everyone in the Heaven and Earth will be perished except those Allah wishes, is told in the verse 39: 68. Read together the verses 27: 87 and 36: 49-50. The verse 14: 48 says: Warn them of the Day when the Earth will be changed to a different Earth and the Heavens as well, and all of them will stand before Allah, the One, the Irresistible. The verse 27: 88 says: These Mountains which you see and think are firmly fixed, will pass away like clouds. Such is the might of Allah, Who has perfected all things. He is aware of what you do. And the verses 101: 1-5 say: The Calamity! What is the Calamity? Ah, how will convey unto you what the calamity is! A day wherein mankind will be as thickly scattered moths. And the mountains will become as carded wool.

When the second trumpet is blown, all of them will be raised from the cemetery and will rush to their Lord just like rushing to a setted pole. The verse 14: 43 says: they will be running in terror with their heads uplifted, staring but seeing nothing and their hearts utterly vacant. The verses 36: 51-52 say: Then a trumpet shall be blown and, behold, they will be raised up from their graves and hasten to their Lord. And with the third trumpet all creatures will be presented before Allah as told in the verse 36: 53. Both the verse 36: 54; 39: 69 say: On that Day no soul will be suffered unjustly and no one will be rewarded except for they were doing. On that Day dominion rests only with the Impartial- Most Gracious. The verse 25: 26 says: That Day will be very strain to the deniers. Read together the verses 25: 27-30. On that Day, the skins, sights and hearings of deniers will witness against themselves as told in the verses 41: 19-24. The verse 25: 24 says: On that day companions of Paradise will be in the best rest houses and they will spend their noon in the best condition. Read together the verses 36: 55-68. See explanation 1: 3; 2: 255; 5: 117- 120; 6: 59.

74. And remember that Ibrahim told to his father 'Aazar': Do you accept idols as deities; indeed I see you and your people in clear astray.

The name of Prophet *Ibrahim's* father is quoted only in this verse in Qur'an. As per the verse 14: 35 it is mentioned what *Ibrahim* prayed: 'Oh my Lord!

Make this land peace and secure, and avoid me and my progeny from serving and worshipping the idols'. As per the verse 19: 42 it is to be remembered what *Ibrahim* told his father: Oh my father, why do you worship to those neither hear nor perceive, and does not benefit you in anyway. As per the verse 43: Oh my father, I have been given some knowledge which has not come to you, so follow me; I will guide you to the Straight path. As per the verse 44: Oh my father, do not serve satan! since he was defiant towards the Impartial. And as per the verse 45: Oh father, by adopting satan as your patron, I fear the punishment of the Most Gracious will be affected on you. Read together the verses 21: 51-73; 26: 69, 104; 29: 16- 27 and 37: 83-113. See explanation 1: 4 and 7.

75. And just like we showed Ibrahim the secret sovereignty of the Heavens and Earth in order to include him among the firm believers.

As per the verse 2: 260 *Ibrahim* had asked, how does Allah give life to the death? So this incident of showing the secret of the universe was occurred after that event. As per the verse 27: 82, being one of the ten signs of the last day an animal will come and say 'humans are not confirmed belief in Our verses', is warned. As per the verse 45: 20 it is told that the Soul of Qur'an is Insight for mankind and It is Guidance and Mercy to confirmed believers. The confirmed belief can be had only with the Soul of Qur'an. The verse 69:51 says, and indeed It is the certainty giving Truth. The confirmed persons are otherwise known as '*Khabeer*' as in the verse 25: 59. See explanation 2: 4; 3: 7 and 6: 27-28.

76. Then, when the night overshadowed him with its darkness, he saw a star. He said: "This is my Lord." But when it set, he said: "I do not love setting things.

The people of that period of *Ibrahim* were not only serving and worshipping the idols, but also were serving, worshipping and fearing non living things like the sun, the moon, stars and various living things. When the night over shaded by the darkness and a star was visible clearly, he invited the attention of the people to the star, and when it set, he said I do not like to consider those which disappear as my Lord. My Lord is Allah who is eternally living, having no sleep and slumber, having no beginning and ending. He is the Dictator Who rules completely with Supreme power.

77. Then, when he saw the moon rising up he said: this is my Lord; and when it set, he said if my Lord does not guide me, certainly I would be among the strayed people.

This verse teaches that the people who maintain and follow the superstitious beliefs based on the sun, moon and stars are gone astray from the Straight path. When we recite in the verse 1: 7, 'and not the way who gone astray', we should bear in mind that do not include us with the people among Muslims who follow and maintain such superstitious belief. See explanation 3: 90; 4: 50 and 51.

78. Then, when he saw sun rising up he said: this is my Lord this is even greater. Then, when it set he said: 'Oh my people, indeed I am innocent of what you associate with Allah.

The style of propagating, calling, policy and wisdom of the Prophets are to be understood from these verses. But this method will be followed only those who know the Soul of Qur'an- the '*Hikmath* -Wisdom. See the explanation 2: 269. The others will adopt style of hypocrites to satisfy the majority and thus to keep the interest of their organizations; they are the party of satan. See the explanation 4: 137-139. It is notable that the stars and the moon are used in masculine gender whereas the sun in feminine gender.

79. Verily, I have turned my face straight forward to the One Who has asunder the Heaven and Earth, and I am not included among the associators.

As per the verses 10: 104- 106 Allah orders Prophet to say: oh mankind, if you are doubt in my *Dheen* -way of life-, I do not live for those you live besides Allah, but I live to Allah alone who shall cause you to die and I am ordered to be among the believers and to turn my face towards Him; you do not ascribe partners in Power and Rights of Allah, you do not call to pray anyone besides Allah who cannot cause you any benefit or harm, If you do so, verily, you will be among the wrongdoers. See explanations 2: 135; 3: 67; 6: 55 and 56.

80. When his people started arguing with him, he told them: "Are you arguing with me concerning Allah, whereas He has guided me? I do not fear what you associate with Him, except my Lord should wish something; the knowledge of my Lord encompasses everything. Will you not make remember others?

When these verses were explained to the Meccan pagans, they argued to Prophet Mohammad such as the people of Prophet *Ibrahim* argued with him. We can see through the verses 3: 65 and 66 ' the Jews and the Christians of *Madeena* in the period of Prophet *Muhammad* also argued with him about Allah just like the people of *Ibrahim* argued with him. We can see the people who associate others with the dominion of Allah in every period saying that the Prophet and the believers were suffering the bad luck due to the curse of idols, honorable men, angles, *Jinns* etc. to whom they invoked and prayed, worshipped, served and devoted offering instead of Allah.

As per the verses 11: 53-56, the people of Prophet Hood say: Oh Hood! you have not brought clear Evidence, we will not be avoiding our deities on account of your words, we will not believe in you. We say that you are suffering from some evil affection of some of our deities. Then Prophet Hood replied, I bear witness Allah alone as Deity, and you witness that I am innocent of what you associate with Him, plot you altogether against me, no need to give me respite, indeed I have entrusted on Allah Who is the Lord of me as well as your, and there is no creature except He holds its forelock. Indeed my Lord is in Straight path. Believers are having the belief that no evil will be taken place without the permission of Allah, Who is the owner and controller of all things and Who has acquainted knowledge of all things. Prophet *Ibrahim* was one among the believing servants as told in the verse 37:111. See explanation 4: 78-79; 6: 37 and 38.

Today the question 'Will you not make remember others?' is to the Muslims only who recite the Qur'an. Among the Muslims the hypocrites and the *fujjar* will not reply to this question, but the believer gives reply to the question by conveying the Soul of Qur'an to entire mankind irrespective of nations or religions. The verse 54: 17 says, verily Allah has made the Soul of Qur'an very easy to understand with hearts, then is there anyone to ready for it? Therefore, the believers by utilizing the Soul of Qur'an as the Criterion and the Balance distinguish their Lord Allah and others, the ability of Allah and others. They by entrusting all affairs in Allah without fearing anyone except Him, will lead a life depending upon only Him, and will walk keeping head upright along the Earth. The verse 32: 4 also ends with the question 'Will you not make remember others?' See the explanation 2: 152; 3: 79, 122 and 4: 116- 118.

81. And how should I fear what you associate with Allah while you do not fear having associated something with Him for which He has

not sent you down any authority? Which of either group deserves more security? If you are knowing.

The challenge made by Prophet *Nooh* to his people just like Prophet *Ibrahim* challenged the people who associate in the dominion of Allah is told in the verse 10: 71 as: Recite to them the history of *Nooh* when he said to his people: "O my people! If my staying with you and remembering you with Allah's verses is unbearable to you, then I entrusted on Allah; so make your designs as well as you have associate with Allah on me, then do not let your plan seeing any gloomy to you, thus execute it against me and give me no respite. The challenge made by Prophet Muhammad on his people is told in the verses 7: 194-195 as, certainly those you call besides Allah are servants just like yourselves. Call to them, and let them answer to you, if you are so truthful. Have they feet to walk with, or hands to hold things with, or eyes to see with, or ears to hear with? Say: "Call all your associates instead of Allah, then plot against me and no need to give me any respite.

The entire mankind belongs to two parties- either Allah's party (58: 22) or satan's party (58:19). All Muslim organizations belong to satan's party and they are the *mushriks* who associate others in the dominion of Allah against the verses such as 21: 92-94; 23:51-53; 30:31-32 and 42:13-15. By the second coming of *Eisa*, all non-Muslim people will recognize *Islam* and *Eisa*. Then the party of believers becomes the major party, and they will kill the hypocrites and those whose hearts contain malice to implement the command of the verses 33: 60-61. See the explanation 3: 103, 4: 159 and 5: 49.

82. Those who believe and do not surround their faith with wrongdoing, such are having more secured and they are the better guided.

Allah has taught the soul of Qur'an to all mankind from the Paradise itself.It is the food,cloth and sight of the human soul. The verse 58: 22 says: You will never find any people who believe in Allah and the Last Day on friendly terms with those who oppose Allah and His Messenger, even though they are being fathers, sons, brothers or their relatives. It is they in whose hearts Allah has inscribed faith and has strengthened them with a spirit of His own. He will admit them to Gardens beneath which rivers flow, to live therein forever. Allah will be well pleased with them, and they will be well pleased with Him. They are the party of Allah. Beware! Surely it is the party of Allah that will be successful. The spirit mentioned in the verses 16: 2 and 42: 52 is the words of Allah mentioned in the verses 18: 109 and 31: 27 which is the explanations of the Qur'an. It will not be completed by speaking or writing. Through the verse 17: 85, Allah commands Prophet to answer for the question about the spirit that it is the matter of my Lord, and you are not given other than something from the knowledge. The believers are the representatives of Allah, they accept Him as their Lord and they live only for Him without fearing anyone besides Him. 'They are in true Guidance' means they are the only people who utilize the Soul of Qur'an which is the True Guidance. No one can be believed without the Permission of Allah as told in the verse 10: 100. Permission of Allah means the Soul of the Qur'an. So belief will not be formed without having the complete Soul of Qur'an. See explanation 2: 186; 3: 145, 5:48 and 54.

83. Such was Our argument which We furnished Ibrahim with against his people. We raise any one We wish in ranks; Indeed your Lord is Wise, well Aware.

Prophet taught that Qur'an will argue in favor or against you, as well as It will witness in favor or against you. The Qur'an will argue and bear witness in favor, and will lead them to the Paradise those who learn, follow and teach It to entire mankind. Whereas It will argue and witness against the hypocrites who hide It and '*fujjar*'who do not try to understand what, what for and why Qur'an. They will not utilize the Soul of Qur'an as the Standard and Balance to identify Allah's path and satan's path; thus they included in satan's party and will return to Hell-'Satan's Paradise'. Prophet taught that Qur'an is from Allah and It will return to Allah. So you make It go ahead in front of you and not leave It to your back; if you keep It in your back It will push you to Hell. But, Muslims of today are neither utilizing the Soul of Qur'an as the Balance and Trust to keep the Universe in its equilibrium, nor allowing other people to utilize It. Thus they become worst than that of Meccan pagans, Jews during the time of Prophet, and they are becoming the only people who have made rejection of Soul of Qr'an their food as mentioned in the verse 56: 82. See the explanation 5: 90 –91; 6: 19 and 26.

84. And We bestowed Is'haq and Ya'qoob on him; each We Guided them and Nooh We had Guided before, and among his descendants were Dawood, Sulaiman, Ayyoob, Yoosuf, Moosa and Haroon; thus We reward those who are living seeing Me.

The verse 16:97 says: Whoever does honorable deeds, whether male or female provided he is a believer, We shall surely grant him a wholesome life in this World, and will certainly reward them in the Hereafter according to their best deeds. Through the verse 39: 10 Allah commands Prophet to say: Oh My servants who believed! Heed your Lord. Those who live seeing Allah in this World will have the best, Allah's Earth is vast. Surely the patient will be paid their rewards without any reckoning. The verses 12: 22; 28: 14 and 37: 110 also end as 'thus We reward those who are living seeing Me'. 'Seeing Me' means those who are living under the Light-the Soul of Qur'an. Not only for Prophets Allah reward in both Worlds, but also for anyone who are utilizing and conveying the Light to entire mankind in order to use It as Balance and Trust to keep the Universe in its equilibrium. The verses 37: 80, 105, 121, 13 and 77: 44 also end as 'verily, thus We reward those who are living seeing Me'. See explanation 2: 112; 3: 134-136 and 6: 53

85. And Zakariya, Yahya, Eisa and Ilyas; each one was among the honorable men.

See explanation 1: 6 and 2: 130.

86. And Isma'el, Alyasa', Yoonus and Looth; and each one We preferred more noble over all the Worlds.

87. And of their forefathers, their descendants and their brothers; We picked out and guided them to the Straight path.

88. That is Allah's Guidance. He thereby guides with any of His servant He may wish. If they have associated others with Him, whatever they were doing would be collapsed.

There is only one path from Prophet Adam to the last, i.e. the Straight path-Soul of Qur'an. The verse 41: 43 says, you have been not told except what was told Messengers before you. Your Lord is master of forgiveness as well as the wielder of painful punishment. See the explanation 2: 2.

All Prophets who make the Qur'an Truth, witness the life of Qur'an and doing deeds under the Light of Qur'an are in the Straight path and belong to the Believer, Allah's party. See the explanation 4: 69. 'Allah leads to the Straight path whom He wishes' means for whom who ask Guidance to Him with the Soul of Qur'an. See the explanation 2: 213. In the verses such as 5: 16; 39: 23; 42: 52; and 46: 10-11 it is told that Allah guides whom He wishes 'by means of It' to the Straight path. 'By means of It' implies the soul of Qur'an. Read together the verses 29: 45; 39: 63; 62: 9 and 63: 9. See the explanation 2: 120-121; 4: 48 and 6: 14.

89. Such are the ones to whom We have given the Book, along with wisdom and Prophet hood; if this people should hide It, then We will entrust It to a people who will not hide It.

Only one Book is sent down from the beginning. 'Wisdom' means the description to understand the matters really or it is the explanation of the Book as intended by Allah. See explanation 4: 105. The verse 25: 33 says: They will not come to you with any question unless We will bring you the Truth and something even finer as a commentary-such that no need to ask such questions by anyone till the Last Day. The Truth mentioned here is the '*Hikmath* verses' and commentary is the Wisdom or explanations. See the explanation 2: 269 and 3: 138. Prophets and Messengers are those who get Inspiration from Allah who received- with that prophesy they lead and guide the servants of Allah. Really Prophecy is also the explanation of the Book. That means Prophets are sent to explain the Book.

This verse teaches that if any people hide the Soul of Qur'an which is the Balance and Trust to keep up the universe in its equilibrium, the Lord powerful for everything will entrust It to another people who will not hide It. See explanation 4:91, 131- 133,150- 151; 5: 67 and 6: 68.

90. Such are the ones whom Allah has guided, so you also copy their Guidance. Say: I do not ask you any reward for it; It is nothing except a Reminder for all the Worlds.

The verse 38: 86 says, you say: I do not ask you for any reward for it, and not I am among boasters who say what they are not doing. The verse 87 says, It is nothing except a Reminder for all the Worlds. None of the Prophets have received any reward for propagating the soul of Qur'an-Allah's Message -to the entire World. The verse 25: 56 says, we have not sent you except as a Herald and a Warner. And the verse 57 says, say: I do not ask you any reward for it except that anyone who wishes to accept a way un to his Lord. Vide verse 26:108 Prophet *Nooh*, Vide verse 127 Prophet *Hood*, Vide verse 145 Prophet *Swalih*, Vide verse 164, Prophet *Looth* and Vide verse 180 Prophet *Shu'aib* told to their own people that I do not ask you any reward for it; my reward only concerns with the

Lord of the Worlds. But today, the boar people mentioned in the verse 25: 18 including the hypocrites and gone astray people who teach mere reading Qur'an without the soul neglecting the Prophet's explanation of the verse 3: 10 are filling their bellies with fire. See explanation 2: 174- 176 and 4:167-169. Both the verses 73: 19 and 76: 29 say, "Certainly, the Soul of Qur'an is a Ticket for those who intend to reach to his Lord". But only the heedful utilize the Qur'an as the Ticket according to the verse 69: 48. Read together the sub heading '*Adhikr*' in the introduction.

Verily, this Qur'an is nothing other than a Remembrance, Reminder, Awareness and Warning. In other words what is meant by '*Dikra*' or '*Adhikr*' is the Soul of the Qur'an which explains everything in one's heart language such as who is Allah?, who is Satan?, where the man was created?, what is their soul?, body?, what is the aim of their appointment on Earth?, who are Angels?, *Jinns*?, Prophets?, Messengers?, who will go to Paradise?, who will go to Hell?, how will be the trial in the hereafter?, What will be the severe punishment in the Hell?, What will be the enjoyment in the Paradise?, who are the disbelievers?, who is believer? Etc. In the verse 36: 69 it is said that this is nothing other than a '*Dhikr*' and a 'clear Book'. *Adhikr* is the soul of Qur'an and the Arabic text is its body. The word '*Adhikr*' is used in Qur'an at least one hundred places such as 15: 6, 9; 16: 43; 21: 7, 50; 29: 45; 36: 11; 38: 1; 43: 36, 44; 62: 9 and 63: 9. In all these verses *Adhikr* is the Soul of the Qur'an in one's hearts language. Allah asks four times repeatedly in *Surath Qamar*, 'certainly We made the Qur'an very easy to understand with one's heart, then who is ready for it?'

The verse 51:55 says; and remind, then surely the Reminding benefits the believers. The verses 87: 9-13 say: So remind, if Reminding will benefit. Anyone who feels afraid will be reminded, while the most unfortunate one shunts It aside, the one who will be roasted in the greatest Fire. Then he will neither die in it, nor will live there. In the verse 89: 23, it is told that on the Day of bringing the Hell, man will become conscious that it was better he might had used the Warning. Therefore, the believers only utilize the Soul of Qur'an. The others who do not utilize It after receiving, will be regretting and wailing at the time of death as well as on the Day of Judgment. The verse 69: 50 says; 'Indeed, It is a cause of sadness upon the disbelievers'. As per the verse 17: 82 It will increase nothing but losses to wrongdoers. And as per the verse 9: 125 it is told that It will not increase to the hypocrites anything except filth over filth. See explanation 5: 10; 6: 24 and 25.

91. They do not consider Allah the way He should be considered when they say: "Allah has not sent down anything to a human being". Ask: "who sent down the Book which Moosa came with, as Light and Guidance for mankind, you publish It on sheets of paper to show It around while you hide a great deal of It; and you have been taught what neither you yourselves nor your forefathers ever knew". Say: "Allah (has sent It)"; then leave them toying away with their speculation.

'They do not consider Allah the way He should be considered' means they do not value Allah the way He should be valued. Or they did not place Allah in the place He should be placed when they say: "Allah has not sent down anything to a human being". The verse 9:115 says, Allah is not apt to let any people go astray once He has guided them, until He makes clear to them what they should guard against; surely Allah has the knowledge of everything. Those who are leading a life of aimless and heedless after receiving the Soul of Qur'an-Guidance- which contains the commands and prohibitions of Lord for enabling them to lead a life as His real vicegerent; and those who are not considering the Soul of Qur'an as the Ticket to the Lord in the Paradise are the people mentioned in the verse who do not consider Allah as He should be considered. Read together the verse 7: 175 and 179. They do not believe in Allah as He should be believed. Those who do not understand what is told in Qur'an, do not have belief according to It, and do not perform deeds according to It are also included in that party. Their deeds like *swalath, fasting, zakath, hajj* etc. will not be accepted as explained in the verse 2:186. In the verse 22: 73 Allah says: Oh mankind! You hear a similitude that Allah quotes; those beings that you invoke besides Allah cannot create even a fly even if they all combined their forces for it. Not only that if a fly snatches anything from their lips, they are even unable to get it back from the fly, both the seeker and sought are weak! Then in the verse 74 says; they do not value Allah the way He should be valued. Certainly, Allah is Powerful for all, Mighty and Unquestionable and Self-sufficient. The verse 39: 74 says; they do not consider Allah the way He should be considered. While on the last day the full Earth will be rolled up in His left hand, and the Heavens will be rolled up in His right hand. Allah is very Glorious from what they ascribe share in His divinity. The verse 40: 16 says; the day on which they come forth openly with nothing of them hidden from Allah, and they will be asked; "to Whom is the Sovereignty?" Reply comes "only to Allah Who rule everything with full Power". See explanation 4: 158.

The hypocrites who hide the Soul of Qur'an knowingly and their blind followers-gone astray people-who reject It mentioned in the verse 1: 7 are included among the aimless and heedless people who do not consider Allah as He should be considered. They are the boar people mentioned in both verses 25: 18 and 48: 12. They are not considering Allah as Impartial when they say Allah is leading His servants to the Hell as well as to the Paradise.

Before Prophet Muhammad, the people of Mecca were commanded to live according to the '*Shareeath*'- practical life way- of Prophet *Moosa*. When Prophet Muhammad deputed to them with the Soul of Qur'an, the Meccan pagans including *Quraish* approached Jew and Christians-the people of the Book- in order to understand and realize the reality of the Qur'an and Messenger. Then Meccan pagans asked them, 'you are already given the Book and also believe in Prophets. So is there any truth in the claim of Muhammad that he is getting divine revelation'. The reply of the Jews for this was 'Allah has not revealed anything on mankind, so Muhammad is telling lie'. Meccan *Mushrik* leaders quoted this reply as a weapon against Prophet Muhammad to make the people turn against him. As a reply for this Allah revealed part of the verse "who sent down the Book which *Moosa* came with, as Light and Guidance for mankind, you publish It on sheets of paper to show It around while you hide a great deal of It; and you have been taught what neither you yourselves nor your forefathers ever knew"..

It is referred in this verse about the '*Thourath*' given to *Moosa* and their attitude towards It. It is understood from this verse that the *Thourath* presented to *Moosa* is also the part of the one Book '*al Kithab*' i.e. 'The Book'. It was also the Light and Guidance to entire people during that period. It is also understood that the *Thourath* was presented on planks –stone discs- and they gradually recorded them in papers, revealed a small part of it to the people while a large part of It they hid from them. In the verse 32: 23 Allah says; and indeed We have given the Book to *Moosa*, so be not doubt about getting such one to you. We have made the book given to *Moosa* true Guidance for children of *Israeel*. See the explanation 3: 3- 4, 5: 19, 48, 68; 6: 7 and 19.

92. And this is a blessed Book We have sent down to confirm whatever came before It, and with It you may warn the mother of countries

and any one around her. Those who believe in the hereafter believe with It and they are steadfast in their swalath.

The soul of Qur'an which is the only Book revealed from the Paradise to Earth as explained in the verse 2: 2, is told as blessed because It teaches mankind about the goal of life and makes them capable of getting success in this World as well the Hereafter. The verses 36: 5- 6 say, this Qur'an which is full of wisdom is sent down from Almighty and Merciful Allah, in order that Prophet has to warn with It a people whom were not warned by their forefathers so that they are heedless. The verse 32: 3 says, do the people say: "He (Muhammad) has forged it?" Nay! It is the Truth from your Lord, so that you may warn a people to whom no Warner has come before you: in order that they may receive the Guidance.

The verse 62: 2 says, He is the One Who has dispatched a Messenger from the unlettered among themselves, to recite his verses to them and purify them and teach them the Book and Wisdom even though previously they were in obvious error; and the verse 62: 3 says, as well as others of them who have not yet joined them. He is the Powerful, the Wise. Since it is mentioned in the verse 62: 3 'as well as others of them', it is clear that only unlettered people in the entire world who do not know the Arabic reading and writing can understand the Soul of Qur'an. The hypocrites and their blind followers who knowingly hide and reject It, will not understand the Soul of Qur'an. See explanation 1: 7 and 6: 89.

The verse 42: 7says, thus I have revealed this inspiration as Arabic Qur'an to warn with this the centre of the country and around her and to warn about a day in which everyone will be gathered, there is no doubt in it, in that day one party will be to the Paradise and other party will be to the Hell. The verse 25:1 says, blessed is the One Who has revealed *Al-Furqan* -the criterion to distinguish right from wrong- to His servant that he may be a Warner to all Worlds. See explanation 5: 48. 'This Qur'an is meant for warning the mother of countries and anyone around her' means the Qur'an is nothing but Reminder for the entire World as told in the verse 6: 90. Read together the verses 7: 158; 21: 107 and 34: 28. See explanation 3: 58 and 5: 60.

As for those who do not believe in the Hereafter, Allah has laid a lid on their hearts and a veil in their ears lest they should understand Soul of Qur'an, is explained in the verse 6: 25. The verses 23: 1- 2 and 9 say; verily those, the successful believers, are humble in their *swalath* and they are doing *swalath* punctually. And as per the verse 20: 14 it is told that *swalath* is to be performed to retain the remembrance of Allah with the Soul of Qur'an. And as per the verse 29: 45, verily the acceptable *swalath* prevents evils and unjust deeds. And vide verses 25: 65- 66 to those who perform *swalath* without taking part the soul will get Hell as penalty. Only with the Soul of Qur'an it can participate the human soul in all their deeds. So the beloved servants of the Impartial are always praying to escape from the Hell 'with the Soul of Qur'an'-the Shield and Safeguard. See explanation 4: 91, 142- 143 and 6: 75.

93. And who is more in the wrong than someone who invents a lie about Allah? Or says: "something has been revealed to me, while nothing has been revealed to him; and who says: "I shall send down the same as Allah has sent down?" If you could only see when wrongdoers are in their death throes and the Angels stretch forth their hands saying: "Deliver out your souls! Today you are awarded the torment of shame because you have been saying something that is not true about Allah. And you have been acting too arrogance for His verses".

'Saying something that is not true about Allah' means to say about Allah without having the Truth- Soul of Qur'an. So to form the belief in Allah and to talk about Allah to others should have His Permission and the real knowledge - the Soul of Qur'an. See explanation 2: 169 and 6: 80. The verse 7: 146 says; I will turn away from My verses those who are arrogant without the Truth, so that even if they see each and every sign they will not believe in It, while they see the Right Way they will not follow It; but if they see a crooked way they will follow it; this is because they denied Our verses and were heedless of them. See explanation 2: 256. As per the verse 16: 28, when the Angels hold the spirit of those who were doing injustice against themselves, they will surrender completely and they will say to the Angels as, we were not doing any evil deeds. Then the Angels will reply, verily Allah knows very well what you have been doing. In the verses 43: 74-78 it is told as, 'when these *Mujrims*-madmen- will be roasted in the Hell tomorrow they will say to the Angel *Malik*- the guard of the Hell- as, Oh *Malik*, let your Lord put and end of us. Then he will reply, you have to stay there as we had come to you with 'the Truth', but most of you were hateful of 'the Truth'. When there is no Soul of Qur'an, the Satan will be with them. Read together the verses 31: 7 and 33: 9. See explanation 4: 97- 99, 5: 80- 81, 6: 21 and 55.

94. And verily you have all come to Us individually now, just as We created in the first place. You have left behind what We conferred on you, nor do We see your intercessors alongside you whom you claimed were associated with you. They have been cut off from you and what you have been claiming has merely led you astray.

This verse points out the death conditions of wrongdoers who are the disbelievers. In the verse 7: 37 it is told, these wrongdoers who invent a lie about Allah or reject His verses after they have received It, at the time of the death shall stand witness against themselves that indeed they were disbelievers. And in the verse 38 they will be told to enter in to the Fire along with the nations of *Jinns* and humankind who have passed away before them. The verse 18: 48 says, on the day of the judgment the deniers will be made stand in row before Allah, and they will be told that you are brought in front of Me just like you were created in the first time, nay, you determined assuredly that the warning what We are saying you will not be fulfilled. In the verse 19: 95 it is said that in the Day of Judgment all will be brought one by one. Read together the verses 18: 100-106, 89: 23 and 24. The believers who live and die as vicegerents of Allah, understand the conditions that will be happened in the Hereafter by utilizing the Soul of Qur'an as Insight and Ticket will be entered directly to the Paradise. Read together the verses 18: 107- 108; 19: 96; 25: 24; 38: 49- 50; 39: 73 and 74. See explanation 2: 154; 5: 119; 6: 23 and 24. In the verse 3: 102 Allah wants believers not to die without in the conditions of being born. It is told in the verse 59: 18 that every Soul has to observe everyday what he has sent ahead for tomorrow. The verse 53: 39 says, no human has anything except what he did with intention. So the deeds done without intention will not be accepted, and also he will be punished for wasting the time merely. In brief, the aim of the life is to utilize all favors, which were neither brought when they were born on Earth, nor will take back when return, construct the Paradise under the light -the Soul of the Qur'an which is the biggest favors. They will be returning to the Paradise seeing Allah with happiness at the time of death as told in the verses 75: 22- 23. Read together the verses 6: 164; 17: 13- 15; 35: 18 and 39: 7. See explanation 2: 94-95; 3: 136, 182 and 6: 50- 52.

95. Verily, Allah splits the seed and kernel; He brings the living from the dead, and He is the one who brings the dead from the living. That is your Allah; then to where you are misled.

Allah is the one Who splits the seed and kernel, germinate and make grow into trees. In the verse 41: 47 it is told that the knowledge about the Hour of doom returns to Him. No fruit comes out from its calyx, no woman conceives pregnancy, does not deliver without His knowledge. On the day they will be called and asked, "Where are My partners?" They will reply, "We declare before you, we are not witnesses to it. The verses 50:7-11 say; and the Earth, how We have spread It out and set upon It mountains and caused to grow in It every kind of beautiful vegetation. All these things are insightful and a reminder for every servant returning to Allah. We send down blessed water from the sky with which We bring forth gardens and the harvest grain, and tall palm trees laden with clusters of dates, piled one over another, a sustenance for the servants; thereby giving new life to dead land. That is how the Resurrection will be of the dead from the Earth. Read together the verses 22: 5, 30: 19, 31: 10- 11 and 36: 33- 36. See explanation 3: 18, 26 and 27.

Then the question "to where you are misled from that Allah?" means, naturally all humans are born as Muslims as told in the verse 30: 30. The Soul of Qur'an is must to exist in that nature till the death. See explanation 2: 136 and 3: 102. The hypocrites-human devils- know the Soul of Qur'an, but do not follow It and hide It from the common people. Thus they are leading the people to the Hell, which is their refuge as told in the verses 9: 67-68; 33: 73 and 48: 6. The verses 28: 62-64 say; On the Day of Judgment Allah will call out them and ask: where are my associates whom you have been claiming? Then the ones against whom the charge will be pronounced will say: "Our Lord, these are the ones whom we misled as aimless! We misled them just as we ourselves were aimless. We absolve ourselves to you, it was not we whom they were worshipping. It will be said to them: Call upon your associates. Then they will call them, yet they will not answer them and they will see the punishment. If only they had utilized the Guidance, they would not have strayed like this. It is told in the verses 43: 36- 38; 50: 27- 29; 59: 16 and 17 that if Jinn comrade is not made as believer with the Soul of Qur'an, he may also cause for your misguidance. Satan's excuse on the Day of Judgment for the misguidance of man can be seen in the verse 14: 22. See explanation 2: 166- 167 and 6: 55.

96. He is the splitter of dawn, and He made night for repose, and made the sun and moon for reckoning time. That is the design of Powerful, the Knower.

The verses 36: 37-40 say another sign for them is night; when We withdraw the daylight from it and behold, they are in darkness. The sun runs along a course of its own, and that is the design of Powerful, the Knower. As for the moon, We have designed phases for it till it again becomes like an old palm frond. Neither it is possible for the sun to overtake the moon, nor for the night to outstrip the day: each floats along in its own orbit. These arrangements will continue till the Day of doom, and on the Dooms day as told in the verse 75: 8, the moon will be eclipsed, and as per the verse 9, the sun and moon will be brought together. The World will be darkened on a Friday when the day is ended, and the alternative change of day and night will become unhappening. In the verse 113: 1, which is presented to get refuge from the sorcery it is asked to pray as, I seek refuge in the Lord who splits the dawn.

The verse 10: 5 says, He is the One Who gave the sun its brightness and the moon its light, established her phases that you may know to count out the years and other such reckoning like days, weeks and months. Allah did not create them except with the Truth. He spells out His verses for people who want to understand. The verse 55: 5 says the sun and the moon move with fixed reckoning. See explanation 2:189.

97. He is the One Who has setup the stars to guide you through darkness on land and sea. We have spell out verses for people who know.

The verses 16: 15 and 16 say, we have established the mountain as nails on Earth so that it might not swing with you. He has also made the rivers flowing on the Earth. He has also made natural way so as to get Guidance to you. He has made on Earth paths, and signs for identifying places. With the stars also they are guided. Allah has made the Earth not in the same shape, but He has made each continent with different symptoms with many advantages. Human-beings are also able to identify the path and destiny with it. The people who have got chance to travel through the desert where these different types of signals are not seen and thereby there are many chances to be misled can only understand the importance of these favors of Allah. Those who sail along the sea where there are no marks of this way can experience largely the importance of stars arrangements made by Allah for the mankind to have guided on desert and sea. Allah who has made arrangements for this physical world has not left you alone without making arrangements for success in the Hereafter. Allah says in the verses 33: 45- 56, Oh Prophet! Verily I have appointed you as a witness informing glad news, giving warnings, reflecting lamp and a caller to Allah with His Permission-the Soul of Qur'an. To know meaning of 'with the permission of Allah' see the explanation of the verse 2: 213. Allah asks through the verses 16: 17and 18, then whether one who creates will be like one who does not create anything? Don't you remember with your heart? If you try to count the favors of Allah you can never do it, verily Allah is Forgiving, Merciful. See explanation 6: 63 and 64.

98. And He is the one Who has produced you from a single soul, and then granted you a settlement on Earth and a resting place after death. We have spelled out Our verses for the people who understand the aim of life.

The verse 67: 23 says, say He is the one who has produced you and granted you hearing, sight and intelligence. But a few are only showing gratitude. Read together the verses 32: 7- 10. See explanation 4: 1; 6: 65. The resting place after death is the godown, the place to keep the dead bodies and from where they will be resurrected on the Day of Judgment. The verse 11: 6 says, no living thing is there on Earth, of its food is not without in the hand of Allah, and Allah knows its abode and its godown; all are recorded in a clear Book. The verse 50: 4 says, We know what is consumed on Earth from his body, all are recorded in a clear Book which is kept with Us. See the explanation 6: 38 and 59.

99. And He is the one Who sends down water from the sky. Thus We bring forth plants of every type with it; We produce green vegetation from it. We produce grain from it piled packed on one another, and from the date palm, clusters close at hand produced from its pollen as well as gardens full of grapes, olives and pomegranates, which are so similar and yet dissimilar, look at their fruit as He causes it to grow and ripen, indeed in that are signs for the people who believe.

Grapes and olives are fruits alike in appearance, but pomegranates are not. Moreover in grapes itself are having different tastes and colors. Like that olives also have different colors. The verses 16: 10 and 11say, It is He Who sends down water from the sky, which provides drinking water for you and brings forth fodder to pasture your cattle. With it He grows for you crops, olives, date-palms, grapes, and every kind of fruit: surely there is a great sign in this for those who utilize their intelligence. All are produced by the One Creator from the same land with the same water. Humans are also brought from the land just like the fruits which become ready to be plucked-harvested, after many processes passed from pollination, flowering, budding, maturing etc. Allah brings human to this World after passing different stages in the womb as explained in the verses 22: 5; 35: 11; 39: 6; 40: 67 etc. Then he or she, after many steps such as laying, crawling, moving on the knee, standing with support and without support, walking, running etc. becomes matured, gets reproduction capacity, then comes to old age, and at last his or her nature becomes like the behavior of the child. The verse 36: 68 says, those to whom We grant long life, We reverse their nature. Will not they utilize their intelligence? The verse 16: 70 says, Allah is the One Who created you, then He causes you to die; there are some amongst you whose lives are prolonged to an abject old age so that they know nothing after having known much. In fact Allah is the All-Knowing, Almighty, at last on death the body made with soil reaches to the godown and dissolves in soil. 'In another time you will be produced from it' as told in the verse 20:55 means in the Day of Judgment you will be resurrected from that 'burial ground'. And that is why for the graveyard it is told 'go down' which means the place where 'bring to keep' and then 'take back'. Read together the verses 50: 11, 42 and 41: 39. See explanation of 2: 28.

100. And they have setup Jinns as associates of Allah, even though He created them. They have even ascribed sons and daughters to Him without having any knowledge. Glory be to Him; exalted is He over whatever they describe.

101. Originator of Heavens and the Earth! How can He have a son while He has no consort? He created everything, and He is the Aware of everything.

Meccan pagans had considered *Jinns* as the sons and the Angels as the daughters of Allah. The Muslims who do not know the Soul of Qur'an are also having such assumptions about Allah, *Jinns* and Angels. This is because of ignoring the Qur'an, which explains everything very clearly. They have become earning the Hell as penalty for their deeds such as *swalath*, *fasting*, *hajj* etc. It is because they are thrown away from the *Dheen-Islam*, such as arrow darts away from the bow. See explanation 2:99; 4:142 and 143. They have become so cheap and vulgar than any other people in the World because of neglecting the Soul of Qur'an which is the Light and Safeguard for all Worlds. Thus they are wandering in darkness and should be entered the Hell by their death as specified in the verses 9:55 and 125. See explanation 6: 26. *Surath Ikhlas* introduces Allah as, "He, Allah is the One. And He is Self-sufficient-Independent of all, while all are dependent on Him. And He neither begot nor is begotten. And there is none comparable to Him. In the verse 42: 11 it is told, 'nothing is there like Him'. The verses 34: 40 and 41 give warning about what will happen in the Hereafter as, "and on the Day when He will gather all his creatures, He will ask Angels; 'was it to you these mankind used to worship? Then the Angel will reply, Glory be to You! You are our patron rather than they; instead they have been worshipping *Jinns* and most of them even believing them". See the explanation 2: 29- 33, 116- 117 and 5: 116- 120.

102. That is your Allah, your Lord. There is no Deity except Him, the Creator of everything. So serve Him. And He is a trustee for everything.

The verse 21: 25 says, We did not send any Messenger before you unless He inspired him with the fact there is no Deity except Me, so serve me! The verse 16: 2 says, He sends down angel with the spirit of the command on any of His servants He may wish: 'warn mankind that there is no Deity except Me, so heed Me!' As per the verse 16: 128 Surely Allah stands with those who are heedful and those who are living under the Light- the Soul of Qur'an. The verse 39: 6 ends as that is Allah your Lord, control belong to Him; there is no Deity except Him, then how are you evaded away. The verse 40: 62 says, that is Allah Your Lord; the Creator of everything, there is no Deity except Him. Then, how are you deluded away from the Truth. Then the verse 63 says, thus those who have repudiated Allah's verses just deluded them.

The verse 39: 62 says, Allah is the Creator of everything and He is the Trustee of everything. The verse 39: 41 ends as you (prophet) are not set up as a custodian for them. Through the verse 10: 108 Allah commands prophet and believer to say as I am not a custodian set up for you. See explanation 2:133; 6: 33 and 66.

103. No powers of vision can comprehend Him, while He comprehends all vision; He is the Subtle, Acquainted.

No one sees Allah with eyes in this World. But one can see Him with hearts utilizing the Soul of Qur'an as Insight. The verse 36: 11 says, indeed you warns only him who follows the Soul of Qur'an and fears the Impartial unseen. To him give glad news of forgiveness and an honorable reward. The verse 67: 12 says, indeed! For those who fear their Lord unseen, for them have forgiveness and a great reward. In both verses 'unseen' means by seeing Allah through the Soul of Qur'an. Thus those who are living under the Light-the Soul of Qur'an are called '*Muhsineen*'. They keep Allah with the Soul of Qur'an in their hearts and they are heedful also. Then those who have seen Allah with hearts using the Soul of Qur'an will see Allah at the time of their death, as told in the verse 75: 23. As the word mentioned in the verse 75: 23 is '*Rabbiha*' means 'her Lord', it is understood that the soul is looking Allah at the time of death. Those who do not see Allah with their heart through the Soul of Qur'an will see satan at the time of their death with sadness as mentioned in the verse 75:24. Such disbelievers' panic condition of death can be seen in the verses 2: 254; 6: 93- 94; 7: 37; 9: 55, 85, 125; 63: 10- 11 and 75: 25- 35.

The verse 31:16 says, Oh my dear son! Lo! Though it is the weight of a grain of mustard seed, and though it is in the layer of a rock, or in the Heavens, or in Earth, Allah will bring it forth. Indeed Allah is the Subtle, Acquainted. The verse 67:14 says, should He not know what He created? And He is the Subtle, the Acquainted. In all the verses 'the Subtle' means the micro knower or the innermost knower of all things. 'The Acquainted' means surrounded or encompassed all things. See explanation 2: 234, 255 and 4: 108.

104. Verily, Insights have come to you from your Lord; then anyone who observes does so for His own soul, while anyone who acts as blindly has herself to blame. I am not any guardian upon you.

In the verse 7: 203 Allah orders Prophet to say, what I follow is the Divine message given to me from my Lord. That is the Insight from your Lord, True Guidance and Mercy for believing people. The verse 45: 20 says, this is the Insight for entire mankind as well as Guidance and Mercy for the people who have convinced belief. In the verse 28: 43 it is said, We have bestowed to *Moosa* the Book which is the Insight, True Guidance and Mercy for entire mankind. As per the verse 17: 102 *Moosa* told to '*Pharaoh*': verily, you know that all these evidences are not sent down except by the Lord of the Heaven and Earth as Insight. And verily I think, Oh *Pharaoh* you are the one to be doomed.

'Insight' is the Soul of Qur'an in ones heart's language. The verse 39:41 says, indeed! We have sent you down the Book with Truth for mankind. Any one who is guided with It, will be so far his sake, while anyone who goes astray will only stray of Its Soul as well. You are not setup as any custodian upon them. As per the verse 7: 179 those who are blind regarding this Insight, they will be filled up in Hell. The verses 18: 100- 101 say, on the Day of Judgment the Hell will be brought near to the disbelievers who had a veil on their eyes against the *Dikree*- the Soul of Qur'an- and were not able to hear the Soul of Qur'an in this World. Read together the verse 50: 22. Insights show to each soul-male or female-their tomorrow's seat whether it will be in the Paradise or Hell. Insights also show one whether he sees Allah or satan at the time of his death as mentioned in the verses 75: 22- 24.

This verse also teaches that either the Paradise or the Hell is prepared here by individual. 'I am not your guardian' means Prophet Muhammad or the believer cannot make anyone to Paradise or Hell. See explanation 2: 272; 4: 174- 175 and 6: 90.

105. Thus We spell out verses so they will say: "you have studied;" and We may explain It to the people who know.

When Prophet introduced Allah and the aim of life to everyone through the Qur'anic verses, deniers said, you really came studied. The verses 25: 4- 6 say, those who disbelieve do say: this is nothing except some lie he has invented; other people have helped him in it. They brought forward something unjust and counterfeit. They also say this is ancient fables written down and dictated to him in the early morning and evening. Say: the One Who knows the secret of Heaven and Earth has sent down It. Indeed, He is very Forgiving and Merciful. The verse 16: 103 says that We already know what they are saying: "indeed it is merely a human being did teach him!" The language of the person whom they hint at is foreign, while this is Arabic. The verse 41: 44 is revealed as a reply to the Mecca *Mushriks'* argument that this Qur'an is in the language of you and us, then, if it is from Allah it should have been sent down in other foreign language. Allah says, if We had made this Qur'an in foreign language, they will certainly ask, why are the verses of It not clearly understood to us? Ha! Foreign Book revealed for Arabs! Allah orders Prophet to say, this is a True Guidance and Healings to those who believe, but for the disbelievers they have a veil on their ears, it is blindness upon them and they are being called from distance. The fact was that the people who knew the illiterate Prophet very well were not ready to recognize the Qur'an. See explanation 2: 121 and 171.

If the believers by quoting the verse 2:186 say that the Soul of Qur'an is a must in order to accept the deeds and to get answered the prayers, the disbelievers of today will repudiate about the Soul of Qur'an asking questions such as; who is your teacher?, where did he learned it from?, Why did not anyone say it before?, Is it not his own opinion? Etc. Asking such questions wrongdoers are actually not ready to accept the Soul of Qur'an. This activity of today's disbelievers is same as that of the disbelievers mentioned in the verse 22: 72 as when Our verses are recited to them with all their clarity, you can notice a denial on the faces of the disbelievers. They can barely restrain themselves from assaulting those who recite Our verses. Say to them: "Shall I tell you something which is worse than that? It is the Hell fire, which Allah has promised to those who reject the Truth; what an evil abode it will be!" This Qur'an is digestive only to those who are naturally good. They will only learn and teach the Soul of Qur'an as told in the verse 56: 79 that none can understand the Soul of Qur'an except the purified. For hypocrites and gone astray people it will increase filth over filth and loss over loss as per the verses 9:125 and 17:82. See explanation 2: 24; 3: 79; 4: 56 and 6: 93.

106. You follow whatever has been revealed to you by your Lord; there is no Deity except Him and avoid anyone who associates others with Allah.

107. If Allah had so wished, they would not have associated anything with Him, we have not set you up as a guardian upon them, nor do you have trustee upon them.

The verse 64: 2 says, 'He is the One Who Created all of you, there is disbeliever among you, there is believer among you. Allah is observing what you do'. The verse 7: 198 says, if you call them to the 'Guidance'-Soul of Qur'an, they will not hear it, they will stare at you, they are not having Insight, and the verse 199 says, you do excuse to them, command them with Soul of Qur'an, and then avoid ignorant people. Prophet's responsibility is to deliver the Message of

Allah to entire mankind as per the verse 5:67. Each individual should ask Guidance to their Lord as explained in the verse 2: 213. Prophet will not be questioned about the inmates of Hell as per the verse 2:119. He has no responsibility over anyone as per the verse 6:104. Then, it is the duty of everyone to identify Allah himself or herself and the aim of life from the Soul of Qur'an and pray to Allah alone, Oh my Lord, increase my knowledge as told in the verse 20: 114, and arrange the life in accordance with the orders and prohibitions of the Soul of Qur'an as far as possible.

The hypocrites are the human devil knowingly hiding the Soul of Qur'an and they will enter the Hell without even trial. The associates are those who are mentioned as gone astray people in the verse 1: 7 and as associates in the verses 33: 73; 48: 6 and 98: 6; and the ones having disease in their hearts as specified in the verses 22: 53; 33: 12, 60 and 74: 31; and are disbelievers as specified in the verses 4: 140; 33: 1, 48; 57: 15; and the '*kuffar*' specified in the verses 9: 68, 73; 66: 9 ; and they are the rejecters specified in the verses 2: 39; 5: 10, 86; 57: 19; 64: 10. Both hypocrites and associates include nine hundred and ninety nine in every thousand are the fuel of the Hellfire from mankind. See explanation 4: 118 and 5: 72.

108. And you do not insult those they appeal to instead of Allah, lest they insult Allah as an enemy without knowing it. Thus We have made their actions seem attractive to every community; then their return shall be to their Lord, so He may notify them how they have been doing.

The believers are ordered not to insult and accuse any great men considering as patrons, intercessors to bring close to Allah whom the associate people appeal instead of Allah. If do so, the anger of the associates will cause effervescent and they will begin to abuse and blame Allah with enmity without realizing the fact. So believers should not cause for it. If Allah had wished He could have gathered all the mankind in True Guidance and had made all as real vicegerent who lives only for Allah. But Allah, as told in the verses 76: 3; 90: 10 and 91:7- 10 has given to every soul two ways-Allah's and satan's. Disbelievers' approach is portrayed in the verse 39: 45 as when those who do not believe in the Hereafter are remembered about the only one Allah, you can see vomiting sensation in their mind; while when others are mentioned instead of Him they are rejoicing! Read together the verses 17: 45 and 46. Today, most of the Muslims who bear the Qur'an like 'donkeys' and do not utilize It as Insight are having this character. That is why in the verse 7: 176 Allah has compared them as 'dogs' which will not have any change whether you attack it or not. As per the verse 6: 43, that satan makes the disbelievers' action seem attractive to them. But the verse 14: 22 says, when the judgment is over, satan will say: "In fact, the promises which Allah made to you were all True; I too made some promises to you, but failed to keep any of them. However, I had no power upon you. I just invited you, and you accepted my invitation. Now! Do not blame me, but blame yourselves. I cannot help you, nor can you help me. I reject what you did before; that you associated me with Allah. Certainly such wrongdoers will have painful punishment. See explanation 2: 113; 5: 105; 6: 97- 98.

Oh Allah, do not include us among such heedless people. Oh Allah include us among the heedful who follow the Soul of Qur'an as it should be followed. And enter us into the Paradise with those who make truth the Soul of Qur'an, Oh the One who sent down the Truth, oh the Lord of the Worlds.

109. And they swear by Allah with their stiffest oaths that if a sign were given them, they would believe with it. Say: indeed signs belong only to Allah. How can I make you perceive that even when they are come them, they will still not believe?

110. And We upset their minds and insights just like they did not believe with It in the first place. We have left them wandering aimlessly in their arrogance.

See explanation 6: 37. Allah says to believers "How can I make you understand that they will not believe though any evidence is brought before them. Prophet Muhammad used to pray in '*sujood*'- prostrate- as "Oh the One, who confound the hearts and insights, make my heart embracing firmly in your *Dheen*- the Soul of Qur'an. In the verse 17: 82 it is told that Qur'an is Healing and Mercy for the believers; whereas It will increase nothing except loss for the wrongdoers. As per the verse 9:124 the Qur'an will increase faith for the believers and they are rejoicing with It, while as per the verse 9: 125 Qur'an will increase filth over filth for the hypocrites and they will die as disbelievers without having the Ticket to the Paradise. See explanation 4:78-79, 143; 6: 4-5, 32-36.

111. And verily, if We were to send Angels down to them, and the dead were to speak them, and We assembled everything before them,

they still would not believe unless Allah so wishes; yet most of them act ignorantly.

The verse 13: 31 says, if there were a Qur'an by which the mountains were moved, or the Earth were cracked open, or the dead were made to speak out! Rather command is wholly to Allah. Do not those who believe despair, because Allah might have guided all mankind had He so wished? Disaster will continuously afflict those who disbelieve because of what they produce or it will settle down close to their home until Allah's promise comes true, indeed Allah does not break any promise. In the verse 15: 14 and 15 say, they did not believe with the Qur'an even though We opened up a gate to Heaven for them and they might keep on ascending into it. They still would say: "verily our eyesight has been dazzled- nay, we are enchanted people. In the verses 10: 96- 97 it is told: "verily, those against to whom your Lords word has been confirmed will never believe until they see painful torment, even though every sign should be brought to them. The verse 10: 33 says, just like that your Lord's word become true upon the transgressors that indeed they do not believe. You have to remember what they prayed as told in the verse 8: 32, "Oh Allah! If this Qur'an is really a Truth from You, then rain down stones from Heaven on us, or give us painful torment". To put it briefly, the disbelievers will never believe even though they see any evidence or sign from Allah. The approach of believers to the Soul of Qur'an is prescribed in the verse 39: 23 as: Allah has sent down the best speech in a Book consistent its verses yet repeating and teaching in different ways. The skins of those who fear their Lord tingle with It; then their skins and hearts are soften up for remembering Allah, that is Allah's Guidance; He guides any one He wishes with It, the Soul of Qur'an; while any one whom Allah lets go astray will none to guide him. The approach of wrongdoers to the Soul of Qur'an prescribed in the verse 32: 22 as who could be more unjust than the one who is reminded in his hearts language with the verses of his Lord and then he turns away from them? Surely We shall take vengeance on such madmen. See explanation 2: 6-7; 5: 51 and 67.

'They still would not believe unless Allah so wishes' means, even if the dead father and mother who have come from the grave and say: 'Oh my son, I am coming from the Hell, so you follow the way of Qur'an', this disbelievers will not follow It. But on the arrival of *Maseeh-A-Ddajjal*, he will alive again the dead father and mother, and that father and mother will say to them, the '*Maseeh-*

A-Ddajjal is your Lord and so believe in him'. They will believe or consider *Maseeh-A-Ddajjal* as their Lord.

By the saying 'Allah wishes' does not mean, Allah is the cause for guidance or astray. Instead He has given every soul both ways of Him and satan by teaching the Soul of Qur'an from the Paradise itself. Therefore each individual by praying 'My Lord, increase me my knowledge' should go through the Soul of Qur'an, and should confirm himself that he is a believer.

The verse 10: 100 says that it is impossible for anyone to believe without the Permission of Allah, and this Qur'an is made as filth for the people who do not utilize their intelligence. The Permission of Allah means the Soul of Qur'an. 'With the permission of their Lord' told in the verse 14: 1 means, each person should ask Guidance to Allah submitting through the Soul of Qur'an after identifying themselves. See explanation 2:27, 213. And as per the verse 58: 22 it is told that faith has been recorded in such believers' hearts and assist them with a spirit from Himself, Allah will be pleased them as well as they will be pleased with Him, those are belonging to Allah's party. Know that indeed Allah's party only be succeeded. As per the verses 8: 2- 4 such believers, if they are remembered about Allah with Qur'an verses, their hearts will be trembled and they will be shivering, and when the Qur'an verses are explained to them, their faith will be increased and they will entrust up on their Lord. See explanation 4: 17- 18; 5: 50, 54; 6: 25 and 36.

112. And thus We have made to each Messenger an opponent, satans from mankind and Jinn, some of whom have inspired others with seductive talk in order to deceive them. If your Lord had so wished, they would not have done so; so leave them alone as well as anything they may be inventing.

This is a verse which teaches that there is satan both in mankind and *Jinn*. It is also told that the satan belonging to Jinn and mankind would stealthy whisper in the chests of mankind as specified in the verses 114: 5 and 6. The hypocrites and their blind followers-gone astray people- are the satans from mankind who do not make their 'soul-mate' believers. The only instrument to make 'soul mate' believer is the Soul of Qur'an which is the food and cloth of human soul. In the verses 41: 26-28 it is told, the disbelievers who prevent the people from the Soul of Qur'an are Allah's enemies. And in the verse 63: 4 it is told, such hypocrites are the enemies of believers and Allah, and Allah has killed them, so the believers have to keep them away. See the explanation 2: 99. The verses 6: 121 says: You don't eat anything on which Allah's name has not being remembered, verily, it produce hypocrisy, and certainly satan will inspire their friends to argue with you; if you obey them you would become among associates. It is understood from the verse 4: 145 that the hypocrites i.e. human satans will be going to the bottom of the Hell without even trial, while the *Jinn* satans will be going to the Hell only after trial as told in the verse 14: 22. It is understood from the verses 43: 36- 38; 50: 27- 29 and 59: 16- 17 that for those who keep away from the Soul of Qur'an, then Allah will entrust the soul mate from *Jinn* to them and those soul mate will hold tight and pull them into the Hell. The verse 7: 202 says, as for satan's brothers, they drag them deeper into aimlessness and never relax their hold.

It is explained in the verses 7: 175; 5: 90- 91; 25: 29; 41: 26- 29 and 58: 19 that the satans belonged to *Jinns* and mankind are preventing the people from the Soul of Qur'an. Those believers who follow quintessence of Qur'an which is the Prophet's complete way of life and entrust in their Lord, satan have not any authority as told in the verse 16: 99. In the verse 7: 179 it is told that, most of the *Jinns* and humans are decided to be filled in the Hell, they have hearts but they do not understand aim of life. They have eyes but they do not see the Insight with it. They have ears, they do not hear the Soul of Qur'an with it, they are like cattle, nay, they are more astray than them and they are the heedless. In the verse 26: 212 it is told that satans are kept away from hearing the Soul of Qur'an. Human satan also will be kept away from the Soul of Qur'an. As per the verses 25: 27-29 warn the scene of wrongdoers wailing tomorrow, by biting their hands and saying, "Oh, he prevented me from the Soul of Qur'an after It had come to me. Certainly, satan is a big betrayer to human beings." See explanation of the verse 2: 102; 4: 118 and 6: 90.

113. Let the vital organs of those who do not believe in the Hereafter incline towards it, and let them feel satisfied with it and acquire whatever they may be acquiring.

Allah has created the mankind and *Jinns* in the nature of freedom. Each soul of men has been given its evil and good as per the verses 55: 1-4; 76: 3; 90:10 and 91: 7-10. The Soul of Qur'an contains both the ways of Allah and satan. Allah has given the power for satan to bring under his control nine hundred and ninety-nine out of every thousand. But humans were given the way for not to involve in the trap of the satan and to control that satan by making him believer with the Soul of Qur'an.

Since the hypocrites knowingly hide the Soul of Qur'an has been killed vide verse 80: 17; are dragging the common people and their soul mates to the narrowed Hell. On the Day of Judgment when it will be questioned about all blessings as per the verse 102:8 on which day the hands and legs, skins and the Earth will reflect, whatever they were earning here; they cannot reply since they didn't spend their blessings to learn and teach the great Bounty-the Soul of Qur'an which is Balance and Trust to keep the Universe in Its equilibrium. The Impartial, Justice Allah will not put anyone in the Hell without witnessing themselves that 'they were disbelievers' as specified in the verses 6:130 and 7: 37.

The meaning of the Arabic word '*Af'edath*' is given as 'vital organs'. '*Af'edath*' is the plural of the word '*Fu'ad*' and which is a process done by the heart and all vital organs. So it can say heed, remembrance, intelligence etc. See the explanation 2: 217, 3:178, 6: 25- 27 and 92- 94.

114. Should I seek other than Allah as a judge? He is the One Who has sent the Book down to you to set things forth in detail. And those whom We have given the Book recognize that indeed It has been sent down from your Lord, with the Truth; so you do not be among a doubter.

Believers are those who utilize the Soul of Qur'an as the Balance and Trust to judge all their affairs. The verse 16: 64 says, We have not sent the Book down to you except for you may clear them what they are differing over, and as a Guidance and Mercy for the people who believe. The verse 39: 41 says, surely We have sent you down the Book with Truth for mankind. Then anyone who is guided will be so for his own sake, while anyone who goes astray will only stray because of It as well. You are not a custodian upon them. Those who do not judge in their individual, family and social life with the Soul of Qur'an are the disbelievers, wrongdoers and transgressors as told in the verses 5: 44, 45 and 47 respectively. The verse 7: 196 says: Indeed, my patron is Allah, Who has sent down the Book and He befriends the honorable men i.e. those who follow the Splendid Book- the Soul of Qur'an. See the explanation 2: 147, 269; 5: 48-50; 6 and 36-38.

115. And your Lord's Word has been completed so far as truly and justly. There is no way to change His Words and He is the all Hearing, all knowing.

The verse 36: 7 says: The word has been proven to be true about most of them yet they still will not believe. And the verse 70 says: This Qur'an is revealed to warn any one who is alive and in order to confirm the Word against disbelievers. It is told in the verse 32: 13: "If We had willed so, We could have given each soul its true Guidance only, but the Words from Me has been come; verily, I will fill the Hell with entire *Jinns* and mankind together". The verses 75: 14 and 15 say: Indeed man holds evidence even against himself although he may proffer his excuses. See the explanation 4: 118.

Words or Statement means the Spirit of the Qur'an i.e. the explanation, which includes the Soul and the meaning of Qur'an. It is understood from the verses 18: 109 and 31: 27 that Words of Allah will not be completed even by writing or saying. Read together the verse 17: 85. 'There is no way to change His Words' means, what is told by Allah, the Knower of all times through His Words- three times knowledge Qur'an- will fulfill without any change. It is told both in the verses 33: 62 and 35: 43 that you will not see the Qur'an, which is Allah's Way and Practice being changed. Therefore, whoever man or woman likes to return to the Paradise, should confirm that he or she is a believer with Allah's Permission-confirming Truth- mentioned in the verse 69: 51. He should lead a life seeing Allah as the Impartial under the Light-The Soul of Qur'an-considering It as the Guidance and Ticket. See the explanation 2: 213; 4: 82 and 5: 13.

116. And if you obeyed most of those who are on Earth, they would lead you astray from Allah's path; they only follow conjecture and are merely guessing.

As among each thousand people, nine hundred and ninety nine are to the Hell, the believers should not follow the way of the majority of Muslims who belong to disbeliever satan's party. "Allah's Way" means the Soul of Qur'an's way from beginning to the last as specified in the verses 41: 41-43. Those who have not the confirming Truth which is the Soul of Qur'an are only following the conjecture and are merely guessing. Yet the hypocrites know all these verses, by hiding this Truth they are dragging the common people to the Hell. The verse 49: 12 says: "Oh you who believe! You abstain from most of the guessing, and some guesses are even sins". That is why without following the Soul of Qur'an after receiving It, the life of such disbelievers and rejecters will be in loss as specified in the verses 2: 121; 3: 4; 39: 63; 63: 9 etc. See the explanation 2: 166- 167 and 4: 135- 140.

117. Verily, your Lord is quite Aware as to who is straying from His path, and He is quite Aware as to who are utilizing the Guidance.

118. So eat from whatever Allah's name has been remembered over it If you are believers with His verses.

Many of the people are keeping conjecture and guessing without having real Knowledge as specified both in the verses 22: 8 and 31: 20. They are blindly following the footsteps of their forefathers as well as hypocrites- human Satan. That is why through these verses Allah is commanding the believers to distinguish Allah's way and satan's way by utilizing the Soul of Qur'an as Guidance and Criterion in order to become and live as the vicegerent of Allah. In the verse 6: 145 it is told that the sacrifice done without Remembrance of Allah as well as the food items offered other than to Allah are forbidden just like the swine's flesh and are filthy as well as inducing hypocrisy. Through the verse 9: 95 Prophet and believers are ordered to abstain the hypocrites as they are filth; and the verse 9: 125 says, the Qur'an will not increase anything other than filth over filth to the hypocrites. The believers, one in every thousand, while reciting the verse 1: 7 are not only praying as "not the way upon whom Allah's wrath happened and the gone astray people" but also will be trying utmost to abstain such satan's friends. See the explanation 1: 170-173; 5: 90 and 91.

119. And what is wrong with you that you do not eat something Allah's name has been remembered over? He has spelled out for you what has been forbidden you except you are compelled to eat. And indeed many people lead others astray through their own passions without having any Knowledge; indeed your Lord is quite Aware as to who are aggressors.

The prohibited food items have been explained in the verse 2: 173. Even the forbidden items of food can be eaten in compulsory circumstances without the intention of eating forbidden food and aggression, is clearly explained. Then the believers should not follow the passions of nine hundred and ninety nine people out of each thousand. 'Knowledge' means the Soul of Qur'an. Even the people who are in proud as educated, but without having real Knowledge- the Soul of Qur'an- which is the great Bounty and benefit in this world as well as the Hereafter are actually belonging to unjust and ignorant as per the verse 33: 72. Read together the '*Amanath*' in the Introduction. Both in the verses 22: 8 and 31:20 it is told that someone are among man who argues about Allah without having any Knowledge or Guidance nor any enlightening Book. The Knowledge, Guidance, enlightening Book means the Soul of Qur'an. Allah asks the prophet as well as the believer through the verse 45: 23 as have you seen someone who has taken his passion as his deity! Allah knowingly lets him go astray and seals off his hearing and his hearts, and places covering over his eyesight. Then who will guide him instead of Allah. Will you not remembering by heart. As per the verses 7: 40-41; 10: 17; 18: 57 and 32: 22 if anyone is remembered with the verses of Qur'an in his hearts language and then neglects It are wrongdoers as well as *mujrims*. See the explanation 2: 208; 5: 77- 82 and 6: 111.

120. And eschew all sins whether open or secret: surely those who earn sin will get due punishment for their acquiring.

The open sins are those deeds that are considered as sin by people generally. The secret sins are those deeds that are done secretly without seeing the people thinking that Allah does not see it. If anyone desired to do a sin, but did not do it; then it will not be considered as a sin; if it is done, the deserving punishment will only be given. But if anyone induces others to do sins, he will get a share in the burden of others' sins. That also become under the open sins. The believer must be vigilant about the heritage- foot steps- that he leaves to his ancestors to be good, under the shadow of Qur'an considering the verse 36: 12. Otherwise he should have to bear the share in the burden of sins of whom he has made astray till the Dooms Day. Therefore, today, the believers have to make meaningful the teaching of Prophet that to lead a life biting the Soul of Qur'an with their molar teeth and thus not to follow the way of the majority Muslims. This verse also teaches that every one will get the reward in the Hereafter only for what he has earned in this life. See the explanation 2: 201- 202 and 261.

121. And do not eat anything over which Allah's name has not been remembered; and indeed it is inducing hypocrisy. And the satans inspire their adherence to argue with you, and if you obeyed them, you would become associates.

Here it is not told that Allah's name mentioned, instead it is told: Allah's name remembered. So the meat will not become permissible to eat by murmuring Allah's name at the time of slaughtering or eating. Therefore the believers will only eat from the meat of over which Allah's name is remembered by hearts: 'This is from you and returns to you' at the time of slaughtering. Otherwise it will induce hypocritical filth and it belongs to the forbidden flesh of swine as explained in the verses 5: 3 and 6: 145. But against these verses the human satan hypocrites teach that the food items will not be forbidden even if they are the Offerings other than to Allah, if Allah's name is murmured at the time of eating it. In their account money earning in anyway such as smuggling, adulteration, interest, lottery, sorcery, black magic, conjuration, bravery, exploitation etc. will not include in prohibited, if a part of such earnings are given as donation for anchorites *Masjid* committee, organizations, orphanages, and giving as help to give dowry in marriage etc. All these can be considered as satan's inspiration to their adherence. To put it brief, if any work doing without participating the soul, that becomes worship to satan. So the Soul of Qur'an is a must to make the soul mate satan the believer in order to maintain the Remembrance of Allah and be heedful, if so any evil will not afflict. See the explanation 4: 78 and 79. This verse teaches the believers not to obey in any case the human satan- hypocrites- who hide the Soul of Qur'an and encourage others to follow the footsteps of satan. The verse also teaches the believers that if they are obeying them, they will be among their associates and losers. See the explanation 1: 7; 3: 86- 91; 4: 140- 145; 6: 106 and 107

122. Is someone who has been dead and whom We revived and granted Light to, so he may walk among people with It, to be compared to someone who is in such darkness he cannot get out of it? Thus anything they have been doing seems attractive to disbelievers.

Here the 'Light' means the Soul of Qur'an. The condition of not having the Soul of Qur'an is like dead. That is why it is warned through the verse 63: 4 that Allah has killed the hypocrites who hide knowingly the Soul of Qur'an; they are the enemies of the believers. See the explanation 2: 159-161. It is told in the verse 14: 1 that this Qur'an is sent down to you to bring out the mankind from the darkness to the Light with the Permission of their Lord. The men who do not utilize the Soul of Qur'an after receiving It are in darkness and also belong to the party of satan; they are showing patience upon fire. See the explanation 6: 36.

For such disbelievers, satan made attractive their deeds is told in the verse 6: 43. As per the verse 12: 3, before getting this Qur'an as a divine Message, certainly Prophet was among the heedless. Then in the verse 7: 205 it is told that, you remember your Lord with your soul every time irrespective of dawn and dusk humbly and fearing in your inner heart without murmuring 'Allah' with tongue; and you do not become among the heedless by thinking that Allah, the Knower of the state of chests, will hear only what is said loudly with tongue. In brief, the Balance and the Criterion to identify Allah and satan, believer and disbeliever, inhabitants of Paradise and inmates of Hell is the Soul of Qur'an itself. In the verse 57: 16 Allah asks: Has not the time come to the believers to be humble with shivering their hearts to the Remembrance of Allah and to the Truth revealed to him for not be like those who got the Book before you! Thus a long period passed over them and so their hearts became hard like stones. Most of them are transgressors. Read together the verses 11: 24; 32: 18; 35: 19-22; 39: 22 and 59: 20. See the explanation 3: 185; 4: 174- 175; 6: 25- 26 and 108.

123. And thus We have placed each town great culprits of madmen, to plot away in it. They are not making plot except against themselves and do not even perceive it.

In the verse 17: 16 Allah says: Yet whenever We want to wipeout some town, We order its extravagant people, then they start transgressing in it; thus the sentence about it is proven to be right and We utterly annihilate it. Allah says in the verses 27: 47- 53, Prophet *Swalih* had been sent to *Thamood* people, but they said to him that we see you and the people with you as ill omen. Then Prophet *Swalih* replied as, your fate is with yourself, nay, you are a people who will be tested. There were nine tribes who were making destruction in the land. They were surely not doing good deeds. They determined to swear a pledge in the name of Allah that we will surely kill *Swalih* and his family in the night and then to say his guardian that we are not witnesses for the destruction of your family, verily, we are the truth tellers. They plotted away, While We plotted too and they did not perceive it. Then see what the consequence of their plotting was. We annihilated them and their people completely, and We saved the one's who believed and were heedful. The verse 13: 33 says, who is there standing over every soul on whatever it has earned, while they give Allah associates? Say "name them or will you inform Him about something on Earth He does not know or Is it just a display of words?" Rather those who disbelieve feel their plot is attractive while they are diverted from the path, anyone whom Allah lets go astray will have no guide. And the verse 42 says, those before them have plotted, even though Allah controls all plotting; He knows what every soul is earning. Disbelievers shall know who has better consequence in the hereafter. Allah says in the verse 14: 46, they hatched their plot while Allah held up their plot, even though their plot had been to move the mountains by means of it!

The hypocrites-the human devil of all periods has played their plots to prevent propagating the Soul of Qur'an. Since the forelock of all such people is under the control of Allah, any of their plots is futile with Him. What Allah warns here is that by exploding the dynamite the mountains may be moved or cracked, but it is impossible to destroy those who propagate the Soul of Qur'an by exploding self-bombs or by any other tactics. The verse 35:10 says, 'for anyone who has been wanted glory, Allah holds all glory: towards Him do wholesome words ascend while honorable deeds also ascend to Him. And those who plot evil deeds will have severe punishment while their very plotting will affect upon them. In the verses 35: 42 and 43 say, yet whenever a Warner has come to them, it only increased their aversion because of how proud they have acted on Earth and plotted evil. Plotting evil engulfs the people who practice it. Are they only waiting for what happen to primitive people? Yet you will never find any change in Allah's practice, nor will you ever find any substitute for Allah's practice.

'The great of the culprits' told in the verse are the hypocrites who are the enemies of Allah- and vice versa. Allah has ordered to kill such hypocrites as per the verse 4: 91 and it is only by their hands the Universe will be wiped out. Read together the verses 43: 74- 78 and 46: 20- 28. See the explanation 3: 54- 55; 5: 67; 6: 26, 55 and 112.

124. Whenever some verse comes to them, they say: "verily we will never believe until we are given the same as Allah's Messengers were given." Allah is the quite Aware as to where He should place His Message; belittlement by Allah and stern torment will strike those that who commits crimes because of what they have been plotting.

'The same as Allah's Messengers were given' means the authority given to *Moosa* such as the Staff becoming snake, and the hand becoming white without any blemish, the ability given to *Eisa* to alive the dead people, to make cure the blind and the lepers, the miraculous sign such as the camel given to Prophet *Swalih*. The Mecca *Mushriks*, when Prophet recites the Qur'an verses told to Prophet that we would not believe in the verses of Qur'an until you bring such miraculous signs. As told in the verses 10: 90- 92, *Pharaoh* said when he was about to be drowned in the sea that I have believed that there is no Deity except the One whom the children of Israel believe in, and I am now a Muslim. Then Allah asked, is it now! You had disobeyed before and being a mischief-maker, however today We will preserve your body so you may be a sign to anyone who comes after you yet, many people are quite heedless of Our signs. The verse 10: 101 says, say: look at whatever exists in Heaven and Earth. Signs and warnings do not benefit any people who do not believe. See the explanation 3: 183, 6: 37-38, 109- 110 and 113.

125. So Allah lays any one's chest open to Islam whom He wants to guide, while he makes the chest of anyone He wants to be led astray seem cramped tight, just as if he were climbing up to Heaven. Thus Allah places filth on those who do not believe.

126. And this is your Lord's Straight path. Indeed We have spelled verses for the people who remember.

The verse 39: 22 says, anyone whose chest Allah has opened up to *Islam* will receive Light from His Lord, it will be awful for those whose hearts have been harden from Allah's Remembrance. Such people are in clear astray. The Light and Remembrance are mentioned here is the Soul of Qur'an. The verse 32:18 says, can he who is a believer be like the one who is a transgressor? Of course, they are not alike. The verses 43: 36- 38 say, he who turns away from the Remembrance of the Impartial, We assign a satan for him, who becomes his soul- mate. And turn such people away from the Straight path, while they think that they are guided aright. Ultimately, when that person will come to Us on the Day of Judgment, he will say to his soul-mate: "I wish that I was far apart from you as the east is from the west: you turned out to be an evil companion." See explanation 4:78. In the verse 94: 1 Allah asks, have not I widen your chest! Allah says in the verse 22: 78; there is no difficult made to you in *Dheen*-Islam. In the verse 9: 125 it is told Qur'an and *Islam* will increase filth over filth to the hypocrites, and they will die as disbelievers. In the verse 10: 100 Allah says, no soul can believe without the Permission of Allah, thus We have made this Qur'an as filth to them who do not utilize their intelligence. The verse 7: 40 says that, those who reject the Qur'an verses and be arrogant about It, doors of the Heaven will not be opened and they will not enter the Paradise till the camel enters through the eye of the tailors' needle. Just like We reward to the *mujrims*. The *mujrims* here mentioned and the *fujjar* mentioned in the verse 83: 7 are the same. And their record will be in '*sijjeen*' in the Hell. The Soul of Qur'an- the Light-is a must to open the doors of Heaven for recording their deeds in '*Illiyyeen*' in the Paradise. In the verse 22: 31 says anyone who associates anything with Allah is as if he had fallen out of the sky and the birds had snatched him away, or the wind had blown him to some far of desert. See the explanation 3: 117.

The Qur'an is received as reply to the servant for his demand through the verse 1:5 as: Guide us along the Straight path. So It is the Straight path to the Paradise. See the explanation 2: 2, 38 and 185. Each soul has been given both the ways of Allah and satan as explained in the verses 2: 28 and 4:1. Therefore by praying 'oh my Lord, increase the knowledge to me' as taught through the verse 20:114, read the Soul of Qur'an is the way of Guidance. Thus be hurry to Allah and reduce the attractiveness of physical life by understanding the aim of life. See explanation 1: 6; 2: 186; 4: 87; 5: 48; 6: 90 and 122.

127. They will have a peaceful home with their Lord; He will be their Patron because of what they have been doing.

The verse 10: 25 says, Allah invites to the home of peace, and guides anyone He wishes to the Straight path. The Soul of Qur'an is the Ticket to the Paradise according to verses 73: 19 and 76: 29. In the verses 74: 49-51 it is told that the disbelievers are fleeing from the Soul of Qur'an just like the frightened wild donkeys fleeing from the roaring lion. Rather, verily, this is a Ticket or Remembrance to those who want to remember Him. It is told in the verses 74: 54- 56 that nay, Indeed It is a Ticket, so let anyone who wishes to remember It, yet they will not remember except however Allah may wish. He is entitled to be heeded as well as entitled to grant Forgiveness. To put it briefly, one can become the believer and represent Allah-the Believer- by the Soul of Qur'an only. Those who are not utilizing the Soul of Qur'an as Ticket after receiving It are representing satan and there by return to the Hell- the house of satan. See the explanation 3: 101- 103, 136, 182 and 5: 54.

Prophet taught to pray after seeking three times forgiveness to Allah just after the *swalath* as: "*Oh Allah! You are the Peace, from You is the Peace, to You the Peace returns, Oh our Lord survive us with Peace, and enter us to the*

House of Peace, our Lord, You are Blessed and the all Highest, Oh the Possessor of Majesty and Splendor."

128. And one day He will summon them all together: Oh assembly of Jinns, you seduced great number from humankind. Then their adherents among humanity will say: "our Lord, some of us have taken advantage of one another, and have reached our deadline which You appointed for us". He will say: the Fire will be your lodging to live in forever, except for whatever Allah may wishes. Indeed your Lord is Wise, Aware.

This scene of reckoning on the Day of Judgment is clearly explained in the verses 34: 40- 42. The verse 40 says, one day He will summon them altogether; then He will ask to the Angels "Are those the one's who were worshiping you?" Then as per the verse 41 they will say: "Glory be to you! You are our Patron rather than they. Instead they have been worshipping *Jinns*; most of them even believed with them. As per the verse 42, then today when some of you will neither control any advantage nor any harm from others, and We will tell those who have done wrong: "taste the torment of Fire which you have been denying." The verse 32: 20 says, and those who have been transgressing the Fire will be their lodging; every time they want to get out it, they will be returned to it and they will be told: "taste the torment of Fire which you have been denying" As per the verses 50: 27-29 the *jinn* soul-mate will deny the responsibility of humans' astray as His soul-mate will say: "Our Lord! I did not mislead him. But he was gone too far astray." Allah will say: "Do not argue with each other in My presence. I had already sent the warning ahead to you. My words will not be changed with in My presence, nor am I unjust towards my servants". The verse 59:16 and 17 say, their parable is like the satan who says the man to disbelieve, but when man becomes a disbeliever, he says: "I am innocent of you; I fear Allah, the Lord of Worlds." The end of both will be that they will be tossed in the Fire, to remain there forever. Such will be the reward for wrongdoers. Therefore, since man is taught the Soul of Qur'an and is deputed as the vicegerent of Allah to the Earth, it is his responsibility to make his soul-mate believer with It. See explanation 4: 118.

The hypocrites and the aggressive leaders will be eternal in the Hell. But the common people of Muslims who follow and imitate the leaders blindly by misunderstanding that they are the scholars may be entered in the Paradise after suffering the punishment of the Hell for many years by recommendation of the believers. That is the indication of the usage 'except whom Allah may wish' in the verse. "Your Lord is the Wise, Aware" implies Allah has the three times knowledge who is encompassed all things and about everyone such as whether he will make the Paradise or Hell, how he is caused to live in the path of Hell, who made him astray or whether he made astray himself etc. Then those who succeeded are seeing Allah by heart and are praying, oh my Lord! I am the servant, you are the Owner, and so you do not include me among the losers. See the explanation 2: 27 and 6: 111.

129. Thus We let some wrongdoers manage others because of what they have been earning.

In the Hell, the wrongdoer human will get the wrongdoer *Jinn* as friend like he has in this World. So human has the duty to make his soul-mate as believer with the Soul of Qur'an. If they have earned Hell in this World, they will have to taste it in the Hereafter. As per the verse 43: 67 on the Day of Judgment all the relations except the relations under the shade of Qur'an, will be in mutual enmity. As per the verse 43:39 it will never benefit you today to have any partners in torment since you have already gone wrong. Through the verses 43:43 and 44 say, then you hold on to whatever has been revealed to you; verily you are on a Straight path and it is a Reminder for you and your people, and both of you (you and your people) will be questioned about It. See explanation 2: 254; 6: 19-21, 125 and 126.

130. "Oh assembly of Jinns and humankind! Have not Messengers from among yourself come to relate My verses to you, and warn you about a meeting of this Day of yours?" They will say: "we bear witness even against ourselves" Worldly life has deceived them, and they will bear witness against themselves that indeed they were disbelievers.

As per the verses 7: 35 and 36; oh children of Adam! whenever any Messengers from among yourselves come to relate My verses to you, then any one you does follow and reforms will have no fear upon them and for them not grieved; while those who reject My verses and act too haughty towards them will become inmates of the Fire; they will remain there forever. Here mentioned rejecters who reject My verses are the *fujjar* and who act too haughty towards them are the hypocrites. As per the verse 4: 145 the hypocrites will be on the lowest depth of the Fire while as per the verse 39:71 the *fujjar*-disbelievers- will be led to the Hell after reckoning is over. The verse 39: 59 says; Rather, My verses came to you, yet you rejected them, and acted so proudly and you were among disbelievers. The verses 67: 8- 10 say: when the group of disbelievers is thrown to the Blaze, Its keepers Angels will ask them 'hasn't the Warner come to you?' then they answer, 'yes verily, there had come the Warner, but we rejected them, we had told them that Allah has not sent down anything and you are none except liars'. In the Hell they will wail themselves as, Oh, if we had heard the Soul of Qur'an, or utilize our intelligence, then we would not have been the inmates of the Blaze.

As per the verse 7: 37, both wrongdoers- hypocrites and gone astray people- will bear witness against themselves at the time of death that indeed they were disbelievers. It is told in the verse 7: 38 that the disbelievers will be entered into the Hell soon after their death. If the Soul of Qur'an is not taught to the offspring by parents, they will be gathered together in the Hell with the *Jinns* and human cursing their forefathers. When the parents and their children are gathered in the narrow Hell, the children will say to Allah pointing their parents as 'Oh Lord! These are who made us astray, and so give them double punishment in the Hell'. Read together the verses 33: 66-68 and 38: 59-64. See the explanation 3: 196-197; 4: 150- 151; 5: 86; 6: 25- 26 and 36.

131. That is because your Lord will not destroy any towns unjustly while their people are heedless.

The Impartial Allah will never admit anyone into Hell without witnessing that 'I was a disbeliever.' The verse 36: 6 says, the Qur'an is revealed in order to warn a people whose forefathers have not been warned, and hence they are heedless. Therefore, the hypocrites who are knowingly hiding and the gone astray people who are rejecting the Qur'an verses are inmates of Hell from among mankind. See explanation 2: 39 and 6: 47

As per the verse 12:3 before the revelation of Qur'an Prophet was heedless and as per the verse 7:205 it is told that you should not belong to the heedless since you have been received the Soul of Qur'an. To put it brief, the Soul of Qur'an should have to be received in order to Punish the Impartial Allah anyone as mentioned in the verse 17: 15. See explanation 2: 38. The believer, one among every thousand to the Paradise will utilize the soul of Qur'an as the Shield and Safeguard from all calamities and disasters as well as the Hell. They will not hide or reject It. Instead, will convey It to entire mankind with the intention of making them Heedful. Thus they are acting as the helpers of the Impartial. Allah says in the verse 8: 33 that He will not punish them as long as the prophet is living with them, and as long as they are seeking forgiveness to Allah. 'As long as Prophet is living with them' means 'as long as there is a believer who witnesses the life of the Prophet', as explained in the verse 2: 143. See explanations 3: 106; 5: 48, 51and 6: 122.

132. And everyone will have ranks according to what they have been doing. And your Lord is not heedless of what they are doing.

The verse 64: 2 says, "He is the one Who created you. Then there is disbeliever and there is believer among you and Allah is observant of anything you do". This verse also teaches that the Paradise or Hell is preparing by individual, and there will be no chance to escape by accusing, cursing and blaming others for his bad fate. Allah says in the verse 36:54, on that Day no soul will be harmed in any way, and you will be rewarded only for what you have been doing. The verse 34:33 ends with a question that will they not be rewarded for just what they have been doing. Through the verse 83:36 Allah asks, are not disbelievers being compensated for just what they have been doing! So the believers by understanding the aim of life prepare the Paradise in this World utilizing the Light- Soul of Qur'an. And they will be in a state of mind that Allah is always observing everything without sleep or slumber as told in the verse 2:255. Anything which is happened in the Heaven and Earth are recorded in the Book as per the verses 9:51; 10:61; 11:6; 22:70; 57:22 etc. By understanding that Book is the Soul of Qur'an itself they will make It argue and witness in favor of them, and they will keep up *swalath* in order to maintain the Soul of Qur'an. See the explanation 2: 140; 3: 185; 6: 91- 92 and 104.

133. Your Lord is Self-Sufficient, the Master of Mercy; if He so wished, He would remove you and bring replacement for you in any way He wishes, just as He has produced you from the offspring of other people.

See the explanation 4: 133. Through the verse 39: 53, Allah ordered Prophet Muhammad to say; My servants who have acted extravagantly against themselves, still do not despair of Allah's Mercy, verily, Allah forgives all offences; He is the Forgiving Merciful. To identify the offences one should read the Soul of Qur'an and admit them to his Lord by heart, as 'I am the servant and you are the Lord, many offences have been happened from me, there is no one to forgive them other than You, so forgive to me all my offences. Not only that, but reminds others about their offences by teaching the Soul of Qur'an and thus make them aware of Allah, the aim of life and thus motivate them to live abstaining from the offences. Then Allah will convert the offences, which were happened during the ignorant time in the absence of the Soul of Qur'an as virtues. The verses 39:55-59 say; follow the best way what is revealed to you from your Lord-the Soul of Qur'an, before the scourge comes to you all of a sudden while you do not even perceive it. Lest someone should say: 'Alas! I neglected my duty towards Allah and I was one of those who mocked at His revelations.' Or lest he should say: `If Allah had guided me, I would have been one among the heedful.' Or lest he should say upon seeing the punishment: `I wish I had another chance, I would certainly be among the one who live under the Light". Then Allah will say to him: "Nay, My verses did come to you; but you rejected them, and were arrogant with them and you were among the disbelievers. See explanation 4:17-18 and 85.

"The character of the beloved servants of Allah is prescribed in the verses 25: 68-70 as, who do not invoke any other Deity with Allah, nor kill any soul which Allah has made sacred, except for a just cause, nor commit fornication-he that does this shall be punished for his sin, and his punishment shall be doubled on the Day of Resurrection and in disgrace he shall abide forever, except the one who repents, becomes a true believer, and starts doing good deeds; for them Allah will change his evil deeds into good, and Allah is Most Forgiving, Most Merciful. Prophet taught that, 'the Qur'an is the prosperity, there is no poverty after It, there is no prosperity without It'. Prosperity means self-sufficient. So anyone holdfast the Soul of Qur'an, he will become self-sufficient. The verse 43: 32 ends, as your Lord's Mercy is better than anything that they are gathering. Here 'The Mercy' means the 'Truth' mentioned in the verse 43: 30 and the Qur'an itself mentioned in the verse 43: 31. Read together the verses 10: 58 and 38: 8. See explanation 3: 58 and 79.

Only the believers remember and represent the 'Believer'-Allah- as it is commanded by the Soul of Qur'an, whereas those who hide Qur'an verses are hypocrites and transgressors who have forgotten Allah and themselves, as explained in the verse 2:99. The verse 24:55 says, Allah has promised those of you who believe and do honorable deeds that He will surely make them vicegerent on Earth as He made their ancestors before them, and that He will establish for them their religion, the one which He has chosen for them, and that He will change their present state of fear into peace and security. Let them serve Me and do not to associate anything with Me; and if anyone rejects faith after this, such are the transgressors. If all the people become hypocrites, the World will be wiped out. The verse 46:35 ends with a question, "then shall any be wiped out except the people of transgressors". Today, since Muslims all over the World made rejecting the Soul of Qur'an as their food as told in the verse 56: 82; It is the responsibility of believers to convey Allah's Message which is the Balance and Trust to keep the universe in its equilibrium to other people than Muslims. See the explanation 4: 113; 6: 89 and 111.

134. What you are promised is surely coming; you will never avert it.

'You will never avert it' means 'you cannot escape from the grasp of Allah, you cannot make Him surrendered, hide from Him or you cannot make Him weak'. The 'promise' means those one who received the Guidance and follow It can enter the Paradise and those who hide and reject It will be the inmates of Hell. See explanation 2:38-39. The verse 62: 8 says to tell wrongdoers: "The death from which you are running away, will surely overtake you: then you will be sent back to Him Who knows the unseen and the seen; and He will tell you all that you have been doing." The verse 32: 20 says, but those who transgressed shall be cast into the Fire. Whenever they try to escape from it, they shall be pushed back into it, and it will be said to them: "Taste the punishment of the Fire which you used to reject." The verse 67: 27 says, but, when they shall see it close at hand, the faces of the disbelievers will turn black with gloom, and it will be said to them: "This is which you were hastening for." See the explanation 3: 30, 136 and 182.

135. Say: oh people, act according to your situation, indeed I am too acting; then you will know who will have the best consequence as a result. Surely He will never lead such wrongdoers towards prosperity.

Prophet and believers who follow the Soul of Qur'an are ordered to say the disbelievers who reject the Soul of Qur'an; to leave me to live in my way, and you live in your way. We can wait and see who will get success in this World as well as in the Hereafter; in any case the wrongdoers will never get success. Allah orders Prophet and believer to say through the verses 39: 39- 40: "O my people! If you do not believe me, then do whatever you want in your positions and so shall I. Soon you will find out, as to whom shall come the disgraceful scourge and who shall get the everlasting punishment'. Through *Surath Al-Kafiroon* Allah orders the Prophet and the believer individually to declare the disbelievers as: Oh disbelievers! I do not serve what you serve, nor are you serving what I serve. I will not worship what you have worshiped; neither will you worship what I worship. You have your way of life while I have Real way of life. See explanation 3: 19. The verse 25: 63 says, true servants of the Impartial are those who walk on the Earth in modestly and will ask: "how do you do when ever ignorant men address them". Through the verse 28: 55 the behavior of believers is told as; when they hear vain talk, they withdraw from it saying: "Our deeds are for us and yours for you; peace be on to you: we do not desire the way of ignorant". The verse 9: 105 says; tell them: "Do as you will. Allah, His Messenger and the believers will now keep a watch over your conduct; then you shall be returned to His court Who knows the seen as well as unseen, and He will inform you of all that you have been doing." Through the verse 10: 41, Allah demands believers to tell the disbelieving rejecters, "to me my deeds, and for you your deeds." You are innocent anything I do, while I am innocent of what you are doing". About the hypocrites and disbelievers Allah says through the verse 41: 40 as certainly the ones who distort Our verses are never hidden Us. Is someone who will be cast in to the fire better, or someone who will come safely through on Resurrection Day? Do whatever you all may wish: He is the observant of anything you do. Read together the verses 11: 93, 121 and 32: 29- 30

The verse 91: 15 ends as the '*Thamood* people did not fear the consequence of killing that camel.' As a *Mouidhath* of this we can consider that today's Muslims by hiding the great sign- the Soul of Qur'an- not fearing the consequence of it became the wrongdoers. Through the verse 7: 176 Allah has told that their similarity is that of a dog, to which no change can be seen whether it is attacked or not. In the verse 62: 5 Allah has said that their similarity is that of a donkey which bear weight without knowing about it and that of Jews bearing *Thourath*. That verse ends as, 'Allah will not guide such a wrongdoing people.' In the verse 17: 82 it is told, Qur'an is the Healing for diseases and Mercy to the believers, and to the wrongdoers It will not increase except loss over loss. See the explanation 2: 254; 4: 140, 5: 50-51 and 6: 81- 82.

136. And they grant Allah a share in what He has produced such as crops and livestock, and they say: "This is Allah's" according to their claim, and: "This is for our associators." Anything that is meant for their associators never reaches Allah, while what is Allah's reaches their associators; how evil is whatever they decide.

When it was asked to Meccan *mushrik* who is the Creator of the Heaven and Earth? They will answer: 'Allah'. They also agreed the fact that it is Allah Who causes to germinate the seeds and to attune the cattle for them. But they considered the Angels, *Jinns*, great persons etc as Allah's associators and intercessors forgetting the truth that they are the creatures of Allah. Then they reserved a share from their crops and cattle to the associators other than they reserved besides Allah for receiving benediction, and for not to affect curse of them. The share reserved for Allah was being the gratitude for getting such benedictions. The second share offered to the associators was to exist the kindness and sympathy of them. The verses 39: 2 and 3 says; certainly We have sent the Book down to you with the Truth, so serve Allah sincerely devoting entire life to Him. Pure religion belongs to Allah! The Ones who takes on other patrons instead of Him claim: "we do not serve them except to bring us closer to Allah in homage". Allah will judge among them about whatever they have been differing over; Allah does not guide anyone who is a disbelieving liar. If we take the Soul of Qur'an as Insight we can see that today, the Muslims who bear the Qur'an like donkeys are the advanced people in the society having all such superstitions just like Meccan associates. That is why they are mentioned as the boar, worthless people who neglect the Soul of Qur'an both in the verses 25: 17-18 and 48: 6. Read together the verses 14: 28. See the explanation 2: 166-167.

"Anything that is meant for their associators never reaches Allah, while what is Allah's reaches their associators" means, if the fruits of trees between the two shares are fallen to Allah's share, then they will take it and add to the share of the associators, whereas if the fruits are fallen to the share of partners, they by considering Allah as self sufficient rich and leave the fruits to remain in the share of the associators. If the water for irrigation less, then they give preference to the land offered to the associators fearing the omen of them. See the explanation 6: 80-82. Such disbelievers' character is portrayed in the verse 36:47 as: Whenever they are asked: "Spend out of what Allah has given you". The disbelievers say to the believers: "Should we feed those whom Allah can feed Himself if He so wishes? You are quite obviously in error!" See the explanation 2: 266, 276 and 5: 64.

Today, most of the Muslims are also maintaining such superstitious belief. Prophet taught that there are only three mosques to visit seeking virtue in the World. They are '*Masjidul Haram*' at Mecca, '*Masjidunnabavi*' at Madeena and '*Baithul Muqaddas*' at Palestine. But the strayed Muslims who without making pilgrimage to the above mosques, they visit different national mosques such as Ajmeer, Nagoor, Muthuppetta, Ervadi, Bheemappalli, Puthanpalli, Mamburam etc. believing that there is virtue in visiting there. They also encourage others to visit these places seeking virtue. They are the associates who ascribe others in the dominion of Allah and there by they have become the disbeliever satan's party. See the explanation 3: 31-32 and 4: 80. So the believers by understanding that all these astray are the part of the prediction made by Prophet that the Dark Age will come back stronger than that period, have to turn in to the Soul of Qur'an and holdfast It with the molar teeth. See the explanation 4: 51; 5: 40, 103; 6: 94, 125 and 126.

137. And even so, their associators have made killing their children seeing attractive to many associates, to lead them on to turn back and to confuse their religion for them; if Allah so wishes, they would not do so; so leave them alone and whatever they are inventing.

'The associators who made attractive killing the children of the associates' are both Jinn and human satans. See the explanation 6: 112. There were three types of killing among Meccan mushrik. They are: (1) Burying the daughters: - 'the mightier has the holding power' - was the darken justice existed among them. The difficulties for growing up the daughters keeping their chastity, and by seeing the negligence and injustice suffered in their married life, the Meccan *mushrik* buried their daughters alive. The verses 16: 58 -59 say: If anyone of them was informed glad news about a newborn daughter, his face becomes black with gloom. And he feels like choking he hides from people because of the bad news that he has just received. Will he hold to her and feel disgraced, or bury her in the dust? What an evil decision they take! But today, due to the non-Islamic dowry system and the customs of huge ornaments and other formality at the time of marriage and after, the parents become sad while hearing the glad news about new born daughters, and some of them even would have proposed to kill the baby during the pregnancy itself if they realized the baby is female. Today among the community, Muslims- the boar people- mentioned in the verse 25:18 who read such verses of Qur'an are having such evil customs and practices more than that of any other people. The reason for that is they lead a life apart from the Soul of Qur'an. (2) Killing children fearing poverty: - Because of limited food and accommodation facilities they had killed both male and female children. They killed their sons not to do illegal intercourse with the fathers' wives when they grow and become adult. The verse 17: 31 says: And do not kill your children for fear of poverty; We shall provide for both them and you. Surely killing them is a great blunder. (3) Killing children as sacrifice: - This was done in order to satisfy their associators whom they ascribed as divine other than Allah to escape from their curse and anger and to achieve treasures as blessings. See the explanation 6: 43, 107 and 108.

Killing children ignoring all these verses is the part of obeying the satan. That is meant by saying 'to turn back them from their religion', in the verse. While there is no one has the right and power to select the children, to kill them is satanic and even shameful to the wild animals. When Allah as per the verse 51: 55 told that *Jinns* and humans are not created except for serving Me alone, without giving chance to serve Allah for the child by such assassinations, they are destroying the Earth itself. The believer only shows and leads the Qur'anic culture, which gives peace and tranquility to the coming generation, considering the verses 4: 85 and 36: 12. As far as believer is concerned, the real life starts after death. And he by teaching the children to lead a life under the Soul of Qur'an here, a share of the reward will be received even after his death. That is the meaning of Prophet's teaching: "*By the death of one, everything will be broken to him other than his useful knowledge of Soul of Qur'an, ever existing charity and the honorable children doing good deeds and praying for him.*" See the explanation 2: 187; 4: 118; 5: 32 and 33.

'To confuse their religion for them' means, the Meccan *mushrik* had claimed that they were the followers of Prophet *Ibrahim* and *Isma'el*. There were pleasantly saying that the life style they practiced was the real life style of those Prophets as well as Allah satisfied. But they had departed from the way of life of those Prophets. Instead they ascribed new rights and customs that were not taught by Prophets. In *Ka'ba*, which was constructed for worshipping Allah alone, they installed about 360 idols including Prophets *Ibrahim* and *Isma'el*.

Today, the customs and believes of Mecca *mushrik* and the people of the Book Jews and Christians revealed by Qur'an are seen only in Muslims, even more than today's Jews and Christians. That is because they transgress as well as run away from the Soul of Qur'an. They have darted away from *Islam* as Prophet taught that by reading Qur'an without the Soul will depart from *Islam* as the arrow darts from the bow. See the explanation 6: 26.

'If Allah has wished, they would not do so' means, everyone is taught the Soul of Qur'an containing true and false ways, and Allah will not change any people or individual till they change themselves, as told in the verses 8: 53; 13: 11 and 76: 3. See the explanation 2: 21- 24, 28, 256 and 257. The verse 7: 180 says: Allah has the finest names, so you appeal to Him by such name; and leave those who distort against His Names alone; they will be rewarded for whatever they have been doing. In other words leave the human satan, hypocrites and their blind followers-*fujjar*; and you do strenuous strive against them with the Soul of Qur'an. See the explanation 1: 7; 4: 63 and 6: 88- 90.

138. And they say: "This livestock and crops are taboo; only someone we wish to may eat them", according to their claim. There are some livestock whose backs one is forbidden to ride as well as other livestock over which Allah's name has not been remembered, as something invented despite Him. He will reward them according to what they have been inventing.

The implication of 'this livestock and crops are safe taboo' means, Meccan *mushriks* had made some conditions to use the fruits and cattle ascribed by them as offering to their associators, and were not permitted to eat them except some persons like priesthood persons had only permission to use it. These are some ascribed laws made by those transgressors. There are some such customs among the Muslims of today. The verse 5: 3 says: All foods that are offered in the name of anyone other than Allah are hypocritical and filth. See the explanation 6: 119- 121.

'There are some livestock whose backs one is forbidden to ride' is just like they considered as prohibited to ride and bear weight on the cattle that they intended to sacrifice on *Hajj* days. They considered as prohibited riding on animals and to bear weight on them which were offered as '*Baheera*', '*Sa'eba*', '*Waseela*', '*Ham*' etc. as explained in the verse 5: 103. But Allah rectified all these evil customs by revealing His verses. About sacrificial animals, Allah revealed the verse 22: 33 as: You have advantages in them for a fixed period, then their place shall be at ancient house'. See the explanation 2: 194. Just like they did not memorize the name of Allah when they were riding on horses, milking their cattle, slaughtering and eating them on account of that, through the verse 6: 118 it is revealed: If you are believers you have to eat from which Allah's name is remembered on it. And through the verse 119 it is asking: 'Why don't you eat from the food on which Allah's name is memorized while you are explained what is prohibited to you'. And in the verse 121 it is told that you do not eat from the food on which Allah's name has not been remembered. See explanation 2: 208 and 4: 136.

Today the Muslims who are following these types of evil customs have not any verse or even a word as proof from the Qur'an. What they have to say is: We are following forefathers' traditions without any change. Through the verse 43: 21 Allah asks: Or have We given them a Book already which they try to hold on to? The verse 22 says: Moreover they say: "Surely we found our forefathers in such a custom, and we are merely being guided along their tracks". The verse 23 says, and just saying we have not sent any Warner in to a country previous to you unless its high livers said: "We found our forefathers with such a customs, and we are merely being led along their tracks. Then as per the verse 24, Prophet asked: 'Will you follow your forefathers' way even if I bring you better Guidance than what you see from them?' They would say: "Verily we reject anything you are sent with". The verse 25 says: Then We have been avenged them; see what consequence was for those who rejected Our verses. See the explanation 4: 174- 175; 5: 104 and 6: 122- 124.

139. And they say: What is in this livestocks' uterus is reserved exclusively for our men folk, and forbidden to our wives. Yet if it is still born, then they may be partners in it. Evil reward them for their description; indeed He is Wise, Aware.

The meat of the baby cattle growing in the uterus of the offered livestock were allowed to eat only for the men folk among them. But if that baby cattle is died in the uterus, then its meat can be edible for both men and women. That means if a thing is good it is reserved for male, whereas if it is bad, it belongs to female was their unwritten law. So through the verse Allah warns: He will punish for following such customs and superstitions foot forwarded by satan. The unwritten habit exists today among some Muslims that the ladies have to eat the food only from the remaining of the gent's food after they have eaten; is belongs to the above said bad custom. They do not consider the command of the verse 24: 61 that the gents and ladies of believers can eat together in a group or by taking individual food from the same tray as much as they like and can eat it separately. The verse 49: 10 says: Indeed believed men and women form a brotherhood, so reform in between your brothers and sisters and heed Allah so that you may find Mercy. Both men and women believer are having the conscious that there is installed the software of computer on their neck as told in the verses 17: 13-14 and 45: 28-32. See the explanation 5: 50 and 6: 55.

140. Verily, those who have stupidly killed their own children without having any knowledge and have forbidden something Allah has provided them with, inventing lies about Allah have lost; they have gone astray and have not accepted the Guidance.

While it is told in the verse 5: 32 that the killing one without just cause is equal to killing the entire mankind, or it is told that beloved servants of the Impartial will never kill any soul without justice, and then it is a big offence to kill the children. It is also a big offence to ascribe food allowed to them by Allah as forbidden inventing lies upon Allah; since the forbidden items of food are already explained through the verses 2: 173 and 5: 3. Those who follow such satanic footsteps are following the satan's way and their abode will be the Hell. About the inmates of Hades, it is prescribed in the verses 37: 69-74 as: Indeed they discovered their forefathers have been misled and yet they went hurrying up alone in those footsteps. And most primitive men went astray before them even though we had sent warners out among them yet see what the consequence was for those who were warned except for Allah's sincere servants- that are only one in every thousand as explained in the verse 4: 118. Nobody can blame even the satan for their misguidance. As per the verse 14: 22 satan will say: I had no authority over you except that I called you and then you responded to me, so do not blame me but blame yourselves. Then no one can escape from the Hell by blaming forefathers or saint persons also. This verse warns that today's Muslims by following the customs and practices against the Soul of Qur'an are leading the World to darkness and even destruction. If the majority people who have not received the Qur'an hate *Islam* seeing the worst lifestyle of Muslims, the Muslims themselves should bear the punishment for it. See the explanation 1: 7; 3: 86- 91; 4: 167; 6: 26 and 133.

141. And He is the One Who produced gardens, both trellised and not trellised, and date palms and field crops whose food taste different, as well as olives and pomegranates which are so alike and yet so unlike! Eat some of His fruit as they ripen, and give away His due on their harvest day. Yet you do not spendthrift, surely He does not love the spendthrifts.

The verses 36: 34-35 say: "We have placed gardens of dates and grapes on Earth and make springs flow forth from it so they may eat His fruits which their own hands did not produce so, will they not give thanks? Allah feeds the people various fruits that they have not produced with their hands. Allah produces the trellised crops like grapes, bitter gourd, snake gourd, green gram, cucumber etc. and not trellised crops with stalk and stems trees like ladies finger, brinjal, and the field crops like rice, wheat, maize etc. See the explanation 6: 99. Allah is the Lord of all things including mankind. That is why it is told in this verse that eat some of 'His fruits' as they ripen and give His due i.e. 'Poor people's right' when they are plucked or harvested. Thus this verse teaches us that all grains, corns and fruits that are cultivated have the *Zakath*- welfare tax- compulsory due to the Creator. It is to be given to the poor when the crops are harvested. If it is cultivated by watering, then the portion of *Zakath* is 5% of total production. While it is cultivated with natural watering, then proportion of *Zakath* is 10% of total production.

"You do not spendthrift" means, you don't do anything against the do's and don'ts of Qur'an forgetting the Creator. Always must be in the awareness that Allah is observing and you are under His control. It is told in the verse 59: 19 that, if anyone forgets Allah, they are forgetting themselves; and they are the transgressors. The verse 9: 67 ends as: 'Indeed the hypocrites are the transgressors'. In the verses 68: 17- 32 it is told about a garden, the crop of which was destructed. They, without saying any exemption (without saying 'If

Allah intends') said with stress that we would harvest our matured crops in the coming dawn. But when they were in sleep some Angels of their Lord ruined that garden just like it was harvested. In the morning land lords started to their field for harvesting. They reached there hiding, bowing and silently for not seeing any destitute. They were in the confidence that they can harvest their crops successfully. But on seeing the ruined field they said: 'Verily, we are astray, nay we are prevented'. Then a person with justice asked, 'why don't you glorify Allah?' They replied: 'Our Lord is Glorious; verily we have become the wrongdoers'. Thus they mutually said: Oh alas! We have become trespassers. And so we can refuge to our Lord; our Lord may give us something better than this. Read together the verses 18: 32-44. See the explanation 2: 266- 267 and 3: 92.

142. Of the livestock you have, some for transportation and for meat. And used for bedspread. Eat anything Allah has provided you with and do not follow the footsteps of satan; surely he is an open enemy of yours.

The verse 16: 66 says, certainly, you have a good lesson to learn in livestock: We let you drink what comes from their bellies in between the cud and blood; pure refreshing milk for those who drink it. The white colored pure milk is in between green colored dung and red colored blood. The verse 16: 80 says: Allah has granted you your houses as homes to live in quietly, and granted you the skins of livestock to make houses which find so light on the day you pack them up to move elsewhere and the day you come to a halt. From their wool, their fur, and their hair come furnishings and commodities for a while. The verses 36: 71-73 say: 'Don't they see how We have created livestock for them out of what Our own hands have made and they are masters over them, we let them tame them: "Some of them are to be ridden, while others they eat; they receive benefits and drinks from them, then will not they act grateful?" With the horn of cattle we are making knife handles and with the skins of them footwear, bags etc. are making. In sugar factories their bones are also using. The 'catgut' used for stitching the wounds after the operation is made from the stomach and entrails of the cattle. 'Gelatine' for capsule is taken from their fats. 'Insulin' used by the diabetic patients is also had made from the cattle. To prepare B.C.G. vaccine, even cattle were used. In the modern age, for meat and other purposes cattle are produced by 'cloning processes. Read together the verses 23: 19- 22.

In brief, it is only Allah Who is the Lord and Donor of all favors such as agriculture, gardens and livestock. So they have to be used according to His do's and don'ts revealed through the Soul of Qur'an. So to showing gratitude other than to Allah and following customs and limitations beyond Allah's command will become overtaking Allah and imitating satan's footsteps. Allah has given them for us as food and for some other uses, and not for considering them forbidden through evil customs. The conditions and limitations ascribed by humans on the foods which Allah has given according to their own will and wishes, are satisfying satan who is the enemy of Allah. See the explanation 2: 168- 169, 208- 210; 4: 116- 121 and 6: 112- 116.

143. Eight exist in pairs: two pairs of sheep and two of goats. Asks: Does He forbid either males or both females or what the female's wombs contain? Inform me according to the knowledge if you are so truthful.

144. And camels also come in twos and cow in twos. Ask: "Did He forbid either males or both females, or what both female's wombs contain? Were you witnesses when Allah instructed you concerning this?" Who does more wrong than some one who invents a lie about Allah in order to lead mankind astray with out having any knowledge? Indeed Allah does not guide such wrongdoing people.

Those who speak about Allah without having the Soul of Qur'an and those who bring into practice the evil customs for that have not even a word from Qur'an as proof, as mentioned in the verse 4: 174; are leading the people without knowledge from Allah's path to the path of satan. These types of hypocrites will be entered to the Hell even without trial as told in the verse 4: 145; 5: 13 and 51. About this type of wrongdoers Allah says through the verses 22: 8 and 31: 20, there are among men who argue about Allah without having the real Knowledge, True Guidance and enlightening Book. Here mentioned 'real Knowledge', 'True Guidance' and 'enlightening Book' means 'the Soul of Qur'an' itself. It is foolish illusion that to consider as forbidden the males and females as allowed from the same livestock or the vise versa, or an animal is allowed whereas its kid is forbidden. How can one having intelligent, can think that Allah has given these types of meaningless and bloody irrelevant command and prohibitions? Therefore, the reason for quoting about the foolish illusions of the Arabs and forefathers in the Qur'an is to get lesson from those verses for the people of all times. And there by they have to understand similar examples and similitude from their life and should abstain from all such types of superstitions and evil customs. Thus they can lead a rightful life under the shadow of the Qur'an in this World and can return to the Paradise- the peaceful home by using the Soul of Qur'an as Ticket, as told in the verse 76: 29. Those who bring into practice anti-Qur'anic commands and prohibitions are the aggressors, and they will have to bear the burden of punishment for making astray the people having no knowledge. See the explanation 4: 85; 5: 57, 64- 67 and 6: 136- 139.

145. Say: I do not find anything forbidden in what has been revealed to me for anyone needing to eat something, unless it is something that has died, or flowing blood or pork meat that is so filthy, Or hypocrisy inducing offering that has been consecrated to someone besides Allah, then concerning anyone who is obliged to do so without either intending to disobey or exceeding his barest needs, indeed your Lord is Forgiving Merciful.

What to be noted in this verse is that those things offered to someone besides Allah are told together with pork meat, and both are filthy and hypocrisy inducing. In all other verses where the forbidden foods are explained, it is mentioned the 'blood'. But here, is told 'flowing blood'. See the explanation 5: 3, 90- 91 and 6: 121.

146. We have forbidden upon those who are become Jews everything having a claw, and in the case of cow, sheep and goats We have forbidden them their tallow, except it is located in their backs or intestines all what is mingled with their bones. That is how We have rewarded them because of their insolence, and indeed We are Truthful.

The verse 16:118 says: And We forbade for those who became Jews, what We have already told you about; We did not wrong to them but they were wronging themselves. In *Islam*-the natural religion, the forbidden things are the same in all periods. But just like different types of evil customs and practices were attributed and made in all sectors of the life, the priests and anchorites were attributing artificial laws in the matter of the forbidden foods also as told in the verses 3: 93; 4: 160 and 161. In this verse Allah told as 'We forbade'. That means Allah forbid a thing not only by sending a Messenger with Book, rather it is also His practice to appoint evil leaders - devil hypocrites who exploit the people when they become transgressed. Thus they forbid the good foods and things to such people. While the 'forbidden' made through the Messenger with Book is the blessings of Allah, the 'forbidden' by the insolent hypocrites and priests told here is as Allah's punishment and curse and that is from the satan as told in the verse 4: 78 and 79. The verses 9: 30-31 say; the Jews say: "*Uzair* is the son of Allah," and the Christians say: "*Maseeh* is the son of Allah." That is what they say with their mouths, imitating the sayings of the former disbelievers. Allah has killed them! How perverted they are! They (Jews and Christians) have taken their scholars and monks as their Lords instead of Allah, and *Maseeh*, the son of *Maryam.* Yet they have been ordered to serve only Allah alone; there is no Deity except Him. Glory be to Him ahead of whatever they may associate with Him. See the explanation 4: 136- 139; 5: 48; 6: 118, 123 and 131.

147. So if they should reject you, then say your Lord possesses boundless Mercy and His scourge will not be withheld from mad people.

After explaining and quoting many superstitions of Meccan *Mushriks* and previous people of Book Allah says; those who abstain from transgress and disobedience and thus making their life only for Allah and turn to Him in all matters, to such people can enter in the wide Mercy of their Lord. But today, Muslims who bear the Book for entire mankind, without trying to understand Its contents have become more transgressed and heedless. As a result, to such wrong and mad people Allah will revenge as told in the verses 7:40-41 and 32: 22. The opposite of the word '*Mujrim*' is '*Mukhbith*' or '*Muhsin*'. '*Mukhbith*' means surrender to Allah by mind, words and deeds. Read together verses 22: 34 and 35. '*Muhsin*' means one who lives under the Light-the Soul of Qur'an. Read together the verse 22: 37. See the explanation 2: 99; 6: 26, 33 and 55.

148. Those who associate others in their worship of Allah will say; "if Allah had so wished, neither we nor our forefathers would have associated anything with Him nor have forbidden anything". Even so did those before them reject us until they tasted our scourge. Say: "have you any knowledge? Then bring it here for us why, you only follow conjecture; you are merely guessing.

The verse 16: 35 says, those who associate others with Allah say: "if Allah so wished neither we nor our forefathers would have served anything besides Him, nor would we have forbidden anything besides Him". Thus have those before them done! Need Messenger do anything except to convey the Message clearly? And in the verse 10: 18 says, instead of Allah they serve what neither harms nor benefits them, and they say: "these are our intercessors with Allah". Say: "do you inform Allah about something in Heaven and on Earth that He already does not know?" Glory be to Him; exalted is He over whatever they associate with Him. In the verse 49: 16 Allah says to ask, "Would you teach Allah something concerning your religion? Allah knows whatever is in Heaven and on Earth. And Allah is Aware of everything. See explanation 6: 116.

The verse 45: 22 says; Allah has created the Heaven and Earth with the Truth in order to reward every soul for whatever it has earned, and they will not be unjust. And the verse 23 says: 'Have you seen some one who has taken his whims as his Deity? Allah knowingly lets him go astray and seals off his hearing and his heart, and places a covering over his eyesight, and then who will guide him instead of Allah. Will you not remember with hearts? And the verse 24 says; and they say: "nothing exists except our Worldly life! We die and live, and nothing except the time destroy us"; they have no knowledge about that; indeed they are not doing except the conjecture. And the verse 25 says; and when our clear verses are recited to them, they have no argument except to say: "bring back our forefathers if you are so truthful."

Today, all members of different Muslim organizations are ascribing partners in Allah's Power and Right. Through the verse 3: 103 Allah has ordered to holdfast the Soul of Qur'an altogether and to become a single party as told in the verse 5: 56. By ignoring verses such as 2: 213 and 23: 51-53, the leaders of various Muslim organizations are asking 'then is not the organization necessary?' They also say; 'if Allah has not wished there would not have different organizations and we would not have followed forefather's way'. The hypocrites also claim that, it is Allah only who shares His servants to the Paradise and Hell. By saying so they do not approve the good name of Allah 'Impartial'. They speak to believers with an attitude that if the forefathers have gone to Hell we are also ready to go the Hell. Due to the ignorance of the Soul of Qur'an they do not know the fact that the Paradise or Hell is to be earned by everyone from this World. See the explanation 2: 6-7, 286; 3: 136, 182 and 6: 22- 27.

149. Say: "Allah holds the convincing argument; if He so wished, He would have guided every one of you.

The Soul of Qur'an is the final Evidence of justice that reaches to reality. Prophet taught: *Qur'an is an argument for you, or against you.* Allah says in the verse 36: 70; the Soul of Qur'an is revealed to give warning for one who is alive and to become truth the word of punishment on disbelievers. Everyone is given evil ways and straight way as explained in the verse 4:1. Then Qur'an will argue for those who response in the manner to be responded, and thus lead a life according to Its do's and don'ts. Then the recited Qur'an will argue against those who follow the way of forefathers -the satan. See the explanation 2: 256, 4: 118 and 6: 88- 90.

150. Say: "Produce your witnesses who will testify that Allah has forbidden this"! If they so testify, still you do not testify with them nor follow the whims of those who reject Our verses and those who do not believe with the Hereafter, setup others equal to their Lord.

If they understand the responsibility of the witness and if they are conscious that 'Allah is the witness' and He is observing all, they will fear to tell false that Allah has ordered these evil customs in the case of food, and they will stand as witness only for about they have real knowledge. If they do not understand the responsibility of the witness and if they are not reluctant shame to stand false witness in the case of Allah, they may do so. Then what the Prophet has to say is, Prophet and believers do not participate in it. The meaning behind the demand not to stand witness with them is do not approve their belief if they stand witness for it. But this demand is for only to make turn back anyone of them having any fear about Allah and Hereafter to the True Guidance. In the verse 25: 43 Allah asks Prophet; Oh Prophet! Have you seen one who has selected his own whims as Deity, could you be a disposer of affairs for him. In the verse 44 it is told: or do you calculate or think that most of them are hearing and thinking? They are not like other than the cattle, nay, they are astray than them. And in the verse 72 it says, the beloved servants of the Most Gracious who consider Allah as Impartial are not standing for 'false witness', and if they happened to walk across any futility things, they will be passing by it with dignity. See explanation 2:120 and 6:1.

151. Say: "come close, I will recite what your Lord has forbidden you: do not associate anything with Him; and treat under the shadow of Qur'an with both your parents. Do not kill your children because of poverty; We shall provide for you as well for them. You do not approach to shameful things that are either open or secret. Do not to kill any person whom Allah has forbidden, except with a Truth. That are the things He has instructed you, with, so that you may become utilizing your intelligence.

152. And do not approach an orphan's wealth before he comes of age, except in the best in the manner. Grant full measure and weight with the Justice. We do not assign any person to do except he can cope with. Whenever you speak, be just even though it concerns a close relative. Fulfill Allah's covenant. That are the things He instructed you with so that you may become remembering with heart.

The contents of the verses 17: 23-25 are the same. Believers are with the belief that Allah is the only Lord of all creatures including humans. Those who represent Allah will only serve Him. Prophet taught: "*No obedience is there to any creature disobeying the Creator*". The verses 31:14-15 say, We have commissioned every man to look after his parents, his mother carries him in her womb while suffering weakness upon weakness and then weans him for two years. That's why We commanded him: "Give thanks to Me and to your parents, and keep in mind that, to Me is your final return. If either of them should strive to make you associate anything with Me which you have no knowledge about, do not obey them; however you should still treat both of them under the Light-the Soul of Qur'an- in this World, and you follow the one who has turned to Me. After all, to Me is your return; then I will notify you about whatever you have been doing." See explanation 4: 36, 48 and 135. Allah is the Creator and the protecting Guardian who feed all, while father or mother has no right to select their children or vice versa. So the father and mother have no power or right to kill their children fearing poverty. Read together the verses 6: 94, 136 and 137.

Any deed considered as humiliating, abusing, disgraceful and anti natural are heinous and shameful. The Holy Qur'an has taught that adultery, fornication, sodomy, nakedness, saying slander, marrying the wife of son in the case of father and the wife of father in the case of son etc. are shameful deeds. Prophet has taught that thefts, drinking intoxicating liquor, begging etc. are shameful deeds. All types of sexual deeds, obscenity, indecent, vulgar etc. are also included in shameful deeds. Allah orders us not to do such shameful deeds either openly or secretly.

Since the soul of all creatures is belonged to Allah, killing any creature unjustly is equal to kill Him. While comparing the killing of other creatures, to kill the humans is a great sin, because the humans are appointed as the vicegerent of Allah. And if one kills a believer who is the real vicegerent of Allah, then the Hell is compulsory to him as his reward, and the anger and curse of Allah is fallen upon him. And also a great severe punishment is kept ready to him as told in the verse 4: 93. 'Without the truth' means do not kill against the orders and prohibitions of the Soul of Qur'an. See the explanation 2:147 and 3: 60. The justifying killing is explained in Qur'an. If one deliberately kills a human, then the retribution for it may be to kill the assassinator as per the verse 2: 178- 179. As per the verses 2: 191- 193 fighting and killing are allowed till the freedom is attained to live according to the 'religion' accepted by Allah. It is necessary to kill the hypocrites who make the Islamic country violent and noisy and there by try to subvert (overthrow) the country as per the verses 4: 91 and 5: 32-33. Prophet taught that the killing is permissible in two situations. (1) Adulteration of married man and woman. (2) To become '*Murthadd*' - going out from *Dheen*. All these punishments have to be executed by the group of believers. In the verse 24: 55 it is told that if there is a group of believers, they will get the ruling power. But today as there is not a group of believers or Islamic rule anywhere in the World, it is impossible to implement this law. The people of the World know 'what the Islamic rule is' only after the arrival of *Eisa* again. Therefore today what believers have to do is strive with the Soul of Qur'an against the hypocrites and the *kuffar* who hide It. Remember that these hypocrites and *kuffar* are from the Muslims only. Read together the verses 9: 73 and 25: 52.

It is told in the verse 4: 10 that those who eat the wealth of the orphan are filling their bellies with fire. 'Grant full measure and weight with the Justice' means 'to weigh with the Soul of Qur'an'. Both in the verses 42: 17 and 57: 25 that Qur'an is the Balance. Then anything will become just and witnessing Allah only when it is weighed by the Soul of Qur'an as told in the verse 5: 8. That is the meaning of what is said, 'Those who do not judge with what Allah has sent down - Qur'an, are the disbelievers, wrongdoers and hypocrites' as told in the verses 5: 44, 45 and 47 respectively. See the explanation 2:185; 4: 6- 9 and 6: 104.

'We do not assign any person to do except he can cope with' means justice should be shown as much as possible and also that Allah will not take action on anyone for any fault done by mistake or not deliberately. It is told in the verses 83: 1-3 that the Fire Street named '*wail*' is for those who make short in measurement and weight. Such people when they buying things weigh and measure accurately, at the same time when they sell the things they make shorten in the measurement and weight. See the explanation 2: 286.

It is told in the verses 4: 17- 18 that repentance will be benefited only for those who do evils because of ignorance. If one speaks with others he must order for goodness and must prohibit evils. That means everyone should advise to live following the commands and prohibitions of the Soul of Qur'an. In other words it means that everyone must be vigilant what he speaks is being recorded in everyone's record of deeds tied up in their necks as per the verses 17:13-14, and he should have to read that record in the Hereafter to Allah in the presence of whole people irrespective of father, mother, brother, sister, son, daughter etc. In the verses 26: 214-215 say, you warn the nearest of your family, and make your wings down to the believers who follow you. See the explanation 4: 135.

'The agreement made with Allah' means the covenant made with Allah in the Paradise when He asked, "Am I not your Lord" every one answered 'yes, our Lord, we bear witnesses as told in the verses 7: 172-173. Those who live a life keeping that covenant when they are reminded about it through the Soul of Qur'an are the heedful, and they will be only returned to the Paradise. See the explanation 2: 26-28. Those who do not fulfill the covenant made with Allah even after it is reminded are the madmen and transgressors. The verses 36:59-62 give warning about the conditions of such madmen, on the Day of Judgment. Allah will ask, "Oh the children of Adam, had not I taken the covenant that you do not serve for satan? Verily he is your enemy. You serve only for Me, that is the Straight path. The satan has made astray most of you. Then were you not thinking with your intelligence?" See the explanation 2: 44, 152; 4: 36-38 and 6: 90.

153. And verily, this is My Straight path, so follow It and do not follow other paths which will separate you from His path. That is the things He instructed you with so that you may become the heedful.

As per the verses 15: 39- 43 Satan said to Allah: "My Lord, you have made me aimless astray, so I will take in my custody by making everything on the Earth to them decorated and I will make aimless astray all of them other than the servants who do serve only to You". Then Allah replied: "This is the Straight Path with Me, certainly you have not any influence on my servants who serve only to Me as My real vicegerent-except those who live aimlessly". Then what promised you and all your followers is the Hell. The way to Allah from the period of Adam to the Last day is the same-The Soul of Qur'an. Those who follow that way belonged to Allah's party as explained in the verses 3: 19; 5: 55 and 56 will go to Paradise. All other ways are to the Hell and the followers of these ways are belonged to the party of satan as explained in the verses 2: 174-176 and 4:118. 'The Straight path' means the Splendid Book-Soul of Qur'an-mentioned in the verses 41: 41-43. See the explanation 1:5; 3:103; 4: 133; 6: 125 and 126.

Prophet used to make 'pledge' after explaining these three verses i.e. 151, 152 and 153 from those who came to embrace *Islam*. Prophet taught: those who live maintaining this pledge have been deserved reward from Allah. And whoever breaches do's and don'ts of these verses will get shameful Punishment in this World itself, and in the Hereafter they will get severe punishment.

154. Then We gave Moosa the Book as complete Our favor upon those who would do good to others, and an analysis of everything, as well as Guidance and Mercy, so that they may believe about the meeting of their Lord.

The Book given to Moosa was also explaining all things completely as well as true Guidance and Mercy. It was given to lead a life accordingly and there by to become ready to answer before Allah about the life of this World. But only the believers consider It as Guidance and Mercy. See explanation 3: 3-4. In the verses 46: 10-12 it is told: Have you ever thought while this Qur'an is from Allah and you deny It, and one from children of Israel does witness for a Book like this. They believe in It. If you are denying It proudly, certainly Allah will never lead to True Guidance such wrongdoers. Moreover, the disbelievers will say to those who believed in the Qur'an, we would have become believers in this Qur'an very earlier than you if there had any virtue in It. What happened to them was that they were not only guided with this Qur'an, but they also said that Qur'an was ascribed tales of ancient time. Before that there is the Book of *Moosa* that is '*Imam*'-Leader and Mercy, while this Qur'an is the one which make it True. And also It is in Arabic language that is a warning to the wrongdoers and a blessing to the believers. See the explanation 2: 121; 5: 48 and 6: 38.

155. And this is a blessed Book We have sent down. So follow It and be heedful so that you may be blessed.

156. Lest you say: "verily the Book was sent down to only two factions before us, and we have been heedless of what they study".

157. Or you may say: "verily, if the Book had been sent down to us, we would be better guided than they are". Then Evidence has now come to you from your Lord, as well as Guidance and Mercy. Then Who is more in the wrong than some one who rejects Allah's verses and even evades them? We will reward those who evade Our verses with the worst torment because they were so evasive.

See the explanation 2: 2. The verse 7: 204 says, whenever the Qur'an is being recited, listen to It carefully and keep silent, so that you may be blessed. The verse 24: 56 says, keep up *swalath*, pay the welfare tax, and obey the Messenger so that you may be blessed. The verse 36: 45 says, when they are told "heed what lies in front of you and what is behind you so that you may be blessed" the disbelievers should not consider It. The verses 46: 29-30 say; remember how We brought to you a group of *Jinns*, who when they reached the place where you were reciting the Qur'an, said to each other: "Be silent." When the recitation was over, they returned to their people as warners. They said "Oh our people! We have just heard a Book sent down after *Moosa* confirming what came before It, guides one to Truth and to a Straight Path. The Qur'an in Arabic language is given to you for not saying as, You gave the Book for the two factions before us, while we were not aware about what they learnt and taught from It. According to the verse 41: 44, Allah has sent down this Qur'an in Arabic language which was the language of illiterate Prophet's people for not to have a chance to say as 'why is the verses of It not clear, what a wonder! We, the Arabs are given a Qur'an in non-Arabic language'. It is Guidance and healing for those who believe, but the disbelievers are with a lid in their ears about the Qur'an, they are also blind about It. They are like ones who are being called from a distant place. The Qur'an is also sent down for not boasting by any one as, 'if we were given a Book, certainly we would have become the best guided'.

'The Evidence, Guidance and Mercy told in this verse are the Soul of Qur'an itself. The Knowledge, Guidance and the Enlightening Book mentioned in both verses 22: 8 and 31: 20 is the Soul of Qur'an. The Book, Truth and Balance mentioned in the verse 42: 17 is also the Soul of Qur'an. Evidence, the Book, Balance and Justice mentioned in the verse 57: 25 is the Soul of Qur'an. 'Truth', '*Mouidath*', '*Dhikra*'-reminder- mentioned in the verse 11: 120 is the Soul of Qur'an. '*Mouidath*', Healing for the disease of dilemma, Guidance and Mercy mentioned in the verse 10: 57 is also the Soul of Qur'an. It is said in the verse 34: 38 that those who rush to overtake Our verses will be gathered in the Hell for the punishment. The verse 45: 31 says, but as to those who disbelieved, Allah will say: "Were My verses not recited to you? But you showed arrogance and became a people of mad". Today the only verses of Allah are the Qur'an. And so today the biggest transgressors are those who hide and reject It and falsify It by leading a way of life just opposite to the do's and don'ts of It. Against them the Qur'an will argue and witness, and push them in to the bottom of the Hell. Read together the verses: 21: 24, 50 and 28: 48-50. See the explanation 3: 138; 5: 72 and 6: 90- 92.

158. What they are waiting except the Angels come to them or your Lord come, or for some of your Lord's signs come? On the Day when some of your Lord's signs arrive, belief in them will not benefit any person who has not believed in them already, nor earned some good through his faith. Say: "you wait; indeed we too are waiting".

In the case of individual 'the Day Allah comes' means his death, while in the case of 'entire mankind' it is the Day of Judgment. The coming of the Angels also happens on the death for the individual, sending down the punishment for the people, or the Doom's day for the entire mankind. Read together the verses 23: 99-100; 25: 21-30 and 39: 55-59. As far as the people is concerned, 'some signs from your Lord' means the punishment such as draught, epidemics, Earthquake, scarcity, disturbances with locust and lice, war, flood, cyclone, Tsunami etc. As for the entire mankind it means the ten important signs of the Last day. Prophet taught that *Last hour will not happen till those ten signs are appeared.* They are rising of the sun from the west as explained in the verse 2: 258, smoke which will spread through out the Earth as told in the verse 44: 10, coming of monster as told in the verse 27: 82, appear of Gog and Magog as told in the verse 21: 96, appear of *Maseeh-A-Ddajjal* as explained in the verse 4: 159, second arrival of *Eisa* as told in the verse 43: 61, the Earth downing to deepness in three places (one in east, other in the west, and third in Arabian peninsula) as mentioned in the verses 28: 81 and 67:16 and the fire from Yemen leading the people to "*Mahshara*' (Summoning place for the Day of Judgment) as told in the verses 21: 97 and 23:104. There will be no chance to believe by seeing any sign as told in the explanation of the verses 4: 17 and 18. The verses 25: 21 and 22 say; those who do not expect to meet Us say: "Why are not the Angels sent down to us, or we are allowed to see our Lord?" Certainly they are too proud of themselves, and have revolted around quite insolently! On the Day when they see the Angels, it will not be a Day of rejoicing for the madmen; rather they will cry: "May there is a stone barrier between us and the Angels of punishment."

The verses 32: 29-30 commands to tell them: "On the Day of victory, to accept the faith will not benefit those who have disbelieved, nor will they be allowed to wait. Shun them and wait; they will be waiting too". On the day the sun rises in the west all the people will be ready to believe. Prophet taught: "*the belief of anyone on that day will not be useful to him and belief or repentance when the Rooh departing from the throat also will not be useful*". See explanation 2: 210, 254; 6: 93-94, 111 and 130.

159. Verily, those who made divisions in their religion and form sects, you should have nothing to do with them in any way. Their case returns entirely to Allah; soon He will notify them about whatever they have been working.

In the verse 32: 25 it is told, verily on the Day of Judgment your Lord will take decision among them in what about they were being divided. The verse 39: 46 is also with the same Message. In the verse 39: 69 it is told; the Earth will glitter with the light of its Lord, their record of deeds will be presented, Prophets and witnesses will be brought and decision will be taken among them with the 'Truth'. And to no one will be shown any unjust. In the verse 70 it is told that 'every soul' will be given completely what it did and Allah knows what they are working. The verse 16: 64 says, we have not sent down this Book for except to clear in what the people are divided, and surely it is the Guidance and Mercy to the believers. See the explanation 2: 113, 176, 213 and 6: 153.

160. Anyone who comes with a fine deed will have ten ... while anyone who comes with an evil deed will only be rew... with its like; they will not be treated unjustly.

Prophet taught: verily, your Lord is very Merciful to you. Anybody intended to do a fine deed but he did not do it, It will be recorded as a virtue to him. If he does that fine deed, it will be recorded to him as virtue from ten to seven hundred times or even without any limit. Anybody intended to do an evil, but he did not do, will be recorded him as one virtue. But if he does that evil, it will be recorded to him as only one evil. See the explanation 2: 261; 4: 85 and 100.

161. You say: verily, my Lord has guided me along a Straight path, leading to an established religion, the creed of Ibrahim, the straight forward, and he was not among the associates.

The verse 16:123 says; then we inspired you: "follow the creed of *Ibrahim*, the straight forward; he was not among the associates. The verse 22:78 says; and strives for Allah's sake, in the way it should be striven; He has chosen you and has not laid upon you any hardship in concerning the religion -life way- of your forefather *Ibrahim*. He has named you Muslims both previous and in this Book now, so that the Messenger may be a witness for you and you may act as witnesses for mankind. Then keep up *swalath*, pay the welfare tax and hold fast with Allah; He is your Protector, what a splendid Protector and what a splendid Supporter! See the explanation 2:135; 3: 101-102; 6: 79 and 105- 110.

162. You say; certainly my swalath, my devotion, my living and my dying belong to Allah, Lord of the Worlds.

The word '*Nusuk*'- devotion- has the meaning sacrifice and worship. As per the verse 2: 128 Prophet *Ibrahim* and *Isma'el* prayed as; 'teach us our ceremonies and turn towards us, You are so Relenting, the Merciful'. In the verse 22: 34 Allah says; we have granted sacrifice to each society so that they may remember Allah's name over any heads of livestock He has provided them with.

In Qur'an the word '*Manasik*' is used for deeds of worships. But the disbelievers taught by Prophet through the explanation of the verse 3: 10 give meaning worship to the word '*Ibadath*'. Actually '*Ibadath* means to lead a life as Allah's real vicegerent by submitting his whole life to Him, or make live Allah- the Believer, as mentioned in the verse 59: 23. Whereas others make living

... disbeliever- as per the verse 2: 34, and their whole life is becoming as ...oadath' to satan. They are the madmen and their consequence is warned in the verses 36: 59-62. See explanation 1: 4; 2: 131 and 152.

163. No associate has He, with that am I commanded, and I am the first of the Muslims.

'With that am I commanded' means I am ordered for not to ascribe any partner to Allah. See the explanation 2: 132; 3: 102 and 6: 151-153.

164. Ask: "should I seek some other Lord than Allah, while He is Lord of everything? And each soul is not earning except for its own self, while no burdened soul shall bear another's burden. Then your return will be unto your Lord, so He may inform you concerning whatever you have been differing over.

See explanation 6: 158-159. This verse also teaches that each individual is earning Paradise or Hell in this Worldly life either by utilizing or rejecting the Soul of Qur'an. In the verses 17: 13- 15; 35: 18; 39: 7 and 53: 38 it is said, 'no bearer of burden shall bear the burden of others'. It is understood from this part of the verse 'no bearer of burden shall bear the burden of others' that the '*Sabiqeen*' who will go to Paradise without even trial and not bearing any burden, will have the power to do recommendation as they are make living Allah, Qur'an and Prophet. From the verse 9: 65 it can be understood that Allah, Qur'an and Prophet are the same. See the explanation 1: 1; 2: 286; 4: 48- 51; 6: 31 and 104.

165. He is the One Who has placed you as vicegerents on Earth, and raised someone of you higher than others in rank. So He may test you by means of what He has given to you. Verily your Lord is swift in punishment; yet He is Forgiving, Merciful.

See the explanation 2: 30. Allah says in the verse 102: 8 that, then on the Day of Judgment all of you will be questioned about all favors. The verse 93: 11 says: And then you declare the favors of your Lord. The greatest favor is the Soul of Qur'an. It is the 'Trust' and 'Balance' to keep the Universe in its equilibrium. Read together the verse 33: 72. Everyone should have to identify himself, the Creator and the aim of life by utilizing the Soul of Qur'an as Insight and Criterion. The Soul of Qur'an which is the best favor of Allah is the instrument to remove the poverty, to make easy the protection of the orphans, indigence, to have peace and calm on Earth to establish human unity by implementing Justice and thus avoid the bloodshed and mischief. That is the implication of the teaching of Prophet that '*Qur'an is the prosperity, there is no poverty after that, and there is no prosperity without It'*. It is the Safeguard and Shield against the Hell as well as all the disasters and calamities for body and wealth. Since Soul of Qur'an is the Permission of Impartial Allah, without It nobody will become believer, as told in the verses 10:100 and 14:1. And if anyone utilizes It as the Permission of Allah, he can decided even his own death as told in the verse 3: 145. 'Jihad' means utilize all the strength and power to fulfill the aim of life. Today it can possible by learning, following and propagating the Soul of Qur'an to entire mankind irrespective of nation or religion. The walking, sitting, laying, speech, thought etc. of Prophet was the Qur'an. When *Ayisha*, the wife of Prophet, was asked about the character of Prophet, she replied: 'It is Qur'an'. The verse 68: 4 says about Prophet: Indeed you are of the highest noble character. See the explanation 2: 146. We, the believers should also have the character of the Qur'an. Then only we will become the vicegerent of Allah- 'the believer' as per the verse 59: 23. If anyone lives ignoring the Soul of Qur'an after receiving It, against them the great people and even Prophet will complain that this people were living worthlessly and they neglected this Qur'an as per the verses 25:18 and 30. Allah says by calling the mankind through the verse 49: 13 that verily We have created you from a man and a woman. You are made as clans and societies in order to identify each other. The most honorable among you near Allah is one having '*Thaqwa*'-the True way of Soul of Qur'an. Prophet taught: Allah divided His mercy into one hundred parts. He kept ninety nine parts with Him, and only one is sent to the Earth. See the explanation 3: 78- 79; 4: 37- 39; 5: 94 and 6: 52- 54.

Oh Allah! Our Lord, Who has the Supremacy, Who is the Dictator and the most Powerful, guide us with the Soul of Qur'an to the Straight path in the matters in which the people are divided. Verily there is none other than You to guide. Oh Allah You bless us, Your servants, to lead a life as Your real vicegerent showing gratitude to all Your favors and remembering You always- in walking, sitting and laying with the Reminder. Oh Allah, bless us to follow the Soul of Qur'an in the right way as it should be followed and thereby to make the Qur'an as witnessing and arguing in favor of us, and not against us. Oh the Merciful Allah! You make us among those who enter the Paradise with the Merciful Qur'an and enter the Paradise with foremost, virtuous and prosperous people.

With the name of Allah, the Impartial, the compassionate.

7. Al-Ahraf

This *Surath* is revealed in the last phase of Prophets Meccan life and is closely connected with the previous *Surath Al An'am*. In volume, it is the second large *Surath* consisting of 206 verses, after the *Surath Al Baqara*. It is mentioned about some persons on heights, who identify those who go to Hell and Paradise, came the name of Surath *Al-Ahraf.* It is told in the verse 203 that Qur'an is the '*Baswaer*'- Insight to identify Allah, satan, the physical structure of body and Soul of men, the goal of life, what is, what for and why Qur'an and to see each individual whether his seat is in Paradise or Hell in the Hereafter.

The verses 172-173 explain where the mankind was first created and what covenant was taken from all of them individually by the Lord. Those who do honorable deeds here utilizing the Soul of the Qur'an as the Light and Proof shall have weight in their scale, and all others' work will be in vain and shall go to Hell, told in the verses 7: 8- 9; 35- 36; 146 and 147. It is described in the verses 11- 33 the creation of Adam, prostration of Angels except *diabolies* who refused to be among who prostrate. It is told in the verse 37 that those who do not follow the Qur'an after getting It will witness themselves at the time of their death that they were disbelievers. It is told in the verse 40 that those who reject the Qur'an after getting It and treat Them with arrogance are the madmen, and they will not enter the Paradise until the camel can pass through the eye of a tailor's needle. It is told in the verses 49- 51 that when the companions of Hell ask water to the companions of Paradise, they will reply, both these things are forbidden to them since they rejected the verses of Qur'an. The historical incidents of former people of prophet *Nooh, Aa'd, Thamood*, *Looth* and the people of prophet *Shuhaib* are quoted through the verses 59-102 and it is commanded to learn lesson from them. The historical incidents of prophet *Moosa* and *Pharaoh* are quoted through the verses 103- 136. It is quoted through the verses 138-171 about the Children of Israel, prophet *Moosa* was given the Book, and when he went to accept the Book they molded and worshipped a calf. The anchorites who hide the verses of Qur'an after receiving It and the laymen who try not to understand It are compared to that of a dog which does not change its attitude whether it is attacked or not. The verses 197- 200 teach to turn away from the ignorant, and be the one who should not maintain suggestions from satan. As per the verse 201 the heedful by utilizing the Soul of Qur'an as Insight will identify the way of Allah from the ways of satan. The verse 206 commands to prostrate before Allah with those who prostrate and to glorify Him. The first prostration of '*Thilawath*'-recitation- comes in this *Surath.* And it is the one among the three *Suras* in which come the prostration of '*Thilavath*' at the end of the *Surath*. The other *Suras* are '*Annajm*' and '*Al-Alaq*'.

With the name of Allah, the Impartial, the compassionate,

1. Alif-Lam-Meem-Swad.

Description of the historical incidents came to Prophet Muhammad from Allah through Angel *Jibreel*. See the explanation 2: 1. The letter '*Swad*' stands for the description of historical events of former people of prophets *Nooh, Hood, Swalih, Looth, Shu'ayb* etc. It may be the alphabet 'Swad' from the word '*Yaquswoona*' in the verse 35; or '*Faqswuswil Qaswaswa*' in the verse 176.

2. A Book sent down to you, so do not let your chest feel it is under any constrained because of It, In order that you may warn by means of It; a Reminder for believers.

Allah says in the verses 20:1- 3 by calling Prophet *Muhammed*, 'We have not sent the Qur'an down to you in order to upset you, but only as a Ticket for some one who act cautiously. The Soul of Qur'an is the Ticket to return to the Paradise as told both in the verses 73: 19 and 76: 29. It is told in the verse 22: 78 that Allah has imposed no distress of you in religion; life way of your forefather *Ibrahim*. It is told in the verses 26: 3- 4 that it may be you will kill yourself with grief that they do not become believers. Certainly if it were Our will We could send down to them from the sky a sign to which they would bend their necks in humility. The verse 36: 76 says let not their speech then grieve you, verily We know what they hide as well as what they disclose. The verse 18:

6 says you would only perchance, fret yourself in to death, following them in grief, if they believe not in this speech. Read together the verses 10: 65; 11: 13 and 14: 17. The Qur'an is sent down not for upset, sorrow, distress and not for to be oppressed by others, lest It is sent down as a Mercy, Guidance, Admonition for believers in order to walk upholding the head wherever and whenever on Earth. It is the unbreakable rope from Allah to Earth, but it is a Warning for the disbelievers. See the explanation 3: 79; 5: 48 and 6: 155- 157.

3. Follow whatever has been sent to you by your Lord. And do not follow any Patrons besides Him; Yet how seldom do you remember.

The verse 39: 55 says: And follow the best that was sent down to you from your Lord before the torment comes on you of a sudden, while you perceive not. Read together the verses 39: 17- 18, 22- 23, and 31- 33. It is asked in the verse 42: 9, what? Have they adopted other patrons instead of Him? But it is Allah- He is the only Patron; He revives dead; He is capable of everything. See the explanation 2: 257. It is told in the verse 12: 103 that, yet most men will not become believers, no matter how eager you may be. And the verse 106 says, most of them do not believe with Allah unless they associate others with Him. That means only one from each thousands lives remembering Allah as His vicegerent and the remaining 999 will be transgressors, forgetting themselves and Allah. See the explanation 2: 99,152and 4: 118.

Here in this verse it is told to follow what is sent down from your Lord instead of saying to follow Allah. It is told in the verse 7: 196 that my Patron is Allah, who sent down the Book and He will befriend the honorable men. Therefore, those who holdfast the Soul of Qur'an are only in the part of Guidance. See the explanation 4: 174 and 175.

4. How many towns have We wiped out? Our scourge come upon them at dead of night or while they were speaking in daytime.

5. When Our scourge came to them, their appeal was merely to say 'we have indeed been wrongdoers'.

The verse 32: 26 says: Does it not guide them How many generations We have wiped out before them in whose dwellings they now walk around in? That contain signs, so will they not listen? It is told in the verse 50: 36 how much generation have We wiped out before them. They were much braver than they are and stormed through the land. Yet had they any escape? The verse 22: 45 says, How many towns have We wiped out while they were doing wrong. Their rafters have fallen in, their wells have been abandoned and many impressive Palace as well. The verse 21: 11 says: how many a town which had been doing wrong did We demolish, and rose up other people in its stead? Then as per the verse 21: 14- 15 They cried: Ah! Woe to us! We were indeed wrongdoers, until they were utterly destroyed. See the explanation 2: 57; 6: 43-47 and 131- 133.

6. Then We will question those to whom messengers were sent and We will question the messengers also.

In the verses 39: 69 it is told that the book mentioned in the verses 17: 13-14 will be laid open. Prophets and witnesses will be brought in and judgment will be made with the Truth among them and they will not be harmed. Therefore those who utilized the Soul of Qur'an as a Balance in this world shall have weight in their Balance in the Hereafter. The duty of prophets and believers is to deliver the Message commanded as per the verse 5: 67. It is told in the verses 41:19-24; 36: 65 and 99:4 that those who do not utilize the Soul of Qur'an after receiving It, their own skins, sights and hearings, hands and legs and even Earth will witness against them. See explanation 1: 3; 4: 41- 42; 5: 109 and 6: 165.

7. Then, We will relate about them with Our knowledge, and We were not been absent.

The meaning of what is told in the verse 'We shall relate about them with our knowledge' is not that Allah will say their history to everyone separately. Instead He will produce the scroll which have fastened in every man's neck as an illuminating spread Book and will be told to each individual 'read your own record and it is sufficient yourself this day to make out an account against you' as told in the verses 17: 13-14. The verse 18: 49 says, the Book will be produced and you will see the *mujrims*-the madmen-apprehensive about Its contents, they will say "ah! Woe to us! What a book is this? it omits nothing either small nor large unless it is accounted for". They will find whatever they have done presented there even though your Lord will not harm anyone. The verse 45: 28 and 29 say, You will see every nation crouching; each nation will be called to appear before its book; "today you will be rewarded for whatever you have been doing this book of Ours will pronounce the Truth about you; We have been recording whatever you have been doing". See explanation 2: 255; 5: 105 and 6: 59.

8. The weight in that day will be for the Truth. Those, whose scales are heavy such will be Succeeded.

9. While those, whose scales are, light such are the ones who have lost their Souls because they had been treating wrongfully towards Our verses.

'*Haq*' -Truth- is the Soul of Qur'an as explained in the verses 2:147 and 3: 60. The verses 23: 102-103 say that then those whose Balance is heavy- they will be successful. But whose Balance is light will be the one who have lost their Souls; their abode will be the Hell. The verses 101: 6- 7 say: then, he whose Balance will be heavy, will be in a life of good pleasure and satisfaction. And in the verses 8-9 it is told that but he whose Balance will be light, fell into '*Haviya*'- Blazing Hell. Believers are those who weigh all their deeds with the Soul of Qur'an, which is the Balance, in the worldly life itself considering the verses 16: 64; 18: 103- 106; 39: 69 and 75. If anybody shows hatredness and blindness towards the Soul of Qur'an, It will witness and argue against them. Therefore, the hypocrites who hide knowingly the Soul of Qur'an leading the '*fujjar*'- disbelievers- to a life just opposite to that of Qur'an will go to Hell without even trial as explained in the verses 2: 175 and 4: 145. The disbelievers who did not try to understand what is, what for and why Qur'an after receiving It will be led to Hell in groups after the trial as told in the verse 39: 71. See the explanation 2: 186; 3: 136 and 6: 49.

10. Certainly We have established you on Earth and granted you means by which you can live on It. Yet seldom are you grateful.

The verses 20: 124- 127 say 'whosoever turns away from the Soul of Qur'an, for him has a life narrowed down in this world. We shall raise him up blind on the Day of Judgment. He will ask: Oh my Lord! Why have You raised me up blind while I had sight in the material world? Allah will reply, thus did you when Our verses come unto you, forgot them, so this day you also be forgotten. It is told in the verse 16: 72 that those who pretend blindness towards the Soul of Qur'an in this world will be blind in the Hereafter and most astray from the Guidance. Those who do not utilize the Qur'an after getting It will be seized to Hell prone on their faces- they will be in an evil plight, and as to path most astray told in the verse 25: 34. See the explanation 2: 22- 24; 6: 25- 26 and 55. 'Yet seldom are you grateful' told in this verse and 'Yet how seldom do you remember' told in the verse 3 are the same.

Oh Allah! Include us among the ones who always remember and grateful towards You and include not us ungrateful and disbelievers who lost everything.

11. Certainly, it is We Who created you; then We shaped you. Then We told the Angels prostrate before Adam and they prostrated, not so Iblees who did not join among the prostrated.

Allah says in the verses 15: 28- 31, Behold, your Lord said to the Angels I am about to create man, from sounding and nasty smelling clay from mud molded into shape. When I have fashioned him and blown into him from My spirit, fall you down in obeisance unto him. So the Angels prostrated themselves all of them together, not so Iblees, he refused to be among the prostrated. see the explanation 2: 28 and 4:1. Here there is a possibility to misunderstand that *Iblees* is an Angel, since it is told to prostrate by calling Angels. But *Iblees* was one of the *Jinns* as told in the verse 18: 50. And he was among the disbelievers as told both in the verses 2: 34 and 38: 74.

Before men, the *Jinns* were the vicegerents of Allah on Earth. *Iblees* was the leader of *Jinns*. They were created before men as told in the verse 15: 27. When the *Jinns* become rebellious transgressors, Angels destroyed them under the leadership of *Iblees*. The leadership was given to *Iblees* because he was a believing independent creature. Allah does not command to mankind and Jinn, because they are independent creatures and have freedom to select either Guidance or evil way. On the contrary the Angels are liable to obey the commands of Allah and have no freedom. Read together the verse 66: 6. Not only that the majorities in that assembly were the obedient Angels. Only *Iblees* was present as an independent creature. That was why the address became by calling the Angels.

12. Allah asked: what prevents you from prostrating when I have commanded you? Iblees said: I am better than he. You did create me from fire and him from clay.

As per the verses 15: 32- 33 Allah asks, Oh *Iblees*! What happened to you for not being among those who prostrated themselves? Then he replied, I am not one to prostrate myself to man whom You did create from sounding clay from mud molded into shape and as per the verse 38: 75 Allah asks, Oh *Iblees*! What prevents you from prostrating yourself to one whom I have created with My hands? Are you haughty? Or are you one of the high ones. Through the verse 38: 76 *Iblees* replies I am better than he. You created me from fire and him You created from clay.

13. Allah said: get you down from here; you have no chance to act as so haughty here superiority. Get out, certainly you are among the one's who selected humiliation themselves.

The verses 15: 34- 35 say, and then get you out from here, for you are rejected and accursed. And the curse shall be on you till the Day of Judgment. The same matter is repeated in the verses 38: 77- 78. He was expelled from the Paradise because he became haughty and arrogant being without depending Allah. As a result, he became a desperate *Iblees*, trying to make others desperate by deceiving. Consequently he became satan-devil- prevented from mercy. Those who have a mustard seed of haughtiness in their heart cannot enter into the Paradise. The Soul of Qur'an is the Light to burn the haughtiness. See the explanation 4: 138- 139. The hypocrites who seek power to people forgetting Allah shall go to Hell without trial.

Oh Allah! Include not us haughty and arrogant, include us humble and fearing only You. See the explanation 2: 165- 167.

14. He said; give me respite till the Day they are raised up again.

As per the verse 15: 36 he said, Oh my Lord! Give me then respite till the Day they are raised up again. It is also repeated in the verse 38: 79.

15. Allah said: be you among those who have respite.

Allah says in the verse 15: 37, respite is granted to you. This is also repeated in the verse 38: 80. *Iblees* asked to Allah, Oh my Lord! since my forelock is in Your hands as told in the verses11: 55- 56; Is it Your Will that I did not prostrate? Therefore give me respite. Thus Allah gave respite to him and told when I give a child to Adam; you will be also given a child. By using those children you make abode in hearts of men and travel through their blood. The Soul-mate or *Jinn* comrade of men are the children of that satan. Actually the Soul of Qur'an is his food and cloth. See the explanation 2: 152; 3: 58 and 4: 38.

16. He said, since you have made me aimless, I will waylay them along Your straight way.

As per the verse 15: 39 *Iblees* told that Oh my Lord! Since You have let me go aimless astray, I shall make things on Earth seem attractive to them; I will mislead them all. As per the verses 38: 82- 83 satan said, with Your influence I will make them all aimless astray except the one among them who are your sincere servants. The straight way means the Soul of Qur'an as explained in the verses 6: 125- 126. See explanation 5: 90- 91 and 6: 88- 90

17. I will come upon them from in front of them and from behind them, on their right and on their left. You will not find that most of them are grateful.

The verse 15: 40 say, except your chosen servants among them who live only for You. The verse 76: 3 say, certainly We gave freedom to man either to select the way of grateful or ungrateful. Satan will not approach Muslims who already became *mushriks* by forming different organizations; lest satan approaches the believers belong to the single party of Allah. But upon the believers who utilize the Soul of Qur'an as Safeguard and entrust in Allah-the Lord of the Worlds, satan has no power as told in the verse 16: 99. As per the verse 26: 212 the satans are repelled even to hear the Soul of Qur'an. Not only the men devils hypocrites and *Jinn* devils but all things on Heaven and Earth are commanded to submit before the believer who learn and teach the Soul of Qur'an and thereby keep the Universe in its equilibrium. They are the one who help the Impartial, Lord of the Worlds. See explanation 2: 102, 3: 191 and 4: 118.

18. Allah said, get out of here despised, rejected! If any of them follow you – I will fill Hell with you all.

The verses 15: 41- 43 say, this will be a Straight path up to Me, you will not hold any authority over My servants except for some one who may follow you from among those who are aimless astray. Hell is promised for all of them together. The verses 38: 84- 85 say, this is the Truth, and the Truth what I say I shall certainly fill Hell with you and those who follow you all. About a scene is warned through the verse 14: 22 that after the trial, satan will say; I had no authority over you except to call you, but you listened to me, then reproach me not, but reproach your own Souls. Read together the verses 32: 13- 14, 11: 118 and 119. See explanation 1: 7, 2: 166 and 167.

19. And Oh Adam! Dwell you and your wife in the Paradise and eat wherever you wish; yet do not approach this tree, lest both of you should become wrongdoers.

The verses 20: 117- 119 say, then We said: Oh Adam! Verily, this is an enemy to you and your wife; do not let him turn either of you both out of the Paradise, If so you will become unlucky. You have so much in the Paradise that you need go neither hungry nor naked; you will neither thirst nor feel sun's heat. See explanation 2: 35.

20. Then satan whispered to them, to show them both their private parts, that had hidden to either of them. He said: your Lord only forbids you this tree, so that you will not become two Angels, or lest you both become immortal.

The verses 20: 120- 121 say, but satan whispered to him; he said 'Oh Adam! Shall I lead you to the tree of immortality and such kingdom that will never disappear? So they both ate some of it and so their private parts become apparent to them. They set to patching themselves over with leaves from the Garden. Adam had disobeyed his Lord and become aimless. See explanation 2: 36 and 6: 112.

21. And he swore to them, 'I am a sincere counsellor with both of you.

22. He led them on by deceiving once they had tasted the tree, their private parts became apparent to both of them and they started to patch together leaves from the garden for themselves. Their Lord called out them: "Did I not forbid you that tree and tell you both that satan is an open enemy of yours?"

The verse 20: 122 says, later on his Lord chose him. He relented towards him and guided him. See the explanation 2: 37.

23. Both they prayed: Our Lord, we have wronged our own Souls. If You do not forgive us and grant us mercy, we will be among losers.

It is told in the verse 39: 63 that those who hide the verses of Allah, such are the only losers. As per the verse 11: 47 prophet Nooh prayed, "my Lord, I take refuge with You from asking you something I have no knowledge about. If You do not forgive me and show me mercy, I may become among losers. See explanation 2: 121; 3: 4 and 6: 156.

24. Allah said: "get you down with enmity between one another. Yet you may have residence and means of livelihood for a while".

The verse 20: 123 says, get you down both of you altogether from the Paradise with some of you enemies of others. Should Guidance ever come to you from Me, who follows My Guidance shall never stray away nor become unlucky. The '*Huda*' -Guidance- mentioned here and in the verse 2: 38 is the same. Today it is the Splendid Book-Soul of Qur'an- mentioned in the verses 41: 41-43 to entire mankind. See the explanation 2: 185. By saying 'with enmity between one another' means the disbelievers from men especially hypocrites are enemies to believers from men. And moreover the satans from *Jinn* are also enemies to man. The hypocrites are the enemies of Allah and believers as told in the verses 41: 28 and 63: 4. It is the duty of man to make his Soul-mate believer by supplying the food and cloth of the Soul- the Soul of Qur'an. See explanation 3: 182, 185; 6: 98 and 112.

25. He said: 'you will live on it and you will die on it, and from it will you be brought forth again.'

Allah sent down Adam and Eve bodily keeping all human beings on his nape from the Paradise to Earth. They ate leaves, fruits and vegetables which have the same components of Earth. From which blood is formed, and from blood, sperm is formed. Thus the bodies of human beings are formed from a drop of semen emitted from father's '*swulb*' and mother's '*thara-ib*'. Read together the verses 86: 5- 7. As per the verse 76: 2 human body are created by mingling sperm and ovum of male and female respectively. Allah creates mankind in the wombs of their mothers in stages one after another. He fashioned in due proportion and in the fourth month, Allah takes the Soul from father's nape and blown to the embryo through an Angel. By that the baby gets the '*Rooh*' (Soul+Life). Read together the verses 39: 6, 32: 7- 9. Though the *Rooh* -spirit- of Adam was blown directly by Allah, the rooh of prophet Eisa was blown through Angel *Jibreel* (Gabriel) and the *Rooh* of mankind is blown by special Angels.

The good name of Allah '*Musawir*' means the one who balances the Soul and body. Read together the verse 59: 24.

The body of human beings created from the earth. At the time of burial, the Muslims utter the verse as 20: 55: 'from It (Earth) did We create you and into it shall We return you and from it shall We bring you out once again', by throwing a handful of soil in three times. The body created from soil is a vehicle for *Rooh* to travel. The death occurs when the spirit-Soul +life- depart from body. Men will be resurrected from their burial ground blowing *Rooh* again to it. That is the meaning of what is told in the verse 81: 7 that when the Souls joined to their bodies. Thus, the creation of mankind took place in the Paradise whereas the first birth and second death occurs on Earth. The second birth will be taken place on the Day of Resurrection. See the explanation 2: 28 and 4:1.

26. Oh children of Adam! We have sent you down clothing with which to conceal your private parts and to dress up in. Yet the clothing of heedfulness is the best. That is from the verses of Allah, so they may remember by heart.

The Arabic word '*reesh*' means feathers and scales of birds and animals. Here it means clothes for human being. It is the raiment for protecting and adorning. The clothing of heedfulness is the Soul of Qur'an which is the food, cloth and sight of the Soul. See explanation 2: 2. This clothing of the Soul is stripped off when Adam couple disobeyed the commands of Allah in the Paradise. As per the verse 11: 88 Prophet *Shu'ayb t*old his people, Oh my people! Have you considered while I bear any explanation from my Lord and He has provided me with the best sustenance from Himself. 'The best sustenance' mentioned here is the Soul of Qur'an. The verse 20: 131 ends as 'Your Lords provision is better and everlasting' the provision mentioned here is the Soul of Qur'an. See the explanation 4: 3; 5: 48 and 6: 90.

27. Oh children of Adam! Do not let satan tempt you just as he expelled your parents out of Paradise, stripping them of their clothing in order to show them their private parts. He and his tribe watch you from where you do not see them! Certainly We have appointed satans as patrons for those who do not believe.

Satan prevents from the Soul of Qur'an, in order to prevent from the remembrance of Allah. Thus he permits not to wear the raiment of truthfulness. See explanation 5: 90 and 91. The verses 16: 99 and 100 say that no authority has satan over those who believe and put their trust in their Lord, his authority is over those only who take him as patron and who join partners with Allah. As per the verse 26: 212 the satans are too withdrawn to hear the Soul of Qur'an and the verse 56: 79 says the Soul of Qur'an will not understand to those who are not purified i.e. disbelievers. So to the believers the purified, one in every thousand will consider the Soul of Qur'an as the food, cloth and sight of his Soul mate-jinn comrade- satan's have no any influence. Read together the verses 23: 97-98; 43: 36-37. In other word the believers are the one who utilize the Soul of Qur'an as Safeguard and Shield. All the parties except the party of Allah mentioned in the verse 58: 22, are belonging the party of satan mentioned in the verse 58:19. See the explanation 2: 257; 5: 55- 56 and 6: 158.

28. Whenever they commit any shameful act, they say: 'we found out our forefathers were performing it and Allah has ordered us to do so'. Say: 'verily Allah never orders any shameful act. Do you say something you do not know about Allah?'

This verse was revealed to reprove an immodest custom of the pagan Arabs, who used to encompass the ka'ba nakedly both men and women. They were doing so in order to become as a new born baby. By doing so, they were in false proud that they follow suit their forefathers and Allah has ordered them to do so. See the explanation 5: 104- 105.

Today, the conditions of Muslims, who bear the Qur'an without knowing its contents, are more astray than that of pagan Arabs or any other people. They are in forefront in all evils than that of other communities and behind in doing honorable deeds. In the religion of *Islam* all observances like birth, marriage, death etc. are very easy and logic. But today all these observances are very difficult and unjust in the Muslim community. In the verse 29: 45 it says, 'surely the *swalath* restrains from shameful and evil deeds'; but today it has become a mere bodily exercise, as a result, they indulged in all satanic footprints like smuggling, interest, gambling, hawala, hoarding, black-market, adulteration, deception, breaking promise, false witnessing, robbery, murder, theft, rape, fornication, sodomy, sorcery, killing, squandering, misery etc. They are in forefront in leveling the mountains which are fixed as nails on Earth, filling the cultivating land and construct buildings and there by destroying its equilibrium. This is because they bear the Qur'an as the donkey bears its burden. Read together the verse 16: 61. The disbeliever satan commands to their patrons disbelievers to say about Allah which they do not know. See explanation 2: 169- 170; 6: 144 and 157.

29. Say: my Lord has ordered to observe with justice. Keep your faces set towards Him at every time and places of swalath and appeal to Him; making your religion sincere even as He created you in the beginning, so shall you return.

It is commanded the human being to live as vicegerents of the Creator on Earth keeping the do's and don'ts of Him. The Justice mentioned in this verse is the Soul of Qur'an. Read together the verses 4: 135 and 5: 8. Not only during *swalath* and prayer but all the times one should have the remembrance of Allah as per the verse 2: 186; 3: 191; 4: 103 and 62: 10 in order to get reply the prayer. As per the verse 20: 14 the intention of performing *swalath* is mentioned as you keep up *swalath* to maintain My remembrance or the Soul of Qur'an. 'Even as He created you in the beginning, so shall you return' means 'men will be resurrected in the Hereafter as they were created in the material world.' On that day, everyone individually shall account before the Creator about each and every seconds of their life after the age of fifteenth. See the explanation 1: 4; 6: 94 and 130.

30. One party has He guided while another party ought to be allowed to go astray: they have adopted the satans as patrons instead of Allah, and reckon they are guided.

The guided party is the party of believers and they will utilize the Soul of Qur'an mentioned in the verse 2: 38 as Guidance. And the party who ought to be allowed to go astray is the disbeliever satan's party. They are the hypocrites who hide knowingly and the gone astray people who reject the Soul of Qur'an after receiving It as mentioned in the verses such as 2: 39; 5: 10, 86; 57: 19 and 64: 10. Through the verse 18: 103 Allah commands prophet to ask, shall we tell you of those whose works are in vain? And in the verse 104 it is told that those whose effort lead them astray during the worldly life, while they reckoned they are producing something fine. And the verse 105 says, they are the ones who have disbelieved with their Lord's verses and about meeting Him; their actions will prove to be useless, and We shall set up no weighing in for them on the Resurrection day. See the explanation 1:7; 4: 118; 6: 43; 7: 8 and 9.

31. Oh children of Adam! Wear your best cloths to every places of prostrate. Eat and drink, yet do not overdo things; He does not love the extravagant.

Wear your best cloths includes wearing complete dress, cleaning body, using perfumes etc. places of prostrate means the places of performing *swalath* irrespective of *masjid* or any other places except the graves and lavatory. Prophet taught that for his community all places except graves and lavatory are *masjids*. See explanation 2: 114. Due to the ignorance of the Soul of Qur'an, Muslims-the boar people mentioned in the verses 25: 18 and 48: 12 wear their tidy and beautiful cloths in the functions like marriages and appearing before the material administrators. But they stand before the King of the Kings at the time of *swalath* wearing soiled and untidy cloths and even wearing *dhothies* and *lungies* neglecting these verses. Prophet taught one should not approach *swalath* by eating onions as per the command of this verse. One should not approach *swalath* while smoking or having the smell of sweat or having other nasty smell even performing *swalath* individually. See explanation 4: 43.

It is Allah who bestowed all the sustenance for men to utilize. Therefore, those who show niggardliness after getting it, are the disbelievers as told in the verses 4: 37 and 38. But if they utilize it overdoing without the remembrance of Allah, they will become the brothers of satan while satan is to his Lord ungrateful disbeliever as told in the verse 17: 27. Read together the verses 25: 67 and 92: 5- 21. See explanation 2: 187 and 7: 26

32. Say: Who has forbidden Allah's amenities which He has produced for His servants and the wholesome things from His provision? Say, they are, in the life of this world, for those who believe and exclusively for them on the Day of Judgment. Thus do We explain the verses in detail for the people who know.

As per this verse Allah's pleasure in utilizing the amenities and sustenance which He produced is the believers who are serving Him as his vicegerents. But Allah, as the Impartial and most Gracious, give sustenance in abundance to the disbeliever satan and his party members since they shall have Hellfire in the Hereafter. Read together the verses 39: 7 and 43: 33-35. The believers by understanding the verse 102: 8 then, you shall be questioned that day about all blessings, utilize all the amenities and wholesome things by weighing with the Soul of Qur'an in the worldly life. See explanation 1: 2; 5: 100; 6: 91 and 92.

33. Say: My Lord has only forbidden shameful deeds whether they are open or secret; sins and trespasses without any Truth and that you should associate anything with Allah, for which He has not sent down any authority; and that you should say something you do not know concerning Allah.

If an offence is done knowingly and deliberately it will be considered as 'sin', whereas if it is done unknowingly by ignorance it is considered as 'error'. 'Trespasses without Truth' means act transgressly without Justice or to pretend as anchorites, showing envy, vain glory, boasting etc. without having the Truth- the Soul of Qur'an. It is told in the verse 7: 146 Allah will turn away those who pretend arrogantly as anchorites on Earth without the Soul of Qur'an. See explanation 3: 79; 4: 48; 5: 30; 6: 151 and 152.

34. To every community has its term; so whenever their deadline comes, they will not be postponed it for an hour, nor will they advance it.

See explanation 2: 254 and 6: 2.

35. Oh children of Adam! Whenever any messengers from among yourselves come to relate My verses to you, then anyone who become heedful and reforms on them there shall be no fear and for them will not be grieved.

Since it is mentioned here the word '*rusul*'-messengers- Plural of '*rasool*'-messenger; some rejecters of faith propagate that there shall come messengers after Prophet Muhammad by distorting the verse knowingly. The verse addresses as 'Oh, Children of Adam' not as 'Oh, You who believe', but they claim the addressing as 'oh, you who believe' falsely. From Adam to *Nooh* only prophets were deputed. From *Nooh* to *Muhammad* about three hundred and thirteen messengers were appointed. These transgressors hide what is told in the verse 33: 40 that *Muhammad* is not the father of any of your men, but he is the messenger of Allah and the seal of the Prophets. That means after *Muhammad* there will be neither messenger nor even Prophet. Those who present Prophet *Muhammad* exclusively for Muslims as against the verses such as 7: 157- 158;

21: 107; 25: 1; 34: 28 etc. are also strayed people and they are the only inmates of Hell from mankind since they hide and reject the Qur'an verses. See the explanation 2: 24, 185; 3: 78; 4:155-159 and 171- 173.

36. While those who reject Our verses and treat them with arrogance, such are the inmates of the Fire; they will remain there forever.

Rejecters of the Qur'an verses are the gone astray people and the one who treat them with arrogance are the cursed hypocrites mentioned in the verse 1: 7. To such disbelievers at the time of death Allah will say 'you were among the disbelievers' as per the verse 39: 59. And they are the '*mujrims*' as per the verses 7: 40; 10: 17; 36: 59-62 etc. See explanation 2: 39; 4: 150- 151; 6: 25 and 26.

37. Who is more in the wrong than someone who invents a lie about Allah or rejects His verses? For such, have been given their portion from the Book until when Our messengers of death arrive and hold their Souls, they will ask: "where are whatever you used to appeal to instead to Allah?" They will say: they have left us in the lurch, and they shall bear witness against themselves that they were indeed disbelievers.

The verse 36: 70 says, this Qur'an is revealed in order to warn to anyone who alive and for justifying the sentence of punishment on the disbelievers. The verse 69: 50 say, certainly this Qur'an is a cause of sorrow for the disbelievers. Allah, the Impartial never lets anyone enter to the Hell unless he confesses himself that he is a disbeliever. Then the verses 43: 30- 31 say, but when the Truth - Qur'an- came to them they said, this is sorcery, and we do reject it. Also they say: why is not this Qur'an sent down to some great man of either of the two cities -*Mecca*, *Tha'if*. The verse 45: 11 says this is Guidance and for those who hide the verses of their Lord, for them have filthy painful torment.

Today, the Book is only the Soul of Qur'an. 'The one who invent lie about Allah' are the hypocrites who hide and distort the verses of Allah knowingly. And those 'who reject the verse of Allah' are the gone astray people who blindly following the hypocrites without trying to understand what is, what for and why Qur'an. Both categories from among Muslims only and at the time of death they will witness against themselves that indeed they were disbelievers. The verses 9: 55 and 85 says, about the hypocrites do not let their wealth and children astonish you; Allah only wants to punish them by means of these during this world, and let their Souls perish while they are disbelievers. If the verse 9: 84 is ending as: and die while they were transgressors about hypocrites; the verse 9: 125 ends as: they will die while they are disbelievers. When the believers recite the verse 1: 7, "not the path upon whom Your wrath happened, they shall have in their mind the hypocrites; 'and who gone astray' they shall have in their mind the *fujjar*-who eat the body of Qur'an. See the explanation 2: 254; 3: 10 and 6: 130.

38. He will say: "Enter the Fire along with the nations of Jinns and human kind who have passed away before you." Every time one nation enters it, it will curse its sister nation until, when they have all gathered together in it, the last of them will say to the first: "our Lord, these people have misled us, so give them double torment from the Fire!" He will say: "each shall have double, even though you do not realize it".

It is the duty of the parents to teach the Soul of Qur'an, which is the Ticket to Paradise, to their children before their fifteenth age. Otherwise, when they all gathered together in the Hell, the children shall tell against their parents: "our Lord these have misled us, so give them double torment from the Fire!" Today the Muslims who read these verses but without teaching the Soul of Qur'an give material education to their children and vainglory in it, have to beware of this warning 'each shall have double, even though you do not realize it' means, they shall have their own punishment for not utilizing the Soul of Qur'an, in addition to this they shall have punishment for not giving It, to their Soul-mate as well as children. Each and every adult is constructing Paradise or Hell here as explained in the verses 3: 136 and 182. See explanation 4: 85 and 6: 26.

After explaining the torment for the arrogant people in the verses 38: 55-58, Allah says in the verse 59 this troop has to join with you. Then the troop already reached in the Hell will say: "They are not welcomed to here. Certainly they shall all burn in the Fire." The verse 60 says, the followers shall say to them: "Indeed you have no welcome either. You have prepared it for us; what an awful plight". As per the verse 61 the followers shall say: "Our Lord, who ever prepared this for us, give them double torment in the fire". As per the verses 62-63, the companions of Fire- the hypocrites and their blind followers, '*fujjar*'-will say what is the matter with us that we do not see any men whom we used to consider as evil persons? Did we take them for laughing-stocks or has our eyesight failed to notice them? As per the verse 64 "that is true: the people in the Fire will just argue away". See explanation 2: 166- 167; 6: 89 and 90.

39. And the first of them will tell to the last: "you had advantages over us." So taste torment because of what you have been earning.

The meaning of what the parents will tell to their children that 'you had advantages over us' is that we had no classes where the Soul of Qur'an is explained, we had not received the Book- the Soul of Qur'an in our hearts language, during our period facilities like Radio, Tape recorder, Video, TV. Computer etc. to hear and see the Soul of Qur'an were not become general. We had no financial capacity to utilize them, and you had all these facilities. But, you did not utilize these facilities particularly to learn and teach the Soul of Qur'an. Therefore, you shall have to taste the torment which you have been earning. The Phrase 'You had advantages over us' also has the meaning that 'no advantage had you over us'. That is instead of having all the advantages you didn't utilize the great Bounty- the Soul of Qur'an as Insight to identify the aim of life. To put it brief nobody can blame others. It is warned through the verse 14: 22 that on the Day of Judgment after the trial satan will say: 'Do not blame me, you blame yourself. No chance will be there to blame parents as told in the verse 7: 173. See explanation 2: 140- 141; 6: 94 and 104.

40. Certainly those who reject Our verses and feel too arrogance towards them, the gates of Heaven will not be opened for them, nor will they enter the Paradise- until a camel can pass through the eye of tailors' needle. Thus We reward Mujrims.

Here and in the verse 7: 36 those who reject the Soul of Qur'an are the *fujjar* and those who feel too arrogance for the verses are the hypocrites. Both categories belong to *Mujrims*. See explanation 6: 55. After describing the death scene of a wicked Soul Prophet recited this verse. Only those who burn their arrogance with the Soul of Qur'an, which is the Light from the Light of Heaven and Earth- Allah- and then die as a newborn baby can only enter the Paradise. See explanation 3: 101-102; 4: 174 and 175.

All mankind are created in the Paradise. Read together the explanation 2: 28, 38 and 4: 1. The Soul and the deeds of believers will be recorded in the book '*Illiyyeen*' in the Paradise and that of *fujjar*- rejecters in the book-'*Sijjeen*' in the Hell, as told in the verse 83: 7 and 18. Prophet physically went to Paradise and made conversation with Allah, on the day of '*Isra'-wal- Mi'raj*'; the believers have to go to Paradise by Souls during "*Athahiyyath*" in *swalath* by utilizing the Soul of Qur'an, the Light as vehicle. For that purpose Prophet *Muhammad* was taken to Paradise and ordained five times *swalath* as explained in the verse 17:1. All the deeds without testifying with the Soul of Qur'an will only ascend up to the Heaven, then it will fall into the *Sijjeen* as told in the verse 22: 31. See the explanation 2: 186 and 4: 48.

The '*Mouedhathul Hasnath*' of this verse can be understood as follows: Certainly those who recite the verses of Allah and make It truthful, the gates of Paradise are kept opened for them and they will be entered in It without trial. Thus We reward to those who live seeing Allah under the Light- the Soul of Qur'an.

41. They will have a cradle with Fire in the Hell, while over them their will hang on awnings. Thus We reward wrongdoers.

The wrongdoers mentioned here are the '*mujrims*' mentioned in the above verse. The verse 32: 22 says, who is more in wrong than one to whom are remembered the verses of his Lord in his heart's language and then turns away there from? Indeed We shall revenge to such '*mujrims*'. See the explanation 6: 21, 25 and 7: 37.

42. And those who believe and perform honorable deeds- We never assign any Soul more than it can cope with. Such will become inhabitants of the Paradise; they will live in It forever.

The believers mentioned in this verse have just opposite character of those mentioned in the verses 36 and 40. Today, to perform honorable deeds means to mould the belief under the Light of Qur'an and propagate the Message of It to others. That is the reality what Prophet taught: The best one among you is one who learns and teaches the Soul of Qur'an. The meaning of Prophet's teaching on the day of *Hajjathul Vida'* that the believers should stay biting the Soul of Qur'an with molar teeth during the Last Days, is also nothing else. See the explanation 2: 38, 285- 286; 6: 151 and152.

43. And we will strip away any rancor in their chests. Rivers will flow beneath them and they will say: "Praise be to Allah Who

led us to this! We would never have been guided if Allah had not led us to this. Our Lords messengers have brought the Truth". They will hear some one call out: "Here is the Paradise; you may be inherited because of what you have been doing".

The believers have to strip away any envy and rancor between them with the Soul of Qur'an and should unite as one body. See the explanation 3: 9-10 and 101-103. In the verse 59: 10 it is told that the believers who came to *Islam* after the '*Muhajirs*' and '*Ansars*' will pray: "Our Lord forgive us and our brethren who have preceded us in faith, and do not place any rancor in our hearts concerning those who believe. Our Lord, indeed You are Compassionate, Merciful".

The Paradise can only be inherited by working here under the Light of Qur'an. In other words the men, who were created in the Paradise, are deputed to Earth in order to prepare the Paradise here. The verse 32: 19 says: For those who believe and convey the belief to others shall have Paradise as hospitable homes for what they were doing here. As per the verses 10: 9-10 believers' prayer in the Paradise will be: Glory be to You, Oh Allah, while their greeting in it will be: 'peace' and the close of their appeal: "Praise be to Allah, Lord of the Worlds". See the explanation 1: 1 and 3: 136.

44. And the inhabitants of the Paradise shall call out to the inmates of the Fire: "We have found out that what our Lord promised us is true. Have you found what your Lord promised you to be true?" They will say: "Yes"! Then an announcer among them will call out: "Allah's curse rests on wrongdoers".

45. Who obstruct Allah's path and try to make It crooked, and are disbelievers in the Hereafter.

Allah's curse shall have on those who utilize not the Soul of Qur'an, hide and thus forbid to others. They distort the verses against the will of Allah. They are the transgressors, wrongdoers and disbelievers. The verses 11: 18-19 say: Who does more wrong than those who invent a lie against Allah. They will be brought before their Lord, and the witnesses will say: These are the ones who lied against their Lord. Behold, the curse of Allah is on wrongdoing people. The wrongdoing people are those who forbid the men from the path of Allah- the Soul of Qur'an- try to twist It and denied the Hereafter. See the explanation 1: 7; 2: 79; 5: 57 and 6: 47.

46. Between them both there will be a barrier on the heights above there will be men who recognize everyone by their features. They will call out to the inhabitants of the Paradise: "Peace be upon you!" They have not yet entered It, even though they long to.

47. When their sights are shifted towards the inmates of the Fire, they will say: "Our Lord do not place us alongside such wrong doing people".

As per the verse 57:12, some day you will see the believing men and the believing women with their light streaming on a head of them and off to their right: "Your good news today, Paradise beneath which flow rivers, to live in forever!" That will be the splendid achievement. The verse 13 says: That Day the hypocritical men and hypocritical women will tell the ones who believe: "Wait for us; we need to borrow a light from you. It will say: "Go on back the way you came, and request a Light. So a wall will rise up between them with a door in it: inside there will be mercy while out side facing there will be torment. The verse 14 says that the hypocrites will call out to them: "Were we not with you?" They will say: "Of course, but you tempted one another, and let yourselves waver and doubt your guessing has deceived you till Allah's command came along. The deceiver satan has even deluded you concerning Allah. And the verse 15 says: So today no ransom will be accepted from you or from those who disbelieve: "Your lodging shall be the Fire; it is your patron and what an evil returning place! Read together the verses 9: 67-68; 33: 1, 73; 48: 6 and 98: 6. See the explanation 5: 51 and 7: 37

48. The men on the heights will call out to some men whom they will recognize by their features; they will say: "Here not benefited your multitude and how proud you were acting".

As per the verse 37: 50-51 then the inhabitants of the Paradise will step forward to ask one another, one of them will speak up and say: There was a friend for me. As per the verse 52, who used to say do you among the Truth convinced? As per the verse 53, when we have died and become dust and bones, will we be called to account about this life? As per the verse 54 He will say: "Would you just take a look? As per the verse 55, so he did look down and will see him in the middle of Hades! As per the verse 56 he will say: "By Allah, if it were possible to you, you would have also seized me to it. As per the verse 57 if it were not for my Lord's favor, I would have been made to appear there. As per the verses 58-59, are not we mortal except for our first death? And will we not be punished. The verse 60 says indeed this is the only splendid achievement. As per the verse 61, it will be told for such as this let workers have to work. Just like no mortal in the Paradise there will be no mortal in the Hell also as told in the verse 87: 13. Then he will neither die in it nor yet live there. The verse 20: 74 says that everyone who comes to his Lord as a *mujrim* will have Hell, he will neither die nor yet does he live. As per the verse 4: 56 in the Hell when the skins are roasted through, new skins will be substituted in order to taste the torment. See the explanation 2: 6-7; 4: 60-65; 6: 116 and 7: 49.

49. (Pointing to the inhabitants of the Paradise) Are those the men about whom so you swore Allah would not confer any mercy on them? Are told enter the Paradise; no need for you to fear nor should you feel sadden.

The disbelievers mock and ridicule the small band of believers and over joy with their huge multitude and organizational arrogance in this World. Here it is portrayed the scene of such disbelievers coming in the Hereafter. See the explanation 2: 212. The inmates of the Hell will say, as per the verses 38: 62-64, what happened to us that we see not men whom we used to number among the bad ones? Did we treat them in ridicule or have our sight failed to perceive them? That is true- the mutual recrimination of the people of the fire. This is not the character of non Muslims- Christian or Hindus- who are in majorities, but this is the character of hypocrites and *fujjar* among the Muslims who received the Soul of Qur'an but not utilized and they are belong to satan's party belonging different organizations. See the explanation 2: 38; 4: 112-113; 6: 109-110; 7: 40 and 41.

50. The inmates of Fire will call out to inhabitants of Paradise: "Pour some water over us, or anything which Allah has provided you with!" They will say: "Allah has forbidden either of them to disbelievers.

51. Who have taken their religion as a time pass and for amusement; Worldly life has deceived them. Today We shall forget them just as they forgot about meeting of this Day of theirs and they were repudiating with Our verses.

The pathetic condition of inmates of Hell between the inhabitants of Paradise is portrayed here. That may be in between the parents in the Hell and the children in the Paradise or vice versa. As per the verses 20: 124-127 any one who fail to utilize the Soul of Qur'an after receiving It will have a meager livelihood and We shall summoned him as a blind person on Resurrection Day. He will say: "My Lord! Why have you summoned me as a blind person when I had sighted". Allah will say: "thus did our verses come to you, and you forgot them; just like that you have been forgotten this Day". Thus We reward any one whoever does think and not believe in his Lords verses. Torment in the Hereafter will be even more severe and everlasting. See the explanation 2: 85; 5: 57 and 58. As per the verse 32: 14 it will be said to the inmates of Hell; so have a taste, since you have forgotten about the meeting on this Day of yours! We have likewise forgotten you. Taste the torment of eternity because of what you have been doing. Read together the verse 39: 71.

As per the verses 41: 26-28 the disbelievers- enemies of Allah, who obstruct others from the Soul of Qur'an will be rewarded the Fire! They will find a home there forever as a reward because they were repudiating Our verses. No one will repudiate to Our verses except the disbelievers and wrongdoers is told in the verses 29: 47, 49 respectively. Read together the verses 25: 27-30. See the explanation 5: 44 and 45. The verse 31: 31-32 say that have you not seen ships sailing along at sea because of Allah's favors, so He may show you some of His Signs? Verily in that are Signs for everyone who is patient and grateful. Whenever waves cover them like awnings, they appeal to Allah sincerely; submitting all life to Him! Yet once He delivers them to land, some of them select middle way in between belief and disbelief. And no one will repudiate Our verses except treacherous and the ungrateful. Read together the verse 35: 32. See the explanation 4: 150-151; 6: 31-33, 70; 7: 37 and 38.

52. And We have brought them the Book; We have spelled it out knowingly as Guidance and Mercy for the people who believe.

The verse 35: 14 ends as no one notifies to you except the One Who is acquainted of all times. The verses 7: 203; 12: 111 and 16: 64 also end as: Qur'an is a Guidance and Mercy for the people who believe. The verse 10: 57 ends as Qur'an is a Guidance and Mercy for those who believe. The verse 27: 77 says: Certainly Qur'an is a Guidance and Mercy for believers. See the explanation 1: 2; 3: 7 and 6: 155-157.

53. What they are waiting except for Its interpretation? The Day Its interpretation comes along, those who have already forgotten It will say: "Our Lord's messengers did bring the Truth! Have we any intercessors to intercede for us? Or should we be sent back, then we would do work so differently from the way we have been doing." Certainly, they have lost their own Souls and what they have been inventing has left them in the lurch.

One third of the Qur'anic verses are to be materialized in the Hereafter. The believers by utilizing the Insight which is the Soul of Qur'an will foresee the forthcoming events in the Hereafter; and they earnestly pray in their mind not to include among the disbelievers who should face such a pathetic, terrible and horrible condition in the Hereafter. The believers having the aim of life will construct Paradise here in this World and will inhabit the Paradise by their death. The disbelievers who repudiate with the verse of Qur'an, and not utilize the Soul of Qur'an as a Ticket to Paradise will go to the Hell by their death. This verse portraits the terrible and horrible condition of disbelievers in the Hereafter. Allah, the Lord of all Worlds, may send the people who did not receive the Qur'an to any other Worlds which are neither Paradise nor Hell. Allah- the Just, Impartial will not send anyone to Hell unless and until he witnesses against himself that he was a disbeliever. See the explanation 2: 146-148; 6: 27-30, 94 and 111.

54. Certainly your Lord is Allah, Who created the Heavens and Earth in six days, and then He mounted on the throne. He wraps night up with day time, seeking it automatically. The Sun, Moon and Stars are regulated by His command. Surely creation and command belongs to Him. Blessed be Allah, the Lord of the Worlds.

The One Who created all things has the Power and Right to issue the commands and prohibitions to the creatures as well as to survive or destroy them. Then, if there is Lord besides Allah to issue the commands and prohibitions and another to survive or destruct, the life will become awkward. The verse 40: 64 ends as: That is Allah, your Lord; so blessed Allah Lord of the Worlds. In the verses 23: 12-14 after explaining the creation of men, Allah says: Then blessed be Ailah, the most excellent Creator among the creators.

It is only Allah Who created not only the Heavens and Earth but all between them including mankind in six days. The verse 32: 4 says: Allah is the One, Who created Heaven and Earth as well as whatever lies in between them in six days. Then He mounted on the throne. You have neither patron nor any intercessor besides Him. Then will you not make remember others with their mind? Read together the verse 25: 59. See the explanation 1: 1; 2: 29 and 4: 133.

55. Appeal to your Lord beseeching and in private, He does not love those who are aggressive.

In the verse 40: 60 says: Your Lord has said: "Appeal to Me, I shall respond to you the ones who are too proud to serve Me will enter Hell abjectly. See the explanation 7: 13. But two conditions are mentioned in the verse 2: 186 to respond for the appeal. One should call Allah submitted by the Soul of Qur'an earnestly by heart, as proving that He knows the state of the chests, otherwise their responds will be to the call of satan, and the satan himself will say that fact on the Day of Judgment as told in the verse 14: 22. Moreover their worship will turn to satan as told in the verse 36: 60-62. Read together the verse 13: 18. As per the verse 7: 205 do remember your Lord within your own Soul, beseeching and fearfully without pronouncing 'Allah' by your tongue. As per the verse 19: 3 *Zakariya* appealed to his Lord with a suppressed cry for a child.

'Certainly He does not love those who are aggressive' means, He does not like the heedless people who pray very loudly convincing men. The people who recite the Qur'an without knowing Its contents are *fujjar,* the transgress hypocrites who do not pray sincerely and they are those who have forgotten Allah. See the explanation 2: 99, 152 and 7: 26-30.

56. Do not mischief on Earth after its reformation, and appeal to Him out of fear and expectation; indeed Allah's Mercy lies close to those who live by seeing Him.

The verses 32: 15 and 16 say that the only ones who believe in Our verses are those who drop down in prostration whenever they are remembered with them, and glorify their Lord's praise and they do not act so proudly. They slip away quietly from their beds to appeal to their Lord in fear and expectation, and spend whatever We have provided them with. See the explanation 2: 11 and 12.

Prophet taught to pray always as follows, Oh Allah! I seek your Paradise and the words and deeds which will bring close to It, and seek refuge to you from the Hell and the words and deeds which will bring close to it. Oh Allah! Make me among the beseechers, fearful and heedful. And not include me among aggressive, transgressors and heedless. See the explanation 2: 112; 6: 52, 63-64, 124 and 7: 40.

57. He is the one Who sends winds to announce His Mercy directly, so that whenever they lift up the heavy clouds, We drive them along to a dead country side and send down water from them; and thus We bring forth every kind of fruit. Thus We bring forth the dead too; so you may remember this in mind.

The verse 30: 46 says, it is one of the signs, that Allah exists, that He sends the winds as a herald of glad tidings, giving a taste of His Mercy. The verses 50: 7-11 say: And the Earth We have spread it out and set there in mountains as nails and grown every kind of beautiful thing in pairs on it as an Insight and Reminder for every repentant servant. We have sent down blessed water from the sky and We grow gardens with it as well as grain to be harvested, and soaring palms which have compact clusters as sustenance for servants. We have revived a dead country side with it; thus will your coming-forth be. The verse 30: 19 says that He brings forth the living from the dead and brings forth the dead from the living, and He revives the Earth following Its death, and thus you will be brought forth again. The verse 30: 24 says among His signs how He shows you lightening for both fear and expectation. He sends water down from the sky so He may revive the Earth with it following its death. In that are signs for the people who think utilizing their intelligence. It is told in the verse 24: 43 that He sends down hail stone from the Sky Mountains: "and He strikes anyone He wishes with it and wards it of from anyone He wishes. A flash from His lightening almost takes one's sight away! The mountains in the sky mentioned in this verse revealed before 1400 years is only discovered after inventing the aeroplane in 1902. Therefore this type of the Qur'an verses denote that Qur'an is from the One who acquainted three times-the past, present and future and making truth the verse 41: 53 as We will show them Our verses on the horizons as well as with in themselves, until it becomes clear to them that It is the Truth, does your Lord not suffice as a witness for everything? The verses 30: 48-50 say: Allah is the One Who sends the winds to blow the clouds along He spreads them out in the sky just as He wishes, and breaks them up into fragments so you see a shower of hail-stone coming from inside them when He strikes any of His servants who

He wishes with it, they are over charmed, even if before it fell on them they had felt despair. Then look at the traces of Allah's Mercy, how He revives the Earth following its death. Surely that is the Reviver of the dead; He is capable of everything. The verse 43: 11 says that Who has sent down water from the Sky in due measure just so have raised up a dead land with it; thus you all will come forth too. Read together the verses 13: 17; 22: 5; 25: 48-49; 39: 21 and 41: 39. See the explanation 6: 125-126, 141; 7: 3 and 26.

58. A good land brings forth with its Lord's permission, while whatever is sterile will produce only grudgingly. Thus We spell out verses for people who act grateful.

The good land is compared to believers and the bad land is compared to disbelievers. The believers shall make their deeds under the Light, of the Soul of Qur'an in order to get weight in their Balance in the Hereafter. See the explanation 7: 8-9. The deeds of disbelievers will be in vain and they will include among the losers of goal of life, since they hide and reject the Soul of Qur'an after receiving It. The verses 14: 24-27 say: Do you not consider how Allah makes up a parable? A good word may be compared to a good tree, whose root is firm and whose branches soar up in to the sky, it yields its food each season with its Lords Permission. Allah composes parables for mankind so that they may be remembered by mind. A bad word may be compared to a bad tree: it will be uprooted from the face of the Earth; it has no foot hold. Allah braces those who believe with firm with speech during Worldly life and in the Hereafter, while Allah lets wrongdoers stray away. Allah does whatever He wishes. See the explanation 2: 264-266; 5: 100; 7: 10 and 32.

59. We sent Nooh to his people and he said: "Oh my people serve Allah alone, you have no other Deity than Him. I fear the torment of an awful day".

60. The chiefs of his people said: "Indeed we see you are in manifest astray".

61. He said: "Oh my people! No, trace of astray lies with me, but I am a messenger from the Lord of Worlds".

62. I transmit my Lords Messages to you, and counsel you sincerely. I know something you do not know from Allah.

63. Are you surprised that a Reminder should come to you from your Lord through one of your own men, in order to warn you and you may become heedful with It, and so that you may be received Mercy?

The messengers of all time brought the same Message. That is the Reminder which is the Soul of Qur'an. It is for warning entire mankind of surviving, to become heedful by keeping Allah in hearts and in order that they may be blessed. See the explanation 2: 285-286; 3: 132; 6: 157 and 7: 2.

64. But they rejected him and We delivered him and those with him in the Ark, but We overwhelmed in the flood those who rejected Our verses. They were indeed a blind people.

See the explanation 6: 11 and 47. Prophet *Nooh's* history of events are portrayed in the verses 10: 71- 73; 11: 25- 49; 21: 76- 77; 23: 23- 30; 26: 105-120; 29: 14- 15; 36: 41; 37: 75- 82; 54: 9- 17 and 71: 1-28.

65. To the Aa'd people We sent Hood, one of their own brethren. He said: Oh my people! You live only for Allah. You have no other Deity except Him. Will you not then keep Him in your heart?

66. The chiefs of disbelievers among his people said: Ah! We see you are in folly and think you are one among the liars.

67. He said: Oh my people, There is no folly in me, but I am a messenger from the Lord of all Worlds.

68. I deliver unto you the messages of my Lord. I am to you a sincere and trustworthy advisor.

69. Are you surprised that a Reminder from your Lord should come to you through one of your own men, so that he may warn you? Remember when He made you inheritors after the people of Nooh and gave you stature tall among the nations. Remember Allah's marks, so that you may prosper.

All the men are created in Paradise and are deputed to the Earth in order to live as the vicegerents of Allah. But only believers bear His representation. The disbelievers bear the representation of satan and therefore they will gather together in the Hell with satan. See the explanation 2: 30; 4: 118 and 6: 133.

70. They said: "Have you come to us so we will serve Allah Alone? And forsake whatever our forefathers have been serving? Bring us whatever you threaten us with, if you are among the truthful.

The disbelievers and hypocrites in every time even today say in the same manner. The verse 17: 45- 46 say, whenever you read the Qur'an, We place a hidden curtain between you and those who do not believe in the Hereafter. We place wrappers over their hearts lest they comprehend It and dullness in their ears, when you mention your Lord Alone in the Qur'an they even turn back in disgust. The verse 39: 45 says, 'whenever Allah Alone is remembered, the hearts of those who do not believe in the Hereafter shrink with aversion, while when others are remembered instead of Him, behold, they are overjoyed. Read together the verse 18: 57. Muslims who read these verses are in forefront to invoke others like *Badr* Martyrs, sheik Muhyudheen, Ajmeer Khoja etc. instead of Allah. As per the verse 25: 18 on the Day when all the creatures are summoned, these great people will be against them and will say 'they people were a boar people who were living forgetting the Soul of Qur'an. And as per the verse 25: 28-29 say, this wrong doing people will bite their hands and will cry as, it is too bad for me! If I had not adopted so and so as a close friend, he led me astray from the Soul of Qur'an even after It had reached to me. Satan is ever a betrayer to man. And as per the verse 25: 30 the Messenger will say, 'Oh my Lord, my own people were fleeing from this Qur'an neglecting. The verse 43: 44 says that indeed It is a Reminder for you and for your people, and you will all be questioned. See the explanation 6: 25 and 26.

71. He said: blight and wrath from your Lord have already fallen on you. Are you arguing with me about some names that you and your forefathers have made up? Allah has not sent down any authority for them. Then you just wait, I am waiting along with you.

As for the reply of the disbelievers' question through the verse 32: 28 that when will this victory for believers be if you are so truthful? Allah order to reply through the verses 29-30 as, 'on the Day of victory, their accepting faith will not benefit those who have disbelieved, nor will they be allowed any delay. Neglect them and wait; they will be waiting too!' See the explanation 4: 33; 6: 19, 22-24, 158 and 159.

72. So We saved him and those who adhered to him, by Our Mercy and We cut off the roots of those who rejected Our verses and were not believers.

For further information about prophet *Hood* and his people read the verses 11: 50- 60; 26: 123- 140; 46: 21- 28; 54: 18- 22; 69: 4 and 6- 8. By Our Mercy means Allah's Permission- the Soul of Qur'an. See the explanation 3: 97 and 6: 45.

73. To Thamood We sent Swalih their own brethren. He said: Oh my people, you serve Allah Alone! You have no other Deity than Him. An evidence has come to you from your Lord: This camel belonging to Allah is a sign for you, So leave her grazing on Allah's Earth and do not let any harm touch her lest some painful torment should seize you.

74. And remember how He made you inheritors after the Aa'd people and settled you on the Earth: you build palaces and castles in its plains and curve out homes in the mountains. So remember the marks from Allah and refrain from evil and mischief on Earth.

75. The chiefs among his people who were puffed up with pride, asked the ones who were esteemed weak, even though they still believed: 'Do you know whether swalih is a messenger from his Lord?' They answered, 'we are believers in whatever he has been sent with'

76. Those who acted proudly replied, 'we are disbelievers in whatever you believe with'.

77. Then they ham-strung the camel, object to their Lord's command insolently, and said: 'Oh swalih bring us what you promise us with, if you are among the messengers'.

78. Where upon a terrible catastrophe affected them, so one morning they lay covering in their homes.

79. Then he turned away from them and said: 'Oh my people, I have delivered my Lord's Message to you and counseled you sincerely, but you do not like sincere reformers'.

For further details about this event read together the verses 11: 61- 68; 26: 141- 151; 54: 23- 32 and 91: 11- 15.

80. And there was Looth when he told his people: do you indulge in a shameful practice such as no one in the world has ever indulged in previously?

81. For you approach men lustfully instead of women! Rather you are a dissipated people.

82. His people's answer was nothing except to say: run them out of your city: they are persons who are trying to keep pure.

83. Then We saved him and his family except his wife; she was one of those who lagged behind.

84. And We sent a rain down on them: Look, what was the consequence for such mujrims?

For further information read together 11: 69- 83; 15: 51- 77; 26: 160-175; 27: 54- 58; 29: 28- 35; 51: 24- 37 and 54: 33- 40. For *mujrims* see the explanation 6: 55 and 7: 40.

85. To the Midian We sent Shua'yb their brother. He said: Oh my people, you serve Allah Alone You have no other Deity besides Him. Now come to you evidence from your Lord. So, offer full measure and weight, and do not reduce people the things those are their dues and do no mischief on Earth after its reformation. That will be best for you if you are believers.

86. And do not lurk along every road, threatening and blocking anyone off from Allah's way who believe in Him, and seeking to make It crooked. And remember when you were few and We multiplied you. And see what the consequence of those who did mischief was.

See the explanation 7: 44 and 45.

87. And if there is a faction of you who believes in what I have been sent with, and another faction which does not so believe, still be patient until Allah judges between us. He is the best of Judges.

88. The chiefs of his people, who had acted proudly said: 'Oh Shua'yb we will run you out of our city as well as those who believe along

with you; or else you will return to our tradition and observances!' He asked: even though we detest it?

Though there is not any compulsion in religion as explained the verse 2: 256, the policy of hypocrites who are falsely priding towards the believers who holdfast the Soul of Qur'an and keep aloof from the flow of the Muslim majority is the same as in the above said verses. See explanation 2: 166- 167; 6: 123 and 124.

89. We should invent a lie against Allah if we returned to your religion after Allah saved from It. There is no means for us to return to it unless Allah, our Lord should wish us to; our Lord comprises everything in knowledge. On Allah have we relied? Our Lord, really deliver from us our own people; You are the best deliver.

Read together the verses 11: 84-95 and 26:177-190. See the explanation 2: 255; 3: 7 and 6: 59.

90. The chiefs of his people who disbelieved said: if you follow Shua'yb, you will then be losers only.

91. So an Earthquake caught them, and one morning they lay covering in their homes.

If read together this verse and 7: 78 we can understand that both *Thamood* and *Midian* people were destroyed in the same manner.

92. Those who rejected Shua'yb became as if they had never been in the homes where they had flourished; those who rejected Shu'ayb were only the losers.

As per the verse 90 above the hypocrites among them told: if you follow Shua'yb, you will then be losers only. But as per this verse the hypocrites and their followers who rejected him became the losers both in this world and in the Hereafter. If we take the Soul of Qur'an as *mouidath*- admonition- we can see that today's hypocrites who pretend false proudly as scholars and the disbelievers who follow them are having the same attitude towards the believers who holdfast the Soul of Qur'an. Their mutual dispute, cursing and accusation in the Hereafter is explained in the verses 2: 166 and 167. See the explanation 7: 38- 40.

93. So he turned away from them and said: 'Oh my people, I have delivered my Lord's message to you and counseled you sincerely. Then why should I grieve over a disbelieving people?

Certainly Allah will not guide a people who hide the Soul of Qur'an which is the Message of Allah. See the explanation 5: 67.

94. We have never sent a prophet into any city unless We first seized its people with suffering and hardship, so that they might be humbled.

95. Then We turned evil into good so that they were thriving and saying, both hardship and happiness befell to our ancestors. So We seized them suddenly while they did not even perceive it.

Here, after describing the history of events of several Prophets separately, Allah says the procedure that He takes when He deputed Prophets all time. See the explanation 6: 42- 44. Whenever Prophets were deputed to any people, they were afflicted different kinds of adversities in order to make them humble to hear the Messages from their Lord. See explanation 2: 155-157. The verses 8: 2-4 says, verily the believers are those who, when Allah is remembered have a tremor in their hearts, and when they hear His verses recited in their hearts language, their faith will be increased and they will entrust everything in their Lord.

If they do not ready to accept the Truth even after these adversities, they will be tested with prosperities. See explanation 6: 123- 124. Thus, when all the people became transgressors by forgetting Allah and the aim of life, punishment seized them suddenly. See explanation 6: 47. Prophet taught, Catastrophes purifies the true believer until he is completely clean from sins. But the hypocrite is like a donkey. It does not know why its boss tied or let it free. Read together the verses 10: 21; 16: 112; 30: 41 and 44: 10- 14. See explanation 6: 42-47.

96. If the people of the cities had believed and followed the Soul of Qur'an, We would have showered blessings from Heaven and Earth on them. But they rejected, so We seized them because of what they had been acquiring.

See the explanation 2: 57; 5: 65 and 66.

97. Do the people of cities feel secure from Our mights striking them at dead of night while they are asleep?

98. Or do the people of the cities feel secure from Our mights striking in bright day light while they are playing around?

The verses 67: 16 and 17 say, do you feel secure that He, Who is in the Heaven will not cause you to be swallowed up by the Earth when it shakes? Or do you feel secure that Who is in Heaven will not send against you a catastrophe so that you shall know how was My warning? The verse 16: 45 says, do then those who device evil plots feel secure that will not cause the Earth to swallow them up or that the wrath will not seize them from direction they little perceive? See explanation 7: 4 and 5.

99. Do they then feel secure from Allah's design? No one can feel secure from the plan of Allah except the people who will lose out.

The verse 14: 46 says, all the times the rebellious people make plots against the Truth, but their plots were nothing in the sight of Allah, even though they were so strong to shake the mountains. That means, if anybody devises plots against the Truth, it will act as a boomerang. Thus, no one will device against the Truth except the people who are to be perished. See explanation 3: 54; 6: 123 and 124.

100. To those who inherit the Earth in succession to its previous possessors, is it not a guiding lesson that, if We so willed We could punish them too for their sins and seal up their hearts so that they could not hear.

The verse 32: 26 says, does it teach them a lesson, how many generations We destroyed before, through whose dwelling places they walk. Verily, in that are signs. Do they not then listen? The verses 22: 45 and 46 say, how many cities have We wiped out while they were doing wrong, they tumbled down on their roofs. And their wells have been abandoned and impressive palaces as well? Have they not traveled around the Earth, so they may acquire hearts think with or ears to listen with? It is not their eyesight which is blind, but their hearts in their breasts which are blind. The hypocrites are not ready to amend their way of life and mould the belief even they know the Soul of Qur'an. The character of hypocrites displays through the verses 63: 2 and 3 as, 'They adopt their pledge as a shield and thus obstruct Allah's way, they are evil because of what they have been doing. That is because they have believed, then disbelieved; so their hearts are sealed off and so they do not understand anything. As per the verse 67: 10 when they will be thrown to the Hell they will lament to its keepers, had we but listened the Soul of Qur'an or used our intelligence we would not be among the companions of the Blaze. See explanation 2: 6- 7; 4: 78 and 6: 25.

101. Those are the cities, We have related news concerning to you: their Messengers came to them with Explanations, yet they were not any mood to believe in something they had already rejected. Thus Allah seals off disbelievers' hearts.

The verses 40: 78 says, We have sent messengers before you, some of whom We have told you about, while We have not told you about others. No messengers can bring any sign unless it is with Allah's Permission. Once Allah's command comes matters will be decided with the Truth and the quibblers will lose out. Read together the verses 40: 82- 85. The characters of the disbelievers who knowingly hide the Soul of Qur'an in all periods can be seen among the hypocrites of today. The 'Explanations' mentioned in the verse is the Soul of Qur'an. See the explanation 2: 54; 4: 91 and 6: 89- 90.

102. We did not find most of them fulfilling the covenant. Instead We found most of them as transgressors.

See the explanation 2: 26- 27, 99 and 5: 49.

103. Then after them, we dispatched Moosa with Our signs to Pharaoh and his chiefs, and they mistreated them. See what the consequences of mischief-makers were.

Even though *Pharaoh* saw all the signs he did not become believer, but he became more transgressor. Then Allah wanted *Moosa* to pray against pharaoh as per the verses 10: 88- 89. Then according to the verse 10: 90 when his *Rooh* - spirit- reached in his throat he said: 'I believe that there is no Deity except the One whom the children of Israel believed, and I am among the one who submitted all to Allah'. As per the verse 91 Allah ask, 'what! Now, you had disbelieved before and been a mischief maker'. In the verse 92 Allah said, 'however We will preserve your body in order to be a sign to anyone who comes after you. Yet many people are quite heedless about Our verses'. The verse 8: 54 says, just like *pharaoh's* companions and those who lived before them, they had rejected their Lord's verses, so We let them perish because of their offences and let *pharaoh's* companions drowned. They were all such wrongdoers. See the explanation 2: 10- 11 and 6: 93.

104. And Moosa said; Oh pharaoh! I am a messenger from the Lord of the worlds.

105. It is only right for me to say nothing except the Truth about Allah. I have brought you Evidence from your Lord, so send the Children of Israel with me.

106. He said; if you have brought any sign, well produce it then if you are so truthful.

107. He tossed his staff down. All of a sudden it became a real snake.

108. Then he pulled out his hand from the pocket. It was white to the onlookers.

109. The Chiefs among Pharaoh's people said; indeed he is a learned magician.

110. He wants to drive you out of your land; so what do you command?

111. They said: 'put him and his brother off, and sent recruiters out through the cities.

112. Who will bring in front of you every clever magician?'

113. The magicians came to Pharaoh. They asked, 'will we have some reward if we are the winners?'

114. He said; 'yes, you will become among courtiers.

115. They asked, 'Oh Moosa! Will you throw down or shall we be the ones to throw first?'

116. He said, 'you throw first!' So when they threw, they charmed the people's eyes and terrified them. They brought a mighty sorcery.

117. We inspired Moosa with; 'Throw your staff', it swallowed up whatever they had trumped up.

That means the snakes formed from their sticks and ropes were because of the ability of satan. In other words satan was making them to imagine as snake. But it was because of Glorified Allah's ability that the staff of *Moosa* became snake. There the Angels were present. By seeing the Angels, satan withdrew, so the snakes formed by sorcery due to the ability of satan, was disappeared. As per the verses 20: 65- 69 the magicians asked, 'Oh *Moosa*, either you will throw or shall we be the first to throw?' *Moosa* told, 'rather you throw first' you should have seen their ropes and rods! it appeared to him as if they were moving around because of their magic, so *Moosa* conceived a fear within himself. We said: 'do not be afraid, you will come out on top! Throw down what is in your right hand, so It will swallow up anything that they have produced. What they have produced is only some magicians' trick and no magician shall succeed any matter was ever he goes. See explanation 2: 102; 4: 18 and 118.

118. Thus the Truth prevailed and what they have been doing collapsed.

119. Those men were defeated and were turned back belittled.

120. And the magicians fell down in prostration.

121. They announced; we believe with the Lord of the all worlds.

122. The Lord of Moosa and Haroon.

123. Pharaoh asked: "have you believed with Him before I permit you to! This is some scheme which you have hatched in the city in order to drive its people out. You will know its consequences!

124. I will cut off your hands and legs on opposite sides; then I will crucify you all"

125. They answered; "surely, we will have to be returned to our Lord.

126. You have no reason to take revenge on us except for that we believed in our Lord's signs once they were brought us. Our Lord, Pour patience upon us, and you gather us up as submitted all to You!

Read together the verses 20: 72- 73 and 26: 48- 50. In the verse 3: 193 it is told that the prudent people will pray as, 'and gather us up at death with the virtuous'. Only one out of every thousand will only be raised up to the Paradise at their death. All others who received the Soul of Qur'an will be entered to the

Hell at their death. See the explanation 4:118 and 7: 40. But virtuous who were living under the Soul of Qur'an here will be raised up to '*Illiyyeen*' at their death. That is why the magicians prayed as 'raise us (gather us) '. One of the disciples of *Eisa*, *Surjas* who was crucified in the cross was raised up near to **Eisa** as soon as his death. Prophet *Eisa* was raised up to the second Heaven bodily as explained in the verses 3: 55 and 4: 155- 159. The magicians, who asked the reward before understanding the Truth, became ready to be crucified avoiding the worldly life. That means, believers who have the aim of life do not consider death as a loss. But disbelievers who are aimless of life consider death as a loss, and they fear death. See the explanation 2: 154 and 7:43

127. And the chief of the Pharaoh's people asked; Are you leaving freely Moosa and his people to ruin the earth and forsake you and your deities? He replied; surely we will slay their sons, and we shall spare their women; we have irresistible power on them.

See the explanation 2: 49; 6:17 and 18.

128. Moosa told his people: "Seek help from Allah and be patient; Indeed the Earth belongs to Allah. Anyone He wishes from His servants will inherit it. And the best consequence belongs to the heedful.

The verse 21:105 says: We have written in the Psalm following the Reminder: "My honorable servant shall inherit the Earth." According to the verse 39: 74 companions of the Paradise will say tomorrow: 'Praise is to Allah who has truly fulfilled the promise given to us, He made us to inherit the Earth. And now we can dwell in this Paradise as we please. How excellent is the reward for the workers!' Believers are with a firm belief that mankind is deputed to Earth in order to prepare the Paradise from this world itself .So they are working in this world to fulfill this purpose. Through the verse 24:55 Allah has promised to the party of believers to implement a '*Dheen*'- way of Life- they satisfied. The heedful and honorable people are those who follow and propagate the Soul of Qur'an to entire world irrespective of nations or religion. See the explanation 3: 136 and 6:155-157.

129. They said: "we were oppressed before you came to us, and after you have come to us." He said; perhaps your Lord will wipe out your enemy and make you vicegerents on Earth, so He may observe how you are acting.

The man created in the Paradise is deputed to Earth in order to undergo trial. See explanation 2:157 and 5: 94. Mankind is deputed to live here as representative of Allah by using the Soul of Qur'an, but the believers are only bearing the representation as it should be. See the explanation 2:283. Allah's representatives are those who keep the Truth Allah with the Truth-Soul of Qur'an and will remember Him in all their standing, sitting and laying in a manner that Allah is seeing them everywhere. Whoever forgets Allah, he is the hypocrite. See the explanation 2: 99; 6:89 and 90.

130. And We afflicted Pharaoh's people with several years of trial and shortage of fruit, so they might remember with heart.

131. Thus whenever something fine came to them, they said, 'this deserves to us', and while if something evil afflicted them, they took it as an omen connected with Moosa and whoever was with him. Did not their omen only lie with Allah? Yet most of them are not knowing.

The disbelievers of today as well as of those of all periods are saying in the same manner. In the verse 36: 18 the people on whom three Prophets were sent told; you are our evil omen, indeed if you not desist, we will surely stone you, or grievous torture will befall on you by our hands. In the verse 19 Prophets replied; your evil omen lies with yourselves, do you say so when you are being admonished? Nay, you are a people of transgressing. It is told in the verse 17: 13; 'every ones fate is fastened around his neck'. As most of the people do not know the Soul of Qur'an, they do not know this fact. They do not believe the Truth that 'goodness and evil are from Allah', and so these people are blaming others for their evils. See the explanation 4: 78- 79; 6:103 and 104.

132. And they said; 'No matter what sign you may bring us to charm us with; we will never believe with you'.

133. So We sent on them flood, locust, lice, frogs, and blood on them as distinguishing signs, yet they still acted proudly and were mad people.

The verse 17: 101 says that Israel children were given nine clear signs. They were (1) the Staff which will form as serpent. See the verse 7: 107. (2) The hand which will become shiny as sun when pulled from the pocket. (3) Years of famine, draught with scarcity of water. See the verse 7: 130. (4) The failure of the sorcerers of the world. See the verse 7: 119. (5) Flood (6) disturbance of Locusts. (7) Insects that spread diseases in human and animals. (8) Abandon of Frogs (9) Changing of water to Blood and there by scarcity of water to drink and wash, as told in this verse. These were the trials told in the verse 130. Insect includes flea spreading infectious diseases as well as destroying agriculture, louse, chicken louse, chuffs etc. Another disaster was abandon of frogs by which people were in difficulty to sit or walk anywhere. Prophet prohibited killing the frogs in a large number which may cause to stop their praising of Allah. 'Changing of water in to blood' means the water for drinking and washing became blood. But they were not ready to receive any lesson from these signs of Allah. He destroyed them since they became mad. See the explanation 6: 55 and 7: 40.

134. Whenever some disaster fell upon them, they said; Oh Moosa! Appeal to your Lord for us with the pledge you have with Him; If you lift the disaster from us, we will believe in you and send the children of Israel away with you.

135. Yet whenever We lifted the disaster from them for a period which they were to observe, why, they failed to keep it.

136. We avenged ourselves on them and drowned them in the deep, because they had rejected Our verses and been so heedless of them.

Today, 'the signs' are the verses of Qur'an which explain all these things in heart's language. In the verse 32: 22 it is told: 'who could be more wrong than the one who is reminded with the verses of his Lord in his heart's language, and then turns away from them? Surely We shall take revenge on such mad men'. The verse 18: 57 is also having the same Message. See the explanation 6: 25 and 26. The verse 36: 6 says, this Qur'an is sent down to warn a heedless people who are not warned by their forefathers. In the verse 12: 3 it is told that before receiving this Qur'an even prophet was heedless. The verse 7: 205 says; after receiving the Qur'an you should not be among heedless. Read together the verses 7: 179; 10: 7 and 92. See the explanation 6: 21, 93 and 157

137. We let a people whom they considered to be inferior inherit the Eastern and Western parts of land which we had blessed. Your

Lord's finest word was accomplished for the children of Israel when they had been so patient. And We destroyed everything Pharaoh and his people had been producing and whatever they had been building.

About this event Allah says in the verses 28: 5 and 6; yet we wanted to endow those who were considered inferior on Earth, and to make them in to leaders and make them inheritors. We established them on Earth, showed *Pharaoh* and *Haaman* as well as their troops about the happening of which they were bewaring. Through the verses 44: 23- 31 Allah says to *Moosa*: "Travel with My servants at night for you will be followed. Leave the sea parted; they are an army to be drowned. How many gardens and fountains have they left behind! And crops and splendid position and noble dwelling places they were delighted with. Even so We let other people inherit from them. Neither Heaven nor Earth wept over them, nor were they allowed to wait. Thus We saved Children of Israel from heinous torment from *Pharaoh*, who was haughty, so dissipated. Allah says through the verses 32: 23- 24; verily, we gave *Moosa* the Book, so you do not be in doubt about receiving such a Book. We granted It to the children of Israel for Guidance. We even set some of them up as leaders to guide people at Our command, once they were patient and convinced about Our verses. The only instrument to confirm belief is the Soul of Qur'an and It is the Shield and the Safe guard from all disasters and calamities as well as Hell. See the explanation 2: 4, 61; 7:35 and 36

138. And We led the Children of Israel across the sea. Then they came upon a people who were dedicated to some idols they had. They said; "Oh Moosa! Make a Deity for us like the deities they have". He said: "Indeed you are a people who act ignorantly.

139. Anything those people are busy at is doomed and whatever they had been doing is absurd".

140. He said: "Should I seek something instead of Allah as a Deity for you, while He has preferred you above all the worlds?

Allah saved *Moosa* and children of Israel across the sea. While they were looking, Allah drowned *Pharaoh* and his troops in the sea. After this event *Moosa* and children of Israel were continuing the journey, they reached at a people dedicating their idol. It was then they demanded a deity like that. They had been engaged in idol and cow dedication for years in Egypt, and they were ignorant about one Deity to whom they have to serve. That is why in the continuing verses Allah quotes the favors He has bestowed on them and criticizes their defiant behavior. But today due to the ignorance of the Soul of Qur'an, the character and behavior of Muslims in all over the world can be seen more badly than that of children of Israel of that period. They are the only people about whom Prophet as well as the great people like *Badr* martyrs, heedful persons will say on the day of Judgment that they were a worthless boar people who lived ignoring the Soul of Qur'an. They do not understand or enquire two conditions told in the verse 2: 186, which is compulsory to form the belief about Allah and the deeds be accepted. For more details about '*Ilah*'-Deity- read explanation 2: 133 and 6: 102.

141. And remember when We saved you from Pharaoh's people. He subjected you to cruel torment by killing your sons and spared your women. That was a serious trial from your Lord".

See the explanation 2: 49 and 50.

142. We did appointed thirty nights for Moosa and completed them with ten; the appointment with his Lord was completed in forty nights. Moosa said to his brother Haroon: Rule my people in my stead and set a good example; don't perceive the mischief makers' course.

Allah invited *Moosa* to Mount *Seena* for giving commandments for children of Israel. And then *Moosa* appointed his brother *Haroon* as his representative to lead his people along the Straight path. For further details read together the verses 20: 83- 85.

143. When Moosa came for Our appointment and his Lord spoke to him, he said; 'my Lord, show Yourself to me, so I may look at You.' He said; 'you will never see me, but look at the mountain. If it remains in its place, then you shall see me'. When his Lord displayed His Glory to the mountain, He left it flattened off, and Moosa fell down stunned. When he came back to his sense he said: 'Glory be to you! I have turned to you and I am the first of the believers!

No one can see Allah with the eyes from this physical world, but can see him by heart through the Soul of Qur'an. That is the meaning of 'Insight' given to the Soul of Qur'an. See the explanation 6: 104. Believers can see Allah with eyes from the Paradise. But the disbelievers can't. The verse 83:15 says; indeed the *fujjar* will be screened of from their Lord on that Day. It is told in the verse 59: 21 that if We had sent this Qur'an down on a mountain, you would have seen it solemnly splitting open out of awe for Allah. These are the parables We make up for mankind so that they meditate and reflect. By reading together these two verses it can be understood that Allah is in the Soul of Qur'an and both Allah and Qur'an are same. See the explanation 3: 101- 103; 5: 48; 6: 115 and 157.

'Glory be to you' said in the verse by *Moosa* means 'you have no comparison, example, similitude, no one is like you, nothing is like you, we cannot see you with eyes in this world etc. See the explanation 2: 33. Here, Prophet *Moosa* declares that 'I am the first of the believers' means *Moosa* is not the first believer among the mankind, but he is the first believer of that period. As per the verse 10: 104 Prophet *Muhammad* is ordered to declare that I am ordered to be among the believers. As per the verse 37: 81 it is told that *Nooh* was among our believing servants. And as per the verse 122 it is told that both *Moosa* and *Haroon* were our believing servants. See the explanation 1: 6.

144. He said; "Oh Moosa, I have selected you ahead of mankind for My messages and for My word; So accept whatever I may give you and be among the grateful".

At that period Allah's messages and words were *Thourath* given to *Moosa*. But today it is only the Soul of Qur'an for entire mankind. See explanation 2:185 and 6:38. Grateful people are those who follow and propagate the messages of Allah to entire mankind. All other Muslims who do not utilize It themselves and not allow to utilize others are ungrateful and transgressors. See the explanation 5: 67and 6: 26.

145. And We inscribed for him on stone disks for instructions and as an analysis of everything: "So hold to It firmly and command your people to hold it in the best manner. I shall show you the home for transgressors.

We can understand from Bible that it was recorded in two stone disks. *Thourath* was the part of '*Al kithab*'- The Book. Today 'the *Mouidath*'- instruction- is the Soul of Qur'an only for entire mankind. See the explanation 3: 138 and 6: 157. The verse 39: 17 ends as 'so proclaim good news to My servants' and in the verse 18 says 'who listen the Statement and follow It in the best, such are the ones whom Allah has guided and such are prudent persons.' Read together the verse 39: 55. Prophet Muhammad has taught in his departure pilgrimage itself that the believer should bite the Soul of Qur'an with his molar teeth during the last days when the hypocrites knowingly hide It and they will be hurrying to ruin the world. See the explanation 2: 2; 3: 58; 4: 91 and 5: 82

146. I shall divert those from my verses who are arrogant on Earth without having the Truth. Even if they saw every sign they still would not believe in them. If they saw the right way, they would not accept It as the way; while if they so anyway of wrong, they would accept it as the way. That is because they have rejected Our verves and being heedless of them.

'Without having the Truth' means without having the Soul of Qur'an. If anyone having the proud that he is a scholar without the Soul of Qur'an which is the Prosperity, Safeguard and Shield from the Hell will be among the arrogant hypocritical anchorites whom Allah has killed as mentioned in the verse 63: 4. See the explanation 2: 256; 3:79; 4:82 and 7: 140.

147. Those who reject Our verses and the fact of meeting in the Hereafter will see their deeds futile. Will they not be rewarded except for what they have been doing?

The verse 34: 33 also ends as 'will they not be rewarded except for what they have been doing?' The verse 76: 4 says: We have kept prepared shackles, chains and blaze for disbelievers. The disbelievers include the hypocrites who knowingly hide the Soul of Qur'an and the *fujjar* who try not to understand It and thus reject It. As per the verse 7:176 both of these people are compared to a dog which will not change its attitude whether it is attacked or not. Therefore if anyone utilizes the Soul of Qur'an as Insight and Criterion he can understand that both of them will be resurrected as dogs in the Hell. See the explanation 2:166-167 and 5:60. The verse 36: 54 says: on that Day, no soul will be wronged in anyway and you will be rewarded only for what you have been doing. This verse also teaches that Paradise or Hell is earning individually. See the explanation 2: 28; 6: 31, 88; 7: 8-9, 35 and 36.

148. People of Moosa, after he had gone designed a calf made out of their jewelry, having a body that mooed. Did they not see that it neither spoke to them nor guided them along any way? They adopted It and thereby became wrongdoers.

While the children of Israel were in *Seenai* desert *Moosa* had gone to *Thwoor* Mountain in order to accept the appointment by Allah as told in the verse 7: 142. During that time the people of *Moos*a under the leadership of *Samiriyy* threw their jewels in to a fire pit. Then by melting the jewels he made for them a statue of the calf. Then satan gave it the mooing sound. And *Samiriyy* told them, that is the Deity of yourself and *Moosa*. *Moosa* forgot to tell it. Read together the verses 20: 87 and 88. The verse 20: 89 says; did they not consider it would not talk back to them, nor control any harm or advantage for them? See the explanation 2: 254; 4:118 and 6: 52.

149. When the matter was dropped in their hands and they realized that they had gone astray, they said: "if our Lord does not show us Mercy and forgive us, we will be among the losers".

As per the verses 41: 41 and 42 the Soul of Qur'an is the Splendid Book no false hood shall approach It from either in front of It or behind It. Since It is a revelation from the One who is Wise, Praiseworthy. Then after receiving this great Mercy which is the Balance and Trust to keep the Universe in its equilibrium whoever hide or reject It will be the losers in this world as well as in the Hereafter. See the explanation 2: 121; 7: 23 and 53.

150. And when Moosa returned angrily, sorrowful to his people, he asked: 'What an evil representation you have accepted after I had gone? Have you tried to hurry up your Lord's command?' He dropped the disks, and seized his brother by the head pulling him towards himself. He said: Son of my mother! The people made me weak and almost killed me. So do not let any enemies rejoice over me nor place me with such wrong doing people.

As per the verse 20: 85 Allah said to *Moosa*: We have tested your people in your absence and *Samiriyy* has led them astray. Then as per the verse 86 when *Moosa* returned to his people angry, sorrowful he asked: "My people, did your Lord not make you a handsome promise? Did the agreement seen too long in reaching you, or did you want anger from your Lord to settle upon you, so that you broke your promise with Me. As per the verse 90; before *Moosa* returned to them *Haroon* had already told them: "Oh my people, you are only being tested by means of the calf. Your Lord is the Impartial most Gracious, so follow me and obey my command". Then as per the verse 91 they said: "We will never quit from devoting it until *Moosa* returns to us". As per the verses 92- 93 *Moosa* asked: "Oh *Haroon*, what prevented you when you saw they had strayed from them follow me? Did you disobey my order?" As per the verse 94 *Haroon* replied: "My brother from mother side! Don't seize me by my beard and by my head! I dreaded you would say that you have brought dissention to the children of Israel and did not wait for my words".

Some hypocrites of today are quoting the above reply of *Haroon* to argue that '*shirk*'-associate partners to Allah's dominion- is allowable for the existence of organizational set up. But they pretend as they have not seen what *Haroon* told in the verse 20: 90 that 'Your Lord is Impartial most Gracious'- which means He is not making anyone either to Paradise or to Hell. At the time of the creation itself in the Paradise He gave to each soul its way to the Paradise as well to the Hell. See the explanation 2: 28 and 4: 1. Moreover, these hypocrites do not see what *Haroon* told to *Moosa* that they made me weak and almost killed me. So do not let any enemies rejoice over me nor place me with such wrong doing people. Actually there are only two parties. Allah's party which includes the believers from Adam till the Last day as told in the verses 5: 56 and 58: 22. All others who received the Soul of Qur'an but reject and hide It become '*mushrik*' and party of satan as told in the verse 58:19. The human devil hypocrites by hiding the verses such as 2: 137, 176; 3: 103; 6: 158- 159; 23: 51- 53; 30: 31and 32 encourage communal unity among Muslims. See the explanation 4: 138-139. They never disclose to the people the teaching of prophet that in every thousand, nine hundred and ninety-nine are to Hell being as the explanation of the verse 4:118. Due to the ignorance of the Soul of Qur'an, Muslims are indulged in terrorist and mischief making activities all over the world. But these hypocrites who are killed by Allah as per the verses 63: 4 and 80:17 are keeping silence just like they have not any responsibility. They are the real enemy to the Believer Allah and His representatives i.e. believers. Due to this, by the second coming of *Eisa*, they will be killed to implement the order of the verses 4: 91; 9: 123, and 33: 61.

From this verse It is very clear that in the anger of Allah to behave angrily to others even with elder brothers is allowed and also throwing the Book Qur'an. That is the meaning of what prophet taught: '*no one of you become a believer until you like others in the pleasure of Allah; show anger to others in the anger of Allah; give anything for the satisfaction of Allah, and not to give anything in the wrath of Allah*'. See the explanation 3: 159; 4:63,135 and 6: 116.

151. He said: "My Lord! Forgive me and my brother, and let us enter in Your Mercy! You are the most Merciful of those who show Mercy.

Believers when praying 'enter us in Your Mercy' have to bear in mind that the Mercy is the Soul of Qur'an. So they have to read the Soul of Qur'an praying as 'Oh my Lord! Increase the knowledge to me'. See the explanation 2: 255 and 7:52.

152. Certainly to those who took the calf overwhelmed wrath from their Lord and disgrace in this world. Thus we reward those who invent lies.

The hypocrites of all periods are inventing and telling lie upon Allah. The verse 10: 17says: who is more wrongdoer than the one who invent falsehood upon Allah or reject His verses? Indeed, Allah will never lead to success such mad people. See explanation 2: 79; 6: 93 and 7: 37.

153. As for those who perform evil deeds, then repent later on and believe, your Lord will later on be Forgiving, Merciful.

See the explanation 2: 159- 162; 4: 146- 147; 7:146 and 147.

154. When his anger had subsided, Moosa picked up the disks, in which We inscribed Guidance and Mercy for those who revere their Lord.

The 'Guidance and Mercy' said in the verse is the Soul of Qur'an. During that period the Guidance and Mercy was the *Thourath*, today it is the Soul of Qur'an only for entire mankind. See explanation 6:157. On the Day of Judgment each and everyone will be given the 'Record of deeds' as told in the verses 17: 13 and 14. According the verse 45: 29 it will be told to each individual; this is Our Book, which will reflect the Truth about you, We had been inscribing all that you were doing in the worldly life. Hence, whoever is heedful to inscribe the readable matters in his computer fastened around his neck should think, speak and do deeds under the Soul of Qur'an. Only such will get the Book of deed on right hand on the Day of Judgment. See the explanation 6: 89-90; 7:42 and 43

155. Moosa chose his people seventy men, for an appointment with Us. When the tremor seized them, he said: "My Lord, even though

You may have wished to wipe them out and myself as well earlier, are you wiping us out just because of what some fools among us have done? It is only your manner of testing: You let anyone You wish to, go astray by means of it, and let anyone you wish to be guided. You are our patron, so pardon us and show us Mercy; You are the best among the pardoners.

See the explanation 2: 55- 56, 286; 4: 153 and 154.

156. Prescribe a fine thing for us in this world and in the Hereafter; Let us be guided towards you!" Allah said; I afflict anyone I wish with my torment while My Mercy embracing everything; I shall prescribe it who for those who are heedful, pay the welfare tax and who believe in Our verses.

Allah's Mercy is the Soul of Qur'an which is the Guidance containing all the parables and instructions for entire mankind as told in the verses 2: 185 and 6: 38. The heedful means those who follow the Soul of Qur'an as it should be followed. See the explanation 2: 5, 38, 201- 202; 7: 32- 36, 146 and 147.

157. For those who follow the messenger, the unlettered prophet whom they will find written down in the 'Thourath' and 'Injeel' with them. He commands them to be decent and forbids them dishonor. He permits them wholesome things and prohibits them evil things, and relieves them of their burdens and shackles which have lain upon them. Therefore those who believe with him, strengthen him and support him, and follow the Light which was sent down with him; such will be the only prospers

The verse 48: 29 says, Muhammad is Allah's messenger while those who are with him should be strict with disbelievers and merciful among themselves. You will see them bowing heads obcying, prostrating, craving bounty and pleasure from Allah. The mark from the trace of prostration can be seen on their faces, such is their description in *Thourath*, while their description in the *Injeel* is like a field crop which puts forth its shoots so it swells up, till it grows thick enough to stand straight on its stalk in the way farmers admire, so that disbelievers are exasperated by them. Allah has promised forgiveness and a splendid reward to anyone those who believe and perform honorable deeds. See the explanation 2: 143; 3: 79 and 5: 48. 'Decent things' means the commands of the Qur'an or the way of Allah. 'Forbids dishonor' means the prohibitions of Qur'an or the ways of satan. Both can be implemented by teaching the Soul of Qur'an. That is the meaning of prophet's teaching *among you the best one is the one who learns and teaches the Soul of Qur'an.* See the explanation 7: 54. 'He permits them wholesome things and prohibit them evil things' means prophet who make them clear what is pure and what is impure as the explanation of the Soul of Qur'an in which is the knowledge of the Three times Knower- Allah. The verse 16: 114 says, so eat any lawful wholesome things Allah has provided you with, and be thankful for Allah's favor if you have been serving Him alone. See the explanation 2: 173 and 5: 100. 'Relieves their burdens' means by teaching the Soul of Qur'an help them to lead a simple, natural and peaceful life; removing the non-Islamic customs and formalities and the other footsteps of satan. See the explanation 2: 168 and 169. 'The shackles fastened on them' means due to the ignorance of the aim of life there were violence, rioting, murders everywhere, so one cannot travel through the towns with peace and tranquility. The condition of the pagans during that period is described in the verses 36: 8 and 9 as We have placed shackles around their neck which reach up to their chins, so that their heads are forced up without moving to anywhere; We have placed a barrier before them and another barrier behind them, and have covered them up, so they do not notice anything. The verse 36: 10 says, it is all the same for them whether you warn them or do not warn them, they still will not believe. And in the verse 11 says you will only warn someone who follows the Soul of Qur'an and dreads the Most Gracious even though He is unseen, proclaim the forgiveness and generous reward to him. Thus with the Soul of Qur'an -The Light- Prophet made them a best community by burning -removing- their false pride, arrogance, defiance, darkness, rejection etc. see the explanation 3: 103- 104 and 6: 151-153.

'Islam', the only way of life Allah satisfied was completed by the '*Hajjathul Vida*'-departing pilgrimage-, gradually began untie the rope. Today, Muslims who keep false pride that we are the followers of prophet and Qur'an are inventing different kinds of anti-Islamic customs and formalities. If we see through the Soul of Qur'an, the Insight we can see that Muslims all over the world are involved in more forbidden dishonor and worst deeds such as terrorism, robbery, bloodshed, theft, smuggling, murdering, drug addiction, gambling, sodomy, fornication, adulteration, dissension of human unity, selfishness than any other people in the world. Thus, they are hurrying to destroy the Earth by hiding the

Soul of Qur'an which is the Balance and Trust to keep the Universe in its equilibrium. See the explanation 4: 175- 176, 5: 15- 16; 6: 157 and 7: 40.

158. Say: Oh mankind, for all of you I am but a messenger from Allah, Who holds control over Heaven and Earth. There is no Deity except Him; He gives life and brings death. So believe in Allah and His messenger, the unlettered Prophet who himself believes with Allah and His words. Follow It so you may be guided.

The verse 34: 28 says, We have not sent you except for the whole mankind as a Herald and Warner to every single human being, even though most men do not realize it. The verse 21: 107 says We have not sent you except as a Mercy for all the worlds. The verse 25: 1 says blessed is the one Who has sent down the criterion on His servants in order he may warn all the worlds. Then without witnessing the life of Prophet revealed by the Soul of Qur'an among mankind, thus considering the Qur'an and Prophet is only for Muslims are really not believe in the Oneness of Allah and they will be the losers in the Hereafter. See explanation 2: 121 and 6: 104. The people who do not identify Allah, satan, Prophet, themselves and the aim of life because of not receiving the Soul of Qur'an as explained in the verse 2: 146, Allah will not punish such people, is told in the verses 17: 15, 34: 32, 41: 41. See explanation 2: 38. Muslims who after receiving the Soul of Qur'an, do not identify and make identify others about Allah and His messenger, shall have to bear the life burdens of them, is told in the verse 6: 26. See the explanation 7: 8-9, 37 and 136.

'Unlettered messenger and Prophet' about Prophet Muhammad is told only in this two verses in Qur'an. The preposition 'It' mentioned in the verse is the 'The Light' which is sent down with him. We can see that Allah, Qur'an and Prophet, is the same from the verse 9: 65. Therefore, Muslims who do not learn and teach the Soul of Qur'an, are hiding Allah and His Messenger in It and they are the True disbelievers, wrongdoers, transgressors, *mujrims*, aimless, heedless and losers of both in this life as well as the Hereafter. See explanation 4: 150-151; 7: 146 and 147.

159. Out of Moosa's people there are who guided by means of the Truth and dealt justly by means of It.

The 'Truth' mentioned in the verse means the only Book: Today it is the Soul of Qur'an, as explained in the verse 2: 2; 7: 8-9. Those who do not judge with the Soul of Qur'an in individual family, and social life, they are disbelievers, wrongdoers, transgressors as told in the verses 5: 44-45, 47 respectively. See the explanation 4: 135 and 5: 2.

160. We split them up into twelve tribes, communities, and inspired Moosa when his people asked for water: "Strike the rock with your staff." Twelve springs gushed forth from it. Each tribe was specified its own drinking place. And We shaded them with clouds and sent down 'manna' and quail for them: "Eat some of the wholesome things which We have provided you with". Yet they did not wrong Us, but they themselves were doing wrong.

See the explanation 2: 57-60; 5: 63-64; 6: 144; 7: 94 and 95.

161. And remember when they were told: "Reside in this town and eat wherever you wish in it, and say: Relieve us! And enter the gate in a prostrate manner. We will forgive you your mistakes; We will increase more to those who are living seeing Me".

See explanation 7: 137, 150 and 155.

162. But those among them who did wrong changed the statement in to something else than what had been told them; so We sent a plague from Heaven upon them because of their wrong doing.

See the explanation 5: 20-25.

163. Ask them, about the town which lay facing the sea, when they act as aggressors in the matter of Sabbath. Their fish came to them swimming on the surface on their Sabbath day, while any day other than the Sabbath, it did not come to them. Thus We tested them because they had been acting so transgress.

See the explanation 2: 65-66; 5: 60 and 94.

164. Also remember whenever a community among them asked: "why do you admonish a people whom Allah will destroy any how or punish them severely?" They said: "to gain absolution from your Lord, and they may become heedful."

The people of the town were in three categories. (1). those who are doing forbidden deeds insolently. (2). those who kept quite even seeing such insolence. (3). those who commanded with the best and forbid with the evil. Here, the second category people are asking to the third category then the third category people reply to the second category that we advise them in order to get absolution from your Lord, and if they may become heedful by omitting transgression and aggression, it will be better for them. See the explanation 5: 105.

Since the Soul of Qur'an is revealed as the Balance to keep the Universe in its equilibrium, there is no virtue today in reciting Qur'an even to those who knows the contents. When the believer says that the only way to postpone the Dooms day is to learn and propagate the Soul of Qur'an, to entire mankind irrespective of nation and religion, the hypocrites and disbelievers among Muslims will ask: "what for it? Is it already decided by Allah? Is it possible if you alone thinking? Today is it possible to implement the do's and don'ts of Qur'an? Such inmates of Hell do not consider the Soul of Qur'an as 'the *Mou'idhath*'. The reply to them is explained in the verses 4: 63, 5: 60, and 7: 176.

165. Then when they forgot what they have been reminded of, We rescued those who had forbidden evil while We seized those who were doing wrong with dreadful torment because they have been acting so transgress.

Allah rescued the third category who had forbidden the evils. And Allah seized the second category that was wrongdoing with dreadful torment since they were not hesitating the evil even by mind. See the explanation 4: 140; 7: 59.

166. Thus when they became insolent about what had been forbidden them, We told them: "Become apes detested."

The first category of people when they were insolently doing what had been forbidden to them repeatedly, Allah transformed them as detested apes maintaining the Soul of human and turning the body in to Monkeys. Thus made that event as an illustration of what had come before them and what would come after them, and as a good advice for the heedful as told in the verse 2: 66. See the explanation 4: 47. If it is the question that why the hypocrites of today who hide and twist insolently the Qur'an verses are not changed in to apes and pigs as happened just like the Jews before? The answer is that Allah, the Omniscient by making Prophet to pray as, "You don't make such type of punishment to my community during this worldly life"; accepted the prayer. See explanation 6: 65. More over if such type of punishment is implemented; the world will not be ended at the fixed time. See the explanation 5: 60. Prophet taught that; "there will be a group in my community who exists in the truth till '*Maseeh-A-Ddajjal*', appears as the first signs of Doom's Day. Their enemies can not do any harm to them. They will be involved in propagating the Soul of Qur'an to entire mankind". See the explanation 3: 79, 5: 67. Only the believers have to face the trial of '*Maseeh-A-Ddajjal*'. The only way to survive his trial is hold fast the Soul of Qur'an with the molar teeth. All Muslims who neglect the Soul of Qur'an should be subjected to the trial of '*Maseeh-A- Ddajjal*. Allah, without delay will bring *Eisa* for the second time to this world in order to clean the disbelief and to enlighten Islam once more which will be extinguished completely by the arrival of *Maseeh-A-Ddajjal*. Thus, he will introduce Prophet Muhammad as merciful to entire worlds as told in the verse 21: 107, who has been made falsehood by Muslims of today. Then as explained in the verse 3: 19, *Islam* the only lifestyle which Allah satisfied for entire mankind will be implemented. After *Eisa's* death the world will again become dark and all other symptoms will be appeared. It is told in the verse 46: 35 that if there is no one to command virtue and to forbid the evil and thus all people become transgressors then the end of the world will be happened. See the explanation 4: 91,133; 6: 158-159; 7: 157 and 158.

167. Then remember your Lord announced that He would raise someone against them who would impose the worst torment on them until Resurrection Day. Indeed your Lord is quick in Retribution, while He is Forgiving, Merciful.

The verse 17: 4 says, We decreed in the Book concerning the children of Israel: "you will create havoc on Earth twice and display great haughtiness. Read together the verses 17: 5-7 and 104. It is told in the verse 5: 64 that Allah has cast enmity and hatred among the Jews till the last Day. Every time they kindle the fire of war, Allah has extinguished and they strive to create havoc on Earth. See the explanation 5: 78-80. Jews were scattered wandering through out the world until 1947. They were creating wickedness and havoc activities such as kidnapping embassy officials, conducting bomb blast and other terrorist activities. Thus without bearing their havoc, America and Britain were compelled to make the nation Israel for them. Today, among all people of the world including Jews, Muslims, due to their negation of the Soul of Qur'an and following the same life way of those Jews, they are suffering humiliation throughout the world, and are being tortured by others. At the end of the encounter between Muslims and Jews of today, '*Maseeh-A-Ddajjal*' will come as the leader of the Jews. Then Jews will get the ruling power and dignity over whole world. Hypocrites-the human devils will welcome and help the '*Maseeh-A-Ddajjal* the satan who comes in the human form. But without delay, Allah will bring *Eisa* and he will kill '*Maseeh-A-Ddajjal* and Jews leaders. Then the control of the whole world will become to believers under the leadership of *Eisa* and they will implement the command of the verses 33: 60-61 by killing hypocrites and their blind followers as well as seventy thousand Jews leaders, the agitators mentioned in the verse. See the explanation 4: 159; 5: 98 and 6: 123-127.

168. We split them up in to nations on Earth. Some of them are honorable while some of them are otherwise. We have tested them with fine things and evil things so that they may return to the aim of life.

The verse teaches that Allah makes 'trial' to the mankind in order to think about the aim of life by hold fasting the Soul of Qur'an and return to the Straight path. But there will be no trial for hypocrites who are already killed by Allah due to their transgression knowingly as explained in the verse 2: 99. The verse 32: 21 says still We shall let them taste worldly torment rather than Supreme torment, so they may yet turn back to the aim of life. The verse 30: 41 says mischief has appeared on land and at sea because of what man's hands have accomplished. So He may let them taste something of what they have earned, in order that they will back to the aim of life. The verse 32: 15 says, indeed, the only ones who believe in Our verses are those who drop down in prostrate whenever they are reminded of them in their heart's language and glorify their Lord's praise and they do not act so proudly. See the explanation 7: 95 and 145.

169. Successors replaced them afterward Who inherited the Book, taking on the vanities of this lowly place and saying: "it will be forgiven to us" if a vanity likes it were given them again, they would accept it. Was not an agreement concerning the Book accepted by them: that they would tell nothing except the Truth about Allah? And they studied what was in It. The home in the

Hereafter is better for those who are heedful. Will you not utilize your intelligence?

After the codification of Qur'an, it is the only Book for entire mankind. See the explanation 7: 157 and 158. Then Muslims, the inheritance of the Book are involved today in all havoc by rejecting the do's and don'ts of the Book and are in a belief that they will get forgiveness. Just like the Jews at the time of Prophet, their false belief is that We are Allah's beloved people, and so whatever evil we did, Allah will forgive us. Because of this false belief, they do not repent to Allah. Instead they are involved in more evil deeds shamelessly and aimlessly. Actually, they are the bearer of the Book which is enough to make them leaders of the world; but their cheap thought and short sight about future do not induce them for anything except for gaining the profits of worldly life. Thus they have become a heedless and aimless people. Instead of witnessing the Qur'anic and Prophet's life among mankind, they became cheap as dogs of this world. Read together the verses 7: 175-176; 8: 22; 9: 68 and 73. 'Was not an agreement concerning the Book was accepted by them: that they would not tell nothing except the Truth about Allah' means anywhere in the Book it is not told that the Ticket of salvation is given to any particular community and if you do anything, you will get forgiveness any how, instead what is told in the verses 4: 123 and 124 is: The final result will neither be in accordance with your desires nor in accordance with the desires of the people of the Book. He who does evil will be requited with evil, he will find no protector or helper besides Allah -And those who do honorable deeds, whether male or female provided that he or she is a believer shall enter the Paradise and will not be harmed a speck. See the explanation 2: 62, 94-95. While covenant has been taken from them that they should not tell about Allah except the Truth, what right they have to say anything about Allah which He has not told? Through the verses 22: 8-9 Allah says; yet there are some among people who argue about Allah without having any Knowledge, Guidance and Enlightening Book -the Soul of Qur'an. They are preventing people from the path of Allah bending to one side. They have humiliation in this worldly life and We will taste them the torment of burning on Resurrection Day. See the explanation 3: 7, 187; 4: 140 and 7: 28-30.

170. And those who holdfast with the Book and keep up the swalath; surely We shall never futile the reward of such reformers.

Allah says that first preference should be given to the Soul of Qur'an, and then only for *swalath*. *Swalath* is performed to maintain Soul of Qur'an, as told in the verse 20: 14. The verse 29: 45 says, recite whatever has been revealed to you from the Book, and keep up *swalath*, indeed *swalath* will restrain from shameful and evil deeds and the Soul of Qur'an which makes remembrance of Allah is the most important and Allah knows whatever you industrialize. The verse 35: 29 says; surely the ones who recite Allah's Book, keep up *swalath* and spend something secretly and publicly from what He has provided for them, can hope for a business which will never worthless. Through the above verses as well as in all other verses of Qur'an, propagation of Qur'an is commanded first, and then only performing *swalath* is to be done. But today the Muslims, who have already become the disbelievers and fuel of the Hell as per Prophet's explanation of the verse 3: 10; are giving importance for the *swalath* with body without participating their Soul than the 'propagation' of Qur'an neglecting the verses 8: 2-4, 39: 17-18, 22-23, 32-34, 53-60, 41: 40-44 etc. See the explanation 3: 78; 4: 56; 5: 48 and 7: 149. Let us pray as: oh Allah! Include us among the ones who help you by conveying the Soul of Qur'an-the Balance and Trust- to entire mankind in order to keep the Universe in its equilibrium.

171. Remember when We suspended the mountain over them as though it was an umbrella and they thought it was going to fall down on them: "Hold on firmly to anything We have given you and remember what is in it, so that you may become heedful".

See explanation 7: 2, 155-156,167.

172. Also remember when your Lord took their offspring from the children of Adam's nape, and made them bear witness about themselves: "Am I not your Lord?" They said: "Of course, We testify to it!" Lest you might say on Resurrection Day: "We were heedless about this".

173. Or lest you say: "Indeed, it was our forefathers who associated others with Allah previously; and we were offspring following them. Will you then destroy us out because of what futile men have done?"

174. Thus do We spell out Our verses so that they may return to aim of life.

All men (souls) from Adam to the Last Day were created in the Paradise from a single soul while He created Adam itself. See the explanation 2: 28 and 4: 1. Through the verses 82: 6-8 Allah asks, oh man, what has lured you away from your generous Lord, who created you, fashioned you and proportioned you in number in what ever shape He wished? He has put your frame together. Then Allah placed them in the nape of children of Adam till the Last Day in proportional fixed number. Here note that it is not told "from the nape of Adam" instead it is told "from the napes of children of Adam. Then Allah made covenant from each individual by asking: "Am I not your owner Lord?" - Creator, Guide, Authority to make alive as well as die. All replied individually: "of course, we testify to it", thus they witnessed themselves. It is called the 'covenant'. Then Allah says that the aim of the covenant made with each individual is lest any one might say on Resurrection Day: "we were heedless about this or lest any one say: "it was only our forefathers who associated others with Allah previously, we were offspring following them, will you then destroy us out because of what futile men have done? In other words each Soul has to reply to His Lord about each moment of her worldly life after the age of fifteenth. See the explanation 2: 27; 3: 90-91 and 7: 37-39.

As per the verse 36: 59 on the Day of Judgment it will be told to the *mujrims* who were not utilizing their intelligence during the worldly life; step aside today! As per the verse 60, Have I not made a covenant with you, oh children of Adam, not to serve satan, he is an open enemy of yours. And as per the verse 61 it is told that you serve Me Alone that is the Straight path. The question asking there 'have I not made covenant with you, Oh children of Adam, not to serve satan' does not mean such a covenant was made. Instead, whoever lives without remembering the covenant made with Allah mentioned in this verse is serving the satan and is living here as his vicegerent. It is told in the verse 4: 118 that satan will bring under his control nine hundred and ninety nine out of every thousand from men. See the explanation 1:4 and 7: 27-30. Through the above verses Allah warns that no one can escape from the punishment by blaming his parents. As per the verse 14: 22 it is told that no one can escape by blaming satan itself. And as per the verses 2: 166-167, no one can escape by blaming the scholars, leaders and great persons. The most Gracious –Impartial Allah, has given each Soul its way to Hell and its way to Paradise at the time of creation in the Paradise itself. So nobody can blame his Lord also as told in the verses 2: 286; 3: 30 and 6: 104. The verse 40:78 ends as, when Allah's command comes matters will be decided with the Truth- the Soul of Qur'an, and that is where the futile men will lose out. See the explanation 7:48-51. The Soul of Qur'an is called '*Adhikr*' because It reminds the previous as well as the coming facts. Just like this, Allah explains His verses in order that man has to return the covenant made with Him, the aim of life and to his Lord in the Paradise. But only the believers approve this fact and they will holdfast the Soul of Qur'an -*Adhikr*. It is the permission of Allah to become believer and to enter the Believer's house- the Paradise. That is why if any misfortune or even death strikes them, they say by mind: "we belong to Allah and will be returning to Him!" Such are the patient people whose prayers are accepted by their Lord and granted Mercy and are having confirmed to be guided. See the explanation 2: 62, 177; 5: 48; 7: 10 and 168.

175. And recite news to them about some one to whom We gave Our verses. He slipped away from them, so satan followed him and he became aimless of life.

Here it is mentioned about the hypocritical anchorites who neither follow nor convey the Soul of Qur'an after knowing It. They are the human satans mentioned in the verses 6: 112 and 114: 6. They prevent layman from the Soul of Qur'an. The condition of such laymen is warned in the verse 25: 29 as; they will say on the Day of Judgment: woe to me, would that I had never taken such a one as leader and friend, he did prevent me from the Soul of Qur'an after it had come to me. Read together the verses 41: 26-29. If anyone neglects the Soul of Qur'an, Allah will appoint for him a satan as Soul mate as told in the verse 43: 36. As per the verses 58: 15-19, such 'satan possessed hypocrites' will obstruct others from the Soul of Qur'an. Allah has kept prepared severe torment for them; with them anything they do is evil. They have taken their pledge as a shield and obstruct Allah's way. They will have heinous torment. Neither their wealth nor their children will help them out in any way with Allah. Such will become the inmates of the Fire; they will remain there for ever. On the Day when Allah raises them all up together, they will swear to Him just as they have sworn to you in the worldly life; they reckon that they are in some truth. Indeed, they are such liars! satan has won over them and caused them forget from remembering Allah, such are the satan's party. Beware; verily the party of satan will be the only losers. See the explanation 6: 158-159, 7: 26 and 27.

Example for their swearing during their speech they will say to lay men, even if you read the body of Qur'an simply without trying to understand Its soul, you will get the reward. Then in the Hereafter they will swear to Allah that 'I did not say them you need not to study the soul, but I was telling them to familiarize Qur'an for reading first and then try to study the meaning -the life, but not the Soul. It was only a technique. But what he is doing is just opposite to that Allah's teachings through Prophet. If any one reads Qur'an without the participation of heart, he will dart out from *Islam* as the arrow dart out from the bow. See the explanation 2: 6-7, 140-145; 5: 90-91 and 7: 40.

176. If it had been Our wish, We might have raised him up by means of It, but he clung to the Earth and followed his own whim. His similitude is that of a dog. If you attack it, it lolls out its tongue; or if you leave it free it still lolls out its tongue. That is the similitude of the people who reject Our verses. Therefore you tell them such parables one by one in order that they may meditate and reflect It.

Here, the anchorites who live only aiming the material life hiding the Soul of Qur'an after receiving It, is compared to a dog which never changes its way of life whether attacked or not. The people who try not to understand and utilize the verses of Qur'an are also compared to a dog. If you pelt it, it will bite it thinking that it is a piece of bone, even after that it will wander through Earth. Another desire of dog is to satisfy its sexual thirst. This character is also seen mostly among these anchorites. See the explanation 4: 63 and 7:169. Another place where dog mentioned in Qur'an is in *Surath Al kahf* (dog of people of the cave). There the dog is mentioned honorably. The dogs used for hunting, the dogs helping the police to catch the criminals as well as the dog used as the security for house and properties are also not considered as the worst beast. But the dog mentioned in this verse is about the man, who will not change his attitude whether is warned or not. And he is not only useless for anyone but also hated by everyone. See the explanation 5: 60- 63; 7:146 and 147. All the creatures like dog, pig, donkey, bandicoot, monkey etc. will be resurrected on the Day of Resurrection and after testifying their agonies they suffered in this world from mankind; they will be turned to dust. Read together the verse 78: 40. But the disbelievers from *Jinns* and mankind will be resurrected in the bodily shape of dog, pig, bandicoot, snake, scorpion, monkey, donkey etc. in the Hell –the house of disbeliever satan.

In the verse 62: 5 those people who reject and belie the verses of Qur'an is compared to Jews and Donkeys. That verse ends as Allah will not guide such wrongdoing people. It is told in the verse 32: 22 that who does more wrong than one to whom are recited the verses of his Lord in hearts language and then turns away there from? Certainly We will take revenge with such *mujrims*- mad men, who have intelligence but not utilize. The verses 53: 29-30 say, shun those who turn away from the Soul of Qur'an and those desire nothing but the life of this world. That is the total goal of their knowledge, certainly your Lord knows best those who are gone astray from His path and He knows best those who received Guidance.

Allah ordered Prophet to say through the verse 13: 27, certainly, Allah leaves to astray whom He wish, but He guides to Himself those who turned to Him in repentance and ask Guidance. It is told in the verse 14: 2 and 3 that these sorts of rejecters shall have '*Wail*'- a severe torment part of Hell as they prefer the life of this world to the Hereafter, who obstruct men from the path of Allah seeking to make It crooked. They went far astray from the path. See the explanation 7: 44 and 45. It is told in the verses 16: 105-107, certainly those who invent falsehood against Allah, do not believe in the verses of Qur'an; verily they are the liars. Anyone, who after accepting faith in Allah, utters disbelief except under compulsion, and his heart remaining in firm in faith-but such as open their chest to disbelief- on them is wrath of Allah and theirs will be a dreadful punishment. This is because they prefer the life of this world to the Hereafter. Indeed, Allah will never guide such disbelievers. The verse 5: 67 says, Oh messenger! Deliver whatever has been sent down to you by your Lord, if you do not do so, you will not have conveyed His Message. Allah will defend you from mankind. Indeed, Allah will never guide such disbelievers. Such disbelievers mean who hide the Soul of Qur'an knowingly. Through the verse 9: 23 Allah says, Oh you who believe! Do not take your fathers and brothers as protectors if they prefer disbelief instead of belief. Anyone of you who chooses them as protectors, such are only the wrongdoers. See the explanation 2: 254; 5:51, 7: 40 and 41. The verse 59: 21 also ends as 'in order that they may meditate and reflect It'. 'To meditate and reflect to others' means to inform others about the consequence if the Soul of Qur'an is hidden and neglected, such that they may also convey the Message to others and thus make the Soul of Qur'an witness and argue in favor of them, instead that of against. 'By means of It' told in the first part of the verse means the Soul of Qur'an by which one will get dignity and proud, and can enter the Paradise without even trial. See the explanation 3; 79; 4: 167; 7: 37 and 143.

177. How evil is the comparison of people who reject Our verses; it is their own Souls they do wrong.

For those who received the Soul of Qur'an, if not utilized or not given others to utilize, It will stand witness and argue against them. Since Soul of Qur'an is the Balance to keep the Universe in its equilibrium and a weapon to stop blood-shed, and thus to maintain the life in peaceful condition, then if it is not utilized by themselves and not allowed others to utilize It, the consequence is the humiliation in this worldly life and the severe punishment in the Hereafter. See the explanation 2: 85, 7: 8-9, 146 and 160.

178. Anyone whom Allah guides has been really guided; while those He lets go astray, such ones will be the only losers.

Through the verse 30: 29 Allah asks: Who will guide someone whom Allah has let go astray? As per the verses 39: 36-37 Allah says: "Anyone whom Allah lets go astray will have no guide and none can mislead anyone whom Allah guides". By quoting such verses the hypocrites teach their people that Allah is the authority for making one to the Guidance or to astray, all good and bad comes from Allah, He is the One who decides Paradise or Hell to anyone, and we have not any role in our Guidance or earnings. But in the verse 16: 37 Allah says; "even if you are eager to guide them, Allah still does not guide someone who gone astray himself. And they will have no any helpers". The Impartial Most Gracious has already taught each the Soul of Qur'an which contains the Guidance -the way to Allah and the futile - the way to satan, when the mankind was created in the Paradise itself. Read together the verses 55: 1-4; 90: 10 and 91: 8. See the explanation 2: 28 and 4:1. Mankind and *Jinn* are created with freedom to select either true Guidance or astray as per the verse 76: 3. As per the verses 14: 1 every one should ask Guidance to their own Lord. In other words the guided one will live by seeing and depending Allah in all their standing, walking, sitting, laying etc. See the explanation 2: 213. As per the verse 4: 78; all good and bad are from Allah. And as per the verse 4: 79 all good are from Allah, and all bad are from man itself, i.e. all bad are from satan. So, one who has not made his Soul mate a believer with the Soul of Qur'an will be strayed. Allah deputed mankind to the Earth with freedom of choice in order to undergo trial. See the explanation 5: 94. Paradise or Hell is earned by oneself as explained in the verses 3: 30, 136, 182 and 185. See the explanation 2: 152; 5: 48; 6: 157

and 7: 136.

The verse 17: 67 says; "whenever some adversity strikes you at sea, any one you appeal to besides Him leaves in the lurch; yet whenever We saved you safely to land, you turn away evasively, and man has been so ungrateful! As testifying this verse, men say by forgetting his aim of life: Our destiny is determined only by Allah. We have no any role in it. But in order to get any benefit or employment in this worldly life such people are ready to hard work, suffer any difficulty, spend wealth, time, influence etc. And they are not sitting idle saying that it is the duty of government to give us job and it will get when its time comes. He acquires enough educational qualifications for the post and gives application in time. Instead of using all power, abilities, influence, wealth etc. for the achievement of permanent Hereafter life he is expressing opportunism by saying that Allah is Merciful, so let Him give what He wishes. This is called the hypocrisy. Such hypocrites are denying the good name of Allah the Impartial. See the explanation 2: 200-202; 7: 150 and 151.

179. Certainly, We have destined many Jinns and human beings for Hell; they have hearts with which they do not understand the aim of life, and eyes with which they do not see the Insight, they have ears with which they do not hear the Soul of Qur'an. Such persons are like livestock; rather they are even worse than them, such are the only heedless.

This verse does not mean that *Jinns* and men are created only for filling the Hell. Instead as told in the verse 2: 24 the disbelievers who hide and reject the Soul of Qur'an after receiving It -which is the food, cloth and sight of the Soul as told in the verse 7: 26 are only the fuel of the Hell together with the stones. Each man has a Soul mate, and then whoever makes his Soul mate a believer with the Soul of Qur'an, can only enter the Paradise. Read together the verses 43: 36-38; 50: 27-29; 59: 16 and 17. See the explanation 4: 118.

The men to be filled in the Hell have hearts, but they do not understand the aim of life using the Soul of Qur'an a Criterion and Insight. Allah has given hearts for men as well as all other creatures, but the intelligence is given only to men. Instead of saying that 'they do not think', it is told 'they do not understand with hearts' does not mean that 'they do not think about means of lively hood, about the benefits worldly life, about gaining and retaining positions and status; but it means they do not understand about the aim of life utilizing the Soul of

Qur'an or do not try to understand what is, what for and why Qur'an and will not realize the fact that the aim of fourth stage of man in this world is to earn for the seventh stage of life in the Paradise. As per the verse 54: 17 the Soul of Qur'an is made very easy to understand by one's heart. But the people who are decreed for filling the Hell will not be ready for it, instead they will acquire all educational qualifications in order to get employment in worldly life; and are leading a life as the dog of this world. In order to achieve the Paradise they will not try to understand and follow the Soul of Qur'an which is the Ticket to the Paradise. Such fleeting men are not ready to be patient until the prophecies of Qur'an are come true in the Hereafter. So they want to fulfill all their ambitions soon in this world itself. That is why in the verse 7: 176 it is told as he clung to the Earth. See the explanation 6: 25, 65 and 7: 53. It is notable that in the verse it is not told 'they have eyes, with which they do not see', instead what told is 'they have eyes with which they do not see the Insight; that is they will see everything except the Soul of Qur'an. See the explanation 2: 6-7 and 6: 104.

'They have ears with which they do not hear' means they will hear everything except the teaching of the Soul of Qur'an. As per the verse 67: 10, such disbelievers will say to the keepers of the Hell: "If we had only listened, the Soul of Qur'an or utilized our intelligence, we would not have become the inmates of the Blaze. Through the verse 25: 43 and 44 Allah asks: have you seen someone who has taken his own whim as his deity? Would you act as a trustee for him or do you reckon that most of them do hear or even utilize their intelligence? They are just like livestock –indeed they are even further strayed from the Path. Through the verse 45: 23 Allah asks: Have you seen someone who has taken his own whim as his deity? Allah knowingly let him go astray and seals off his hearing and his hearts, and places a covering over his eyesight. Who will guide him instead of Allah? Will you not remember by hearts? As per the verse 69: 48 the heedful only utilize the Soul of Qur'an as the Ticket. See the explanation 4: 140; 6: 36-38 and 7: 40.

'*Ghaveen*'-aimless and '*Ghafileen*'-heedless: See the verses 7: 175 and 179. *Ghaveen* means those who lost the aim of life. *Ghaveen* are the hypocrites who knowingly hide the Soul of Qur'an, are killed by Allah and will go to Hell even without trial, whereas the *Ghafileen* are the heedless or *fujjar* who follow blindly the aimless hypocrites. And they will be led to the Hell after trial. Both the *Ghaveen* and *Ghafileen* will blame, argue, curse and abuse one another in the Hell as explained in the verses 2: 166-167. Both include in '*mujrims*' as told in the verses 7: 40; 10: 17; 45: 31 etc. As per the verse 10: 33 the aimless will not then believe, where as the verse 36: 6 says; the Qur'an is revealed in order to warn a people who are not warned by their forefathers, so that they are heedless. While *Ghaveen* are those human satan who hide what the Prophet taught and Allah has ordained through the Qur'anic verses that only one out of every thousand is to Paradise and nine hundred and ninety-nine are to Hell, as explained in the verse 4: 118. The heedless are those who follow simply the path of the majority of the forefathers, and there by belong to the party of satan. For both aimless and heedless Allah will not respond to the prayer and accept any deed since they do not fulfill two conditions explained in the verse 2: 186. The aimless know '*Thilavath*' –recitation of Qur'an with response by mind to the verses as it demands as explained in the verse 2: 44 Whereas the heedless know only '*Qira'th*' i.e. mere reading by which they will dart away from *Islam* just like the arrow darts from the bow. The read Qur'an will witness and argue against for both the aimless and heedless. The *Ghafileen* mentioned in the verse 16: 108 are *Ghaveen*, because it is told that their hearts, hearing and eyesight Allah has sealed off. See the explanation 2: 6 and 7. It is told in the verse 20: 121 that Adam had disobeyed his Lord and became *Ghaveen* where as Prophet Muhammad was among *Ghafileen* before receiving the Qur'an, is told in the verse 12: 3. Adam disobeyed immediately after teaching the Soul of Qur'an in the Paradise where there is no chance to do sins. But Prophet Muhammad is deputed as the last Prophet to the world and he came in a dark ignorant age. Through the verse 7: 205 Allah commanded Prophet and the believer not to be among the *Ghafileen.* To put it briefly, the *Ghaveen* cannot be reminded with the Soul of Qur'an whereas the *Ghafileen* can be reminded. The *Ghafileen* after reminding is not returned to the Soul of Qur'an will be destined in the Hell.

The believers always will pray as: *Oh Allah let us not make among both Ghaveen and Ghafileen; include us among those who follow the Soul of Qur'an as it should be followed. Oh Allah, Enter us to the Paradise among those Sabiqueen who enter the Paradise without trial and the heedful who enter the Paradise after trial with the Ticket, Oh the One Who sent down the Ticket, Oh the Virtuous, Merciful!*

180. Allah has the finest names, so you appeal to Him by such name; and shun those who distort against His Names alone; they will be rewarded for whatever they have been doing.

The names of Allah taught by the Soul of Qur'an are known as the finest name. Through the verse 17: 110 Allah wants to say: you appeal by calling Allah or by calling *Rahman* -the Impartial- whichever name you may invoke He still has the finest names. Do not shout in your *swalath* nor say it under your breath; seek a course in between. The verse 59: 24 says; 'He is Allah, the Creator (who creates the Soul), the Maker (who made the body), the Shaper (balanced the Soul with the body) His names are the finest. Whatever is in Heaven and Earth glorifies Him and He is the Powerful, the Wise". Those who invoke any creature other than Allah at the time of accident, sufferings etc. are only calling the satan, is told in the verse 4: 117. Those who give Allah's name such as '*Moulana*' -our patron- to any of His creature and argue that it is allowable to give such names to others are the human satan, hypocrites. So this verse teaches the believers to shun such hypocrites. "They will be rewarded for whatever they have been doing" means they will be sent to depth of the Hellfire. The verse 41: 40 says; the ones who distort our verses are never hidden from Us; then, is someone who will be cast in to the Fire better, or someone who will come safely through on Resurrection Day? Do whatever you may wish, He is observant anything you do. See the explanation 2: 286; 3: 78 ; 7: 50 and 51.

181. Some of those whom We have created, form a community which guides men by means of the Truth and deal justly by means of It.

See the explanation 7: 159. The aim of life is to distinguish the Creator through the Soul of Qur'an. The Truth means Allah and the Soul of Qur'an. So 'guided with the Truth' means follow the commands and prohibitions of the Soul of Qur'an. 'Deal justly by means of It' means encourage others to utilize the Soul of Qur'an as the Balance and Trust. See explanation 5:8; 6: 1; 7: 8 and 9.

182. And those who reject Our verses, We shall bring them step by step close to destruction in ways that they do not recognize.

See the explanation 2: 38-39; 6:89-90 and 165.

183. And I grant them respite; indeed, My scheme is strong.

A prayer taught through '*Hadeeth Qudsee*' is; Oh the Strong, Oh the Undefeatable, avoid from me the evils of the wrongdoers. See the explanation 2: 256; 3: 177-178; 4: 56 and 7: 30.

184. Have they not ever meditated? There is no madness in their companion; surely, he is none except a plain Warner.

'Their companion' specified in this verse is about Prophet. Through the verse 34: 46 Allah commands to tell the Prophet: "I advise only one thing to you that you stand up in pairs or singly for Allah; then meditate whether there is any madness with your companion. He is none except a Warner to you before the coming of severe torment. As per the verse 15: 6 the disbelievers were saying: Oh you to whom the Soul of Qur'an has been sent down, indeed you are a madman. That means they were ascribing that the Qur'an has been sent down through *Jinns*. As a reply to this ascription it is revealed the verses 26: 210-212 as: "the devils did not descend with It: It does not suit them too, nor can they possible to it; they are too averted from even hearing It." It can be seen in the explanation of the verses 7: 175 and 176 that satan prevents men only from the Soul of Qur'an. As per the verse 81: 22 Allah says, your companion is not madman, and as per the verse 25 it is not the words made by some outcast satan and as per the verse 27 It is nothing except a Reminder for all the worlds. The verses 25: 56 and 57 say; We have not sent you except as a Herald and a Warner. Say: "I do not ask you for any payment for It except that anyone who wishes to accept a way unto his Lord". The verses 53: 2-4 say: Your companion is neither strayed nor has he become aimless. He does not pronounce from some whim; it is nothing except an inspiration that is revealed to him. See the explanation 5: 90-91 and 7: 2.

185. Have they not observed the sovereignty over Heaven and the Earth and whatever Allah has created of any sort, that perhaps their dead line may be approaching? In what talk after this will they believe?

As it is explained in the verses 3: 190 and 191 the prudent persons will meditate about the creation of the Heaven, Earth and all things including mankind in between them and thereby discover the Creator. They will conclude the fact that these are all created with truth and not in futile. The aim of the creation of all these things and themselves if not recognized by utilizing the Soul of Qur'an as Insight, they will have to return to the Fire. Therefore they will remember

Allah in all standing, sitting and laying on their sides through the Soul of Qur'an. Thus they will make the Soul of Qur'an as Witness, Argument and Intercede in favor of them. It is told in the verse 42: 29 that the creation of Heaven and Earth as well as any living creatures He has spread in both of them are the evidence for the Creator's- Allah's- presence, and He is capable of gathering them in whenever He wishes. The verse 44: 38 and 39 say: We did not create Heaven and Earth and anything in between them just by playing around. We have not created them both except with the Truth, even though most of them do not realize it. The verse 45: 22 says: Allah has created Heaven and Earth with the Truth, in order to reward every Soul for whatever it has earned, and they will not be unjust. So these verses teach us Allah- Who created the Heaven, Earth and everything in between them is in order to undergo test the men who will serve Him unseen and who are serving the cursed satan. The verse 45: 12 and 13 say: Allah is the One Who has subjected the sea to you, so that ships may sail on it at His command and you may seek His bounty and even feel grateful. Also He has subjected whatever is in Heaven and whatever is on Earth to you; certainly, it all comes from Him. In that are evidences for the people who meditate things over. See the explanation 5: 94; 6: 75 and 160.

The prudent persons will learn about any creature and themselves and there by they will discover the Glorified Creator. Through the verse 88: 17 Allah asks that do they not observe how camel has been created. So the reply of the believer will be: 'Glory be to You, Oh our Lord!' That means, I saw the Creator behind the camel by using the Insight. He is the Glorious One not having any comparison, similarities, examples and He is capable of everything. The verse 39:18 says: Those who listen the speech- Soul of Qur'an- and follow It in the best manner, such are the ones whom Allah has guided; and such are prudent person. See the explanation 7: 69 and 74.

'Have not they observed that their dead line may be approaching' means, the dead line of every person is decreed and it may happen at any time. Allah by calling the believers through the verse 59: 18 says: Oh you who believe, heed Allah and each soul should observe whatever it has prepared for tomorrow, and heed Allah, and Allah is acquainted of anything you do. Prophet taught that "*the decree will not be changed except by praying by oneself*". But to respond the prayer, there are two conditions specified in the verse 2:186. All these verses teach that we should be always heedful and aim full of life; and not to be among the heedless, aimless of life and gone astray from the Straight path-the Soul of Qur'an. See the explanation 2: 152; 4:1; 7: 157 and 158.

The verse 77: 50 also ends as: 'in what speech after this will they believe'? The verse 45: 6 says: Those are Allah's verses which We recite to you with the Truth, so in what speech will you believe after Allah and His verses? The verse 53: 31 says: Allah possesses whatever is in Heaven and whatever is on Earth, in order to reward the ones who commit evil according to whatever they have done while to reward the ones who act best with the Best, i.e. who lived under the shadow of Qur'an here, they will inherit the Paradise from where the Qur'an is sent down. See the explanation 2: 94-95; 4: 122; 7: 35 and 36.

Oh Allah, nobody can become a believer without the Soul of Qur'an which is Your Permission, speech. So make us believers with It and to live aim fully, and to leave the World being Muslim- submitting all to Allah.

186. Anyone whom Allah lets go astray will have no Guide; He leaves them wandering aimless.

See the explanation 2: 15; 6: 111; 7: 180.

187. They may ask you about the Hour: "When will It take place". Say: "Knowledge about it rests only with my Lord; He didn't disclose Its time except Himself". Things will seem heavy in Heaven and Earth; it will not come to you except all of a sudden. They will even ask you as if you are the custodian of It. Say: "Knowledge about It rests only with Allah, though most people do not realize it".

The verse 33: 63 says: People will ask you about the Hour, say: "Knowledge about It rests only with Allah. What will make you realize that perhaps the Hour is near?" The verse 41: 47 says: To Him should knowledge about the Hour be referred, no fruit comes forth from its blossom and no female conceives nor gives birth without His knowledge. The Day when He calls out to them: "Where are My associates?" They will reply: "We assure You there is not a witness among us". The verses 54: 49 and 50 say: We have created everything in due proportion, no need to implement Our command except the twinkling of an eye. Once, Angel *Jibreel* came to Prophet, then after asking about '*Eeman*'-belief- and '*Islam*'-submission of everything to Allah- asked about the Hour. Then Prophet replied: "The one who is asked does not know than the one who asks". The verses 36: 49

and 50 say: They will not observe except a single blast to catch them while they are arguing away. They will not even get chance to make a bequest, nor will they return to their family. The verse 39: 55 says: And follow in the best manner whatever has been sent down to you from your Lord before torment or death comes upon you suddenly while you do not perceive it.

Things will seem heavy in Heaven and Earth. The scene of the Hour is described through the verses 22: 1-2 as: Oh mankind, heed your Lord! Indeed the quaking at Hour will be a serious thing. On the Day when you see It, every breast feeding mother will neglect whatever she is feeding. And every pregnant female will miscarry. You will see the men intoxicated while they are not intoxicated. But Allah's torment is severe! The verse 76: 27 says: Indeed those people love a fleeting show, and leave a heavy Day behind them. The heavy Day mentioned here for individual is day of death and in the case of entire mankind it is the Dooms Day. The character of virtuous is described in the verses 76: 7 and 11 as: They always keep their word and dread a Day- the evil of which is widespread. They offer food to the needy, orphan and captive out of love for Him, even though they are in need of food, with a mind that we are only feeding you for Allah's sake. We want neither reward from you nor any thanks. We indeed fear a gloomy dismal Day from our Lord, so Allah will Shield them from that Day's evil, and procure them splendor and happiness.

During the period of prophet the soul of Qur'an is not codified. But today the Splendid Book- the Soul of Qur'an- mentioned in the verses 41: 41-42 is formed. Since the Soul of Qur'an is explained everything and It is the knowledge of the three time Knower - past, present and future. Those who knows the well versed knowledge or the deep knowledge in the Soul of Qur'an, knows the time of Hour and when the Testament of mankind will be stoped and when and where the Last days signs appear etc. and he will be the last Forerunner who enter the Paradise without trial. By considering Allah as Impartial he will convey and propagate the Soul of Qur'an to entire mankind irrespective of nations or religion. After his departure to the Paradise only, the first sign of Last Day-the appearance of satan in the shape of man as *Maseeh-A-Ddajjal*- will take place. See the explanation 3: 7; 4:158-159 and 6: 59.

188. Say: "I have no power to acquire benefit or avert any harm from myself except whatever Allah may wish. If I had known the unseen, I would have tried to increase good things for me, while no evil

would even touch me. I am none except a Warner and Herald for the people who believe".

Read together the verses 10: 15-16; 17: 73-75 and 90-93. Since the Soul of Qur'an is the Prosperity, Mercy, Bounty, Insight, Safeguard and Shield the one who utilize It as it should be utilized may increase and achieve good things and will not touch evil or any accidents. Such person is the Forerunner who extends the life of the Universe by propagating and conveying the Soul of Qur'an as Balance and Trust to entire world. See the explanation 3: 128-129; 5: 48 and 6: 104.

189. He is the One Who created you from a single Soul, and made its mate from it, so he may dwell with her comfortably. Once he has overlapped her, she conceives a light burden and walks around with it; when she begins to feel heavy, they both appeal to Allah, their Lord: "If You grant us an honorable child, we will be among grateful".

The life in the Paradise will be immortal and eternal. The deed 'overlap' should give the status of the life in the Paradise and will help to discover the Creator. So in Islam it is the greatest form of serving Allah. That is the only deed in which both Souls become one. The verse 30: 21 says, it is the evidence for the presence of Allah that He has created spouses for you from among yourselves in order that you may overlap yourself comfortably with them. He planted love and mercy between you. Indeed in that are signs for the people who meditate and reflect. See the explanation 4:1 and 7: 26.

190. Once He gives them an honorable child they both setup associates for Him despite what He has given them. Exalted is Allah over anything they may associate with Him.

Today this verse reveals the behavior of Muslims except believers. They pray to Allah for an honorable child. And if they get a healthy, non handicapped child, parents may intend to go to the places of great person's graves and offer devotion to them by calling name and giving first food to the child in presence of such great persons. All such superstitious activities are done with an attitude that they got the child as the mercy of such great person. Actually satan makes alluring such customs and traditions to convert them disbelievers as told in the verse 19: 83. The verses 39: 64- 67 say: "are you ordering me to serve somebody besides Allah? You know- nothing. Yet there has been inspired in you as well as to those before you: 'if you associate anything with Allah, your deed will be futile and you will be among the losers'. Rather you should serve Allah alone and be among the grateful." They have not valued Allah the way He should be valued. The whole Earth will hold within His hand on Resurrection day, while Heaven will be folder up in His right hand. Glory be to Him; exalted is He over anything they may associate with Him! See the explanation 6: 121; 136-137 and 7: 28-30.

191. Do they associate something with Him that has never created anything, while they themselves have been created?

The verses 16: 20-22 say, those whom they invoke instead of Allah do not create anything, while they themselves have been created; they are dead, lifeless, they do not even perceive the times when they will be raised up. Your Deity is the One Deity only! Those who do not believe in the Hereafter have hearts which refuse to accept and they are over proud. See the explanation 2: 165; 6: 36 and 7: 36.

192. And they have neither the ability to help them, nor can they help themselves!

The verses 36: 74-76 say, yet they have adopted other deities instead of Allah so that they may be helped, they do not have the ability to help them, and in the Day when all will be gathered they will be an army against them. Then do not let their statement sadden you; We know what they are keeping secret and what they are disclosing. The verses 46: 5 and 6 say, who is further become astray than the one who appeals to someone instead of Allah who will not respond to him until the Resurrection Day and they are heedless that they are been appealed to. When mankind is summoned, they will become enemies of theirs and renounce their own worship. Through the verses 10: 34 and 35 Allah command to ask: "has any of your associates ever created anything, and then repeated it?" Then to say: "Allah begins with creation; then repeats it again; how is that you shrug Him off?" Ask: "thus anyone of your partners guides one to Truth?" Say: "Allah guides to Truth. So whether the One who guides to Truth is worthier to be followed or the one who does not guided unless he himself is guided? What is the matter with you? How did you decide things?" As per the verse 10: 36 Allah says, most of them not follow except the conjecture; however guessing is not a substitute for the Truth. Indeed Allah is Aware of whatever they are doing. The verse 22: 73

ends as, both the seeker and to whom he seeks are weak. All such '*shirk*' happening in Muslim community is due to the ignorance of the Truth which is the Soul of Qur'an. See the explanation 1: 4 and 6: 21-24.

193. If you invite them to Guidance, they will not follow you; it is the same for you whether you call them or you keep silent.

Here mentioned 'you' means the believers. If they call the associates to the Soul of Qur'an and Allah they will not come. Or otherwise not the idols they dedicate. So in the case of believers to call the associates or not call them is the same. In the verse 36: 10 says: it is same in the case of them whether you warn or not warn them, they will not believe. Then in the verse 11 says, indeed you warn the one who follows the Soul of Qur'an and fear the Most Gracious by seeing through the Soul of Qur'an. Proclaim forgiveness and generous reward to him. See the explanation 2: 6-7; 7: 2, 150, 180 and 181.

194. "Indeed those you appeal to besides Allah are servants just like yourselves. Then appeal to them so they may respond to you if you are so truthful!

Here mentioned 'you' is about the associators. They invoke besides Allah to someone who are creatures just like them. Those who invoke other creatures instead of Allah, is not appealing to anyone other than disbeliever satan, is told in the verse 4: 117. See the explanation 4: 172.

195. Have they feet to walk with, or hands to grasp things with, or eyes to see with, or ears to hear with?" Say: "you call your associates besides Allah; then plot away against me, and no need to give me any respite".

By calling the associates asking the associators they invoke besides Allah have feet to walk with, or hands to grasp things with, or eyes to see with, or ears to hear with; then Allah commands the Prophet and believer to challenge them; that to say the associates: you and your associators altogether gather and plot against me, and no need to give me any respite to implement your plot. Such challenge made by *Ibrahim* to his people can be seen in the verses 6: 80 and 81 and *Nooh's* challenge in the verse 10: 71, and Hood's in the verses 11: 55-56 to their people. See the explanation 7: 176-179.

196. Indeed, my patron is Allah, the One Who sent down the Book. He chooses as friends the honorable.

The verse 42: 6 says, those whom they adopt as patron instead of Him, will still have Allah as an overseer, while you are not the custodian setup over them. The verse 29: 9 says, we will let the ones who believe and perform honorable deeds enter in among honorable people. The verses 48: 5-6 say, for that He may admit believing men and believing women in the Paradise beneath which rivers flow, to live there forever, and to cancel out their evil deeds for them. That will be a Supreme achievement with Allah. And He may punish hypocritical men and women as well as associating men and women who conjecture such evil about Allah; on them will fall and evil turn of fortune. Allah has become angry with them and has cursed them and kept prepared Hell for them how evil is such returning place! The aim of the revelation of the Book is to identify the Creator, Allah. Then who believe in Allah as introducing by the Book and who following the do's and don'ts of it, are the honorable people. See the explanation 2: 186. Allah's party includes all Prophets, those who make the Truth truthfulness, those to whom the Truth will witnesses in favor and honorable men who reform the people with the Truth from Prophet Adam to the last Day is the only party of believers, told both in the verses 5: 56 and 58: 22. The verse 28: 85 says, the One Who has charged you with the Qur'an will return you to the best destination. Say: "my Lord is Quite Aware as to who has brought Guidance and who is in clear astray. See the explanation 1: 6; 7: 157 and 170.

197. And those you appeal instead of Him neither have the ability to help you, nor can they help themselves.

If appeal to anyone besides Allah, they cannot help the caller as well as themselves. Through the verse 17: 56 Allah command to say: "invoke those whom you claim to have besides Him: they do not control any means of removing harm from you, nor for changing it. Then the verse 57 says, such are those whom they appeal to, seek way approach to their Lord, trying which of them shall be the nearest. They hope for His Mercy and fear His torment. Indeed your Lord's torment is something to beware of! The verses 26: 91-102 say, the Hades will appear for the aimless. Then will be asked: "where is whatever you where serving instead of Allah will they help you, or even help themselves? So they will be toppled in to It, both they and the aimless ones as well as all the armies of *Iblees*. They will say while they quarrel away in It: "by Allah, we were in such manifest astray when we put you on the same footing as the Lord of the Worlds!" It has only being '*mujrims*' who have led us astray; now here We have no intercessors nor any bosom friend. If we only had another chance, we would then be believers. See the explanation 5: 36; 6: 25-30 and 7: 37-40.

198. If you call them to the Guidance, they will not hear, and you will see them looking at you, while they are not seeing.

Here also 'you' mean the believers. When the believer calls the associates to the Soul of Qur'an they will not even listen to the calling. They will only stare to the caller but not ready to see and hear the Soul of Qur'an, the Insight. The verse 22: 72 says; whenever Our verses are clearly recited to them, you will recognize the disgust on the faces of those who disbelieve; They almost pounce up on those who recite Our verses to them. Say: "shall I announce something even worse then that to you, the Fire!" Allah has promised It to those who disbelieve. How evil is such returning place! The verse 68: 51 and 52 say; The ones who disbelieve almost trip you up by glaring at you, whenever they here the Soul of Qur'an, and they say: Indeed he is possessed one. But it is nothing less than a Reminder to all the worlds. See the explanation 2: 18-19; 6: 36 and 7: 179.

199. Practice forgiveness, command decency and avoid ignorant people.

200. If some tempt from satan should prompt you, seek refuge with Allah; indeed He is All Hearing, All Knowing.

It is told in the verse 25: 63 that the beloved servants of the Impartial who walk modestly on Earth and peacefully say: "how do you do!", whenever ignorant men address them in a dispute manner. i.e. they will peacefully say: "you can go in your way". The verse 41: 34 says a good deed and evil deed are not alike: repel evil with something that is the best –the Soul of Qur'an, and notice how someone who is separated from you because of enmity will become a bosom friend. Then the verse 35 says, and that will not attain except those who preserve patients themselves and will not it be achieved except the luckiest one who accepts the Soul of Qur'an as Good admonition. As per the verse 36 Allah says, nevertheless if some impulse from satan should prompt you, then seek refuge with Allah, indeed He is the only All Hearing, All Knowing. Command decency means command with the best that is with the Soul of Qur'an as mentioned in the verses 92: 6 and 9. It is told in the verse 11: 114 that indeed the good deeds remove evil deeds. 'The good deeds' means the deeds under the light of the Soul of Qur'an.

In order to become a believer, one should be satisfied in Allah's satisfaction, and be angry in Allah's angry. Allah's satisfaction means the command of the Soul of Qur'an. Allah's angry means the Prohibition of the Soul of Qur'an. Since the Soul of Qur'an is a clear decisive statement, as per the verse 86: 13 then, an amusement approach to it is not permitable. Through the verse 56: 81 asks to disbelievers "are you consider this speech as lubricant!" That means for Allah's sake one should talk, keep quite and be patient. As per the verse 9: 73 it is the inevitable duty of believers to do Jihad to the *kuffar* and hypocrites and show angry with them since they hide and reject the Soul of Qur'an, and help satan to obstruct the people from the Straight path. But it should be considered the fact that there is no compulsion in '*Dheen*'-Religion as explained in the verse 2: 256, and should deal accordingly to any people. In brief, the believers are those who live for Allah as His real vicegerent. So they lead a life according to the Soul of Qur'an in order to witness the Prophet's life among the mankind. See the explanation 2: 143. As per the verse 23: 96 it is ordered to repel evil with the Best- Soul of Qur'an, and as per the verses 97-98 to pray: "my Lord, I seek refuge with You from the devil's promptings and I seek refuge with You my Lord lest they approach me. See the explanation 3: 159; 4: 63-64; 5: 50 and 6: 54.

201. Indeed the ones who are heedful, whenever some impulse from satan should prompt them, they remember Allah in mind and thus they are granted Insight.

'Those who are heedful' means the one who keeps Allah in their hearts with the Soul of Qur'an as explained in the verse 2: 38. They make their Soul mate believer with the Soul of Qur'an. But a satanic temptation from outside afflicted them; soon they remember Allah by heart. Then they recognize the way of Allah and the way of satan and accept the True way of Allah. The Soul of Qur'an is the Insight and the Criterion to distinguish the way of Allah and the way of satan. The one, who apart from the remembrance of Allah or from the Soul of Qur'an undergo temptation of the satan. It is told in the verse 25:73 that the servant of the Impartial whenever reminded with their Lord's verses do not fall down deaf and blind upon them. Read together the verses 8: 29; 20: 124-127; 32: 15; 38: 1, 8; 41: 44; 43: 36 and 58: 19. See the explanation 2: 152; 6: 68; 7: 170, 175 and 176.

202. While the satan's brothers, they will drag them deeper into aimlessness; then never relax their efforts.

Yes, satans either from *Jinns* or from mankind who are the hypocrites- will drag their followers from the Straight path to the path of Hell. As per the verse 4: 118 it is the character of satan that he will make aimless nine hundred and ninety nine out of each thousand of men and their Soul mates. If they once hold one, relax not their holdings in such a way that one cannot return to the Straight path –the way of Allah. It is told in the verse 17: 27 that indeed spend thrifts are the devils brethren, and satan has always been ungrateful towards His Lord. Today we can see Muslims; the people of the Book are in front of all evil deeds of satan and extravagant comparative to others all over the world. The reason for that is they neither use the Soul of Qur'an nor give others to utilize as the Guidance to the Paradise and Balance to keep the Universe in its equilibrium. As per the verse 41: 29, the ones who disbelieve will say: "Our Lord, show us which *Jinns* and humans have misled Us; We shall trample on both of them with our feet, since we were underdogs blindly followed them. See the explanation 1: 7; 6: 112; 7: 146 and 147.

203. If you had not brought them any verse, they would ask: "why did not you get It together?" Say: "Surely, I follow only what has been inspired to me by my Lord. This is an Insight from your Lord, as well as Guidance and Mercy for the people who believe".

As per the verses 25: 32-33, Those who disbelieve say: "why hasn't the Qur'an being sent down to him as a single book, it has been done like that in order to embrace your mind by It; and we would phrased orderly your life . And they will not come to you with a question unless we will bring you the Truth and the best commentary such that nobody has to ask such question till the Last Day. It is told in the verse 17: 82 that "in Qur'an there is Healing and Mercy for those who believe; but for disbelievers It causes nothing but loss over loss. Read together the verse 41: 44. In the verse 9: 125 it is told that for the hypocrites, who knowingly hide It, Qur'an will add filth to their existing filth; and they will die as disbelievers. See the explanation 6: 155-157; 7: 35-37 and 52.

204. Whenever the Qur'an is being recited, listen to It attentively and keep silent, so that you may be received Mercy.

It is a command to the believers that, they should keep quiet and hear attentively the Qur'an whenever or wherever It is being recited. In *swalath*, while *Imam*- leader- recites the Qur'an, the followers shouldn't recite but should hear attentively and should respond with mind according to the content of the verse. To have such a habit, one should know the Soul of Qur'an. That is what Prophet taught: Don't recite Qur'an even in *swalath* without having the contents. '*Thilavath*' is the reciting of Qur'an with response. See the explanation 2: 44. If anyone does not respond to the Qur'an because of his unawareness about Its soul, then that Qur'an which he heard and his skin will witness against him on the Day of Judgment as mentioned in the verses 17: 36 and 41: 19-24. See the explanation 2: 285; 4: 43; 6: 36; 7: 157 and 158.

205. And remember your Lord within your own soul, beseeching and fearfully, without raising your voice, both in the early morning and in the evening; and you do not belong to among the heedless.

"Remember Allah in the morning and evening" means remember Allah always in heart irrespective of morning or evening. Read together the verses 2: 152; 3: 190 and 191. It is told in the verse 12: 3 that before getting the Qur'an, you too were among heedless. By saying: 'Do not be among heedless' means one should know that Allah knows the status of the hearts and He is acquainted of everything. Then don't be among those who think that Allah will hear prayer only when spelled by tongue. Here it is ordered to prophet and the believers that do not be heedless after receiving the Soul of Qur'an. The verse 36: 6 says: This Qur'an is revealed in order to warn the heedless people who were not warned before.

In *swalath*, all the prayers except the reciting of Qur'an should carry out with the heart not by the tongue. Prophet taught that those who recite Qur'an without knowing Its soul-even if it is in *swalath* will dart from the *Dheen* as an arrow dart from its bow. The prayers after completing the *swalath* also should carryout with the heart. Moreover it should not be like the prayer of Meccan *mushriks*. The verse 8: 35 says about their prayers as: their prayers and *swalath* are nothing but whistling and clapping. Those who utilize the Qur'an as an Insight can realize that, today the Muslims all over the World is deviated to the darkness than that of the previous periods due to their ignorance of the Light, the Soul of Qur'an. See the explanation 6: 93; 7: 179 and 180.

206. Surely those who are with your Lord do not feel too proud to serve Him; they glorify Him and prostrate before Him.

The Angels- who are closer to Allah- always obey Allah and prostrate before Him by praising Him. Believers who represent Allah from among the men have high grade than any other creatures. So they will be in front to prostrate before Allah than any other creatures. Deviating from being servant of Allah is the character of satan, and that will cause disgrace and downfall. Therefore, the believers who expect greatness and superiority will give up the character of satan and will come forward than the Angels to become closer to Allah. They themselves are the "*Sabiqs*"- foremost people- who enter the Paradise without trial. By the prostration he proves that he has not fallen in arrogance and has not deviated from obeying the Lord; but is the one who serves only Allah and bows head only in front of Him. That dignity and position can only be achieved by learning and propagating the Soul of Qur'an that is the way of serving Allah and witnessing the prophet's life. See the explanation 3: 79 and 5: 48.

Allah says in the verse 32: 15 that surely those who believe in Our verses, whenever they are reminded with It in their hearts' language, will fall down in adoration by praising and glorifying the Lord, And they will not puff up with pride. Once the companions of prophet asked to him "Are there is two prostrations in *Surath Hajj* and is it compulsory?" Then Prophet replied: Yes, there is, those who are unable to prostrate shouldn't recite It. In the verses 22: 18 and 19 Allah says: Did you not see that all things are in Heaven and Earth, the Sun, the Moon, the Stars, the Hills, the Trees, the Animals, a great number among the mankind; and a great number who are liable to affect punishment prostrate to Allah. And such as Allah shall disgrace, none can raise to honor. Surely Allah carries out all that He wishes. These are the two groups who dispute in front of Allah. Then for the disbelievers will be cut out a garment of fire and over their heads will be poured out boiling water. Thus disbelievers who prostrate unwillingly also will get Hell as hospitable homes. See the explanation 2: 186 and 3: 97.

There are fifteen places of prostration in Qur'an. Beside here, the other verses are 13: 15; 16: 50; 17: 109; 19: 58; 22: 18, 77; 25: 60; 32: 15; 38: 24; 41: 38; 53: 62; 84: 21 and 96: 19. Prostration is compulsory while reciting all these verses. If anyone recites these verses and doesn't prostrate, he is the disbeliever and transgressor. Sometimes, if the verse of prostration comes while Prophet carrying out "*Khuthuba*"- Friday ceremony- of *swalath*, he used to prostrate by coming down from the dais and continue '*Khuthuba*' after prostration. Once while carrying out the '*Khutuba*' for '*Jumua*', prophet recited the verse 38: 24 and came down from the dais and prostrated. Companions also did so. On another occasion, when the mentioned verse recited, the companions prepared for prostration. Seeing this, prophet came down from dais and did prostration. After that he came up to the dais and told that the prostration mentioned here is compulsory for prophet *Dawood* whereas about us it is for expressing our gratitude.

For the prostration of '*Thilawath*', there is no condition as in the case of the prostration in *swalath* such as having ablution and facing '*Qibla*'. Whenever one reaches the verse of prostration while reciting Qur'an, on the same place and same condition itself he should fall down. It aims that falling down in front of Allah. Those who drive vehicles should at least bow their heads without considering the direction; even it is towards east, west, north or south. See the explanation 2: 177.

Only the prostration of '*Thilawath*' is single. All other prostrations in *swalath* are two times. Prophet taught that *during the last Period their single prostration will be best for them than getting the Earth and all things on it*. It is to be remembered that prophet has taught at '*Hajjathul Vida*' itself, that one should live by biting the Splendid Book-Soul of Qur'an, mentioned in the verses 41: 41-42, with his molar teeth. Hence today, the most important thing is to live by reciting the Soul of Qur'an and doing prostration. In other words, that will be the way of life which is going to be practiced on the second coming of *Eisa*. *Surath Alaq* ends by the verse; 'then you prostrate in adoration and become closer to Allah.' Prophet taught that *prostration is the place in which the servant is closer to Allah than any other time*.

In prostration of '*Thilawath*', after glorifying and praising Allah three times as, "Oh Lord! The highest, you are Glorious", one can pray as, "Oh Allah, I prostrated for You, believed with You, submitted completely to You. I prostrated to You with face, You created it, You are the One Who fashioned it, You made it its beautiful form and made sight and hearing in it. Allah is the best beautiful Creator than any other creators, Who is so blessed."

While saying about prostration along with Angels, may glorify as, 'the Glorified and Sanctified Lord of us, the Lord of Angels and *Jibreel*! If it is like the verse 22: 77 commanding for prostration, then one can pray as, 'Oh Allah! Include us among the one who bow and prostrate, and serve only to You, and who praise You and Glorify You. Enter us in the Paradise along with the winners with utmost Mercy-the Soul of Qur'an. Oh the Impartial, Most Merciful! See the explanation 2: 33 and 4: 158 to understand the method of glorifying Allah.

Oh Allah! Make me not among the disbelievers who hide and reject the Soul of Qur'an. Oh Allah! Make me not among the wrongdoers who do not utilize and not give others to utilize It. Oh Allah! Make me not among the transgressors who twist and hide the verses. Oh Allah! Make me not among the aimless who knowingly neglect the Soul of Qur'an. Oh Allah! Make me not among the heedless who try not to understand the soul of Qur'an. Oh Allah! Make me not among the mujrims who do not utilize their intelligence. Our Lord! Do not turn us into a trial for the wrongdoing people! Save us with your Mercy from such disbelieving people.

Oh Allah! Make me not among the despairs, unjust, guessers, doubtful, skeptical, quandary, ridiculers, mischief makers, extravagant, aggressors, trespassers, terrors, forgetters, evil doers, false prouder, haughtiness, quibblers, associators, distorters, repudiators, dissipaters, cheaters, traitors, insolent, and life losers.

Our Lord! Make us the Soul of Qur'an as a Shield and Safeguard throughout our life. Make It as witnessing and arguing in favor of us and not against us. Oh Allah! Help us to utilize the Soul of Qur'an as a Ticket, Guidance, Balance, Criterion, Trust and Light.

QUR'AN SURATHS		NO. OF VERSES
1. Al-Fathiha	(Introduction)	7
2. Al-Baqara	(The Cow)	286
3. Ali-Imran	(Imran's Family)	200
4. Annisa	(Women)	176
5. Mae'da	(The Heavenly food tray)	120
6. An-am	(livestock)	165
7. Ahraf	(The Heights)	206
8. Anfal	(Booty)	75
9. Thouba	(Repentance)	129
10. Yoonus	(Name of a Prophet)	109
11. Hood	(Name of a Prophet)	123
12. Yoosuf	(Name of a Prophet)	111
13. Ar-ra'd	(Thunder)	43
14. Ibrahim	(Name of a Prophet)	52
15. Al-hijir	(Stone land)	99
16. An-Nah'l	(The Bee)	128
17. Isra'	(The night journey)	111
18. Al-Kah'f	(The Cave)	110
19. Maryam	(The name of Jesus' mother)	98
20. Twaha	(Another Name of Prophet Mohemmed)	135
21. Ambiya'	(Prophets)	112
22. Al-Hajj	(Pilgrimage)	78
23. Mu'minoon	(Believers)	118
24. An-Noor	(The Light)	64
25. Furqan	(The Criterion)	77
26. Shuara'	(Poets)	227
27. An-Naml	(The Ants)	93

28. Al-Qasus	(Narration of historical incidents)	88
29. Ankabooth	(The Spider)	69
30. Ar-Room	(The Romans)	60
31. Luqman	(The name of a person who had been given wisdom)	34
32. Sajadha	(Prostration)	30
33. Ah'zab	(The Confidarates)	73
34. Saba'	(Country of Sheeba)	54
35. Fathir	(The Originator)	45
36. Yaseen	(Oh... Man!)	83
37. Swaffath	(Ranged in Ranks)	182
38. Swad	(Historical incidents)	88
39. Zumar	(Groups)	75
40 Mu'min	(The Believer)	85
41. Fussilath	(Spelled out)	54
42 Assura	(Consultation)	53
43. Zukhruf	(Adornments)	89
44. Dukhan	(Smoke)	59
45. Jasiya	(Crouching)	37
46. Ahquaf	(Dunes)	35
47. Muhammad	(Name of a Prophet)	38
48. Fath'h	(Victory)	29
49. Hujurath	(The Inner apartments)	18
50. Qaaf	(The letter Qaaf)	45
51. Addariyath	(winnowing)	60
52. Athwoor	(The Mount)	49
53. Annaj'm	(The Star)	62
54. Qamar	(The Moon)	55
55. Ar-Rahman	(The Impartial)	78
56. Al-Waqia	(The Inevitable event)	96

57. Hadeed	(Iron)	29
58. Mujadila	(The pleading woman)	22
59. Hash'r	(Gathering)	24
60. Mumthahana	(Examining woman)	13
61. Swaff	(Battle Array)	14
62. Jumu'a	(Assembly for prayer)	11
63. Munafiqoon	(Hypocrites)	11
64. Athagaboon	(Mutual Loss and gain)	18
65. Thwalaq	(Divorce)	12
66. Thaharim	(Prohibition)	12
67. Mulk	(Dominion)	30
68. Qalam	(Pen)	52
69. Al-haqa	(The sure Realily)	52
70. Ma'arij	(Staircases upword)	44
71. Nooh	(Name of a Prophet)	28
72. Jinn	(Sprites)	28
73. Muzammil	(Folded up in garments)	20
74. Muddazir	(Folder in garments)	56
75. Qiyama	(Resurrection)	40
76. Insan	(Every man)	31
77. Mursalath	(Sent Forth)	50
78. Naba'	(Great News)	40
79. Annaziath	(Soul snatchers)	46
80. Abasa	(He Frowned)	42
81. Thakhwir	(Folding up)	29
82. Infithwar	(Bursting apart)	19
83. Muthafifeen	(Reducer in weigh and measure)	36
84. Inshiqaq	(Spliting open)	25
85. Burooj	(Constellations)	22
86. Athwariq	(The night comer)	17

87. A'la	(The Highest)	19
88. Gasiya	(The Pall)	26
89. Faj'r	(Day break)	30
90. Balad	(Countryside)	20
91. Ashams	(The Sun)	15
92. Al-lail	(The Night)	21
93. Adhuha	(The Morning Bright)	11
94. Asharh	(The expansion)	8
95. Atheen	(The Fig tree)	8
96. Alaq	(The clot)	19
97. Qad'r	(Power)	5
98. Bayyina	(Evidence)	8
99 Zalzala	(The Earth quake)	8
100. Adiyath	(The Chargers)	11
101. Al-Qaria	(The terrible event)	11
102. Athakasur	(Competition)	8
103. Al-as'r	(Eventide)	3
104. Humaza	(Gossipmonger)	9
105. Feel	(Elephant)	5
106. Quraish	(Quraish)	4
107. Ma'un	(Alms giving)	7
108. Al-Kauzar	(plenty)	3
109. Kafiroon	(Disbelievers)	6
110. An'Nasr	(Divine support)	3
111. Mazad	(Palm rope)	5
112. Ikhlas	(Sincerity)	4
113. Falaq	(Dawn)	5
114. An-Nas	(Mankind)	6
	TOTAL VERSES	**6236**